Inequality in Canada

Third Edition

Inequality in Canada

A Reader on the
Intersections of
Gender, Race,
and Class

Edited by
Valerie Zawilski

OXFORD
UNIVERSITY PRESS

Oxford University Press is a department of the University of Oxford.
It furthers the University's objective of excellence in research, scholarship,
and education by publishing worldwide. Oxford is a registered trade mark of
Oxford University Press in the UK and in certain other countries.

Published in Canada by
Oxford University Press
8 Sampson Mews, Suite 204,
Don Mills, Ontario M3C 0H5 Canada

www.oupcanada.com

Library and Archives Canada Cataloguing in Publication

Inequality in Canada : a reader on the intersections of gender, race, and
class / edited by Valerie Zawilski. — Third edition.

Previous edition published by Oxford University Press, 2009.
Includes bibliographical references and index.
ISBN 978-0-19-901331-9 (paperback)

1. Equality—Canada—Textbooks. 2. Canada—Social conditions—1991—Textbooks.
I. Zawilski, Valerie Sarah-Elizabeth, 1957-, editor

HN110.Z9S6 2015   305.0971   C2015-904243-7

Cover image: Steven Puetzer/Getty Images

Oxford University Press is committed to our environment.
Wherever possible, our books are printed on paper which comes from
responsible sources.

Printed and bound in the United States of America
1 2 3 4 — 19 18 17 16

Contents

PART SIX   Canada and Global Inequality

Contributors

Sedef Arat-Koç is Associate Professor in the Department of Politics and Public Administration and a member of the Yeates School of Graduate Studies at Ryerson University.

Deborah Barndt is Associate Professor in Environmental Studies and Coordinator of the Community Arts Practice Certificate Program at York University.

Henry M. Codjoe is Adjunct Professor of Sociology of Education at Dalton State College, Georgia, USA.

Linda Cornwell is the Program and Communications Manager of the Women's Health in Women's Hands Organization in Toronto.

George Sefa Dei is Professor of Sociology in the Social Justice Education Department at the Ontario Institute for Studies in Education, at the University of Toronto.

Ann Doris Duffy is Professor of Sociology in the Critical Sociology and Social Justice and Equity Studies Program and an affiliated faculty member of the Labour Studies Program at Brock University.

Evelyn Nakano Glenn is Professor of Gender and Women's Studies in the Ethnic Studies Department and Asian American Studies Program at the University of California, Berkeley.

Jana Grekul is Assistant Professor of Sociology and Director of the BA Criminology Program at the University of Alberta.

Julia Hemphill is a research consultant in Oakville, Ontario.

Laura Lee Howard is Past Executive Director, PEI Association for Newcomers to Canada, Maritime Centre of Excellence for Women's Health.

Samantha Hudyma is a PhD Candidate in the Social Sciences at York University.

Sarah Hunt is an alumna of Simon Fraser University's Geography Department and a community-based independent researcher and teacher in British Columbia.

Helen Jefferson Lenskyj is Professor Emerita of Sociology in the Sociology Department and Social Equity Studies in Education Program at the University of Toronto.

Meg Luxton is Professor of Sociology in the School of Gender, Sexuality and Women's Studies at York University.

Ann Kim is Associate Professor of Sociology in the Sociology Department at York University.

Anna C. Korteweg is Assistant Professor of Sociology in the Sociology Department in Mississauga at the University of Toronto.

Kari Krogh is Assistant Professor of Disability Studies and Senior Fellow at Ryerson University.

Robin LeDrew is Chair of the Monashee Arts Council in British Columbia.

Marian MacKinnon is Associate Professor of Sociology at the University of Prince Edward Island.

Nancy Mandell is Professor of Sociology in the School of Gender, Sexuality and Women's Studies at York University.

Patricia A. Monture-Angus was Professor of Native Studies at the University of Saskatchewan (deceased November 17, 2010).

Jennifer J. Nelson is Assistant Professor in the Department of Public Health Sciences at the University of Toronto.

Valerie Preston is Professor of Geography in the Geography Department at York University.

Colleen Reid is Instructor in Child and Family Community Studies at Douglas College, British Columbia.

Goli Rezai-Rashti is Professor of Sociology in the Faculty of Education at the University of Western Ontario.

Carla Rice is Associate Professor and Canada Research Chair in Care, Gender, and Relationships in the College of Social and Applied Human Sciences at the University of Guelph.

Bernard Schissel is Professor of Sociology and Head of the Doctor of Social Sciences Program at Royal Roads University, British Columbia.

Daiva K. Stasiulis is Professor of Sociology and Graduate Program Coordinator at Carleton University.

Wangari Esther Tharao is the Program and Research Manager of the Women's Health in Women's Hands organization in Toronto and a PhD student at the University of Toronto.

Njoki Nathani Wane is Associate Professor and Director of the Office of Teacher Support in the Department of Sociology and Equity Studies in Education, at the Ontario Institute for Studies in Education at the University of Toronto.

Terry Wotherspoon is Professor of Sociology and Head of the Sociology Department at the University of Saskatchewan.

Nira Yuval-Davis is Professor of Sociology and Director of the Research Centre on Migration, Refugees and Belonging (CMRB) at the University of East London, UK.

Preface

While it remains a relatively new direction in critical inquiry, intersectional theorizing in Canada rests on a strong and well-established research foundation. Since the first edition of this text was published in 2005, intersectional theorizing has now, in 2015, entered mainstream sociology and is also used in other fields of inquiry, including psychology, anthropology, social work, health, political geography, masculinity studies, and women's studies. According to Lesley McCall, intersectionality is "the most important theoretical contribution that women's studies, in conjunction with related fields, has made so far" (qtd in Yuval-Davis 2012, 2). Driven by dual commitments to scholarship and humanitarian social change, many Canadian scholars have dedicated their efforts to understanding how and why social inequality is socially reproduced in Canada. In seeking published work in five substantive areas and working with just four requirements for the selection of articles—they had to be Canadian, and/or transnational, recent, and about inequality—I was led to innumerable databases, abstracts, publishers' websites, journals, reference lists, course outlines, libraries, and consultations with colleagues. I soon learned that the desire for a strong representation of women and for work that was derived from a critical perspective was, as it had been for the first and second editions of this text, easy to satisfy: these characteristics described most of the work I liked. I also sought out regional representation and especially Aboriginal voices. Finally, with the requirement that each reading examine intersectional forms of social inequality, I discovered I had created a robust and highly rigorous set of criteria to guide me through what would otherwise have been an overwhelming body of work. What I have produced is, I believe, a unique collection of essays on social inequality in Canada, all of which share a critical analysis of injustices manifest across a range of social processes and across interlocking systems of gender, race, age, sexuality, disability, geography, and class. The sections—family, education, health, social justice, and Canada and global inequality—have been structured to reflect these relationships and interrelationships. New to this third edition of the text are a number of recent readings that reflect growing concerns about the globalization of social inequality in the world today. These readings include chapters on decolonizing sex work, aging and economic security, women's work and health, the politics of belonging, and gender politics and the Olympic industry.

While all the individual essays are important in their own right, I make no claim that the collection is in any way exhaustive. I am well aware of omissions, and I apologize to those scholars whose work ought to be included here but is not for reasons of accessibility, permissions costs, or length. Nor could I include many of the "classic" works on this topic (some, but not all, made it to one of the annotated lists of readings included at the end of each chapter). This undertaking has also drawn my attention to the need for further research in certain areas. Indeed, some glaring gaps became apparent as I read widely to find work that satisfied the criteria I had set out. For example, more Canadian work is required on intersectionality and health, especially in the subfield of gerontology, and on intersectionality and globalization looking beyond the problem of labour. On the other hand, I was very encouraged to see the large number of critical Canadian writings on intersectionality and social justice. The literature on education is almost as rich. Other areas outside my arbitrary purview are also in need of further attention; these include intersectionality and the media, urban culture, social policy, criminology, and the arts, to name a few. Finally, though intersectional theorizing is more widely known and is more likely to be used by scholars throughout the world than it was 10 years ago, there is still a need for more integration of feminist and anti-racist writings in "mainstream" textbooks in the social sciences. I am indebted to acquisitions editors Suzanne Clark and Darcey Pepper, developmental editor Heather Macdougall, copy editor Joanne Muzak, and production coordinator Lisa Ball at Oxford University Press for the thoughtful advice and the collegial support that they provided. I would also like to thank the reviewers for their ideas and insights, which helped to guide the direction that the third edition of this book has taken. I am optimistic that the outcome will have some influence on the study of social inequality in Canada. In particular, I hope that this field of inquiry will stretch well beyond what Daiva Stasiulis calls the "trinity" of gender, race, and class to encompass issues of sexuality and ability (both physical and emotional), as well as the dynamic categories of religion, nationality, ethnicity, masculinity, and immigration. While these issues are not neglected in this reader, I admit they are not thematically prominent. What I have here is neither the initiation nor the conclusion of an intellectual endeavour. I hope to join those social critics who are currently engaged in cultivating research programs to address questions of inequality and the complex dimensions of power relations. I also share with them the animation of a "language of possibility" toward the integration of critique, alliance, and struggle.

Valerie Zawilski
August 2015

Reviewers

We gratefully acknowledge the contributions of the following reviewers, whose thoughtful comments and suggestions have helped to shape this new edition:

Barbara Heather, Grant MacEwan University
Satoshi Ikeda, Concordia University
Julie McMullin, Western University
Barbara Perry, University of Ontario Institute of Technology

Introduction

I f social inequality is inevitable—given that it is a pervasive element in all social relationships and is embedded in the social structures of all societies—why do scholars spend time and energy seeking ways to eliminate this complex social phenomenon? Its inevitability notwithstanding, if we can understand how inequality is generated and how it is socially reproduced, then we can use our knowledge to at least reduce it, even if we cannot eradicate it entirely. As individuals, as members of a group, and as citizens of a state, we can contest acts of social injustice against vulnerable populations, support the civil rights of all peoples of the world, and try to prevent further discrimination against those who are constructed as "other(s)."

The body of the other(s) may vary to some degree from culture to culture and from country to country, but internationally, sociologists now recognize a global pattern. Other(s) are people who are most likely working as low-cost manual or semi-skilled labourers in substandard working conditions and living in conditions that would be described as absolute or relative poverty. In many cases, these other(s) are racialized women. An older woman who lives in poverty, who is physically or mentally challenged, and who belongs to a marginalized ethnic or religious group has limited life choices and opportunities, and is an example of a victim of social inequality based on various intersections of age, gender, disability, class, and race.

In the field of social inequality, three traditional modes of thinking have evolved, each one contributing to a large body of research: thinking on class, thinking on race/ethnicity, and thinking on gender. In the 1970s, sociologists such as Nicos Poulantzas and Eric Olin Wright, who studied social inequality issues, engaged in a Marxian analysis of class that examined trends and patterns of inequality in the wages and occupations of the proletariat and the bourgeoisie. Canadian scholars such as Monica Boyd, Peter Pineo, Wallace Clement, Edward Grabb, Robert Brym, David Livingstone, James Curtis, John Goyder, and Carl Cuneo investigated patterns of social mobility in the Canadian population by examining relationships among the variables of income, socio-economic status, social class, levels of education, prestige, and wealth status.

In 1965, John Porter's book *The Vertical Mosaic* examined questions about race, ethnicity, and class. Porter proposed that Canada had fostered a social hierarchy, in which people of British descent were most likely to belong to the class of economic and political elites, while Aboriginal men and women occupied the bottom tier. Porter's work sparked a national debate, and with the advent of Canada's multiculturalism policy in 1971—just as the country was welcoming greater numbers of racialized immigrants from Asia and Africa—the field of social inequality exploded with studies on race and ethnic relations in the 1970s and 1980s. Race and ethnic relations became a subdiscipline of social inequality in which Leo Driedger, Raymond Breton, Jeffery Reitz, Warren Kalbach, Wsevolod Isajiw, Anthony Richmond, Victor Satzewich, Peter Li, and B. Singh Bolaria began to question economic and political policies and practices that encouraged institutionalized forms of economic, political, and social discrimination against immigrants and racialized minorities. In the 1980s and 1990s, scholars who worked within the subdiscipline of race and ethnic relations expanded their areas of interest to include demographic diversity, residential segregation, prejudice and discrimination, and problems of racism and equality (Driedger 2001).

In the 1970s and 1980s, successive federal governments added to Canada's body of multiculturalism laws, developing a social policy that symbolically sought to eradicate racism on an everyday level by educating people about tolerance and encouraging a dialogue of difference. At the same time, the feminist movement began to flourish within sociology, and Canadian feminist scholars such as Dorothy Smith, Margrit Eichler, Mary O'Brien, Bonnie Fox, Meg Luxton, Pat Armstrong, and Roxanna Ng moved beyond a Marxian analysis of class. This group of sociologists looked at the relationship between gender, paid and unpaid labour, and women's rights in the labour force. As more women began to join the labour force, feminists asked why women were expected to work a "double-duty day," toiling for low wages in often undesirable jobs, only to return home to perform several hours of household chores. Canadian feminist scholars extended their inquiries into the underlying reasons for women's social inequality to examine how the patriarchal state sought, through the male-dominated medical system, to control women's reproductive rights and to medicalize women's life cycles and bodies, encouraging "body work."

In the first reading of Part One, George Sefa Dei builds on the questions that feminist scholars have asked about gender- and class-related issues. He proposes an integrative anti-racism studies program that would examine the dynamics of *social difference*, a category that includes, in addition to class, race, ethnicity, and gender, such variables as sexual orientation, religion, language, and physical ability. He describes the need to develop an anti-racism program, in response to the conflict that arises out of processes of domination and struggle, and are the result of oppressions that are polyvocal and overlap and intersect on multiple sites. Dei suggests that "lived experience is the starting point to understanding oppressions." Thus, understanding the historical, social, and political origins of oppression not only on the local or regional level but also on national and transnational levels is the foundation for developing an anti-racism discourse in Canadian society. In addition, Dei argues that in order to explain how the politics of difference is used to oppress people, the material conditions and the hegemonic group's access to power and privilege must be understood. Economic restructuring on the local and global level has heightened our awareness of difference not only in Canada but throughout the world, Dei claims. Subsequently, marginalized people such as racialized minorities and immigrants are held responsible for the economic shortcomings of the state, and reductionist arguments pit class against race. Dei concludes this chapter by stating that anti-racism education must deal simultaneously with social inequalities embedded within class, ethnicity, culture, (dis)ability, sexuality, and gender discrimination in the classroom, in the home, in the workplace, and in community actions and groups.

Understanding social inequality through intersectional theorizing is the focus of Daiva Stasiulis's chapter. According to Stasiulis, intersectional theorizing has not attained a privileged voice within feminist theory; however, there is a trend in feminist debate to *move beyond* the race–gender–class trinity and understand the impact of other forms of social division and oppression of women on multiple levels. Stasiulis describes two currents in intersectional theorizing. The first is a discourse emphasizing race, yet Stasiulis (like Dei) cautions against race essentialism. The second acknowledges that racial discrimination is not a prominent issue for the many people in the world who primarily experience religious, linguistic, or ethnic discrimination. It is these social variables that become part of their intersectional "triad." Stasiulis concludes the chapter by warning that religious/ethnic/national issues for women may be prone to a form of cultural essentialism that does not recognize variation between and among ethnic groups. Stasiulis argues against this process, suggesting that boundaries between ethnic and cultural groups are dynamic rather than static. Moreover, women's roles in negotiating their identities and altering their social and material conditions should be recognized by the social actors themselves and by the scholars who study them.

Reference

Driedger, L. 2001. "Changing Visions in Ethnic Relations." *Canadian Journal of Sociology* 26, 3: 421–51.

The Intersections of Race, Class, and Gender in the Anti-Racism Discourse

.... *George Sefa Dei*

The anti-racist discursive framework articulates that the study of racism must pay particular attention to the experiences and knowledge of the oppressed while simultaneously examining the benefits and privileges that accrue to the dominant from their oppression. Anti-racism works with the understanding that the self and subjectivity matter in terms of the ways knowledge is produced and disseminated locally and internationally. Anti-racism also emphasizes that bodies and identities (race, class, gender, sexuality, [dis] ability, etc.) are linked in the production of knowledge and, specifically, interpretations of experience. Consequently, the learner cannot distance herself/himself from a study of racism and social oppressions. The anti-racist discourse offers ways to understand the processes of racializing subjects through history and social systems. It is argued that racial dominance is an integral part of social inequity, and that there is the salience of the white body/racial identity in a white supremacist society. In discussing racism and oppressions, the anti-racist approach engages an understanding of the asymmetrical power relations that exist among us. As noted elsewhere (Dei 1994), the politics of anti-racism requires that race be kept in the foreground in the axis of oppression. The contemporary challenge as we seek to uncover and address oppressions is how we can theorize and engage the politics of social movements broadly and yet keep certain goals at the centre.

The engagement of the multiple sites of oppression (race, gender, class, disability, sexuality, etc.) in anti-racist work is critical given that oppressions are relational and intersecting. Thus we cannot deal with one oppression and leave others in intact. To say oppressions are relational is to argue oppressions are not parallel. Similarly, oppressions are multiplicative (not additive). Oppressions are interactive (not dual/double). Oppressions are intersecting (not oppositional). Oppressions are embedded (not dichotomous). Oppressions are enmeshed (not isolated). Oppressions are polyvocal (not univocal). Oppressions are best understood as "and/ with," not through an "either/or" approach. Lived experience is a starting point to understanding oppressions. An emphasis on history and context is key. But it is important always to link the understanding of social oppressions to institutions and to the working of the local and global political economies. All discursive analysis of oppression maintain blind spots. But not to recognize and acknowledge such shortcomings is to continue to reproduce hegemonic knowledge. For the anti-racist worker, the challenge is to always maintain a critical gaze on the oppressions within oneself first. It is equally important that as we engage the multiple sites of oppression, we also recognize the saliency and severity of issues for certain bodies. In effect, while acknowledging the myriad forms of racism, the saliency of skin colour (anti-black racism) in a racialized society cannot be denied. But race and racism as we know are not just about skin colour. Racism can be effected along lines of class, gender, sexuality, disability, religion, and sexuality. So how do we proceed in such analysis?

In this chapter I develop a case for why the analysis of race and racism cannot stand alone in the intellectual and political pursuit of an educational transformation that undermines social oppression. King (1994) asserts the need for a new theoretical synthesis to rewrite knowledge in the academy. This is in part because of the incapacity of existing theory to provide a more complete account of human and social development. Legitimate concerns are being raised, particularly by marginalized and minority groups in society, about how conventional discourses do not adequately inform knowledge producers and consumers about the totality of human experiences. We need to reject "essences/totalizing discourses" (King 1994), and work to articulate comprehensive forms of knowledge that reveal an understanding of how our multiple identities and subject positions affect our very existence. Russo (1991) quotes Evelyn Glenn in a poignant remark that our individualities, "histories and experiences are not just diverse, they are intertwined and interdependent."

The understanding of gender identities is critical for anti-racist work. For the anti-racist worker a key question is: how is race lived through the lens of gender (and by extension social class, disability, sexuality, etc.)? The significance of gender for anti-racism work is that gender is a form of identity and a basis of knowledge production. Gender is a fundamental principle of social organization and identity formation in societies. Gender is also about embodiment and how bodies are read. Gender is a basis of political mobilization. The entanglements of gender and power demand that we do not decouple gender and race in anti-racist work. In other words, we must recognize gender as a social relation of power and privilege that shapes, structures, and is informed by culture, experience, and history. The social categories of gender, class, race, disability, etc. are not mutually exclusive categories. For example, one's blackness cannot erase one's femaleness or (dis)ability. Race does not exist outside of gender, sexuality, class, or vice versa. There are gender differences around how race and racism are experienced. There is a specificity to black women's experiences. Bodies matter and body image and representation are key sites of anti-racism investigation.

Like gender, race also intersects with sexuality. One should exercise some caution not to phrase the challenges oppressed peoples face as "problems" as stemming from our "cultural/sexual/class/linguistic differences." Many times these challenges stem from the power of "common sense"/"hegemonic

thinking," which are presented as rigid orthodoxies/ideologies. There are sexual differences around how race and racism are experienced. Bodies matter and body image and representation are key sites of anti-racism investigation. Sexuality is about the state of being, the manner or characteristic of "sexual"; it is about the constitution of sexual orientation. We must understand the extent to which the violence of history has shaped fears and anxieties about sexuality.

For example, in examining black and Asian femininity, we see how problematically notions of sexual promiscuity and fantasies idealize discourses (e.g., Jezebel/Hottentot). Sexuality is also context- and culture-bound, meaning we must be careful that we do not assume the markers of Western sexuality for all peoples. But this is not to say sexuality has no place in anti-racist analysis. As a constitutive part of our identities, sexuality is socially constructed, politically constitutive, and relational. Sexuality is significant for anti-racist work because it is an expression of self, feelings, body, and image. Sexuality also helps in destabilizing notions of the essential subject. There is the question of political disaggregation of identities—blackness/whiteness/indigenity—as such notions are marked and demarcated by sexuality and sexual politics. There is a political project of decolonization around how we come to engage sexuality in anti-racist work for transformation. I am referring here to an earlier observation and acknowledgement of the ways the gay and lesbian space and presence (along with black feminisms) has altered "the public face of Black politics" (Mercer 1996, 128). In such work we see a linking of sexual politics and black liberation. Educational studies have revealed the complex ways homophobia and misogyny are linked in everyday schooling interactions (see Archer 2001). Anti-racist discourse and practice calls us to challenge the racist construction of blacks' bodies as "somehow intrinsically more homophobic by virtue of being supposedly closer to nature and hence less civilized" (Mercer 1996, 121).

Increasingly, critical anti-racist work is broaching the intersections of race and masculinity in terms of the ways notions of manhood are racialized (see Archer 2001; Archer and Yamashita 2003). Seeing schools as masculinizing agencies is to explore the ways school policies and practices (curriculum, pedagogy, and instruction) reinforce certain notions of what it means to be a man. There are also hierarchies of masculinity in school and society, and anti-racist focus is to examine which forms of masculinity are granted the most power and privilege, and on what basis, and using who or what as a reference point. Anti-racist research is also exploring whether or not there is a connection between masculinity and school-based violence (McCready 2008, personal communication).

In anti-racist work we must also ask new questions about the ways all differences that are equally salient are constructed. For example, what are the identifications of "disability" that can be employed in critical anti-racist studies? Disability is gendered, raced, classed, sexualized. Disability can be understood through lenses of religion, language, age, ethnicity, etc. Disability is also about the use of language and what is intended to be conveyed. As Titchkosky (2007) asks, what do terms like the "vulnerable," "weak," "special needs," "elderly and infirm" come to signify in everyday discourse? Is the disability the "Other" to "normalcy"? Are some differences constructed as if they are "natural"? What is concealed in such undertakings? Disability is also about inclusion/exclusion in schooling and the questions of power, knowledge, and making of the normality lodged differently for groups (see Ferri and Connor 2005). Disability categories are thus key ways racism is practised and how critical anti-racism can be pursued. Schools are about exclusion/inclusion and how and what we (as educators) choose to notice and not to notice. In other words, again as Titchkosky (2007) argues, "disability is used as a metaphor of choice to discuss problems," and also a metaphor that "disappears from the social landscape as a form of human existence" (137). Given that disability discourses implicate the processes of schooling,

we need to bring a critical integrative lens to the pursuit of anti-racism. For example, "special education" classes are filled with racialized students as are all other institutions of social control under the name of "disability," especially under "crazy" and mentally impaired (see also Ferri and Connor 2005). Disability categories help us to explain racist ideologies. For example, "disability" is a way to "naturalize" some humans as not-quite-human. Consequently, disability and anti-racism must be approached through intersectional analysis.

The Notion of "Integrative Anti-Racism"

I am introducing the notion of **integrative anti-racism studies** to address the problem of discussing the social constructs of race, class, gender, and sexuality as exclusive and independent categories. Elsewhere (Dei 1994), I have defined integrative anti-racism as the study of how the dynamics of social difference (race, class, gender, sexual orientation, physical ability, language, and religion) are mediated in people's daily experiences. Integrative anti-racism is also an activist theory and analysis that must always be consciously linked to struggles against oppression. Integrative anti-racism acknowledges our multiple, shifting, and often contradictory identities and subject positions. Borrowing from critical **postmodernism** and anti-colonial thought, integrative anti-racism rejects metanarratives or grand theories. Integrative anti-racism, in effect, calls for multiplicative, rather than additive, analyses of social oppression. It is conceded that an additive analysis denies the complexity of experiences that can, and must, be examined, explained, and addressed.

Integrative anti-racism provides an understanding of how different forms of social oppression and privilege have been historically constituted. It identifies how forms of social marginality and structured dominance intersect and shift with changing conditions in society. Since one of the key objectives of the transformative project of anti-racism is to critique and deal with human injustice, all the different forms of oppression, defined along racial, ethnic, class, (dis)ability, and sexual lines, must be problematized. We cannot hope to transform society by removing only one form of oppression. There is a common link between all oppressions in the material production of society; all forms of oppression establish material and symbolic advantages for the oppressor. Any resistance to bringing the diverse and varied forms of social oppression into the anti-racism debate should be exposed both for its myopic focus and its capacity to politically paralyze social movement building. It is also destructive to fight against one form of oppression while using patterns of another to do so. An example would be a white male adult using the strap on a white child to teach the child not to be racist against a black child. This tactic may punish racist behaviour, but it leaves physical violence as a method of controlling others and adult authority over children solidly in place.

An understanding of how race, class, gender, (dis)ability, and sexuality are interconnected in our lives will work against the construction of hierarchies of social oppression. Such hierarchies can take the form of a naive relativism and divide and fragment a movement. Racism, sexism, heterosexism, and classism function in myriad forms. Integrative anti-racism therefore seeks a non-hierarchical discussion of social oppressions without assuming that all forms of oppression are unified, consistent, and necessarily equal in their social effects. This understanding follows from a recognition of the theoretical inadequacy of singular, exclusive constructs when it comes to explaining the diversity of human experiences of oppression. There is also an awareness of the need to reject "dichotomous logic ... [that] oversimplifies and limits the scope of analysis" (Sullivan 1995; see also Stasiulis 1990; Brewer 1993; Grewal and Kaplan 1994; Dua 2007; Lawson 2008; Hall 2002; Archer and Yamashita 2003; Fenelon and Brod 2000; Rothenberg 2007). These critiques arise out of an analytical context in which the complexity of peoples' historical and daily experiences are continuously distorted. For example,

too often intellectual discourses conflate race with black(ness) and gender with women (Carby 1982). At times too, the "conflation of race and class has been found to engender anti-Semitism by obscuring the range of class positions occupied by Jews in North America" (Sullivan 1995; see Nestel 1993).

Brewer (1993) critiques dichotomous/binary oppositional modes of thought, which employ *either/or* categorizations rather than *both/and* perspectives when theorizing the simultaneity, embeddedness, and connectedness of myriad oppressions. An integrative anti-racism approach is based on the principle that myriad forms of oppressions are interlocked and that a study of one such system, racism, necessarily entails a study of class, gender, sexual inequalities, homophobia, and ableism (see Mercer and Julien 1988). The complex nature of oppressions, and the interchangeability of the roles of "oppressor" and "oppressed" in different situations, necessitate the use of an integrative anti-racism approach to understanding social oppression. This approach is informed by the knowledge that individual subjectivities are constituted differently by the relations of race, class, gender, age, disability, sexuality, nationality, religion, language, and culture.

The following discussion of integrative anti-racism primarily (but not exclusively) focuses on the three basic categories/constructs of race, class, and gender. Belkhir and Ball (1993) make the interesting argument that, while "religion, sexual or political preference, [and] physical ability" are important issues affecting the human experience and condition, they are often the result of the primary ascribed statuses of race, class, and gender. They add that the complex mixture of these social constructs "above all else influences our socialization, emotions, thought process, ideology, self-concept, and our social identity." The authors further point out that "issues like religion, sexual or political preference, and physical ability may certainly be examined more thoroughly through the interactive and triadic relation of race, [gender], and class" (1993). But I would argue that sexual orientation, ability, and religion can play primary roles in a person's lived experiences, particularly given the prevalence of heterosexism, homophobia, and anti-Semitism which are particularly significant in, but not exclusive to, Euro-Western influenced societies (see also Fanon 1967). In fact, the matrix of oppression must simultaneously engage all oppressions. And a strategic decision to highlight a particular oppression (even as we understand the intersections with other oppressions) is itself an acknowledgement that we all continually maintain blind spots in our intersectional analysis.

The study of integrative anti-racism raises some important questions about social inequality: How are class divisions maintained and produced in the face of emerging and complex social identities? What qualifies as "difference" among the factors that shape and define human relations in racialized, classed, sexualized, and gendered contexts? How will a conception of interlocking systems of oppression that reinforce each other and have multiple effects on individuals avoid points of conflict? How can we prevent differences from becoming sites of competition for the primacy of one subordination or oppression over another? How do we challenge discursively imposed social identities? Perhaps most of these questions will only be answered in the actual process of doing educational and political work.

In order to respond effectively to some of these questions, it is important that we view integrative anti-racism as a critical study of the social and material relations of the production of social oppressions. We must understand the material conditions for the persistence and reproduction of racism, sexism, classism, homophobia, ableism, and other forms of social oppression. The political and academic goal of integrative anti-racism is to address all oppressive relations constructed along lines of difference. An integrative approach to understanding social oppressions must thus examine closely the *politics of difference*, recognizing the materiality of human existence, that is, the material consequences of myriad social identities and subjectivities. The roots of social oppression lie in

material conditions and the access to property, privilege, and power (see Joyce 1995; Ng, Staton, and Scane 1995; Rothenberg 2007; Dua 2007; Hall 2002; Archer and Yamashita 2003; Fenelon and Brod 2000). All social relations are firmly embedded in material relations. All social relations have material consequences. The politics of integrative anti-racism arise from the collective position of material disadvantage that many people find themselves locked into, and the desire to work for a just redistribution of material means.

Notwithstanding the possible tensions between bland talk about diversity and the real question of power asymmetries around the notion of difference, it is important that the social categories of race, class, gender, sexuality, and (dis)ability are not seen as competing for primacy. There is a natural contestation that must be accepted and struggled with and against if the fight against oppression is to be successful. The study of race, class, gender, (dis)ability, and sexuality in critical anti-racism work should be pursued as an integrated approach to understanding the lived (social and material) realities of people. A foregrounding of race in the integrative anti-racism approach should not mean the exclusion of class, gender, and sexual orientation. Integrative anti-racism has to address the intersectionality of class, gender, and sexual orientation (sexuality). Classism, sexism, and homophobia do not disappear because race has become the central focus. The lived experience of those who face racism daily from others is one where they must also face inter/intra-racial classism, sexism, and homophobia. I have more to say about this later in this chapter.

How do the complex politics of social difference articulate with material-economic interests? Rizvi (1995) rightly calls on educators to avoid a celebratory approach to social difference which may only serve the hegemonic interests of industrial capital. For example, the state's approach to multiculturalism adopts a superficial definition and treatment of culture, as reflected in the celebratory practices of the "saris, samosas, and steelbands syndrome" (Donald and Rattansi 1992).

Events like international cultural days can constitute opportune times for big business to make huge profits without any fundamental challenge to power relations in society. For example, the initial movement to bring multiculturalism into the classroom did not address the lived experiences of peoples of colour; rather, such a move focused on the more simplistic "getting to know you" move of consuming and observing "ethnic foods," dancing, and dress. As we examine how difference is perceived in society, Rizvi (1995) suggests certain fundamental questions should be asked. For example, why the focus on difference? In whose interests is difference being presented and for what material purposes and consequences? We might also ask about the timing and sequencing of the uses and constructions of social difference. What qualifies as difference? No doubt there are some powerful academic and political forces more than ready to co-opt the language of difference and diversity to serve their own material needs and concerns.

bell hooks cautions against constructing a politics of difference in the academy to serve the intellectual interests of an emerging postmodern discourse. She argues that postmodern theory should not simply appropriate the experience of otherness to enhance the intellectual discourse of postmodernity. Postmodern theory should not separate the "politics of difference from the politics of racism" (hooks 1990). Integrative anti-racism must be critical of how current articulations of multiple identities are/can be manipulated in the space of dominant, hegemonic discourses, particularly in academia (see Carty 1991a; Bannerji 1991a).

An integrative approach to anti-racism must examine conventional understandings of the politics of identity. Hall offers one such critique when he references Marxian theory on identity; he talks about the fact that there are always "conditions to identity which the subject cannot construct" (1979; see also Hall 1991). Bhabha also writes about the fact that "the visibility of the racial/cultural 'other' is at once a point of identity" (1994). Hall and Bhabha make different but connected

points. On the one hand, identity construction is a point of power and, therefore, difference. To claim difference is to have the power to claim one's difference as identity. On the other hand, as Hall points out, one is never entirely in control of the mechanisms of identity construction, like language, for example. However, one is not entirely controlled by the identity construction of others either. Bhabha is suggesting that the identification of others is also the moment of self-identification. Identities are not static; we are forever negotiating who and what we are. Social identities are constructed beyond notions of race, class, gender, sexuality, language, and culture to the actual practices engaged in by people in the course of daily social interactions. It is crucial to a progressive politics of identity to understand that identity is not entirely dependent on categories of difference because social practice transgresses these boundaries all the time. We are not entirely constrained by the categories of race, class, and gender. They are coercive and resilient structures in our lives, but they do not define the limits of social action. Our identities, then, are made in social interaction in concert with and using categories of difference and identity. In order to effectively organize for political change, we first have to recognize and understand that identity is defined by who the individual is, how the individual self is understood in relation to others, and how such constructions of social identities match or do not match what people actually do in their daily lives.

Of equal importance, a politics of identity involves politicizing identity. It moves beyond the mere recognition and acknowledgement of identities to engage in effective political action. Identity must provide the basis for political struggle, but as others have pointed out, identity itself is not political action (Bourne 1987; Train 1995). While not dismissive of the utility of its strategic politics, the conventional "identity politics" prioritized an essentialized, ahistorical, and non-materialist identity. Train (1995) argues that "identity politics" eliminated the political by focusing too much on the personal. It is important for a distinction to be made between "who am I?" and "what is to be done?" (Bourne 1987). These two questions are connected. One needs to know the self in order to engage in political action. But change cannot happen simply from knowing oneself. We have to find answers to the questions, "what is to be done and how?"

Thus, in a sense, the importance of adopting an integrative approach to anti-racism studies is captured in the intersections between issues of identity and social practices. The study of the concept of race is a study of representation as defined by identity, identification, and social practices. Racism, as a set of material practices, is about unequal power relations. It is also about how people relate to each other on the basis of defined social identities and identifications. These reasonings implicate how we organize politically for change; they move us beyond questions about *who we are* to discussions about *what we do*. We must search for connections between identity and social practices (see Britzman 1993). Our everyday local social networks are increasingly structuring and governing our daily experiences.

Below I will explore this topic further in the context of six interrelated key issues underlying integrative anti-racism studies. The *first* is an understanding of *the process of articulation* of social difference. Integrative anti-racism speaks to the need to examine the social categories of difference in order to understand their points of "articulation" and connection with each other. The articulations of race, class, gender, (dis)ability, and sexuality produce sites of complex human social differences, rather than sites and sources of a celebratory approach to diversity. They are "rupturing these social categories"; thus, we need to recognize, understand, and engage our multiple subject positions and to work for alternative futures. Feminist writers such as Carby (1982), Mohanty (1990), Collins (1990), hooks (1990), Carty (1991a, 1991b), Bannerji (1991a, 1991b), Mullings (1992), and Rothenberg (2007), among many others, have articulated varying ideas about multiple subjectivities to illustrate the intersections of oppressions in the everyday experiences of so-called women of colour.

Many, if not all, of these authors speak from their embodied selves while making the connections between their individual and collective identities and their own experiences.

Integrative anti-racism is a critical analysis of how current understandings of the dynamics of social difference relate to issues of identity and subjectivity. It moves away from establishing a hierarchy of difference and an exclusive and problematic concern with the "other." Integrative anti-racism does not see the *self* as that which *other* is not. Human experiences are dialectically shaped by questions of social difference, by history, and by socio-political contexts. The existence of multiple identities has some significance for how individuals live their lives and relate to each other in society, and how individuals come to understand society and work collectively for change.

Belkhir and Ball (1993), in their interesting discussion of the dynamics of social difference, point out the complex mixture of race, class, and gender, and how these categories influence everything we do as humans. Our social world is structured by power relations of race, ethnicity, class, gender, and sexuality (see also Collins 1993; Roscigno 1994). Individuals do not simply and solely fit into one specified category as an oppressor or the oppressed. One can be oppressed and an oppressor at the same time and at different times.

For example, as an anti-racist educator, I must acknowledge my own privileged middle-class background when speaking to students about oppression. There is the question of the relational aspect of oppression, there is the "nonsynchrony of oppression" (McCarthy 1988), and there is the problematic of a discourse of "humanization as a universal without considering the various definitions this term may [acquire]" from individuals of different positionalities and from diverse social groups (Weiler 1991). I have to be aware of how my views as I present them in the classroom, by way of instruction or through interaction with students, could be maintaining social privilege and power. My power as a black, middle-class, heterosexual male teacher may often work to make me forget that, while I am debating and struggling against race oppression, I might be marginalizing women and other peoples oppressed by reason of, for example, their class or sexuality. Such understandings are fundamental to any attempt to theorize the connections between social differences and oppression in the integrative anti-racism discourse.

Each individual goes through a variety of experiences in a lifetime, and theoretical articulations of social reality have to reflect the intersections of such various experiences. For example, when a Southeast Asian male executive living in Canada loses his job and eventually goes on welfare, his lifetime experiences, relating to all his subject positions, come into play. We cannot essentialize race, class, and gender categories. These are socially constructed categories whose social meanings and actualities in the daily experiences of peoples not only overlap but also shift in time and space. We need to understand the systemic and structural character of these social categories and how they function as social ideologies (see King 1994).

Fumia (1995) brings an interesting perspective to discussions of articulations of identities and political action, stressing the importance of knowing our multiple subject positions and the frustrations associated with this practice. In identifying herself as a "middle-class white female," she talks about her frustrations with the term. She asks: "How do those words locate anyone? Middle-class white female conflates differences in economics, subjectivities, and colours. Yet, because my life intersects with enough of the stereotypical aspects of the category, how do I position myself elsewhere?" (1995). For me, Fumia's question is important as it draws attention to the difficulty of placing individuals into neatly conceptualized boxes that will allegedly capture the complexity of their identities and experiences. If this is a difficult project for individuals, how can we then engage in academic discussions as if everything about our world is so neatly packaged and stationary?

It is thus important for an integrative approach to social oppression to disaggregate social categories such as race, class, gender, (dis)ability, and sexuality along multiple dimensions to see, for example, how race articulates with other forms of oppression. Joyce (1995) posits that, as a white person, she has unearned privileges and material advantages because of the physical characteristics that Euro-Canadian/American society deems as "racially white and of highest value." But she argues that the material consequences of being a woman is the absence of power and a lack of resources that one collectively shares with other women. Women, she points out, experience a "relative position of structurally and materially less power and privilege" than men in a particularly sexist, patriarchal society (ibid.). However, to be a woman of racial minority background is to have even relatively less material power and privilege in a patriarchal, white-dominated society. But even among women of racial minority backgrounds, class differences can be apparent. For example, there are differences in terms of those occupying relative positions of wealth and influence (e.g., a bank executive or university professor) and those who are employed in jobs with lower status and are paid barely enough to support the household they head.

The significance of adopting an integrative perspective of anti-racism is illustrated by the unique oppressions that black working-class women, for example, experience in Euro-Canadian/American societies. Black feminist scholars (hooks 1988, 1992; King 1988; Collins 1990; Dill and Zinn 1990; Carty 1991a, 1991b; Zinn 1991; Wane, Deliovsky, and Lawson 2002; McClaurin 2001; Brand 1991; Massaquoi and Wane 2007) have argued that the unique oppression experienced by black women has to be understood in the context of how the dialectical relationships of race, class, and gender are played out in women's daily lives. The social construction of a black, working-class mother's position in North American society has been one of the ways for mainstream society to maintain hegemony over production relations within the white hetero-patriarchal, capitalist system (Carty 1991a, 20). Black, working-class women have historically and contemporarily been constructed as a source of labour for the state. The historical role and position of black "immigrant" nurses in the reproduction of economic wealth for the Canadian state is a well-documented example that race cannot be understood outside of gender and class constructions (Calliste 1991, 1993a, 1993b, 1994).

As Zinn (1991) has shown, it is not simply that gender cannot be understood outside of race and class. Gender is experienced differently within each racial framework and class group. Subordinate racial groups of all classes are subject to racial oppression and, while members of dominant racial groups may be oppressed by means of gender oppression, their membership in a racial group is not a source of oppression. Furthermore, class and gender differences in society are complicated by the harsh realities of intra-group oppression among members of the same socially constructed racial framework.[1] The exploitative working conditions of many "immigrant women" working in the homes of middle-class families in Canada are a well-documented case. The task of integrative anti-racism is to unravel these interlocking systems of oppression in order to be able to intellectually articulate and engage in meaningful and progressive political action to address social injustice and oppression.

The *second* and related issue of interest in integrative anti-racism studies is the relevance of *personal experiential knowledge* and the specific ways our multiple subject positions and identities affect our ways of creating knowledge. Knowledge is produced out of a series of socio-political arrangements, such as the particular intersections of social oppressions. Lived, personal experience is central to the formulation of any social knowledge. Matsuda (1989) discusses the importance and relevance of seeing the world as experienced by the oppressed if we are to achieve effective political action and change. However, as Burbules and Rice (1991) caution, we must guard against an over-valorization of personal experiential knowledge in which "external" forces mediating and/or impinging upon such knowledge are considered "coercive and imperialistic." We must also resist

the temptation of presenting ourselves as not-to-be-questioned voices of authority merely because we are speaking from experience.

Sullivan points out that an integrative theory of anti-racism "draws on the actual lived experiences of individuals as a basis for intellectual inquiry" (1995) and engagement in politics of change. The work of feminist scholars Weiler (1991), Russo (1991), and Collins (1990) shows that the personal experiences and a self-reflective critique of the experiential reality are important bases from which to pursue integrative anti-racism work. Weiler speaks about the different kinds of knowledge that can be uncovered when women question their daily experiences and their collective experiences with regard to the interlocking systems of oppression. She makes reference to the everyday experiences of so-called women of colour and of lesbian women "whose very being challenges existing racial, sexual, heterosexual, and class dominance [and] ... leads to a knowledge of the world that both acknowledges differences, and points to the need for an integrated analysis and practice" in relation to the interlocking systems of oppression (Weiler 1991; see Combahee River Collective 1981).

Collins (1990) and Russo (1991) also argue that experience and practice are the contextual bases of integrative anti-racism knowledge; they link this practice and experience to theory. Both authors call for a self-reflective critique and validation of personal experiences of the relational aspects of difference as part of the process of creating theoretical and practical knowledge for social transformation. Individuals must be able to articulate and critically reflect upon their own experiences and their accumulated personal knowledge about the workings of the inner self and questions of identity, in order to work collectively for change (see also hooks 1993, 1994).

The *third* issue concerns developing an understanding of how *differential power and privilege* work in society. The study of the dynamics of social difference is also a study of differential power relations. Power relations are embedded in social relations of difference. Thus, an understanding of the intersections of difference is more than a preparedness to hear each other out. It involves more than providing the means and opportunities for subordinated groups to empower themselves and find creative solutions to their own concerns. It is about ensuring that all social groups have decision-making power; safety provisions; and equitable access to, and control over, the valued goods and services of society with which to attain human dignity and individual and collective survival.

Therefore, an integrative approach to anti-racism studies explores the use of power to differentiate, discriminate, and establish material advantage and disadvantage among and between peoples and groups. Social power and economic advantage are intertwined. Understanding the relational aspects of social difference means delving into the critique of micro and macro structures of power, and how these structures mediate people's daily experiences. It draws attention to the larger socio-political contexts in which the fragmented categories of race, class, gender, and sexuality intersect in daily social practices. Attention is paid to the material needs of individuals and groups in society and how these needs are sanctioned and stratified through social relations of domination and subordination. For example, it is about understanding how the hegemony of the market economy affects the schooling experiences of minority youth. How this is manifested in schools can be attested to in the differential positions that students occupy according to their race, ethnicity, class, gender, and sexual orientation. Many studies demonstrate a clearly disproportionate representation of African-Canadian/American students from working-class backgrounds in vocational courses rather than in the "academic" courses which lead students into universities (Oakes 1985; see also Fine 1991).

Integrative anti-racism examines the power of subordinated groups to resist positions of marginality through individual agency and collective will. It interrogates how groups positioned differently in society can nevertheless come together on the basis of a common abhorrence of social oppression and fight the prevailing culture of dominance. While recognizing the power of human agency, an integrative anti-racism approach also locates significant responsibility for change in the arena of those who control the structural means to effecting fundamental change in society, that is, those who control the apparatus of the state. This is an example of where the intersections of social class become important. Social power is generally in the hands of the ruling class, which comprises mostly white heterosexual males. It is thus difficult to speak about power and not highlight class. The bourgeoisie will not give up power easily since it will not be in their interest to do so. This means it will take the collective effort of the relatively powerless groups to work and bring this change about.

The *fourth* issue of concern relates to the *saliency of race* in an integrative anti-racism discourse. In recognizing the centrality of race and its "immediacy in everyday experience" (Omi and Winant 1994), integrative anti-racism also acknowledges the co-determinant status of race, class, and gender dynamics. Integrative anti-racism is based on the understanding that race relations in society are actually interactions between raced, classed, and gendered subjects. Thus, in theorizing integrative anti-racism, race becomes the main point of entry through which the varied forms of social oppression can and must be understood.

While it is true that we live in a society structured by relations of race, ethnicity, class, gender, sexuality, and ability, among others, we nevertheless make political choices every moment and every day of our lives. Giving saliency and centrality to race and racial oppression in a critical anti-racism educational practice should not be seen as an attempt to hierarchize and/or privilege one form of social oppression over another. It is *a political decision*. Admittedly, selecting one form of human experience as a point of entry may render another experience invisible. Yet, we cannot adequately simultaneously explore all experiences with the same vigour and intensity. Therefore, we should attempt to capture, as much as possible, from the points where they intersect with one particular form of social oppression the diversity and multiplicity of human experiences. Racism should neither be subsumed nor separated from all forms of oppression. Bannerji's (1993) work is exemplary in this regard when she discusses racist sexism and sexist racism. The fight for equity should not be seen as a zero sum game that pits blacks against whites, women against men, heterosexuals against homosexuals, Christians against non-Christians, Canadian immigrants against First Nations peoples.

But, as we recognize the matrix of domination and subordination, and conceptualize racism, sexism, and classism as interactive, interlocking, and mutually reinforcing systems of oppression, we must also validate the saliency and visibility of certain forms of oppression (see Collins 1993). For how can we understand and transform social reality without recognizing or acknowledging that certain forms/systems of domination and oppression are more salient and visible than others for different groups in different contexts? How do we explain the situational and contextual variations and intensities of different forms of oppression? For example, how do we account for the fact that a single, black, middle-class woman is kept out of a white neighbourhood when trying to rent or buy a house because of her race and gender? Are we not trivializing social oppression by claiming that we are all oppressors and oppressed?

The answer to this last question is complex and deserves further comment. As Bunch (1987) has pointed out, when individuals identify themselves according to their victimization as a member of an oppressed group, there is less ability for them to see their own agency and power to effect change. Others may also begin to identify themselves as "victims of oppression" and fail to see the severity of other forms of oppression because they are so narrowly focused on their own victimization. This is problematic, particularly when that form of oppression may not have a material basis but is experienced more as a hurtful, restrictive practice. For example, black students can use discriminatory words or engage in discriminatory actions (such as telling white students that they cannot join in a basketball game because they cannot slam-dunk), which may not have material consequences for white students. My point is that black racism does not deny material wealth to whites.

Nevertheless, the concept of oppression may be helpful for those who are highly privileged in society and are just beginning to learn what social oppression really is. It helps these individuals to place their own grounded experiences of oppression, no matter how comparatively trivial in relation to more widespread and sustained forms of oppression that marginalized groups regularly experience, in a webbed system of domination/subjugation. To find one's place in the web, these individuals must begin to see the whole web and how various oppressions are played off each other horizontally to keep the systems of oppression in place. It is thus a useful beginning to allow each individual to talk about his or her own oppressions. It provides an opportunity to make that first crucial step, which is to enter into the discussion about oppression. Issues about the location of multiple identities, and analysis of the implications, intersections, and variable degrees of material consequences of different oppressions can be pursued once the concept of oppression is connected to one's personal experience and that experience is located in the total web of systemic oppressions.

Historically, in movements for social change, race concerns have always been pushed to the background or denied. So the decision to recognize the saliency and centrality of race is, in part, taken to ensure that race as an issue in the struggle for change is not lost. Similarly, in a hetero-patriarchal capitalist society, gender, sexuality, and class issues are conveniently denied. But there have been, and continue to be, insidious attempts to misplace race and racism from social critique and political agenda for change. An example of this is the constant questioning of "what does race mean?" or the declaration that "racism does not exist" or "we are all one race." Integrative anti-racism will thus have to contend with the ways that all of us are burdened with this history of racism as a social, material, and political practice, as well as the ways we come to know, understand, and interpret racism. Racism and its varied manifestations have to be front and centre in the anti-racism discourse. For anti-racism work to be truly "anti-racist," it must evoke its conceptual grounding: that is, claim the centrality of race; the relative saliencies of different identities; the situational and contextual variations in intensities of oppression; the severity of issues for different bodies; and the idea that at any given moment, oppressions may not be equal in their consequences. Are there different articulations of racisms within social class, sexuality, and gender categories? (See Anthias and Yuval-Davis 1992.) In coming to understand the dynamics of social difference, individuals can and will articulate similar ideas differently given their social realities. This requires that, to avoid negating or denying certain aspects of our experiences, we are able to discuss these experiences, showing their intersections with our multiple subjectivities.

A conceptual and analytical distinction must be made between anti-oppression and anti-racism studies. While there are broad similarities and points of connection between "*integrative anti-racism*" and "*anti-oppression*" studies, there are important distinctions between the two. The integrative anti-racism approach sees race as both the first point of entry and a point which does not lose its position of centrality during subsequent analyses of intersecting oppression. Joyce (1995) argues that "anti-oppression education does not presume a single central point of entry nor a central point of analysis . . . It presumes multiple positions of identity by which an individual enters the discourse on social oppression [and] . . . some of those identities are individually experienced as central, and some are marginal" (1995). As individuals, we possess diverse identities that variously describe who and what we are, and what we politically and consciously choose as our points of entry into discussions about oppression. In anti-oppression studies, race is one of many entry points. But it is important we also recognize that "some forms of oppression have a

particularly substantial material base" when compared to others (ibid.). For example, the impact of institutionalized racism on the job opportunities and wages of marginalized racial groups has a material impact that is different from the impact of racist language. In deciding on our entry points, we must make explicit our subject locations and the relative power, privileges, and disadvantages, as well as the experiential knowledge and the political assumptions that we bring to the discussion. What is important in this discussion is the convergence and alliance between integrative anti-racism and anti-oppression studies. We must speak of and act on the alliances in these struggles if successful change is to happen.

Social oppression is a topic that elicits pain, anger, shame, guilt, fear, and uneasiness in people. People are likely to engage the subject from diverse vantage points. For me, the experience of racism, while not diminishing its connections with other forms of oppression, runs deep. I know more about racism, perhaps, than I do about other forms of oppression, not simply because I have chosen to take the time to learn about racism, but more so because it has been a very significant part of my experience, particularly in North America (see also hooks 1984). There is a prior personal and collective history that cannot be ignored. We have to deal with the historical fact that, in past academic discussions about myriad oppressions and other "isms," the topic of racism has often been pushed to the background or omitted altogether. This is what informs Enid Lee when she strongly recommends that we put "racism at the foreground, and then include the others by example and analysis" (Rethinking Schools 1991) to illustrate the powerful connections to other forms of oppression.

The foregoing discussion also indicates that while educators stress integrative and relational aspects of difference (race, class, gender, [dis] ability, and sexuality), they must be critical of postmodern discourse that will deny the saliency of racial oppression in the anti-racism political project. Racism is what most educators and many other people are either afraid to talk about or continually and conveniently choose to ignore. While the integrative anti-racism strategy is to ensure that race is not given an exclusive pre-eminence, it must also avoid a "political paralysis" (Roman 1993) in the struggle for change. As educators, we can make pragmatic choices as to how to take up and centre race analysis for political education and for educational advocacy. It should also be possible for educators and members of society to engage in a theoretical discussion of race issues that speak foremost and most appropriately to social reality and economic materiality.

The *fifth* concern involves extending discussions about integrative anti-racism to include *global political economic* issues. Central to this is building an understanding of how current processes of **globalization** relate to questions of identity and social practice in Euro-Canadian/American contexts. My objective is not to re-engage in any detail the classical debates about whether or not race, gender, and sexuality can be understood in terms of the analytical approach of historical materialism, or whether race, gender, and sexuality must be accorded an analytical status separate and distinct from class (Marx 1853; Simmel 1950; Gabriel and Ben-Tovim 1979; see also Miles 1980). I am more interested in showing how global political economy issues (Stasiulis 1990; Satzewich 1990) relate to the integrative anti-racism dialogue and the political struggle for social change. A biological-genetic explanation of race (and gender) emerged prior to the institutionalization of capitalism and slavery. This fact neither denies the centrality of slavery in the development of capitalism, nor the significant role of capitalism in institutionalizing racism (see Cox 1948, 1976; Williams 1964).

We know that the concept of race has a global, modern, and world-historical dimension. So how do we concede to the reality of race today? Race as materially consequential signifies that even when it lacks a "scientific status" and/or analytical clarity, race "is all too real" in terms of its material, political, and social currencies. The reality of race recognizes that it acquires a relative autonomous status and has its own internal dynamics outside class, gender, sexuality, (dis)ability, etc. The theorization of race as a system of power and domination allows us to engage the ways Marxist and neo-Marxist (materialist) analyses present a global theory of oppression as an overarching historical perspective for understanding race and racism. Racism cannot solely be attributed to capital/economics. Racism cannot be seen simply as a function of capitalism. While race is powerfully lodged in class relations, we must ask questions about its genesis. Does the function of a phenomenon explain its origins? What about the evidence of pre-modern, pre-capitalist prejudices against people of colour, especially blacks? Or, what about the expressed trans-historical, trans-class, and trans-local European cultural, religious, and moral superiority (see also Fanon 1967)? Admittedly, the concept of historical materialism is key to understanding the relations of race, class, and capital. Securing material advantage has its **social dynamics** and politics. While there is a "materialism of the body" given the material conditions under which subjects reproduce themselves as constitutive bodies, the claim that the material is simply economics can be problematic and limiting. We must see the "material" in terms of a sociological and empirical understanding that can be other things as well as "material." No doubt, the notion of "race as consequential" is a materialist interpretation. Such understanding, however, helps move beyond the "material and physical" to the spiritual, ideological, and non-material. Similarly, exploitation in the case of race has other dimensions (spiritual, mental, psychological, etc.) besides the extraction of surplus value in the relations and mode of production (i.e., economistic reading).

Although race is not class, we cannot polarize these two terms nonetheless. White racial privilege is trans-class as much as trans-gender and trans-sexual. Similarly, language, religion, disability, culture, etc. can be racialized. As noted already, race is also contingent upon other identities—class, gender, sexuality, (dis)ability, language, religion, etc. Anti-racist analysis challenges the thesis that poverty is an independent variable. It critiques an understanding that poverty is a result of inherent characteristics of individuals and groups, such as bad genes or low I.Q. Poverty is not a result of low motivation and the lack of self-discipline, or due to poor work habits, self-indulgence, and a failure to pull oneself up by the bootstraps. Anti-racism challenges the individualization of poverty and instead focuses on how the organization of the economic and political systems cause poverty and socio-economic inequity in the first place. That is, anti-racism sees poverty as a by-product of changes in society (e.g., economic and political changes engendered by globalization/global capital). Poverty results from the imbalance/inequity in the influence different sectors, actors, groups, and communities have in society. Poverty is a consequence of the unequal distribution of social wealth and resource.

In linking race and class, anti-racism, therefore, focuses on the "making of the racialized poor"—the processes for the creation of high unemployment, the processes of legitimizing the underutilization and non-recognition of (foreign) credentials and skills, etc. An anti-racist analysis raises questions about local group access to education and the extent to which the craze to maintain "safe schools," through student expulsions and the exclusion of other bodies from educational environments through the high legal fees, work to create and cement a stratified society. The "prison industrial complex," where society builds prisons rather than schools to keep certain bodies in/out and the way society offers differential access to health care needs, requires that we bring a critical race-based analysis to the social organization of knowledge. Through a race-base prism we can understand the impact of official policies on racialized bodies (e.g., immigration and resettlement, education, human rights, national security, youth and criminal justice) and how racialized bodies and communities become cheap and vulnerable sources of labour. Today, particularly in North America, we are re-living the consequences of race-based policies through the impact of government decisions on the racialized poor (e.g., rising immigration fees and workplace closings);

the exploitation of the working poor from racialized communities to serve the needs of the labour market; as well as the sourcing of cheap labour, underpaid and without benefits (see also Colour of Justice Network 2008).

Neo-Marxist analysis of society may inform the progressive politics of integrative anti-racism change. All current forms of social oppressions are the products of a system of capitalist insurgence and domination. In fact, many scholars have pointed to the need for the critical analysis of race, class, and gender intersections to be placed in the context of global capitalism (see, for example, Bannerji 1991a; Carty 1993). Local problems of race, class, and gender relations have their global dimensions. It is for these reasons that a narrow conception of integrative anti-racism politics must be rejected. Ongoing processes of restructuring capital at global, regional, and national levels are having a deleterious impact on the ability of many individuals and groups to meet basic economic and material needs. A consequence of modern capital flows and exchanges, particularly the globalization of capital, is the growing **feminization** of poverty and the racialization of working-class politics. Working-class politics is now "race sensitive." Much work is currently being done to address racism within working-class groups, and some ruling groups are using race and racism as a way to divide working-class movements. There are mounting antagonisms and competitions between and among groups, communities, and nations over access to, and control over, drastically maldistributed economic and productive resources.

Undoubtedly, globalization, defined as a process of increased social, political, and economic international integration, driven primarily (but not exclusively) by the interests and dictates of modern industrial and transnational capital, has produced some challenges that need to be addressed by anti-racism education. Globalization is the new justification used by Euro-Canadian/American society for asserting its political and economic dominance over Indigenous and colonized peoples. Globalization has resulted in a crisis of knowledge about human society, a crisis manifested in the contradictions and tensions of a competitive knowledge economy, the internationalization of labour and the concomitant struggles over power-sharing among social groups. Globalization has also accelerated the flow of cultures across geographical, political, and cultural borders. Cultural borders can be marked by a language or concentrations of one racial or ethnic group within a diverse population, or by more malleable cultural forms like dress and music. Cultural borders are not necessarily materially or geographically constrained. Any agenda for educational and social transformation must be able to deal with the dilemmas and contradictions inherent in the trend towards cultural homogenization, cultural differentiation, and cultural revitalization in our societies.[2]

These are far-reaching concerns because the knowledge crisis is not restricted to the so-called metropolitan centres of the world. Within local communities, as Zarate (1994) points out, the crisis of knowledge can be seen in the fragmentation of traditional values and beliefs, the erosion of spirituality, and the distortions in local, regional, and national economies. The commodification of knowledge and culture across space and time also has implications which reach far beyond jeopardizing the integrity of local cultural production. For example, the so-called developing world continues to vigorously confront current insidious attempts at cultural, economic, and political recolonization, which take the form of educational reforms driven by the interests of corporate, transnational capital. The workers in the Chiapas resistance against the Mexican government and the **North American Free Trade Agreement** (NAFTA) are an example of a developing nation confronting the invasion of capitalist practice and ideology. This example is particularly significant in that the resistance comes from subordinated groups in Mexico and demonstrates the similarity of interests among the ruling classes of different countries.

The harsh economic lessons of globalization clearly point to the urgent need for a new approach to education that responds appropriately to the challenge of difference and diversity in communities internationally. In Euro-Canadian/American circles, current academic and political projects of rupturing hegemonic social science paradigms have added fuel to the demand of marginalized communities for education to respond to the pressing concerns of racism, sexism, classism, and other forms of oppressive and discriminatory practices that diminish our basic humanity. In fact, anti-racism education emerged as a consequence of the ongoing transformations in social science epistemologies to offer alternative readings of how, as social beings, we live our lives in multiracial, multi-ethnic, pluralistic communities.

Each individual in society lives and experiences different material realities. Nevertheless, we are all governed by a set of socio-political and structural conditionalities. There must be some awareness on the part of anti-racism educators and practitioners of the structures, constraints, limitations, and possibilities embedded in the wider social contexts. This awareness is fundamental to political work for an alternative society (see Brewer 1993). For example, the practice of integrative anti-racism education needs to recognize at all levels the forces of political rigidity and economic constraints that obstruct the envisioning and actualization of alternative social formations.

There are substantial socio-economic and demographic changes taking place internationally, nationally, and locally that have significant consequences for human interactions and relations. Codjoe lists some of the changes as "a general shift in the national [economies] from goods-producing to service-intensive industries; an increasing bifurcation of the labour market into low-wage/high-wage sectors; technological innovation; the relocation out and/or de-industrialization of the manufacturing sectors of major cities; and a re-constitution of the social composition of the work force which now consists mainly of women and minorities" (1995). These developments have implications for social relations defined along lines of difference. Particularly, the economic recession in North America and most of Europe in the 1980s provided the "scene for the re-emergence of race as a salient issue in political and public debates" (ibid.) when unemployment and poverty forced people to look for scapegoats for the economic hardships. One look at the policies of the Mike Harris–led Ontario government of the mid-1990s shows how those in power can use seemingly neutral economic problems to attack the rights of marginalized groups.

Economic depression has heightened an awareness of "otherness" among some members of white Canadian society, making racial minorities the focus of people's anger. The transition from industry-based economies to high technology economies continues to create economic turmoil due to high unemployment rates and poverty. Class differences have been accentuated, and the working class are fearful of what the future holds. Classism is gaining currency just as much as racism, sexism, homophobia, and xenophobia.

The current ultra-conservative rhetoric, utilizing racist code words to blame racial minorities and women for the most recent economic problems, has an appeal to many lower-middle- and working-class whites (particularly males) in Euro-Canadian/American society. But there are clear examples in the apportioning of blame of the intersections of class, race, and gender. Many white women do not accept the blame, just as some black men may accept the rhetoric blaming women for some societal problems. This is because of the prevailing economic climate of diminishing wages, increasing unemployment, and economic insecurity (see Apple 1993). In particular, dominant group members of middle-class backgrounds see their privileges under assault and their class positions weakening in the face of globalization and the downward trends in national economies. This may, in part, explain the election of the Progressive Conservatives in the 1995 Ontario provincial election as they basically promised to punish the poor and protect the "beleaguered middle-class" in their election campaign.

Within the Canadian context, many people, irrespective of class, racial, and gender backgrounds, are threatened by national and international economic insecurity. Whites, particularly men, have more to lose since economic disparities rely upon racist and patriarchal power structures which provide unequal access to opportunities and resources. In a context of political and economic insecurity, those with the highest vested interest in maintaining material advantage are the most likely to feel threatened by further destabilizing forces that question their advantage. They speak up to protect the status quo.

In the Euro-Canadian/American context this is made apparent by voices of criticism over such issues as employment equity and **affirmative action policies**. Agents of oppression become very defensive about being exposed and will use whatever (considerable) means in their power and influence to bury, hide, and deflect their agency. Examples of such strategies appear in the "take the offensive," blame someone or scapegoat the poor, blacks, women, and feminism's attitude in order to avoid responsibility for agency as part of the "oppressor" group. Others deny the inequality or divest themselves from membership in the oppressing group and instead focus on individual agency. Other strategies include shifting the frame of reference of debate completely to nullify or stymie the argument so as to maintain control of the agenda. Sometimes, too, those who wield power and have the means to do so will attempt to silence opponents or critics or even have someone else speak on their "behalf." Others will plead the cause of "fairness" or "reasonableness" in order to fall back into normalcy and the familiarity of existing conditions. My argument is that, rather than question the Canadian government's economic policies and the activities of private and corporate organizations, some Canadians, especially those feeling most threatened, decide to vent their anger on "immigrants," racial minorities, the working poor, those who are not employed, and women.

Therefore, discussions of racism and public discourses which blame marginal and disempowered groups for economic problems must recognize institutionalized poverty through bringing class issues seriously into the anti-racism debate (see Troyna 1993). Integrative anti-racism cannot sufficiently deal with the problem of racial oppression without simultaneously confronting the structural problems of economic poverty, cultural sexism,[3] and capitalist patriarchy. Integrative anti-racism must interrogate how current social formations continue to reproduce conditions of abject poverty in the midst of affluence and plenty for a few. In doing so, it must guard against reductionistic arguments that pit class against race. Such arguments fit well with the ideological position that class inequality is the fundamental problem of human social relations. And the neo-conservatives would argue that, through paid labour and hard work, people can overcome racial subordination. But, class relations are not only sustained by material (economic) relations. Class is also a social identity constructed through ideological and symbolic practices.

Race, class, gender, and sexuality mutually affect each other. An integrative anti-racism approach must reject analyses which reduce racial subordination to economics. Rather, it must examine how people relate to the processes and struggles over the control of the means of production and reproduction. Such an inquiry reveals the exploitative character of the current social formation and the nature of individual and collective action developed around questions of individual and collective identity and social practice. No doubt, economic relations and imperatives influence the production of racial and gender ideologies, just as gender and racial structures can be understood only in the context of a historically constituted set of economic formations. Integrative anti-racism must speak to working-class concerns (e.g., equity, poverty, class bias in institutional structures, and educational practices) in a way that recognizes the intersections of difference.

The examination of relations between different social groups is not synonymous with the political project of explicating the reasons why these groups exist in the first place (see McAll 1992).

In all social formations, dominant groups exert their power through the systematic reproduction of the sources of their economic and political advantage. The linkage between cultural, social, and economic power ensures a sustaining of the hegemonic relationship which allows for the appropriation of the wealth, knowledge, and property of a weaker group. Racism, sexism, and classism are ideological practices developed through a false sense of superiority of certain members of society. Using the power of "public opinion," popular culture and religious teachings on morality to create "false senses" is a strategy of domination.

Admittedly, the mode of reproduction of racism, sexism, homophobia, and so forth cannot be explained with reference to capitalism alone. While all social formations have been good at maintaining subordinate and dominant relations, it appears, however, that post-industrial economies have systematically cultivated relations of domination between and among social groups to serve particular material and ideological interests. West (1987) has asked for an understanding of how racist beliefs form part of the common-sense knowledge of various social formations, how racist ideologies operate in everyday practices and constructions of identities, how state bureaucratic structures continually regulate the lives of racial minorities in particular, and how those minorities resist state repression, domination, and class exploitation. To respond to these questions, we have to examine how racism, capitalist patriarchy, and other forms of gender and sexual oppression work jointly in the lived experiences of people (see Stasiulis 1990). We must be able to articulate an alternative form of global education that connects issues of global economic oppression, capitalist patriarchy, human rights, environmental racism, and international development, and respond to the urgent need to build coalitions across national borders to deal with global social injustice. Such global education will stress the mutual interdependence and interconnections among nations and peoples in a common struggle for change.

The question today is not whether capitalist social formations need racism and other oppressions to reproduce wealth and material advantage for their most privileged members. It is a question of *how* and *why*. Racism and patriarchy continue to be powerful ideologies and social practices that serve the interests of modern industrial capital (see Williams 1964). Racism, sexism, and other forms of oppression, constituted along the lines of difference, function as effective social barriers. These practices help segment the labour force. As others have repeatedly argued, racism and sexism regulate the labour force not only by consigning people to particular roles and responsibilities in production relations, but also by the very practice of systemic exclusion from sharing in the material and social goods of society. But, above everything else, racism and other forms of oppression serve to maintain and reproduce the capitalist system.

Finally, the related *sixth* issue concerns how educators, students, and community workers can engage in a progressive politics for *social transformation*, utilizing the integrative anti-racism approach. A more genuinely integrative anti-racism approach to social change requires focusing on the utilization of the relative power and privilege constituted around notions of race, class, gender, and sexuality, and prioritizing all forms of oppression. Privilege and oppression, as Dahan (1992) points out, co-exist in our individual and collective lives. By virtue of one's race, social class, gender, and sexual orientation, it is easier or more difficult to access the dominant culture and the associated economic and political capital in Euro-Canadian/American contexts.

In the struggle for social transformation, public policy must not be confused with political action and, conversely, action should be seen as a precursor to effective change. For change to take place, integrative anti-racism discourse and practice must be grounded in people's actual material conditions. The political, communicative, and educational practices of integrative anti-racism call for people to work together to develop a "community of differences"; that is, a community in which our differences help to strengthen us collectively to develop some degree of a shared commitment to justice and social transformation. Social transformation is possible when solidarity is understood to mean constructing coalitions among and between difference, and coalitions come to be openly defined in terms of relations of power (see Joyce 1995). Without a doubt, struggles against race, class, gender, and sexual discrimination generate distinct versions of what justice should look like (see Troyna and Vincent 1995). But the goal of coalition building is to educate each other so that there is, or can be, a common view of justice. The struggle against injustice implies a struggle for justice. We cannot, as a society, choose to ignore injustice.

As we struggle for change through the politics of an integrative anti-racism approach, we must continually guard against what Mohanty has observed as the "erosion of the politics of collectivity through the reformulation of race and difference in individualistic terms" (1990). This means that definitions of identity should extend beyond references to personal experience and make connections with the wider community. We cannot reject the politics of identity and difference. And we cannot simply engage in what can be called "politics of the moment" or situational politics. Integrative anti-racism must ground the new politics of change in an understanding of the history of colonialism and re-colonization, as well as of how global capital (through processes of economic domination) continually produce definitions of "valid" knowledge about ourselves and society.

The politics of integrative anti-racism change can start in the classroom, in the home, in the workplace, and in community actions and groups. There are some pedagogical and communicative challenges to the pursuit of an integrative anti-racist perspective. As already discussed, there is always the temptation to prioritize race and overlook the embedded inequalities which flow from class, ethnicity, culture, gender, sexuality, and religious and language disparities, many of which are refracted through the official and hidden curriculum of the school and society. Since anti-racism education has to deal simultaneously with race, class, gender, and sexual orientation, the anti-racist pedagogue, trainer, and/or activist should necessarily be anti-classist, anti-sexist, and anti-homophobic in her or his social practices. For anti-racism teachers, an awareness of the link between personal identity, experience, and authority is crucial.

There must be congruence between the theory and practice engaged by anti-racism educators and practitioners. For example, the teacher's theoretical viewpoint of anti-racism education and the classroom atmosphere (e.g., that of an anti-authoritarian, democratic environment) that is nurtured should be closely aligned in order to make change happen. This is particularly true in the context of an anti-racist pedagogy that questions privilege, attempts to create a critical and powerful voice for students, and develops their sense of critical judgement, while at the same time attempting to provide an openness to teaching that is non-universalizing.

Notes

1. See the film *My Beautiful Laundrette* (1985), directed by Stephen Fears, for a representation of these complex relations.
2. As groups are formulated and reformulated within different relations and categories, there is an inevitable homogenizing of groups of people. Larger groups of people are grouped under broad terms. *The Global Economy* is one such term. This epithet constructs us all as being involved in a seamless world economy, all sharing and producing the material goods of our collective labour. Cultural differentiation is a concomitant social process. While we may all be part of "the global economy," certain factions of our society get singled out for not contributing to this world of plenty. Racist, sexist, and classist ideologies mobilize popular sentiment against these "troublemakers" and every other group scrambles for a moral high ground. This is the negative side of cultural differentiation. There are also processes of cultural differentiation that serve to empower marginalized groups as they claim space in the public consciousness.
3. By "cultural sexism" I am referring to patriarchal tendencies and practices embedded in upholding certain cultural traditions that are disempowering to women.

References

Anthias, F., and Nira Yuval-Davis. 1983. "Contextualizing Feminisms: Gender, Ethnic, and Class Division." *Feminist Review* 16: 62–75.

———. 1992. *Racialized Boundaries: Race, Nation, Gender, Colour, and Class and the Anti-Racist Struggle.* New York: Routledge.

Apple, Michael. 1993. "Rebuilding Hegemony: Education, Equality, and the New Right." In Dennis Dworkin and Leslie Roman, eds, *Views beyond the Border Country.* New York: Routledge, 91–114.

Archer, L. 2001. "Muslim Brothers, Black Lads, Traditional Asians: British Muslim Young Men's Construction of Race, Religion and Masculinity." *Feminism and Psychology* 11, 1: 79–105.

Archer, L, and H. Yamashita. 2003. "Theorizing Inner-City Masculinities: 'Race,' Class and Gender and Education." *Gender and Education* 15, 2: 115–32.

Bannerji, Himani. 1991a. "But Who Speaks for Us?: Experiences and Agency in Conventional Feminist Paradigms." In Himani Banerji, Linda Carty, Kari Delhi, Susan Heald, and Kate McKenna, eds, *Unsettling Relations: The University as a Site of Feminist Struggles.* Toronto: Women's Press, 67–108.

———. 1991b. "Racism, Sexism, Knowledge, and the Academy." *Resources for Feminist Research* 20, 3/4: 5–12.

———, ed. 1993. *Returning the Gaze: Essays on Racism, Feminism, and Politics.* Toronto: Sister Vision Press.

Belkhir, Jean, and Michael Ball. 1993. "Editor's Introduction: Integrating Race, Sex, and Class in our Disciplines." *Race, Sex, and Class* 1, 1: 3–11.

Bhabha, Homi. 1994. *The Location of Culture.* London: Routledge.

Bourne, Jenny. 1987. *Homelands of the Mind: Jewish Feminism and Identity Politics.* London: The Institute of Race Relations, Race, and Class, Pamphlet No. 11.

Brand, D. 1991. *No Burden to Carry . . . Narratives of Working Women in Ontario.* Toronto: Women's Press.

Brewer, Rose M. 1993. "Theorizing Race, Class, and Gender: The New Scholarship of Black Feminist Intellectuals and Black Women's Labour." In Stanlie James and Abena Busia, eds, *Theorizing Black Feminisms.* New York: Routledge, 13–30.

Britzman, Deborah. 1993. "The Ordeal of Knowledge: Rethinking the Possibilities of Multicultural Education." *Review of Education* 15: 123–35.

Bunch, C. 1987. *Passionate Politics: Feminist Theory and Action.* New York: St Martin's Press.

Burbules, Nicholas C., and Suzanne Rice. 1991. "Dialogue across Difference: Continuing the Conversation." *Harvard Educational Review*, 61: 393–416.

Calliste, Agnes. 1991. "Canada's Immigrant Policy and Domestics from the Caribbean." *Socialist Studies* 5: 136–68.

———. 1993a. "Race, Gender, and Canadian Immigrant Policy." *Journal of Canadian Studies* 28, 4: 131–48.

———. 1993b. "Women of Exceptional Merit: Immigration of Caribbean Nurses to Canada." *Canadian Journal of Women and the Law* 6, 1: 85–102.

———. 1994. "Race, Gender, and Canadian Immigration Policy: Blacks from the Caribbean 1900–1932." *Journal of Canadian Studies* 28, 4: 131–47.

Carby, Hazel. 1982. "White Women Listen! Black Feminism and the Boundaries of Sisterhood." In Paul Gilroy at the Centre for Contemporary Cultural Studies, ed., *The Empire Strikes Back*. London: Hutchinson, 212–35.

Carty, Linda. 1991a. "Black Women in Academia." In Himani Bannerji, Linda Carty, Kari Dehli, Susan Heald, and Kate McKenna, eds, *Unsettling Relations*. Toronto: Women's Press, 13–44.

———. 1991b. "Women's Studies in Canada: A Discourse and Praxis of Exclusion." *Resources for Feminist Research* 20, 3/4: 12–18.

———. 1993. "Introduction: Combining Our Efforts: Making Feminism Relevant to the Changing Sociality." In Linda Carty, ed., *And We Still Rise: Feminist Political Mobilizing in Contemporary Canada*. Toronto: Women's Press, 7–21.

Codjoe, Henry M. 1995. "Experiences of Black/African-Canadian High School Graduates in Alberta's Public School System: A Multi-Case Study." PhD research proposal, Department of Education Policy Studies, University of Alberta.

Collins, Patricia Hill. 1990. *Black Feminist Thought*. London: HarperCollins.

———. 1993. "Toward a New Vision: Race, Class, and Gender as Categories of Analysis and Connection." *Race, Sex, and Class* 1, 1: 25–45.

Colour of Justice Network. 2008. "The Colour of Poverty." Toronto. http://cop.openconcept.ca/. November 2008.

Combahee River Collective. 1981. "Combahee River Collective Statement." In C. Moraga and G. Anzaldua, eds, *This Bridge Called My Back*. New York: Kitchen Table-Women of Color Press, 210–20.

Cox, Oliver. 1948. *Caste, Class, and Race: A Study in Social Dynamics*. New York: Monthly Review Press.

———. 1976. *Race Relations: Elements and Social Dynamics*. Detroit: Wayne State University Press.

Dahan, Carole. 1992. "Spheres of Identity: Feminism and Difference: Notes by a Sephardic Jewess." *Fireweed* 35: 46–50.

Dei, George J.S. 1994. "Reflections of An Anti-Racist Pedagogue." In Lorna Erwin and David MacLennan, eds, *The Sociology of Education in Canada*. Toronto: Copp Clark Pitman, 290–310.

Dill, B.T., and M.B. Zinn. 1990. *Race and Gender: Re-visioning Social Relations*. Memphis: Center for Research on Women, Memphis State University, Research Paper No. 11.

Donald, James, and Ali Rattansi, eds 1992. *Race, Culture, and Difference*. Newbury Park, CA: Sage.

Dua, E. 2007. "Exploring Articulations of 'Race' and Gender: Going Beyond Singular Categories." In Sean P. Hier and B. Singh Bolaria, eds, *Race and Racism in 21st-Century Canada: Continuity, Complexity, and Change*. Peterborough, ON: Broadview Press, 175–96.

———. 2008. "Thinking Through Anti-Racism and Indigenity in Canada." *The Ardent Review* 1, 1: 31–5.

Fanon, Frantz. 1967. *Black Skin, White Masks*. New York: Grove.

Fenelon, J.V., and R. Brod. 2000. "Ideologies of Reverse Discrimination: Race, Gender, Class, Age Analysis." *Race, Gender and Class* 7, 2: 149–78.

Ferri, B.A., and D.J. Connor. 2005. "Tools of Exclusion: Race, Disability, and (Re)segregated Education." *Teachers College Record* 107, 3: 453–74.

Fine, Michelle. 1991. *Framing Dropouts: Notes on the Politics of Urban Public High School*. New York: SUNY Press.

Fumia, Doreen. 1995. "Identifying Sites of Anti-Racism Education. Everyday Lived Experiences Seen as the Micropolitics of Institutionalized Racialized Practices." Unpublished paper, Department of Sociology in Education, Ontario Institute for Studies in Education (OISE), Toronto.

Gabriel, John, and Gideon Ben-Tovim. 1979. "The Conceptualisation of Race Relations in Sociological Theory." *Racial and Ethnic Studies* 2, 2: 190–212.

Grewal, Inderpal, and Caren Kaplan. 1994. "Introduction: Transnational Feminist Practices and Questions of Postmodernity." In Inderpal Grewal and Caren Kaplan, eds, *Scattered Hegemonies*. Minneapolis: University of Minnesota Press, 1–36.

Hall, Stuart. 1979. "Ethnicity: Identity and Experience." *Radical America*. Summer: 9–20.

———. 1991. "Old and New Identities: Old and New Ethnicities." In A. King, ed., *Culture, Globalization, and the World System*. New York: SUNY Press, 41–68.

Hall, K.Q. 2002. "Feminism, Disability and Embodiment." *NWSA Journal* 14, 3: vii–xiii.

hooks, bell. 1984. *Feminist Theory: From Margin to Center*. Boston: South End Press.

———. 1988. *Talking Back: Thinking Feminist, Thinking Black*. Toronto: Between the Lines.

———. 1990. *Yearning: Race, Gender, and Cultural Politics*. Boston: South End Press.

———. 1992. *Ain't I a Woman: Black Women and Feminism*. Boston: South End Press.

———. 1993. *Sisters of the Yam: Black Women and Self-Recovery*. Toronto: Between the Lines.

———. 1994. *Teaching to Transgress: Education as the Practice of Freedom*. New York: Routledge.

Joyce, Moon V. 1995. "Approaches to Anti-Racist/Anti-Oppression Education: Implications for Employment Equity Interventions." Unpublished paper, Department of Sociology in Education, OISE, Toronto.

King, D. 1988. "Multiple Jeopardy, Multiple Consciousness: The Context of a Black Feminist Ideology." *Signs* 14, 1: 42–72.

King, Joyce E. 1994. "Perceiving Reality in a New Way: Rethinking the Black/White Duality of Our Time." Paper presented at the Annual Meeting of the

American Educational Research Association, New Orleans, 4–9 April.

Lawson, E. 2008. "The Politics and Pedagogy of Crash in the Postmodern Era: A Black Feminist Reflection." In P. Howard and G.J.S. Dei, eds, *Crash Politics and Antiracism: Interrogations of Liberal Race Discourse*. New York: Peter Lang Publishing, 71–90.

McAll, Christopher. 1992. *Class, Ethnicity, and Social Inequality*. Montreal: McGill-Queen's University Press.

McCarthy, Cameron. 1988. "Rethinking Liberal and Radical Perspectives on Racial Inequality in Schooling: Making the Case for Nonsynchrony." *Harvard Educational Review* 58, 3: 265–79.

McClaurin, Irma, ed. 2001. *Black Feminist Anthropology: Theory, Politics, Praxis, and Poetics*. New Brunswick, NJ: Rutgers University Press.

McCready, L. 2008. Personal communication. OISE, Toronto.

Marx, Karl. 1853. "The Future Results of British Rule in India." *New York Daily Tribune* 8 August.

Massaquoi, N., and N. Wane, eds 2007. *Theorizing Empowerment: Canadian Perspectives on Black Feminist Thought*. Toronto: Inanna Press.

Matsuda, Marie. 1989. "When the First Quail Calls: Multiple Consciousness as Jurisprudential Method." *Women Rights Law Reporter* 11, 1: 7–10.

Mercer, K. 1996. "Decolonization and Disappointment: Reading Fanon's Sexual Politics." In Alan Reed, ed., *The Fact of Blackness: Fanon and Visual Representation*. Seattle: Bay Press, 114–31.

Mercer, Kobena, and I. Julien. 1988. "Race, Sexual Politics, and Black Masculinity: A Dossier." In Rowena Chapman and Jonathan Rutherford, eds, *Male Order: Unwrapping Masculinity*. London: Lawrence Wishart, 97–164.

Miles, Robert. 1980. "Class, Race, and Ethnicity: A Critique of Cox's Theory." *Ethnic and Racial Studies* 3, 2: 169–81.

Mohanty, Chandra Talpade. 1990. "On Race and Voice: Challenges for Liberal Education in the 90s." *Cultural Critique* 14: 179–208.

Mullings, Leith. 1992. *Race, Class, and Gender: Representations and Reality*. Memphis: Center for Research on Women, Memphis State University.

Nestel, S. 1993. "Facing Foreclosure: A Jew in the Classroom." Unpublished essay, Department of Adult Education, OISE, Toronto.

Ng, Roxana, P. Staton, and J. Scane, eds 1995. *Anti-Racism, Feminism, and Critical Approaches to Education*. Toronto: OISE Press.

Oakes, Jeannie. 1985. *Keeping Track: How Schools Structure Inequality*. New Harlem, CT: Yale University Press.

Omi, M., and H. Winant. 1994. *Racial Formation in the United States from the 1960s to the 1980s*. New York: Routledge.

Rethinking Schools. 1991. "An Interview with Educator Enid Lee: Taking Multicultural, Anti-Racist Education Seriously." *Rethinking Schools* 6, 1 October–November: 1–4.

Rizvi, Fazal. 1995. "Commentary on Panel Session: 'Equity Issues in Education.'" Annual Meeting of the American Educational Research Association, San Francisco, 18–22 April.

Roman, Leslie. 1993. "White is Colour! White Defensiveness, Postmodernism, and Anti-racist Pedagogy." In Cameron McCarthy and Warren Crichlow, eds, *Race, Identity, and Representation in Education*. New York: Routledge, 71–88.

Roscigno, Vincent. 1994. "Social Movement Struggle and Race, Gender, Class Inequality." *Race, Sex, and Class* 2, 1: 109–26.

Rothenberg, R.S., ed. 2007. *Race, Class and Gender in the United States*. 7th edn. New York: Worth Publishers, 131–8.

Russo, Ann. 1991. "We Cannot Live without Our Lives." In Chandra Mohanty, Ann Russo, and Lourdes Torres, eds, *Third World Women and the Politics of Feminism*. Bloomington: Indiana University Press, 297–313.

Satzewich, Vic. 1990. "The Political Economy of Race and Ethnicity." In Peter Li, ed., *Race and Ethnic Relations in Canada*. Toronto: Oxford University Press, 209–30.

Simmel, Georg. 1950. "The Stranger." In K.H. Wolf, ed., *The Sociology of George Simmel*. New York: The Free Press.

Stasiulis, Daiva K. 1990. "Theorizing Connections: Gender, Race, Ethnicity, and Class." In P.S. Li, ed., *Race and Ethnic Relations in Canada*. Toronto: Oxford University Press, 269–305.

Sullivan, Ann. 1995. "Realizing Successful Integrative Anti-Racist Education." Unpublished paper, Department of Sociology in Education, OISE, Toronto.

Titchkosky, T. 2007. "Pausing at the Intersections of Difference." In *Reading and Writing Disability Differently: The Textured Life of Embodiment*. Toronto: University of Toronto Press.

Train, Kelly. 1995. "De-Homogenizing 'Jewish Women': Essentialism and Exclusion within Jewish Feminist Thought." MA thesis, Department of Education, University of Toronto, Toronto.

Troyna, Barry. 1993. *Racism and Education: Research Perspectives*. Toronto: OISE Press.

Troyna, Barry, and Carol Vincent. 1995. "Equity and Education: The Discourses of Social Justice." Paper read at the Annual Meeting of the American Educational Research Association, San Francisco, 18–22 April.

Wane, N., K. Deliovsky, and E. Lawson. 2002. *Back to the Drawing Board: African-Canadian Feminisms*. Toronto: Sumach Press.

Weiler, Kathleen. 1991. "Freire and a Feminist Pedagogy of Difference." *Harvard Educational Review* 6, 4: 449–74.

West, Cornel. 1987. "Race and Social Theory." In M. Davis, ed., *The Year Left 2*. New York: Verso, 73–89.

Williams, Eric. 1964. *Capitalism and Slavery*. London: Deutsch.

Zarate, Jose. 1994. "Indigenous Knowledge and Anti-Racist Education: Reaching Out to People and Cultures." *Orbit* 25, 2: 35–6.

Zinn, M.B. 1991. *Race and the Reconstruction of Gender*. Memphis: Center for Research on Women, Memphis State University, Research Paper Number 14.

Questions for Critical Thought

1. The author argues that individuals should talk about their personal experiences of oppression as a first step toward anti-racism practices. What is your own experience of oppression? How may someone who has not experienced oppression join such a discussion? What could be their contribution to such a discussion?

2. The author provides examples of defensive positions taken by socially dominant groups against equity measures like employment equity. Which of these have you observed? Do you support the author's explanation that defensiveness emerges from perceived threats to the power occupied by socially dominant groups? What would you do if you witnessed a racial incident in the classroom, in the community, or on the streets of your town or city?

3. The author recommends that teachers interested in incorporating anti-racism in their classroom practices be aware of their personal identity, their experience, and their authority. Is it possible for a member of the socially dominant group to assume such a role? What tensions may arise in this case? How should such a teacher respond to accusations of oppression in the classroom?

4. Dei argues for the salience of "race" while advocating for an anti-racism practice that integrates the intersections between race, class, and gender. How might this be done? Is it possible to highlight racism and avoid emphasizing "one subordination or oppression over another"? How can alliances between different oppressed groups be created? Can you think of organizations that have created alliances between oppressed groups? Have they been successful in raising awareness about the multiple sites of oppression that people experience?

5. How does oppression occur on a global scale? What are the social, political, and economic conditions giving rise to such oppression? That is, how is oppression manifest in social relations and social organizations in different locations? You might begin with the social institutions found in this book, then consider broader issues like international development, free trade, human rights, the environment, and security/military issues.

Feminist Intersectional Theorizing[1]

.... *Daiva K. Stasiulis*

Theoretical efforts to understand the intersections among social relations, such as race, gender, and class, have arisen within a tumultuous political and intellectual terrain. In the 1980s, within the North American and Western European left, the socialist certainty of the primacy of social class as the major basis for social division and solidarity in progressive struggles was shattered by events such as the fall of the Berlin Wall, the disintegration of the Soviet Union, and the embrace of capitalist economic goals by a formerly communist China. Preceding these formative events, beginning in the 1960s, social movements were organized to further the goals of civil rights, feminism, environmentalism, gay and lesbian rights, disability rights, ethnocultural and indigenous rights, national liberation, and racial and cultural justice. These movements claimed a status equal to or exceeding that of labour movements and a new prominence in defining progressive and largely "identity-based" politics. Yet they also faced formidable challenges in reconciling the needs, conflicts, and contradictions that arose from the diversity and complexity of the collectivity they claimed to represent with their frequently reductive analysis of oppression based on a *single* social division or form of power (sexism, heterosexism, racism, etc.).

Intersectional theorizing understood the social reality of women and men, and the dynamics of their social, cultural, economic, and political contexts to be *multiply, simultaneously, and interactively* determined by various significant *axes of social organization*. Intersectional theory was largely a response to the reductive tendencies of the theories that informed key progressive social movements, the idea that there is only *one* fundamental axis of social organization and source of oppression.

It is notable that the theories underlying the politics of all the radical social movements had rejected the classical liberal, Eurocentric notion of the individual, isolated from consideration of larger social structures and social divisions. Thus, Marxist and socialist theorizing, which animated class struggles, argued for the central significance of class relations in shaping material life and rewards, consciousness, and collective action. In contrast, feminist theorizing regarded gender as the key division across time and space, which accounted for the most fundamental dynamics of power and domination. While much of the Marxist and early feminist theoretical traditions did not altogether ignore other social divisions, they tended to subsume them within the two supposedly more fundamental singular axes of class and gender respectively.

Within this intellectual and political context, socialist feminism in the 1970s and 1980s represented a major breakthrough in its attempt to theorize the articulation of gender (or sex) and class. In analyzing the relationship between capitalist production and human reproduction, socialist feminists presented a serious challenge to the notion of "genderless" class relations implicit within much of the Marxist and socialist traditions, and "classless" gender relations, which had been a hallmark of a good deal of feminist writing (Armstrong and Armstrong 1986a, 1986b; Barrett 1980; Maroney and Luxton 1987). At about the same time, the "race and class" debates critiqued Marxism's tendency to subsume racism under capitalism and race relations theories' tendency to ignore the significance of class divisions (Gabriel and Ben-Tovim 1978; Hall 1980; Miles 1980; Omi and Winant 1994).[2] Subsequent theorizing about the interlocking oppressions of race, class, and gender, chiefly by women of colour, was critical of liberal, Marxist/socialist, feminist, and anti-racist traditions. These were all guilty of ignoring at least one and sometimes more of the simultaneous and interlocking axes of racial, class, and gender power within a matrix of domination (Collins 1990).[3]

The resounding refusal to produce theory that posited the "categorical hegemony" of class for Marxism/socialism, gender for feminism, and race for anti-racism was a hallmark of writings from black feminist and other racialized women's movements and writings. Beginning in the 1970s, US women of colour presented analyses that exposed the oppressions and agency of black women and other women of colour, and which argued vehemently for the development of integrative analysis and politics based upon the non-separability of race, class, gender, and other social relations such as sexuality. Thus, the "Combahee River Collective Statement" (originally written in the United States in 1977) presents a clear argument for the need to view oppression and political resistance in terms of the simultaneity and interconnectedness of social oppressions:

> The most general statement of our politics at the present time would be that we are actively committed to struggling against racial, sexual, heterosexual, and class oppression, and see as our particular task the development of

integrated analysis and practice based upon the fact that *the major systems of oppression are interlocking*. (cited in Jakobsen 1998, emphasis added)

The turn to intersectional theorizing in such countries as the United States, Britain, Canada, Australia, and New Zealand sought to demarginalize the lives and experiences of oppression among racialized women. The scholarship by and about black women, indigenous women, and other women of colour focused largely on those who historically occupied the lowest rungs of hierarchies within the labour force and state entitlements, and who were subjected to denigrating racialized, sexualized, and class-bound forms of representation. It also represented the defiant reflections on their own conditions of academic women of colour, who failed to find any resonance within white feminist theories about the "generic" woman's oppression in their own lives, or those of their mothers, sisters, daughters, or grandmothers. Written from the standpoint of middle-class white women, the available feminist literature was oblivious to racial hierarchies and systems of domination, which distinguished the experiences of racialized women from those of white women. Much of the intersectional theorizing was forged within the context of women's movements, and the tensions arising out of constructing autonomous identities and politics, in conjunction with multiracial alliances among racially/ethnically diverse women. The fact that so much of the intersectional theorizing has been intimately engaged with the challenge of dealing with "difference," particularity, and power relations among women in women's movements is a major reason why intersectional theory has been pursued so vigorously by feminist theorists and has dwelled so much on the subject of women.[4] This has often been to the detriment of scholarship that examines systematically what is uniquely masculine in racialized systems of domination. In addition, many of the leading male critical race and class theorists have made scant mention of gender, and much of the intersectionality of

gender with other social forces in men's lives has been left unexamined.

The location of intersectional theorizing within feminist debates by no means suggests that intersections among race, class, and gender have attained a hegemonic or privileged status within feminist analyses. Indeed, several women of colour feminists writing in Canada and the United States have concluded quite the opposite, namely, that with a few notable exceptions, much of Euro-American and Euro-Canadian feminist scholarship continues to ignore the intersections of race, gender, and class in its theorizing (Agnew 1996; Carty 1993; Higginbotham 1992; Jhappan 1996). Beyond token mention of "differences" among women that fall along race and class lines, the scholarship of white feminists remains "lily white," "paying lip service to race as they continue to analyze their own experience in ever more sophisticated forms" (Higginbotham 1992). Such white solipsism is decried on the grounds that the unrepresentative theories of female experience and oppression that were produced fail to illuminate the social reality or subjective identities of many, indeed globally the majority of, women. Those left on the margins of these theories include women of colour for whom "race" and racism are always central features of their existence and mediate their experience of other features of their identity and existence, including gender, class, ethnicity, religion, sexuality, disability, etc.

While much of feminist theorizing continues to suffer from racialist biases, there is nonetheless a trend in feminist debates towards intersectional theorizing, which has sought to "move beyond" the race–gender–class trinity and to understand the simultaneous and interactive impact (again chiefly on women's lives) of other forms of social divisions and oppressions, including ethnicity, colonialism, imperialism, nationalism, sexuality, religion, language, culture, citizenship, and disability.[5] The incorporation of these other social relations in intersectional theoretical frameworks has been largely inspired by the tremendously insightful yet limited naming of relevant analytical concepts in the triadic interpretative framework of race, class, and gender. The proliferation of social categories used in intersectional analysis has also been influenced by the interest in postmodernism and its intellectual appeal of fragmentation and "difference." But it is the course of contemporary world events, and the fact that economic globalization has stimulated and fed nationalisms and religious fundamentalisms, ethnic secessionist movements and "ethnic cleansing," homophobias and xenophobias, that has made imperative consideration of these forces within intersectional analyses distinct from yet enmeshed with race, class, and gender. In other words, there is an intimate relationship between the politicization of social identities within various social movements and state politics on the one hand, and the prominence and popularity of these social differences within intersectional analyses on the other.

Faced by a daunting and seemingly endless array of social divisions, intersectional theorists must confront the question, "Is there a parsimonious basis for including or excluding a particular dimension in the matrix of intersectionality?" By the 1990s, some feminists and critical race intellectuals were already expressing derision for the "iron triangle" of race–gender–class (Stimpson 1993), which "threatened to become the regnant cliché … of our critical discourse" (Appiah and Gates 1995; see also Mercer 1994). Similarly, Susan Bordo (1990) lamented "the coercive, mechanical requirement that all enlightened feminist projects attend to 'the intersection of race, class, and gender.' What happened to ethnicity? Age? Sexual orientation? On the other hand, just how many axes can one include and still preserve analytical focus or argument?"

The reasons underlying the inclusion or exclusion of a particular social relation, or combination of social relations, within intersectional analysis will be addressed in this chapter by examining two significant yet contradictory trends within feminist intersectional theorizing. The first is the continued prominence of race and racism and the race–gender–class triad within many contemporary intersectional analyses of women's conditions and politics in diverse societies. After more than two decades of theorizing about differences in experiences and self-understanding among women, and the proliferation of sources of their oppression and self-identification, there are staunchly persistent reasons for giving centrality to issues of race and racism within the matrices of social forces shaping the lives of women. At the same time, some of the limitations of the intersectional theorizing of the relations among race, gender, and class are revealed in the race **essentialism** of some of this literature, whereby a person's or group's oppression and knowledge can be "read off" their position within a given racial hierarchy.

The second trend is towards intersectional analyses that downplay race and focus on social forces of nationalism, religion, ethnicity, and cultural differences. The second part of the chapter examines some of the consequences of the fact that among many peoples and communities in many parts of the world, race is far less salient as a social construction than other social forces (including religion, ethnicity, and nationalism) in the discourses of political movements and the state. The acceleration and heterogeneity of international migration and the resurgence of nationalisms and religious and ethnic movements have brought new issues involving ethnocultural, religious, and national rights and oppressions into discussions of diasporic communities. Secular and ethnically dominant feminists, often caught unaware by the passion of women's attachments to religious and national/ethnic cultures, have had to navigate through the twin shoals of "cultural relativism" (the acceptance that different cultures legitimately diverge on issues such as gender roles and gender equality) and "universalism" (the validation of universal human and feminist rights such as freedom from patriarchy). Some of the new intersectional ways of viewing religious/ethnic/national women's particularity are also prone to cultural essentialism, ignoring the ways in which religious, ethnic, and national cultures are internally heterogeneous, have been constructed historically, and vary across time.

The second part of the chapter therefore focuses on some of the implications for intersectional theories of contemporary developments within, and novel understandings of, women's complicated relationships with nationalisms, religions, and cultural traditions.

As will become clear from my discussion of the persistent salience of race, and the new prominence given to social divisions based on ethnicity, nationalism, religion, and culture within intersectional feminist analyses, the choices academics and activists make for including or excluding particular social divisions are shaped by their location within historically and geopolitically specific contexts. Similar dynamics of inclusion and exclusion, which in one place and time will be constructed as based on racial divisions, will in another place and time be seen as based on ethnic or national differences. Emergent forms of conflict, in some instances built upon historical forms of what Benedict Anderson (1983) calls "imagined communities" (that is, political communities that are imagined by people based upon diverse sets of shared attributes and loyalties), may alter the landscape of "fundamental" axes that make up the matrix of domination shaping the lives of women and men within a particular region. The prominence of particular forms of difference in the subjective identities of individuals and the construction of communities also shifts as people migrate across borders and find themselves in new national and local contexts. This does not only occur because people's (citizenship, class, etc.) status may become transformed when they migrate from one country to another. It also occurs because the significance given to certain social divisions (e.g., indigenous/migrant, North/South) is markedly different in different national contexts. The shifting status of particular social divisions, which unsettles the identities of people across borders, is also unsettling for the stability of particular axes in intersectional theorizing and presents significant challenges for comparative analyses of domination, inequality, and resistance.

Notwithstanding claims for universality, most theoretical conceptualizations are informed by specific historical and geopolitical contexts. Much

of the following discussion will therefore make reference to European colonialism and the historical and contemporary realities of "white settler societies," including Canada and the United States.[6] At the same time, transborder crossings and emergent transnational realities are major influences compelling reconceptualizations of intersectionality of social relations as they are manifested within given national and local contexts.

Part One: The Prominence of Race

Race, gender, and class have been called the three "giants of modernist social critique" (Bordo 1990). All three concepts pertain to seemingly enduring divisions within and between human societies that are integrally related to the distribution of resources and the exercise of power and autonomy. All three concepts provide fundamental axes of social organization of the economy and of relations of production and reproduction, governance, and legal systems, as well as of identity formation. They are all forms of power, privilege, and subordination and "all consist of a field of projects whose common feature is their linkage of social structure and signification" (Omi and Winant 1994).

Race and gender (and less commonly class) have historically been treated in such a manner as to conflate what is natural or biological with the social, and thus are "always in part fixated on the body" (Eisenstein 1996; see also Goldberg 1993). A significant task set by critical race and feminist theorists and historians has been to "denaturalize" these categories to reveal the extreme arbitrariness and tenuousness of links drawn between biological or corporeal distinctions, and social or behavioural differences between racial or gender groups (Gould 1984; McLaren 1990; Scott 1996). The powerful self-interest of nineteenth-century "race science" in reaching foregone conclusions—namely, in establishing the intellectual, moral, spiritual, cultural, and aesthetic superiority of white European upper-class males over "lower races," women, and "lower classes"—was reflected in the twisted choices made of putative indicators. Thus, "for decades the Negro's similarity to apes on the basis of the shape of his jaw was asserted, while the white man's similarity to apes on the basis of his thin lips was ignored" (Stepan 1990). Similarly, when scientists found that the average weight of brains in proportion to body weight was in fact higher for women than for men (a result that undermined the sense of male superiority), they selected other absurd indices such as brain weight in relation to thigh bone weight in order to produce the desired results (Stepan 1990).

Race has received pride of place as the key point of entry within intersectional analysis focused on systems of racial, class, and gender domination. There are historical and political reasons for the more explicit analytical attention given to race than to gender, and the near effacement of class within much of this literature. First, intersectional analysis that linked race, gender, and class was produced beginning in the 1970s by a number of black feminists, women of colour, indigenous women, and Third World feminists.[7] These theorists, critics, and activists passionately challenged the **hegemony** of white, Western feminism and white feminists' problematic claims about the shared oppression and common political interests of all women, regardless of their positions within racial formations.[8] The most extensive critiques of white feminism first came from black feminists and Third World feminists who theorized from the experiences of African-American and other women of colour in the United States, Britain, Australia, New Zealand/Aotearoa,[9] and Canada.[10] The social formation of plantation slavery in the United States, which provided a totalizing narrative of African Americans' racial oppression, became a central trope in the analysis of the racist, sexist, and class-based domination of black women and the oppressive relation of white women vis-à-vis women of colour in the United States and elsewhere. Within a growing body of work that engaged with and developed black feminism, women of colour of diverse national and ethnic backgrounds in these various

societies examined and gave prominence to their own experiences. This scholarship examined these women's relationship to their communities, labour, family, sexuality, reproduction relations, the state, legal systems, and oppositional social movements. I will refer to this body of work as "women of colour feminism."[11] Despite divergences in epistemological frameworks and concrete analyses, the theorizing of racialized women's experience in women of colour feminism has had two common themes.

The first theme is expressed by the main conceptual anchor for the new intersectional theorizing; namely, the understanding of the *simultaneity* of racism, sexism, and class exploitation as interconnecting "systems" of privilege and oppression. Rather than treating race, gender, and class as discrete categories, the thrust of women of colour feminist analyses was to indicate how material structures, discourses, and experiences of gender were racialized, how race was gendered, and how class was overlapped with the logics of race and gender. Marxist or socialist feminist work had recognized that gender as a social relation was constructed in part through class and economic relations, and that the experience of gender subordination and oppression varied within different class and economic contexts. Most of this work, however, had failed to consider how class and gender systems of subordination and exclusion are also structured and informed by racist logics, a fact that is most apparent to those who are subjected simultaneously to all three forms of racial, class, and gender oppression.

For white feminist theorizing and feminist movements, the profound and disturbing implication was the realization that women are not all equally oppressed and that the marked divergences in positionality between white women and women of colour within the matrices of power relations built upon race, gender, and class rendered unrealistic the notions of "sisterhood" or a political community of women. Thus, to speak about or for "women" was no longer a liberating politics but a homogenizing gesture that masked the race privilege of racially dominant women and the racial oppression and marginalization of women of colour.

The second theme common to women of colour feminist scholarship is the prioritization of race and racism despite the general insistence upon the simultaneity of social relations based upon race, gender, and class. Through their writings and political struggles, black feminists, indigenous (including Canadian Aboriginal) women, and other women of colour have typically and repeatedly affirmed that racism rather than sexism is the primary source of their oppression (Agnew 1996; Calliste 1996).[12] While some have insisted that solidarity with the men of their community is critical in ameliorating their oppression, others have emphasized how feminist (or in Alice Walker's terms "womanist") consciousness plays an important role in the autonomous organizing of women with origins in Asia, Africa, the Caribbean, Latin America, the Pacific, the Middle East, and indigenous communities who self-identify by race (Agnew 1996; Walker 1983).

The priority given by women of colour feminism to race and racism stemmed in part from the absence of consideration of racial cleavages and oppressions from prior intersectional feminist theories, notably socialist/Marxist feminism with its focus on the complex interplay of gender and class, patriarchy, and capitalism.[13] As Himani Bannerji (1991) points out, "'Racism' and 'race,' as well as non-white women as producers of theory or politics are generally absent from the textual world of 'Marxist/socialist feminism.'" Many feminists of colour have echoed Bannerji in viewing these omissions as throwing "the whole theoretical and political project of Marxist [and socialist] feminism into question" (1991).

Feminist theory produced by white women, however, has been guilty of more than mere inattentiveness to race and to the unique sources of oppression for women of colour. The objectives and strategies of first-wave feminist theory and politics in the nineteenth century actively reproduced racism. As Mariana Valverde (1991, 1992) points out, the "whiteness" of the social purity, temperance, female suffrage movements led by middle-class Anglo-Celtic women in Canada was more than metaphorical; it embodied assumptions about the moral and cultural superiority of white Christian nations. In the United States, white suffragettes broke their alliance with blacks and cooperated with avowed racists in order to gain the southern (white male) vote for female suffrage (King 1988). Recent feminist historiography has also unearthed the staunch "maternal imperialism" of several white British feminists within British colonial history (Chaudhuri and Strobel 1992). During the 1960s, white feminists appropriated the incendiary metaphors of racism and slavery, as well as the political strategies of the African American civil rights movement to battle their own subordination vis-à-vis white men, but without interrogating their own complicity in racial oppression.

The centrality of racism to the intersectional analyses of black and women of colour feminism stems also, some writers argue, from the perceived salience of racism for women of colour who experience multiple oppressions in institutions such as the workplace. In a context of labour market segmentation by gender and race, women of colour are often assigned positions subordinate to white women in female-dominated occupations. Thus, analyses of the Canadian nursing profession have revealed how black women nurses are oppressed by white female nurses who are viewed as collaborating with management through racialized surveillance and harassment practices (Calliste 1996; Das Gupta 1996). Within white settler societies, much personal domestic and child care service is performed by women of colour from Third World countries such as the Philippines, Jamaica, and Mexico who experience racialized maternalistic forms of oppression from white female employers (Bakan and Stasiulis 1995, 1997). In this asymmetrical relationship between female domestics and female employers/supervisors, shared gender is unlikely to be a source of solidarity, whereas race provides a discourse through which clashing material and often class-based interests are experienced and articulated.

A fuller explanation for the prominence assigned to race and racism over gender and class within the writings of black and other women of colour feminists necessitates further probing of the significance of these phenomena in modern societies. An important question that repeatedly arises in many contemporary societies is why the concept of race has enjoyed such enduring power as a lens through which to differentiate and discriminate among people even long after scientists in the post–Second World War era had repeatedly established that the race concept has no scientific validity.[14] I can think of four ways of explaining the persistence of the race concept. First, race provides a "common-sense" way of seeing and interpreting. Second, race is a means to exclude, dominate, and exploit others and to rationalize these forms of racial power. Third, it evokes a visceral, psychosexual set of responses. Fourth, race is an empowering form of identity and subjectivity. It is significant that each of these partial answers to the persistence of race thinking already suggests intersectional analyses in the sense that relations of race are often simultaneously expressions of relations, beliefs, meanings, and fears pertaining to the social construction and organization of gender, sexuality, and class. Nonetheless, understanding the connections among these various dimensions of social experience and social structure is arrived at by making race "the main point of entry through which the varied forms of social oppression can and must be understood" (Dei 1996, 65). The following discussion addresses each of the four dimensions of race, which together account for the robust power of race within intersectional analyses.

1. Racial "Common Sense"

Racialism, or the construction of racial classifications or taxonomies of humans in terms of phenotypical or morphological differences, has a relatively long history dating back to at least the seventeenth century. Some writers have argued that there was a significant paradigmatic shift in Western European belief systems in the sixteenth and seventeenth centuries from defining the "other" in religious terms (their degree of distance from Christianity) to a more explicit form of racialized "othering," which valorized white European male physical features, ethical values, and aesthetics as the yardstick against which all humankind would be measured (Goldberg 1993).

Scientific and popular thought during the nineteenth century were permeated by race thinking. While the new theories were invested with scientific respectability, their presentation and tone were populist, enabling ideas about race to be easily assimilated into popular culture as a "metalanguage"—one that combines common sense and pseudoscience (Higginbotham 1992). So pervasive did race become in lending meaning "to myriad aspects of life that would otherwise fall outside the referential domain of race" (Higginbotham 1992) that Benjamin Disraeli, a future prime minister of Britain, was prompted to declare in 1847 that, "All is race, there is no other truth" (cited in Young 1995).[15] All fields of nineteenth- and early twentieth-century academic inquiry were obsessed by race theory's assertion of hierarchical differences among human populations. Different "races," "breeds," or "stocks" were assessed as possessing or lacking imprecisely defined qualities such as intelligence, moral virtue, rational capacity, culture, and civilization—all inferred from meticulous measurements taken of skulls, jaws, noses, lips, eyes, brains, stature, skin pigmentation, hair texture, sexual organs, and virtually all body parts.[16]

2. Racial Power

Racism, or the denigration of particular populations through racialized discourses, is generally viewed to have occurred in the context of European empire expansion and enslavement for profit of entire indigenous populations of several continents. The issue of whether racism preceded or was born of colonial capitalist expansion remains an unresolved and vigorously debated issue (see Miles 1982; Solomos 1986; Stasiulis 1990). Earlier Marxist accounts of the origins of racism tended to treat racialist thinking and racism as the products of capitalism or capitalist class struggles (Cox 1948). Such Marxist explanations regarded racial ideologies and subjectivities as by-products of the "more fundamental drama" of capitalism and class conflict. The needs and diffusion of capitalism on an international scale are insufficient explanations for the emergence of racism, however (Omi and Winant 1994). Moreover, the insistence within Marxist approaches that the function of racism was to justify or hide some form of economic exploitation of subordinate social classes or racialized class fractions did not unacknowledge that racism has material effects in its own right in ordering people's lives and access to material resources, citizenship rights, and human dignity (Goldberg 1993; Higginbotham 1992). While Marxist and neo-Marxist approaches to racism have drawn attention to the significant functions of racism in justifying the super-exploitation of colonized and migrant peoples, they provided unsatisfactory accounts for their social oppression, even at the hands of white working classes. In addition, (neo-)Marxist analyses of racism left much of the discursive content of racist ideologies and their internal complex, contradictory, and historically unstable properties unexamined and unproblematized. Even when new meanings are constructed about "race" in general or about particular racial constructs, "the old meanings refuse to die. They rather accumulate in clusters of ever-increasing power, resonance, and persuasion" (Young 1995).

A powerful illustration of the layered discourses that are sedimented into popular racist views underlying white supremacy is provided by Cornel West (1982). West suggests that three white supremacist logics—Judaeo-Christian, Cartesian scientific, and psychosexual—operate simultaneously in European and North American contexts to produce the belief that people of colour are alien and inferior. The justification of "black ugliness, cultural deficiency, and intellectual inferiority" was made possible by the "creative fusion" of Cartesian philosophy, the rise of the new disciplines of phrenology and physiognomy

(the reading of skulls and faces, respectively), and the revival during the Enlightenment of neoclassical aesthetic and cultural norms of human form, proportion, and beauty (West 1982). The advent of modern science, which routinized empirical observation and measurement, concomitantly incorporated Graeco-Roman aesthetic standards and thus played a central role in producing what West calls the "normative gaze" (West 1982). Through this gaze—namely, a specific ideal from which to order and compare measurements regarding "what it is to be human, cultured and intelligent"—all people of colour would be judged and found wanting (1982).

The state is an important focal point for the orchestration of relations of racialized power. In many of the white settler societies, including Canada, the United States, and Australia, a "rearticulation" of the meaning of terms such as "racial equality' is occurring in the political realm while many of the gains made by anti-racist and indigenous rights movements are being dismantled (Omi and Winant 1994; Perera and Pugliese 1997).[17] Within these countries, neo-conservative "colour-blind" strategies, which are detrimental to racialized peoples and minorities because they fail to recognize and ameliorate historical and structural patterns of racial inequality, are gaining ascendancy in state policies and the rhetoric of mainstream political parties and state legislatures. At the same time, attacks are increasing on racialized "others," including indigenous peoples, racial minorities, immigrants, and refugees in efforts to exclude, dominate, and prevent these groups from gaining equality and justice. The fact that the terms of these power-laden dynamics are either explicitly racialized or disguised by "code words" certainly supports arguments for the continued need to provide manifest analytical attention to social divisions of race within intersectional theorizing.[18]

3. Racism and Sexuality

A third explanation for the sustained durability of racialized constructs to this day (despite reasoned arguments about the non-existence of races) resides in what may be viewed as the unconscious, visceral, or prerational responses to racialized others. Numerous influential texts and popular media have fabricated symbols, metaphors, and allegories that together have provided iconographies of colonial rule associating colonized peoples with dirt, sin, criminality, and perversion. Some recent psychoanalytic probings of race thinking have illuminated the psychosexual and erotic dimensions of racism, the ambivalent fusing of desire and repulsion, that accompanied all encounters between colonizers and the colonized, enslavers and the enslaved. This is one area where race tends to subsume or overdetermine other sets of relations such as gender and sexuality, as when Ronald Takaki (1977) asserts that sexual fear in nineteenth-century Europe and North America was basically a racial anxiety. As Nira Yuval-Davis (1997) states, "The embodiment dimension of the racialized 'other' puts sexuality at the heart of the racialized imagery which projects dreams of forbidden pleasure and fears of impotency onto the 'other.'"

Centring on the case of Sarah Bartman, the South African woman who was displayed nude in the British Museum as a living model of the "Hottentot Venus," Sander Gilman (1989) has elucidated the link between sex and race constructed in white colonial fantasies in which blackness evoked an attractive but dangerous sexuality and limitless but threatening fertility. Young (1995) demonstrates how the writings of nineteenth-century race theorists, such as the notorious Count Gobineau (whose work informed the Nazi project of race purification), were obsessed with interracial sex or its consequences, such as the degree to which sexual relations between those who were considered to be of different races would produce healthy offspring. While Gobineau's race theories assumed a natural repugnance between races, they are also predicated on the recognition of race mixing as an inevitable process whose long-term result is "degeneration." Race mixing is compelled by the irrepressible sexual attraction felt by the males of the higher "Aryan" race

for the lower savage races. Young suggests that for Gobineau, interracial sexual desire (the imputed cause of the rise and fall of civilizations) is centred on white males' desire for exoticized black-, brown-, and yellow-skinned females. Racial differences, however, themselves become gendered so that the males of yellow, brown, and black races become feminized, leading to a sadistic interracial homoeroticism in the colonial arena (Young 1995; see also Nandy 1983).

The actual patterns of interracial sexual violence and consensual intimacy were masked by complicated and contradictory stereotypes of the sexuality of males and females from colonized races, as well as of European colonial men and women. One of the most infamous inversions of the actual pattern of sexual relations was the pathologized constructions of the "black male sexual predator and rapist" of "innocent and vulnerable white women" in the southern states of the United States, throughout much of the British Empire, and other European colonies. In diverse contexts such as Southern Rhodesia, Kenya, New Guinea, the Solomon Islands, and India, the images of the primitive sexuality and uncontrollable lust of black men and other men of colour prompted the passage of ordinances for the protection of white women and severe punishments such as the death penalty for sexual assault of white/European women by men of colour (Stoler 1996). In the American South, the popular purchase among whites of the imagined sexual/racial peril led to a savage "orgy" of lynching black men from the late nineteenth century until the 1960s. All these situations had no correlations between actual sexual assault on white/European women by men of colour and the rhetoric of sexual assault and harsh punitive measures. Rather, these race-sex panics were more likely to flare up during periods of the intensification of white settler interests, political insurgence, fear of non-acquiescence to colonial rule, or even labour unrest within European communities (Stoler 1996).

In contrast to the lack of evidence of actual black male sexual violence perpetrated against white women, white/European men's sexual assault of women of colour was commonplace, systematic, and rationalized by the stereotypes of black female sexual natures as licentious and depraved (Davis 1983; Marshall 1996; Ware 1992). Moreover, the sexual assault of black women was not recognized within law as rape and therefore was not legally punishable; rapes of women of colour committed by white men did not result in prosecution or incarceration of the rapists (Stoler 1996).

A legal edifice of **anti-miscegenation** laws in the United States, in place over most of the past 400 years, prohibited marriage between members of the dominant white race and Native, African, Chinese, Japanese, and Filipino Americans. Each of these prohibitions, and a range of atrocities from genocide and lynching to segregation and immigration quotas and exclusion acts, were justified by racialized stereotypes of male and female sexuality in each of these racial/ethnic groups. Often at the centre of many of these laws was the paternalistic construction of the vulnerable and innocent white woman's need to be "protected" by white patriarchy from the "primitive" sexuality of men of colour. In Canada, workplace laws such as the 1923 Women's and Girls' Protection Act in the Statutes of British Columbia embodied similar stereotypes and sought to prohibit the employment of white women and girls in Chinese businesses, which were defined in the statute as places "where morals might be in question" (Li 1988). Another anxiety at the base of such laws was the fear of diluting white male economic power through inheritance patterns resulting from marriages of white males to women of colour (Frankenberg 1993). White women who transgressed racial/sexual boundaries in choosing relationships with men of colour were portrayed as morally "loose" prostitutes and betrayers of their race (Frankenberg 1993). In some European colonies, such as Rhodesia, laws like the Immorality Act of 1916 were enacted, which "made it an offence for a white woman to make an indecent suggestion to a male native" (Stoler 1996).

Racialized depictions of sexuality were also amenable to transformation depending upon changed metropolitan priorities and racial/ethnic and sexual demographics within colonies. Thus, in the process of creating settler colonies, the arrival of large numbers of European women inevitably led to the denigration of previously more positive, albeit ambivalent, images of indigenous and Métis women whose intimate and often long-term relations with European colonial men had long been condoned and even encouraged (Van Kirk 1980). Recent feminist scholarship has increasingly accepted the interpretation that white women aided in constructing the asymmetries in race, gender, and class hierarchies of settler societies and played active roles in creating colonial culture rather than existing only as victims of colonial ideologies exclusively authored by white men (Lake 1993; Stasiulis and Yuval-Davis 1995). Such work has also sought to demonstrate how white women—who were assigned the roles of custodians of a redefined colonial morality, family welfare, and respectability, and mothers of imperial nations—did not alone invent racism but nonetheless were participants in a much broader colonial project of shoring up white prestige and redrawing class lines within these societies (Jolly 1993; Stoler 1996).

4. Racial Subjectivity and Affirmation

A fourth piece of the puzzle as to why race thinking endures despite its lack of scientific validity is the role played by race in constituting subjectivity and agency. Race can be viewed as a "double-voiced discourse"—serving both racial oppression and racial affirmation or liberation (Higginbotham 1992). Race penetrates state institutions, market relationships, mass media, and popular "common sense" in a manner that denigrates, oppresses, and exploits racialized others.

The mythologizing and even essentializing of races can occur in the construction of both dominant and oppressed races. Thus, in Canada, eugenicists in the social purity movement of 1885–1920 were not, Mariana Valverde points out, involved in a purely negative, prohibitory program. Rather, the project, which involved such deplorable acts as the sterilization of Aboriginal and immigrant women and the exclusion of Asians and blacks from settlement, was that of nation building; that is, the construction and strengthening of the white British-Canadian state and civil society according to a pristine, snowcapped, milky white vision of moral health, truth, and beauty (Valverde 1991).

As Etienne Balibar (1991) points out, race thinking is much more than the denigration or elevation of particular groups based on biological or "natural" characteristics. Racialist ideologies are also frequently based on the valorization of "communities of language, of descent, of tradition that fail to coincide with actual nations" (Balibar 1991). Not confined simply to expressing a discourse of degradation, racialist ideologies are infused with strength through certain vitalist metaphors representing energy, initiative, mastery, morality, and domination. Work on the construction of whiteness has revealed how problematic it is to deal with whiteness as a positive identity given white culture's ties to racial domination (Frankenberg 1993; Giroux 1997).[19] Suvendrini Perera and Joseph Pugliese (1997) refer to the "reracialisation" of Australian identity. Certain racialized iconic national figures such as the "Aussie battler" are being reinvigorated by Australian political leaders to articulate the myth of white, mainstream Anglo-Australians as a marginalized, persecuted, and silenced majority taming the landscape and Aboriginals within, and holding forth against the unassimilable, criminalized Asian migrants. More generally, within all European countries and their white settler offshoots, it is difficult to deny that whiteness, which has for so long been associated within Eurocentric thought with moral social, aesthetic, and political supremacy over all racialized "others," is an empowering form of identity not only for white supremacists but for many white people who do not hold extremist racist views.

Thus, race endures because of the complexity and enduring power of racist discourses, the role of racial divisions in organizing relations of production and exploitation, the visceral, psychosexual responses evoked by racial differences, and the psychically and politically affirming properties of racial existence.

The Pitfalls of Race Essentialism

Faced with these staunchly resistant realities of racialized domination, women of colour feminists and other anti-racist theorists have made a strong political and analytical case in placing race within a central position in intersectional theorizing (Calliste 1996; Dei 1996; Omi and Winant 1994). As it is impossible to simultaneously explore all categories of social difference and power with the same intensity, these scholars have strategically chosen to emphasize race and racism to seek to understand, in order to resist, the racialized forms of power that are more visibly salient or more damaging for women (and men) of colour than gender or class in most areas of their lived experience. The priority accorded to race phenomena in intersectional analysis provides the basis for resistance against racial subordination, exclusion, and marginalization. While race (or skin colour) identification was by no means the sole or even defining feature of black feminism, women of colour feminism, and Third World feminism, it was nonetheless the *sine qua non* of the oppositional social movements that formed to contest the matrix of domination, which combined racist, sexist, homophobic, classist, and imperialist logics (Mohanty 1991; Sandoval 1998).

First, the white/colour dichotomy, which is the hallmark of race essentialism, oversimplifies the sources of oppression for women of colour (Jhappan 1996). European/white racism and all whites are constructed as oppressors, regardless of the heterogeneity among whites and among people of colour in class and ethnic terms. Non-European racisms and intragroup subjugation among people of colour and within Asia, Africa, Central America, the Caribbean, the Pacific, and the Middle East are ignored. Racisms woven from Eurocentric threads cannot make sense of the particular racial hostilities in countries where whites are virtually absent, such as the hostility experienced by the Chinese in Malaysia, the denigration of Filipinos in Singapore, the Gulf region countries, and so forth. Yet racial and ethnic othering, hatred, violence, exclusion, and discrimination based on racial/ethnic/religious opposition are global phenomena. Friedman (1995) critiques as Eurocentric "the notion that the West invented racial and ethnic classifications and their institutionalization or has been the only culture to engage in such otherings." Other civilizations, such as the Chinese and Indian, had adopted highly developed conceptions of hierarchies based upon skin colour and racial difference prior to contact with the West (Friedman 1995; Jhappan 1996). Similarly, Radha Jhappan draws attention to the fact that

> many racisms in different parts of the world (such as Japanese racism against Koreans) seemingly have nothing to do with Europeans at all, while others (such as the generalized racism throughout Asia against the many thousands of exported Filipina domestic workers and nurses, and male Filipino labourers exported for the construction and shipping trades) are indirectly caused by European imperialism by virtue of its stunting of economic development in various regions. (1996)

Second, essentialism links racism to skin colour rather than to the structural location of particular groups in concrete and historically specific social relations and to the accompanying discourses that aid in the processes of denigration, subordination, and exploitation. There is ample evidence of the enduring and unique liability of skin colour racism in white settler societies for black women and many other women of colour in the distribution of material rewards, status, and acceptance as legitimate settlers and citizens. Nonetheless, the production of racism through perception of significant skin colour differences is a complicated issue as many collectivities contemporaneously perceived to be white (such as Jews and the Irish) have historically been constructed as black (Gilman 1991; Ignatiev 1995).

Thus, it is problematic to construct people of colour as the exclusive objects of racism and skin colour as a necessary racialized signifier whether one is speaking about Canada or many other societies across the globe. The racisms currently experienced by Eastern and Southern European migrants and refugees, such as Gypsies seeking asylum in Canada from persecution in the Czech Republic and other European countries, are left unaccounted for by skin colour racism.

Indeed, the development of many different racisms in Canada are the product of a long history of European and non-European immigration, which had brought to Canada many waves of peoples who departed from the British model of physical appearance and cultural desirability. Language, religion, and other cultural markers have made diverse groups—including the Catholic Irish in the nineteenth century, the European Jews who unsuccessfully sought refuge in Canada from the Holocaust in the 1930s, and Southern Italians who migrated to postwar Toronto—targets of racist scorn, intolerance, and unequal treatment.

One effect of structural racism in Canada is that in a multiracial, multi-ethnic sex-segregated workforce, particular groups of European immigrant women have historically shared disadvantages similar to those of working-class women of colour, and many continue to do so. The work of several feminist historians and sociologists in Canada have documented the particularized histories of oppression and spirited resistance to gendered, racist, ethnicized, and class-based stereotypes and institutionalized discrimination of European women who had migrated to Canada from Italy (Iacovetta 1986, 1992), Finland (Lindstrom-Best 1988), Portugal (Noivo 1997), and the Ukraine (Swyripa 1993).[20]

Third, an exclusive focus on skin colour racism lends itself to a hierarchization of racial oppression based upon skin colour, rendering many minorities "quite invisible and silenc[ing] the voices of less-coloured or 'differently coloured' groups" such as Arabs and Muslims in North America (Abdo 1993). The homogenization of all whites is matched by the homogenization of all women of colour (Jhappan 1996). This leads to inattention to the specific nature of discursive, structural, and institutional racisms experienced by different groups with common skin colour such as fifth-generation African Canadians who are descendants of African-American slaves, Afro-Caribbean immigrants, and Somali refugees.

Reference to skin colour draws attention to the origins of racism in colonial and imperial relationships, and the fact that many racialized migrants are from areas of the world that were colonized by European powers, and whose development continues to be stunted by Western neo-colonialism and imperialism. However, it is equally important to point out the distinctive and protracted colonial burdens within settler societies borne by indigenous women, such as First Nations women in Canada (*Fireweed* 1986; LaChapelle 1982; Kirkness 1987–88; Turpel 1993). The unique histories of colonial, class, racial and gender oppression of First Nations women and their resistance to that oppression are nurturing grounds for distinctive Aboriginal political concerns such as land claims and self-governance. First Nations women also continue their protracted struggle to deal with gendered and racialized forms of discrimination in the Indian Act, which until recently decreed that marriage to **non-status** men removed status rights for generations of women and their offspring. Bill C-31, the 1985 amendments that were supposed to end gender inequities in the Indian Act, has in fact led to more complicated distinctions between status and non-status Indians across generations. Such neo-colonial, racist, and gendered legislation has produced tensions within First Nations communities (Anderssen 1997).

Part Two: Beyond Race, Gender, and Class

A great deal of recent commentary on the post–Cold War "state of the world" or "postmodernity" has taken note of the current intensity of ethnic, national, and religious assertions of identity, which are frequently expressed in violent terms (Ahmed 1995; Kothari 1997). The tendency to construct national, ethnic, and religious identities in restrictive terms has increased in an era of global restructuring, geopolitical imbalance, and new right ideological attacks on citizenship rights and benefits (Stasiulis 1997). The fact that among the most important differences among women worldwide is their membership in ethnic, national, and religious collectivities has recently captured the attention of feminist theorists of intersectionality (Andrew 1996; Moghadam 1994; Stasiulis 1999; Yuval-Davis 1997). Many of these analyses are particularly interested in understanding how women have organized themselves politically in relation to these intersections (Andrew 1996; Basu 1995).

Just as the definition of race is hotly debated, so too are the definitions of ethnicity, nation, and religion within feminist intersectional analysis. One conceptual problem is that of clearly and unambiguously delineating the distinctions among social relations of ethnicity, race, and nation. For instance, while older definitions of race had emphasized biological referents and solely negative usages and viewed ethnicity in terms of cultural identity and boundaries, more recent definitions have blurred the distinctions between the two concepts. This is partially because racist discourses are increasingly couched in terms of cultural differences rather than notions of biological inferiority and superiority (Anthias 1995). It is also because many collectivities are using both concepts of race and ethnicity in a self-affirming manner to resist assimilation, pursue cultural difference and autonomy, and produce new cultural forms. This means that the same racialized term, such as "black," could be used in different contexts to denote the race or ethnicity of a collectivity. The confusion and conflation between the two terms is quite apparent in Statistics Canada's problematic construction of the racial category of "visible minorities" from ethnic origin categories.[21]

The distinction between race and ethnicity is further clouded by the heinous military and political practices conducted in the name of preserving ethnic divisions and purity, such as the mass rape of women and systematic genocide, given the chilling euphemism of "ethnic cleansing" in Bosnia. In Bosnia, Croatia, Rwanda, Somalia, and other countries that have seen the rise of bloody warfare between collectivities, these conflicts appear to emphasize the "narcissism of minor differences" (Ignatieff 1993). It is difficult to maintain that such ferocious animosities and violence between collectivities are clearly matters of "ethnic differences" rather than racial hostilities. In other words, there is increasingly the sense that the political uses of ethnicity are no more benign than political movements based on preserving racial divisions or supremacy.

The distinction between ethnicity and nation is also murky. For instance, ethnicity is derived from the Greek word *ethnikos*, the adjective of *ethnos*, which refers to a people or nation. The definitional difference is largely a political one in a context where international bodies such as the **United Nations** affirm the right of nations/peoples, but not ethnic groups, to self-determination. Both ethnic groups and nations have been defined with reference to shared cultural attributes such as "heritage" or "tradition," language, as well as material and political dimensions such as territory, the state, biological or genetic "stock," and economic life.

What constitutes a nation and the extent to which it is a particularly modern or even Western phenomenon are thus controversial questions. At one extreme are "the primordialists" (Geertz 1963; Shils 1957; van den Berghe 1979) who claim that nations are natural and universal, an automatic extension of kinship relationships. For primordialists, a nation's historical importance might rise or fall, but it is always there, waiting to be discovered rather than historically constructed. At the other extreme are "the modernists," those who see nationalism and nations as phenomena that are particular to capitalism (Althusser 1969; Hobsbawm 1990) or other modern developments, such as the invention of print (Anderson 1983).

Consistent with Benedict Anderson's (1983) germinal insight concerning the constructed or "imagined" character of nations, Nira Yuval-Davis (1997) differentiates among three major dimensions of nationalist projects. The first is based on the myth of common origins or shared blood/genes (*Volknation*); the second is based on culture or the "symbolic heritage provided by language and/or religion and/or customs and traditions," which then define the "essence" of the nation (*Kulturnation*); and the third is based on common citizenship within a sovereign nation-state (*Staatnation*) (Yuval-Davis 1997). While, of the three, the first dimension of nationalism tends to construct the most exclusionary and ethnically/racially restrictive vision of "the nation," each dimension intersects with gender and other social relations to create hierarchies of belonging to national communities and citizenship entitlements within nation-states.

The intersections between nationalist phenomena and gender relations, and between nationalism and movements for women's liberation have typically manifested an extremely fraught yet intimate relationship. Cynthia Enloe has noted the masculinist and androcentric cast of nationalisms that have "typically sprung from masculinized memory, masculinized humiliation and masculinized hope" (1989). Nationalist politics resonate with masculine cultural themes such as cowardice, bravery, the allure of adventure, patriotic duty, male honour, and the prevention of female shame (Nagel 1998). Notwithstanding the involvement of many women in the front lines of nationalist battles, the military and political leadership is usually overwhelmingly male. While men are the generals and foot soldiers of nationalist battles, women are disproportionately the victims in the political sexual violence of wartime rape or "ethnic cleansing." Alongside children, women form the vast majority (up to 80 per cent) of those displaced in worldwide refugee movements, the outcome in large part of nationalist, interethnic, and religious wars (Rogers 1993).

Anne McClintock has drawn attention to the "family trope" in nationalist narratives of "motherlands," "fatherlands," and of nationalist heroes and heroines who are called "Fathers" and "Mothers" of the nation. The family trope naturalizes the social subordination of women and children within the private domestic sphere of the family/household (McClintock 1993). The most common roles inscribed in nationalist discourses for women are those of Wife and Mother (Moghadam 1994). In the context of military, demographic, and politico-ideological battles fought for the nation, the primary contributions of women become those of biological reproducers of members of the national collectivity, ideological agents for the transmission of national/ethnic identity, values and traditions, and icons of national/ethnic difference (Yuval-Davis and Anthias 1989).

The regulation of women's sexuality and fertility, and their domestication through nationalist projects, contradicts feminist goals that generally seek to free women from biological and domestic strictures or the narrow confines of female-appropriate roles ordained by nature, divine will, tradition, or the goals of national survival (Moghadam 1994). Many nationalisms tend to circumscribe and regulate women's roles, autonomy, and identity, a feature that has also been noted of various religious fundamentalisms, and that puts nationalisms and fundamentalisms in opposition to the goals of women's emancipation (Moghadam 1994). But there are also nationalist struggles, especially involving decolonization movements of indigenous peoples, where women have played key leadership roles and have drawn on ancestral traditions of female power.

Women, and indeed feminists, including those belonging to hegemonic ethnic groups, have also at different times and in different geospatial contexts defined their agenda in terms of women's gender-specific and exalted roles in reproducing their nations. Women of both ethnic majority and subordinated groups may be exhorted to have children or curtail their fertility within state natality policies. Such policies variously emphasize a demographic contest with enemy groups, eugenics, or, as is common in developing countries, a Malthusian discourse (Yuval-Davis 1997).

The already complex relationship between nationalism and feminism, which involves various types of "patriarchal bargains," is further complicated by the reality of competing nationalist and nation-building projects mapped within the same geopolitical space. Whether or not a nationalist movement hinders or furthers a movement towards women's emancipation among women defined as part of that nation is a separate question from whether a nationalist movement may oppress women who are defined as outside that nation, and who may have their own nationalist or communal self-determination aspirations. The answer to the second question depends in part on whether nationalism is inherently exclusionary or whether it is capable of recognizing and validating other nationalist and ethnic minority claims, together with the demands of women's liberation within these competing national/ethnic projects. The degree to which a particular nationalism is open or oppositional to the communal projects of those who are not part of the dominant ethnicity is also dependent on the larger societal project (neo-liberal, social democratic, fascist, and so on) to which the nationalism is wedded.

*   *   *

Conclusion: Relational Conceptualizations of Intersectionality

Which social relations in the seemingly dizzying array of differences should be accorded particular salience or significance in any given theoretical framework is impossible to predict a priori. As Majid (1998b) states, "People occupy different subject positions in various social hierarchies . . . privileges and exclusions; articulations and silences shift across temporal and spatial boundaries." This means that academic efforts to construct general theories of intersectionality inevitably flatten complex heterogeneities and are unlikely to have resonance for all groups of women or men within and across all localities. Do the apparently endless permutations in intersectional analyses mitigate against the production of some level of generalizations and patterning, which would appear to be important for any broad-based theoretical and political project? The current debates that take more demarcated sets of relations into account—e.g., nationalism and feminism, migrant domestic worker relations with employers and states—offer some cause for optimism. The trend towards comparative research of specific yet diverse groups of women (e.g., the scholarship on women and Islam discussed earlier) provides overlapping vocabularies, assumptions, and frameworks that lead to rich forms of intersectional theorizing.

The challenges in capturing those social relations that have material force and meaning in women's lives have stretched intersectional theorizing beyond the triadic formulation of race, gender, and class. Diverse intersectional frameworks reflect the complex and contradictory relations women have with ethnic tradition, religion, nations, and other forms of social differentiation. As the exploration in this chapter of the continued prominence of race has illuminated, however, feminist theorists should not be in a rush to discard the significance of race and racism in women's lives and politics. Even where other social relations such as religion appear to have displaced race from a central position within a matrix of identities and oppressions, this should not be seen to have made race irrelevant. On the contrary, religion, ethnicity, nations, etc., are also constantly racialized as reflected in **Orientalist** constructions, which have portrayed Muslim women as "veiled" and "dark-skinned" and Christian women as "white."

One shared problem among intersectional frameworks that prioritize race or culture is the tendency towards essentialism, the assumptions of hard-and-fast differences between communities or groups regarded as homogenous, bounded, and discrete. Anti-essentializing feminist efforts to theorize the political consequences of national, religious, and ethnocultural diversity require the development of more appropriate conceptual tools. The theorizing of the complex intersectionality within the lives of ethnically and racially heterogeneous women has begun to move away from schemas that speak only of oppression, domination, and victimization while ignoring women's own agency in negotiating their

identities and altering their material and cultural conditions. "Relationality," "positionality," and "relational positionality" are concepts developed by anti-racist and postcolonial feminists to deal analytically with the fluidity of individual and group identities at the crossroads of different systems of power and domination (Bannerji 1991; Brah 1991; Friedman 1995; Mohanty 1991; Shohat and Stam 1994).

Susan Friedman (1995) elaborates on the work on relationality developed by Mohanty and others in viewing the dynamics of contradictory subject positions through narratives or "scripts of relational positionality." Such scripts offer an understanding of "the interplay of privilege and alterity" by acknowledging that power flows in more than one direction so that the oppressed can also be the oppressor, and the victim the victimizer, depending on the particular site of power (race, gender, class, sexuality, religion, etc.) one considers (Friedman 1995). Scripts of relationality are particularly useful in mapping the shifting and contradictory nature of intersectional identities and power arising out of transnationalism—the movement of capital, people, information, technology, culture, and ideology that has increased dramatically over the last three decades (K. Mitchell 1997).

The destabilizing consequences for identity, experience of oppression, agency, and political alliances of shifting positionalities are especially evident for "experienced" international migrants. An example of a person with a contradictory and shifting subject position within a complex set of social relations is

a relatively dark-skinned Brahmin woman who moves back and forth between London and Calcutta. As a Brahmin she is privileged by caste; as a woman, she is oppressed. As a frequent traveller, she is well-off in class terms, but called black by the British and subject to the disorientations of a bicontinental postcolonial identity. As a dark-skinned woman, she is differently disadvantaged within the Indian context of colorism and the British context of racism. (Friedman 1995)

Women who have migrated twice or more to various destination economies have identities not wholly defined by exclusion and domination and are active agents in negotiating their cultural values within different diasporic communities (Bhachu 1996). Bhachu notes that the role of (Asian) migrant women as active agents in transnational diasporas is largely absent from the literature (1996). But in addition, there is a tendency in ethnic relations and feminist literature to essentialize culture, i.e., to treat ethnic minority cultures as clearly organized, homogeneous, fixed, and impervious to all influences except those of the "homeland." As Bhachu argues, "particular ethnicities and identities are not stable, despite a common core of fundamental religious and cultural values that constitute cultural roots but which shift according to the forces operating on them" (1996).

Notes

1. I gratefully acknowledge the helpful comments and insightful suggestions that Yasmeen Abu-Laban, Radha Jhappan, Peter Li, and an anonymous reviewer provided on an earlier draft of this chapter.
2. For summaries and analyses of the race and class debates, see Solomos (1986) and Stasiulis (1990).
3. Patricia Hill Collins uses the term "matrix of domination" to refer to a single, historically created system whereby race, class, and gender (and other axes such as religion, ethnicity, sexual orientation, and age) intersect at the level of personal experience, the group or community level, and the systemic level of social institutions. She contrasts this notion of a matrix to additive models of oppression (Collins 1990).
4. Here I am also referring to women of colour theorists who have distanced themselves from the label of "feminist" because of the white solipsism associated with this term. Some African-American women writers such as Alice Walker (1983) have opted for the term "womanist" to signal their unique positioning in relations of race, gender, and class and their political disaffiliation from the racist and exclusionary nature of hegemonic feminism.
5. Some intersectional analyses are drawing attention to the neglected area of disability. For instance, Meekosha and Dowse (1997) chart some of the ways through which exclusionary forms of citizenship link together gender, nation, and disability.
6. White settler societies are societies in which "Europeans have settled, where their descendants have remained politically dominant over indigenous peoples, and where a heterogeneous society has developed in class, ethnic, and racial terms" (Stasiulis and Yuval-Davis 1995).
7. Precursors to black feminist theorists in the United States included nineteenth-century black suffragettes such as Anna Julia Cooper, who linked struggles against racism and against sexism (Brewer 1993).
8. "Racial formation," as defined by Omi and Winant, refers to "the sociohistorical process by which racial categories are created, inhabited, transformed and destroyed." "From a racial formation perspective, race is a matter of both social structure and cultural representation" (1994).
9. *Aotearoa* is the Maori word for New Zealand.
10. The black feminist literature is extensive. It includes the influential works produced in the United States by Bonnie Dill (1983), Angela Davis (1983), Audre Lorde (1984), Gloria Hull et al. (1982), bell hooks (1981, 1984, 1989), Patricia Collins (1991), Chandra Mohanty (1991), and Patricia Williams (1990); in Britain by Kum-Kum Bhavnani and Margaret Coulson (1986), Amina Mama (1989), Pratibha Parmar (1982), Valerie Amos and Pratibha Parmar (1984); and in Canada by Dionne Brand (1984), Agnes Calliste (1996), and Linda Carty (1991, 1993). The related scholarship by women of colour of various national/ethnic origins and by indigenous feminists is naturally even more voluminous. It is significant that the term "black" has been defined politically and in relation to anti-racist politics to mean descendants of African slaves in the United States, migrants from the Caribbean and South Asia in Britain, peoples of African ancestry (including migrants and their descendants from the Caribbean and the United States) in Canada, and Aborigines in Australia. Recent African refugees and migrants to Canada, such as those from Somalia, Ghana, and Rwanda, are more likely to self-identify as Somali, Ghanian, Rwandan, etc., rather than as black.
11. The labels, such as "non-white," "non-European," and "non-Western," which are in common usage in Europe and its satellites to designate non-hegemonic racial and ethnic collectivities, are Eurocentric and reflect white skin privilege. Minh-ha (1989) has argued that the labels by which many feminists refer to racial differences among women—such as "Western," "non-Western," and "Third World"—"take the dominant group as point of reference, and reflect well the West's ideology of dominance," adding for dramatic illustration that "it is as if we were to use the term 'non-Afro-Asian'... to designate all white people." All umbrella terms tend to homogenize collectivities that have tremendous diversity. For instance, some groups of women have expressed dissatisfaction with the term "women of colour" because it fails to reflect the social context of different communities (Dutt 1996). I use the term "women of colour" here in the knowledge of its limitations, but also to avoid the negative connotations of the "non" terms.

12. I am using the umbrella term "indigenous peoples" (adopted by the World Council of Indigenous Peoples) to refer to all those peoples globally who claim ancestry from the pre-European colonization/settlement period. "Aboriginal" is the term adopted in Canada and Australia. In Canada, the term does not include the Inuit. The term "First Nations" generally refers to those registered under the Indian Act (or "status Indians").

13. The centrality of race within intersectional theorizing has recently been taken up by authors such as Dei (1996) and Calliste (1996), who advocate "integrative anti-racism." As Dei (1996) argued, "The integrative anti-racism approach sees race as both the first point of entry and a point which does not lose its position of centrality during subsequent analyses of intersection oppression."

14. Racism is endemic in the First World and Third World, North and South, East and West, although in some countries race may be less salient than other social divisions, such as religion or ethnicity. Some societies with demographically large ethnic majorities, such as Japan, practise systematic discrimination against particular racialized groups, yet official state discourses are silent about issues such as racial minorities and racial discrimination.

15. The fact that Disraeli was Jewish and subjected to British anti-Semitism might well have raised his awareness of the injuries associated with racialized othering.

16. As Robert Young (1995) put it, "In the nineteenth century racial theory, substantiated and 'proved' by various forms of science such as comparative and historical philology, anatomy, anthropometry (including osteomentry, craniology, craniometry and pelvimentry), physiology, physiognomy and phrenology, became in turn endemic not just to other forms of science, such as biology and natural history, to say nothing of palaeontology, psychology, zoology and sexology, but was also used as a general category of understanding that extended to theories of anthropology, archaeology, classics, ethnology, geography, geology, folklore, history, language, law, literature and theology, and thus dispersed from almost every academic discipline to permeate definitions of culture and nation."

17. "Rearticulation" is the practice of the reorganization and reinterpretation of pre-existing discursive and ideological themes, so that the various elements obtain new meanings or coherence (Omi and Winant 1994).

18. "Code words" are superficially non-racial rhetoric used to disguise racial issues (Omi and Winant 1994). For an analysis of the use of code words in the racialist policies of the Reform Party of Canada, see Kirkham (1998).

19. Henry Giroux (1997) has called for a rearticulation of "whiteness" as part of a democratic cultural politics that might "challenge the conventional left analysis of 'whiteness' as a space between guilt and denial."

20. The flowering of ethnic feminist historiography in Canada has made it possible to replace such clumsy and misleading concepts as double (or triple) oppression (or jeopardy) with increasingly detailed portraits of the social structures, social relations, institutional mechanisms, cultural forms, and discourses that affect the lives of immigrant and refugee racialized/ethnic minority women (see Bakan and Stasiulis 1994; Boyd 1986, 1984; Estable 1986; Foote 1996; Ng and Ramirez 1981; Stasiulis 1987). But detailed case studies that take as their setting the workplace (Das Gupta 1996; Gannage 1987), trade unions (Borowy, Gordon, and Lebans 1993; Lipsig-Mumme 1987), the household (Iacovetta 1986), or the employment agency (Ng 1986, 1988) reveal many other situations in which immigrant and racial/ethnic minority women constitute distinct groups facing circumstances that are sometimes unique and sometimes shared with women of other ethnicities. Such histories also highlight the agency of women as they navigate and resist imperialist, capitalist, sexist, racist, and bureaucratic forms of domination, thus undercutting the image of minority and immigrant women as hapless, passive victims of "tradition" or of a seamless web of oppression.

21. In the 1996 census, Statistics Canada included a new "population group" question to collect statistics on visible minorities required for federal employment equity law. According to employment equity law, visible minorities are those Canadians who are "non-Caucasian in race or non-white in colour." Question 19 in the 1996 census asked: "Is this person . . . White, Chinese, South Asian (e.g., East Indian, Pakistani, Punjabi, Sri Lankan), black (e.g., African, Haitian, Jamaican, Somali), Arab/West Asian (e.g., Armenian, Egyptian, Iranian, Lebanese, Moroccan), Filipino, Southeast Asian (e.g., Cambodian, Indonesian, Laotian, Vietnamese), Latin American, Japanese, Korean, Other (Specify)?" This method of collecting statistics on visible minorities replaced the more complicated formula used in earlier censuses, which relied on data derived from a question on ethnic origin, as well as other questions pertaining to language and religion (A. Mitchell 1997).

References

Abdo, Nahla. 1993. "Race, Gender and Politics: The Struggle of Arab Women in Canada." In *And Still We Rise: Feminist Political Mobilizing in Contemporary Canada*, edited by Linda Carty, 73–98. Toronto: Women's Press.

———. 1994. "Nationalism and Feminism: Palestinian Women and the Intifada—No Going Back?" In *Gender and National Identity*, edited by V.M. Moghadam, 148–70. London: Zed Books.

———. 1997. "Muslim Family Law: Articulating Gender, Class and the State." *International Review of Comparative Public Policy* 9: 169–93.

Agnew, Vijay. 1996. *Resisting Discrimination: Women from Asia, Africa, and the Caribbean and the Women's Movement in Canada.* Toronto: University of Toronto Press.

Ahmad, Aijaz. 1992. *In Theory: Classes, Nations, Literature.* London: Verso.

Ahmed, Akbar S. 1995. "Ethnic Cleansing: A Metaphor for Our Time?" *Ethnic and Racial Studies* 18: 1–25.

Alam, S.M. Shamsul. 1998. "Women in the Era of Modernity and Islamic Fundamentalism: The Case of Taslima Nasrin of Bangladesh." *Signs* 23, 2: 429–62.

Althusser, Louis. 1969. *For Marx.* London: Allen Lane.

Amin, Samir. 1989. *Eurocentrism.* New York: Monthly Review Press.

Amos, Valerie, and Pratibha Parmar. 1984. "Challenging Imperial Feminism." *Feminist Review* 17 (July): 3–19.

Anderson, Benedict. 1983. *Imagined Communities: Reflections on the Origins and Spread of Nationalism.* London: Verso.

Anderssen, Erin. 1997. "Lost Generations: Not Indian Enough by Law." *The Globe and Mail* (17 November): Al, A3.

Andrew, Caroline. 1996. "Ethnicities, Citizenship and Feminisms: Theorizing the Political Practices of Intersectionality." In *Ethnicity and Citizenship: The Canadian Case,* edited by Jean Laponce and William Safran, 64–81. London: Frank Cass.

Anthias, Floya. 1990. "Parameters of Difference and Identity and the Problem of Connections—Gender, Ethnicity and Class." Paper presented at the XII World Congress of Sociology, RC05, Gender, Race and Class Stream, Madrid, July.

——. 1995. "Cultural Racism or Racist Culture? Rethinking Racist Exclusions." *Economy and Society* 24, 2: 279–301.

Anthias, Floya, and Nira Yuval-Davis. 1992. *Racialized Boundaries: Race, Nation, Gender, Colour, and Class and the Anti-Racist Struggle.* London: Routledge.

Appadurai, Arjun. 1991. "Global Ethnoscapes: Notes and Queries for a Transnational Anthropology." In *Recapturing Anthropology: Working in the Present,* edited by Richard G. Fox, 191–210. Santa Fe: School of American Research Press.

Appiah, Anthony, and Henry Louis Gates. 1995. *Identities.* Chicago: University of Chicago Press.

Armstrong, Pat, and Hugh Armstrong. 1986a. "Beyond Sexless Class and Classless Sex: Towards Feminist Marxism." In *The Politics of Diversity: Feminism, Marxism, and Nationalism,* edited by R. Hamilton and M. Barren, 208–40. Montreal: Book Center.

——. 1986b. "More on Marxism and Feminism: A Response to Patricia Connelly." In *The Politics of Diversity: Feminism, Marxism, and Nationalism,* edited by R. Hamilton and M. Barrett, 249–54. Montreal: Book Center.

Bakan, Abigail, and Daiva Stasiulis. 1994. "Foreign Domestic Worker Policy in Canada and the Social Boundaries of Citizenship." *Science and Society* 58, 1: 1–33.

——. 1995. "Making the Match: Domestic Placement Agencies and the Racialization of Women's Household Work." *Signs* 29, 2: 303–35.

——. 1997. *"Not One of the Family": Foreign Domestic Workers in Canada.* Toronto: University of Toronto Press.

Balibar, Etienne. 1991. "The Nation Form: History and Ideology." In *Race, Nation, and Class,* edited by E. Balibar and I. Wallerstein, 86–106. London: Verso.

Bannerji, Himani. 1991 "But Who Speaks for Us? Experience and Agency in Conventional Feminist

Paradigms." In *Unsettling Relations: The University as a Site of Feminist Struggles,* edited by H. Bannerji et al., 67–108. Toronto: Women's Press.

Barrett, Michele. 1980. *Women's Oppression Today.* London: Verso.

Basu, Amrita, ed. 1995. *The Challenge of Local Feminisms: Women's Politics in Global Perspective.* Boulder, CO: Westview Press.

Belkhir, Jean, and Michael Ball. 1993. "Editor's Introduction: Integrating Race, Sex, and Class in Our Disciplines." *Race, Sex, and Class* 1, 1: 3–11.

Bhabha, Horni. 1990. *Nation and Narration.* London: Routledge.

Bhachu, Parminder. 1996. "The Multiple Landscapes of Transnational Asian Women in the Diaspora." In *Re-Situating Identities: The Politics of Race, Ethnicity, and Culture,* edited by Vered Amit-Talia and Caroline Knowles, 283–303. Peterborough, ON: Broadview Press.

Bhavnani, Kum-Kum, and Margaret Coulson. 1986. "Transforming Socialist-Feminism: The Challenge of Racism." *Feminist Review* 23 (June): 81–92.

Bordo, Susan. 1990. "Feminism, Postmodernism, and Gender-Scepticism." In *Feminism/Postmodernism,* edited by L. Nicholson, 133–56. New York: Routledge.

Borowy, Jan, Shelly Gordon, and Gayle Lebans. 1993. "Are These Clothes Clean? The Campaign for Fair Wages and Working Conditions for Homeworkers." In *And Still We Rise: Feminist Political Mobilizing in Contemporary Canada,* edited by L. Carty, 299–332. Toronto: Women's Press.

Bourgeault, Ron. 1983a. "The Development of Capitalism and the Subjugation of Native Women in Northern Canada." *Alternate Routes* 6: 110–40.

——. 1983b. "The Indian, the Metis and the Fur Trade: Class, Sexism, and Racism in the Transition from 'Communism' to Capitalism." *Studies in Political Economy* 2: 45–80.

Boyd, Monica. 1984. "At a Disadvantage: The Occupational Attainments of Foreign Born Women in Canada." *International Migration Review* 18 (Winter): 1091–119.

——. 1986. "Immigrant Women in Canada." In *International Migration,* edited by Rita J. Simon and Caroline Bretell, 47–75. Totowa: Rowman and Allenheld.

Brah, Avtar. 1991. "Difference, Diversity, Differentiation." *International Review of Sociology* 2: 53–72.

Brand, Dionne. 1984. "A Working Paper on Black Women in Toronto: Gender, Race and Class." *Fireweed* 19 (Summer/Fall): 26–43.

Brewer, Rose M. 1993. "Theorizing Race, Class, and Gender: The New Scholarship of Black Feminist Intellectuals and Black Women's Labor." In *Theorizing Black Feminisms: The Visionary Pragmatism of Black Women,* edited by S.M. James and A.P.A. Busia, 13–30. London: Routledge.

Calliste, Agnes. 1996. "Antiracism Organizing and Resistance in Nursing: African Canadian Women." *Canadian Review of Sociology and Anthropology* 33, 3: 361–90.

Cannon, Katie Geneva. 1995. *Katie's Canon: Womanism and the Soul of the Black Community.* New York: Continuum.

Carby, Hazel. 1982. "White Women Listen! Feminism and the Boundaries of Sisterhood." In *The Empire Strikes Back*, edited by Paul Gilroy at the Centre for Contemporary Cultural Studies, 212–315. London: Hutchinson.

———. 1987. *Reconstructing Womanhood: The Emergence of the Afro-American Woman Novelist*. New York: Oxford University Press.

Carty. Linda. 1991. "Black Women in Academia: A Statement from the Periphery." In *Unsettling Relations: The University as a Site of Feminist Struggles*, edited by H. Bannerji, L. Carty, K. Delhi, S. Heald, and K. McKenna, 13–44. Toronto: Women's Press.

———. 1993. "Combining Our Efforts: Making Feminism Relevant to the Changing Sociality." In *And Still We Rise: Feminist Political Mobilizing in Contemporary Canada*, edited by L. Carty, 7–24. Toronto: Women's Press.

Chaudhuri, N., and M. Strobel, eds 1992. *Western Women and Imperialism: Complicity and Resistance*. Bloomington and Indianapolis: Indiana University Press.

Clifford, James. 1994. "Diasporas." *Cultural Anthropology* 9, 3: 302–39.

Collins, Patricia Hill. 1990. *Black Feminist Thought: Knowledge, Consciousness, and the Politics of Empowerment*. London: Unwin Hyman.

Connolly, Clara. 1991. "Washing Our Linen: One Year of Women Against Fundamentalism." *Feminist Review* 37 (Spring): 68–77.

Cox, Oliver. 1948. *Caste, Class, and Race*. New York: Monthly Review Press.

Creese, Gillian, and Daiva Stasiulis. 1996. "Introduction: Intersections of Gender, Race, Class, and Sexuality." *Studies in Political Economy* 51 (Fall): 5–14.

Das Gupta, Tania. 1996. "Anti-Black Racism in Nursing in Ontario." *Studies in Political Economy* 51 (Fall): 97–116.

Davis, Angela. 1983. *Women, Race and Class*. New York: Vintage Books.

Dei, George J. Sefa. 1996. *Anti-Racism Education: Theory and Practice*. Halifax, NS: Fernwood Publishing.

Dill, Bonnie Thornton. 1983. "Race, Class and Gender: Prospects for an All-Inclusive Sisterhood." *Feminist Studies* 9, 1: 131–50.

Duclos, Nitya. 1993. "Disappearing Women: Racial Minority Women in Human Rights Cases." *Canadian Journal of Women and the Law* 6, 1: 25–51.

Dumont, M. 1992. "The Origins of the Women's Movement in Quebec." In *Challenging Times: The Women's Movement in Canada and the United States*, edited by C. Backhouse and D.H. Flaherty, 72–89. Montreal and Kingston: McGill-Queen's University Press.

Dutt, Mallika. 1996. "Some Reflections on US Women of Color and the United States Fourth World Conference on Women and NGO Forum in Beijing, China." *Feminist Studies* 22, 3: 519–28.

Eisenstein, Zillah. 1996. *Hatreds: Racialized and Sexualized Conflicts in the 21st Century*. New York: Routledge.

El Saadawi, Nawal. 1980. *The Hidden Face of Eve*. London: Zed.

Enloe, Cynthia. 1989. *Bananas, Beaches and Bases: Making Feminist Sense of International Politics*. Berkeley: University of California Press.

Estable, Alma. 1986. "Immigrant Women in Canada—Current Issues." A background paper for the Canadian Advisory Council on the Status of Women, Ottawa.

Fincher, Ruth, Lois Foster, Wenona Giles, and Valerie Preston. 1994. "Gender and Migration Policy." In *Immigration and Refugee Policy: Australia and Canada Compared*, vol. 2, edited by H. Adelman et al., 149–84. Toronto: University of Toronto Press.

Fireweed. 1986. *Special Issue on Native Women* (Winter).

Foote, Victoria. 1996. "Refugee Women and Canadian Policy: Gaining Ground?" *Canadian Women Studies* 16, 3: 65–8.

Frankenberg, Ruth. 1993. *White Women, Race Matters: The Social Construction of Whiteness*. Minneapolis: University of Minnesota Press.

Friedman, Susan Stanford. 1995. "Beyond White and Other: Relationality and Narratives of Race in Feminist Discourse." *Signs* 21, 1: 1–49.

Fuss, Diana. 1989. *Essentially Speaking: Feminism, Nature and Difference*. New York: Routledge.

Gabriel, J., and G. Ben-Tovim. 1978. "Marxism and the Concept of Racism." *Economy and Society* 7, 2: 1818–54.

Gannage, Charlene. 1986. *Double Day, Double Bind*. Toronto: Women's Press.

———. 1987. "A World of Difference: The Case of Women Workers in a Canadian Garment Factory." In *Feminism and Political Economy*, edited by H.J. Maroney and M. Luxton, 213–28. Toronto: Methuen.

Gates, Henry Louis, Jr, and Kwame Anthony Appiah. 1995. "Multiplying Identities." In *Identities*, edited by K.A. Appiah and H. Louis Gates Jr, 1–6. Chicago: University of Chicago Press.

Geertz, Clifford. 1963. *Old Societies and New States*. New York: Free Press.

Giles, Wenona, and Valerie Preston. 1996. "The Domestication of Women's Work: A Comparison of Chinese and Portuguese Women Workers." *Studies in Political Economy* 51 (Fall): 147–82.

Gilman, Sander L. 1989. *Difference and Pathology: Stereotypes of Sexuality, Race and Madness*. Ithaca: Cornell University Press.

———. 1991. *The Jew's Body*. New York: Routledge.

Giroux, Henry A. 1997. "White Squall: Resistance and the Pedagogy of Whiteness." *Cultural Studies* 11, 13: 376–89.

Glenn, Evelyn Nakano. 1992. "From Servitude to Service Work: Historical Continuities in the Racial Division of Paid Reproductive Labor." *Signs* 18, 1: 1–43.

Goldberg, David Theo. 1993. *Racist Culture: Philosophy and the Politics of Meaning*. Oxford: Blackwell.

Gould, Stephen Jay. 1984. *The Mismeasure of Man*. Harmondsworth: Penguin.

Hall, Stuart. 1980. "Race, Articulation and Societies Structured in Dominance." In *Sociological Theories: Race and Colonialism*, edited by UNESCO. Paris: UNESCO.

Higginbotham, Evelyn Brooks. 1992. "African-American Women's History and the Metalanguage of Race." *Signs* 17, 2: 251–74.

Hobsbawm, Eric. 1990. *Nations and Nationalism Since 1780*. Cambridge: Cambridge University Press.

hooks, bell. 1981. *Ain't I a Woman: Black Women and Feminism*. Boston: South End Press.

———. 1984. *Feminist Theory from Margin to Center*. Boston: South End Press.

———. 1989. *Talking Back: Thinking Feminist, Thinking Black*. Boston: South End Press.

———. 1992. *Black Looks: Race and Representation*. Toronto: Between the Lines.

Hull, Gloria, Patricia Bell Scott, and Barbara Smith, eds 1982. *All the Women Are White, All the Blacks Are Men, But Some of Us Are Brave*. New York: Basic Books.

Iacovetta, Franca. 1986. "From Contadina to Worker: Southern Italian Immigrant Working Women in Toronto, 1947–62." In *Looking Into My Sister's Eyes*, edited by Jean Burnet, 195–222. Toronto: Multicultural History Society of Ontario.

———. 1992. *Such Hardworking People: Italian Immigrants in Postwar Toronto*. Montreal and Kingston: McGill-Queen's University Press.

Ignatieff, Michael. 1993. *Blood and Belonging: Journeys in the New Nationalisms*. Toronto: Viking.

Ignatiev, Noel. 1995. *How the Irish Became White*. New York: Routledge.

Iyer, Nitya. 1993. "Categorical Denials: Equality Rights and the Shaping of Social Identity." *Queen's Law Journal* 18, 1 (Fall): 179–207.

Jakobsen, Janet R. 1998. *Working Alliance and the Politics of Difference*. Bloomington and Indianapolis: Indiana University Press.

Jayawardena, K. 1986. *Feminism and Nationalism in the Third World*. London: Zed.

Jhappan, Radha. 1996. "Post-Modern Race and Gender Essentialism or a Post-Mortem of Scholarship." *Studies in Political Economy* 51 (Fall): 15–63.

———. 1998. "The Equality Pit or the Rehabilitation of Justice?" *Canadian Journal of Women and the Law* 10, 1: 60–107.

Jolly, Margaret. 1993. "Colonizing Women: The Maternal Body and Empire." In *Feminism and the Politics of Difference*, edited by Sneja Gunew and Anna Yeatman, 103–27. St Leonards, NSW: Allen and Unwin.

Khan, Shahnaz. 1998. "Muslim Women: Negotiations in the Third Space." *Signs* 23, 2 (Winter): 429–63.

King, Deborah. 1988. "Multiple Jeopardy, Multiple Consciousness: The Context of a Black Feminist Ideology." *Signs* 14, 1: 42–72.

Kirkham, Della. 1998. "The Reform Party of Canada: A Discourse on Race, Ethnicity and Equality." In *Racism and Social Inequality in Canada*, edited by Vic Satzewich, 243–69. Toronto: Thompson Educational Publisher.

Kirkness, Verna. 1987–88. "Emerging Native Women." *Canadian Journal of Women and the Law* 2, 2: 408–15.

Kothari, Rajni. 1997. "Globalization: A World Adrift." *Alternatives* 22: 227–67.

LaChapelle, Caroline. 1982. "Beyond Barriers: Native Women and the Women's Movement." In *Still Ain't Satisfied*, edited by M. Fitzgerald, C. Guberman, and M. Wolfe, 257–64. Toronto: Women's Press.

Lake, Marilyn. 1993. "Colonised and Colonising: The White Australian Subject." *Women's History Review* 2, 3: 377–86.

Lazreg, Marnia. 1988. "Feminism and Difference: The Perils of Writing as a Woman on Women in Algeria." *Feminist Studies* 14, 1: 81–107.

Le forum pour un Québec féminin pluriel. 1994. *Pour changer le monde*. Montreal: Editions Ecosocieté.

Li, Joyce. 1995. "Living Between Two Worlds." *Maclean's* 108, 5 (30 January): 32–4.

Li, Peter S. 1988. *The Chinese in Canada*. Toronto: Oxford University Press.

———. 1994. "Unneighbourly Houses or Unwelcome Chinese: The Social Construction of Race in the Battle over 'Monster Homes' in Vancouver, Canada." *International Journal of Comparative Race and Ethnic Studies* 1, 1: 14–33.

Lindstrom-Best, Varpu. 1988. *Defiant Sisters: A Social History of Finnish Immigrant Women in Canada*. Toronto: Multicultural History Society of Ontario.

Lipsig-Mumme, C. 1987. "Organizing Women in the Sewing Trades: Homework and the 1983 Garment Strike in Canada." *Studies in Political Economy* 22 (Spring): 41–72.

Lorde, Audre. 1984. *Sister Outsider*. Trumansberg, NY: The Crossing Press.

McClintock, Anne. 1993. "Family Feuds: Gender, Nationalism and the Family." *Feminist Review* 45: 61–80.

McLaren, Angus. 1990. *Our Own Master Race: Eugenics in Canada, 1885–1945*. Toronto: McClelland and Stewart.

Majid, Anouar. 1998a. "The Politics of Feminism in Islam." *Signs* 23, 2: 277–390.

———. 1998b. "Reply to Joseph and Mayer: Critique as a Dehegemonizing Practice." *Signs* 23, 2: 377–89.

Mama, Amina. 1989. "Violence Against Black Women: Gender, Race and State Responses." *Feminist Review* 32 (Summer): 30–47.

Maroney, Heather Jon, and Meg Luxton, eds 1987. *Feminism and Political Economy*. Toronto: Methuen.

Marshall, Annecka. 1996. "From Sexual Denigration to Self-Respect: Resisting Images of Black Female Sexuality." In *Reconstructing Womanhood, Reconstructing Feminism: Writings on Black Women*, edited by Delia Jarrett-Macauley, 5–35. London: Routledge.

Meekosha, Helen, and Leanne Dowse. 1997. "Enabling Citizenship: Gender, Disability and Citizenship in Australia." *Feminist Review* 57 (Autumn): 49–72.

Mercer, Kobena. 1994. *Welcome to the Jungle: New Positions in Black Cultural Studies*. New York: Routledge.

Mernissi, F. 1992. *The Veil and the Male Elite: A Feminist Interpretation of Women's Rights in Islam*. Reading, MA: Addison-Wesley.

Miles, Bob. 1980. "Class, Race and Ethnicity: A Critique of Cox's Theory." *Ethnic and Racial Studies* 3, 2: 169–87.

———. 1982. *Racism and Migrant Labour*. London: Routledge.

———. 1987. *Capitalism and Unfree Labour: Anomaly or Necessity?* London: Tavistock.

Minh-ha, Trinh T. 1989. *Woman, Native, Other*. Bloomington: Indiana University Press.

Mitchell, Alana. 1997. "Visible Minorities Cluster in Canada's Largest City." *The Globe and Mail* (5 November): A1, A10.

Mitchell, Katharyne. 1997. "Transnational Discourse: Bringing Geography Back In." *Antipode* 21, 2: 101–14.

Moghadam, Valentine M. 1994. *Identity Politics and Women: Cultural Reassertions and Feminisms in International Perspective.* Boulder: Westview.

Mohanty, Chandra Tolpade. 1991. "Under Western Eyes: Feminist Scholarship and Colonial Discourses." In *Third World Women and the Politics of Women*, edited by C.T. Mohanty, A. Russo, and L. Torres, 51–80. Bloomington and Indianapolis: Indiana University Press.

Nagel, Joane. 1998. "Masculinity and Nationalism: Gender and Sexuality in the Making of Nations." *Ethnic and Racial Studies* 21, 2 (March): 242–69.

Nandy, Ashis. 1983. *The Intimate Enemy: Loss and Recovery of Self under Colonialism.* Delhi: Oxford University Press.

Ng, Roxana. 1986. "The Social Construction of Immigrant Women in Canada." In *The Politics of Diversity, Feminism, Marxism and Nationalism*, edited by Roberta Hamilton and Michele Barrett, 269–86. Montreal: Book Center.

———. 1988. *The Politics of Community Services: Immigrant Women, Class and the State.* Toronto: Garamond.

———. 1991. "Sexism, Racism and Canadian Nationalism." In *Race, Class, Gender: Bonds and Barriers*, edited by J. Vorst et al., 12–26. Toronto: Garamond Press and Society for Socialist Studies.

Ng, Roxana, and Judith Ramirez. 1981. *Immigrant Housewives in Canada.* Toronto: Immigrant Women's Centre.

Noivo, Edite. 1997. *Inside Ethnic Families: Three Generations of Portuguese-Canadians.* Montreal and Kingston: McGill-Queen's University Press.

Omi, Michael, and Howard Winant. 1994. *Racial Formation in the United States: From the 1960s to the 1990s*, 2nd edn. New York: Routledge.

Parashar, Archana. 1993. "Essentialism or Pluralism: The Future of Legal Feminism." *Canadian Journal of Women and the Law* 6, 2: 328–48.

Parmar, Pratibha. 1982. "Gender, Race and Class: Asian Women in Resistance." In *The Empire Strikes Back*, edited by Centre for Contemporary Cultural Studies, 236–75. London: Hutchinson.

Perera, Suvendrini, and Joseph Pugliese. 1997. "'Racial Suicide': The Re-licensing of Racism in Australia." *Race and Class* 39, 2: 1–19.

Razack, Sherene. 1994. "What Is to Be Gained by Looking White People in the Eye? Culture, Race, and Gender in Cases of Sexual Violence." *Signs* 19, 4: 894–923.

Rogers, Rosemarie. 1993. "The Future of Refugee Flows and Policies." *International Migration Review* XXXVI, 4: 1112–43.

Sahgal, Gita, and Nira Yuval-Davis. 1992. "Introduction: Fundamentalism, Multiculturalism and Women in Britain." In *Refusing Holy Orders: Women and Fundamentalism in Britain*, edited by G. Sahgal and N. Yuval-Davis, 1–25. London: Virago Press.

Said, Edward. 1978. *Orientalism.* New York: Pantheon.

Sandoval, Chéla. 1998. "Mestizaje as Method: Feminists-of-Color Challenge the Canon." In *Living Chicana Theory*, edited by C. Trujillo, 352–70. Berkeley: Third Woman Press.

Scott, Joan Wallach, ed. 1996. *Feminism and History.* Oxford: Oxford University Press.

Shaheed, Farida. 1994. "Controlled or Autonomous: Identity and the Experience of the Network, Women Living under Muslim Laws." *Signs* 19, 4: 894–923.

Shils, E. 1957. "Primordial, Personal, Sacred and Civil Ties." *British Journal of Sociology* 7: 113–45.

Shohat, Ella, and Robert Stam. 1994. *Unthinking Eurocentrism: Multiculturalism and the Media.* London: Routledge.

Solomos, John. 1986. "Varieties of Marxist Conceptions of 'Race,' Class and the State: A Critical Analysis." In *Theories of Race and Ethnic Relations*, edited by J. Rex and D. Mason, 84–109. Cambridge: Cambridge University Press.

Stasiulis, Daiva K. 1987. "Rainbow Feminism: Perspectives on Minority Women in Canada." *Resources in Feminist Research* 16, 1: 5–9.

———. 1990. "Theorizing Connections: Gender, Race, Ethnicity, and Class." In *Race and Ethnic Relations in Canada*, edited by Peter S. Li., 269–305. Toronto: Oxford University Press.

———. 1997. "International Migration, Rights and the Decline of 'Actually Existing Liberal Democracy.'" *New Community: The Journal of the European Research Centre on Migration and Ethnic Relations* 23, 2: 197–214.

———. 1999. "Relational Positionality of Nationalisms, Racisms and Feminisms." In *Between Woman and Nation: Nationalisms, Transnational Feminism, and the State*, edited by N. Alarcon, C. Kaplan, and M. Moallem. Durham, NC: Duke University Press.

Stasiulis, Daiva K., and Nira Yuval-Davis. 1995. "Introduction: Beyond Dichotomies—Gender, Race, Ethnicity and Class in Settler Societies." In *Unsettling Settler Societies: Articulations of Gender, Race, Ethnicity and Class*, edited by Daiva Stasiulis and Nira Yuval-Davis, 1–38. London: Sage.

Stasiulis, Daiva K., and Radha Jhappan. 1995. "The Fractious Politics of a Settler Society: Canada." In *Unsettling Settler Societies: Articulations of Gender, Race, Ethnicity and Class*, edited by Daiva Stasiulis and Nira Yuval-Davis, 95–131. London: Sage.

Stepan, Nancy Leys. 1990. "Race and Gender: The Role of Analogy in Science." In *Anatomy of Racism*, edited by D.T. Goldberg, 38–57. Minneapolis: University of Minnesota Press.

Stimpson, Catharine R. 1993. "How Did Feminist Theory Get This Way?" In *Politics, Theory, and Contemporary Culture*, edited by M. Poster, 13–40. New York: Columbia University Press.

Stoler, Ann Laura. 1996. "Carnal Knowledge and Imperial Power: Gender, Race, and Morality in Colonial Asia." In *Feminism and History*, edited by Joan Wallach Scott, 209–66. Oxford: Oxford University Press.

Suad, Joseph. 1998. "Comment on Majid's 'The Politics of Feminism in Islam.'" *Signs* 23, 2: 363–9.

Swyripa, Frances. 1993. *Wedded to the Cause: Ukrainian-Canadian Women and Ethnic Identity, 1891–1991.* Toronto: University of Toronto Press.

Takaki, Ronald. 1977. *Iron Cages*. Berkeley: University of California Press.

Thornhill, Esmerelda. 1991. "Focus on Black Women!" In *Race, Class, Gender: Bonds and Barriers*, edited by J. Vorst et al., 27–38. Toronto: Garamond Press and Society for Socialist Studies.

Tu, Than Ha. 1998. "Quebec Rape Ruling Sparks Uproar." *The Globe and Mail* (28 January): A1, A2.

Turpel, Mary Ellen. 1993. "Patriarchy and Paternalism: The Legacy of the Canadian State for First Nations Women." *Canadian Journal of Women and the Law* 6, 1: 174–92.

Unterhalter, Elaine. 1995. "Constructing Race, Class, Gender and Ethnicity: State and Opposition Strategies in South Africa." In *Unsettling Settler Societies: Articulations of Gender, Race, Ethnicity and Class*, edited by Daiva Stasiulis and Nira Yuval-Davis, 207–40. London: Sage.

Valverde, Mariana. 1991. *The Age of Light, Soap and Water*. Toronto: McClelland and Stewart.

———. 1992. "'When the Mother of the Race Is Free': Race, Reproduction, and Sexuality in First-Wave Feminism." In *Gender Conflicts*, edited by F. Iacovetta and M. Valverde, 3–26. Toronto: University of Toronto Press.

van den Berghe, P. 1979. *The Ethnic Phenomenon*. New York: Elsevier.

Van Kirk, Sylvia. 1980. *"Many Tender Ties": Women in Fur Trade Society*, 1670–1810. Winnipeg: Watson and Dwyer.

Walker, Alice. 1983. *In Search of Our Mothers' Gardens*. New York: Harcourt Brace.

Ware, Vron. 1992. *Beyond the Pale: White Women, Racism and History*. London: Verso.

West, Cornel. 1982. "A Genealogy of Modern Racism." In *Prophesy Deliverance! An Afro-American Revolutionary Christianity*. Philadelphia: Westminister Press.

Williams, Patricia. 1991. *The Alchemy of Race and Rights: Diary of a Law Professor*. Cambridge: Harvard University Press.

Wilson, Tikka Jan. 1996. "Feminism and Institutionalized Racism: Inclusion and Exclusion at an Australian Feminist Refuge." *Feminist Review* 52 (Spring): 1–26.

Winter, Bronwyn. 1994. "Women, the Law, and Cultural Relativism in France: The Case of Excision." *Signs* 19, 4: 939–74.

Young, Robert J.C. 1995. *Colonial Desire: Hybridity in Theory, Culture and Race*. London: Routledge.

Yuval-Davis, Nira. 1997. *Gender and Nation*. London: Sage.

Yuval-Davis, Nira, and Floya Anthias. 1989. Introduction to *Woman-Nation-State*, edited by N. Yuval-Davis and F. Anthias, 1–15. London: Macmillan.

Questions for Critical Thought

1. Stasiulis describes gender, race, and class not as static identity characteristics, but as "processes through which people construct and alter their relations to institutions within the economy, state, and civil society with the given means at their disposal." What does she mean? Reflect upon your own gender, race, and class identity. How has it been constructed? How is it related to social institutions, the economy, or the state?

2. Stasiulis states that race may soon be far less salient in shaping identity than other social forces such as nationalism, religion, and ethnicity. Does this reflect your own identity? Do you think it reflects the identities of other groups in Canada? What about people living in other countries; should we actively support people who are experiencing discrimination due to their national, religious, ethnic, or gendered identities? If you think that we should support these groups, how can we do this?

3. Stasiulis asks whether intersectional analysis might prevent the identification of generalizations and patterns among groups. She is concerned that this may interfere with collaborative work for change. Do you think her concerns are legitimate?

4. Stasiulis refers to recent debates on whiteness. What role do you think research on whiteness can play in analyses of inequality? What benefits and risks might arise from such debates?

5. In what ways has traditional sociological inquiry neglected what Stasiulis calls "the non-separability of race, class, gender, and other social relations such as sexuality"? Are some branches of sociology more responsive to intersectional analysis than others? Is there any movement "beyond the race–gender–class trinity"? Which other disciplines in the social sciences are receptive to this form of inquiry? How have they used intersectional theorizing in their research?

Conclusion

In the introductory section of this book on social inequality in Canada, both Dei and Stasiulis have explained how intersectional theorizing examines identities that occur simultaneously and interactively. It is these identities that are involuntarily assigned to a person by society, and that are used to systematically marginalize and to oppress those individuals or groups of people who are deemed to be the social and political "others." The history of colonization and re-colonization of Canada and the role that global capital plays in disseminating knowledge shapes how identity is politicized and articulated not only in Canada but also throughout the world. Various authors in the following sections of this book have focused on different sets of intersectional theorizing in an effort to encourage us to think about social inequality and sites of oppression that move beyond the scope of the race–gender–class triad.

Recommended Readings

Danielle Juteau. 2000. "Patterns of Social Differentiation in Canada: Understanding Their Dynamics and Bridging the Gaps." *Canadian Public Policy/Analyse de Politiques* 26 (supplement): S95–107.

- In this article, Danielle Juteau examines the underlying patterns that produce inequalities in Canada that are related to age, gender, "race," and region. According to Juteau, the relationship between public policy and social inequality could be modified if socio-economic disparity in Canada were reduced.

Celine-Marie Pascale, ed. 2013. *Social Inequality and the Politics of Representation: A Global Landscape*, Washington DC: Sage Publications Ltd.

- This edited text offers numerous examples of analyses, including frame analysis, critical discourse, and conversation analysis. Each chapter explores the politics of exclusion and "othering," both within and across national boundaries in twenty countries from five different continents. Intersectional theorizing and queer theory are used to explain how the social construction of gender, race, class, region, language, religion, sexual, and cultural categories socially and politically reproduce and perpetuate social inequality.

James W. Russell. 2009. *Class and Race Formation in North America*, 2nd edn. Toronto: University of Toronto Press.

- In this comprehensive comparative analysis of Canadian, American, and Mexican history, James Russell traces the social origins of class and racial inequality from the colonial era to the NAFTA and post-NAFTA period. Russell demonstrates that there are diverse ways of thinking about class systems and race that are products of historical circumstances.

Les Samuelson and Antony Wayne, eds 2009. *Power and Resistance*, 4th edn. Halifax, NS: Fernwood.

- This stimulating text looks at how social inequality is socially reproduced in Canada. The readings critically examine issues such as gender, racialization, class, and sexual orientation, and how these categories are sites of social inequality that produce social problems such as poverty, barriers to social justice for Aboriginal people, intimate partner violence, and the privatization of the university system. The authors demonstrate how these social inequalities have been challenged on both an individual and a collective level by Canadians.

Nira Yuval-Davis. 2011. *The Politics of Belonging: Intersectional Contestations*. London: Sage Publications Ltd.

- Nira Yuval-Davis challenges the debates that surround the "politics of belonging." The author critically examines the position of women in the global world and she argues that the construction of political projects of belonging, cosmopolitanism, and the feminist "ethics of care" need to addressed. She suggests the categories of belonging and intersectional theorizing which may include, for example, a person's citizenship or national identity, should be supplemented by collectivities that are differentially located—socially, economically, and politically.

....

Inequality and Family

I n this second section, we present research on the most intimate of social institutions: the family. The notion of family brings to mind a host of contradictory associations—comfort and oppression, reward and hardship, support and degradation—and
many others that fall within the extremes. Moreover, the relationship between family
and inequality for gendered, raced, and classed subjects is neither singular nor universal. Clearly, the family setting is the venue where inequality is produced through
the unfair **division of domestic labour**—even the meaning of such work fluctuates
in a gendered way, as men and women have differing opinions of what constitutes
"**domestic labour.**" Yet the family is also an object of the state's attention, and government efforts to influence family can inadvertently produce and perpetuate inequality
of a racialized nature; for example, the kind, size, or purpose of family may be circum-
scribed by state intervention. Forces of capitalism, colonialism, state formation, and
the transition to industrialism have all had an effect on the formation of family relations and the inequalities attendant upon it; indeed, these forces affect the very meaning of "family."

The relational nature of difference is highlighted in the family: it dovetails with gender roles in both the private and public domains. That is, inequalities of gender, race,
and class are reproduced through the family owing to the power relations in dominant
gendered, raced, and classed groups. While gender may have received a privileged place
in sociological analysis on the family, crucial differences exist with respect to race, sexuality, and class as well. These differences are significant if our goal is to understand
inequality in Canada, a nation that is shaped by a range of intersecting interests. As a
set of social relations, family is part of the construction of these categories of difference.
The chapters in this section show how family can be understood only by looking at the
intersections of gender, race, class, and sexuality, and how they shape differences in
family and inequality.

In most societies in the world, women are culturally expected to be kin keepers and
the primary caregivers of the children in a family. The idea that women should engage
in intensive mothering, which suggests that women should maintain child rearing as
a top priority, has created a social conundrum for women who work both inside and
outside of the home. Colleen Reid and Robin A. LeDrew conclude, after interviewing 70 women in a participatory action research project in four economic contexts in
urban, rural, remote, and reserve communities in British Columbia, that the recent
governmental policy to designate women as "employable" has resulted in an increase

in the feminization of poverty in British Columbia. Women who receive minimal or no social-welfare support from the government cope with the challenges of juggling caregiver overload, paid and unpaid work, precarious employment, multiple jobs, and insecure seasonal work with few benefits. Reid and LeDrew conclude that due to cultural expectations, work disruptions, social and geographical isolation, a lack of employment opportunities, and chronic health problems, women living in these communities will often stay in abusive relationships and continue to work in violent and unsafe workplaces. In the second reading in this section on the family, Valerie Preston, Ann Kim, Samantha Hudyma, Nancy Mandell, Meg Luxton, and Julia Hemphill use an intersectional approach to understand and address poverty among foreign-born seniors. Their findings indicate that foreign-born senior men and especially women experience higher levels of poverty than their Canadian-born counterparts. The authors explain that the gendered life course of immigrant women can include withdrawal from the workplace to care for children, an older age of entry into the workforce and shorter duration in the labour market, part-time labour in service sector jobs with no security and few benefits, single parenting, and being widowed, which are some of the reasons why elderly racialized women have less financial security in their senior years than Canadian-born women. They conclude that the current governmental pension 10-year residency requirement does not consider the challenges and barriers that immigrant women face. They suggest that Canadian pension policies need to address inequalities that occur earlier in the life course of foreign-born women, due to gendered social roles and family obligations.

While regional and federal government social-welfare program cuts and pension policies have had a negative effect on vulnerable populations of women and their families, the governmental policy to sterilize men and women in the province of Alberta between the years 1928 and 1972 has also been the subject of intense scrutiny. In this third reading, Jana Grekul examines the eugenics movement in Canada, which sought to ensure that only mentally capable and competent individuals were creating and establishing families. She discusses the development of the social movement and the role that women played in this movement; she documents the shift in the attitudes of the Eugenics Board—from encouraging the sterilization of mentally defective men who were patients in hospitals in the 1930s to sterilizing younger, mentally normal but "morally abnormal" women in the 1950s.

The Burden of Being "Employable": Underpaid and Unpaid Work and Women's Health

....*Colleen Reid and Robin A. LeDrew*

Since the 1990s globalization and governmental prioritization of economic gain over human development and social justice have been dominant trends in Canada, specifically in the province of British Columbia (BC). In this context, people who were previously seen as unemployable because of parenting, caregiving responsibilities, disability, or ill health were redefined as employable; regardless of the reason, the unemployed are impelled back to work. Through years of involvement with a range of women serving organizations in various locations across BC, we have witnessed the limitations of policies that redefine diverse women as employable. Women continue to juggle paid and unpaid work, precarious employment, multiple jobs, and insecure seasonal work with few work-supported health benefits. Many women are involved in unpaid, underpaid, under-the-table, or illegal work. The Women's Employability and Health Research Project (WEHP) investigated these experiences. We defined employability as the relative chances of getting and maintaining different kinds of employment (Brown & Hesketh, 2004). The research questions guiding this analysis were: (1) What factors shape diverse women's employability across BC? (2) What is the impact of being seen as employable on women's subjective health and well-being?

Literature Review

Employability-Based Approaches

Initially, the concept of employability described a disabled person's capacity for employment. As liberal labour market policies strove to "wean the hardest-to-employ people off long term state programs" the concept shifted to include delinquents, ex-convicts, and eventually women (White, 2001, p. 6). These same market policies also maintained that the state had neither the responsibility nor the capacity to create jobs. The causes of unemployment were conceived in individualistic and behavioural terms: The old problems of demand deficiency and job shortage were dismissed, and policies needed to focus on the motivations and expectations of the "workless class" (Peck & Theodore, 2000, p. 729). Failing to take into consideration the supply and demand of labour perpetuated the idea that credentials, knowledge, and social status alone guaranteed a good position in the labour market (Brown & Hesketh, 2004).

Although women in both developing and developed countries saw significant improvements to their socioeconomic status after World War I, "economic adjustments undertaken globally since the 1980's halted and even reversed this progress" (McDaniel, 2002, p. 127). Employability-based approaches to labour market policy are typical examples of these economic adjustments. Over the past 30 years, many industrialized countries have shifted the responsibility for the social safety net from the state to women's shoulders by classifying women as employable (Baker, 1996; Baker & Tippin, 2002; Day & Brodsky, 2007; Morris, 2000; Porter, 2003; Stratigaki, 2004). However, women face challenges to their employability for societal as well as individual reasons. The unavailability of good-quality child care, the lack of public affordable transportation, and the inflexibility of employment opportunities can hardly be viewed in individualistic terms (Berry et al., 2008). According to Peck and Theodore (2000, p. 731), "employability-based approaches are not sufficient to the task of tackling unemployment, social exclusion, and economic inequality." Certainly, they address neither women's chronic poverty nor the nuances and implications of women's unpaid caregiving work.

Employability and Women's Poverty

For as long as data have been collected, women as a group have experienced poverty and deprivation more significantly, and more deeply, than men. The main causes of women's poverty are labour market inequities, domestic circumstances, and welfare systems (Ruspini, 1999). Almost 24 per cent of Canadian women are raising children on their own, and 14 per cent of single older women are poor, even after governmental taxes and transfers (Townson, 2009). More than 1,772,000 women in Canada live in poverty (Canadian Association for Social Workers, 2009). Women are not only at a greater risk of poverty than men, but their poverty is more persistent over time (Lochhead & Scott, 2000).

Labour market inequities are particularly evident in the highly gendered nature of the Canadian workforce. Men still dominate higher-earnings groups and constitute a relatively small proportion of workers in the lowest-earnings categories (Townson, 2009). The majority of women remain in the lowest earnings categories in increasingly part-time, temporary, or contract, employment (Townson, 2009). Such nonstandard jobs offer little financial security, and few, if any, offer health care or disability benefits. Important parts of the Canadian social security net, such as employment insurance, are "discriminatory in effect" and remain inaccessible to many Canadian women (Porter, 2003, p. 240). Poor women as a group have little recourse to protection through labour laws and are often in compromising positions that threaten their health and personal safety and expose them to violence within the family or community (Townson, 2009).

Women's poverty occurs as a consequence of domestic circumstances, such as divorce and separation, with many BC women falling into the category of being "one man away from welfare" (Reid, 2004). Women's roles as mothers, homemakers, and caregivers also contribute to their poverty (Townson, 2009). Women perform two-thirds of unpaid caregiving work. The enormous demands of unpaid work reduce many women's opportunities to participate fully in the paid workforce. While the costs of raising children have been acknowledged by the addition of the childrearing drop-out provision of the Canada Pension Plan, caregiving for other relatives has not, which contributes to some women's deepening poverty. Canadian policies of **deinstutionalization** and "closer to home health care" in the same era of governmental downsizing have been shown to result in increased caregiving responsibilities for women (Armstrong, 2007; Yalnizyan, 2005). In addition, Canada's aging population and rural-to-urban migration have both been shown to be increasing women's caregiving responsibilities significantly (Joseph, Leach, & Turner, 2007; Lero & Joseph, 2007).

In 1995, the federal Canadian government replaced the Canada Assistance Plan with the Canada Health and Social Transfer (CHST) removing national standards for the delivery of services. In the subsequent decade, the BC government reduced welfare rolls by 54.2 per cent, mainly by increasing restrictions in eligibility (Ministry of Human Resources, 2003). In 2001 and 2002, BC initiated deep cuts in social programs and shifts in social policy. Services that supported women and their children were either cut entirely or reduced significantly. For example, governmental programs in BC redefined lone mothers of children aged three to seven as employable. Governmental downsizing also brought the elimination of many relatively high-paid unionized service sector jobs for women (Fuller, 2005; Laurence, 1992).

The confluence of these policy shifts and economic trends has put diverse women in BC in increasingly precarious positions. Shifting understandings of who is employable force many women, who carry a disproportionate burden of unpaid care work, to take on work that is underpaid, unstable, seasonal, and at times dangerous and illegal.

Women's Health

It is commonly known that although women have a longer life expectancy than men, they suffer greater burdens of morbidity, distress, and disability (Doyal, 1995), including depression; stress overload; chronic conditions, such as arthritis and osteoporosis; and injuries and death resulting from family violence. Varcoe, Hankivsky, and Morrow (2007, p. 5) noted that "in 2000–2001 over 4 million women compared to under 3 million men reported having two or more chronic conditions," and that in that same time frame "500,000 more women than men reported having functional health disabilities." In addition, in Canada, women are poorer than men (Townson, 2009). It is well known that poverty is a determinant of health. Indeed, "living in chronic material deprivation limits access to health promoting services and resources and has a significant impact on women's health behaviours . . . [poverty] leads to shame, stress and depression . . . [and] women living in poverty are often forced to compromise good health choices for bad ones for financial reasons" (Reid, 2007, p. 214).

Women's Employability and Health Research Project (WEHP)

Recognizing the provincial shift toward neoconservative labour market policies, a group of service providers in Metro Vancouver formed the Coalition for Women's Economic Advancement to discuss and take action on their observations of women's worsening situations. Members of the coalition shared anecdotal evidence that changes in governmental policy had resulted in an increasing number of women staying in abusive relationships; getting into sexually exploitive relationships for economic gain; engaging in sex trade work or the underground economy, such as dealing in drugs; relying on their children for

money, food, and shelter; and getting involved in other criminal or marginal behaviour that was directly linked to their deepening poverty. It was also believed that women's worsening economic circumstances were not limited to any particular group of women and that the women affected were diverse ethnically, racially, socially, and geographically.

Coalition members recognized the need to gain a better understanding of women's economic situation in BC. We initiated WEHP and identified two research questions: (1) What factors shape diverse women's employability across BC? (2) What is the impact of being seen as employable on women's subjective health and well-being? In an effort to capture the broad range of women's experience in BC, we selected research communities on the basis of their socio-demographic and geographic diversity. In choosing the research communities, we considered the gap between women's and men's incomes, the sources of income in the community, and the basis for the local economies. The four research communities are here called Rural-Farming, Northern-Resource, Remote-Reserve, and Urban–**South Asian**.

The project was managed by the lead researcher and the project coordinator. Local researchers were hired in each community, in one instance as an individual and in three others as teams of two to four women. The community researchers were responsible for forming and liaising with a local advisory committee, recruiting participants, collecting and analyzing, and writing a final community report. As a project team, we adopted feminist participatory action research as our conceptual and methodological framework (Maguire, 2001; Reid, 2004; Reid & Frisby, 2007). We held a deep commitment to intersectionality as our theoretical lens and identified as an intersectional research team. Together, we examined the ethical dimensions of our work with a particular focus on the implications of maintaining community confidentiality in the context of a project that is action oriented. We gained ethical approval from the Research Ethics Board at Simon Fraser University, where Reid, the lead researcher, was completing her postdoctoral fellowship, and from the Vancouver Foundation, the funding organization. In other venues, we have examined these conceptual, methodological, and ethical issues more extensively (Reid et al., 2010; Reid et al., 2011).

WEHP Research Communities
Northern-Resource

Northern-Resource is a remote community of 25,000 people with a subarctic continental climate. Its population has expanded by 9.3 per cent since 2001, primarily as a result of the robust oil and gas economy. The labour participation rate is 81 per cent, with 88 per cent of the men compared to 73 per cent of the women able to work (Statistics Canada, 2010). The strong labour market is reflected in low unemployment rates. Citizens in this community have one of the highest levels of **disposable income** in the country compared to the Canadian average. However, in this community, the median income for men is more than double that of women (Statistics Canada, 2010).

Rural-Farming

Rural-Farming is a village serving a rural area of approximately 5,000 residents nestled in south central BC. In 2006, the unemployment rate was almost twice that of BC (Statistics Canada, 2010), which may have been due to the seasonal nature of the logging industry as well as the periodic shifts in the resource-based economy. Women accounted for one third of full-year, full-time jobs, compared to men (Statistics Canada, 2010). While Rural-Farming has a lower-than-provincial average wage, women's median income is only 70 per cent of men's locally (Statistics Canada, 2010).

Remote-Reserve

Remote-Reserve is comprised of just under 800 people (Statistics Canada, 2010), including status Aboriginals, **non-status Aboriginals**, and non-Aboriginals. In this community, the employment rate during the high season is 53 per cent in part due to ecotourism and students' summer jobs. The off-season employment rate drops to 30 per cent. Most people who have full-time, year-round jobs work for the Band Council or the Tribal Council. The average educational level of employable community members is Grade 10. The drop-out rate from high school is 57 per cent; the provincial drop-out rate for the general population was 18 per cent in 2006 (Statistics Canada, 2010).

Urban–South Asian

Urban–South Asian, a large community in the southern part of BC, has a population of approximately 400,000. Thirty-eight per cent of the residents are immigrants, and the majority of them are from India, Sri Lanka, and Pakistan (Statistics Canada, 2010). Since 2001, there has been a 14 per cent increase in the population (Statistics Canada, 2010). Urban–South Asian's labour force works primarily in the manufacturing and retail sectors. Employment in Urban–South Asian is highly dependent on work in trades and construction, for which formal training or education may not always be required.

Research Methods
Participants

The local researchers produced a community report to provide in-depth contextual information and relevant data on each research community. From this community snapshot, they then purposefully recruited a broadly representative range of participants. Across the four communities, 70 women participated in the study. The participants were diverse in many ways; they ranged in age from 17 to 74, had various domestic statuses (single, separated, divorced, married, and partnered) although most were mothers, and possessed a range of education and training from not completing Grade 8 to multiple university degrees. The participants worked in various sectors and had a range of jobs from insecure and seasonal to secure and long term. Regardless of their current employment status, all the women self-identified as employable.

Data Collection and Analysis

We gathered qualitative data from 57 semi-structured one-on-one interviews and three focus groups. Our data set consisted of 60 primary documents and 18 sets of field notes as secondary documents. Data analysis was conducted in the local communities by the local researchers. The lead researcher provided a descriptive coding framework, which was used by the community researchers for coding and analysis. ATLAS.ti was used to manage and sort the data. From the inductive and descriptive coding, the local researchers wrote a community report that integrated the contextual information from their communities with the research findings.

We identified intersectional theory as the most appropriate theoretical lens for our work. Intersectionality theory is the study of multiple categories of identity and social relations that intersect with one another to produce systems of power, oppression, and privilege (McCall, 2005). It has grown out of critical feminist concerns about the limits of privileging one category of analysis (e.g., gender) over others (e.g., race, class, sexual orientation, ability, or place) and seeks to understand the fluid ways in which they intersect to shape the reality of women's lives systematically (Canadian Research Institute for the Advancement of Women [CRIAW], 2006). Intersectionality can help illuminate the connections between individual subjectivities and broader social structures, as well as local and global experiences (Shields, 2008). The core purpose of intersectionality theory is to facilitate deep analyses of social justice issues, such as women's employability and health, by interrogating the complex social and power relations that lie at their root (Hankivsky & Cormier, 2009; Shields,

2008). Intersectional frameworks "provide potentially transformative alternatives. They unravel how social categories of difference intersect in constantly changing ways in order to crack open oppressive dialogues, structures, and practices" (CRIAW, 2006, p. 10).

Findings

Investigating the fullness of women's employability through an intersectional analysis explicates the ways in which gender, place, the local economy, and cultural identity intersect and influence each other to shape how women experience employment and how these experiences influence their health and well-being. The findings are divided into two major sections that correspond to the research questions. In the first section, we examine the ways in which gender intersects with location, unpaid caregiving, and culture. The second section describes how women's experiences with employability affect their perceived health and well-being. Intersectional analysis is not additive; rather, it is multiplicative (Phoenix & Pattynama, 2006). As such, the findings build on one another. Rather than provide an analysis that separates out distinct analytic categories, analytic categories that intersect and cross-cut the four research communities are presented sequentially. In other words, the relationships among the analytic categories are presented in the sections of the findings. The intention is to render the fluidity of women's experiences across the four communities and to capture the overlapping nature of the analytic categories.

Women's Employability

Women's employability was shaped by community location, the community's local economy, gender, culture, and caregiving roles and expectations. Although there were some distinct differences between women across the province, there were also remarkable similarities. What follows is an analysis of the women's experiences of employability across the four research communities.

Community Location and Gendered Work

A striking finding was how the remoteness of all but the urban community and the highly gendered nature of well-paying job opportunities curtailed women's earning capacity. In the booming Northern-Resource community, one woman said, "It's a man's world up here . . . and it's really, really hard for women to make it. I see some that will never be able to break out. They have no opportunities, no options, just to stay on that gerbil wheel at 7 or 8 dollars an hour, stuck on there. There is nowhere else for them to go because they don't have the money to get the education."

Northern-Resource offered many well-paying jobs in the oil field outside the town centre, but these jobs were not widely available to women, who worked predominantly in the low-paying service sector in the city. The dearth of well-paying employment contributed to a substantial gender difference in women's ability to earn a living wage. "At one point I was averaging $8,000 a year working and going to school, and my ex-husband was earning $120,000 to $150,000" (Northern-Resource). Of the four research communities, Northern-Resource had the strongest local economy, but despite its prosperity, women in Northern-Resource were not faring well—they did not have access to the same economic opportunities as men, and they also struggled with limited resources in terms of transportation, accessible child care, and services to support them.

At the time of the study, women in Rural-Farming earned an average of 58 per cent of men's wages (Statistics Canada, 2010). For women who were supporting themselves and their families, it was normal to hold multiple part-time jobs. They had few employment benefits (e.g., employment insurance and a pension) and struggled while living in poverty: "I've taken a while to adjust from coming from the big city, Toronto, where I was making $120,000 a year, coming to [Rural-Farming town] making nothing" (Rural-Farming).

Most Remote-Reserve women relied on seasonal, precarious employment at the minimum wage, unless they had the education and training to access the few health or governmental service positions that were available or had the means to start their own businesses. To make ends meet, most women also reported that they worked "under the table." The majority of women in Remote-Reserve, along with most women in the other research communities, faced the burden of making ends meet. The following captures the experiences of most of the participants: "I'm so worried I *have* to get to work, I *have* to make the money, I *have* to pay the bills. And when I'm doing that, two of my kids quit school within like three months of the school being over. And I keep thinking well, maybe if I didn't work so hard or, but I still, I *have* to" (Remote-Reserve).

Cultural Factors Shaped Women's Employability

Cultural factors shaped women's employability in the Urban–South Asian community. For some, immigrating to Canada forced shifts in employment opportunities that had an impact on gender roles and expectations in the family. Like the Remote-Reserve women, these changes in traditional gender roles, which for both groups of women were driven by economic factors but were bound in cultural norms and expectations, were challenging and difficult to negotiate. After immigrating to Canada, some South Asian women had the potential to earn as much or more than their husbands and often found work before the men. Although this potential brought a sense of self-sufficiency and independence to the South Asian women, in many cases it created conflict in their relationships. For the first time, the women earned an income and kept some of it, which undermined their reliance on their male partners as the sole providers.

Some South Asian women were positive about their work prospects. Generally, the younger women and the women who spoke English easily and had a postsecondary education were more optimistic about their work opportunities. These women reported that they were confident that they could find rewarding and financially sustaining employment. One woman said, "I guess I am just lucky. . . . [I] have never had a problem finding a job. I apply to jobs and usually go to the interview and get the job the same day. . . . They [jobs] just pop up in the newspaper or sometimes they come up through friends that I know or people that I know, a lot of networking and sometimes it's through training courses and that sort of thing" (Urban–South Asian).

While some South Asian women spoke of finding work easily and before their husbands did, others, particularly those who were older and had more difficulty speaking English, encountered difficulties finding work, as one woman noted: "At first it was very difficult to find work, and by knowing people, you can work on the farms, and after my hours were done, I collected EI [employment insurance] and then had a little bit of school . . . With knowing friends, we would ask [for work] and they would say they are not hiring" (Urban–South Asian). Older South Asian women spoke about the hardships they had endured to arrive at their current lifestyles: "It is very hard to go to work. Even though I work part time, I work seven days a week" (Urban–South Asian). Still others reported that immigrating to Canada had caused them to lose the careers they had established in India. One woman said that her degree as a registered nurse was not acknowledged in Canada: "[I didn't like Canada when I first moved here] because I was working before, and when I got here [Canada], I did not get the same job [as a registered nurse], and everything else was new to me and it was hard."

Like Northern-Resource, the Urban–South Asian economy was growing quickly; however, half the participants from Urban–South Asian reported struggling to make ends meet. One woman reported that her ex-husband was faring significantly better than she was: "He [ex-husband] is much better off because he does own a property, so that works out a lot better, and the other thing is he has worked full time and put

himself back in school part time and has gotten a second job. So he is far ahead much more than me" (Urban–South Asian).

Another woman spoke of struggling with her family to pay the bills: "My parents make minimum wage, and my dad was laid off for a very long time, so it has been really hard because we do have a house, so we do have a mortgage; it's been hard, and because I haven't had a full-time job, it has been hard on the family . . . We have to live check to check literally."

Domestic Responsibilities

An overwhelming finding from all four communities was the challenge of juggling paid and unpaid work. The women's limited opportunities for jobs intersected with their domestic responsibilities to often prevent them from taking employment. The lack of child care spaces prevented women with dependent children from participating in jobs that were available in the oil field and forest industries. Although four participants had worked in the oil patch before having children, they found it impossible to return to that industry after giving birth. As one woman stated, "The reason I'm taking bookkeeping is because it is something I can do at home while I raise my children. I wouldn't be able to go back to the oil patch because of the hours; . . . It wouldn't be worth it—I would never get to see my kids" (Northern-Resource).

With few opportunities available to women in the lucrative oil field, the Northern-Resource women spoke of being responsible for maintaining their households and child care when their partners were working away from the community. When their partners returned from the oil patch, the women's control over the household shifted dramatically, which was stressful and at times difficult to manage. As one woman put it,

Basically, everything falls on the women's shoulders . . . everything from finances, to running the household, to caring for the children. A lot of these men are gone from three weeks to two months, and they come home and it creates tremendous stress and tension in the home because you're really used to doing everything yourself.

A common term used in Northern-Resource to denote women's status was "oil and gas widow." After a drastic downturn in the forest sector more than 10 years ago, Rural-Farming had an unemployment rate that was three times the provincial average. More recently, unemployment rates for women moved much closer to provincial averages, while unemployment for men remains significantly higher and men's labour force participation is also lower than the provincial rates (Statistics Canada, 2010). With few well-paying local jobs, some men looked for work outside the area, resulting in a gender imbalance similar to that in the Northern-Resource community. Several Rural-Farming women reported that they were managing the homes in their husbands' prolonged absence to Alberta oil fields or northern forestry jobs. As one woman stated, "I do have a husband, but he works in Alberta. He basically lives in Alberta. The job he does now he works 15 days and gets 6 off. But he doesn't come home every time because . . . it is an 11-hour drive. . . . He comes home long enough to get everyone all worked up, (laughs) and then he leaves. And then he waits for 6 weeks and then he comes home again. Of course, nothing is run the way he wants to run it."

Greater Uncertainty and Caregiving in Resource-Based Economies

In both Rural-Farming and Northern-Resource, a reliance on the resource-based economy disrupted normal family functioning and created a set of power dynamics within the family characterized by greater uncertainty and increases in women's caregiving role. Another dimension of shifting gender roles occurred during the economic downturn in Rural-Farming when many men lost their high-paying jobs. More employment options opened for women that were low paying and part time: As one woman said, "At the

forestry I made $12.65 an hour 26 years ago. Now I am offered $10 for the same [job] . . . and I am not working any less."

In Remote-Reserve, there was a sharp reduction in resource-sector jobs in the past 10 years that had been held primarily by men. Tourism and local government jobs became the main sources of income in this small community. In many cases, women found themselves the main breadwinners in the family. At times, this situation caused strain on the couple and jeopardized some women's ability to keep their jobs, as one woman put it: "It [the reduction in resource-sector jobs] has a big impact. I can't go to work, and I have to worry about my kids, and I have to hire someone, right? . . . I think. If he [husband] was able to get more [work] under his belt and feel more self-sufficient, things would go a bit smoother in the house. 'Cause the seasonal work is, when he's off his job, eh, it is the bottle. What else do you have here?"

Limited Access to Training and Education

Caregiving and location intersected to limit some women's access to training and education. The college in a neighbouring town of Remote-Reserve offered some certificate programs, but because of the small population base, courses were often cancelled because of the lack of enrolment. For the most part, women had to leave the community in order to access postsecondary training, at a high cost to themselves and their families. Some partners and families were supportive of women's efforts to improve their employability, but it was equally true that some women had to cut their studies short because their spouses were unable or unwilling to look after the home and children. Indeed, the economic realities for women and men in Remote-Reserve affected the family dynamics, including family transitions and the ability to gain a sense of "readiness" for other employment opportunities. The high unemployment rate in Remote-Reserve was representative of many reserves. Jobs that paid more than the minimum wage required higher skills and education. Although this community was known to be resilient and progressive, many families continued to be affected by the residential school experience and, as a result, experienced unique barriers to realizing their potential fully.

Cultural Expectations Reinforced Caregiving Roles

In Remote-Reserve and Urban–South Asian, women's caregiving roles were reinforced by cultural expectations. Women were expected to play (and expected themselves to play) this role in their families, **extended families**, and social networks. The meaning of family in Remote-Reserve extends to all those related by blood and clan. Women's traditional caregiving role reached well beyond the extended family and, for some, included the majority of the community since most families were interconnected. As one woman stated: "When she's [mom] here, she helps out with my boys a lot because I am a single mom, and she also helps me out financially if I need the help. And my sister does a lot of babysitting for me and helping me with the kids" (Remote-Reserve).

While women can rely on a large network for support, they are likely to be providing care of some sort to one or more people in their community in addition to looking after their immediate families. Local women are also expected to care for grieving families, prepare a deceased person's body for burial, and organize the memorial service when a loved one is lost. These activities take priority over all other activities, including care of one's own family or other responsibilities like work or school. For six consecutive weeks during the project, there was a loss of a community member every week, which left the local women exhausted and the community burned out.

In Urban–South Asian, women's caregiving was also intricately linked with cultural values and norms. In South Asian culture, the family is seen as the fundamental building block from which all else grows. Support and guidance from the family influence every decision an individual makes. Many extended families in India live under the same roof, and most aging parents live with one

of their sons. The son and his family are expected to care for the elders, while married daughters become responsible for their in-laws: "My mom and dad do the housework, and my brother and I bought a house together, and we live together and we work together."

One participant described taking a leave from her paid work to care for her mother for three months while she recovered from surgery: "[Caregiving] would involve taking care of their financial, legal matters, anything that they had, those kinds of documents, or taking them to doctors' appointments, driving them to get groceries, even the basic things . . . It increases the stress level because you are trying to balance your priorities, caring for yourself as well as finding time for your family because you are working full time, that's stressful, and [you] come home and everybody wants stuff done." In this interview, the participant acknowledged that she had moved out of the family home to gain some distance from her parents' demands and expectations. Since she had moved away from her parents, she felt like more of an adult and noticed immediately that her level of stress had decreased. South Asian women's caregiving responsibilities had an impact on both their health and their ability to function in their paid work.

Discussion

Location, caregiving, and cultural expectations had profound impacts on women's employability. In the rural and remote communities, women did not have access to well-paying jobs. They experienced major family disruptions and power dynamics with partners repeatedly absent for lucrative work in the resource sector. In the South Asian and Aboriginal communities, cultural expectations shaped women's employability and caregiving duties, as well as some women's access to training and educational opportunities.

In spite of the diverse research communities, we found remarkable similarities. Many women juggled two or three part-time jobs, managed child care and domestic duties, and worried about paying the bills. The few women who were not in the paid workforce anticipated returning to it when possible; in other words, they considered themselves "employable." In all the communities, the women reported that unpaid caregiving reduced their options for finding work or for training and education that could improve their employability. The women struggled to make ends meet; few had financial security, employment security, health benefits, or plans for retirement. The fact that their work was variously underpaid, precarious, and unpaid, contributed significantly to their impoverishment. They valued both paid and unpaid work even when there was conflict between the two.

Employability and Women's Health and Well-Being

All the participants readily saw a connection between their employability and their health and well-being. In particular, the women spoke of the toll that stress and living in poverty took on their health. They also spoke at length about safety concerns and experiences of violence and discrimination in the workplace.

Women's Concern for Their Health

Although their health issues were diverse, the majority of the participants expressed some concern about their health. In Northern-Resource, seven of the women younger than age 40 had significant chronic health problems, and four others had been diagnosed with a serious disability. In Remote-Reserve, two-thirds of the participants reported significant and persistent health problems. In Rural-Farming, almost 80 per cent of the women had chronic health concerns. In the Urban–South Asian community, only 1 of the 15 women claimed good health.

Women's Employability and Health Status

The vast majority of the participants understood their health holistically and readily saw a connection between their employability and their health status. They spoke of the relationship among role overload, caregiving responsibilities, financial uncertainties, and health and well-being. Many participants identified the stress of balancing work and caregiving as a significant factor that affected their health: "I seriously don't cope, stresswise, coping [sic] my days go from work to kids, work to kids . . . I feel guilty that I'm not enough for them, so I try harder to be with them (Northern-Resource)." Urban–South Asian women spoke frequently about the stress of juggling paid and unpaid work, as this woman did: "My health isn't that good because I have a lot of stress: I have to think of my son, I have to wake him up for school, go to work, then get him from the babysitters, and help with his homework, and if I have schoolwork. I have to do that, and so I have a lot of stress." Although early research suggested that women's participation in the paid workforce appeared to be health enhancing, more recent literature has acknowledged that women's juggling of paid and unpaid work in itself contributes to ill health (Forssén & Carlstedt, 2001; Thurston & O'Connor, 2005).

The Impact of Prolonged Stress and Living in Poverty on Women's Health

The majority of the women earned less than the BC median income, and most were poor as defined by the low-income cut-off. In Rural-Farming and Northern-Resource, the difference between women's and men's median incomes was far greater than the provincial average. In Remote-Reserve, over half the women spoke openly of their struggles with poverty. They told us repeatedly that their health had deteriorated because of prolonged stress and living in poverty. In Remote-Reserve, for example, one-third of the participants reported that their health was affected by their financial situations, including the inability to purchase healthy foods and to afford recreational opportunities, increased stress and worry, and the struggle to afford rising costs of prescription medications. As one woman stated:

"Finances have a big impact on your life emotionally . . . There's nobody happy when finances are tight. And it's really hard on the relationship. Going through the no-money period there was really tough . . . I stress about it [finances]." Women in Rural-Farming reported the same struggles: "You cannot live without money . . . I know I don't eat right. I know I don't exercise . . . I don't have any money . . . It's so interconnected because everything costs money."

Violence, Safety, and Workplace Discrimination

One of the most surprising findings was the number of women from each community who reported significant concerns with violence, safety, and workplace discrimination. "All oppressed groups suffer systematic violence simply because they are members of a subordinate group. Subordinate groups not only experience direct violence, but also live in constant fear that violence may occur" (Mullaly, 2007, p. 268). Violence has strong and negative impacts on women's employability even when the women are well trained or educated (Moe & Bell, 2004). Morrow, Hankivsky, and Varcoe (2004) documented the negative effects of **government downsizing** in BC on women's vulnerability to violence. Even nonviolent workplace discrimination has been shown to have a negative impact on women's health (Pavalko, Mossakowski, & Hamilton, 2003).

Almost a third of the participants had past and direct experiences with violence, and the majority continued to be concerned about their own or their children's safety. One Urban–South Asian woman spoke of the threat she felt from her ex-husband: "[I don't feel safe in my home] because my husband knows where I live, but I know that if something were to happen, I would call 911." Nine Northern-Resource women described a past intimate relationship as physically and/or emotionally abusive. As one woman recalled: "It was January '96, I had stated that maybe we should break up. He came home; he was drugged up on . . . I don't know what it was. It was three weeks

after my hysterectomy that he came home and attacked me with a baseball bat in front of my youngest daughter and another 3-year-old child." Rural-Farming women also reported high rates of violence and abuse. Three teenagers who were interviewed in the Rural-Farming region had already experienced abuse by male relatives. One said: "My uncles were . . . bullies . . . My uncle used to hang me out of a two-story window by my legs," and abusive relationships took their toll on women in marital relationships: "I got beat down . . . I took a welding course, . . . and he made me quit . . . I spent 10 years with him; . . . the last thing he did was beat me up with his new girlfriend."

One-third of the Urban-South Asian women who were interviewed worked night shifts. Many women worked in the janitorial and housekeeping industries, some travelling home by public transportation at two in the morning. Because of their shift work, they knew that they could easily be targets of violence. One woman said, "No I don't feel that way [that my community is safe]. I hear about all the things that are happening, and I get scared. . . . At work when I go from my car to work, I park kind of far away, because inside it's pay parking. So when we walk from our car we feel a little bit scared." Half the participants in Remote-Reserve thought that community safety was an issue because of crime and drugs. As one woman indicated, "I don't feel safe at night because of all the crime and stuff that's been happening around here. . . . I get a little bit worried when I'm out with my friends, that, you know, things are going to happen for the worst."

Historical victimization intersected with geographic isolation and limited work opportunities to keep women in abusive or unhealthy relationships. One Rural-Farming woman stated, "I was in relationships that I knew I shouldn't be in, but I was in them because of the financial burden I would have had with the five kids, with four kids at one time and then five." Another Rural-Farming woman said, "The last relationship I was in, I stayed in it for probably an extra, almost a year, even though I kept telling myself . . . I was trying to fix it, but it just wasn't fixable."

In the Remote-Reserve community, five women commented on violence and its impact on their lives. Three described violence in a personal context, and four described the effects of violence in the context of family and/or community members. One participant said that she had to leave her job and school because of the impact of violence on her family: "I didn't do well because my daughter was being abused physically, emotionally, mentally, [and] there was nobody home for her. And when I went into doing this course, it was all about what I wanted. I didn't think about what was going to happen down the line with my daughter and if she could handle it. It just didn't connect." The woman intimated that it was partially her fault that her daughter suffered while she was working and attending school. She did not consider other factors that may have led to the violence.

All the participants understood the links between their social and economic circumstances and their health. While most were concerned with their health and reported ongoing health issues, they all saw a connection between their employability and their health status. The women's efforts to obtain or maintain paid employment, alongside their considerable unpaid caregiving responsibilities, had profound effects on their psychosocial health and well-being. In addition, many of the women experienced the stress of living in poverty and, for some, the stark reality of living in material deprivation. An unexpected yet significant finding across the four research communities was women's ongoing concerns with violence, safety, and workplace discrimination.

Implications and Conclusion

Adopting an intersectional framework demonstrates the inextricable links among gender, location, unpaid caregiving, and cultural expectations. In multiple and overlapping ways, these factors have intersected with each other and interacted with role expectations and threats of violence and discrimination to limit women's opportunities for well-paid employment across a range of British Columbian communities. Not only has the daily challenge of juggling unpaid and paid work limited women's opportunities financially, but it has resulted in the chronic worry of living in material scarcity.

Currently, policies across Canada, particularly in the province of BC, ignore women's realities. Assuming that most women can be classified as "employable," with no regard for their multiple roles and urban, rural, and remote contexts, has a deleterious impact on their health and well-being. Overwhelmingly, the women we spoke with could not obtain high-paying stable employment or access safe and affordable child care. Many struggled to care for children and other relatives or friends and did so with few or no community supports. Yet rather than challenging their classification as "employable," the women were working hard to secure and maintain employment. Despite their best efforts, they faced increasing difficulties supporting themselves and their families. Employability-based approaches, which focus on getting the indigent to work, do not tackle the systemic problems of demand deficiency and job shortage and are insufficient to the task of tackling unemployment (Peck & Theodore, 2000).

Over the past 20 years, provincial and federal governments in Canada have instituted macroeconomic changes that have resulted in the transfer of the Canadian social safety net from the state to the already-overburdened shoulders of individual women: "In nations such as Canada, with high unemployment, a stagnant economy, vast discrepancies between the wages of men and women, and a severe shortage of affordable and regulated child care, focusing on employability has negative consequences for many individuals as well as social policy development" (Baker, 1996, p. 498). The data for this study were gathered in 2005 and 2006, before the worldwide economic meltdown in 2008 and subsequent economic crises of 2011. Unfortunately, the trend toward neo-conservative labour market policies that individualize systemic issues has firmly taken hold as governments urge "**fiscal restraint**" and "net zero mandates." The result has been women's deepening economic insecurity and deteriorating health and well-being.

Note

The authors are grateful for funding provided by the Social Sciences and Humanities Research Council and the Michael Smith Foundation for Health Research.

The author(s) declared no potential conflicts of interest with respect to the research, authorship, and/or publication of this article.

References

Armstrong, P. (2007). Relocating care: Home care in Ontario. In M. Morrow, O. Hankivsky, & C. Varcoe (Eds). *Women's health in Canada: Critical perspectives on theory and policy* (pp. 528–553). Toronto: University of Toronto Press.

Baker, M. (1996). Social assistance and the employability of mothers: Two models from cross-national research. *Canadian Journal of Sociology, 21,* 483–503.

Baker, M., & Tippin, D. (2002). Health, beneficiaries and welfare to work: Competing visions of employability. In T. Eardley & B. Bradbury (Eds), *Competing visions: Refereed proceedings of the National Social Policy Conference* 2001 (pp. 45–62). Sydney, Australia: University of New South Wales.

Berry, A. A., Katras, M. J., Sano, Y., Lee, J., & Bauer. I. W. (2008). Job volatility of rural, low-income mothers: A mixed methods approach. *Journal of Family Economic Issues, 29,* 5–22.

Brown, P., & Hesketh, A. (2004). *The mismanagement of talent: Employability and jobs in the knowledge economy.* Oxford: Oxford University Press.

Canadian Association for Social Workers. (2009). *Comparing women's income in 2000 and 2005: Improvements and disappointments.* Retrieved from www.casw-acts.ca/sites/default/files/policy_statements/Comparing%20Vision.pdf

Canadian Research Institute for the Advancement of Women. (2006). *Intersectional feminist frameworks: All emerging vision.* Retrieved from www.criaw-icref.ca/sites/criaw/fileslThe%20IFFs-%20An%20Emerging%20Vision.pdf

Day, S., & Brodsky, G. (2007). *Women and the Canada social transfer: Securing the social union.* Ottawa: Status of Women Canada. Retrieved from www.fafia-afai.org/en/women_and_the_canada_social_transfer_cst

Doyal, L. (1995). *What makes women sick: Gender and the political economy of health.* New Brunswick, NJ: Rutgers University Press.

Forssen, A., & Carlsledt, G. (2001). Work, health and ill health: New research makes women's experiences visible. *Scandinavian Journal of Primary Health Care, 19,* 154–157.

Fuller, S. (2005). Public sector employment and gender wage inequalities in British Columbia: Assessing the effects of a shrinking public sector. *Canadian Journal of Sociology, 30,* 405–439.

Hankivsky, O., & Cormier, R. (2009). *Intersectionality: Moving women's health research and policy forward.* Vancouver: Women's Health Research Network.

Joseph. G., Leach. B., & Turner. S. (2007). *Caring at a distance: Working women, rural to urban migration and the compassionate care challenge.* Ottawa: Status of Women Canada.

Laurence, M. K. (1992). Womancare—Healthcare: Power and policy. *Canadian Women Studies, 12.* Retrieved from http://pi.library.yorku.ca/ojs/index.php/cws/article/viewFile/10531/9620

Lero, D., & Joseph, G. (2007). *A systematic review of the literature on combining work and eldercare in Canada.* Guelph, ON: University of Guelph and the Homewood Foundation.

Lochhead, C., & Scott, K. (2000). The dynamics of women's poverty in Canada. Canadian Council on Social Development. Status of Women Canada. Retrieved from www.swc.cfc.gc.ca/

McCall. L. (2005). The complexity of intersectionality. *Signs, 30.* 1771–1800.

McDaniel, S. A. (2002). Women's changing relations to the state and citizenship: Caring and intergenerational relations in globalizing western democracies. *Canadian Review of Sociology/Revue Canadienne de Sociologie, 39,* 125–150.

Maguire, P. (2001). Uneven ground: Feminisms and action research. In P. Reason & H. Bradbury (Eds). *Handbook of action research: Participative inquiry and practice* (pp. 59–69). London: Sage.

Ministry of Human Resources. (2003). *Annual services plan report.* Vancouver: Government of British Columbia.

Moe, A. M., & Bell, M. P. (2004). Abject economics: The effects of battering and violence on women's work and employability. *Violence Against Women, 10,* 29–55.

Morris, M. (2000). *Quick facts: Women, poverty and Canadian public policy in an era of Globalization.* Paper presented to the International Colloquium: Globalization, Societies, Cultures, Congress of the Social Sciences and Humanities, Edmonton, AB. Retrieved from www.criaw-icref.ca/WomenPovertyGlobalization

Morrow, M., Hankivsky, O., & Varcoe, C. (2004). Women and violence: The effects of dismantling the welfare state. *Critical Social Policy, 24,* 358–384.

Mullaly, B. (2007). *The New Structural Social Work.* Toronto: Oxford University Press.

Pavalko, E. K., Mossakowski. K. N., & Hamilton, V J. (2003). Does perceived discrimination affect health? Longitudinal relationships between work discrimination and women's physical and emotional health. *Journal of Health and Social Behavior, 43,* 18–33.

Peck, J., & Theodore, N. (2000). Beyond "employability." *Cambridge Journal of Economics, 24*, 729–749.

Phoenix, A., & Pattynama, P. (2006). Intersectionality. *European Journal of Women's Studies, 13*, 187–192.

Porter, A. (2003). *Gendered States: Women, unemployment insurance, and the political economy of the welfare state in Canada. 1945–1997.* Toronto: University of Toronto Press.

Reid, C. (2004). *The wounds of exclusion: Poverty, women's health, and social justice.* Walnut Creek, CA: Left Coast Press.

Reid, C. (2007). Women's health and the politics of poverty and exclusion. In O. Hankivsky, M. Morrow, & C. Varcoe (Eds), *Women's health in Canada: Critical health theory, policy and practice* (pp. 199–220). Oxford: Oxford University Press.

Reid. C., & Frisby. W. (2007). Continuing the journey: Articulating dimensions of feminist participatory action research. In P. Reason, & H. Bradbury (Eds), *Handbook of action research* (2nd ed., pp. 93–105). London: Sage.

Reid, C., Ponic, P., Hara, L., Kawcesi, C., & LeDrew, R. (2010). Performing intersectionality: The mutuality of intersectional analysis and feminist participatory action health research. In O. Hankivsky (Ed.), *Health inequities in Canada—Intersectional frameworks and practices* (pp. 92–111). Vancouver: University of British Columbia Press.

Reid, C., Ponic, P., Hara, L., LeDrew. R ., Kaweesi, C., & Besla, K. (2011). Living an ethical agreement: Negotiating confidentiality and harm in feminist participatory action research. In G. Creese & W. Frisby (Eds), *Feminist community research: Negotiating contested relationships* (pp. 189–209). Vancouver: University of British Columbia Press.

Ruspini, E. (1999). The contribution of longitudinal research to the study of women's poverty. *Quality & Quantity, 33*, 323–338.

Shields, S. (2008). Gender: An intersectionality perspective. *Sex Roles, 59*, 301–311.

Statistics Canada. (2010). 2006 Community profiles. Retrieved from www12.statcan.ca/census-recensement/2006/

Stratigaki, M. (2004). The cooptation of gender concepts in EU policies: The case of "reconciliation of work and the family." *Social Politics, 11*, 30–56.

Thurston, W. E., & O'Connor, M. (2005). Preventive/health promotion strategies: Health promotion for women. Ottawa: Canada–USA Women's Health Forum.

Townson, M. (2009, September). *Women's poverty and the recession.* Canadian Centre for Policy Alternatives. Retrieved from www.policyalternatives.ca/sites/defaultlfiles/uploads/publications/National_Office_Pubs/2009/Womens_Poverty_in_the_Recession.pdf

Varcoe, C., Hankivsky, O., & Morrow, M. (2007). Introduction: Beyond gender matters. In M. Morrow, O. Hankivsky, & C. Varcoe (Eds), *Women's health in Canada: Critical perspectives on theory and policy* (pp. 3–32). Toronto: University of Toronto Press.

White, D. (2001). To market to market: Employability in the liberal investment. Paper presented at the Conference on Social Cohesion, Université de Montréal.

Yalnizyan, A. (2005). *Canada's commitment to equality: A gender analysis of the last ten federal budgets (1995–2004).* Canada Feminist Alliance for International Action. Retrieved from www.fafia-afai.org/images/pdf/CanadaCommitmentsEquality.pdf

Questions for Critical Thought

1. According to Reid and LeDrew, what are the unintended consequences of being an "oil or gas widow" in the remote north of British Columbia? How does this social phenomenon affect the gendered division of labour within the household?

2. What are the cultural expectations of South Asian and Aboriginal groups? Why are these expectations incompatible with work in the primary labour market? Is this problem more likely to affect one economic or cultural group more than another? Why or why not?

3. Explain Reid and LeDrew's finding that economic constraints, caregiving overload, seasonal work, or a lack of paid labour force women to continue to live in relative poverty and abusive relationships. Is this pattern reflected among members of your immediate or extended family? Is this pattern reflected in your community?

4. The authors suggest that the neo-conservative policies of the government of British Columbia have "transferred the Canadian social safety net from the state, to the already overburdened shoulders of individual women." What are some services that you can think of that could be provided to these women and their families in order to improve their standard of living?

Gender, Race, and Immigration: Aging and Economic Security in Canada[1]

Valerie Preston, Ann Kim, Samantha Hudyma, Nancy Mandell, Meg Luxton, and

Julia Hemphill

Introduction

Although the economic situations of many seniors[2] in Canada have improved since the 1980s, a large population of seniors does not have access to the resources needed to age securely (CASW, 2007; Marier & Skinner, 2008; NACA, 2005). Very old, single women and growing numbers of visible minority and immigrant seniors lack the financial resources that ensure a secure and stable standard of living in old age (Durst, 2005). Much of the literature and many policies address the financial challenges facing each of these groups of seniors separately, as if gender, **ethnoracial** background, and immigrant status can be viewed in isolation from each other. To understand the economic challenges facing immigrant seniors, we adopt an intersectional approach (McCall, 2005) that recognizes how multiple dimensions of social identity, such as immigrant status, gender, and visible minority status, interact to influence seniors' economic security. This analysis therefore takes account of differences in seniors' incomes by considering age-related and gender differences, as well as the effects of visible minority status. In turn, by focusing on how social characteristics interact, current retirement policies, and programs that may have unequal impact on subgroups of seniors are illuminated.

Economic security means that a person has the necessary resources to ensure a stable and secure standard of living. This paper shows how economic security is **racialized**[3] and gendered among aging immigrants in Canada. After a brief review of current Canadian literature on seniors' economic circumstances, the 2006 census information will be used to analyze the variation in the incidences of low income between men and women, and immigrant seniors and Canadian-born seniors. Although income is only a partial measure of economic security, it is one crucial component for which information is readily available. For this study, the percentages of immigrant and Canadian-born seniors who have incomes less than the **low-income cut-off (LICO)** will be compared, followed by a consideration of the percentages of seniors with low incomes from Canada's largest racialized minorities.[4] The conclusions highlight the complex patterns of poverty among immigrant seniors and some of the ensuing policy implications.

The Impacts of Gender, Immigrant Status, and Visible Minority Status

Current understanding of the effects of gender, immigrant and visible minority status on seniors' economic security is based on studies that examine the impact of each dimension of social identity separately. This research shows that seniors have unequal access to the three main sources of retirement income: the **Old Age Security Program (OAS)** and **Guaranteed Income Supplement (GIS)**, the **Canada Pension Plan/Quebec Pension Plan (CPP/QPP)**, and private pension plans and individual savings (CASW, 2007). Over two-thirds of seniors, particularly women, only have access to government-sponsored income security programs and government pensions (NACA, 2005). Furthermore, many immigrants who arrive to Canada in later life never even qualify for these benefits. As a result, many Canadian-born and immigrant women and men have a very low income in their old age.

Poverty also occurs because the value of retirement benefits for many seniors is low. The minimum payments provided through OAS and GIS, sources of retirement income, are very low. For single people, the maximum OAS and GIS payments are just below the after tax low-income cutoff (LICO), a widely used measure of poverty (CASW, 2007). Because benefits from the Canada Pension Plan and the Quebec Pension Plan are based on the length and value of contributions made while active in the labour force, and many women and immigrants have interrupted employment histories and/or low lifetime earnings, the CPP/QPP payments that they receive are limited.

Gender: Women's Financial Insecurity in Old Age

Economic insecurity in old age is a persistent problem for many women. The percentage of female seniors who have low incomes is more than double that of their male counterparts (3.2 per cent of men compared to 8.4 per cent of women in 2005) (CASW, 2007). The gender difference is due in part to women's limited entitlement to government pension benefits. On average, the CPP/QPP replaces only 25 per cent of women's average annual lifetime incomes (CASW, 2007). Women are also more dependent than men on government income security programs. In 2003, women received 55.3 per cent of their total income from OAS and GIS, while only 41.4 per cent of senior men's total income came from the same sources (CASW, 2007).

For women, income security in later life is shaped by gendered life courses (Berger & Denton, 2004; McDaniel & Bernard, 2011; Moen, 2001) and **gender segmentation in the labour market** that systematically impedes their ability to achieve economic security through current retirement income programs. Women who withdraw from the labour market to care for their children and other family members are among the most vulnerable to economic insecurity in old age

(Townson, 2006). The Canadian income retirement system does not acknowledge or compensate women for their years of unpaid care work (McDonald, 2002). The adverse effects of employment interruptions are compounded by women's participation in female-dominated occupations that are often poorly paid. Women are overrepresented in precarious, part-time, and low paid work that reduces their pension contributions (Berger & Denton, 2004; Preston & D'Addario, 2009). Government and private pension plans are earnings-based, penalizing those who work discontinuously and earn low wages (CASW, 2007).

Marital status also influences women's retirement incomes. Many widows suffer economically after the death of their husbands (Bernard & Li, 2006; Li, 2004). The incomes of many widows are "clustered" just above the LICO, leaving them at serious risk of poverty. Without the benefit of a husband's lifetime earnings, single, unattached women are also overrepresented among the poorest elderly (CASW, 2007; Gaszo, 2005).

Immigrant Status: The Poverty of Aging Newcomers

Immigrants also face challenges to achieving financial security in old age. Many spend some of their working lives outside Canada unable to accumulate pension credits (CASW, 2007). The growing earnings gap disparity between immigrants and the Canadian-born means that the average pension contributions of immigrants are also lower than those of the Canadian-born (Elgersma, 2010). As the time required for immigrants to achieve the earnings of their Canadian-born counterparts has increased from five to more than ten years (Frenette & Morissette, 2003), the disparities in pension contributions have also increased. Immigrants' financial security in old age is also constrained by a 10-year residency requirement for OAS.

The International Social Security Agreements (ISSA) that allow immigrants to use pension entitlements from their countries of origin to qualify for Canadian retirement programs and thereby redress disparities in pension benefits operate mainly with European countries (e.g., Germany, Italy, and Portugal). Canada does not have agreements with some major and recent immigrant-source countries such as India and Pakistan (CASW, 2007). One result is that recent immigrants to Canada are more likely than those who arrived earlier to experience financial hardships in old age (Turcotte & Schellenberg, 2007). Although many Canadians are uncertain about their retirement plans, this is particularly true for recent immigrants (Stobert, 2003). Approximately half of all recent immigrants, 47 per cent, did not know when they would retire or planned to never retire and 45 per cent expressed concerns about the adequacy of their financial preparations. There is a large difference between what they want in terms of financial preparation for retirement and their actual financial position (Schellenberg & Silver, 2004).

Race and Ethnicity: The Impact of Visible Minority Status

Visible minorities, both Canadian-born and immigrant, often have differential access to retirement income programs. In general, visible minorities are more likely than whites to face workplace discrimination that reduces their earnings and subsequent retirement incomes (Pendakur & Pendakur, 2002; Ray & Preston, 2009). However, the extent to which these obstacles affect the financial security of racialized immigrants in their old age varies among visible minority groups and over time (Mata, 2010). For example, Caribbean women who entered Canada as **domestic workers** on **temporary work visas** did not qualify for OAS or GIS (Hsuing & Nichol, 2010). In the 1990s, long after the temporary visa program ended, Bakan and Stasiulis (2003) found that Caribbean women who worked as domestic workers were paid lower wages and were less likely to receive benefits than other foreign domestic workers. Kaida and Boyd (2011) also uncovered important

ethnocultural differences regarding intergenerational family transfers that affect financial security in old age. For example, older Filipino, East Indian, and other South Asian women often benefit from co-residence with kin. Although these women appear financially secure because their families care for them, they may have little personal access to money and they also face financial vulnerability if they ever lose family support (Mitchell, 2005).

American studies suggest that minority status may also influence expectations about retirement (Honig, 1996) and the timing and reasons for retirement (Bulanda & Zhang, 2009; Stanford & Usita, 2002). For example, poor health is a more frequent reason for retirement among racial minorities in the United States than among white seniors (Standford & Usita, 2002). These findings suggest that variations in health status across and within ethnocultural groups in Canada (Kobayashi, Prus, & Lin, 2008) may also affect seniors' financial security (Buckley, Denton, Robb, & Spencer, 2006).

By building on research that shows how seniors' economic security varies by gender, immigrant status, and visible minority status, this study compares the financial circumstances of men and women of different ages and distinguishes between white and racialized immigrants and non-immigrants. The analysis highlights the trends in financial security for aging immigrants and the Canadian-born, and identifies disparities in financial security between men and women from different ethnoracial backgrounds.

Data and Methods

There are numerous indicators and statistical measures of economic security and disadvantage; however, there is no official poverty line or rate in Canada (Statistics Canada, 2011). This analysis therefore draws on the definition of economic security proposed by the Canadian Council on Social Development (CCSD):

Economic security refers to an assured and stable standard of living that provides individuals and families with a level of resources and benefits necessary to participate economically, politically, socially, culturally, and with dignity in their community's activities . . . Security goes beyond mere physical survival to encompass a level of resources that promotes and ensures social inclusion. (Tsoukalas & Mackenzie, 2003, p. 3)

The CCSD applies the before-tax LICO measure to operationalize this definition of economic security. LICO is a widely used indicator of poverty in Canada that will also be employed here (CASW, 2007; Kaida & Boyd, 2011; Li, 2004; NACA, 2005; Palameta, 2004). It compares the annual income of an economic family (i.e., related individuals living in the same household) or a single individual to a threshold calculated by using the percentage of income spent by an average family or individual on basic necessities plus 20 per cent. After factoring in family size and population of the city or town of residence, all individuals who live in households with incomes below the threshold identified are classified as falling below the low-income cut-off. In 2006, the before-tax LICO threshold was $39,393 for a family of four living in a metropolitan area with a population of 500,000 or more (Statistics Canada, 2011). In short, falling below LICO suggests that a family is spending a larger portion of its income on food, shelter, and clothing than the average family (Statistics Canada, 2011).

While Statistics Canada does not recognize LICO as a measure of poverty, it is a valid measure of the income needed to live and participate in a community, and identifies those who are living in "**straitened circumstances**" (CCSD, 2007). Families whose incomes fall below the thresholds are spending at least 20 per cent more of their household income on necessities, which limits their participation in everyday activities. LICO is the preferred measure as its wide usage permits comparisons with past and future studies, it is familiar to researchers, and it is a variable in readily available datasets.

Data from the 2006 **Canadian Census of Population Public-Use Microdata File** provide detailed information about the social and economic characteristics of individuals, permitting an examination of low-income rates according to gender, immigrant status, and ethnoracial background. In an examination of trends for adults aged 25 years and over at a national level,[5] this study's weighted analysis[6] distinguishes men and women and the Canadian-born and the foreign-born[7] from each other across 10-year age categories ending with those 85 years and older. Visible minority status that is ascribed to people who are not Aboriginal, not white, not Caucasian, and not of European background is also considered. The statistical data on visible minorities are problematic, although the best available, as they distinguish between presumed physical characteristics (skin colour), cultural affiliations, and countries of origin. The number of visible minority groups and age categories considered at each stage of the analysis varies, reflecting the sample size of each group (a minimum of 18 unweighted cases). For example, among Canadian-born seniors, the study distinguishes between whites, blacks, Japanese, and Chinese, while, for immigrants, several additional visible minority groups are reported since for each age group the number of immigrants in each visible minority group is sufficiently large. Results from tests of statistical significance are provided where relevant.

Disparities in below-LICO rates are suggestive of structural inequalities throughout the life course. In other words, social groups that are more likely to live in poverty at younger ages are also more likely to live in poverty at older ages (Berger & Denton, 2004; Denton & Boos, 2007). However, the data analyzed here are cross-sectional and as such they illustrate patterns of low income across the age spectrum and do not provide a long-term perspective on the trajectories of economic security throughout the life course. Moreover, LICO data indicate only whether an individual falls above or below the cut-off, not how distant a person is from the threshold. Thus, while two groups may have similar below-LICO rates, their incomes may differ markedly. With these limitations in mind, the LICO data here are used to examine some of the gaps between gendered, racialized, and nativity groups by age as they are indicative of the patterns of inequality at a given point in time and allow us to anticipate potential disparities as people age. In much of the analysis, white Canadian-born men are used as the reference group.

Gender and Low Income

Trends in poverty across age groups reflect gender differences in labour market participation and access to retirement income. With the exception of the 45- to 54-year age group, we observe statistically significant (p<0.01, two-tailed t-tests for proportions) differences in low-income rates between men and women across the seven age categories (Figure 1). Among older Canadians, beginning at the age of 55, as people begin to retire and enter old age, the percentage of women with low incomes increases rapidly, from 14.4 per cent for women aged 55 to 64 years to 33.8 per cent for women over 84 years of age. In contrast, poverty

declines initially for men in the older age groups, falling below 10 per cent of all men between the ages of 75 and 84 years, the lowest percentage of all groups. When the prevalence of poverty among men rises for the small number that is 85 years of age or older, the increase is between 5.6 to 14.4 percentage points. The disparity between the percentages of older men and women with low incomes is even more striking when the fact that women tend to live longer than men is taken into account. Thus, the ratio of older women (85 years plus) living in poverty relative to men is about 4.5 to 1.

An examination of marital status indicates the persistence of gender patterns. Among those over the age of 55 years, the smallest gender gaps are for married individuals. At each age group, the below-LICO rates are less than 6 per cent for married men and married women.[8] The below-LICO rates and gender disparities among unattached men and women are noticeably higher than among married older adults. Among the seniors (55 years plus) who never married or were divorced, separated, or widowed, women have higher below-LICO rates than men at each age group, with the exception of single, never-married women 55 to 64 years old. In general, the largest

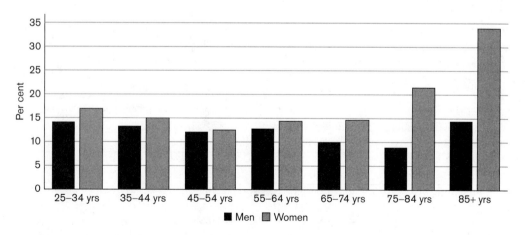

FIGURE 1   LICO rates for men and women by age categories[9]

Source: Preston, et al., *Canadian Review of Social Policy/Revue canadienne de politique sociale*, Nos. 68/69 (2012/2013). "Gender, Race, and Immigration: Aging and Economic Security in Canada," p. 96.

gaps in below-LICO rates can be found among older seniors, between divorced or separated women and men 75 to 84 years old (42.4 per cent and 23.9 per cent, respectively) and between widowed women and men 85 years plus (37.6 per cent and 21.2 per cent, respectively).

Gendered Patterns of Low Income Disaggregated

Visible minority and immigrant status also influence levels of economic security across the life course. We disaggregate the below-LICO rates further by examining their association with visible minority status and immigrant background. These results are presented in Figures 2a, 2b, 3a, and 3b, and the analysis reveals that immigrant experience and racialization influence gendered inequality across the age groups, and that while it is important to examine the gendered patterns of poverty, this practice renders other inequalities invisible. Similarly, an analysis that focuses only on the immigrant experience and racialization renders gender invisible.

Among the visible minority men for whom there are sufficient samples, some interesting patterns emerge. White Canadian-born men tend to have the highest incomes at every age category, as might be expected. Their below-LICO rates are also relatively uniform across the different age groups, falling between 8 per cent and 12 per cent with the lowest rates among seniors aged 65 years and older. In comparison to white Canadian-born men, black men born in Canada have approximately double the below-LICO rates at all ages. While these rates must be interpreted with caution due to the small sample sizes for the older age groups (see Table 1), the pattern suggests that black men experience lifelong disadvantage (Figure 2a). Demonstrating the vulnerability of racialized seniors, the largest disparity between these two groups is found among seniors aged 75 years and older.

Different patterns of low income are evident for Canadian-born Chinese and Japanese men. In the younger age groups, between 25 and 54 years of age, their below-LICO rates are no different from those of white men. However, the oldest Chinese men appear to face higher poverty rates, likely due to earlier barriers in the labour market, but

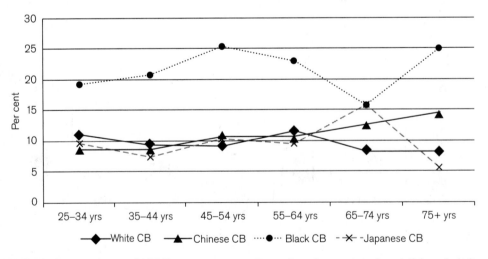

FIGURE 2A Comparison of LICO rates among Canadian-born men by visible minority status

Source: Preston, et al., *Canadian Review of Social Policy/Revue canadienne de politique sociale*, Nos. 68/69 (2012/2013). "Gender, Race, and Immigration: Aging and Economic Security in Canada," p. 97.

TABLE 1   Unweighted frequencies for each visible minority group by age, gender, and immigrant status

	25–34	35–44	45–54	55–64	65–74	75+	Total
Men							
White Cdn-born	37,410	44,104	47,566	33,857	19,235	13,317	195,489
Chinese Cdn-born	546	310	160	47	24	28	1,115
Black Cdn-born	574	231	114	74	38	20	1,051
Japanese Cdn-born	62	66	49	42	44	54	317
White imm.	2,784	5,455	6,375	7,736	5,979	4,882	33,211
Chinese imm.	1,481	2,392	2,259	1,371	919	564	8,986
S. Asian imm.	1,952	2,700	2,059	1,522	827	374	9,434
Black imm.	792	1,209	932	631	318	124	4,006
Filipino imm.	455	706	591	379	163	83	2,377
L. Amer. imm.	510	619	465	252	84	37	1,967
SE Asian imm.	360	500	411	186	85	55	1,597
WA/Arab imm.	671	984	659	345	153	65	2,877
Korean imm.	135	160	228	113	72	18	726
Women							
White Cdn-born	37,602	45,464	49,501	35,024	21,746	20,056	209,393
Chinese Cdn-born	457	274	187	54	38	32	1,042
Black Cdn-born	595	280	142	81	35	34	1,167
Japanese Cdn-born	67	69	48	59	39	48	330
White imm.	3,080	5,629	6,727	7,784	6,154	6,391	35,765
Chinese imm.	1,705	2,846	2,565	1,501	1,050	794	10,461
S. Asian imm.	2,453	2,512	1,947	1,391	804	391	9,498
Black imm.	1,000	1,438	1,021	762	381	221	4,823
Filipino imm.	670	1,141	952	574	271	149	3,757
L. Amer. imm.	604	678	582	247	114	83	2,308
SE Asian imm.	459	527	450	173	110	86	1,805
WA/Arab imm.	778	801	503	284	284	74	2,594
Korean imm.	158	263	268	110	55	43	897

Source: Preston, et al., *Canadian Review of Social Policy/Revue canadienne de politique sociale*, Nos. 68/69 (2012/2013). "Gender, Race, and Immigration: Aging and Economic Security in Canada," p. 98.

these differences are not statistically significant (p<0.05). Among the younger Canadian-born Chinese and Japanese men, the relative parity in low-income rates with white Canadian-born men in 2006 may indicate that low-income rates for men from the two visible minority groups will decline to equalize those for white Canadian-born men in the future. Various factors such as employment conditions, opportunities for career and salary advancement, spending habits, and retirement planning, among others influence the economic security of racialized groups as they age; however, a life course perspective suggests that income during one's paid working life is a good indicator of the potential for economic security in later life. Comparing the four groups of Canadian-born men, it is clear that blacks have the lowest level of economic security.

In an analysis of immigrant men, a different pattern emerges (Figure 2b). Greater variation and greater inequality can be observed in the low-income rates of racialized immigrant groups

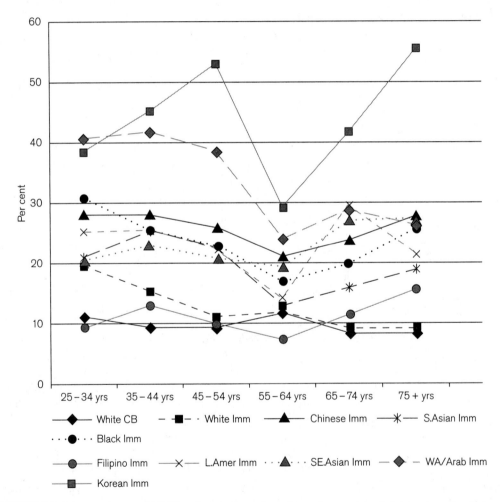

FIGURE 2B Comparison of LICO rates among immigrant men by visible minority status

Source: Preston, et al., *Canadian Review of Social Policy/Revue canadienne de politique sociale*, Nos. 68/69 (2012/2013). "Gender, Race, and Immigration: Aging and Economic Security in Canada," p. 99.

by age, compared to the variation in rates among non-immigrant men. The graph illustrates that, for most groups, the below-LICO rates fall between 10 per cent to 30 per cent with two exceptions, Korean and West Asian/Arab men, who are characterized by higher levels of economic insecurity across all of the age categories. Relative to the reference category, white Canadian-born men, the largest gap falls in the oldest age category for Korean immigrant men, and this difference is statistically significant (p<0.001). Their high rates of poverty across the age groups are not surprising given their high levels of self-employment in small family businesses in the trade and service sectors. These migrant trajectories leave little opportunity for retirement savings and pensions, including CPP/QPP, and this group tends to rely on OAS/GIS upon retirement (Kim, 2010).

Also, despite some narrowing of the "immigrant" **poverty gap** for those 55 to 64 years old, fairly consistent economic disparities with white Canadian-born men across the life stages are evident for all other immigrant groups, with the exception of white and Filipino immigrant men,[10] raising concerns about the persistent poverty of racialized immigrants. Our analysis highlights similarities and differences across racialized immigrant groups. While recognizing that we have not controlled statistically for social, demographic, and economic variables such as marital status, household composition, educational attainment, and labour force participation that affect household income, we offer some general thoughts and explanations for the similarities and differences.

First, those with higher levels falling below the LICO thresholds are racialized immigrants, groups that have experienced a wage gap in the labour market (Galabuzi, 2006; Swidinsky & Swidinsky, 2002). These racialized immigrants also include men for whom English or French is unlikely to be a first language and who would face or would have faced barriers in the primary labour market (e.g., Koreans, West Asians/ Arabs, Chinese, and Southeast Asian, and Latin Americans). Members of such groups would have

turned to self-employment or unstable working conditions, such as temporary, contract, or part-time work. However, the position of black immigrant men, who are predominantly of Jamaican, other Caribbean, or East African origin, demonstrates that these discrepancies cannot solely be explained by language, as they also fall at the higher end of the economic insecurity spectrum with similar rates as their Canadian-born counterparts.

Second, past research has identified the earnings disadvantage of immigrant men who arrive at older ages (Swidinsky & Swidinsky, 2002). Our analysis supports this earlier finding as groups with higher poverty levels are also those whose age at migration structures tend to be older with large proportions of migrants entering Canada as older adults or sponsored older adults with shorter or no employment histories in Canada. For example, over 40 per cent of Korean immigrant men are aged 40 years or older when they arrive in Canada and Chinese immigrant men were also older upon arrival with 27 per cent aged 40 years or older.

Among male seniors, the lowest levels of poverty are observed for Canadian-born whites, Japanese and Chinese men, and immigrant white men. All others have noticeably higher rates of low income (over 15 per cent). Among immigrant men there is also evidence that racialization and migration history may reduce economic security.

Larger disparities are observed between white Canadian-born men and most groups of women (Figures 3a and 3b). Gender differences in low-income rates across the ages can be explained generally by the higher rates for black women born in Canada and immigrant women. White Canadian-born women also have higher levels of low income than their male counterparts, and while they are statistically significant at all age groups (p<0.001), the differences are small for younger and middle-aged women. Among seniors, however, the gaps increase dramatically. A large disparity between Canadian-born white men and women is clearly visible for 65- to 74-year-olds, and the oldest group of 75-year-olds and older (a 16 percentage point difference). The jump in low-income rates for all groups of Canadian-born women relative to white Canadian-born men in the oldest age category is striking, providing further evidence of the complex ways that poverty in old age is gendered and racialized. For white Canadian-born women, inequalities are due mainly to gender while for others they arise mainly from race or from the combined effects of race and gender.

While patterns across the age categories among Canadian-born women are generally similar, black Canadian-born women are distinctive for their higher rates of low income compared to white women born in Canada. Differences are statistically significant across all the age groups except for the oldest seniors. However, among the oldest seniors, the gap is the widest at 14 percentage points, the difference between 38 per cent below-LICO for black Canadian-born women versus 24 per cent for white Canadian-born women in the same age group. Like their male counterparts, black Canadian-born women experience economic insecurity more than other visible minority women born in Canada

(Swidinsky & Swidinsky, 2002). While limited economic opportunities likely contribute to the high rates of poverty, these women are also less likely to be married than white Canadian-born women. Among seniors aged 65 to 74 years, 17 per cent of black Canadian-born women are married while 57 per cent of white Canadian-born women in the same age group are married. Among the oldest black and white women born in Canada whose below-LICO differences are not statistically significant, the percentages of married women are 23.5 per cent and 30 per cent, respectively.

When compared with white Canadian-born men, the patterns of income disparity for immigrant women (Figure 3b) are somewhat similar to those of immigrant men. Immigrant women overall also experience a narrowing of the immigrant poverty gap from the youngest age group to young seniors aged 55 to 64 years, and the gap then widens again for older seniors. Other than for Filipina immigrant women aged 55 to 64 years,[11] all other immigrant women have significantly higher rates of economic insecurity relative to white Canadian-born men ($p < 0.05$). These

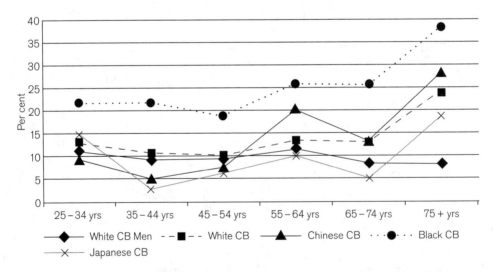

FIGURE 3A Comparison of LICO rates among Canadian-born women by visible minority status

Source: Preston, et al., *Canadian Review of Social Policy/Revue canadienne de politique sociale*, Nos. 68/69 (2012/2013). "Gender, Race, and Immigration: Aging and Economic Security in Canada," p. 101.

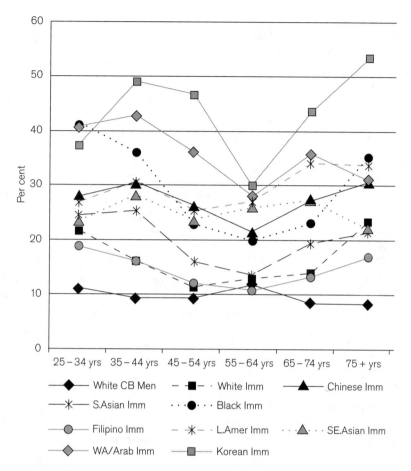

FIGURE 3B Comparison of LICO rates among immigrant women by visible minority status

Source: Preston, et al., *Canadian Review of Social Policy/Revue canadienne de politique sociale*, Nos. 68/69 (2012/2013). "Gender, Race, and Immigration: Aging and Economic Security in Canada," p. 102.

disparities generally exist across all age groups, with the below-LICO percentages rising among the oldest immigrant women in these five visible minority groups: Korean, Chinese, black, Filipina, and white. Below-LICO rates remain similar or drop in the oldest age group (i.e., 75 years plus) for immigrants from three ethnoracial groups, West Asian/Arab, Latin American, and Southeast Asian, but the gaps between all of these groups and white Canadian-born men remain the same. The smallest gap in this age category is elderly Filipinas, who still have more than double the below-LICO rates of white Canadian-born older men. Therefore immigrant woman seniors, like their male counterparts, are at an economic disadvantage relative to men born in Canada. However, the findings become more mixed after a comparison between immigrant women and Canadian-born white women is made; perhaps a more appropriate reference group than Canadian-born white men is needed to illustrate this immigrant effect. A comparison of different groups of immigrant women to Canadian-born white women shows that immigrant women are still likely to have higher rates of economic insecurity at younger ages than Canadian-born white women, but there is some convergence among older women, mainly among white, South Asian, and Filipino immigrants. Similar to their male counterparts, Korean immigrant women stand out for their unusually high levels of income insecurity at virtually all ages, and this is especially true of older women. We draw cautious conclusions based on these findings due to fairly small sample sizes, but a significance test[12] shows that the differences between white Canadian-born women and Korean immigrant women are statistically significant (p<0.001).

The same explanations offered for immigrant men such as period of arrival, age at arrival in Canada, and labour market barriers likely contribute to the heightened rates of poverty for some immigrant women, but all women have the added disadvantage of being more likely to be unattached as seniors. For older seniors, the convergence in percentages with income below the low-income threshold may be explained by the lower labour force participation rate of white Canadian-born women who are now in their seventies and eighties, and their lower likelihood of co-residence with adult children.

As mentioned earlier, some groups of women entered Canada under specific conditions that affect their eligibility for programs. Specifically, Caribbean women who entered on temporary visas as domestic workers were not eligible for income security programs (Hsuing & Nichol, 2010). More recently, women who are entering Canada as live-in caregivers have temporary status for two years, which subsequently reduces their eligibility for CPP/QPP payments (Bakan & Stasiulis, 2003).

Conclusions

This census analysis highlights the need for an intersectional examination of financial security in old age that takes simultaneous account of gender, race, and immigrant status. The percentages of Canadian-born and immigrant men and women from different visible minority groups who have low incomes differ substantially. The large differences between the low-income rates for Filipino immigrants and all other visible minority immigrants underscores the need for detailed and disaggregated analysis of visible minority status and its impacts on immigrants' economic circumstances. There are large differences in the levels of poverty between immigrants and Canadian-born citizens and also across other visible minority groups that need to be examined in more detail. An intersectional analysis that captures the heterogeneity of the Canadian population and their diverse experiences of financial security in old age (Basavarajappa, 2000; CASW, 2007; Strohschein, 2011) would be facilitated by accurate and reliable longitudinal data about the financial situations of seniors in Canada (CASW, 2007; Strohschein, 2011). Such data will help avoid policies that are superficially race- and gender-neutral and that benefit some seniors more than others (Green, 2005).

The consistent differences in poverty related to gender and visible minority and immigrant statuses that we have found across all age groups, suggest that current policies and programs do not take sufficient account of **systemic barriers** faced by newcomers, racialized minorities, and women. Newcomers who work in survival jobs, racialized minorities who experience discrimination in hiring and promotion, and women who move in and out of the labour market suffer financial disadvantages later in life that current retirement programs do not mitigate. This is especially true for the OAS and GIS, universal retirement programs that underpin the economic security of low-income seniors. For example, current policies penalize older adults who continue to work by a dollar for dollar reduction of GIS, imposing the greatest financial loss on low-income seniors who rely on OAS and GIS as their principal income (NACA, 2005). Contribution rules for CPP/QPP also benefit those who work continuously rather than immigrants and many women who need opportunities to accumulate benefits during short periods of labour market participation (CASW, 2007). The value of immigrants' retirement benefits would also improve if there were more international agreements coordinating pension income, particularly with the countries of origin for many of Canada's current immigrants. Lack of information also contributes to older adults' low incomes. Many eligible recipients of GIS and OAS programs, particularly low-income, older adults, do not know how to enrol for these programs. Immigrants in particular need more pension information in their first languages prior to their arrival in Canada. Our recommendations to address these issues run counter to recent policy changes that are moving in the other direction. The increase in the eligibility age for OAS from 65 to 67 will affect the poorest seniors who are disproportionately women and racialized minorities. They will have to rely longer on inadequate social assistance and disability programs before qualifying for OAS.

In our analysis, immigrant women, particularly those who are visible minorities, are the most impoverished seniors. Policies need to be revised so that the effects of gendered social roles and family obligations do not place immigrant women at even greater financial disadvantage than their male counterparts (CASW, 2007; Mitchell, 2005). Reconsideration of the 10-year residency requirement to qualify for OAS and GIS benefits would assist many immigrant men and women, but it would be particularly helpful for immigrant women who are often sponsored by their families

to care for children and other dependents without pay. Even more radical policy changes would enable Canadian-born and immigrant women to contribute to government pensions while they are unpaid caregivers. Such policies should recognize that some men, both Canadian-born and immigrant, are taking active responsibility for the care of children, frail seniors, and other dependants; these policies should be designed to encourage more men to continue on this path (Townson, 2006).

Our findings confirm the need for policies to address inequalities throughout the life course. In old age, Canadian-born visible minority men have higher rates of low-income than white Canadian-born men; however, up to the age of 55, the low-income rates for Canadian-born Chinese and Japanese men are similar to those for white Canadian-born men. These trends suggest that some racialized inequalities may decline in the future, at least for Chinese and Japanese men born in Canada. Overall, our findings draw attention to the diverse and intersecting challenges that racialized and immigrant men and women in Canada must overcome throughout the life course to achieve economic security in old age. Effective policies must respond to inequalities earlier in the life course to reduce current high rates of low income among so many of these older men and women.

Notes

1. We gratefully acknowledge funding from a SSHRC Standard Research Grant and York University; the research assistance of Tracy Nguyen, who assisted with the graphs; and editorial comments from the reviewers and editor, which improved the article. We have benefited from our collaboration with Karen Robson. All correspondence should be addressed to the first author at vpreston@yorku.ca and Geography Department, York University, 4700 Keele St, Toronto, ON, M3J 1P3.
2. Older adults are defined as aged 55 and over. In addition, the terms "seniors" and "older adults" will be used interchangeably in this paper.
3. The term "racialized" refers to those who are visible minorities.
4. Although this paper concentrates on the foreign-born, the authors recognize that Aboriginal peoples are the

most disadvantaged groups in Canada. In addition, older gays and lesbians face challenges in financially securing their retirements; however, due to a paucity of literature, the situations of LGBTQI individuals are not addressed here.
5. The final dataset is weighted and contains a total of 571,367 cases.
6. Unweighted frequencies of each visible minority group by age, gender, and immigrant status are provided in Table 1.
7. This analysis only considers permanent residents. Canada's growing population of temporary residents is excluded since the complexity of their economic circumstances warrants separate analysis and there is little information about this population.
8. Data available upon request.

9. In each figure, the Y-axis refers to the percentage of individuals whose annual income falls below the low-income cut-off.
10. On average, Filipinos in all age groups have higher rates of labour force participation than other immigrants, this may contribute to the relatively low percentage of men with incomes below the low-income threshold (Kelly, 2006).
11. Like their male counterparts, Filipinas in all age groups have higher labour force participation rates than either other immigrant women or Canadian-born women. They also work more hours per week than either of the other groups (Kelly, 2006).
12. As mentioned earlier, the analysis is weighted to represent the entire Canadian population.

References

Bakan, A. & Stasiulis, D. (2003). *Negotiating citizenship: Migrant women in Canada and the global system.* Basingstoke, Hampshire: Palgrave MacMillan.

Basavarajappa, K. G. (2000). Distribution, inequality and concentration of income among older immigrants in Canada. *International Migration, 38*(1), 41–67.

Berger, E. D., & Denton, M. A. (2004). The interplay between women's life course work patterns and financial planning for later life. *Canadian Journal on Aging, 23*(supplement), 81–95.

Bernard, A., & Li, C. (2006). *Death of a spouse: The impact on income for senior men and women.* Analytical Paper, Analysis in Brief. Ottawa: Minister of Industry.

Buckley, N. J., Denton, F. T., Robb, A. L., & Spencer, B. G. (2006). Socioeconomic influences on the health of older Canadians: Estimates based on two longitudinal surveys. *Canadian Public Policy, 32*(1), 59–83.

Bulanda, J. R., & Zhang, Z. (2009). Racial-ethnic differences in subjective survival expectations for the retirement years. *Research on Aging, 31*(6), 688–709.

Canadian Association of Social Workers (CASW). (2007). *Financial security for women seniors in Canada.* Ottawa: CASW.

Canadian Council on Social Development (CCSD). (2007). Backgrounder: Measuring Low Income in Canada. *Urban Poverty Project 2007.* Retrieved from www.ccsd.ca/pubs/2007/upp/measuring_low_income.htm.

Denton, M., & Boos, L. (2007). The gender wealth gap: Structural and material constraints and implications for later life. *Journal of Women and Aging, 19*(3–4), 105–120.

Durst, D. (2005). Aging amongst immigrants in Canada: Population drift. *Canadian Studies in Population, 32*(2), 257–270.

Elgersma, S. (2010). *Immigrant seniors: Their economic security and factors affecting their access to benefits.* Ottawa: The Library of Parliament.

Frenette, M., & Morissette, R. (2003). *Will they ever converge? Earnings of immigrant and Canadian-born workers over the last two decades* (Research Paper 11F0019MIE No.215). Ottawa: Analytical Studies Branch, Statistics Canada.

Galabuzi. G. E. (2006). *Canada's economic apartheid: The social exclusion of racialized groups in the new century.* Toronto: Canadian Scholars' Press.

Gaszo, A. 2005. The poverty of unattached senior women and the Canadian retirement income system: A matter of blame or contradiction? *Journal of Sociology and Social Welfare, 32*(2), 41–62.

Green, C. A. (2005). Race, ethnicity, and social security retirement age in the US. *Feminist Economics, 1*(2), 117–143.

Honig, M. (1996). Retirement expectations: Differences by race, ethnicity, and gender. *The Gerontologist, 36*(3), 373–382.

Hsuing, P. C., & Nichol, K. (2010). Policies on and experiences of foreign domestic workers in Canada. *Sociology Compass, 4*(9), 766–778.

Kaida, L., & Boyd, M. (2011). Poverty variations among the elderly: The roles of income security policies and family co-residence. *Canadian Journal on Aging, 30*(1), 83–100.

Kelly, P. F. (2006). *Filipinos in Canada: Economic dimensions of immigration and settlement* (CERIS Working Paper No. 48). Toronto: CERIS–The Ontario Metropolis Centre.

Kim, A. H. (2010). Filial piety, financial independence and freedom: Explaining the living arrangements of older Korean immigrants. In D. Durst and M. MacLean (Eds), *Diversity and aging among seniors in Canada: Changing faces and greying temples* (pp. 387–408). Calgary, AB: Detselig Enterprises Ltd.

Kobayashi, K. M., Prus, S., & Lin, Z. (2008). *Ethnic differences in health: Does immigration status matter? Social and economic dimensions of an aging population* (Research Paper No. 230). Hamilton, ON: McMaster University.

Li, C. (2004). *Widowhood: Consequences on income for senior women* (Analytical Paper, Analysis in Brief). Ottawa: Minister of Industry.

McCall, L. (2005). The complexity of intersectionality. *Signs: Journal of Women in Culture and Society, 30*(3), 1771–1800.

McDaniel, S., & Bernard, P. (2011). Life course as a policy lens: Challenges and opportunities. *Canadian Public Policy, 37*(supplement), 1–13.

McDonald, L. (2002). *The invisible retirement of women: Social and economic dimensions of an aging population* (Research Paper No. 69). Hamilton, ON: McMaster University.

Marier, P., & Skinner, S. (2008). The impact of gender and immigration on pension outcomes in Canada. *Canadian Public Policy, 34*(supplement), 59–78.

Mata, F. (2010). *Economic vulnerability and ethnicity in Canada's metropolitan workforce: An exploratory analysis of census classifications. Social and economic dimensions of an aging population* (Research Paper No. 10-04). Hamilton, ON: McMaster University.

Mitchell, B. A. (2005). *Canada's growing visible minority population: Generational challenges, opportunities and federal policy considerations.* (Discussion Paper commissioned by The Multicultural Program, Dept. of Canadian Heritage). Gatineau, QC.

Moen, P. (2001). The gendered life course. In L. George & R. H. Binstock (Eds), *Handbook of aging and the social sciences, 5th edn* (pp. 179–196). San Diego: Academic Press.

National Advisory Council on Aging (NACA). (2005). *Seniors on the margins: Aging in poverty in Canada.* Ottawa: Minister of Public Works and Government Services Canada.

Palameta, B. (2004, April). Low income among immigrants and visible minorities. *Perspectives*, 12–17.

Pendakur, K., & Pendakur, R. (2002). Colour my world: Have earnings gaps for Canadian-born ethnic minorities changed over time? *Canadian Public Policy, 28*(4), 489–512.

Preston, V., & D'Addario, S. (2009). Recent migrants in Canadian labour markets: Exploring the impacts of gender and racialization. In S. McKay (Ed.), *Refugees, recent migrants and employment, challenging barriers and exploring pathways* (pp. 139–164). New York: Routledge.

Ray, B., & Preston, V. (2009). Geographies of discrimination: Variations in perceived discomfort and discrimination in Canada's gateway cities. *Journal of Immigrant and Refugee Studies, 7*(3), 228–249.

Schellenberg, G., & Silver, C. (2004). You can't always get what you want. *Canadian Social Trends, 75.* Ottawa: Statistics Canada.

Stanford, E. P., & Usita, P. M. (2002). Retirement: Who is at risk? *Generations, 26*(2), 45–49.

Statistics Canada. (2011). *Low income lines, 2009–2010* (Income Research Paper Series). Ottawa: Minister of Industry.

Stobert, S. (2003, September 2). General social survey: Social support and aging. *The Daily.* Retrieved from www.statcan.gc.ca/daily-quotidien/030902/dq030902a-eng.htm

Strohschein, L. (2011). A life-course approach to studying transitions among Canadian seniors in couple-only households. *Canadian Public Policy, 37*(supplement), 57–71.

Swidinsky, R., & Swidinsky, M. (2002). The relative earnings of visible minorities in Canada: New evidence from the 1996 census. *Industrial Relations, 57*(4), 630–659.

Townson, M. (2006). *Growing older, working longer: The new face of retirement.* Ottawa: Canadian Centre for Policy Alternatives.

Tsoukalas, S., & Mackenzie, A. (2003). *The personal security index, 2003: Five years later.* Ottawa: Canadian Council on Social Development.

Turcotte, M., & Schellenberg, G. (2007). *A portrait of seniors in Canada.* Ottawa: Minister of Industry.

Questions for Critical Thought

1. What do the authors mean by the term "survival jobs?" Can you think of examples of survival jobs? Have you or any members of your family worked in a survival job?

2. Do you think that the 10-year residency requirement before an immigrant is eligible to qualify for the Old Age Security Program (OAS) or Guaranteed Income Supplement (GIS) benefit is fair? Why or why not?

3. Why do certain groups in Canadian society feel threatened by racialized immigrant groups? What are the social, religious, and political origins of these fears?

4. Which countries in the world have international pension agreements with Canada? Why won't some countries agree to this transnational practice?

5. According to the authors' data, Korean men and women experience the highest levels of poverty in their senior years. Why do you think that this is true? Which other groups of visible minority immigrants experience high rates of poverty?

Sterilization in Alberta, 1928–1972: Gender Matters

Jana Grekul

Alberta, Canada, paged a Sexual Sterilization Act in 1928, and up until its repeal in 1972, over 2,800 people were sterilized. Women were overrepresented in the number of **sterilizations** performed. This paper explores how changing understandings of **eugenics** led to a subtle transformation that resulted in a "two-pronged" system that targeted mentally defective men, often a danger to society, and mentally normal but morally abnormal women who consented to sterilization. The end result was success for the movement in terms of the types and numbers of people sterilized, and in the longevity of the program.

In 1883 Francis Galton coined the term "eugenics" to refer to "good breeding" (McLaren 1990; Paul 1995). Genetic theory at the time suggested that "like begets like"; social reformers aimed to control the progression of the human race by instituting policies and legislation that would ensure "fit" members of society would procreate (positive eugenics) while those "unfit" for reproduction would not (negative eugenics). In Alberta and other jurisdictions, parallels were made with the development of crops and breeding of cattle: if science could determine which crops and domestic animals were superior, could we not do the same with the human race? Social engineers worldwide worked to pass laws and create policies that would have "feeble-minded" degenerates confined to institutions and eventually sterilized to prevent the propagation of these unfit members of society.

Perhaps the most notorious example of **social engineering** took place in Germany beginning in 1933. Other jurisdictions, though not as aggressive as the German program, certainly contributed their share to the intended "saving" of the human race. In the United States, over 30 jurisdictions implemented sterilization programs, some active as early as the late 1800s.

Alberta's Sterilization History

In Alberta, beginning in the early twentieth century, individuals and interest groups actively campaigned for the passage of legislation that would require mental health testing before the provision of marriage licenses. Influenced by the international eugenics movement, backed by current genetic theory, promoted by influential, well-respected, and educated prominent citizens, and fuelled by racist sentiments, these initial calls for marriage licensing soon transformed into a movement focused on the passage of sexual sterilization legislation. In March 1928, Alberta's Sexual Sterilization Act was passed. By 1929, the Eugenics Board of Alberta, a four-member decision-making body, had begun the process of determining which feeble-minded Alberta citizens should be prevented from procreating. The only other Canadian province to pass legislation authorizing involuntary sterilization was British Columbia. This province, however, appears to have had a much less aggressive program than that developed in Alberta. Between 1929 and 1972, over 2,800 Albertans were sterilized, many without their knowledge or consent.

Alberta's eugenic history is not news. In 1995, media coverage of the legal battle between Leilani Muir, sterilized without her knowledge as a teenager in the Provincial Training School (PTS) in Red Deer, Alberta, and the provincial government exposed many Albertans and Canadians to a dark period in the province's history. Successful in her battle, Muir received damages close to $1 million and an apology from the province. The issue resurfaced in the media and received public attention again several years later when, after a lengthy battle marred by such antics as Ralph Klein's short-lived invocation of the Charter's notwithstanding clause to thwart victims' attempts for substantial financial compensation,[1] the provincial government and hundreds of plaintiffs agreed to settle out of court. The would-be plaintiffs received over $80 million in damages, and the government issued an apology to the victims of the province's sexual sterilization program.

Academic investigations into the eugenics movement in Alberta provide additional insight into this experiment in social engineering. A number of academic studies over the decades, initially laudatory (Baragar et al. 1935; MacLean and Kibblewhite 1937; Frost 1942), turned into scathing commentaries on an apparatus led by politicians and professionals who had the audacity to play God with people's reproductive rights. A number of studies were produced (McWhirter and Weijer 1969; Christian 1974; Chapman 1977; Caulfield and Robertson 1996; Wahlsten 1997; Park and Radford 1998) that revealed the abuses of the system, the socially constructed nature of diagnosis, and the tendency for the Board to approve sterilizations not necessarily covered under the Sexual Sterilization Act.

In one of the more recent studies, Grekul, Krahn, and Odynak (2004) identify several subgroups, including women, Aboriginals, and teenagers and young adults that were overrepresented in cases sterilized by the Eugenics Board and its affiliated mental health institutions. Evidence also points to a bias toward poorer members of society, all indicators of a trend toward targeting marginalized groups in society. While discrimination against the marginalized is not surprising, one of the perplexing issues surrounding Alberta's sterilization program is why it continued for as long as it did. Grekul et al. (2004) provide a political economy exploration for the over-40-year life span of the Alberta Sexual Sterilization Act and its Eugenics Board, offering suggestions for how and why Albertans were being sterilized long after the

horrors of Nazi Germany's eugenics program were exposed, and after other jurisdictions halted sterilization programs.

This paper explores the role-changing ideas about gender and reproductive responsibility in the province's sterilization program. While the indicators of marginality identified earlier (ethnicity, class) certainly played an important role, we suggest that complex interactions between gender norms, changing constructions of eugenics and sterilization, diagnosis, and consent contributed to the longevity of Alberta's sterilization program and the overrepresentation of women among those sterilized. Patterns in sterilization between the genders differ in significant ways, revealing that women and men were sterilized for different reasons, despite the assumed equal administration of the province's Sexual Sterilization Act. Two professionals affiliated with the Alberta Eugenics Board, a surgeon and a social worker, expressed the difficulty in convincing men to accept sterilization, because "the operation would be a blow to [their] pride or vanity" (MacLean and Kibblewhite 1937, 588). It is this gendered treatment in the process leading up to sterilization and in the justifications for sterilization that are the focus of this paper.

Eugenics Activists and Legislation in Alberta

In the years leading up to the passage of Alberta's Sexual Sterilization Act, "scientific" links between feeble-mindedness and social problems were being made by the experts at the same time media reports contributed to the spreading belief that the province was being overrun by defectives. Noteworthy public figures, many of them female, actively campaigned for such programs during this time. While activists across the country promoted eugenic goals in their provinces (see McLaren 1990 for a detailed history of eugenics in Canada), in Alberta members of the Famous Five, including Nellie McClung, Louise McKinney, and Emily Murphy, heartily endorsed sterilization of society's unfit. Murphy, first female magistrate in the British Empire, was quoted in the *Lethbridge Herald* as reporting that "75 per cent of the cause of feeble-mindedness is due to heredity. The other 25 per cent may be attributed to alcoholism, social diseases, mental overstrain, training children as mediums, drug addiction, cigarettes, etc." (Cairney 1996, 791).

In 1924, the United Farm Women of Alberta (UFWA) actively worked to garner support for sterilization legislation. In her presidential address that year, Mrs Margaret Gunn encouraged the government to pursue a policy of "racial betterment through the weeding out of undesirable strains" (Christian 1974, 9). She "brushed aside civil libertarian opposition by arguing that 'democracy was never intended for degenerates'" (Christian 1974, 9). The legislation passed in 1928 and allowed for the sterilization of inmates of mental health institutions who were eligible for discharge. A four-person Eugenics Board was created to determine if sterilization was appropriate for each case considered. In order for sterilization to occur, all four members had to unanimously agree to authorize the sterilization, and the patient had to give his/her consent unless mentally incapable, in which case consent from the next of kin had to be obtained.

What some find unsettling is the consistent, energetic, and determined involvement of women in the North American eugenics movement, especially in light of the fact that many of their "sisters" were directly targeted by the segregation and sterilization programs. From today's vantage point, it is perhaps easier to understand women's involvement in the birth control movement during this time because this movement's objectives, on the surface at least, represent a move toward greater female control of their own bodies. However, birth control advocates did not all share the same objectives and many were also eugenicists. In fact, the relationship between the birth control movement and the eugenics movement was conflicted at best (McLaren 1990; Paul 1995).

Once the Act was passed, women's involvement continued to provide strength to the eugenics movement. Appointed Secretary to the Eugenics Board, Mrs J. Field was an active and ardent supporter of the sexual sterilization of "misfits" and played an active role in the UFWA's campaign. Social workers, many of whom were female, participated in the presentation of patients to the Board and also provided follow-up reports following sterilization, based on visits to the homes of patients who had been sterilized. Of the 21 Board members over the years, at least five were women.[2]

The social and political context of the time suggests that women's involvement in the movement was largely based on their role as protectors of hearth and home. The cult of domesticity placed responsibility for healthy children and functional homes squarely on the shoulders of middle-class women. It may not be surprising, then, that these women actively promoted the sterilization of individuals deemed unfit to reproduce, who would threaten the sanctity of marriage and family life and who ultimately had the potential to "undo" all the hard work and accomplishments of the suffragists, child savers, and other activists. The "sisters" referred to earlier were not really their sisters; most of the feeble-minded came from the lower social ranks of society. The middle-class females who worked tirelessly for social reform perceived a marked divide between themselves and their working class counterparts, as is evidenced in the documents produced by Alberta's eugenics program.

Data Sources and Eugenics Procedure in Alberta

The Eugenics Board and its affiliated mental health institutions maintained individual patient files for the 4,785 people who ever appeared before the Board. From this information, a *basic data file* was constructed that contains the name, Eugenics Board number,[3] birth date, date of presentation and sterilization, and gender of all patients. In addition to this, a more detailed database containing information gleaned from the patient files was built.[4] Each patient file contained what is termed a *presentation summary*, a one-page highlight sheet, documenting the diagnosis, family history, sexual history, criminal record, psychometric test scores, education level, economic history, and reason for sterilization for patients. The presentation summary accompanied each patient to the Eugenics Board meeting at which his/her case was presented and discussed. Patient files were stored in the Provincial Archives following disbandment of the Eugenics Board in 1972, but in 1987 a decision was made by the Archives administration to destroy the majority of records, keeping only 20 per cent, or what amounts to one out of every five files. The second database used in this study, comprised of 861 cases, draws on information from this "*1 in 5 sample*."[5]

The process for "presenting" a patient for sterilization was developed at the initial meetings of the Eugenics Board of Alberta and changed very little throughout the years of the Board's operation. Patients who fit the criteria for sterilization set out in the Sexual Sterilization Act were presented to the Board upon the advice and selection of the superintendent of the institution in which they resided. The Board, following a brief interview with the patient, would unanimously reach a decision regarding sterilization: whether the patient should be "passed clear" for sterilization, "passed" with some condition attached (i.e., "patient consent required"), or not passed. In 1937, the Act was amended to permit the sterilization of mental defectives without their consent.

Ultimately, 64 per cent of all women ever presented were sterilized, while 54 per cent of men presented were sterilized. If we look closely at the activities of the Board and its affiliated institutions, as revealed through our analysis of documents and case files, changes in constructions of how eugenics was defined during this time facilitated the endurance of the Alberta eugenics system by directing its activities toward certain individuals.

Explaining the Role of Gender in Sterilization

Sterilizations in the province were performed from 1929 until 1972 when the newly elected

Conservative government made repeal of the Act their first order of business. A combination of social, economic, professional, and political factors contributed to the continuation of the province's sterilization program in the wake of the revelation of Hitler's program, the horrors of which shamed other jurisdictions into terminating their own eugenics programs. However, Alberta's peak "sterilization years" occurred in the 1950s and 1960s, long after such revelations and stoppages. Why? Likely contributors to the longevity of the Alberta program include a highly conservative authoritarian Social Credit government with little regard for external criticism and a heavy reliance on "expert" opinion; the niche carving of various helping professionals whose mandate was to rid the province of defectives; elected government officials who were also **charismatic** religious leaders and who mixed their conservative politics with their religious sermons; and an economic boom that distracted Alberta citizens from the goings-on behind closed doors (Grekul et al. 2004). All contribute to a valid, tenable interpretation.

However, missing from this analysis is the significant contribution of changing sterilization goals occurring at the time. As Kline (2001) astutely points out, eugenics in the United States did not die following its negative publicity in the 1940s. The kind of eugenics that Hitler practised was abhorred and flatly rejected. But a different kind of eugenics was much more palatable. The goal was no longer sterilizing the unfit as much as it was encouraging the fit to have children (and through counselling, encouraging the unfit to choose not to procreate). Morphing the emphasis from negative to positive, eugenicists were able to reach more people, more often women, under the auspices of "family planning" and "reproductive morality." Ultimately, in terms of consequence if not "methodology," the goal was the same as it was pre-1940s: saving the race from degeneration.

The emphasis became one of "intelligent parenthood," "marital/parental counselling," nay *convincing* individuals into making wise decisions regarding their reproductive potential. Kline

(2001) documents this subtle, but significant, shift in the eugenics program in the United States. Our data do not support the kind of explicit shift Kline describes.[6] Rather, the data indicate that in the province there emerged over time two categories of negative eugenics: voluntary and involuntary. Both genders were subject to involuntary sterilization, while women were also more likely to submit to voluntary sterilization. Evidence for this "two-pronged" eugenics program, which likely also contributed to the longevity of the Alberta sterilization program, and which sets it apart from its American counterparts, is discussed next.

Probability of Presentation and Sterilization

Women were overrepresented in presentations to the Board, as Grekul et al. (2004) establish by comparing the gender distribution of the Alberta population based on census data to the number of women presented to the Eugenics Board during this time. They also show that this overrepresentation was not the result of more women being resident in the province's mental health institutions. While the probability of presentation for men housed in mental health institutions was 0.024, for women it was 0.048; in every decade women faced a higher probability of presentation than their male counterparts. In other words, mental health personnel working in the institutions, making decisions about which patients to present to the Eugenics Board, were twice as likely to suggest that women should be sterilized. During the span of operation of the Eugenics Board, approximately 46 per cent of the cases presented were men compared with 54 per cent women. Significantly, 58 per cent of the 2,834 individuals sterilized by the Board were women.

But the story is complicated. The province's sterilization activities experienced two peaks, one between 1934 and 1939 and another in the late 1950s (Grekul et al. 2004). A partial explanation for the pattern relates directly to the nature of the "feeder institutions," the institutional populations

from which Eugenics Board patients were drawn in the province. In the early years of the eugenics program, Oliver and Ponoka, both mental health institutions whose wards were primarily adults suffering from mental illness, were the most active presenters. However, by the 1950s, the PTS and, later, Deerhome in Red Deer, training schools responsible for children diagnosed mentally defective, replaced Oliver and Ponoka as most prolific in terms of presentations and sterilizations. The emphasis switched from adult defectives to defective children. This is reflected in the overrepresentation of children in the latter decades of the Board's operation.[7]

Consent and Diagnosis

Consent presents an interesting twist on the activities of the Eugenics Board. Following the amendment to the Sexual Sterilization Act in 1937, consent was no longer required for mental defectives. Children were more often diagnosed as mentally defective (Grekul et al. 2004). Following 1937, and allowing for a time lag for practice to follow policy, it should not be surprising to find a preponderance of sterilization cases from the PTS and Deerhome (institutions that primarily housed children and adolescents) in the 1950s and 1960s. In explaining the increased activity of these institutions, the activities of one individual, Dr LeVann, Superintendent of PTS, warrants mention. LeVann actively pushed the Board in the direction of sterilizing children at younger and younger ages (Grekul 2002; Grekul et al. 2004).

While age and consent emerge as correlates of sterilization, evidence also exists for a relationship between gender and patient diagnosis. More men than women were diagnosed as mentally defective (60 per cent versus 51 per cent), yet more women than men were sterilized (58 per cent of the people sterilized were women). The men presented were less likely to be legally capable of consenting to their sterilization. The women, however, were more likely to be relatively "normal" in that their consent was legally required. There is also a temporal dimension to this relationship. In the 1930s and

1940s, consent was more likely to be required from a man than a woman before sterilization. For example, in the 1930s, of all cases requiring consent, 64 per cent were men, while 41 per cent were women. However, these proportions changed dramatically over the next decades. Following the amendment to the Act in 1937, which made consent unnecessary for mental defectives, overall cases requiring patient consent declined. However, in the 1950s, of those cases where patient consent was required, 38 per cent were women while 18 per cent were men; by the 1970s, the proportion of cases in which patient consent was required dropped to 18 per cent for females and 5 per cent for males. Despite the overall decrease in cases where consent was required over the decades, women were far more likely than men to have a consent requirement attached to the Eugenic Board's decision regarding sterilization.

The comparative lack of mental defective diagnoses (and the concomitant ability to consent to sterilization) among women suggests they were perhaps not "abnormal" in a psychiatric sense, but rather in a social sense: they violated the norms of proper feminine behaviour and therefore would not be suitable mothers. As Carey (1998) found, American eugenics campaigns focused on male misbehaviour considered dangerous to society, while female misbehaviour was not so much disruptive to public safety as it was to notions of appropriate gender roles and norms. In other words, in order to "warrant" sterilization, male behaviour had to fall on the extreme end of a continuum of deviant behaviour. This was reflected in the tendency to sterilize male criminals, homosexuals, and rapists, all of whom were thought to be a risk to others. Females, on the other hand, were more likely to be sterilized for normative violations that made them risky to themselves or society's moral order.

Diagnoses and consent suggest the possibility of a similar pattern in Alberta. Men at the more extreme end of the deviance continuum, who were publicly dangerous (i.e., mental defectives, criminals, homosexuals, molesters), and women who exhibited less publicly dangerous but more socially dangerous behaviours were presented.

This amounts to a change over time toward a greater emphasis on involuntary sterilization for men and voluntary sterilization that targeted non–mentally defective women. The fact that more women were sterilized in the end indicates that perhaps they, not deemed mentally defective and therefore capable of making decisions on their own, were persuaded to choose sterilization in the name of reproductive morality, to protect future generations by choosing sterilization. As the bearers of children and primary caregivers, females have a more onerous burden in terms of decision-making responsibility: decisions that would affect family histories and the future of the race were borne on their shoulders.

We find more support for the presentation and sterilization of women who were socially problematic in their documented "family histories," a section contained in patient presentation summaries where mental health professionals compiled information on the genetic conditions that plagued the families of individuals presented to the Eugenics Board for sterilization. From the start, the mental health professionals and Eugenics Board used leniency in interpreting the Sexual Sterilization Act. Figure 1 shows the distribution of "family history" comments for the 861 cases in the "1 in 5" sample. Most noteworthy is the fact that for 326 cases (38 per cent of the total), the Eugenics Board was explicitly told by the institutions/individuals presenting the cases that there was *no* history of mental illness in the family. If we include the cases where the patient denied such a history and where no information was available, we account for 47 per cent of all cases. And if we add in the comments about alcohol/**promiscuity**/character defects and comments about health and family problems, we now include almost two-thirds (62 per cent) of all the "family history" comments in the "1 in 5" sample. In only a minority of cases (38 per cent in total) was the Board presented with evidence of suspicious or problematic family history. As we see below, some of this evidence was not particularly

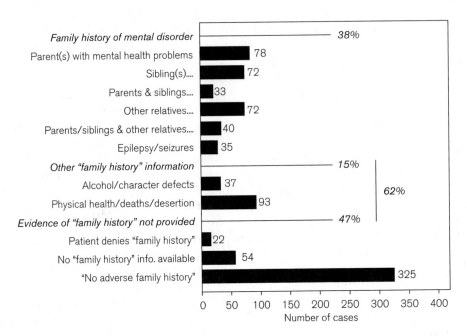

FIGURE 1   "Family History" of Feeble-Mindedness or Psychiatric Disorder (1 in 5 sample)

Source: "1 in 5" files; grouped comments about "family history" as recorded on "presentation summary" sheet (N = 861).

convincing. Even so, the Eugenics Board passed virtually all the cases that were presented to it and typically did so with the explanation that sterilization would ensure that the mental disability would not be passed on to future generations.[8] In other words, evidence for a eugenics campaign that focused solely on genetic/mental disorder is lacking. So, what did inform the eugenics campaign in Alberta?

Kline (2001) argues that in the post–World War II era, as US eugenics campaigns shifted their emphasis from negative to positive, the focus shifted from genetic to environmental "disorders." In Alberta also both genders were subject to environmental eugenic expectations. The family history information, originally intended to document instances of hereditary diseases in a person's family history, was in reality an opportunity to document any hint of family or behavioural dysfunction or a straying from the norms as defined by middle-class society.[9] In other words, the family history section of the presentation

summary was a place where sexual misbehaviour, alcoholism, poor performance in school, unemployment status, distant relatives' escapades, and a great deal else was recorded. While the family histories of both genders contained information not directly related to **genetics**, but related to environmentally "dysgenic" influences, the family histories of female patients were characterized by an emphasis on sexually appropriate (or inappropriate) behaviours that far outweigh in emphasis any of the other social dysfunctions in their lives. In other words, despite the overall trend toward environmental as opposed to strictly genetic problems, there are also significant differences in the gendered emphases of these documented family history flaws.

Promiscuity in particular appears as a concern pertaining primarily to female patients. During the 1930s, in 8 per cent of the female family histories (*n* = 125) but in only one of 115 male cases (0.8 per cent) was mention made of promiscuous behaviour on the part of the patient or a family member.

Importantly, promiscuous behaviour appears to be a catchall for a variety of non-normative behavioural expectations for women. One patient's mother was "married three times and weighs over 250 lbs" (EB#373). Another patient's family history includes "six children, each with a different father" (EB#641). A maternal grandmother "had four illegitimate children, of whom the patient's mother is one" (EB#912). Another patient's mother "was running about with various men" (EB#629). Yet another has a mother who "has lived as a common-law wife with several men" (EB#1321). One woman is a "patient with a promiscuous mother whose present whereabouts are unknown" (EB#252). The reason for sterilization for this case is "family history." These examples reveal an emphasis on the best environment for raising future citizens. This precludes the "promiscuous" environments apparent in the cases cited above, and of many of the female patients who would be primary caregivers to children.

In addition to the gendering of promiscuity ("promiscuous" behaviours of the kind cited above did not appear in male patient case files), eugenicists were concerned with a variety of other behaviours deemed unsuitable for females. Many comments pertain to women being hysterical, experiencing depression after childbirth, being nervous and worrisome, or otherwise weak. The mother of one patient "had a short mental breakdown, with depression at the menopause" (EB#349). In another family history both of the patient's parents are living and well, "except that the mother is passing through the change of life" (EB#891). Another mother "became mentally ill following child birth" (EB#707). Thus, "female problems" largely based in women's sexuality and reproductive roles are relevant to family history, again revealing not only hereditary but environmental concerns and gender expectations on the part of the mental health workers constructing these case files.

Perplexing is the inclusion of sexually based behaviours in the "family history" section of the presentation summaries, when in fact a separate section on these summary sheets entitled "Sexual history" existed. Perhaps when it came to female patients, sexuality was the overriding concern for the mental health professionals compiling these histories. Records of sexual behaviour entered into *both* sections because the sexuality and reproductive capacity of these women were foremost in the professionals' minds. While alcoholism and crime frequently appeared in the family histories of male cases, female cases were dominated by discussions centring on sexual issues. This is significant to our discussion for two main reasons. First, the family history section was to document instances of hereditary taint; sexual issues were documented elsewhere on the summary. Second, the fact that sexual abnormalities crept into the family history section for female patients and not their male counterparts is evidence for the strong influence of appropriate sexual behavioural dictates that we suggest influenced the greater likelihood of sterilization for female patients.

Sexual History

Sexual history, like family history, is composed of paragraphs written by institutional staff members and recorded on the presentation summaries. Because the Eugenics Board was concerned with the reproduction of "inferior" members of the race, it follows that they would be concerned with sexual behaviours. Second, the Eugenics Board and the institutions, as we have seen so far, were very concerned with moral and deviant behaviours, intricately connected to sexuality, and particularly as they relate to females.

In a significant number of male and female cases presented in the 1930s, there is nothing "wrong" sexually with the patients. In 52 per cent of female cases there is either nothing wrong sexually with the patient, the patient's life is "normal" and "marriage is happy," the "children are normal," there is "no sex interest," or there is no information recorded. For males, the number is lower, but still high: 44 per cent.

In the remaining sexual histories, a majority of the females presented to the Board had some history of "promiscuity." In fact, 32 per cent of the 125 female sexual history write-ups in the 1930s make some mention of promiscuous behaviour. Female cases from the 1930s read as follows: "History of sex interest and promiscuity. History of two pregnancies. Was admitted previously on account of sex delinquency" (EB#l65); "Promiscuous: yes. Has been for sometime" (EB#197); "Apart from her sexual promiscuity, there is no history of immorality and no complaints of other immoral behaviour. Patient has had six children, all by different fathers" (EB#259). Another patient "admits sexual indiscretion with four or five different boys" (EB#403). Yet another patient "has no control at all and is a menace wherever she is placed" (EB#409). Gendered expectations include an ability to embody sexual restraint. Failure in this regard was a contributing cause for presentation and possible sterilization.

Promiscuity appears in male cases as well. Mentioned in 29 per cent of the 115 male cases from the 1930s, it is reported, for example, that one patient "has been quite sexual, living with prostitutes and other women" (EB#240). However, while rates of promiscuity reporting are similar for both genders, the nature of the promiscuous behaviours differs: for women the issue is multiple sexual partners outside of marriage and often resulting in illegitimate children; for men it includes sex with prostitutes. By the 1950s, there are only three cases of recorded promiscuity for males, while promiscuity emerges as a theme in 26 per cent of female cases.

Not only were actual or suspected sexual activities recorded in the sexual histories, but the *potential* for sexual activity was also included. In many female cases no delinquency was reported. Yet the Board made sterilization decisions based on the *possibility* of particular behaviours. This trend began early in the 1930s with case 209: "No special sex interest. No history of sex delinquency. Is quite suggestible, *could* be easily led into anti-social conduct" (italics added). Another patient is "unmarried and shows no active interest in the opposite sex, but *would probably* respond passively and rather easily to approaches" (EB#277) (italics added). This potential for sexual behaviour

or victimization appears in the female cases only in the 1930s: six per cent of female sexual histories mention this issue. The issue does not appear at all in the male cases.

There is mention of criminal behaviour and sexual assault in the sexual histories of the male cases. In comparison with the relative lack of evidence of females being sexual offenders, 6 per cent of male cases exhibit such behaviours. For example, one patient "practiced elicit sexual offences. Misled other children" (EB#379). Another patient has been accused by his brother of assaulting his niece (EB#445). One patient appears to have been causing problems within the institution: "became an active masturbator and on several occasions was found in bed tampering with other boys" (EB#463). Another's sexual history is quite telling: "history of unmoral conduct since early life, sex interest quite pronounced. He has also exhibited a tendency to sex perversions. Once sent to Portage La Prairie for sex misdemeanours. One or two episodes since admission to PMI [Ponoka Mental Institution]" (EB#725). Still another patient was serving a 25-year sentence for raping a 13-year-old girl (EB#793). Another was "sentenced to six months at Ft. Saskatchewan in October 1935 for buggery" (EB#1230). While the concern with female patients was their actual or potential sexual deviance in the form of premarital or extramarital relations and illegitimate births, for males, criminal behaviour was the concern.

While gendering of the content of the sexual histories is significant and points to the greater focus on gender-typed norms, the style and format of the sexual histories is also gendered. The frequency of the kind of detail evidenced in the 1930s does not appear with the male sexual histories by the 1950s and 1960s. The majority of the male sexual histories become one-line sentences that read as follows: "patient shows no interest in the opposite sex" or some variation on this general format. In fact, of the 98 male cases presented in the 1950s, 57 cases are of this format. In other words, the majority of write-ups for males for this variable indicate very brief phrases and descriptors compared with female cases. Overall, for the

male sexual histories there is either no information, or no mention of criminal sexual behaviour
(assault, incest) or institutional misbehaviour of a
sexual nature (homosexual or heterosexual).[10]

The average length for a male write-up in the
1960s is about two or three lines. For females, the
average is about eight lines. Female sexual history
write-ups include more details about all aspects
of the patient's life. All that is female is in some
sense sexual, even for the younger female patients.
In the female sexual history write-ups, we read
about ethnicity, religious concerns, abortion, husbands' and fathers' alcoholism, contraceptive use,
worry on the part of the patient about becoming
pregnant, and abusive husbands, to name a few
topics. These types of social concerns are not
mentioned in the male write-ups. Another glaring
difference is the mention in the female sexual histories, but not in the male histories, of economic
situation and occupational status. In this sense,
the female histories have not changed much over
the years, but the male sexual histories have. Male
histories became shorter, documenting only the
most extreme cases of sexual deviance.

Related to this, the "potential for sexual behaviour" is still a greater concern for female patient
histories. Only three of the write-ups for males
(about 3 per cent) include mention of this concern, but for females, close to 10 per cent of the
write-ups contain reference to this potential.
Promiscuity remains a concern primarily for
female patients (23 per cent), while it is barely
mentioned for males (2 cases out of 77).

The Changing Face of Eugenics

Grekul et al. (2004) identify several subgroups that
were targeted by the eugenics program in Alberta.
Women comprised one such group. In this paper
we set out to describe some of the processes that
contributed to female overrepresentation in both
presentations and sterilizations. Female probability of presentation to the Eugenics Board was
double the odds of presentation for males; women
made up a greater proportion of people eventually

sterilized at the hands of the Eugenics Board.
Changes in emphasis of North American sterilization programs are implicated in our explanation
of the gendered results of the Alberta program
and in its long life.

Kline describes a transformation from negative
to positive eugenics in the United States, post–
World War II, which explains the continuation of
professional influence on reproductive control in
that country. In addition to a political economy-
based explanation (Grekul et al. 2004), it is worth-
while to consider, as we have in this paper, the
role that changing constructions of both gender and sterilization played in the longevity of
Alberta's program. While our data do not support a change from negative to positive eugenics
of the type Kline describes, it does seem that the
negative eugenics program morphed into a two-
pronged approach to reproductive control over
marginalized populations. Although women outnumbered men in sterilizations in every decade,
consent and diagnosis interacted with gender
over time to create a situation where mentally
defective males (and females) were sterilized primarily without their consent, while non–mentally
defective women consented to sterilization. At
the same time, official "reasons for sterilization"
as recorded on patient files gradually changed
from an emphasis on genetically based reasons
to reasons that incorporated notions of "intelligent parenthood," signalling, it seems, a change
in emphasis from genetic to environmental concerns on the part of mental health professionals.

In the original legislation, individuals were to
be sterilized if it could be shown that "the patient
might safely be discharged if the danger of the
procreation with its attendant risk of multiplication of evil by transmission of the disability to
progeny were eliminated." Rife with hereditary
disease references that would instill fear in the
province's citizenry and mental health practitioners, this official reason for sterilization is
indicative of the eugenic movement's emphasis
on negative eugenics.

Part of the 1937 amendment to the Act broadened the reason for sterilization to include cases

where "the exercise of the power of procreation by any such psychotic person involves the risk of mental injury, either to such person or to his progeny." This reason for sterilization was most popular over the years of operation of the Eugenics Board, being cited in 46 per cent of the cases presented for sterilization where reasons for sterilization were provided. The addition of this modification suggests a concern with halting the reproduction of individuals "incapable of intelligent parenthood," another frequently used reason for sterilization (in 24 per cent of cases where reasons for sterilization were provided) couching eugenic ideals in terms less fear-inducing, but rather indicating a concern for the potential parents and their offspring. Importantly, "risk of mental injury" can transpire from either genetic or environmental factors.

In plotting the "evolution" of "reasons for sterilization," during the 1930s about 10 per cent of reasons made some reference to a family history of mental health problems or feeble-mindedness compared with only 2 per cent of the 1940s cases. In later decades, the reasons for sterilization never contained this type of genetically based information. Post-1940s, the shift in Alberta was toward an emphasis on environmental factors that would negatively affect children. Further proof of this unstated objective is evidenced in patient family and sexual histories. We saw above that in the vast majority of cases the "family history" section of the presentation summaries revealed no evidence of genetic disorder. And standards for normalcy were different for men and women. Women's family histories were "marred" by evidence of promiscuity, illegitimacy, flirting, dancing, and the potential for sexual indiscretions. For women, the bar was set much lower in terms of behaviours warranting sterilization. Carey (1998) suggests, and our findings concur, that women's deviance comprised behaviours that would not even register on the mild end of the deviance scale for men. These activities were indicative of the potential for women's reproductive immorality and therefore served as criteria for presentation to the Eugenics Board. Suspicious male family histories were characterized by criminal acts or severe sexual indiscretion. Sex, promiscuity, and reproduction did not bear the same meaning or repercussion for men as it did for women.

The implications of these trends are that women were sterilized for "lesser" reasons, or more aptly, for transgressions that more directly relate to appropriate gender role expectations. The window of deviance was much narrower for women. Importantly, this window remained narrow from the inception of the Act in 1928 until its repeal in 1972. Men were not subject to similar sexual social stricture.

Interestingly, women's sexual histories were remarkably similar to their family histories; the two were conflated. In other words, for females, sexual behaviours defined their existence: to be female was to be sexual. To be feeble-minded was to be sexually deviant. In addition, the women (and men) usually experienced social class problems: they were poor. Class, too, is sexualized. These are *poor* feeble-minded women who are oversexed. It is *poor* women who have the most uncontrollable sexual urges. Returning to our discussion earlier of middle-class female social reformers, they likely had little sympathy for these women: they were not sisters at all. In fact, female eugenics activists contributed significantly to the construction of their reproductively prolific, whorish sisters as responsible for the imminent downfall of the human race.

While the involuntary negative eugenic bent of the Alberta program certainly contributed to the significant number of adolescents and young adults sterilized, particularly in its later years, evidence for a voluntary negative eugenics influence also exists. Gender emerged as a key variable early on in the Alberta eugenics movement. Key activists, campaigning for passages of the Sexual Sterilization Act, were women. During a time when women were deemed protectors of hearth and home, the savers of children, the gender that would clean up society by eradicating alcoholism, prostitution, and a variety of social problems, it seemed natural that they would also influence the direction of evolution by controlling reproduction.

Perhaps it should not be surprising that women who were deemed "normal" by psychiatric standards were nonetheless brought into the mental health system and encouraged to opt for sterilization. Maybe it is even less surprising that they, burdened with the fate of the race on their shoulders, agreed to the sterilization procedure.

Conclusion

The story of eugenics in Alberta is a complicated one. This paper adds to the discussion the importance of changing eugenic constructions and how they contributed to the longevity of the province's sterilization program. Initially setting out to sterilize individuals marred by hereditary taint, the legislated reasons for sterilization changed to address less obviously hereditary environmental concerns. The end result was a two-pronged eugenics program. Negative eugenics, the original basis for the Act, continued through the years largely through the work of individual superintendents of institutions who held onto the belief that mentally defective children required sterilization without consent as did mentally defective adult males and females.

However, interesting is the concomitant second prong of the eugenics program with its emphasis on environmental reasons for sterilization that broadened the scope of the Act and facilitated the sterilization of more people, and in many cases women deemed "normal" by psychiatric standards but whose social background negated their ability to provide a "proper" environment in which to raise children.

Significantly, in the early years of the eugenics program in the province, when the focus was on the danger of passing on genetic disorders to progeny, women's family histories contained evidence of their sexually inappropriate behaviour, as did their sexual histories. As the emphasis toward environmental eugenics occurred, women's family and sexual histories continued to evince support for their sexually inappropriate behaviours. In others words, whether the eugenic

focus was genes or environment, it was women's sexual behaviour that was scrutinized. Men's sexual behaviour was not similarly scrutinized. In fact, as we saw earlier, by the 1960s, men's sexual histories became brief and relatively inconsequential to their overall personal history. On the other hand, women's sexual histories remained lengthy, detailed accounts of sexual indiscretions that hardly warranted mention in the write-ups of their male counterparts.

There are, of course, several other issues that warrant mention because they may in part explain some of the disparity in the sterilization program's handling of the genders. Most obvious is the fact that reproductive biology dictates that it is women who have the babies. As a result it makes sense that to some extent women would be overrepresented in sterilization cases. This reality also helps to explain, at least to some extent, the greater focus on sexual history and sexual behaviour in the case files of female patients, although it cannot explain the interaction between consent and diagnosis, and the changes that occurred over time. An additional point that merits discussion is the difference between "eugenics" and "sterilization"; the two are not identical. Eugenics implies state control over the reproduction of those deemed undesirable. Sterilization, on the other hand, refers simply to reproductive control and can be conducted for a variety of reasons, including individual birth control, or on a broader level, saving the government money by reducing the number of children born who might require state care or assistance. It is entirely possible that some of the women who were sterilized sought the operations as a form of birth control, willingly and voluntarily.

Another question worth pondering concerns the temporal dimension that interacts with gender, consent, diagnosis, and sterilization. The argument presented in this paper is that over the decades changing gender norms resulted in the presentations and sterilization of mentally normal but sexually deviant women. How is it possible that gender norms influenced the sterilization of women in the 1960s but not the 1930s? A possible answer to this question may lie in the broader social context of the respective time periods. In the 1930s traditional gender norms dominated: women "knew their place" and acted accordingly. However, with the tumultuous 1960s, the women's movement and the sexual revolution, traditional gender roles were increasingly questioned and challenged. In the politically conservative province of Alberta, run by an authoritarian Social Credit regime for four decades, led by premiers who were also fundamentalist religious leaders, it seems plausible that the province's mental health professionals would and could draw on sexual sterilization legislation in an effort to control the mentally normal women who were challenging gender norms and the establishment.[11]

Eugenics in Alberta was about many things. It was about power, status, control, deviance, class, immigration, and racial purity. But it was also and significantly about gender. Although we have presented data in this paper that suggest women were more likely to be mentally capable of consenting to their sterilization, further research might explore the dynamics of consent. When pressure exists to conform to familial, social, sexual, and societal norms governing appropriate behaviour, it seems that a logical extension of this pressure might appear in the form of pressure to be "reproductively responsible." How many of the women consented because mental health professionals were able to convince them that they were in fact "incapable of intelligent parenthood" and would be doing society and the race a favour by consenting? In such instances, the line between voluntary and involuntary consent is blurred, as is the line between sterilization and eugenics.

Notes

1. Within 24 hours of making this suggestion, as a result of public outcry, Klein and his Conservatives were forced to rethink their position.
2. This information is based on the minutes of the Eugenics Board. Board members were often identified by initials and last name only. These five women were identified as such based on their identification as "Miss" or "Mrs.," and the provision in some instances of full first names. It is possible that some of the members identified by initials only were also female, so our count may actually under-represent the number of female board members.
3. Numbers in brackets indicate Eugenics Board Numbers assigned to patients by the Board. Each patient received such an identification number. Although we cite real cases, we have modified the original EB numbers using a formula in order to protect anonymity of patients.
4. These databases, constructed on the advice of the legal firms representing the victims of the sterilization program, rely only on the information available in the Muir exhibits, to which we were allowed access by the kind permission of Ms Muir (*Muir v. Her Majesty the Queen*).
5. A case-by-case examination of the Eugenics Board numbers for these 861 cases indicates they are a reasonable representative "1 in 5" sample of the basic database. With the exception of 96 missing cases from 1945, the 861 remaining cases appear to be a systematic sample. Until 1944, one in six cases was kept; starting in 1945, one in five was retained.
6. It is possible that additional historical documents may support a parallel emphasis on positive eugenics in the province. However, our data deal directly with the activities of the Eugenics Board and its affiliated mental health institutions, which conducted their activities in accordance with the Sexual Sterilization Act, based in principle on a negative eugenics program.
7. As Grekul et al. (2004) illustrate, Ponoka and Oliver, institutions that primarily catered to adult populations, presented approximately 90 per cent of patients to the Eugenics Board in the 1930s and 1940s. By the 1960s, the PTS and Deerhome, institutions that housed children, adolescents, and young adults, were responsible for presenting almost 60 per cent of all patients presented to the Eugenics Board.
8. In the end, the Eugenics Board of Alberta approved sterilization in 99 per cent of cases.
9. This content analysis is based on the 845 presentation summaries that contained family history information.
10. Homosexuality during this time period was a criminal offence in Canada, which may help explain why such behaviour was included in the sexual histories.
11. Grekul et al. (2004) discuss the significance of the authoritarian nature of the Social Credit government. Unresponsive to outside criticism, and heavily reliant on experts, the government was run by charismatic premiers, Aberhart and then Manning, who were also religious leaders in the province. The result was a marked lack of public criticism of government policies and practices, including the sterilization program.

References

Baragar, C.A., G.A. Davidson, W.J. McAllister, and D.L. McCullough. 1935. "Sexual Sterilization: Four Years Experience in Alberta." *American Journal of Psychology* 91: 897–923.

Cairney, Richard. 1996. "'Democracy Was Never Intended for Degenerates': Alberta's Flirtation with Eugenics Comes Back to Haunt It." *Canadian Medical Association Journal* 155: 789–92.

Carey, Allison C. 1998. "Gender and Compulsory Sterilization Programs in America: 1907–1950." *Journal of Historical Sociology* 11: 74–105.

Caulfield, Timothy, and Gerald Robertson. 1996. "Eugenic Policies in Alberta: From the Systematic to the Systemic?" *Alberta Law Review* XXXV: 59–79.

Chapman, Terry. 1977. "The Early Eugenics Movement in Western Canada." *Alberta History* 25: 9–12.

Christian, Timothy J. 1974. "The Mentally Ill and Human Rights in Alberta: A Study of the Alberta Sexual Sterilization Act." Unpublished research report, Faculty of Law, University of Alberta, Edmonton, AB.

Frost, E. Mary. 1942. "Sterilization in Alberta: A Summary of the Cases Presented to the Eugenics Board for the Province of Alberta from 1929 to 1941." Master's thesis, University of Alberta, Calgary, AB.

Grekul, Jana. 2002. "The Social Construction of the Feebleminded Threat: Implementation of the Sexual Sterilization Act in Alberta, 1929–1972." PhD dissertation, University of Alberta, Calgary, AB.

Grekul, Jana, Harvey Krahn, and Dave Odynak. 2004. "Sterilizing the 'Feeble-Minded': Eugenics in Alberta, 1929–1972." *Journal of Historical Sociology* 17: 358–84.

Kline, Wendy. 2001. *Building a Better Race: Gender, Sexuality, and Eugenics from the Turn of Century to the Baby Boom*. Berkeley: University of California Press.

McLaren, Angus. 1990. *Our Own Master Race: Eugenics in Canada, 1885–1946*. Toronto: McClelland & Stewart.

McWhirter, K.G., and J. Weijer. 1969. "The Alberta Sterilization Act: A Genetic Critique." *University of Toronto Law Journal* 19: 424–31.

MacLean, R.R., and E.J. Kibblewhite. 1937. "Sexual Sterilization in Alberta: Eight Years' Experience, 1929 to May 31, 1937." *Canadian Public Health Journal* 587–90.

Muir v. Her Majesty the Queen. 1995. Trial Exhibits.

Park, Deborah C., and John P. Radford. 1998. "From the Case Files: Reconstructing a History of Involuntary Sterilisation." *Disability and Society* 13: 317–42.

Paul, Diane B. 1995. *Controlling Human Heredity: 1865 to the Present*. Atlantic Highlands, NJ: Humanities Press.

Wahlsten, Douglas. 1997. "Leilani Muir versus the Philosopher King: Eugenics on Trial in Alberta." *Genetica* 99: 185–98.

Questions for Critical Thought

1. Since the Second World War, the discussion about the practice of eugenics has been largely focused on Nazi Germany in the 1930s and 1940s. Why has this discussion not included Canada?

2. At what point, according to the author, did the intersections of gender, poverty, education, ethnicity, race, and mental health predispose certain social groups to be the target of the eugenics movement in Alberta? How did the nature of this movement shift and change from the 1930s to the 1950s? Why did this happen?

3. According to Grekul, controlling women's bodies was central to the eugenics movement in the 1950s. What social, economic, and political factors influenced the development of this movement in Alberta? What role did postcolonialism play in supporting the eugenics movement? What role does postcolonialism continue to play in controlling women's bodies in Alberta and in other provinces in Canada?

4. Several prominent Albertan women were supportive of the Sexual Sterilization Act of 1928, according to Grekul. Why is this a social contradiction? What information did the Eugenics Board use to convince women to consent to sterilization in the

1950s? How can this be explained in terms of intersections of social inequality and patriarchy?

5. Why did the sterilization of people continue until 1972? What role did human rights groups and the de-institutionalization movement have in changing this practice? Do you think that involuntary or "coerced" sterilization should be considered a crime against humanity? Why or why not?

Conclusion

As a presumed haven of dominant norms and the reinforcement of cultural mores, the family, as a result of its social construction and purpose of reproduction, can be a source of inequality for individuals and groups, particularly for racialized immigrant women and their families and those individuals who are deemed to be mentally or morally unfit. The "family" is not a natural institution. It is created by power relations produced through political, historical, and social forces. The workings of labour markets, nation building, migration patterns, culture, and more currently, globalization, shape the family. As a result, not only is the makeup of the Canadian family changing but also its very meaning is contested. These chapters have described this social phenomenon through research on the family and inequality as it intersects with gender, race, age, region, and class.

Recommended Readings

Rachel Epstein, ed. 2009. *Who's Your Daddy? And Other Writings on Queer Parenting*. Toronto: Sumach Press.

- This interesting and diverse collection of essays from Canada, the United States, the United Kingdom, and Australia examines a broad range of themes, including bisexuality, fertility issues, adoption, race relations within families, and the experiences of single mothers and gay fathers.

Martha Friendly and Susan Prentice. 2009. *About Canada: Childcare*. Halifax, NS: Fernwood.

- This text asks why Canada does not have publicly funded early childhood education and care facilities for children while other countries do. The authors argue that early childhood education is important to children's development, and they propose that making such programs available is important to working parents. Friendly and Prentice suggest that this is a political issue that needs to be publicly addressed, and that early childhood education should be part of an integrated system of services provided by the state.

Marla H. Kohlman, Dana B. Krieg, and Bette J. Dickerson, eds 2013. *Notions of Family: Intersectional Perspectives*. Bingley, UK: Emerald Group Publishing Limited.

- This edited volume examines new and original research on the intersections of gender, class position, race, sexuality, and other demographic characteristics that simultaneously affect the social construction of family dynamics in the United States. The book includes chapters on African Americans' and Latinas' mothering scripts, work-family schemas of black, middle-class mothers, and homeless mothers in San Francisco.

Sheryl Nestel. 2006. *Obstructed Labour: Race and Gender in the Re-Emergence of Midwifery*. Vancouver: UBC Press.

- Sheryl Nestel examines the changing nature and subsequent regulation of midwifery in Ontario, and shows how qualified racialized women are excluded from playing a significant role in the health care professions. Nestel examines the success of the midwifery and education program in Ontario, and discusses the emergence of "midwifery tourism," whereby Canadian women have been able to exploit the knowledge and services of experienced midwives from the global South.

Amber E. Kinser, ed. 2008. *Mothering in the Third Wave*. Toronto: Demeter Press.

- This collection of readings about mothering brings together feminist theory and the politics of resistance. The authors discuss the tension surrounding the idea of "postfeminism" and the benefits and challenges to having various feminisms that inform a diverse spectrum of narratives about the mothering experience. The authors examine unclear boundaries that define the family and the ambivalence that has emerged in shaping feminist mothering.

Eleanor Leacock. 2001. "Women in an Egalitarian Society: The Montagnais-Naskapi of Canada." In *Family Patterns, Gender Relations*, 2nd edn. Edited by Bonnie Fox. Don Mills, ON: Oxford University Press.

- Eleanor Leacock examines the egalitarian family and gender relations of the Montagnais-Naskapi (now known as the Innu) people of Labrador. She contends that the fur trade, combined with the attempts at conversion to Christianity by Jesuit priests, introduced a system of patriarchy, and economic and social inequality, to the Montagnais-Naskapi Nation.

PART THREE

....

Inequality and Education

O ur notions of gender, race, and class are shaped by a range of social institutions. In turn, they help to shape those institutions. Education, for example, may promote social difference through curriculum materials, interactions between students and teachers, methods of student assessment, and the way different groups of students are assigned to academic or applied educational streams. At the same time, students (and educators) who have experienced gender, racial, or class inequality have at times held the educational system to account by challenging unjust treatment. Students and their communities have resisted and effected change to inequities in curriculum, texts, programs, and funding allocations and priorities. However, cuts to education funding make advances such as these difficult to sustain, and in fact threaten to erase many of the gains that have been made. Further advances towards equity and justice for marginalized groups in the schools depend on the power dynamics of conflicting interest groups: students, parents, teachers, the public, the state, business, and the labour market.

The chapters in this section illustrate the tensions that exist in formal education in Canada. How, for example, can education be associated with both equality and inequality? With social mobility and opportunity for disadvantaged groups and with the maintenance of inequality? With expectations that education fulfill both social objectives and economic objectives? With the desire for education to be its own end and grant intrinsic rewards and the desire for education to be the means to an end with extrinsic rewards? As the following chapters show, these tensions define the practice of education in Canada today and in the past. They particularly affect those stationed on the "other" side of social difference.

Contradictions in the purposes of education and the effects of racial domination is the theme of the first reading. Bernard Schissel and Terry Wotherspoon argue that residential schools for First Nations students were part of a state policy to force Native peoples to assume a subordinate place in Canada's industrializing and developing labour market. Since Native peoples were not regarded as participating fully in society, residential schools were seen as training grounds for the cheap surplus labour required for Western expansion and new resource industries. Cultural genocide was the objective of the policy, and was ensured by racism, rigid discipline, forced labour, and physical and sexual abuse.

Following this historical portrayal of inequities in Canadian schools, the subsequent readings describe the issues of racial, gender, and religious discrimination occurring in Canadian schools today. Henry Codjoe considers racism against black students. Differential treatment in the schools, racial stereotypes, curriculum bias, low teacher expectations, and a hostile school environment are the factors that often result in low black academic achievement. Codjoe follows some high-achieving, post-secondary black students who succeeded despite the racism they faced.

Njoki Nathani Wane substantiates Codjoe's conclusions as she examines the lack of interest in or information about not only black people but specifically African women in Ontario's high school curriculum. She points out that there is a blank spot in Canadian history, which is socially reproduced in Ontario schools. Wane challenges the concept that African women were passive victims of social inequality as she briefly outlines the historical development of black feminist thought and resistance in Canada. In her conclusion she discusses the contemporaneous role that African-Canadian women are playing in social consciousness–raising by writing about their identities within the transhistorical context of their foremothers.

Another minority group that is systematically ignored and experiencing particular inequities in Canadian schools is female Muslim students (thus challenging a critique limited to gender/race/class). Goli Rezai-Rashti shows how religious stereotypes and other forms of racism and sexism affect these young women. Western feminism doesn't adequately address their experiences, and seemingly liberal-minded educators unfairly expect them to defy their culture and families, argues Rezai-Rashti. Female Muslim students are caught between two different ways of life, Western culture and Islam. Choosing between them results in costs that are often overlooked by Western feminists. In these chapters, the rhetoric of equal opportunity and the right to freedom from discrimination conflict with inequities of sexism, racism, and classism.

The Legacy of Residential Schools

....*Bernard Schissel and Terry Wotherspoon*

Introduction

Our intention in this chapter is to describe the history of Aboriginal education in Canada in **residential schools** in order to explain better education's historical role in the subjugation of Aboriginal people. Our approach is twofold: to describe history through the eyes of the survivors in both primary and secondary accounts; and to place this history in an explanatory context that includes issues of state hegemony over First Nations people and the Euro-Canadian quest to industrialize Canada.

Most clearly, our arguments are based on the contention that the history of the relations between Aboriginal peoples and formal education in Canada is largely a history of cultural genocide. This fact is becoming increasingly clear as First Nations survivors of residential schools are making their voices heard in two ways. First, continuing lawsuits against the federal government and churches of Canada are based on a quest by residential school survivors for compensation for sexual and physical abuse in residential schools. Second, a growing body of relatively new research is documenting not only the abuses against Aboriginal children and youth but also the connections among those abuses, the historical official policy of assimilation, and the current dilemmas faced by Aboriginal peoples and communities.

The journey that we embark upon here is one framed by Santayana's aphorism that if we do not study and reflect upon history, then we will be condemned to repeat it. The history of such genocide might best be described in terms of cultural destruction, although there are writers of Aboriginal ancestry who believe that the history of residential schools is a history of absolute genocide. What we study here is the worst and most blatant form of schooling—as a tool of control, exploitation, and destruction. The residential school system attempted to assimilate Canadian First Nations children into a Euro-Canadian culture and economic system, ironically through the practice of isolating them for gradual integration at a later phase of development. In this quest, what it meant to be of First Nations ancestry was obliterated and replaced with a rigid code of temporal, linguistic, and religious/moral conduct that fed the political and economic needs of an expanding, colonizing economic Goliath. We demonstrate through this historical account that until recently the role of education in the lives of Aboriginal peoples in Canada has not changed significantly since the early twentieth century. What changes have occurred are of form and degree; the impact of those changes has remained largely unchanged. School, for the most part, has been a place where Aboriginal children have done less well than their non-Aboriginal counterparts and where public explanations for this fact have been reduced to issues of race, class, and culture. Later, we consider how the media played a role in constructing social problems faced by Aboriginal peoples as problems resulting from lack of educational success.

We draw for the information in this chapter on some very poignant and valuable sources, including Jim Miller's *Shingwauk's Vision: A History of Residential Schools in Canada*, Roland Chrisjohn's *The Circle Game*, Isabelle Knockwood's *Out of the Depths*, and Helen Cote's graduate thesis, "Damaged Children and Broken Spirits: An Examination of Attitudes of Anisnabe Elders to Acts of Violence Among Anisnabe Youth in

Saskatchewan." The latter two works, both of which are first-person accounts of victimization and exploitation as opposed to official accounts based on a polemic of educational rights, connect the damage wrought by the education of Indian children with the modern-day dilemmas faced by Aboriginal peoples. The historical and autobiographical accounts that we draw on focus attention on a theoretical perspective that goes beyond understanding the exploitation of Aboriginal children and youth in residential school as a result of internal colonialism (Frideres 1998; Miller 1996) or cultural genocide (Chrisjohn and Young 1997). This historical perspective, then, is based on a theory of absolute genocide in which the destruction of culture and the enslavement or protracted physical destruction of a people are a planned state project. Canada's First Nations peoples were in the way of the relentless onrush of capitalist and industrial expansion (York 1992). By the late nineteenth century, their protracted destruction was undertaken most forcefully with compulsory Euro-Canadian education. The legacy is one of continuing harm, albeit in a more subtle guise. This chapter is an attempt to understand how modern universal education is a logical political-economic extension of the residential school era in the "development" of Canada.

We acknowledge, however, that a somewhat dated body of "neo-colonialist" literature, written mostly by non-Aboriginal social commentators, stands in contradiction to the history we present here. This literature is based on several partial or incomplete sources: individual histories of missionaries among the "Indians" (e.g., Nock, *A Victorian Missionary and Canadian Indian Policy* [1988]); American history applied to the Canadian context (e.g., Coleman, *American Indian Children at School, 1850–1930* [1993]); and literature reviews of selected scholarly works that "prove" that despite what has happened to Aboriginal people in the past, they have become like white people and that is the only reality we need to face (e.g., Richards, "Reserves Are Only Good for Some People" [2000]). These works represent for us an ongoing scholarly and social discourse that

is a fundamental part of the injustice Aboriginal people suffer. Nock's work tells us that there were good missionaries; Coleman tells us, in a traditional anthropological paradigm, that Aboriginal students in boarding schools in America were ambivalent about their experiences; and Richards describes how even the most progressive scholars perceive modern-day Aboriginal culture as rightly assimilated into the socio-economic system through which we all gain advantage. Certainly there are truths in these works. It would be naive to assume that all missionaries were bad, that all children in residential school suffered severely, or that assimilation is not part of the reality for race relations in Canada.

In practice, as with most forms of formal education, residential schooling and its outcomes and consequences have had mixed and often contradictory significance. Many government and educational officials, even if they had low estimations of the capacities of Aboriginal children, were committed to offering training, skills, and discipline that would be useful for integration into selected strata within Canadian society. In most cases, students were expected to combine studies with practical training oriented to domestic work, farm labour, or other trades. This meant that students' academic progress was limited, often complicated further by the absence of meaningful employment opportunities out of school. In a few instances church officials sponsored students to continue their studies at the post-secondary level, but state authorities were more likely to place severe restrictions on registered Indian students' abilities to advance their education and frequently refused students' requests for more formal education (Barman et al. 1986; Stevenson 1991). Residential schools, despite their damaging consequences for community relations, sometimes constituted a basis for friendships, personal connections, resistance, and political organization (Fiske 1996). Accounts of residential schooling are further mixed by acknowledgement that schooling (though not necessarily in the form that it took in residential schools) was sought, or at least regarded as a necessary evil, by many

Aboriginal people as a vehicle through which their children and communities would gain a chance to survive in a modernizing world (see, for example, Treaty 7 Elders and Tribal Council 1996). Moreover, not all Aboriginal children experienced residential schooling—not all children, and especially Aboriginal children, attended any kind of school regularly in the late nineteenth and early twentieth centuries; residential schools were not a factor in many communities, which often had day schools; and the federal government was not responsible for the education of non-status and Métis children.

Nonetheless, the overall impact of residential schooling, hidden until recently in denial, isolation, or sublimated memories, has been highly destructive for individuals, their families, and Aboriginal communities in general. By focusing on a few successes or good stories, the social commentators/historians who cast a positive light on residential schooling either miss or fail to acknowledge the socio-economic forces that continue to put Aboriginal people in their "place."

We emphasize, in addition and without apology, that if we continue to ignore the voices of those most damaged, we are part of the problem and not part of the solution. The strong works we include in this chapter are written largely, although not entirely, by Aboriginal people and, most importantly, by Aboriginal scholars/writers who have tried to make sense of their first-hand experiences of oppression. Some of the works that we do not discuss in this chapter, such as Celia Haig-Brown's *Resistance and Renewal: Surviving the Residential School* (1988) and Linda Jaine's *Residential School: The Stolen Years* (1993), incorporated some of the initial autobiographical accounts by Aboriginal writers and stand as further testimony to how important the first-hand Aboriginal experience is in taking a radical new view of Canadian history. We would be remiss as non-Aboriginal writers if we did not defer to the wisdom and knowledge of Aboriginal writers as the most valid chroniclers of their own oppression. We also wish to state that the conventional literature that we mention above stands in stark contrast to some very fine

legal writers who, as knowledgeable observers of the law, present a history of Aboriginal–European relations in Canada that is consonant with the writings of Aboriginal people. We refer specifically to Thomas Berger (1991), a lawyer and judge who has been involved in Royal Commissions on Northern development and who has written an important legal-historical work on Native rights in the Americas, *A Long and Terrible Shadow: White Values, Native Rights in the Americas, 1492–1992*; Patricia Monture-Angus (1999), a Mohawk legal scholar and activist who documents the colonialist nature of the Canadian legal system in *Fire in My Soul: A Mohawk Woman Speaks*; Rupert Ross (1992), who practises law in northern Manitoba and who describes the human rights damages incurred by Aboriginal people as they come into contact with formal law in *Dancing with a Ghost and Returning to the Teachings*; and Judges A.C. Hamilton and C.M. Sinclair (1991), who led the Manitoba Aboriginal Justice Inquiry.

Indoctrination and Destruction of Self, Community, and Family

To understand how education, both historically and in contemporary circumstances, has helped to maintain state control over Aboriginal peoples, we need to discover what was lost to First Nations communities through compulsory education. It is important to realize that all cultures and civilizations have some form of education, and that pre-contact First Nations peoples had forms of education, though they might be unfamiliar to many Canadians. Their education was based on experiential, informal learning that was integrated with life and was not based on notions of competition for marks or grades or on attaining specified levels of achievement. Education was preparation for life. This stands in contrast to public or formal education systems today that originated in the nineteenth- and twentieth-century residential schools and the manual labour schools developed by Egerton Ryerson and other prominent school promoters. The implicit assumption in this institutional education paradigm is that education prepares the developing child for the labour market. Interestingly, Aboriginal peoples' current struggles to reclaim their culture and dignity often involve reclaiming traditional forms of learning.

> The dignity of Aboriginal culture was lost initially through forms of discipline in residential schools that attacked the implicit sense of autonomy in Aboriginal cultures.
>
> The ethic of non-interference is the essence of Aboriginal cultures, and is probably one of the oldest and one of the most pervasive of all the ethics by which we Indians live. It has been practiced for twenty-five or thirty thousand years, but it is not very well-articulated. . . . This principle essentially means that an Indian will never interfere in any way with the rights, privileges, and activities of another person. . . . Interference in any form is forbidden, regardless of the following irresponsibilities or mistakes that your brother is going to make. (Ross 1992)

This fundamental principle of life was extended to children and stood in direct contrast to the use of coercion, physical or emotional discipline, ridicule, or any other form of behaviour modification that came to be the trademark of both residential schools and, in a more muted form, modern-day conventional education.

That Aboriginal cultures cherished individual autonomy and expression was manifested in an ethos of learning described as the three "L's—looking, listening, and learning" (Miller 1996). This method of acquiring knowledge relied on the use of models and illustrations through storytelling and rested on a belief system that the eldest in the community had the wisdom to offer and that they were to be listened to with respect. As such, the process of learning was devoid of coercion and routine and respected the giver and the receiver. The acquisition of vocational and life skills was based on observation and emulation and was carried out in a context without institutional

structure and that blended education and play. This system stands in stark contrast to modern-day conventional education that is highly routine, tends to divorce education from fun, and is eminently institutionalized.

For children from societies in which education occurred in informal and informally structured ways, the schooling regime that the abortive missionary efforts of New France attempted to impose on them was simply unbearable. The alien quality of regimented hours, indoor classrooms, structured lessons, and a competitive ethos were for most of these children foreign, stressful, and painful in the highest degree (Miller 1996).

The imposition of a compulsory system of formalized education created not only generations of traumatized children and youth, but also young people who were unable to survive in either world. They were inculcated with Euro-Canadian values and regimens that, they were told, had to become part of the way they lived. This newly acquired code of conduct left many students marginal from both cultures; they were unable to fit into their culture of origin and were always outsiders in the dominant Euro-Canadian society. When those sorts of emotional confusion are added to the loss of the traditional lands and territories, the individual's sense of self is under extreme stress. York (1992), in *The Dispossessed*, describes how rapid industrialization and the expropriation of Aboriginal lands and communities in Canada in the 1850s and 1860s eroded Aboriginal communities to the point of extinction.

In a section on children and gas-sniffing, York (1992) makes connections between industrial exploitation and education in the context of Aboriginal Australians:

> For centuries, the Children of Elcho Island were educated by their relatives. Today the Western educational system has intruded, cutting across the responsibilities of the aboriginal adults and placing a barrier between man and boy . . . The aboriginal adolescent is doubly excluded. On the one hand he is blocked from sharing in the benefits of European society by educational deficiencies

and by the fear of breaking step; on the other, he is ambivalent about many of the old ways. Some he has forgotten altogether. . . . Gasoline sniffing is a result of the disorientation of the Murngin adolescents. . . . Adolescents reflect the conflicts of a people.

In this simple, poignant example, we see how cultural invasion through education had a direct and profound effect on the welfare of children and youth. The problem of gas-sniffing is ubiquitous among exploited communities in North America and Australia and the question is still being asked why gasoline-sniffing has taken over the lives of young people in communities like Elcho Island in Australia or Davis Inlet, Labrador.

On 26 January 1993, six Inuit youth in Davis Inlet tried to commit suicide together by sniffing gasoline. Their attempt at collective suicide was thwarted by an addictions counsellor who heard the youth declare that they wanted to die. Subsequently, 14 youth from this small community were airlifted south for medical treatment, but the legacy of colonization and government neglect remained. Ninety-five per cent of the adult population were addicted to alcohol, 10 per cent of the children and youth were chronic gasoline-sniffers, and 25 per cent of the adults had attempted suicide. Nearly a decade later, the trauma for Davis Inlet has grown. In November 2000, 20 Innu children were airlifted to the Goose Bay treatment centre as an interim reaction to another epidemic of gas-sniffing among the children. Of the 169 children aged 10–19 living in Davis Inlet at the end of 2000, 154 have attempted gas-sniffing and 70 of them are chronic sniffers. The socio-economic reality for Davis Inlet, like that for many other northern Aboriginal communities in Canada (York 1992), is one of historical resource exploitation and/or community relocation, and the imposition of "industrial education."

Helen Cote, an Anisnabe elder and scholar from Saskatchewan, presents another dimension of the problem as she explains how her family became unrecognizable to her after she and her siblings were forcibly removed to residential school. Her father, who had never had a drink in his life, began to drink after his children were taken, and his alcohol abuse resulted in the destruction of his marriage. In returning to her family of origin after years of absence, she was not only a different person to her family but her family was no longer there, at least as a loving, nurturing unit. The historical works and personal stories of the connection between education and family illustrate a fundamental reality of forcibly imposed, compulsory education. Inappropriate education not only destroys children and youth, it also destroys families and communities. Whether such communities were doomed to destruction because of unbridled resource exploitation from the 1940s onward is a subject that might also be debated. But, it is clear that a Euro-Canadian-based compulsory education model imposed on Aboriginal peoples certainly contributed to a type of cultural genocide that some commentators argue still exists.

Indentured Labour

The question remains, then, that if the government of Canada and various churches and agencies undoubtedly saw this destruction taking place, how could they persist with a system that they knew full well would destroy culture so completely? The answer lies in some critical work that has linked the role of residential schools and government policy bent on the forced assimilation of Aboriginal people to the facilitation of a growing industrial-based labour market. The most critical of these works (York 1992; Satzewich and Wotherspoon 2000) make the argument that policies towards Aboriginal people, including education policy, were a calculated, albeit veiled, expropriation of Aboriginal rights and indenture of Aboriginal peoples, linked with the expansion of industry and resource markets. Even the Royal Commission on Aboriginal Peoples (1993) was clear in its assessment of imposed education:

> Put simply, the residential school system was an attempt by successive governments

to determine the fate of Aboriginal people in Canada by appropriating and reshaping their future in the form of thousands of children who were removed from their homes and communities and placed in the care of strangers. Those strangers, the teachers and staff, were, according to Hayter Reed, a senior member of the department in the 1890s, to employ "every effort . . . against anything calculated to keep fresh in the memories of the children habits and associations which it is one of the main objects of industrial education to obliterate." Marching out from the schools, the children, effectively re-socialized, imbued with the values of European culture, would be the vanguard of a magnificent metamorphosis: the "savage" was to be made "civilized," made fit to take up the privileges and responsibilities of citizenship.

In essence, the expressed intent of residential school policy was to destroy a culture and rebuild Indian children as active participants in the industrial economy, if not remove them as impediments to economic development. The unapologetic attempt to destroy culture was an extreme expression of an assimilationist mentality that persists to the present. The patriarchal nature of education as part of this assimilationist movement began essentially with the development of manual labour schools proposed by Egerton Ryerson. Ryerson and other representatives of parochial institutions developed industrial labour schools for Aboriginal children based on principles of basic education, hard work, and religious devotion, values that were held sacred by the Euro-Canadian middle class. The order of the manual labour school was the principle of "half-day" in which the student would be exposed to academics in the morning and would spend the rest of the day acquiring the practical labour skills—farming and mechanics for boys and domestic skills for girls—that would allow them to exist in an industrialized world. Clearly, one of the expressed purposes of the half-day system was to allow students to contribute to the maintenance

and expansion of the school. Ultimately, Ryerson and other government officials envisioned the residential labour schools as potentially self-sufficient. As the self-sufficiency of these schools did not come to fruition, the expense of maintaining them was downloaded by the government to the Christian churches.

It is at this point in the history of Aboriginal education in Canada that historians tend to disagree. The conventional historical accounts generally focus on the assimilationist demands of the federal government as part of a program whereby the schools would function as instruments of economic and cultural absorption. Moreover, the mandate of the missionary movements in Canada was to induce conformity not only to religious beliefs but, more importantly, to the daily rituals of obedience and subservience. Indeed, the same values and expectations applied to white society, especially the working classes. Government officials saw parochial residential schools, then, as "social laboratories in which a people's beliefs and ways could be refashioned" (Miller 1996). This reading, although not entirely inaccurate, presumes that an assimilationist mentality pervaded the ways of thinking of government and religious bureaucrats.

While this may have been true, in part, a more careful and complete reading of this history focuses on the physical and sexual exploitation that occurred almost regularly in most residential schools. For example, the forced schooling of registered Indian children at the end of the nineteenth century was based on a system of apprenticeship that provided free child and youth labour for farms, industries, and households (Miller 1996). As we shall see, this sort of servitude was common among all marginalized groups, including impoverished immigrant white children. This involuntary servitude extended well into the middle of the twentieth century with the system of outing in which Aboriginal children in residential schools were sent to work on farms and in domestic situations as seasonal free labour. Miller (1996) documents how, in many cases, all able-bodied students were pulled out of school to help with the local harvest or to engage in the cutting of wood prior to winter. Similarly, girls were extracted from school to work in local homes under the guise of work experience. However, school and government officials believed that domestic labour would not only provide badly needed labour for the community but that it would keep girls "out of trouble" from the sexual advances of peers and from potentially compromising innocent schoolteachers. This racist and ageist belief system condemned not only Aboriginal children and youth as sexually volatile but also placed the blame for sexual indiscretion squarely on the shoulders of the children and youth as potential predators and teachers as potential victims. The attendant presumption was that girls and boys, because of their sexual volatility, could not be trusted to be together. While this was true in non-Aboriginal schools also, the mistrust of children's sexuality was particularly acute in residential schools. Physical distancing was the practice based on a long-standing mistrust of children and youth as incompletely socialized beings. Interestingly, the distancing of girls and boys in education persists somewhat today in school settings where physical education and sex education classes are segregated, where sports teams are stratified by gender, and where technical and academic subjects are typified by high enrolments of one or the other gender.

The system of free child and youth labour was important to the vitality of local communities to the extent that communities aggressively lobbied to have schools established in their areas (Miller 1996). The city of Brandon, in 1891, for example, offered a free site to secure a Methodist residential school. Civic officials saw the industrial or boarding school as a mechanism to "generate employment, a demand for goods, and a revenue for their community" (Miller 1996). As importantly, the desire for free child and youth labour among these aggressive and growing communities was left unspoken but was nonetheless part of the compulsion to attract residential schools. Furthermore, as Ottawa realized that Indian boarding schools were becoming a burden to

the taxpayer, a per capita funding formula was introduced that would decrease spending and enhance revenues. The only way this could happen, in reality, however, was for principals of the schools to reduce spending on food and to increase the labour of the students. As a result, the schools became increasingly unattractive to Aboriginal parents: "More labour was expected of students, while simultaneously the school sought to limit the food they were receiving. . . . Many Indian groups were more reluctant than ever to surrender their children to the school" (Miller 1996). As a result, missionaries pressured Ottawa to introduce compulsory attendance in Indian schools. This became a reality in 1894 and 1895 with amendments to the Indian Act that gave Indian agents the authority of the law to force Indian children under 16 to go to school.

The conditions of children in residential schools deteriorated dramatically after the turn of the century as compulsory attendance and fiscal priority created schools that were inadequate physical facilities and unprepared and incapable of caring for the health problems of children. Denominational rivalry and competition for students as commodities were responsible for the plague of ill health that beset Indian children. As government official R.H. McKay grudgingly admitted, "The existence of the school is made to depend on the Government Grant, and if healthy children cannot be secured then the unhealthy are taken in to the destruction of all" (cited in Miller 1996).

This system of child and youth slavery under the guise of mandatory education had historical parallels with other social histories of children in Canada. At the same time, and extending well into the twentieth century, the treatment of immigrant Irish children in Canada was no less savage. Well into the twentieth century, youth who were apprehended by legal authorities were largely white male youth who had little schooling, were poorly nurtured, and who lived primarily on the streets. These "street urchins" or "street arabs," as they were called at the time, came from impoverished urban families who either were of first- or second-generation immigrant backgrounds. Further, between 1873 and 1903, over 5,000 children came to Canada from the slums and orphanages of Great Britain (Carrigan 1998). The policy of importing disadvantaged children reflected a mutual agreement between the governments of Canada and Britain to help "solve" the wayward children problem in Britain while providing "indentured servants for Canada's bourgeoisie and as free labour for Canada's expanding industrial sector involving agricultural settlement, the fur trade, and westward expansion" (Schissel 1993). The reality for most of these children, however, was that they lived at the mercy of their adoptive families in Canada, and the historical records suggest that they were, in general, highly exploited (see, for example, Kramer and Mitchell 2002).

The rise of public panic over a growing youth problem in Canada at the turn of the century coincided with the exploitation of children and youth as a form of slave labour. Thus, the movements to free children and youth from the shackles of exploitation took two contradictory forms. The child-saving movement was at the same time bent on preventing the exploitation of children and youth on the streets and in industry, and a movement that, through legislation such as the Juvenile Delinquents Act (1908), tended to label the working and marginal classes as inferior and potentially criminal (Schissel 1993). Children "at risk" were identified by their social characteristics and were to be "saved" by their bourgeois benefactors. The **moral panic**—that a growing subpopulation of children and youth was becoming increasingly criminogenic and posed an immediate threat to individual and collective welfare—became legitimated by public policy. West (1984) observes,

> Whereas, during early industrialization, children were grossly exploited for low wages, their partial humanitarian exclusion from the labour market had by the end of the nineteenth century made them an expendable surplus population, a nuisance about which something had to be done. Burgeoning slum

areas, the enforced idleness resulting from the passage of the anti-child labour legislation, "foreign" immigration, and fears of impending social disorder through epidemics and street crime focused attention on the working-class young (although there were other problems, such as alcoholism, poverty, urban boredom . . .).

In the middle of nineteenth century, Egerton Ryerson and other social reformers who were influential in the development of residential schools for Aboriginal peoples were also of the opinion that Canada was vulnerable to evils of immigrant children and youth. His expressed opinion was that immigrants from the Irish famine "accompanied by disease and death" were likely the "harbingers of a worse pestilence of social insubordination and disorder" (Prentice 1977). As with residential schools for Aboriginal children, social reformers such as Ryerson envisioned universal compulsory education as the panacea for crime, delinquency, and other forms of social unrest at the hands of the marginalized. The justification for forced compliance was easy—the children and youth who fell prey to the law and ended up in youth and adult institutions were identifiable by their socio-economic and racial backgrounds. The tenor of the times dictated that problems of crime and deviance were easily explained by the incompleteness of those who were different. Beginning with John A. Macdonald's move to establish off-reserve residential schools in 1879, a similar belief system framed the movement to force Indian children into a European educational system. Macdonald's appointee, Nicholas Flood Davin, set out to establish a policy of "aggressive civilization" for Aboriginal peoples based on an expressed belief that "western Indians were merely at an earlier stage of evolution than their white brothers and sisters" (Miller 1996).

This is where we see the historical role of education as purposeful of more than assimilation. In fact, education was part of the post hoc justification for enslavement of children and youth in an expanding industrial Canada.

Immigrant children were a source of free domestic and agrarian labour. Aboriginal children in residential schools were similarly a source of free labour for the expansion of Christianity and for the subordination of First Nations people who were "in the way" of Canadian industrialization. Whether educators were deliberately or inadvertently compliant with industry in the exploitation of the labour of children and youth, what started as the use of an untapped labour supply turned into a protracted attack on Aboriginal communities (York 1992) and an ongoing denigration of the poor and marginalized through institutions like the law. It is no coincidence that in the early twentieth century publicly financed correctional facilities for juvenile delinquents were developed to assist schools in controlling young offenders who were on the streets and were neglected (West 1984). It is also no accident that residential schools were based on the utopian models of prisons that advocated hard labour, discipline, religion, and solitary meditation. The original Cherry Hill and Auburn prisons in the United States and Kingston Penitentiary in Canada were based on penal philosophies that advocated strict discipline, hard labour, and meagre living conditions. In the end, the residential schools were run like modern-day youth and adult prisons in Canada in which time is rigidly controlled, segregation is used as punishment and "rehabilitation," and the authority structures are unyielding (Morin 2001).

In Saskatchewan, the majority of prisoners are of Aboriginal ancestry and there is some evidence that modern-day prisons house the irreparably damaged products of residential schools. Although residential schools have been closed for several decades, Cote (2001), a survivor of residential school who has interviewed other survivors, shows how victimization in childhood impairs the ability to be effective and happy parents. As she argues, she and her peers were so damaged by the experiences of forced education that they became chronically involved in the criminal justice system to their own detriment but also to the detriment of their children and grandchildren. Her arguments, then, are based on an understanding of the history of forced education as part of the "history of genocide." Whether such a historical reading is accurate or not is debatable, but what cannot be questioned is the veracity of victims of residential schools, who understand their personal histories as encompassing an attack on themselves and a fatal assault on their culture.

Educational Ideology and the Legitimation of Coercion

The discourse of education is fraught with elaborate rationalizations that perpetuate the philosophy that no one can survive in the modern world without basic conventional education. The extension of this axiom is that the moral obligation of any modern state is to provide its citizens with equal opportunity through established, customary education. The moral view of education as mandatory contains an interesting contradiction, as we shall see as we explore the historical legitimation for residential schools. The arguments are that moral obligation drives the teacher/administrator and moral learning is the result for the student.

The belief that morality and education are inextricably intertwined provided the basis for the involvement of churches in the operation of residential schools. The federal government, in 1879, commissioned a study headed by Nicholas Flood Davin (cited in Miller 1996) to provide a template for establishing residential schools in western Canada. The ensuing report provides a not-so-outdated logic for the forced education of Indian children:

These new establishments should be denominational for two reasons. First, it would be irresponsible to deprive Indians of "their simple Indian mythology" by a process of "civilization" without putting something positive and uplifting in its place. Second, reliance on churches would make it less difficult to find teachers with the essential combination of learning and virtue, and, moreover, to secure their services at a rate of remuneration less than the teachers' qualifications, pedagogical and moral, would otherwise command ... to teach semi-civilized children is a more difficult task than to teach children with inherited aptitudes, whose training, moreover is carried on at home.... The advantage of calling in the aid of religion is that there is a chance of getting an enthusiastic person, with, therefore, a motive power beyond any pecuniary remuneration could supply.

The discourses of learning and virtue, of family involvement, and of the dedicated teacher with missionary zeal are part of the logic of compulsory education that frames education policy today. The presumptions are:

1. that teaching is a moral crusade and that the best teachers are on a moral mission of which money is not a part;
2. that aptitude is inherited and that aptitudes are more prominent among certain sectors of the society;
3. that the best families help in the schooling of children at home; and that compulsory education has a spiritual/moral element that is required by all children, but especially those children most unlike the norm.

All of these elements, in some form or another, frame modern-day education exemplified by family values rhetoric in political debates, by a collective common-sense perception that teachers are underworked and overpaid, and by the continued lobby to keep or reintroduce Christian prayer in schools (despite the fact that such a practice violates the Charter of Rights and Freedoms).

The ideology of education lived, as well, in the labour-school mentality of residential advocates and practitioners. The survivors of residential school we consulted are unanimous in their belief that the schools were primarily about exploiting labour. Isabelle Knockwood describes her and other Mi'kmaw children's experiences in residential school in Nova Scotia. She is very clear that schools deliberately did little to educate Mi'kmaw children because they needed the children and youth to carry out manual labour. She describes how the farm and the physical plant of the school were maintained by the exploited labour of students at the expense of their education:

The older boys who tended the furnace never went to classes except of course Sunday school. The other boys who were not working in the barn were taken out of school during the coal-shovelling season for weeks at a time until all the coal was put in the bins. Then they returned to classes only to be called out again to work in the fields spreading manure, picking rocks, harvesting vegetables, or slaughtering animals. Their classroom hours were very irregular and an afternoon session once or twice a week was the average. Full-time barn and furnace boys worked fifteen hours a day, seven days a week. (Knockwood 1992)

She also describes vividly how many of the girls in residential school suffered the same types of work exploitation as domestic help and how an inordinate number of girls and boys were hurt on the job, some severely. A parallel epidemic of injuries of children and youth in employment has been documented in more recent times for agricultural labour and for the fast-food industry (Schissel 2003; Parker 1997; Dunn and Runyan 1993).

The question remains how a so-called civilized society, especially one that had been assumed to be highly moral and virtuous, could treat children as if they were unworthy of human rights. This is the point at which the rhetoric of labour, education, and racism comes to the fore. Compulsory schooling was a highly effective ideological system of self-justification, and it drew upon racist and religious/moral beliefs to indict First Nations families and their children and ultimately to confine them to a white world. Indian children were not only considered intellectually inferior to their Euro-Canadian counterparts, but their morality was constantly diminished as a justification for educational control. Schools were seen as social laboratories in which education and hard labour were considered panacea for cultural inferiority. Residential school administrators as well as government officials often held the belief that the Indian child had the capacity to be a responsible citizen but lacked the morality that education would induce. As Miller (1996) contends, "it seemed clear to many missionaries that the innately intelligent Native children lacked only instruction and enhancement of their underdeveloped moral senses. . . . Native morality was sufficiently debased to justify missions in general and residential schools for their children in particular."

One of the great ironies of forced education and one of its tragic legacies is that ambiguous attitudes about the capabilities of Aboriginal children resulted in schools that were largely dysfunctional pedagogically. This was the result of institutionalized bigotry that had, at its core, a system of education based on curricula that were ineffective and intentionally dismissive, a system that was staffed by teachers who were poorly trained, incompetent, and in some respects morally bankrupt, and a system based on severe degrees of reward and punishment that violated the human dignity of the schools' charges. Knockwood (1992) describes the reality of punishment for Aboriginal children in residential school:

I remember those horrifying years as if it were yesterday. There was one nun, Sister Gilberta, she always passed out the punishment. Every day, she would take me into the bathroom and lock the door. She would then proceed to beat me thirty times on each hand, three times a day, with a strap. She would count to thirty, out loud, each time she hit me. It's an awful way to learn to count to 30. My older sister, Grace, learned to count to 50.

I never understood why I had to get those beatings, but at the age of 37, I realize it had to be because I spoke my language. To this day,

I can't speak my language very well. But I do understand when I am spoken to in Micmac.

Why was our language and culture such a threat that it had to be take away from us with such vengeance?

To be taught your language with respect and kindness by your people, then to have the White Man pull it from your heart with meanness and torture. Some people wonder why we are so tough, because we had to, we had no choice.

I have polio and it affected my bladder and as a child, I wet my pants a lot. I received extra beatings for that too.

Once I was thrown across the dorm floor by Sister Gilberta. At the age of six, it seemed far away. I bounced off the wall at the other end of the dorm. I was sore on one side of my body for a few days.

Cote (2001) further illustrates how punishment was often sexualized to provide the most devastating form of opprobrium:

As we approached the school I became more excited, talking as loudly as I could. The priest turned me over to a nun, who took me upstairs to the infirmary and took my clothes off. She went to fill a bath tub with water. She was very rough, told me to shut up and called me a dirty, filthy, little Indian. My family had never told me to shut up. When I was first told to shut up, it shocked me. Where did she get all these terrible words from? She was pulling my hair, and kept telling me to shut up and stand still. I fought back. Nobody was going to treat me like dirt. When I protested that she was hurting my head by pulling my long hair, she became more angry and pulled my hair harder. I jumped up to leave, but she knocked me down in the tub. I could never have guessed in a million years what she would do next. She began to scrub me up and down my body, separated my legs and began poking her fingers in my vagina. I was shocked and I protested more by jumping out of the tub and yelling. She slapped me in the face and pulled my hair harder, calling me a dirty little savage. "We have to clean you inside and out." She held me down under water several times while she continued to beat me. She almost drowned me. I am sure she would have if I had continued to resist her. Even today, I have nightmares about escaping from water. Such fear of water has been so terrifying for me that I have never learned how to swim.

These graphic accounts of horror are part of a massive body of evidence that residential schools were not places of socialization and learning but rather places where abject behaviourism and sexual exploitation became the institutional mode of operation (Cote 2001; Jaine 1993; Miller 1996; Milloy 1999; Haig-Brown 1988; Knockwood 1992). Education and care were secondary to order, discipline, and sexual exploitation, and this was further evidenced by staff that were poorly qualified and who received little scrutiny upon hiring. As Miller (1996) observes, the use of incompetent or poorly trained teachers was noted as early as 1890 and continued until the 1960s. Residential schools were considered a last resort for most teachers, and the ones that were drawn to Aboriginal schools because of missionary zeal often felt that "the proper missionary spirit was more important in a potential teacher than normal school or university training in teaching methods" (Miller 1996). Governments, in their determination to download the financial burden of residential school education to the churches, were all too willing to participate in this implicit policy of inferior education for Aboriginal students. Both governments and churches realized that qualified teachers were expensive and that the pittance the federal government provided for residential schools necessarily dictated that qualified teachers were unaffordable.

The lack of qualified staff and institutionalized racism conspired to create a further dilemma for the lives and futures of the students. Schools unwittingly or knowingly created curricula that focused on the institutional needs and deficient requirements of unqualified teachers. Therefore, no attempt was made to incorporate issues sensitive to the socio-cultural background of the students. Specifically, course content focused on Euro-Canadian history and settlement; the Indian in Canada, in this "white" history, was always posed as the enemy. Despite the fact that many educational officials were aware of the need to incorporate Aboriginal culture and sensitivity into curricula, the pedagogical materials were decidedly Euro-Canadian, with little recognition of the role of First Nations people in Canadian history as other than "the enemy." As Milloy (1999) argues, "The literary curriculum was education's own worst enemy. The textbooks that were no different from those used in provincial schools were, therefore, particularly unsuitable.... Devoted teachers with imagination can make some use of them, [but] . . . in the hands of uninspired teachers they are deadly." More importantly, the academic rigour and content of residential schools' curricula were compromised by the philosophies and morality of labour. The moral content of nebulous curricula was that moral redemption could not be found in books but could only happen through the learning of labour. At the turn of the century, the Department of Indian Affairs stated explicitly that the school program aimed to "develop all the abilities, to remove prejudice against labour and give courage to compete with the rest of the world" (Miller 1996). In the next 30 to 40 years, the philosophies of hard work and moral education drove curricula to focus more and more on "vocational education" that culminated in half-day schools in which formal education occurred for half a day and labour occupied the other half. Indeed, this educational regimen resulted in extracting free labour and not in imparting vocational learning. Egerton Ryerson's model of education for Indian communities was that the half-day system would eventually make schools self-sufficient and independent of public revenues (Miller 1996).

The entire system of "miseducation" resulted in generations of Aboriginal children who were not only forcibly disconnected from their culture, but who also were relegated to educational failure. Research conducted in the 1980s (Barman et al. 1986) has shed light on the degree of educational failure. For example, between 1890 and 1950, depending on the decade, between 60 and 80 per cent of Aboriginal children in federal day and residential schools failed to advance past Grade 3. Further (Barman et al. 1986), in 1930,

> three-quarters of the Indian pupils across Canada were in grades one to three, receiving only basic literary education. Only three in every 100 went past grade six. By comparison, well over half the children in provincial public schools in 1930 were past grade three; almost a third were beyond grade six.

Clearly, the system of federal education of Aboriginal children was devoted to the continuing relegation of generations of Aboriginal people to the margins of society.

The claim has been made that modern-day schools are, in part, institutions of social placement and social reproduction in which implicit and explicit educational streaming of students leads ultimately to selected socio-economic strata. Certainly, the devastation wrought by residential and industrial schools left Aboriginal children socially marginalized or excluded. Helen Cote (2001) describes how residential schooling contributed to socio-economic marginalization for a damaged people:

> We were not a threat to anyone. In that residential school we lived in fear. When we left that residential school, some of us promptly killed ourselves, or drowned our sorrows in drugs and alcohol. We went away to hide from our people, being too ashamed to look at them. Some of us died with our shame, therefore leaving our shame to be lived on in our children and grandchildren. The cycle continues because we have no money to improve our lives. They have taken our land, our powers and have killed our wills to live.

The residential school system not only reproduced the Indian as savage but resulted in an epidemic of socio-cultural devastation that, as Cote and others have argued, continues today.

The Modern Legacy

The period of education that we have just described, which lasted, ostensibly, until the end of World War II, has been labelled, rather benignly, as the paternalistic phase. Until 1945, Native schooling was "education in isolation." During this period, schools and hostels for Indian children were established, but scant attention was paid to developing a curriculum geared to either their language difficulties or their sociological needs. A few Indian bands established schools for their children on the reserves, but the majority of them had neither the financial resources nor the leadership to establish and operate their own schools. Provincial governments were too preoccupied with their own priorities to become involved in Indian education. Missionaries provided a modicum of services, but their "noble savage" philosophy effectively insulated the Indians from the mainstream of society (Special Senate Hearing on Poverty 1970, quoted in Frideres 1998).

This official view of the history of residential schools as paternalistic stands in contrast to some of the works we have discussed in this chapter that describe a much more malevolent government bent on appropriating land by destroying the inhabitants of that land. This view is shared by observers such as Chrisjohn and Young (1997), who argue quite strongly that

> residential schools were one of many attempts at the genocide of the Aboriginal Peoples inhabiting the area now commonly called Canada. Initially, the goal of obliterating these peoples was connected with stealing what they owned (the land, the sky, the waters, and their lives, all that these encompassed); and although this connection

persists, present-day acts and policies of genocide are also connected with the hypocritical, legal, and self-delusional need on the part of the perpetrators to conceal what they did and what they continue to do.

The subsequent historical period, described euphemistically as the "democratic ideology" (Frideres 1998) was based on an "open-door" policy in which Aboriginal children could attend schools off reserve. The impetus for this policy came from a realization that the cultural and personal destruction wrought by residential schools could no longer be tolerated or at least rationalized. However, the enduring belief in integration and assimilation still framed educational policy change. The 1967 **Hawthorn Report**, authored by anthropologist Harry B. Hawthorn, who was appointed by the federal government to conduct an inquiry into the economic, political, and educational needs of Canada's Native population, explored the underprivileged place of Aboriginal peoples in Canadian society. One of its central mandates was to assess the failure of education for Aboriginal people and to provide a framework for upward mobility for First Nations citizens. The philosophy that framed this project was decidedly assimilationist, with the enduring expectation that for First Nations people to become productive citizens, they had to be schooled in the ways of industrial white society. Part of the rhetoric of this policy was that indigenous ways stood in the way of personal and social progress. Although couched in politically astute terminology, the discourse of public policy was framed around ethnocentric propositions that were hidden by a discourse of progress and mobility. The following excerpts from the Hawthorn Report (1967) illustrate how government policy attempted to be culturally sensitive and somewhat self-reflective but really condemned First Nations culture in the process:

The background of the stress on schooling and its results is interwoven with needs for better employment, better health and livelihood, more capital for enterprise, and a greater share in the governmental and political life of Canada. . . . The fuller achievement of goals in many of these areas is ordinarily and obviously dependent on a certain level of schooling. . . . Indians must receive some wider responsibilities and a fuller place in Canadian life in order that learning can have enough meaning for their children. The child at school needs to see while he learns that an Indian can do other things besides logging, trapping, fishing, or small farming.

What the school wants the child to be like above all is the ideal middle-class Canadian child. At this point and in this study we do not propose to weigh the values of Indian childhood and the values of middle-class Canadian childhood and attempt to say which is better. . . . But since the Indian child often lacks a spokesman, and since later in the Report we comment unfavourably on aspects of his life which we think are harmful to him, we will note here that the qualities of independence, self-reliance, and non-competitiveness which he commonly brings to school are not negligible ones, and in some of the major countries of the world would fit him well for life. But these qualities do not fit as well in a contemporary Canadian school, and the child's lack of many items of knowledge possessed by the ordinary White child is very unfitting in that context.

Being an Indian has become an uncertain thing. The child entering school finds that out for the first time, and is offered no way to resolve the uncertainty. In some ways his situation is like that of children from many other minority families except that the other parents are likely to have insisted that their home values have an esteemed historical past, written down and accepted, and their children may soon grow to know that they can cite authority for speaking, acting, and looking as their families do.

The questioning of Aboriginal people and culture lies in a discourse of difference. Aboriginal children, despite their admirable qualities of independence, self-reliance, and non-competitiveness, are not quite appropriate for Canadian schools/society. The authors of the report, despite the fact that they declared Aboriginal people to be "citizens plus," maintained that teachers face considerable challenges in having Aboriginal children in their classrooms and that these teachers must "continue to take refuge in the 'rightness' of their ways and struggle onward in the task of 'helping children overcome their Indianness'" (Hawthorn 1967). Quite clearly, the report implies that in order to partake of the Canadian way, the child must learn to abandon his/her native ways. Apparently "logging, trapping, fishing, and small farming" are inferior pursuits in the Canadian industrial model. We do not have to analyze any more deeply the language of the report to uncover a view that applauds the "noble savage" child while maintaining that such a child is better placed with children from other cultures. Verna St Denis, a Canadian Aboriginal scholar, has recently produced a treatise on the Hawthorn Report and identifies the assimilationist nature of the document and how, despite its expressed good intentions, it was based on a body of knowledge that failed to incorporate the knowledges of Aboriginal people and focused on the "psychology of Indian people." St Denis argues that the report is a typical example of policy that blames the victim by focusing on the Indian psychology and the culture of Indian people as primarily responsible for educational failure (St Denis 2002). The final implication is a warning that, to survive, the Indian child and his/her family must adapt to the values and pursuits of the white Canadian world. The "democratic phase" in Aboriginal education in Canada was, quite clearly, assimilationist more than it was democratic.

The historical reality is that, despite the general belief that the residential school program was largely a failure and that integration was consistent with national education policy, the residential school system persisted for four decades

into this "democratic" period. As Milloy argues, however, the residential schools changed from places of education to places of child care. This newly adopted welfare role was based on a rather general belief that "their parents would not be able to 'assume responsibility for the care of their children,' upon which integration/closure policy depended" (Milloy 1999). In fact, the rhetoric of public policy at the time was that Aboriginal parents were to be rated as to their worthiness to raise children, and their children were subsequently judged as to their welfare needs. The criteria for assessing neglect and worthiness, however, were strongly biased in favour of non-Aboriginal values based largely on the concept of the nuclear family. The characteristics that became part of the social service files of indicted families included "father shiftless . . . unmarried mother . . . very large family . . . very poor home" (Milloy 1999). Many of the traits of Aboriginal families in trouble were often connected to economic conditions and ultimately to the marginality of Aboriginal communities. However, the files of Aboriginal families that remained in the public archives were stories of impaired people. Milloy observes that "the official view seemed to be that the need for welfare and residential placement was not a product of economic circumstances but of parental moral shortcomings" (1999). The grim result of all of this is that, in the 1960s and 1970s, upwards of 50 per cent of children in residential schools were there because they had been judged to be neglected and their families were assessed as inadequate. Obviously, the official judgments surrounding Aboriginal family morality had a strong class bias.

Ironically, the day school system that accompanied the persistent residential school system and that became a large part of Aboriginal education from the 1950s on still lacked adequate teachers and adequate curricula. As the Royal Commission on Aboriginal Peoples showed, despite efforts to attract more competent staff through competitive salaries and the abandonment of the half-day system, by the 1980s the Department of Indian Affairs had ongoing trouble recruiting and keeping teachers in both day and residential schools. In addition, as the Commission declared, "both the curriculum and the pedagogy made it difficult for the children to learn.... Although the department admitted in the 1970s that the curriculum had not been geared to the children's sociological needs, it did little to rectify the situation" (Royal Commission on Aboriginal Peoples 1993). While there was a growing body of evidence on culturally inoffensive teaching materials and on the impact that such material had on Aboriginal children, none of this research informed the decisions of educational policy makers. The Royal Commission's summary statement on this matter (Royal Commission on Aboriginal Peoples 1993) suggests without equivocation that current educational policy in Canada fails to meet the cultural, spiritual, and educational needs of Aboriginal children:

> The majority of Aboriginal youth do not complete high school. They leave the school system without the requisite skills for employment [and] without the language and cultural knowledge of their people. Rather than nurturing the individual, the school experience typically erodes identity and self-worth. Those who continue in Canada's formal education systems told us of regular encounters with racism, racism expressed not only in interpersonal exchanges but also through the denial of Aboriginal values, perspectives, and cultures in the curriculum and the life of the institution.

Harold Cardinal (1977) warned several decades ago that "the problem here is simple but frightening. Children who are bussed off to provincial schools very quickly wind up not being able to talk to their own parents." Knockwood (1992) describes how "many had difficulties when they left school finding an identity and place in the world.... Some went home to the reserves after being discharged from the school only to find out that they didn't fit in." They were not only jettisoned from white society but were treated often as outsiders in their home communities,

especially when they attempted to criticize those communities based on their experiences on the outside: "when they tried to point out the social ills at home, they were told 'You don't belong here. Go back to where you came from.' Even those of us who had parents who welcomed us home were suspended in limbo, because we could no longer speak Mi'kmaw" (Knockwood 1992).

The Legacy

The legacy of Aboriginal residential schools in Canada can be understood at both a simple and a complex level. The simple level involves understanding federal control of Aboriginal education as part of colonialist expansion and Canadian national policy of development and industrialization in which Aboriginal people and their cultures, existing in their current state, were posed as an impediment. Our intention in this chapter, however, has been to show that the history of Canadian Aboriginal education must be understood at a more complex level and that the interpretations of the history and the motives of a colonizing Euro-Canadian society are most profoundly presented through what has been described as "standpoint epistemology." This position suggests that the best and most valid interpretations of socio-historical events come from the oppressed, because they understand the lived reality of the oppressed. By presenting the works of survivors of residential schools within a broader political economic framework, we not only draw on their experiences to support our polemic, but we accept their insights as the most important reading of history. The legacy we present in the sections that follow is a composite of their stories and our critical reading of Canadian history.

Damaged Generations

First, and most importantly, generations of abuse by commission or omission in residential schools have left an infamous legacy for Aboriginal communities. Cote (2001) and Knockwood (1992) describe how their treatment has resulted in generations of damaged peoples. The writing of Helen Cote (2001) depicts how the enormous and ongoing involvement of Aboriginal people in the justice system can, in most cases, be linked to abuse in residential school. Her story is one of how physical and emotional torture not only damages the spirit, but also distorts the world view to a point at which the damaged spirit will do anything to escape the horror of the past. She, her parents, and her siblings escaped into a world of substance abuse that literally killed many of them. Knockwood reveals, on the other hand, how abuse in residential schools instilled a fear of touching in the survivors to the point where they hated to show physical affection. The most devastating effect of this was borne out in parenting practices described by a woman survivor:

> Today I have a hard time, I don't want any-body to touch me unless I'm really close to them. I even have a hard time shaking hands. I want to be close to my family, but they're like me, afraid to hug me. The closest thing they ever tell me is, "See you tomorrow." (Knockwood 1992)

Her mother also had been a student at the school and she writes of how her mother's reticence to talk resulted from experiences in school.

The Destruction of Culture and Spirituality

"Those who ran the school tried to rob us of our collective identity by punishing us for speaking our language, calling us 'savages' and 'heathens'" (Knockwood 1992). Through the direct attack on culture and spirituality, the residential school system created children and youth who were welcome in neither Aboriginal nor white cultures. When children returned home and criticized the home community, they were, at worst,

shunned as outsiders or, at best, left in limbo as their new experiences and new language made them foreigners. The Royal Commission on Aboriginal Peoples (1993), in reference to a small group of former "successful" residential school students whose opinions were canvassed by the Department of Indian Affairs in the 1960s, noted that "the former students consulted in 1965 were unanimous in the opinion that for most children, the school experience was 'really detrimental to the development of the human being.' Isolated from both the Aboriginal and non-Aboriginal community, schools were 'inclined to make robots of their students,' who were quite incapable of facing 'a world almost unknown to them.'"

Education as a Class Weapon

We commented earlier in this chapter that the Canadian state, through the Department of Indian Affairs, created dossiers on Indian families and assessed children into categories of appropri-ateness for school. These files, in large part, were based on evidence about the level of privation in which the family (or the community) lived, and the discourse about child welfare became a language of indictment of poverty. In the end, families and children became identified and blamed for being poor. The culture of poverty mentality that framed government and church thinking drew on educa-tion to create a self-fulfilling prophecy whereby poor children from poor families could not pos-sibly succeed in educational institutions built upon middle-class parochial values and temporal demands. Chrisjohn and Young (1997) argue that

> "Limited" education has been a policy of European religious institutions long before Columbus, the tactic serving in earlier eras to establish and maintain the within-society colonization known as class through obfus-cations such as the "doctrines" of Innate Depravity, Original Sin, and the Divine Right of Kings, and the promise of "something bet-ter" in the "next" world. This long history of

the use of education as a weapon of oppression has largely been concealed, and though sometimes barbed with religion, sometimes predominantly secular, the weapon was, as was the case with Indian Residential Schooling, generally fashioned cooperatively by church and state. This "moralistic camouflage" has served both to isolate historically the aims and achievements of Indian Residential Schooling (thus contributing to its systematic misunderstanding), and to prevent the various victims of this strategy from comparing notes and making common cause.

The Pathology of Oppression

In the 1950s and 1960s, as the Canadian state searched its collective soul for answers to the "problem of Indian education" much of the rhetoric of change and improvement involved the quest to pathologize the effects of residential schooling. The "Residential School Syndrome" (Chrisjohn and Young 1997) became the mantra of a society hoping to gain political absolution by treating its victims as sick and in need of care and therapy. As determined by many institutions concerned with issues of medicine and deviance, the sick person needs to accept the sick role before he or she is deemed worthy of therapy. This was the case for many survivors of residential school who readily took part in psychotherapy as part of the solution. While the efficacy of psychotherapy is not in question here, the state's role in promoting a sickness model as the starting point for resolution is. The syndrome mentality shuts down other avenues of explanation; it prevents us, at least at the political level, from considering more structural/political sources of damage and victimization and, as Chrisjohn and Young (1997) state, "The meaning of Indian

Residential Schooling is not the pathology it may have created in some Aboriginal peoples; it is the pathology it reveals in the 'system of order' giving rise to it."

The Defamation of Children

The final legacy of the residential school period is the most difficult to chronicle and, yet, is likely the most traumatic for all cultures. In Aboriginal societies, children are regarded as a precious gift and are central to their world view. The reasoning behind this is simple—the destiny of a culture is closely bound to the welfare of its young. Education, of course, is inextricably bound to the welfare of children and youth, especially insofar as it prepares for life and not just work. Traditional Aboriginal philosophies of education were based on the assumption that education is lifelong and that teaching should prepare young people to participate fully in the spiritual, cultural, physical, and emotional life of the society. In an educational context like this, the concepts of "failure" and "pass" are irrelevant. In fact, the competitiveness of conventional education is anathema to learning. In this light, then, what the residential school experience did was to reroute Aboriginal children from a true apprenticeship for living to a false apprenticeship for democratic and labour force participation. One of the tragedies of this transformation is that the costs of failure are immense and Aboriginal children were consigned to failure. In final analysis, the combination of failure and abuse led to a massive devaluation of children from their accustomed place in cultural life. This devaluation was especially acute in the eyes of the children themselves. They have been removed from a place of privilege and care to a place of defamation and abuse.

References

Barman, Jean, Yvonne Hébert, and Don McCaskill. 1986. "The Legacy of the Past: An Overview," in Barman, Hébert, and McCaskill, eds *Indian Education in Canada: Volume 1: The Legacy*. Vancouver: University of British Columbia Press, 1–22.

Berger, Thomas. 1991. *A Long and Terrible Shadow: White Values, Natives Rights in the Americas, 1492–1992.* Vancouver: Douglas & McIntyre.

Cardinal, Harold. 1977. *The Rebirth of Canada's Indians.* Edmonton: Hurtig.

Carrigan, D. Owen. 1998. *Juvenile Delinquency in Canada: A History.* Concord, ON: Irwin Publishing.

Chrisjohn, Roland, and Sherri Young. 1997. *The Circle Game: Shadows and Substance in the Indian Residential School Experience in Canada.* Penticton, BC: Theytus Books.

Coleman, Michael C. 1993. *American Indian Children at School, 1850–1930.* Jackson: University Press of Mississippi.

Cote, Helen. 2001. "Damaged Children and Broken Spirits: An Examination of Attitudes of Anisnabek Elders to Acts of Violence amongst Anisnabek Youth." MA thesis, University of Saskatchewan.

Dunn, K., and C. Runyan. 1993. "Deaths at Work Among Children and Adolescents." *American Journal of Diseases in Children* 147: 1044–7.

Fiske, Jo-Anne. 1996. "Gender and the Paradox of Residential Education in Carrier Society." In Christine Miller and Patricia Chuchryk, eds, *Women of the First Nations: Power, Wisdom, and Strength.* Winnipeg: University of Manitoba Press, 167–82.

Frideres, James S. 1998. *Aboriginal Peoples in Canada: Contemporary Conflicts,* 5th edn. Scarborough, ON: Prentice-Hall Allyn and Bacon Canada.

Haig-Brown, Celia. 1988. *Resistance and Renewal: Surviving the Indian Residential School.* Vancouver: Tillacum Library.

Hamilton, A.C., and Murray Sinclair. 1991. *Report of the Aboriginal Justice Inquiry of Manitoba.* Winnipeg: Queen's Printer.

Hawthorn, H.B. 1967. *A Survey of the Contemporary Indians of Canada: Economic, Political, and Educational Needs.* Ottawa: Indian Affairs Branch.

Jaine, Linda, ed. 1993. *Residential Schools: The Stolen Years.* Saskatoon: University Extension Press, University of Saskatchewan.

Knockwood, Isabelle. 1992. *Out of the Depths: The Experiences of Mi'kmaw Children at the Indian Residential School at Shubenacadie, Nova Scotia.* Lockport, NS: Roseway Publishing.

Kramer, Reinhold, and Tom Mitchell. 2002. *Walk Towards the Gallows: The Tragedy of Hilda Blake, Hanged 1899.* Toronto: Oxford University Press.

Miller, J.R. 1996. *Shingwauk's Vision: A History of Native Residential Schools.* Toronto: University of Toronto Press.

Milloy, John S. 1999. *A National Crime: The Canadian Government and the Residential School System, 1879 to 1986.* Winnipeg: University of Manitoba Press.

Monture-Angus, Patricia. 1999. *Journeying Forward: Dreaming First Nations' Independence.* Halifax, NS: Fernwood Publishing.

Nock, David. 1988. *A Victorian Missionary and Canadian Public Policy: Cultural Synthesis and Cultural Replacement.* Waterloo, ON: Wilfrid Laurier University Press.

Parker, D.L. 1997. *Stolen Dreams: Portraits of Working Children.* Minneapolis: Lerner Publications.

Prentice, Alison. 1977. *The School Promoters: Education and Social Class in Mid-Nineteenth Century Upper Canada.* Toronto: McClelland & Stewart.

Ross, Rupert. 1992. *Dancing with a Ghost: Exploring Indian Reality.* Markham, ON: Octopus Publishing.

Royal Commission on Aboriginal Peoples. 1993. *Aboriginal Peoples in Urban Centres: Report of the National Round Table on Aboriginal Urban Issues.* Ottawa: Minister of Supply and Services Canada.

St Denis, Verna. 2002. "An Exploration of the Socio-Historical Production of Aboriginal Identity: Implications for Education." PhD thesis, Stanford University.

Satzewich, Vic, and Terry Wotherspoon. 2000. *First Nations: Race, Class and Gender Relations.* Regina: Canadian Plains Research Centre.

Schissel, Bernard. 1993. *The Social Dimensions of Canadian Youth Justice.* Toronto: Oxford University Press.

Stevenson, Winona. 1991. "Prairie Indians and Higher Education: An Historical Overview, 1876 to 1977." In Terry Wotherspoon, ed., *Hitting the Books: The Politics of Educational Retrenchment.* Toronto and Saskatoon: Garamond Press and Social Research Unit, 215–34.

Treaty 7 Elders and Tribal Council. 1996. *The True Spirit and Original Intent of Treaty 7.* Montreal and Kingston: McGill-Queen's University Press.

West, W. Gordon. 1984. *Young Offenders and the State: A Canadian Perspective on Delinquency.* Toronto: Butterworths.

York, Geoffrey. 1992. *The Dispossessed: Life and Death in Native Canada.* Toronto: Little, Brown and Co.

Questions for Critical Thought

1. Why was residential schooling introduced by the Canadian government? How was residential schooling justified in its day? Which organizations were administering residential schools and what were the goals and priorities of the organizations?

2. Why do Schissel and Wotherspoon argue that the residential school system was a deliberate form of cultural genocide? To whom are they directing their argument? What is the other "side" of that argument? Can you think of other groups in Canadian society who have experienced a form of cultural genocide? Can you think of other groups of people who have experienced cultural genocide in other countries in the world?

3. For Schissel and Wotherspoon, what is the link between the abuses experienced at residential schools and the ongoing social problems found in Native communities today? Are you supportive or critical of their argument? Has the Idle No More social movement in Canada been successful in raising public awareness about the legacy of residential schools? Why or why not?

4. Why are the authors critical of the approach to healing "Residential School Syndrome"? What would a more appropriate approach be in light of these criticisms?

5. Today there are numerous lawsuits in the courts seeking settlements for the abuse of Native people in residential schools. What degree of responsibility should churches and the government assume for these damages? What is a fair monetary settlement? Should any other reparations be made?

Fighting a "Public Enemy" of Black Academic Achievement: The Persistence of Racism and the Schooling Experiences of Black Students in Canada

... Henry M. Codjoe

The most important issues facing [black] students and that present enormous difficulties in adaptation are the structural and attitudinal barriers within the education system itself. Systemic racism and the differential treatment of [black] students by teachers, administrators, and other students is a significant problem that directly contributes to the lack of achievement. (Yon 1994)

Introduction

As my opening quotation demonstrates, structural and institutional dimensions of racism continue to affect adversely the educational achievement of black students in multi-ethnic societies like Canada. Indeed, it has been rightly observed that the psychological effects of racism on the education of black youths remain greatly underestimated. The problem is exacerbated by neo-conservative thought that "the racism/discrimination explanation of black underachievement is no longer viable" (Harrison 2000); and that "black culture" is mainly responsible for black underachievement. I reject this view, as numerous studies have shown ways in which racism and other forms of discrimination affect black students and their learning (Gougis 1986; Taylor 1991; Walters 1994; Alladin 1996; Steele 1997, 1999; Solorzano 1997). For example, Taylor (1991) found out that, to the extent that teachers harbour negative racial stereotypes, the black student's race alone is probably sufficient to place him or her at risk for negative school outcomes. Yet, despite attempts to address the issue, persistent racism in the lives of black learners in North America endures. If we are to address the chronic academic underachievement of black students, then teachers, parents, and school administrators must tackle aggressively the issue of racism and the negative thoughts associated with it. As Dei (1996b) correctly notes, "to deal with the [racist] concerns expressed by students, educational institutions and school administrators should increase efforts to develop race and antiracism policies." This is critical, especially in Canada where racism as a social issue continues to endure but is denied (Moodley 1985; Reitz and Bretton 1994; Clarke 1998; Chigbo 1989; Codjoe 2001).

Just like other Western societies, race continues to be a problem in Canada. Like the United States, Canada is a race-conscious society (Barrett 1987; Campbell 1989; McKague 1991; Lewis 1992; Cannon 1995). The concept of race persists, and its permanent feature is shown by "the presence of a system of racial meanings and stereotypes, of racial ideology" (Omi and Winant 1998, 17). This form of modern racism, as Flecha (1999) calls it, "occurs when the rules of the dominant culture are imposed on diverse peoples in the name of integration ... and presumes that different races have unequal levels of intellectual, cultural, economic, and political progress, rather than simply different ones." Racism is manifested when the "ideology that considers a group's unchangeable physical characteristics [is] linked in a direct, causal way to psychological or intellectual characteristics,

and that on this basis distinguishes between superior and inferior racial groups" (Feagin and Feagin, in Codjoe 2001). Within current North American educational practices, the image of the black student as an academic failure is thus viewed in this context, and it is "manifested in discriminatory treatment by teachers, counsellors and administrators, and in curriculum and school practices that excluded Black students" (James and Brathwaite 1996; Head 1975; D'Oyley and Silverman 1976). I contend that because black youth abound in many North American secondary schools, colleges, and universities, the issues of race and racism must be significant issues of discussion and policy making in the education of youths. On this, I agree with Giroux (1994) that

within the next century, educators will not be able to ignore the hard questions that schools will have to face regarding issues of multiculturalism, race, identity, power, knowledge, ethics, and work. These issues will play a major role in defining the meaning and purpose of schooling, the relationship between teachers and students and the critical content of their exchange in terms of how to live in a world that will be vastly globalized, high tech, and racially diverse than any other time in history.

Research

Having lived in North America for more than 20 years, first in Canada and now in the United States, and been involved in the education system as a student and a professional, I have developed a strong interest in the education of Africans in the diaspora. It is this interest that inspired my research into the educational experiences of African-Canadian youth at the University of Alberta, Edmonton, Canada (Codjoe 1997, 1998, 1999). My research was part of a larger and comprehensive study of factors underlying successful educational attainment of Canada's black youth. I was motivated in part to do the study because studies rarely document and investigate the successful educational experiences of black students in North America. The tendency, as the research in North America shows, is to emphasize the poor academic performance of black students. This has led to the observation that "the disproportionate school failure of minority-group children has become one of the most active research issues in education as researchers attempt to understand the underlying causes and to provide policymakers and educators with reliable and useful information" (Ogbu, in Foreword to Solomon 1992).

As well, just like other Canadians of African origin interested in research in the Canadian public school system (e.g., Thakur 1988; Brathwaite 1989; James 1990; Dei 1993, 1994; D'Oyley 1994), I was disturbed by the "marginality and depersonalization" of Canadian students of African origin. There is what Dei (1996b) has termed a "racial, cultural and gender 'othering' of [black] students." Black educational theory and practice have not been a priority in mainstream Canadian education. For example, the theoretical knowledge about education of African-Canadian children advanced in Ontario by such black theorists as Carl James (1990), Enid Lee (1992), and Patrick Solomon (1992), to name a few, is rarely read or cited by Euro/Anglo-Canadian scholars in critical ways that challenge the status quo. In fact, there is minimal educational literature about black students in Canada (Henry 1993).

My research presented a small but positive effort to highlight certain aspects of the black educational experience not commonly known to the public. It was trying to speak "about the silences that often are registered but not so often highlighted and analyzed" (Sultana 1995). As Orange (1995) points out,

> Concerned educators and administrators must first believe that we can win against the enemies of Black achievement, then be willing to keep trying until we do win. The educational imperative is that paying

attention to Black students may garner the attention of significant others who can be helpful but who may not otherwise pay attention. We must know that Black children—all children—are more than worthy of our efforts.

Indeed, one of the greatest myths promoted about people of African origin is that, as a people, they lack "the values of scholarship and study" and that they see "academic achievement as a form of 'acting White'" (D'Souza 1995). This perception of blacks as genetically inferior when it comes to academics is reinforced in the minds of some educators and the public at large, partly because of the achievement levels of young blacks in the school systems and the overemphasis in the literature of school failure and underachievement among black youth. But as Macias (1993) reminds us, black underachievement is a "complex social [phenomenon that] must be explained within a historical, socio-structural view." Nonetheless, "scholars" like Herrnstein and Murray (1994) and D'Souza (1995) continue to produce "research" that continues to denigrate African peoples. Reed (1993) correctly perceives this as "propaganda in which one denigrates the achievements of those considered an enemy, or problem people." With this in mind, my study, carried out in Alberta, western Canada, focused on the successful secondary school experiences of black students. The primary purpose of the study was to examine the experiences and **narratives** of black/African-Canadian students in order to learn and document some of the significant factors that influence and contribute to black educational achievement. The basic issue and common concern, which underlined the research, was the academic and personal success of black students. I do not intend to share all the research findings of my study here. What I want to do here is to highlight a major aspect of the study—the institutional dimensions of racism—that speaks to what it means for Africa's youth to be educated in North American elementary, middle, and secondary schools.

Methodology

The sample for my study was drawn from a population of black students in the metropolitan area of greater Edmonton. It was not a random sample, but rather, I sought—with the help of black youth, community, and student groups—black students for this purpose. I did this because, unlike cities like Toronto, Halifax, or perhaps Montreal, there is no concentration of black students in specific areas of Edmonton. I chose the students from an extensive list of individuals supplied to me by a black community group. There were 30 students on the list, and later, more responded to requests to take part in the project. Since I could not involve all 30 and more students, my first task was to make a selection of the required number of students needed for the study. After some discussions with a number of the students and advice from my dissertation supervisor, I selected 12 students from the pool. The major reason or rationale for choosing these students is that they were those who showed more awareness of the issues concerning black education and could articulate their feelings, experiences, and thoughts as compared to the other students. Although I chose participants mainly on the basis of race, academic success, and urban experience (Edmonton), there were other important criteria. Chief among them were (1) successful graduation from an Alberta high school and entry into one of Alberta's colleges or universities; (2) gender; (3) place of birth or country of origin; (4) student availability and willingness to participate in the study; and (5) that they were conversant with black educational and other social issues. My primary aim here was to ensure a wide range of the black student experience in Edmonton, as well as to keep the study at a manageable size, making in-depth inquiry possible.

The sample selected four students who had been born or who had origins in continental Africa, four born in the Caribbean region, and four born in Canada. They were young men and women who had had a variety of experiences in schools in Canada and, in some cases, in other countries as well. About half graduated from high school in the last two years before I conducted my study, the other half graduating in the last three or more years. The participants represented a number of linguistic and social class groups, as well as both sexes, and there were an equal number of men and women. They were also first-, second-, or third-generation Canadians and came from a variety of socio-economic backgrounds. Some of the students were from single-parent families, although the majority was in two-parent families. In this way, I can argue that my student sample provided important dimensions of the diversity within the black community.

The one common characteristic of my student sample—which may not be true of many of their peers—was that they could be considered "successful" students. As Nieto (1992, 1994) points out in a similar study, although there may be disagreements about what it means to be successful, the students in my sample had been able to develop both academic skills and positive attitudes about themselves and about the value of education. They generally had excellent grades, had graduated, and were enrolled in Alberta's post-secondary institutions. In fact, all but two enrolled at the University of Alberta, and two have actually completed a first degree. In retrospect, I agree with Nieto's (1992) observation that "it seemed logical that students who are successful in school are more likely to want to talk about their experiences than those who are not." The students' perspectives provide an opportunity to

> explore what it was about these specific students' experiences that helped them become successful in school, focusing on home, school, and community resources, attitudes, and activities.... By focusing on successful students, we can gain a clearer understanding of the conditions, experiences, and resources in their schools, homes, communities that have helped them succeed. (Nieto 1992)

To seek answers to the questions posed by the research, I utilized a **qualitative research** method. With the help of an interview guide, I conducted in-depth personal interviews with the 12 informants. My questions were not necessarily structured as interview questions as I permitted questions to emerge from my discussions and interactions with the participants. Indeed, I gave informants the opportunity to introduce new and other themes that would throw light on the black experience in Alberta schools. There were both individual and focus group interviews. In the former, each student participated in about an hour-long semi-structured interview. In the latter, I used the interviews to encourage students to build on and react to comments of their peers, creating a dialogue around each question. I used open-ended questions in both the individual and focus group interviews because they are "important when you want to determine the salience or importance of opinions to people, since people tend to mention those matters that are important to them" (Spencer 1995, ii). Data from the individual and focus group interviews were further supplemented and corroborated by secondary data to give a holistic picture of the black school experience in Canada. There was so much interest in the subject matter that it led to many hours of non-structured, informal conversations and discussions after the structured interviews. Because some of these informal conversations contained important information that was not recorded during the structured interviews, I wrote and kept a notebook for later use. In the end, the study used four distinct sources of data: (1) 12 individual students' interviews; (2) two focus groups interviews with students; (3) personal notes based on informal conversations and discussions; and (4) summary and reading notes from a variety of secondary published written material. All these personal memos, observer comments, conversations, and students' interview transcripts make up what has been referred to as the case study database (Yin 1984). The student interviews generated perceptions about ethnic and racial identity, self-esteem, personal academic expectations and achievements, home-cultural expectations, multiculturalism, racism,

stereotypes, parental influence, knowledge of black culture and history, school experiences, peer groups, extracurricular activities, and more.

My overall data analysis drew on the student narratives as well as relevant secondary sources and my own experiences. My theoretical and empirical support for my study came from the broader theoretical framework of schooling, education and social reproduction theories, multicultural/anti-racist education, race/class and social conflict, sociology of education, international and global education, black sociology, and sociological/political analysis of the experiences of racial and cultural minorities in the West.

Finally, a quick note on the definition of "black" used in my study. I used the term *black* to mean "all Black peoples of African descent—continental Africans and those of the African diaspora—and their world views in my notion of 'Africanity' or 'Africanness'" (Dei 1994). It is based on the philosophical foundation and belief that "people of African descent share a common experience, struggle, and origin" (Asante 1985; see also Henry 1993). In this context, it is realized "that there exists an emotional, cultural, intellectual, and psychological connection between all Africans, wherever they may be" (Dei 1994). I also used the term "black" interchangeably to mean "African-Canadian," "African-American," and "African." My use of the term "black" did not include others sometimes called "black" in the UK (e.g., Asians) or other "people of colour" as used in the United States to refer to all other racial/ethnic groups other than whites. The term preferred by the students in this study and which many used to describe themselves was "African-Canadian."

Research Findings: Racism and the Schooling Experiences of Black Students in Canada

Although the primary focus of my study was successful black student experiences, it became clear during the interviews that these students had to contend with, cope with, and overcome what might be described as "racialized barriers," that is, "the pervasive incidence of discrimination and demarcation predicated on assumptions of 'race' ... often embraced by groups which we call 'Black' and 'White'" (Small 1994). In this regard, five primary concerns pervade the student narratives about their school experiences in Canada and form a significant part of the study: differential treatment by race; negative racial stereotyping; the lack of representation of black/African perspectives, histories, and experiences; low teacher expectations; and what can be described as a hostile school environment. All constitute part of the racism and racist behaviour in schools. Indeed, they point to the structural and institutional dimensions of Canadian racism. Let me expand on these concerns as my main focus for this article, using the narratives of the students and other supporting research as points of illustration, discussion, and analysis. Before I do that, a brief discussion of the relevant aspects of the Canadian school system would be in order.

Under Canada's federal system of government, enshrined in the Constitution Act, 1867 (formerly known as the British North America Act), education falls under provincial jurisdiction. As a result, a variety of curricular programs and school systems exist to meet regional, linguistic, and religious (separate) needs. Nonetheless, in general, the Canadian educational structure is remarkably similar (Wotherspoon 1987). For example, every province provides three levels of education: elementary, secondary, and post-secondary. The language of instruction in Canadian schools is either English or French, and in some jurisdictions both. School systems are generally given public support, but there are also private schools. Elementary school usually starts in the first grade and ends in the eighth or ninth grade, depending on the province. Secondary school begins in Grade 8 or 9 and continues through Grade 11 or 12. Post-secondary institutions range from one to three years for (community) colleges and three to four years for university programs.

Racism and Racist Attitudes

The successful educational experiences of the black students I interviewed for my study did not come easily. All the students in the study said they experienced racism (both subtle and overt) in one form or another. Their experiences show racism and racist attitudes in school and out of school, the impact of racism on them, and how they coped with it. Ama (I have used pseudonyms to ensure anonymity of participants) recalled the difficulty of dealing with racism for the first time. Having been born in West Africa and remembering "how so nice we're to White people," she could not believe, when she came to Canada, "there's just a reverse and you think, how can anybody be so mean?"

> When we first came to Canada, when I was going to school I'd see these three kids walking way down the road, and then I'd hear "nigger," then they'd run away. I was hurt, I can't believe it. I've never done anything wrong to these people. I can't believe this is happening. I came home and again it's usually through the parents; my parents talking to me, going, "Well, you can't always take these things and internalize it, you have to get over it. These people just don't know." (Codjoe 1997)

For Abena, born and raised in Alberta, racism started very early for her in Grade 1. She recalls the experience:

> I was just minding my own business and there was a boy a few grades older than me. Every day he would come and harass me, call me "nigger." And so from day one, I kind of knew that I wasn't going to be accepted. I found the older I got the less overt it was. . . . I had a close group of friends that I was always with. That group was there for me. (Codjoe 1997)

Racism also started young for Alberta-born Kwadjo and his brother, who were the only black children in the school. He sadly remembers how "people would stick their tongue out at me; and I've been spit on the forehead and I've been called liver lips" (Codjoe 1997). What was especially galling for him was that one of the name-callers was "a kid that was Black too. He was kind of light-skinned Black and one of his parents was White so maybe he had perception problems or something of who he was" (Codjoe 1997). In some other ways, the racist attitudes take on dimensions that are least expected, as illustrated in this personal narrative by Kwabena, an African immigrant:

> What I always did, especially in class, was I'd always want to be the best or do the best in the classroom, disprove all those beliefs that Blacks can't do this, can't do that. A lot of cases, I'd come up with the top mark and a lot of students would be surprised. I remember in one of my math classes, I had one of the highest marks, and this one girl came up to me and she goes, "You got the highest mark." I'd go, "Yes I did." She goes, "I didn't think that was right." "Why not?" She says, "I thought you were dumb originally, and stupid." I just laughed but I just brushed it off. [These incidents] always make me try to do my best and disprove that Blacks can't be smart like Whites. (Codjoe 1997)

Kofi, another African-born student, also tells about his experience in an English class in high school. He prided himself on his command of the English language because of the rigours he underwent in his native country before coming to Canada. He was always arguing with his teacher. In the end, he believed it was because "I think she had a problem with someone from Africa challenging her in class" (Codjoe 1997). Having an African student excel in English in her class was just too much. It was just unthinkable. Echoing this experience, Kwesi, born and schooled in Alberta, makes the important point that sometimes it is that "silent treatment" that is at the heart of racism for black students in the secondary school system. He emphasizes,

I don't think most of the teachers that I had would ever have thought of themselves as bigots. None of them would have said "Oh, I hate this group," except as a joke. They would have all thought of themselves as very enlightened people who believed in social justice and equality. Now whether they truly did or not is a different matter. So I didn't ever have a teacher say to me, "You can't do this," or "You won't be any good at this." But I look at the difference between what I do as a teacher now and what they did. I don't think in the twelve years that I was in public school I had a single teacher tell me that I should pursue an English degree or I should pursue a History degree or I should become a doctorate of such and such. Not one of them encouraged me. I'm always telling students, "You should go into this in university" or "You'd be really good at that, you have talent here, or you have ability, apply yourself, you'll be great." I don't remember one teacher ever telling me that or that I should be a writer—none of them. (Codjoe 1997)

Words cannot describe the psychological damage, emotional pain, and the personal humiliation conveyed in these student narratives. Indeed, most of the students interviewed expressed the impact of racism on them. For example, Kwame, born in Alberta, described how

to this day, it [racism] still affects me. It was a big hindrance. I dropped out twice as a direct result of that and other stuff, like problems in high school with security guards and principals, and when one Black person does something the whole Black population in the school gets to go to the principal's office and stuff like that. You get fed up and want to quit. (Codjoe 1997)

Another student, Kwadjo, also states how racism affected him:

It [name-calling] affected me, but then I got past it. It made me angry because in the beginning I heard it so much. So I thought the majority of people must think that I'm like this and I know I'm not like this but nobody will listen to me. Then it got to the point where I realized that my overt concern for what they were saying in a way represented my actually caring about what they thought, which I didn't. So my realization of the fact that I didn't really care what they thought helped me sort of push them back into the corner and get on with whatever I wanted to do. (Codjoe 1997)

In all these instances, the students described how they coped with the racism they faced and how it did not stop them from achieving academic success. This is how Akosua, born in Canada and adopted by white parents, described how she coped:

When I was younger, basically I tried to pretend I didn't hear it [the name-calling in school]. I actually wrote poetry and that kind of thing and humour has always been a big part of my life. I always had my nose in a joke book or something so I think part of it I responded to with humour and part of it I sort of pretended I didn't hear it but I would write poetry and I've got quite a bit of poetry written. I think at first I just pretended I didn't hear it and I would be suffering inside by not say anything, and then when I got older I think I dealt with it with humour and I think because my parents really tried to give us the confidence [to cope with it]. I think, I don't know when the big revolution of "Black is Beautiful" was, but I know our parents really tried to make that a big point to us. I think we felt beautiful even though we didn't necessarily look it, we felt it because I think that they gave us that, they helped us to get that confidence and so even when somebody was saying something to me, like even when I got older, it really just started to roll off my back. (Codjoe 1997)

The role played by parents was particularly effective in coping with racism. Just like Akosua, Ekua (born in Alberta of mixed African and Canadian parentage) noted how her mother, a teacher

always helped me, especially in elementary school, because I had to deal with a lot of name calling: "Nigger," "Blacks are coming," "What did your mom do, did she stick you in an oven, cooked you too long?" and all that kind of stuff. I'd come home crying and she'd be the one saying, "Oh don't listen to them, you are way better than any of them could possibly be, just keep your head up." My dad would always share information with us and he'd explain it [racism] to us so we could understand. So I think that [parental support] helped. (Codjoe 1997)

In addition to parental support, the determination to succeed and prove blacks are capable of academic success also helped students to cope with racism. Ama explains,

I think it just helped me be stronger in determining that no, this was not going to make me go the other way, I'm going to show them that I can do this and I'm better than anything they are. (Codjoe 1997)

This point of view is also supported by another student who said,

I hated it when people would tell you that you can't do well and you initially never did well in the first place either because they told you you weren't able to do well or just because you had no reason for doing well in the first place. Personally, I've always had that inspiration or motive to be the best I can and do the best I can no matter what was involved. What I always did was to be the best or do the best in the classroom. I always have that desire to do as good as I can. (Codjoe 1997)

Others said they coped by being "very antisocial" and being with black friends for emotional support.

Negative Racial Stereotyping

In addition to experiencing racism, the students interviewed believe that part of the barriers they have to deal with as black youth in Alberta's school system is negative societal labelling and stereotyping of black people. The student narratives and discussions—both during the individual and focus group interviews—confirm that there was a general and deep concern about how black students were viewed by society in general. There was the sentiment expressed that "to a certain extent, society as a whole has placed us [black students] in a position [that makes] some of us feel like we weren't supposed to be able to make it because that's the way it is" (Codjoe 1997). During the focus group discussions, many of the students felt that the media has contributed to the negative stereotyping of black students. It was the view of some that images of black people from the United States broadcast into Canadian homes have compounded an already serious situation. Indeed, the student narratives showed "how everyday interactions are loaded with assumptions made by educators and mainstream society about the capabilities, motivations, and integrity of low-income children and children of color" (T.M.B. 1995, 206). For example, Akosua recalls the time when her teacher asked her to leave the class because the class wanted to discuss slavery and would not want to offend her by that discussion:

I know when I was in elementary school here in grade five, we had to do school reports and someone did a report on slavery and the teacher asked me if I wanted to leave while they discussed it so I wouldn't have to hear it. At that time I really didn't have much of a Black identity and I don't think I had a lot of confidence in myself. I was the only Black student for miles. I don't even remember at this point whether I stayed or whether I left. It seems to me I was in the Library when they did do it and I think I sort of had a confused look and he [teacher] said maybe you'd feel better if you

did leave and I think I did end up going to the Library while they discussed it. (Codjoe 1997)

Furthermore, I noted a conversation I had with one of the students, Ekua, whose experience again shows how teachers steer blacks into roles best suited to their "natural ability." According to Ekua, she had mentioned to her science teacher that she would like to study medicine. Sounding incredulous, the teacher suggested she look to another career as he wasn't sure a black could study to become a doctor. Luckily for Ekua, her parents helped her overcome the hurt the teacher's expression conveyed about her academic abilities. I am pleased to say that Ekua is completing her first degree in science and on her way to becoming a doctor. This anecdote brings to mind another point raised by the students in their narratives. As I previously noted, almost all the participants attended the University of Alberta. Time and time again, some expressed the view that people are shocked to see black students in university. It just does not fit the prevailing stereotype about black academic success. According to one such narrative,

To this day, people are shocked [to see black students on campus]. There are a lot of Black students in university and we all hang out in one section.... They're shocked that we're all here. They still to this day don't think we all go to university, but we do and most of the Black students here are not the bottom level. At the university [grade] level, they're not just passing, most of them are getting 7s and 8s and going into Law, Medicine and stuff like that. They're succeeding well and this is from all backgrounds not just the African nations, but the Caribbean and students born in Canada. (Codjoe 1997)

Another student also recalls the incident in his senior high years when some of his schoolmates expressed amazement to see black students enrolled in mathematics and science classes:

I think I was with another Black student and we saw that we were being followed by some students. They were wondering what we were doing or where we were going. So they walked around and still followed us into the math class. Then they confronted us in person. We were told we're not supposed to be doing math and science. We are supposed to be playing sports and stuff like that. We were absolutely shocked by this, and I think that just serves to show that there's a lot of stereotyping involved. It is the case of portraying Blacks as just entertainers or sports people. It serves to portray us as just being that sort of way instead of being a scientist. (Codjoe 1997)

As we can see, "the stereotyping involved here is systematic, elaborate and based on assumptions of separate racialized groups possessing distinct mental and physical abilities" (Small 1994). No wonder that the most talked-about and discussed issue by the study participants regarding stereotypes and black students was the perception of blacks as athletes. The students believe that the general view of blacks as only excelling at sports has contributed to the perception of the black student as an academic failure. One student put it thus:

In North American society, Black kids are supposed to be good in things like basketball. A lot of who you see up there, they're either rappers or basketball stars or involved in some area of sports. The only time you see more Black people on television in Canada is during the Olympics. That's something that I could never fully understand. (Codjoe 1997)

He further elaborates on this point by noting that

Paul Robeson was a football star, he was an actor, he was a writer, he was a singer, he was a man of letters in college; he was, I think a lawyer, too. He went to Rutgers and

Columbia. His grades rank the highest in the school's history. It's like, we have to focus on the fact that he was a football star in College. The man did so much more and there's so much more than physical exertion but if you're Black it's considered that's what you're supposed to do. (Codjoe 1997)

Consequently, these students viewed sports with some contempt, and as one described, as a way out, tried to avoid sports altogether even though she liked sports. In fact, the stereotypes of blacks as nothing more than athletes bothered her so much that

I didn't want to do track anymore because of this. You see lots of Black people doing track and field. It's not a bad thing, but I always wondered, "Did they do anything else other that this?" It is this focus that bothered me. Even if I could throw, I could do that better than most of the other things I did, but I thought what if this is all I'll be doing. Before I know it, I'll be pushed into it more than anything else. [So] even though I liked sports, it was not really my number-one focus. It's always been education—reading, learning, the sciences. (Codjoe 1997)

Biases in School Curriculum and Textbooks

Perhaps no other area in the education of black students in Canada attracts more concern than the attention on the curriculum. As James and Brathwaite (1996) correctly note, "the curriculum concerns are some of the most damaging elements in our students' schooling, and this is an area that has attracted much attention in the Black community and among educators." Not surprisingly, it was also an area that generated the most discussion, and sometimes anger and emotion, among the students in my study. In fact, the question of racial bias in the curriculum content as well as Eurocentrism in school courses and texts were also recurring themes in the student narratives. All complained that the curriculum had little relevance for their lives and, as one of them put it,

> I really didn't feel as though I got any education from school as far as Black education was concerned. . . . I didn't learn anything about Black history in high school. There was no subject [in black studies] for you to take, and in regular social studies classes they didn't discuss anything Black or African. They might have said something about slavery once or twice but they didn't really say anything in depth and they didn't say anything positive. (Codjoe 1997)

This theme was echoed again and again by the students. Having grown up outside Canada before immigrating to Alberta with her parents, Akosua thought courses in Canadian schools would be more inclusive and reflect all of its people. However, she found out in high school that

> Canadian history just seems to be concerned about White Canada. Except maybe the States because they're so close to the States, they're not really concerned about other countries. I never knew anything about the history of Blacks in Canada until I joined Ebony [a black youth club in Edmonton]. That's when I started to realize, "Oh, Blacks have been here for this long." I've talked to some Black families too here in Alberta and found that their roots have been here for a long time and it's like I never knew. (Codjoe 1997)

Kwabena, also born outside Canada, found that

> A lot of the history was about World War I, World War II—European history. There was very little African history. You find that a lot of the students hardly knew anything about Africa whatsoever. All they knew was what they saw on TV or what portrayed Blacks in the most negative way. (Codjoe 1997)

One student found this Eurocentric emphasis "frustrating" at times

> because we heard so much about the French and English and stuff. Amazingly, they don't even talk very much about the Natives. You'd think there'd be a lot more on that. It is frustrating because I mean the Blacks here did contribute a lot. We [blacks] were one of the first immigrants here in Canada. I do feel that there should be a lot more mentioned about us, most definitely. (Codjoe 1997)

This last point was often mentioned by the black students born in Canada. They are hurt by what one of them, echoing Willis (1995), called "a sin of omission." For example, Abena, born in Alberta, narrated that

> in some of my classes, in social studies, when they did mention anything that had to do with Black people, it was generally that the Blacks came over. They were slaves. In English you'd read a book, Tom Sawyer or something, and it is "Nigger this," "Nigger that," every second word and I found that in the end, I started to verbalize how, why do you always portray the negative aspects of Black life. I found that a lot of my teachers just would almost automatically say something and they'd turn to me because they would expect me to give them a response because I wasn't going to be quiet about it. So, I thought it just made me more outspoken in the end, which was to my benefit. It made me learn more about Black history, on my own than in school. (Codjoe 1997)

For Kwesi, also born in Alberta, making some sense of this, he said he does not think "the big problem is that the teachers are hidden Klansmen, [although] you still find teachers who have really bigoted attitudes and that sort of thing." He believes that "the real problem is that we're just invisible to the curriculum." He explains further:

I took social studies in high school and the history course—that was supposed to be an enriched history course. The history course was actually subtitled, "History of Western Europe." They didn't even make a secret out of it. So all the civilizations of the earth that were brown and black were left out. We didn't discuss China until the twentieth century. The first mention of Africans was not Egypt, or Nubia or Mali or Songhai or great Zimbabwe. The first mention was the slave trade. (Codjoe 1997)

On this last point, it also came out unanimously during the focus group discussions that black education in Alberta's schools, if mentioned at all, "tends to start and stop with Martin Luther King. That's about it. There are a whole lot of other historical Black figures—music, science, you name it. Even in this country alone, there are a lot nobody knows about" (Codjoe 1997).

I was curious to know how all this made them feel in class and school and so I asked them to tell me about it. Interestingly enough, although they were hurt and marginalized by the whole experience (one dropped out of school because of this, although returned later), most told me they were not surprised. They had expected it. They had been forewarned. As one said,

I wasn't really surprised because I remember actually being told by someone before I went to [mentions school attended], I was told, "You're not going to learn anything about Black education." In fact, they said something about how the teachers there weren't very fond of Black students. (Codjoe 1997)

A few said they were "furious" because "if you're willing to learn about other cultures, my culture might as well be known too" (Codjoe 1997). One or two started to get into arguments with their teachers. Kwame relates one such experience:

One time, I got into a big argument with a teacher. We were doing the history of the world. When it came to the history of Africa, the teacher said Africa's history started from 1773 when the White man came. I said this is foolishness. Africa's history didn't start with the arrival of the White man. I pointed out to the teacher that when it came to do the history of Russia he talked about way back in when they were still in [inaudible], that's their history. But when he talked about the history of Africa the only thing he talked about was when the White man came. That's my experience with Black things in Alberta's schools. Always, it's not Black things. It's when the White people came and how the Black people kind of fitted in. That's about it. (Codjoe 1997)

But perhaps the most important aspect mentioned by the students was the damage the impact of the absence of black studies in the school has on black students. This comment was typical:

There was nothing on anything that was Black-related or Black successful in the academic area. I think if there was, even if it was just a small thing, a Black child would feel that they had something to associate themselves with in the academic sense. This would make them more motivated to achieve as well, 'cause right now they just feel that maybe some kids feel that education is a White thing. But it's [education] not something that they should be ashamed of. (Codjoe 1997)

Another added,

I'm no academic genius but when you have a sense of what your people have done it helps you get through the school system too. It helps you get through different things because you feel that your people have made a contribution to where you are. (Codjoe 1997)

What I found remarkable about these students was that though the schools made no effort to introduce or teach them about black studies, they made the effort on their own and, as one said, "I learned about Black history more on my own than in School" (Codjoe 1997). Some regretted this and commented that "it's not fair that they should have to learn their own history outside school, when European history is being taught in school" (Codjoe 1997).

Low Teacher Expectations

In looking at what actually happens when teaching occurs, there is a growing body of research and evidence to suggest that a teacher's expectations, encouragement, attitudes, and evaluations primarily influence students' perceptions of themselves as learners, and that a student's social class, race, or ethnicity is a major determinant of teacher expectations. Some of the students I talked to mentioned teacher expectations and attitudes as one of the racialized barriers they faced while going through the Alberta public school system. I must say that not all of them had negative experiences with teachers. About half had positive and supportive teachers. However, they all related that although they were academically successful themselves, they were aware that some teachers' expectations often doomed their peers to failure.

For the students who said teachers had low expectations of them, their narratives and experiences fall into two areas. One relates to how some of their teachers were not "sympathetic" and often did not encourage them to develop their full potential. Looking back now, they wished their teachers had encouraged and helped them as they did with white students. The other area in which students spoke about their negative experiences with teachers had to do with what appears to be the surprise on their teachers' faces when they handed in papers or assignments where they had excelled. Often, the teachers would not believe the student had actually done that paper. As one put it, "a lot of times, I'd do well in Math and Biology and they'd be surprised. I wondered why that was the case but I was told by my parents to do my best"

(Codjoe 1997). Another related how he had turned in an English essay. His writing and presentation was so well done that his teacher did not believe a black student could write that well. He had to remind his teacher about the rigour and discipline of essay writing in his native country—an experience that he brought to Canada and which he had used so well. Related to this incident was the one related by Ekua, where her teachers had told her she could not aspire to become a doctor because of her race and gender. Here is how she related her experience:

What also threw me is I had other teachers, who because I wasn't doing well in their particular class, told me I couldn't do what I wanted to do. One particular teacher, I remember, my Chemistry teacher. I remember he told me that, there was no possible way, he even told my dad, that I could never become a doctor because I just couldn't get the Chemistry in high school. At first it hurt . . . then later on it made me angry. So what happened was I figured, I said some day, maybe he could come into a hospital room and I'd be the doctor that would be assigned to him. So I figured, I got to go, I got to go. I had a Math teacher, he said the same thing, that maybe I should find something else, secretarial. (Codjoe 1997)

Ekua's experience is somewhat similar to Kwesi's, who told me that he

always did enjoy the sciences . . . and did very well in physics but I had a very bad experience with a math teacher [who doubted my abilities] in junior high and for two years in a row. That undermined my math ability, and if your math ability is undermined, then your physics ability is undermined. (Codjoe 1997)

Alienating School Environment

Finally, apart from the racism, the negative racial stereotypes, an alienating curriculum, and teachers who do not expect much of them, black students are also faced with another racialized barrier: that of a school environment that I can describe as "essentially solitary," unsupportive, alienating, and perhaps racially hostile. As expressed by the students in the study, the most difficult aspect of the school environment they experienced was the social isolation and loneliness as the only black students in predominantly white schools and the lack of support of those around them. Because the black or African population in Alberta is very small, all the students said they faced "intense isolation and deprivation" in school. Sometimes they were abused and racially harassed. Not able to make or form friendships with other black students made the isolation worse and demoralizing, particularly for the students who attended schools in the Catholic (separate) system. This is how one described his experience:

In school, I was faced with isolation, intense loneliness, deprivation. That's really unfortunate. In all of elementary school and junior high, I never had an African peer in my grade level, ever. In high school there was one girl who was in my grade level and then there were, I think, one or two kids older than me and as I got up to grade 11 and 12, there were some kids younger and that was it. I did not have any African peer friends and that was really distressing for me. (Codjoe 1997)

For those like Adwoa, who was coming to Canada for the first time,

adjustment was difficult when I first came here. It was a difficult adjustment through until high school. In elementary I was the only Black girl in my school, in junior high there

TABLE 1   Racialized barriers that impede the academic achievement of African-Canadian students

Anti-black racism	*Low teacher expectations*
Name-calling ("Nigger")	Differential/discriminatory treatment
Racial hostility and slurs ("liver lips")	Lower expectations and insensitivity
Prejudice	Doubting of academic capabilities
Discrimination	No encouragement
Devalued position/status in Canadian society	Expect less academically from black students
	Receives "silent treatment" from teachers
Negative racial stereotyping	*Alienating school environment*
Social stigma (black students seen as "athletes" and "entertainers")	Only black student in a predominantly white student body
Stigma of intellectual inferiority ("can't do math or sciences"; "could never become a doctor")	Social isolation and loneliness
	Lack of black friends/peers
Streaming and tracking ("steering black students into roles suited to their 'natural ability'")	Lack of black role models (teachers, counsellors, administrators)
Black students as troublemakers	Difficult adjustment period
Racially biased curriculum/texts	
Eurocentric (monocultural) curriculum	
Lack of relevancy to black students' lives	
Invisibility of black/African studies	
Negative references to African-Canadians	

Source: Partly adapted from *Black Learners Advisory Committee Report on Education*, 1994: 40.

were about two others. I got called names and stuff like that. It was difficult and it did affect me drastically in that, in grade 12, I almost did not graduate. I was hardly at school. (Codjoe 1997)

Another aspect of the isolation the students related was the fact that most of them went through their entire public schooling in Alberta without ever having known or been taught by a black teacher or counsellor. For example, one said, "I didn't really have a Black teacher of my own until I was in university" (Codjoe 1997). Another said, "Since I've been in Canada, I've never had a Black teacher" (Codjoe 1997). On the other hand, Abena, who had a black teacher, recounted how it had an impact on her:

My grade one teacher was Black. In elementary school there were two Black teachers in that school. But I'm really glad that I actually did have Miss Buchanan as my grade one teacher because I just felt a little bit more comfortable going into the whole school system because it was somebody in a position of authority, who was like me, so I didn't feel entirely isolated. I really appreciated that experience. (Codjoe 1997)

Having black teachers in the school system was seen by all as critical. As one commented, "The school system should have a bit more Black teachers. Some Black teachers who are sympathetic, knowing the Black history, the Black background, would be quite helpful" (Codjoe 1997). Talking about counsellors, another said, "if I were to go up to a Black counsellor, I'd relate more than if it were a White person. I think a lot of Black teachers or a lot of Black counsellors would be way easier to relate [to]. I think there should be more Black counsellors in school" (Codjoe 1997). Indeed, the loneliness and isolation made these black students "shy and silent" and "nice and polite," with the effect that, "by and large [they could not make] positive contributions in class. . . . So when the situation required them to set an example of

being extroverted, they couldn't do it" (Codjoe 1997). It had a negative impact on their education.

Discussion

The student narratives provide evidence of the persistence of racism in Canadian schools. This case study strengthens other research findings in Canada regarding the structural and institutional dimensions of racism in Canadian society (see, for example, Oake 1991; Talbani 1991; Walker 1991; Lewington 1993; Henry et al. 1995; Dei 1995b). In fact, one picks up similar concerns in interviews with other black students about their school experiences in Canada. For example, a year-long study in Manitoba concluded that "racism is running rampant in Winnipeg schools and is forcing many Black students to drop out of the system." About 81 per cent of more than 200 black students interviewed by the study authors identified racism as a major barrier blocking integration of blacks into the Winnipeg school system. According to Jean-Joseph Isme, one of the authors of the report, "Racism is one of the major causes of dismissals and suspensions of Black youth from schools," and "the impact of racial insults on the mental health of [black] youths cannot be ignored" (Codjoe 1997). A similar study in Ontario discovered that

Black students encounter discrimination daily on an individual level. They must deal with racial slurs, vicious graffiti, [and] ostracism on the part of their fellow students. Many feel that it is no use complaining to the authorities about this, since they believe that the teachers and the administrators are themselves racist. (Towards a New Beginning 1992)

The psychological effects of racism on black youths remain greatly underestimated (Walters 1994). Studies point out numerous ways in which racism and other forms of discrimination affect black students and their learning. For example, Taylor (1991) found out that, to the extent that teachers harbour negative racial stereotypes, the black student's race alone is probably sufficient to place him or her at risk for negative school outcomes. Teachers who harbour racist attitudes can affect students in a more personal way as low expectations, hostility, and differential treatment can adversely affect blacks in the classroom. Secondly, results of experiments have confirmed that racism creates what has been described as an "environmental stressor" for black students that can adversely affect their academic performance. It has been found that racial prejudice increases emotional stress of blacks over and above that experienced by other groups in North America, and that

> that stress is likely to adversely affect students' daily academic performance by reducing their willingness to persist at academic tasks and interfering with the cognitive processes involved in learning. As this process continues over a long period, Blacks do not develop the cognitive skills that are necessary for high academic achievement. (Gougis 1986)

Furthermore, according to this study,

> recurring thoughts and feelings associated with race prejudice contribute to a reduction in their [black students'] motivation to learn and to increased interference with the cognitive processes involved in learning. As this process continues over the years, its effects are cumulative. On the average, Blacks will have spent less time trying to learn academic material and will have made less efficient use of their cognitive skills (attention, rehearsal, recall) in doing so. (Gougis 1986)

Gougis (1986) thus concludes that, although "the academic performance of both Blacks and Whites is affected by stress, Blacks are burdened with the added stress of [racial] prejudice throughout their academic careers. Their academic performance is more impaired." Irvine

(1990) also adds that "racism and the devalued position of Blacks in our society cannot be ignored as a primary contributing factor to Black underachievement."

Besides the daily encounters of racism, the black student experience in Canada also includes "stereotyping by the dominant power groups whose attitudes are reflected in institutions such as education, the media, and the law" (Brathwaite 1989; see also Yon 1994; Dei 1996b). Indeed, the same concerns about social stereotyping narrated by the black students in my study have been borne out in many studies and reports (James 1994; Spencer 1995; Lendore-Mahabir 1995; Dei 1995c). For example, in his study, *Drop Out or Push Out?*, which examined the attitudes of 200 black and non-black students toward school, Dei (in Sarick 1995) recounts the experience of a black student who narrates why he dropped out of school:

> I can tell you the reason why I dropped out. The school I went to, they made me feel like I wasn't smart enough to do the stuff. They told my parents to send me to a technical school. They treated Blacks like we had no brains . . . and that the Chinese were smarter, the Whites were better, so I just said "Forget it."

Similarly, in her interviews with black students in Edmonton secondary schools, Spencer (1995) also found that

> some students felt there were specific stereotypes that related to their academic potential. As one student stated: "[We have to] . . . show them that Black people are not drug dealers, pimps, whores, not just sports people, rappers, and singers. We are people that have high intelligence. They see us as someone who can do great 'slam-dunks.'"

According to Spencer, "several students felt even though the teachers did not express any open animosity or direct negative verbal comments, they had to try extra hard to prove themselves in order to overcome the stereotype of Blacks as being non-academic."

Indeed, stereotypes have been found to play a significant role in inter-group relations and serve an important function in the maintenance of racism (Laroque 1991). When it comes to the stereotypes about black intellectual capabilities, I share C. Steele's (1992) contention that "the culprit I see is stigma, the endemic devaluation many Blacks face in our society and schools. Blacks fail in school for reasons that have little to do with innate ability or environmental conditioning. The problem is that they are undervalued." According to C. Steele (1992), this devaluation "grows out of our images of society, and the way those images catalogue people," and furthermore, terms like "prejudice" and "racism" often miss the full scope of racial devaluation in our society. Logan (1990) elaborates:

The negative stereotypes connected with education and learning begin at the elementary and secondary school levels and continue beyond college. Black children attend schools where most of their peers, if not themselves, are labelled by the professionals as "culturally deprived," "high-risk," "learning-disabled," "stupid," and "crazy" by their classmates. Even when such descriptors do not fit students, the prevailing attitudes still affect their well-being. The negative stereotypes continue and are reinforced through the curriculum and by the school's faculty. From the perspective of teachers and administrators, the tendency is to expect less academically from the Black student and to assume that nearly every Black student does not meet the standard academic requirements.

S. Steele (1989) has referred to this presumption of black academic inferiority as "stereotype vulnerability"—implying that "everywhere in this new world her skin color places her under suspicion of intellectual inferiority" (C. Steele 1992). The consequence has been that some black students perform poorly in school because they buy

into the stereotype that they cannot compete academically with white students. As well, the psychological costs are such that the burden of stereotypes depress black academic performance and impose on black students a self-doubt and aversion to academic competition. Indeed, black students who have never been victims of racism can perform below expectations academically because of negative stereotypes (Dei 1993; Gose 1995; Miller 1995). In carrying out further research in this area, Steele and Aronson (1995) have recently employed the term "stereotype threat" to account "partly for the relatively poor performance of any group widely considered deficient in some ability, such as women in science" (Steele and Aronson 1995).

Unfortunately, many, including educators, still believe that black students' school failure is related to their inferior intelligence and their own inadequacies and problems (Macias 1993). The so-called "deficiency approach" alleges the genetic and cultural inferiority of the black "race" and has been used historically to support decisions that emphasized vocational education for black children at the expense of providing them with a liberal education. This has been extremely damaging to the educational advancement of blacks as it has provided a rationale not to invest as much in the education of minority children as in white children. As well, this kind of reasoning locates the source of black academic achievement within the "skill deficits" and cultural background of the black student and thus participates in "blaming the victim" (Tyack 1974; Selden 1978; Boykin 1986; Erickson 1987; Irvine 1990; Strickland 1994; Carlson 1995; Miller 1995; Orange 1995). It is perhaps no coincidence that one of the contemporary manifestations of the racialized obstacles faced by black students today is the pervasive streaming of them into the Basic and General levels of education—resulting in negative consequences as these lower academic tracks and labels become self-fulfilling (Black Learners Advisory Committee [BLACK] Report on Education 1994; see also Oakes 1985; Sium 1987; Hayes 1996). At the same time, if black students are not "streamed" into basic or vocational education, the prevalent stereotype still holds that they have a natural ability to excel at sports. Here, physical prowess becomes one of the stereotypes around which "blackness" is constructed. Thus, it has been observed that "PE teachers widely assume that Blacks are naturally better at sports, and promote Black participation as an alternative success system for these pupils, as a way of integrating them into the school culture and of gaining prestige for themselves and the school" (quoted in Small 1994). Spencer (1995) suggests that "this stereotype tends to reinforce the idea that physical prowess is divorced from intellectual ability" and falls "prey to the dualism of Western philosophy, where things are seen as 'either or'"—thereby promoting the stereotype of the athletic black male who doesn't excel academically.

Apart from the negative stereotyping, the continued marginality of black students has created the situation in which these students lack any sense of identification and connectedness to the school. As a racialized barrier, Alberta's secondary schools have failed to respond to the direct needs of the black student and to incorporate black people's history and experiences into the existing curriculum. This "sin of omission," as Willis (1995) calls it, has "[allowed] the cultural knowledge of culturally and linguistically diverse children to be ignored, devalued, and unnurtured as valid sources of literacy acquisition." According to Giroux (1986), "the issue here is that the school actively silences students by ignoring their histories . . . by refusing to provide them with knowledge relevant to their lives." Indeed, there is a feeling among black educators, students, and parents that because the school curriculum is one of the most important elements of education and is the carrier of the philosophy, culture, and national agenda of any country, the mismatch between black students' cultures and that of Canadian schools goes a long way to "reinforce feelings of limited self-worth and cultural isolation by ignoring the historical contributions of African Canadians or devaluing their culture" (BLAC Report on Education 1994). The culture in

Canadian schools, according to Hoo Kong (1996), is that, "in general, textbooks tend to present the perspectives of White, upper-class, Anglo- and French-Canadian males. Consequently, many textbooks do not acknowledge African-Canadians as active participants in the shaping of our nation's history." In reference to these important omissions from Canadian school curricula, Winks (1971) further observes,

Indeed, most White Canadians would not have learned that there were Negroes in Canada at all had they relied upon their formal schooling. Textbooks forgot that Black men existed after 1865, and only a few Canadian books gave even passing reference to the influx of fugitive slaves in the 1850s. Most did not mention Canada's own history of slavery, and none referred to Negroes— or separate schools—after discussing the American Civil War.

This impact of the exclusion from the curriculum on black learners has been analyzed by numerous educators and summed up by Asante (cited in BLAC Report on Education 1994) as follows: "Lacking reinforcement in their own historical experiences, they [black students] become psychologically crippled, hobbling along in the margins of the European experiences of most of the curriculum." As a matter of fact, the monocultural content of the school curriculum, including testing and grouping practices, and the expectations of educators for black and minority children, have been established as the major barriers to educational achievement and equality (King 1993). Research by Hale-Benson (1986) provides compelling evidence that the under-representation of black culture in the curriculum, and the resulting curricular and instructional inequalities, foster mediocre classroom experiences for black children and erect barriers to their academic achievement. I would argue that this "exclusionary curriculum" constitutes a "hidden curriculum" because it "often reinforces society's prejudicial view that

Black children, particularly low-income Black children, are incapable and inferior" (Irvine 1990). I agree with Yon (1994) that "the hidden curriculum has received less attention than the formal curriculum because it addresses what is essentially intangible, the very ethos of schooling that is difficult to pin down." My point here, and again agreeing with Yon (1994), is that "the school's hidden curriculum can cause students to feel marginalized. This is the aspect of schooling through which the subtle and sometimes unintentional forms of racism manifest themselves" (see also Gay 1988).

Furthermore, when one looks at the education of black students in Canada, the evidence indicates that some teachers, it seems, often have lower expectations of black students. In fact, research and experience have shown that black students encounter and still face two institutional barriers: "teacher insensitivity and low expectations which result in differential treatment. Black students feel ignored by their teachers. They *feel invisible in class, unimportant*" (BLAC Report on Education 1994; original emphasis). In my study and others, black students express the belief that white teachers view them as academically inferior, discourage their interests in academic subjects, stream them into vocational and athletic activities, and respond to them less positively than to their white counterparts. Consequently, these "negative expectancies militate against the [black] students' development and reduce their intellectual performance to a point that ultimately may cause them to forfeit a successful academic experience" (Boateng n.d.; see also Good and Brophy 1973; Garcia et al. 1995; James and Brathwaite 1996). Very often, many teachers will say "they are colour blind, that they see the person, not the person's colour" (Richardson 1995). But this approach obscures the fact that, indeed, teachers hold biased and racist views and stereotypical expectations of different groups, and that they consciously or unconsciously have different expectations that are race-related which affect the way they subsequently interact with students (Braun 1976; Singh 1986; Yon 1994). As Banks

and Banks (1991) point out, "many teachers are unaware of the extent to which they embrace racist and sexist attitudes and behaviours that are institutionalized within society."

Finally, the quality of the school context or environment is an important factor that has implications for school success for black students. In fact, students' perceptions of the school environment have been known to be positively correlated to their school success. As Maharah-Sandhu (1995) remarks, "if the child feels alienated, and cannot see his/her world view represented in the school experience, it is unlikely that there will be equality of educational outcome." But the school environment often becomes another barrier for blacks as they face an acute sense of isolation; indeed, many black students do not seem to have a sense of belonging or ownership and thus feel alienated from the public school. The continued marginality of black youths within the school system has created the situation in which these students lack any sense of identification and connectedness to the school (see Maharah-Sandhu 1995). This has led to concerns by black parents and communities regarding such issues as the absence of black teachers and top administrators in schools (Dei 1995b). So long as cultural domination remains a fact of life for black and minority students, Sleeter (1991) argues that minority students may need to develop a strong sense of group identity and action, including commitment to common goals, awareness of conflict against a dominant group, and effective organization in order to overcome the impediments of the dominant culture. As well, "strategies should recognize the value of bicultural and multicultural identities of individuals and groups, as well as the difficulties confronted by those who live in two or more cultures" (Reynolds 1993).

In a way, the students' narratives, although subjective, lend empirical support to the existing knowledge on race and education and inform the (re)theorization of race, difference, and schooling in North America. In one important respect, they show, for example, that the socio-cultural "skewing" towards a white, majority population operates at many levels within the educational hierarchy, from teaching to research about teaching and schooling. Pedagogical discourse derives in part from an academic tradition created and shaped by western European and Anglo-American thinkers. For instance,

> the language in which we discuss our issues is a language permeated with ideas, beliefs, values, and positionings that have been formulated by the dominant majority. Terms such as "multiculturalism," "diversity," "ethnicity," "race," and more have been defined and discussed by White, upper-middle-class, male academicians and politicians. Women and minorities who engage in this discourse must do so using a language formed by those who, historically and currently, occupy power positions in our society. (Estrada and McLaren 1993)

It is what Apple (1992) has called the "selective tradition," i.e., "someone's selection, someone's vision of legitimate knowledge and culture, one that in the process of enfranchising one group's cultural capital disenfranchises another's." The point here is that, all too often, "legitimate" knowledge does not include the historical experiences and cultural expressions of labour, people of colour, and others who have been less powerful (Roman and Christian-Smith, with Ellsworth 1988). For example, the absence of black knowledge in many school curricula is not a simple oversight. Its absence represents an academic instance of racism, or what has been described as "wilful ignorance and aggression toward Blacks" (Pinar 1993). Indeed, Apple (1990) has argued that the selection and organization of knowledge for schools is an ideological process, one that serves the interests of particular classes and social groups. At the same time, he also notes that this does not mean that the entire corpus of school knowledge is "a mirror reflection of ruling class ideas, imposed in an unmediated and coercive manner." Instead, "the processes of cultural incorporation are dynamic, reflecting both continuities

and contradictions of that dominant culture and the continual remaking and relegitimating of that culture's plausibility system." The foregoing analyses lead us to the following neglected questions. How has certain knowledge come to be more appropriate for school curriculum content than other knowledge? By what mechanisms have certain realms of knowledge been given higher status than others? Whose class and social interests have been served by the form and content of schools? Why are the views and concerns of black people so often ignored in the school curriculum? (Apple 1978; Minnich 1990; Sarup 1991). The students' narratives suggest that minority youth have begun to offer a more systematic challenge to the structure of existing school knowledge and the assumptions and practices that undergird the curricula of schools and universities in Northern industrialized societies. This is very encouraging.

Summary and Conclusions

In summary, I have tried to show through my research, and strengthened by other studies, how certain racialized barriers affect or impede the academic success of black students. It is my view that the psychological effects of racism on black students remain greatly underestimated. From my study, I can conclude that how African-Canadian students experience their schooling and education is filtered by their race, and, contrary to what is normally believed, racial identity does make a difference. Regardless of the level of awareness of their racial background and gender, black students in Canada's schools cannot ignore their racial identity, as the dominant group will always view them as "the other"—Canadian citizenship notwithstanding. Consequently, I also conclude that since racism permeates every aspect of our lives, race must be taken into account in developing a meaningful theory of social reproduction through schooling (see Solomon 1992). Educators must play an important role in engaging students in discussions about racism. As James (1995) puts it, "our aim must be to provide an educational climate where difficult issues can be taken up, and all students can voice how they see the issues that affect their aspirations." Most particularly, Roman (1993) suggests that

White educators have a responsibility to challenge and work with racially privileged students to help them understand that their (our) attempts to assume the positions of the racially oppressed are also the result of our contradictory desires to misrecognize and recognize the collective shame of *facing* those who have been *effaced* in the dominant texts of culture, history, and curricular knowledge. (original emphasis)

I believe, therefore, that by exploring such issues as racism and discrimination and raising awareness to the impact of racism on the educational opportunities of black students, we can develop a theory and practice of education that is multicultural, anti-racist, comprehensive, pervasive, and rooted in social justice. Commenting on the whole black school experience in Canada, Solomon (1992) observes,

Black students in White dominant school structures have not benefited from Canada's policy of multiculturalism. Despite this national policy, dominant-group educators continue to embrace an ethnocentric approach to **pedagogy** within schools. Although the official policy is multiculturalism, these responses show that the dominant teaching paradigm within Canadian classrooms is cultural assimilation. Teachers are socializing racial and ethnic minority children into the dominant, mainstream culture.

On this note, I share Dei's (1996b) conclusion that "on both analytical and practical levels, [the students' narratives] bring to the fore the dilemma of searching for an appropriate centrality of the experiences, histories, and cultures of the diverse student body in curriculum and classroom pedagogical practices to facilitate youth learning." In

fact, making black culture empowering in schools now appears to be an indispensable and critical part of any large-scale program of black political and economic advancement (Asante 1992; Boateng 1997). The current system of schooling and education has to be radically transformed in order to reverse the inferiorization of black youths by the historically Euro-centred school system. It is encouraging to note that several attempts are currently under way to develop programs emphasizing black history and culture (D'Oyley 1994; James and Brathwaite 1996). Particularly instructive here is the focus on an anti-racist education within a multicultural education framework. This helps us to understand "the processes of public schooling [and] acknowledge[s] the role the educational system [plays] in producing and reproducing racial, gender, and class-based inequalities in society." The anti-racist framework "also acknowledges the pedagogic need to confront the challenge of diversity and difference in Canadian society and the urgency for an educational system that is more inclusive and is capable of responding to minority concerns about public schooling" (Dei 1993: 49; Dei 1996a). Anti-racism, then, acknowledges the reality of Canadian racism and other forms of social oppression (e.g., class, gender, sexual orientation) in the organizational life of the school and the potential for change (Thornhill 1984; Dei 1995a, 1995b).

Talking about change, it is also quite clear from our discussion that many Canadian teachers lack relevant training in black history, race relations, and cross-cultural understanding and have little appreciation of the enormous challenges and difficulties black students face on a daily basis. They make things worse by the tendency to view and treat all students the same. But same does not mean fair and very often this "colour-blind" approach serves only to deny black students their rights to define who they are and the experiences that they bring to school. To educate black learners successfully, teachers need to be trained to successfully teach a multicultural and anti-racist curriculum. This includes developing "a sense of responsibility to becoming sensitive to their students' emotional, psychological, and physical needs. In addition, teachers must hold similar expectations for all their students and provide Black students and their parents with positive feedback and reinforcement" (BLAC Report on Education 1994). To enhance the academic performance of black and other minority students, they must also "provide each learner with academically rich and challenging material and opportunities for growth and learning commensurate with his or her potential" (Garcia et al. 1995). Particularly, teachers must have positive attitudes toward racially visible students and have high expectations of African-Canadian youth. Furthermore, teacher education institutions have to tackle fundamental issues of inequity. I believe that student teachers' attitudes, understanding, and knowledge are not sufficiently coherent or informed to tackle racial and gender inequalities within schools and classrooms. One way to alleviate this is to ensure that teachers can transmit a sense of tolerance to their class by recognizing their own biases. Also, hiring and promotional practices of school boards should give more consideration to visible minorities. It is important that schools reflect the community's composition, as well as provide positive role models for all students. Black teachers are important for they contribute much to society and all areas of education and serve as role models for all children and youth (King 1993; McCarthy and Crichlow 1993; Siraj-Blatchford 1993; Lyons and Farrell 1994). Finally, teachers' expectations of poor academic work from black students stem from how these teachers view their relationships with black parents. It is reasonable to conclude that if so many teachers are inadequately prepared to interact with a culturally diverse student body, they would be less prepared to negotiate with students' parents. Indeed, as Boateng (n.d.) points out,

> there are many teachers who are hesitant about communicating students' progress to parents for fear that parents would turn a deaf ear to the reports. This expectation is contrary to all reports which suggest that

the Black family is the motivating force that inspires children to value education, even in the face of all the negative stereotypes perpetuated by White teachers. It is critical that teachers understand and capitalize on the significance of the Black family and eliminate the myth that this powerful unit is capable only of transmitting a "culture of poverty." It is the Black parent who helps the child to understand that excellence in education is the foundation for success in society. (See also O'Malley 1992; Perry 1993)

In this respect, my study was a departure from many others, because while addressing racialized barriers in the education of black students, it also provided personal insights to help us gain an understanding of how some black students have succeeded in school in spite of the odds against them. It was a departure from previous research, which has almost always focused on describing and explaining the students who are academically successful in school and determining what factors are associated with their success. Yes, black students face and must contend with racism, but contrary to popular opinion and research, not all of them make poor choices about education. In spite of the racism, black students also can develop successful academic skills (Slaughter and Epps 1987; Pollard 1989). A positive black racial identity, enhanced with an awareness, pride, and knowledge of black and African affairs, is crucial to school success. In fact, it is the antidote to and the coping mechanism for the daily doses of racial hostility and humiliation. The implication—and an important one—is that minority status and identity do not and should not always lead to negative educational outcomes. Indeed, the students in my study represent what Mehan (1996) calls "the current generation of minorities [who] reflects a faith in the potential of schooling to solve or at least deal with social problems." He adds that "although they feel victimized by systematic discrimination, they do not dismiss schools. Indeed, they express confidence that schools are or can be sites that foster the opportunity for children to succeed." In all of this, we can benefit and learn from the spirit of striving and the determination to succeed which characterizes so much of the black experience in North America (Small 1994). Certainly, my study contributes to this undertaking; but more research is needed. The students in my study make up part of the Canadian black population that will not be considered *indigenous*; i.e., those who have lived in North America for many generations like the African-Canadian population in Nova Scotia, or African-Americans in the United States. They are primarily children of Caribbean and African immigrants who immigrated to Canada in the 1960s and 1970s. This begs for some questions for future research. For example, did the backgrounds of these students

as Canadian "voluntary immigrant minorities" play a part in their academic success? Would they have succeeded if some of them came to Canada as refugees, like the Ethiopians and Somalis? Would that have made any difference? Or, would they have achieved the same success if they lived in the United States, or in Ontario, where there is a large black immigrant population? Would the same results be achieved if a second or later generations of these students' families and school experiences were studied across time? And would cultural differences diminish as these black students move from being first or second to third and fourth generation individuals? These are important new questions that need to be further explored for a fuller understanding of the black educational experience in Canada.

References

Alladin, I., ed. 1996. *Racism in Canadian Schools*. Toronto: Harcourt Brace & Company Canada.

Apple, M.W. 1978. "Ideology, Reproduction, and Educational Reform." *Comparative Education Review* 22, 3: 367–87.

———. 1990. *Ideology and Curriculum*, 2nd edn. New York: Routledge.

———. 1992. "The Text and Cultural Politics." *Educational Researcher* 21, 7: 4–11, 19.

Asante, M.K. 1992. "Afrocentric Curriculum." *Educational Leadership* 49, 4: 28–31.

Asante, R.G. 1985. "Afrocentricity and Culture." In M.K. Asante and K.W. Asante, eds, *African Culture: The Rhythms of Unity*. Westport, CT: Greenwood Press, 3–12.

Banks, J., and C.A. McGee Banks, eds 1991. *Multicultural Education: Issues and Perspectives*, 2nd edn. Boston, MA: Allyn & Bacon.

Barrett, S.R. 1987. *Is God a Racist? The Right Wing in Canada*. Toronto: University of Toronto Press.

Black Learners Advisory Committee. 1994. *BLAC Report on Education: Redressing Inequity: Empowering Black Learners*. Vol. 1: Summary. Halifax: Black Learners Advisory Committee.

Boateng, F. 1997. "Reflections on Education: A Call for a Creative African-Centered Approach." *Ghana Review International* 42: 21–2.

———. n.d. *Equalizing Opportunities for Black Students in School District 81: Concerns and Recommendations*. Spokane, WA: Black Education Association of Spokane.

Boykin, A.W. 1986. "The Triple Quandary and the Schooling of Afro-American Children." In U. Neisser, ed., *The School Achievement of Minority Children:*

New Perspectives. Hillsdale, NJ: Lawrence Erlbaum Associates, 57–92.

Brathwaite, K. 1989. "The Black Student and the School: A Canadian Dilemma." In S.W. Chilungu and S. Niang, eds, *African Continuities*. Toronto: Terebi, 195–216.

Braun, C. 1976, "Teacher Expectations: Socio-psychological Dynamics." *Review of Education Research* 42: 185–213.

Campbell, M. 1989. "Fighting Back: Canadian Blacks Have Become Alarmed over a Recent Series of Race-related Incidents." *The Globe and Mail* 21 January: D1–2.

Cannon, M. 1995. *The Invisible Empire: Racism in Canada*. Toronto: Random House.

Carlson, D.L. 1995. "Constructing the Margins: Of Multicultural Education and Curriculum Settlements." *Curriculum Inquiry* 25: 407–31.

Chigbo, O. 1989. "Land of 'Smiling Racism': Canada's Image as a Racially Tolerant Society Is a Myth." *West Africa* 20–26 March: 438.

Clarke, G.E. 1998. "White Like Canada." *Transition* 73: 98–109.

Codjoe, H.M. 1997. "Black Students and School Success: A Study of the Experiences of Academically Successful African-Canadian Student Graduates in Alberta's Secondary School." PhD dissertation, Faculty of Education, University of Alberta.

———. 1998. "Pre-college/University Education of Ghanaians and other Africans in North America: A Canadian Perspective." *Ghana Review International* 52 (June): 10–11.

———. 1999. "The Schooling Experiences of African Students in Canadian Schools." *International Journal of Curriculum and Instruction* 1: 67–94.

———. 2001. "Can Blacks Be Racist? Reflections on Being 'Too Black and African.'" In C. James and A. Shadd, eds, *Talking About Identity: Encounters in Race, Ethnicity and Language*. Toronto: Between the Lines, 277–90.

Dei, G.J.S. 1993. "Narrative Discourses of Black/African-Canadian Parents and the Canadian Public School System." *Canadian Ethnic Studies* 25: 45–65.

———. 1994. "Afrocentricity: A Cornerstone of Pedagogy." *Anthropology and Education Quarterly* 25: 3–28.

———. 1995a. "African Studies in Canada: Problems and Challenges." *Journal of Black Studies* 26: 153–71.

———. 1995b. "Examining the Case for 'African-Centred' Schools in Ontario." *McGill Journal of Education* 30: 179–98.

———. 1995c. "Report's Critics Can't Ignore Student Alienation: OISE Study Found Sense of Exclusion Among Minorities." *The Toronto Star* 8 December.

———. 1996a. *Anti-racism Education: Theory and Practice*. Halifax: Fernwood Publishing.

———. 1996b. "Black/African-Canadian Students' Perspectives on School Racism." In I. Alladin, ed., *Racism in Canadian Schools*. Toronto, Harcourt Brace & Company, 42–61.

D'Oyley, V., ed. 1994. *Innovations in Black Education in Canada*. Toronto: Umbrella Press/National Council of Black Educators of Canada.

D'Oyley, V., and H. Silverman, eds 1976. *Black Students in Urban Canada*. Toronto: TESL Talk, Ministry of Culture and Recreation.

D'Souza, D. 1995. *The End of Racism: Principles for a Multicultural Society*. New York: The Free Press.

Erickson, F. 1987. "Transformation and School Success: The Politics and Culture of Educational Achievement." *Anthropology and Education Quarterly* 18: 335–56.

Estrada, K., and P. McLaren. 1993. "A Dialogue on Multicultural and Democratic Culture." *Educational Researcher* 22 (April) 3: 27–33.

Flecha, R. 1999. "Modern and Postmodern Racism in Europe: Dialogic Approach and Anti-racist Pedagogies." *Harvard Educational Review* 69: 150–71.

Garcia, S.B., C.Y. Wilkinson, and A.A. Ortiz. 1995. "Enhancing Achievement for Language Minority Students: Classroom, School, and Family Contexts." *Education and Urban Society* 27: 441–62.

Gay, G. 1988. "Designing Relevant Curricula for Diverse Learners." *Education and Urban Society* 20: 327–40.

Giroux, H.A. 1986. "The Politics of Schooling and Culture." *Orbit* 17, 4: 10–11.

———. 1994. "Doing Cultural Studies: Youth and the Challenge of Pedagogy." *Harvard Educational Review* 64: 278–308.

Good, T.L., and J.E. Brophy. 1973. *Looking in Classrooms*. New York: Harper & Row.

Gose, B. 1995. "Test Scores and Stereotypes: Psychologist Finds That Blacks, Females Are Vulnerable to Lowered Expectations." *Chronicle of Higher Education* 18 August: A31.

Gougis, R.A. 1986. "The Effects of Prejudice and Stress on the Academic Performance of Black-Americans." In U. Neisser, ed., *The School Achievement of Minority Children: New Perspectives*. Hillsdale, NJ: Lawrence Erlbaum Associates.

Hale-Benson, J. 1986. *Black Children, Their Roots, Culture and Learning Styles*. Baltimore: Johns Hopkins University Press.

Harrison, L.E. 2000. "Why Culture Matters." In L.E. Harrison and S.P. Huntington, eds, *Culture Matters—How Values Shape Human Progress*. New York: Basic Books, xvi–xxxiv.

Hayes, D.W. 1996. "Athletes, Outcasts and Partyers: Academic Excellence Rarely Seen on the Big Screen." *Black Issues in Higher Education* 12, 23: 26–8.

Head, W. 1975. *The Black Presence in the Canadian Mosaic: A Study of Perception and the Practice of Discrimination against Blacks in Metropolitan Toronto*. Toronto: Ontario Human Rights Commission.

Henry, A. 1993. "Missing: Black Self-representations in Canadian Educational Research." *Canadian Journal of Education* 18: 206–22.

Henry, F., C. Tator, W. Mattis, and T. Rees. 1995. *The Colour of Democracy: Racism in Canadian Society*. Toronto: Harcourt Brace & Company.

Herrnstein, R., and C. Murray. 1994. *The Bell Curve: Intelligence and Class Structure in American Life*. New York: Basic Books.

Hoo Kong, N.A. 1996. "Confronting a History of Exclusion: A Personal Reflection." In K. Brathwaite and C.E. James, eds, *Educating African Canadians*. Toronto: James Lorimer & Company, 58–68.

Irvine, J.J. 1990. *Black Students and School Failure: Policies, Practices, and Prescriptions*. New York: Praeger.

James, C. 1995. "'Reverse Racism': Students' Response to Equity Programs." *Journal of Professional Studies* 3: 48–54.

James, C.E. 1990. *Making It: Black Youth, Racism and Career Aspirations in a Big City*. Oakville, ON: Mosaic Press.

———. 1994. "I've Never Had a Black Teacher Before." In C. James and A. Shadd, eds, *Talking about Difference: Encounters in Culture, Language and Identity*. Toronto: Between the Lines, 25–140.

James, C.E., and K. Brathwaite. 1996. "The Education of African Canadians: Issues, Contexts, and Expectations." In K. Brathwaite and C.E. James, eds, *Educating African Canadians*. Toronto: James Lorimer & Company, 13–31.

King, S.H. 1993. "The Limited Presence of African-American Teachers." *Review of Educational Research* 63, 2: 115–49.

Laroque, E. 1991. "Racism Runs through Canadian Society." In O. McKague, ed., *Racism in Canada*. Saskatoon: Fifth House Publishers, 73–6.

Lee, E. 1992. *Letters to Marcia: A Teacher's Guide to Anti-racist Education*. Toronto: Ontario Cross-Cultural Communication Centre.

Lendore-Mahabir, M. 1995. *Issues Associated with Racial Intolerance and Inequality and Proposals for Their Resolution*. Edmonton: Council of Black Organizations.

Lewington, J. 1993. "Ontario Attacks Racism in the Classroom." *The Globe and Mail* 16 July.

Lewis, S. 1992. *Consultative Report on Race Relations.* Toronto: Ontario Ministry of Citizenship.

Logan, S.L. 1990. "Promoting Academic Excellence of African-American Students: Issues and Strategies." *Educational Considerations* 18: 12–15.

Lyons, C., and M. Farrell. 1994. "Teaching Tolerance: Multicultural and Anti-racist Education." *McGill Journal of Education* 29: 5–14.

McCarthy, C., and W. Crichlow. 1993. "Introduction: Theories of Identity, Theories of Representation, Theories of Race." In C. McCarthy and W. Crichlow, eds, *Race, Identity, and Representation in Education.* New York: Routledge, xii–xxix.

McKague, O., ed. 1991. *Racism in Canada.* Saskatoon: Fifth House Publishers.

Macias, J. 1993. "Forgotten History: Educational and Social Antecedents of High Achievement among Asian Immigrants in the United States." *Curriculum Inquiry* 23: 409–32.

Maharaj-Sandhu, S. 1995. "Anti-racist Curriculum in an Ethnocentric Society." *Multiculturalism* 16: 14–16.

Mehan, H. 1996. "Commentary: Constitutive Processes of Race and Exclusion." *Anthropology and Education Quarterly* 27: 270–8.

Miller, L.S. 1995. "The Origins of the Presumption of Black Stupidity." *Journal of Blacks in Higher Education* 9: 78–82.

Minnich, E.K. 1990. *Transforming Knowledge.* Philadelphia: Temple University Press.

Moodley, K. 1985. "The Predicament of Racial Affirmative Action: A Critical Review of 'Equality Now': Report of the Special Committee on Visible Minorities in Canada." In K. Moodley, ed., *Race Relations and Multicultural Education.* Vancouver: Centre for the Study of Curriculum and Instruction, University of British Columbia, 111–23.

Nieto, S. 1992. *Affirming Diversity: The Sociopolitical Context of Multicultural Education.* New York: Longman.

———. 1994. "Lessons from Students on Creating a Chance to Dream." *Harvard Educational Review* 64: 392–426.

Oake, G. 1991. "Racism Hits Edmonton Schools." *Toronto Star* 12 December.

Oakes, J. 1985. *Keeping Track: How Schools Structure Inequality.* New Haven: Yale University Press.

O'Malley, S. 1992. "Demand Quality Education, Black Parents Told." *The Globe and Mail* 20 August.

Omi, M., and H. Winant. 1998. "Racial Formations." In P.S. Rothenberg, ed., *Race, Class, and Gender in the United States—An Integrated Study,* 4th edn. New York: St Martin's Press, 13–22.

Orange, C. 1995. "Precursors, Perceptions, Probabilities, and Peers: Enemies of African-American Achievement." *NASSP Curriculum Report* 25.

Perry, T. 1993. "How Racial and Ethnic Family and Community Characteristics Affect Children's Achievement: The African-American Experience." *Research and Development Report* 3 (March). Baltimore: Center on Families, Communities, Schools and Children's Learning.

Pinar, W.F. 1993. "Notes on Understanding Curriculum as a Racial Text." In C. McCarthy and W. Crichlow, eds, *Race, Identity and Representation in Education.* New York: Routledge.

Pollard, D.S. 1989. "Against the Odds: A Profile of Academic Achievers from the Urban Underclass." *Journal of Negro Education* 58: 297–308.

Reed, I. 1993. *Airing Dirty Laundry.* Reading, MA: Addison-Wesley.

Reitz, J.G., and R. Bretton. 1994. *The Illusion of Difference: Realities of Ethnicity in Canada and the United States.* Toronto: C.D. Howe Institute.

Reynolds, A.J. 1993. "Distinguishing Characteristics of Children at Risk Who Are Successful in School." Paper presented at the 1993 Annual Meeting of the American Educational Research Association, Atlanta, 12–16 April.

Richardson, R. 1995. "Let No One Off the Hook." *Canadian Forum* 74, 841: 36–8.

Roman, L.G. 1993. "White is a Color! White Defensiveness, Postmodernism, and Anti-Racist Pedagogy." In C. McCarthy and W. Crichlow, eds, *Race, Identity, and Representation in Education.* New York: Routledge, 71–88.

Roman, L., and L. Christian-Smith, with L. Ellsworth, eds 1988. *Becoming Feminine: The Politics of Popular Culture.* Philadelphia: Falmer Press.

Sarick, L. 1995. "Studies Examine Hurdles Facing Black Students." *The Globe and Mail* 21 December: A3.

Sarup, M. 1991. *Education and the Ideologies of Racism.* Stoke-on-Trent: Trentham Books.

Selden, S. 1978. "Eugenics and Curriculum: 1860–1929." *The Educational Forum* 43: 67–82.

Singh, A. 1986. "Effects of Teacher Perception on Achievement." In R.J. Samuda and S.L. Kong, eds, *Multicultural Education Programmes and Methods.* Toronto: Intercultural Social Sciences Publications, 89–104.

Siraj-Blatchford, I., ed. 1993. *Race, Gender and the Education of Teachers.* London: Open University Press.

Sium, B. 1987. "Streaming in Education and Beyond: Black Students Talk." *Orbit* 18: 20–1.

Slaughter, D.T., and E.G. Epps. 1987. "The Home Environment and Academic Achievement of Black American Children and Youth: An Overview." *Journal of Negro Education* 56: 3–20.

Sleeter, C. 1991. "Multicultural Education and Empowerment." In C. Sleeter, ed., *Empowerment through Multicultural Education.* Albany, NY: State University of New York Press, 157–71.

Small, S. 1994. *Racialized Barriers: The Black Experience in the United States and England in the 1980s.* London: Routledge.

Solomon, P. 1992. *Black Resistance in High School: Forging a Separatist Culture.* Albany: State University of New York Press.

Solorzano, D.G. 1997. "Images and Words that Wound: Critical Race Theory, Racial Stereotyping, and Teacher Education." *Teacher Education Quarterly* Summer: 5–19.

Spencer, J.R. 1995. "Under the Gaze: The Experiences of African-Canadian Students in Two Edmonton High Schools." Unpublished MA thesis, Department of Educational Policy Studies, University of Alberta.

Steele, C.M. 1992. "Race and the Schooling of Black Americans." *The Atlantic Monthly* April: 68–78.

———. 1997. "A Threat in the Air: How Stereotypes Shape Intellectual Identity and Performance." *American Psychologist*: 613–29.

———. 1999. "Thin Ice: 'Stereotype Threat' and Black College Students." *Atlantic Monthly* 284, 2: 44–54.

Steele, C.M., and J. Aronson. 1995. "Stereotype Threat and the Intellectual Test Performance of African Americans." *Journal of Personality and Social Psychology* 69: 797–811.

Steele, S. 1989. "The Recoloring of Campus Life: Student Racism, Academic Pluralism, and the End of a Dream." *Harper's Magazine* 278, 1665: 47–55.

Strickland, D.S. 1994. "Educating African American Learners at Risk: Finding a Better Way." *Language Arts* 71: 328–36.

Sultana, R.G. 1995. "Ethnography and the Politics of Absence." In P.L. McLaren and J.M. Giarelli, eds, *Critical Theory and Educational Research*. Albany: State University of New York Press, 113–25.

Talbani, A.S. 1991. "Education and Ethnic Minorities in Canada: South Asian Students in Quebec Schools." PhD dissertation, Faculty of Education, McGill University.

Taylor, A.R. 1991. "Social Competence and the Early School Transition: Risk and Protective Factors for African-American Children." *Education and Urban Society* 24: 15–26.

Thakur, A. 1988. *The Impact of Schooling on Visible Minorities: A Case Study of Black Students in Alberta Secondary Schools*. Nanaimo, BC: Malaspina College.

Thornhill, E. 1984. "Fight Racism Starting with the School." *Currents: Readings in Race Relations* 2, 3: 3–7.

T.M.B. 1995. Review of *Other People's Children: Cultural Conflict in the Classroom*, by Lisa Delpit. *Harvard Educational Review* 65, 3. http://hepg.org/her-home/issues/harvard-educational-review-volume-65-issue-3/herbooknote/other-people-s-children_293.

Towards a New Beginning. 1992. *The Report and Action Plan of the Four-Level Government/African Canadian Community Working Group*. Toronto.

Tyack, D. 1974. *One Best System: A History of American Urban Education*. Cambridge, MA: Harvard University Press.

Walker, S. 1991. "Schools Don't Do Enough for Blacks, Educators Say." *Toronto Star* 15 April.

Walters, T.S. 1994. "Multicultural Literacy: Mental Scripts for Elementary, Secondary, and College Teachers." *Equity and Excellence in Education* 27: 45–52.

Willis, A.I. 1995. "Reading the World of School Literacy: Contextualizing the Experience of a Young African American Male." *Harvard Educational Review* 65: 30–49.

Winks, R. 1971. *The History of Blacks in Canada*. New Haven: Yale University Press.

Wotherspoon, T. 1987. "Conflict and Crisis in Canadian Education." In T. Wotherspoon, ed., *The Political Economy of Canadian Schools*. Toronto: Methuen, 1–15.

Yin, R.K. 1984. *Case Study Research: Design and Methods*. Newbury Park, CA: Sage.

Yon, D. 1994. "The Educational Experiences of Caribbean Youth." In F. Henry, *The Caribbean Diaspora in Toronto: Learning to Live with Racism*. Toronto: University of Toronto Press, 120–47.

Questions for Critical Thought

1. What characteristics of these black students could account for their academic success, despite the racism they encountered? Do they indicate personal, family, or community factors? What role do intellectual, emotional, spiritual, or economic factors play?

2. What aspects of the "hidden curriculum" could affect black students? How is racism manifested in the hidden curriculum? How can teachers, students, guidance counselors, parents, community workers, social and health care workers contest the "hidden curriculum"?

3. Why are some teachers committed to "colour-blindness"? Are you "colour blind"? Are members of your family, your friends, and your community "colour blind"? Why or why not?

4. Codjoe notes the diversity of his sample of students, yet he draws no conclusions based on gender or class differences. Why do you think Codjoe made no effort to make these distinctions? Do you expect differences in experiences would emerge if more attention were paid to gender, class, and ethnic differences?

5. Do you think similar conclusions would be drawn about successful Aboriginal students? About white students of low socio-economic status? Can you think of examples of people that you know who have been able to successfully overcome the social barriers that they have experienced and navigate their way through the school system? Why have they been successful?

The Persistence of Colonial Discourse: Race, Gender, and Muslim Students in Canadian Schools

..Goli Rezai-Rashti

Towards a Conceptual Framework: Islam, Race, Gender, and the Public School System

In recent years there have been two important challenges to academic and political thought that have helped in understanding the complexities of dealing with issues of racism and sexism in relation to Muslim women. First, especially among women from Muslim countries,[1] there is increasing academic interest in issues of gender and Islam. Second, the criticisms addressed to Western feminism by mainly black and third world women have generated a wealth of literature that has contributed to make the multi-positionality of women's issues across the globe more visible (hooks 1981, 1990; Collins 1990, 1998; Bannerji et al. 1991; Bannerji 1993; Mohanty 1991; Ng 1993). However, most of these discourses have had very little impact on education, especially at the public elementary and secondary school level. Partly, this is because most of these new academic discourses do not focus on education and the life experiences of young women in the school system. The failure to engage in these areas has worked to reinforce colonial attitudes on the

part of educators towards Muslims, especially in their views on gender issues in Muslim culture. In fact, it appears as if this colonial perception has been reinforced by various changes in the last two decades. Recent events in the Islamic world (i.e., the Iranian Revolution, the Gulf War, the Taliban regime in Afghanistan, and the controversy over Salman Rushdie's *Satanic Verses*) and the Western media's distorted coverage of almost anything Islamic have contributed to the persistence of long-held stereotypical attitudes. As Said (1981) argues,

> [There] is no relation between the term "Islam" in common Western usage to the enormously varied life that goes on within the world of Islam, with its more than 800 million square miles of territory, principally in Africa and Asia, and its dozens of societies, states, histories, geographies, and cultures. The term "Islam," as it is used today, seems to mean one simple thing but in fact is part fiction, part ideological, and part minimal designation of a religion called "Islam."

This devastating combination shapes the force of colonial attitudes. In this chapter, I do not intend to talk about Islam and Muslims as a uni-fied and essentialist category, as I am well aware of the different histories, nationalities, and experi-ences of Muslims and Muslim women. In reject-ing the essentialist notion of Muslims, I agree with Hall's (1996) argument on the problematization of the "essential black subject." Hall discusses the importance of recognizing the extraordinary diversity of subjective positions, social experi-ences, and cultural identities that comprise the category "black." Referring to the need to prob-lematize and make more complex the imperatives of identity, Hall talks of it as "the end of innocence." As well, he insists upon the recognition that the central issues of race always appear historically in articulation with other categories and divisions and are constantly crossed and re-crossed by the categories of class, gender, and ethnicity. Some feminists have argued specifically along these lines, among them Najmabadi (1991), in a self-criticism of her own earlier work:

> In the literature on Islam and Islamic posi-tions on women, in sources both sympa-thetic and hostile, including some of my own earlier writings, there is a tendency toward an essentialist conception of Islam, reducing Islam to a given set of doctrines, with a set of edicts on women, and attributing the current practice and ideology of Islamic movements to the implementation of these doctrines.

This monolithic conception of Islam has been part of Western colonial discourse since the beginning of colonization in Muslim coun-tries. The rise of the fundamentalist movement has reinforced such a monolithic conception of Islam. More importantly, this **essentialist col-onial discourse** does not address the question of how religion is used for political purposes and how people in positions of power are able to interpret and reinterpret the Islamic texts. This essentialist concept of Islam negates the sense of agency and looks at Muslim women as somehow trapped in fixed Islamic doctrines and edicts.

In his work *Culture and Imperialism* (1993), Said also discusses the complexities surround-ing issues of identity and rejects accordingly the fixed, essentialist, and single notion of identity:

> No one today is purely one thing. Labels like Indians, or women, or Muslim, or American are not more than starting points, which if followed into actual experience for only a moment are quickly left behind. Imperialism consolidated the mixture of cultures and identities on a global scale. But its worst and most paradoxical gift was to allow people to believe that they were mainly, exclusively, white, or black, or Western, or Oriental.

This more recent non-essentialist conception of identity has not, however, had an impact on the essentialist Western Orientalist views held pre-dominantly in North American societies towards women in Muslim cultures. I have found that in the education system there is a persistence of colonial discourses in relation to Muslim female students. Educators, administrators, and students alike still rely on the old **stereotypes** as well as on the more recent popular images of Muslims por-trayed by the media.

One of the main signifiers of Western stereo-types of Islamic societies is Islam's alleged repres-sive treatment of women. Muslim women are perceived as subjugated, veiled, secluded, and oppressed beings in need of rescue. These ideas have a long history dating back to the late nine-teenth century when Europeans established themselves as colonial powers in Islamic societies. As Kandioti (1991) argues, "there is a consensus among scholars that the age-old antagonism between Islam and Christendom, much of it a history of colonial domination, created an area of cultural resistance around women and fam-ily." As part of their "civilizing" mission, both colonial administrators and the Christian mis-sionaries tried to reform the sexual relations and family traditions of Muslims. Thus, any discussion of feminism, women's issues, and concerns in Muslim countries creates tension and resistance because of the experience of colonization. These discussions are usually seen as part of the strategy of cultural imperialism to undermine the culture and tradition of the independent Muslim nations. This situation has created enormous difficulties for women in the Muslim world. If they raise women's issues, they are perceived to be allying themselves with imperialism and betraying their traditional religion and culture. The extraordinary challenge for women is to raise feminist issues in such a way that they will not be dismissed as part of the colonial and imperialist strategies.

This is a complex situation for women not only in Muslim societies but also within diasporic Muslim communities in the North American context. Women are forced to deal with the tensions and contradictions of having to discuss the "woman question" and "feminist issues" without betraying their Islamic culture and religion. Feminists from and within Muslim societies have to create a delicate balance between reclaiming a national identity, reaffirming progressive elements of their indigenous culture, and struggling for the creation of a just society (Moghadam 1991).

In the following section, I discuss some of these issues as they pertain to the lives of young Muslim women in the Canadian school system.

Remnants of Colonialism in School Practices

As mentioned earlier, women's "mistreatment" within Islamic culture is one of the main signifiers of Muslim inferiority in Western culture. Based on years of experience in the school system in the areas of anti-racism and feminism, I have seen how gender issues in the Islamic religion are the target of severe criticisms and grave misunderstandings. In dealing with teachers, students, and administrators, I find their interactions with Muslim students to be based largely on stereotypes of Muslims that are reminiscent of the colonial era. Muslim girls who wear the veil are automatically considered passive and oppressed, and educators

often seem to hold the view that these girls have been forced by their oppressive parents to wear the veil. Guidance counsellors dealing with Muslim girls take their stories about their repressive parents at face value without even bothering to corroborate the students' claims with the parents themselves.

Many teachers are not aware that Western feminist views have themselves been rightly criticized for their lack of sensitivity to issues of race and culture. Well-meaning teachers (both men and women), appropriating the language of feminism while oblivious to the full range of issues and situations that women experience in other cultures, continue to make open remarks about gender oppression in such cultures. This is an interesting phenomenon because some of the teachers who are critical of gender oppression in other cultures are, in contrast, quite uncritical of feminism, the feminist movement, and gender oppression within their own Western cultures. There seems to be a predominant perception that women in Western societies are already liberated and have achieved equality, and other women need only follow the same path if they want to be liberated and experience equality.

In trying to address the situation, I have found that multiculturalism and anti-racist advocates were similarly unable to respond to it effectively. Although the anti-racism approach is more progressive in terms of dealing with issues of power relations, it nevertheless shares some of the same limitations of multiculturalism when dealing with gender issues in other cultures. Both lack, above all, an analysis of internal power dynamics and conflict within the collective communities.[2] In recent years, the work of authors who have written extensively on the question of identity and representation, such as Hall (1996), Bhabha (1994), Yuval-Davis (1997), Rattansi (1992), Britzman (1998), McCarthy (1998), and Yon (1996) constitute a good starting point for the critique of both multiculturalism and anti-racism approaches. Racism, according to Hall (1996), operates "on the one hand by constructing impassable symbolic boundaries between racially constituted categories, and on the other hand, by using its typical binary system of representation which constantly marks and attempts to fix and naturalize the difference between belongingness and otherness." The tensions, confusions, and contradictions in the lives of young Muslim women are a result of dealing with such opposing poles of belongingness and otherness.

The discussion about the alleged repressive treatment of women in Islamic religion and culture can best be described in this context. Gender issues in Muslim cultures are one of the most important elements of signification and categorization of their otherness, since gender issues have become one of the foundations of racialization of Muslims (both men and women) in Western societies. Islam provides a fascinating example of how ethnicity, community, and gender can collide in strange and unexpected ways (Ali 1992).

Tensions and New Understandings

When discussing gender issues in Muslim cultures, I am not suggesting, as some Islamists do, that there is no sexism in Muslim religion and cultures. Similarly, I am not working with a romanticized vision of Islam, one which does not take into account dilemmas, tensions, and lived experiences of Muslim women. In a troubling way, both Islamist as well as Western discourses "fall into the same pitfall in cross-cultural affairs, comparing one's ideal to someone else's reality" (Haddad and Esposito 1998). This illustrates the complexity of the situation. On the one hand is the predominance of old colonial ideas among educators; on the other hand are the internal conflicts and power differences within Muslim communities. Muslim communities, however, like all other communities, are not immune from internal conflicts based on gender and social class differences. It is interesting to notice, however, that in the everyday practices of schooling, Muslim students are generally perceived and treated in ways that are congruent with firmly held perceptions

of the inferiority of their religion and cultures. The following examples illustrate the complexities of these encounters and interactions.

Educators who work with youth and adolescents are aware that intergenerational conflict between teenagers and their families is common.[3] A normal occurrence such as this is seen and interpreted in dramatically different ways when the youth involved happens to be a young woman from a Muslim background; more often that not, educators view the problem as a cultural one. It is immediately communicated to the student that her culture is backward. In this colonial logic, the best way to "solve" what is a common generational conflict is to break with the "old" cultural tradition and adopt the cultural ways of the "new country." Culture is thus both problem and solution, a dynamic that of course sustains colonial representation of one culture as saviour.

Ideas such as these are often conveyed to the student openly and with a sense or belief that the teacher, principal, or the guidance counsellor is defending the democratic rights of the student. Students who complain that their parents do not allow them to go out after school, or that they are not allowed to date, are sometimes advised to leave their homes and get into a social assistance program in order to live independently. This is certainly a huge undertaking for some of these young women who have lived all their lives with their extended families and have no experience of living on their own. On numerous occasions, educators make remarks about how in "backward" cultures parents have "conditional love" for their children. By this they mean that these parents only love their children if children obey their parents' rules fully.

Students are also well aware of the stereotypical attitudes of educators and sometimes take advantage of a situation. For example, one day I was consulted by a school to find out if it was true that in Muslim culture girls cannot study mathematics. Surprised by the question, and after some discussion with the Grade 7 student, I found out that she was using Islam as an excuse for not attending the math class and had readily convinced the principal of the school about this cultural rule. The student was certainly aware of the educators' attitudes towards Muslims and Islam; she also knew that any remark about the culture, however ridiculous, would be seen as acceptable provided that the remark could constitute Muslim culture as illogical and superstitious.

Erroneous understandings of Islam also assume the inferiority of Muslim culture vis-à-vis Western culture. At a high school meeting, the discussion turned to whom to invite as guest speakers. Very confidently, the vice-principal suggested the name of an East African woman, claiming that she was an excellent speaker because "she is so modern and westernized."

While these scenes of misrecognition abound, another tension seems to structure the ways Muslim girls are treated in school settings. This tension concerns the growing fundamentalist movement across the globe, and the increasing number of Muslim families influenced by the movement who are immigrating or entering Canada as refugees. Some of these families use the official discourse of Canadian multiculturalism as a way of enforcing their traditional ideas around gender codes. For example, some families will impose religious restrictions towards sports (such as swimming), learning to play certain musical instruments, and the imposition of certain types of more repressive arranged marriages. These families also bring with them some fixed notions of Muslim female identity that should not be exempt from criticism. As Yuval-Davis (1997) argues, "multiculturalism can have detrimental effects on women in particular, as often 'different' cultural traditions are defined in terms of culturally specific gender relations, and the control of women's behaviour is often used to produce ethnic boundaries."

In my work with some Muslim families, I have observed a clearly differential treatment between male and female children. While girls are asked to observe the Islamic veil and "look authentic," and have restrictions placed on their social interactions, boys are relatively free to choose Western clothing and to go out and socialize with others.

Likewise, similar patterns of differential treatment shape the lived experiences of many of these families. For example, while mothers are expected to "look authentic" and act as the gatekeepers of the culture and tradition, fathers wear Western suits and blue jeans. In a discussion about his request that his daughter not be in the same class as Jamaican girls (who, according to him, were "sexually loose" and a "bad influence" on his daughter), an East African father, dressed in blue jeans and a black leather jacket, looked at me and asked if I was from a Muslim background. When I responded "yes," he immediately questioned my identity by stating that I didn't look like a Muslim woman—like him, I dress in Western clothes.

The state policy of multiculturalism gave permission for these expressions of essentialist, ahistorical, and monolithic concepts of the culture and identities of minority and dominant groups. Minority ethnic communities, in the multicultural perspective, are constructed as static and two-dimensional, like an exquisite Indian miniature compared to representations of a heroic conquest in European art (Ali 1992). A study of the Muslim South Asian communities in England illustrates how it has been implicitly and explicitly perceived that with multiculturalism, minorities can be given limited autonomy over internal community affairs, such as religious observance, dress, food, and other supposedly "non-political" matters, including the social control of women. For fundamentalists working with rigid and static notions of culture and identity, control of women is basic to the construction of a social order. The overall effect of fundamentalist movements has been detrimental to women, limiting and defining their roles and activities, and actively oppressing them when they step outside their preordained limits (Yuval-Davis 1997).

Without going into extensive debate about the nature of fundamentalist movements around the world, it is important to mention that these movements are political in nature. It has been rightly argued that with globalization and a growing sense of disempowerment at the political level, more and more people feel the need for a "symbolic retreat"[4] to the past in order to face the future. As Yuval-Davis (1997) tells us,

> The myth of common origin and a fixed immutable, ahistorical, and homogenous construction of the collectivity's culture is used in a similar way to that of religious **fundamentalism**. Indeed, religion often plays a central role as cultural signifier in these cultural fundamentalist constructions.

Student Voices and Feminist Discourse

From 1996 to 1997, I conducted a year-long focus group of 12 young Muslim women (16–18 years old) from various cultural and racial backgrounds. We met as a group for two hours every week and discussed their complex daily encounters at home and in school. Their stories and their life experiences made me realize the formidable task faced by Muslim women having to struggle at various levels. On the one hand, they often have to deal with sexism within their families and communities; on the other hand, at school, they are under tremendous pressure to assimilate, to leave home, and to abandon their "oppressive" religion and culture. It was quite evident from our discussions that these young women desired neither to leave home and their "oppressive" parents, nor to fully assimilate into the Western way of life. While there was a strong sense of community affiliation, there was at the same time admiration for some of the personal freedom experienced by Western women. These students brought with themselves a counter-narrative of both their collective community culture and the dominant culture of their schooling. Literally, they were struggling with their identities. Theirs is, as Bhabha (1994) tells us, a counter-narrative emerging from those national and cultural hybrids who have lived, because of immigration and exile, in more than one culture. Such hybrids both evoke and erase the totalizing boundaries of their adoptive nation. Theirs is a process—in the word of Hall (1996)—of "cultural diasporization."

At the secondary school level, as mentioned earlier, educators (who often do not identify themselves as feminists) appropriate the language of feminism in order to criticize repressive treatment of gender issues in students' cultures. Many of these teachers hold an essentialist view of women, and their oppression, as stable, homogeneous, and undifferentiated. This is not to say that oppressive treatment of women in other cultures should be immune from criticism. Rather, gender issues should be discussed with the complexity, coherence, and cultural sensitivity necessary to avoid reinforcing distorted information, over-generalizing, or suggesting that choices around gender are always clear-cut.

Furthermore, educators have to become more aware that earlier feminist movements have been criticized for their lack of analysis of race and culture as an integral part of understanding gender relations. While much can be learned from Western feminism, it is important to realize that it is just one version of feminism and cannot be forced upon every minority woman. The notion of the universality of Western feminism needs to be challenged. Ahmed (1992) has convincingly exposed some of the limitations and ethnocentrism of Western feminism:

> As the history of Western women makes clear, there is no validity to the notion that the progress of women can be achieved only by abandoning the ways of an androcentric culture in favour of those of another culture. It was never argued, for instance, even by the most ardent nineteenth-century feminists, that the European women could liberate themselves from the oppressiveness of Victorian dress only by adopting the dress of another culture. Nor has it ever been argued, whether in Mary Wollstonecraft's day, when European women had no rights, or in our own day and even by the most radical feminists, that because male domination and injustice to women have existed throughout the West's recorded history, the only recourse for Western women is to abandon

Western culture and find themselves some other culture. The idea seems absurd, and yet this is routinely how the matter of improving the status of women is posed with respect to women in Arab and other non-western societies.

It has only recently been acknowledged that feminists from the third world, black women, Muslim women, and other marginalized women have challenged the essentialist notion of Western feminism. This is an important development that challenges and disrupts the taken-for-granted notion of gender issues in other cultures. Feminist theorists are becoming increasingly aware of the pitfalls of essentialism. The challenge seems to be the application of these theories to the level of practice, as many educators are not yet aware of these recent developments in feminist theories.

The Official Discourse of Anti-Racism: Dealing with Issues of Race and Gender and Their Connections

In Ontario, both multiculturalism and anti-racism have failed to respond to the complex issues of articulation of race and gender at both policy and curriculum levels. Within multiculturalism there have been implicit and explicit assumptions of cultural homogeneity in which gender relations were perceived as the essence of the culture. In fact, under the policy of multiculturalism, schools continue to promote existing assimilationist policies and, at best, only engage themselves with non-political forms of "cultural awareness," such as workshops and other add-on changes to the overall school's practices and curriculum. This leads to the view of the problem of racism as an outcome of individual attitudes, caused by a lack of familiarity with various cultures, that students bring to schools; little or no attention is paid to the significance of power relations (Rezai-Rashti 1995). It is certainly a mistake to suppose that

those who support multiculturalism assume a civil and political society in which all cultural identities would have the same legitimacy (Yuval-Davis 1997). In multiculturalism policies, the naturalization of the Western hegemonic culture continues while the minority cultures become reified and differentiated from normative human behaviour.

In 1991, political changes resulted in school boards being mandated to develop and adopt, by 1993,[5] a policy on anti-racism and ethnocultural equity. Policy/Program Memorandum No. 119 of the Ministry of Education and Training (1993) stated, "there is a growing recognition that educational structures, policies, and programs have been mainly European in perspective and have failed to take into account the viewpoints, experiences, and needs of aboriginal peoples and many racial and ethnocultural minorities." This statement confirmed that anti-racist and ethnocultural equity education goes beyond multicultural education, with its focus on teaching about the cultures and traditions of diverse groups.

However, the progressive nature of this policy, in terms of raising the issues of power differences among groups, did not make it immune from criticism. Like multiculturalism, anti-racism policy holds an essentialist and unproblematic concept of culture and identity in which ethnic and racial collectivities are still seen as stable, homogeneous, and undifferentiated. Such construction does not allow space for internal power conflicts within minority communities; for example, conflict along the lines of class, gender, and culture. It is interesting to note that in the 50-page document produced by the Ministry of Education and Training (1993) that outlines a policy for the school boards, only once is the word "gender" mentioned: "The impact of racism becomes compounded when two or more factors, such as race, gender, disability, sexual orientation, etc., are present in the same situation." Thus, while the policy puts into place the potential to confront certain forms of racism, it still assumes a hierarchy of race, gender, disability, and other significant issues. In this case, gender is used in a rhetorical form to acknowledge the awareness of gender dynamics, without having any significant role in the policy.

As can be seen, official multiculturalism and anti-racism discourses cannot sufficiently respond to the daily issues that Muslim girls have to negotiate. In my discussion of Muslim women's issues in the school setting, I tried to begin to look at the complexities of dealing with issues of race and gender in the complex articulation of religion, gender, and culture, especially in relation to diasporic Muslim communities within the education system. My comments should then be seen as a starting point to further engage educators in a positive dialogue around complex issues of identity, race, class, gender, culture, religion, and sexuality. We need to move beyond simplistic and fixed notions of race and identity in education, constructions that serve to perpetuate and naturalize the history of colonial relations. Educators will have to do more than notice individuals in trouble. They will need to question their own conceptualizations by encountering critiques of colonization and universal impulses of feminism and by listening differently to the lives of Muslim women and girls.

Notes

1. Some of these recent writings are D. Kandioti, ed., *Women, Islam and the State* (Philadelphia: Temple University Press, 1991); D. Kandioti, ed., *Gendering the Middle East: Emerging Perspectives* (Syracuse: Syracuse University Press, 1996); L. Ahmed, *Women and Gender in Islam* (New Haven: Yale University Press, 1992); F. Memissi, *The Veil and the Male Elite: A Feminist Interpretation of Women's Rights Movement in Islam* (New York: Addison-Wesley Publishing Company, 1991); L. Abu-Lugbod, ed., *Remaking Women: Feminism and Modernity in the Middle East* (Princeton: Princeton University Press, 1998); H. Badman and N. Tohidi, eds, *Women in Muslim Societies: Diversity within Unity* (Boulder, CO: Lynne Rienner Publishers, 1998).

2. See the debate in England over the opening of segregated Muslim girls' schools in which two well-known anti-racist theorists, Troyna and Carrington, engaged themselves in discussion with Walking and Brannigan, 1986 and 1987. "Anti-racist/Anti-sexist Education: A Possible Dilemma," *Journal of Moral Education* 16, 1.

3. I agree with the assertion made by Avtar Brah (1992) who, in studying the women of South Asian origins in England, argued that there is no evidence to suggest that conflicts among South Asian families are much different from those in white families. Asian parents tend to be portrayed as "authoritarian," "conservative," and supposedly "opposed to the liberating influences of schools." Yet, there is as much variation among Asian parents on issues concerning the education of their children as it can be expected in any other group of parents.

4. This term was first used by Stuart Hall, and then used by Yuval-Davis in *Gender and Nation* (1997).

5. The political changes in Ontario in recent years have had a significant impact on the education system, especially on issues of race and culture. The province's last Conservative government introduced drastic changes to the education system that are beyond the scope of the present study.

References

Abu-Lugbad, L., ed. 1998. *Remaking Women: Feminism and Modernity in the Middle East.* Princeton: Princeton University Press.

Ahmed, L. 1992. *Women and Gender in Islam.* New Haven: Yale University Press.

Ali, Y. 1992. "Muslim Women and the Politics of Ethnicity and Culture in Northern England." In G. Sagal and N. Yuval-Davis, eds, *Refusing Holy Orders: Women and Fundamentalism in Britain.* London: Virago Press.

Bhabha, H. 1994. *The Location of Culture.* London: Routledge.

Bannerji, H., ed. 1993. *Returning the Gaze: Essays on Racism, Feminism and Politics.* Toronto: Sister Vision Press.

Bannerji, H., L. Carty, K. Dehli, S. Heald, and K. McKenna, eds 1991. *Unsettling Relations: The University as a Site of Feminist Struggle.* Toronto: Women's Press.

Bodman, H., and N. Tohidi, eds 1998. *Women in Muslim Societies: Diversity within Unity.* London: Lynne Rienner Publishers.

Brah, A. 1992. "Women of South Asian Origin in Britain: Issues and Concerns." In P. Braham, A. Rattaosi, and R. Skellington, eds, *Racism and Antiracism: Inequalities, Opportunities and Politics.* London: The Open University Press.

Britzman, D. 1998. *Lost Subjects, Contested Objects: Toward a Psychoanalytic Inquiry of Learning.* Albany: State University of New York Press.

Cohen, P. 1992. "'It's Racism What Dunnit': Hidden Narratives in Theories of Racism." In J. Donald and A. Rattansi, eds, *"Race," Culture and Difference*. London: The Open University.

Collins, P. Hill. 1990. *Black Feminist Thought: Knowledge, Consciousness, and the Politics of Empowerment*. New York: Routledge.

———. 1998. *Fighting Words*. Minneapolis: University of Minnesota Press.

Haddad, Y., and J. Esposito, eds 1998. *Islam, Gender, and Social Change*. New York: Oxford University Press.

Hall, S. 1996. "New Ethnicities." In D. Morley and K. Chen, eds, *Stuart Hall: Critical Dialogues in Cultural Studies*. London: Routledge, 442–51.

hooks, b. 1981. *Ain't I a Woman: Black Women and Feminism*. Boston: South End Press.

———. 1990. *Yearning: Race, Gender and Cultural Politics*. Toronto: Between the Lines.

Kandioti, D. 1991. *Women, Islam and the State*. Philadelphia: Temple University Press.

McCarthy, C. 1998. *The Uses of Culture: Education and the Limits of Ethnic Affiliation*. New York: Routledge.

Memissi, F. 1991. *The Veil and the Male Elite: A Feminist Interpretation of Women's Rights Movement in Islam*. New York: Addison-Wesley.

Ministry of Education and Training, Ontario. 1993. *Antiracism and Ethnocultural Equity in School Boards: Guidelines for Policy Development and Implementation*.

Moghadam, V. 1991. "Islamist Movements and Women's Responses in the Middle East." *Gender and History* 3, 3: 268–84.

Mohanty, C. 1991. "Under Western Eyes: Feminist Scholarship and Colonial Discourse." In C. Mohanty et al., eds, *Third World Women and the Politics of Feminism*. Bloomington: Indiana University Press. 51–80.

Najmabadi, A. 1991. "Hazards of Modernity: Women, State and Ideology in Contemporary Iran." In D. Kandioti, ed., *Women, Islam and the State*. Philadelphia: Temple University Press, 48–76.

Ng, R. 1993. "Sexism, Racism, Canadian Nationalism." In H. Bannerji, ed., *Returning the Gaze: Essays on Racism, Feminism and Politics*. Toronto: Sister Vision Press.

Rattansi, A. 1992. "Changing the Subject? Racism, Culture and Education." In J. Donald and A. Rattansi, eds, *"Race," Culture and Difference*. New York: Sage Publication.

Rezai-Rashti, G. 1995. "Multicultural Education, Anti-racist Education, and Critical Pedagogy: Reflections on Everyday Practice." In R. Ng et al., eds, *Anti-racism, Feminism, and Critical Approaches to Education*. Westport, CT: Bergin & Garvey.

Sagal, G., and N. Yuval-Davis. 1992. *Refusing Holy Orders: Women and Fundamentalism in Britain*. London: Virago Press.

Said, E. 1978. *Orientalism*. London: Routledge & Kegan Paul.

———. 1981. *Covering Islam: How the Media and the Experts Determine How We See the Rest of the World*. New York: Pantheon Books.

———. 1993. *Culture and Imperialism*. New York: Alfred A. Knopf.

Troyna, B., and B. Carrington. 1987. "Antisexist/Antiracist Education—A False Dilemma: A Reply to Walking and Brannigan." *Journal of Moral Education* 16, 1: 60–5.

Yon, D. 1996. "Identity and Differences in the Caribbean Diaspora: A Case Study from Metropolitan Toronto." In A. Ruprecht and C. Taiana, eds, *The Reordering of Culture: Latin America, the Caribbean and Canada in the Hood*. Ottawa: Carleton University Press, 479–98.

Yuval-Davis, N. 1997. *Gender and Nation*. London: Sage Publications.

Questions for Critical Thought

1.   In what ways are Muslim women and Islam in general stereotyped in Western culture? Do you think the diversity in Islam and roles for Muslim women are sufficiently understood in the West? Do you think that Muslim women experience racial profiling in Canadian society? Why or why not?

2.   In what ways do young Muslim women experience both racism and sexism? How does the school system reinforce their inequality? How does the university do so? Should the university accommodate the specific needs of ethnic minorities, or should it treat all groups the same?

3.   What are these young Muslim women's responses to the pressure to assimilate to Canadian norms? What problem does this dilemma create for these young women? Can you think of an example where a Canadian Muslim woman has been able to balance her cultural identity with her civic identity? Can you think of an example where a Canadian Muslim woman has not been able to balance her cultural and civic identity? Why or why not?

4. How could equity education policies be changed to become more sensitive to young Muslim students? What would other groups of students stand to benefit from such a change? How could it benefit white Euro-Canadian students?

5. Why is Western feminism problematic for combating Muslim women's oppression? What changes need to take place to make feminism more responsive to the lives of non-Western women?

African Women and Canadian History: Demanding Our Place in the Curriculum

.... *Njoki Nathani Wane*

For as long as Europeans have called Canada home, so too have Africans. This fact, often marginalized if included at all, serves as an entry point for understanding Canada's past and the silence and selective memory that informs dominant understandings of Canadian history. Africans are one of Canada's founding people—alongside the French and British. Working from a black feminist discursive framework, this chapter articulates and centres some of our history as African women in Canada in order to establish a better footing for black feminist struggles today. The first section of this chapter briefly outlines the ideas, struggles, and resistance at the heart of black feminism in Canada. The second section, with a focus on education, looks at the way the invisibility of African-Canadian women has been constructed by different aspects of the Canadian colonial encounter. Included in this section is a comparative analysis of numerous curriculum documents to demonstrate the way African people are excised from history within the Ontario educational system. The third section is a timeline of events and achievements affecting or effected by African-Canadian women. The fourth and final section of this chapter examines some of the missing history of African-Canadian women's history. My aim in this article, which is based on some of the data collected for my research on African-Canadian feminisms,[1] is to provide a preliminary context on which to theorize African-Canadian women's

organizing. We must draw a clear link between the deepest roots and the tallest branches in order to understand the tree.

Missing Pieces: African Women in Canadian History

This misconception continues . . . and means that Black children entering the schools have no sense of Blacks being here for generations and, hence, that there is a 400-year presence and contribution of African-Canadians in this country. These children naturally feel invisible and marginalized. Of equal importance to us is that such a distorted sense of history minimizes the claims of African people to a role in the making of Canada. Further, this distortion suggests that racism is a new phenomenon in this country. (Bristow et al. 1994, 3)

Nine years and one month before Rosa Parks sparked the Montgomery Bus Boycott by refusing to move from the European section of the public bus, Viola Chambers found herself in jail for sitting in a Europeans-only section of a Nova Scotia theatre. The 31-year-old African-Canadian woman was not so quietly protesting Canadian racial segregation. Although the details of her trial (she was given no council) read like so many miscarriages of justice facing blacks at the time, her story is important because it provides a chronological anchor from which to begin analyzing and understanding the history of African-Canadian women and African-Canadian feminism. Viola Chambers's story connects with the voices of African-Canadian women who participated in my research and who provided detailed accounts of their activism, which does not make it into the Canadian history books (although it has been dramatized on CBC).

In my research, I asked participants[2] about their early experiences of activism. D.J. states,

> I can still remember like it was yesterday.... I was holding my mother's hand and walking to Maple Leaf Garden[s] with all these fellow Torontonians ... and everyone was yelling and screaming.... This particular rally was protesting against [Governor] George Wallace [of Alabama, who was advocating segregation]. That was in 1962.... From a twelve or eleven-year-old perspective ... I thought there could have been 200 people, maybe more.... This was a major event for me.... From that point I started to be black conscious and very involved with a number of organizations. I became more conscious of what my mother's group of women were doing in the Canadian Negro Women Club.

Talking to D.J. indicated that she did not always feel a sense of belonging in Canada. Stories of black women's activism were not part of the curriculum in her schooling. However, she was quick to add,

> Despite racism, I feel that I am Canadian, and have to be involved in issues of social justice, not necessary for me but for those to come after me.... I have to follow my mother's and my aunt's footsteps.

D.J.'s mother and aunt were both active in their communities around social justice issues. Their histories, and the histories of other black women, and men, before them, have not been acknowledged as part of the Canadian past. Although at times scared and intimidated, D.J. has not backed away from her involvement in feminist organizing and activism. She sees it as an extension of the work her mother's generation began:

> Looking at African Canadian women and their work ... it is something we did, we do not have to name it ... or claim it to be feminist.... Women of my mother's generation worked, advocated, organized.... They got things done.... Did they name it? Not necessarily.... Feminist organizing or feminism is not just about work and organizing.... Feminism to me is an independent spirit, and a way of trying to connect and correlate what you believe in terms of action ... that is in terms of black consciousness.

For all intents and purposes, the history of African-Canadians is a secret. Africans, if such a diverse group can be so called, are one of Canada's founding people—alongside the French and British. Unlike the European powers, however, they did not widely participate in the slaughter or domination of First Nations peoples. Instead, they decided, in many cases, to work with Aboriginal peoples toward their mutual freedom. The history of African-Canadian women specifically has been thrown further down the well than the history of African-Canadians in general. Ours is a forgotten past. This construction of a **blank spot** on the map of our history impacts our understanding of the present and of our identities within the present. When dominant history denies us access to our past, belittles that past, or ignores it, we suffer amputation from the very roots meant to give us life. History is a contested discursive terrain upon which many of the epistemological battles of the present are fought. The silence around the history of black people in this country is evidence of the ongoing colonial encounter that constitutes the Canadian national project.

African Canadian Feminism in Canada

While mainstream feminism responds largely to the oppression faced by European middle-class women, its gaze has missed the racial oppression experienced by women of African ancestry. African-Canadian feminism has thus arisen out of the wisdom, abilities, and efforts of women of African ancestry on the one hand, and out of the neglect of European feminist movements (first, second, and third wave) on the other. The emergence of African-Canadian feminism arose as a response to the unavailability of space outside of mainstream women's feminism and African-Canadian men's sexism (Hull and Smith 1982). This is clearly articulated by Carie in her comments related to her involvement with the National Action Committee on the Status of Women[3] (NAC):

> I think what was important for me was to examine the work of [the] feminist movement in terms of . . . the whole discussion of women issues, to really see which women had power and which women were benefiting from the movement. . . . When the leadership changed, the dialogues changed, and the priorities changed as well. . . . A woman of colour was the President. . . . Many women of colour demanded visible and tangible results. . . . The change in [NAC] leadership created . . . I think space for different issues to be taken up. . . . For instance . . . how were we integrating the issues of immigration, domestic workers, women who were on contract? How were we seeing issues of poverty? What was our relationship historically with other women? . . . And so there were [a] number of issues that black feminists prioritized, issues we had to deal with. . . . Here was an opportunity, to take up different issues. . . . Some women left the movement . . . others stayed.

For Carie, women's issues vary according to race, geographical location, status, class, etc. The multiple oppressions of racism, homophobia, ableism, sexism, classism, and ethnic discrimination facing women of African ancestry are different from those experienced by European women and African-Canadian men. The African-Canadian women who therefore got involved with the NAC wanted to address all these issues, as they affected black women in Canada, and this created a rift between white women and women of colour. As a result, some white women as well as some women of colour left the movement when Joan Grant Cummings assumed leadership of NAC. According to Carie,

> Some women of colour left . . . for different reasons. Also some women of European ancestry left to start other organizations and to focus on what they felt were their priorities. . . . I stayed. . . . Yes, I wanted to work on certain issues that were affecting many young women of colour. . . . I wanted to represent the youth.

From my interview with Carie it was clear that African-Canadian feminism addresses the experiences and realities of women of African ancestry, providing them with a concrete and secure forum in which to express, organize, and resist. Transhistorical, colonial, and neo-colonial relations in the Canadian context are unique inasmuch as people in this country have resisted these relations in specifically Canadian ways. The socio-racial makeup, as well as the economic, immigration, and cultural priorities of the Canadian state, serve to create distinct conditions of oppression and resistance in the Canadian context. African-Canadian women experience these variegated relations of oppression in tangible ways. It follows that this distinct yet dispersed community of women has suffered, organized, and resisted in unique ways; thus, African-Canadian feminism in Canada is distinct from that of our sisters to the South and elsewhere around the world. According to Tiara,

African Canadian feminist thought is layered and requires more textual analysis of women's experiences. I am not looking for a feminism that addresses only sexism or classism or homophobia.... We need a feminism or framework or theory that addresses all oppressions, oppressions which may be very difficult to articulate sometimes—for example, post-traumatic slavery.

In the mainstream feminist movement, African-Canadian women did not have a public voice, and as a result of these exclusions, women of African ancestry have developed their own strategies of social resistance.

Theories of resistance and collectivism intersect to provide a firm foundation for a collective and united understanding of black Canadian feminism. While all African-Canadian women experience the world they inhabit differently, they face common struggles in the Canadian context specifically, and the North American context more generally. Canadian black feminist thought is thus a creation of historical and contemporary forces that interweave with the lives of women of African ancestry (see also Wane 2007). These forces are mainly experiential in nature; that is, our experiences at school, at work, at home, on the streets, and our history, as well as those of our mothers and grandmothers, share commonalities.

Legacies Denied: African-Canadian Invisibility within Education

African-Canadian women, condemned by their colour and **caste**, became part of the slave trade in which approximately 15 to 20 million Africans were shipped abroad (Steady 1987). African women were controlled by the slave trade, even after its abolition, to continue reproducing for the system in both the United States and Canada. Women of African ancestry were contained and maintained within marginalized positions, suffering economic exploitation and occupying low

economic positions (Collins 2000; Steady 1987). As in many places in Africa today, women of African ancestry in Canada are the first to be under- or unemployed, and to be underpaid for their labour (Steady 1987). In disparate communities from coast to coast, African-Canadian women have organized, resisted, and identified their struggle in opposition to racist, sexist, and Eurocentric oppression for the last 400 years. Our textbooks, founding mythology, and dominant history have on the whole denied, ignored, and thus marginalized the presence, struggles, and accomplishments of African women in Canada. For example, the work of women like Catherine Albuquerque is rarely mentioned or taught. Women of African ancestry have ways of theorizing these omissions, as eloquently articulated by Shiea:

African Canadian women have always had different ways of organizing their feminist activities or theorizing their exclusionary experiences . . . starting with Catherine Albuquerque who built a school for African children in a church log house in the early nineteenth century—that is, African Canadian feminist organizing to me should be written all over feminist books.... It is hard to capture African-Canadian feminist organizing and how it has manifested itself over the last 100 years, however, we know it is there and we know it is growing—that is why we are sitting here today talking about it. It is a journey that doesn't really get captured in mainstream theories. I said to myself each person is a chapter in itself on black Canadian feminist organizing.... Your whole life is one project that you can look at in a story.... How do I look at this experience? How do I look at what happened to me when I came here 30 years ago, connect that with what is happening to me now?

Every February—"Black History" month—African-Canadian men and women are invited into many classrooms around the country. African faces magically appear on walls and in texts, along with profiles of various non-threatening African people, like black activist Elijah McCoy, only to disappear as quickly as they appeared, with the arrival of March. Beyond this "celebration" of various African individuals as a sort of pause within the broader Euro/Canadian focus of our schools, people of African ancestry remain outside Canadian history. Cleavage between oneself and one's history produces spiritual dislocation. Separation from one's past has a direct correlation to one's ability (or inability) to relate to the present. The silence around our histories is instructive, reinforcing the message that our histories are neither relevant nor valid. The implication is that if the wisdom and accomplishments of our past are not worthy of validation, then neither are our contributions in the present. Silence begets silence, and this also has implications for how we come to understand and theorize our place from a feminist standpoint. This point was elaborated on by Naid:

Being involved in this [research] project has made me realize the roles played by such feminist activists as MaryAnn Shadd. It has made me revisit feminist historiography that emphasizes the stories of women—however, these stories, unless they are told in such a way that all voices are included [means that] feminist history is not inclusive.

The paucity of historical accounts suggests the lack of a starting point for Caribbean feminists, African-American feminists, and African-Canadian feminists. Part of the challenge is to root our thinking about African-Canadian feminism in Canada in this historical context. Before we move to look at this history, however, it is critical to look at some of the tools that construct this silence. One is a perpetual Canadian self-identification and definition in oppositional relation to the United States of America. Canadians often define themselves by virtue of that which most of all we are not: American. The mythical construction goes something like this: It was the United States that had slavery and segregation

and whose horrid race-relations paradigm necessitated the famous civil rights movements of the 1960s. It is the United States who imposes its will globally, and the United States whose attitudes of manifest destiny define the nation to its very core. Canada (we/us) on the contrary is a tolerant place, where different cultures are welcomed and encouraged to retain and celebrate their culture. Canada needed no Malcolm X or Martin Luther King Jr for the problems they sought to resolve were never ours to begin with. Finally, Canada is a peacekeeping nation whose international interests extend only as far as our willingness to help others around the world!

In reality of course, slavery played an integral part in Canada's development as a wealthy colony/country. Segregation and civil rights movements played out from coast to coast in this country, and our contribution as peacekeepers (if such a thing ever existed) has morphed into a role as junior partner in the US imperial project, in line just behind the United Kingdom and Australia. As Arlo Kempf argues,

We must inform our understanding of the present with a critical transhistorical perspective, by challenging popular Canadian misunderstandings of historical racial oppression. For example, how is it we celebrate Canada for its role in the Underground Railroad but forget that upon arrival from the United States, Africans escaping to Canada were faced with many of the same forms of racial oppression from which they were fleeing? This is why, after coming out on our end of the Underground Railroad, so many went back to the States. (Kempf 2008)

Our educational systems provide powerful answers to this question, with examples of the processes of historical validation and omission. Although the **androcentrism**, **Eurocentrism**, and heterosexism that characterize our curriculum as a whole is instructive about domination on a number of levels, most striking is the treatment (or lack thereof) of African-Canadians in the provincially mandated curriculum of the Ontario government. The following data are taken from the curriculum documents that outline precisely what students are to be taught in given courses, grades, and subjects.

As a professor who prepares student teachers, I felt compelled to examine Canadian history. Also, in my interviews with women teachers, I asked them to elaborate about black Canadian women and their inclusion in Canadian education textbooks. (Canadian history is introduced in the curriculum in Grade 1, then 6, and is continued in Grades 7 and 8.) Learning expectations for all courses in Ontario are expressed through specific categories, with overall learning expectations for a given course (or grade) listed at the beginning of the expectations section. These curriculum guidelines for Ontario schools outline the major themes to be addressed in the delivery of the course. Specific learning expectations follow and expand upon the overall expectations, which are more numerous and provide the details of what is to be taught. If the overall expectations are the skeleton, the specific expectations are the meat on that skeleton.

A close reading of the policy document containing the expectations for social studies (Grades 1 to 6) and history and geography (Grades 7 and 8) reveals that of 18 overall expectations, none refer to black Canadians or African-Canadians, let alone African-Canadian women. Of 86 specific expectations, two refer to Africans in Canada. Finally, there is no reference whatsoever to slavery (Ministry of Education and Training 2004). In the secondary panel (high school), history is offered as part of the Canadian and World Studies discipline, the main goals of which (according to the curriculum document) ensure that students:

1. Develop the knowledge and values they need to become responsible, active, and informed Canadian citizens in the twenty-first century;
2. Apply the knowledge and skills they acquire in Canadian and World Studies courses to better understand their interactions with the natural environment; the political, economic, and

cultural interactions among groups of people; the relationship between technology and society; and the factors contributing to society's continual evolution. (Ministry of Education and Training 2005b, 14)

What is relevant here is the degree to which the curriculum intends to develop students as citizens and cultural actors within Canada. The education outlined in the curriculum is thus not simply fact memorization, but rather part of a culturally aware project of character building. When I asked Kris, one of the women teachers, about this omission, she said,

As an African Canadian woman, teaching in one of the elementary schools here, I was aware of these absences, however, I did not even think of women as a category, let alone, African Canadian feminist organizing. . . . This interview has given me ideas for my Grade 7 class next year. One of the assignments will be to research all African Canadian women's heroic acts in Canada. You know, I am a fourth generation [Canadian] from Nova Scotia and my grandparents always talked about the great women in our family. . . . However, I was so brainwashed that I did not want to think about it let alone research my history. . . . All through my life . . . I have been running away from myself. . . . I did not want to identify with African history . . . It was slave history . . . I wanted people to know me as Kris and that I had deep roots in Canada. . . . I guess as a teacher, I have no excuse. . . . I can always find ways of including African people's history.

The only mandatory Canadian history course in the secondary curriculum is *Canadian History Since World War I*, a course students usually take in Grade 10. An examination of the curriculum reveals that of 14 overall learning expectations, none make reference to black or African people. Of the 54 specific learning expectations, one makes reference to African-Canadians and one makes reference to Continental Africa—the latter referring to the AIDS crisis (Ministry of Education and Training 2005a).

In a culturally diverse society we must look critically at any cultural character building that ignores an entire people. Students have the opportunity to study Canadian history again in Grade 12, with *Canada: History, Identity and Culture*, although this is an elective course. The exclusion of people of African ancestry persists in this course as well. Despite a title that might indicate culturally inclusive course content, of 21 overall learning expectations, none makes any reference to African-Canadian people. Of 68 specific expectations, only three make reference to African-Canadian people, two of which are under immigration sections. There is no reference whatsoever to slavery. Interestingly, the same policy document outlines the expectations for the Grade 11 American history course, and makes numerous references to slavery in the United States (Ministry of Education and Training 2005b).

The omissions are not only a characteristic of the province's history curricula but also of other disciplines. Indeed, in the entire Grades 11 and 12 social science curriculum, among hundreds of expectations, there is only one that makes reference to Continental Africans or African-Canadian people or their achievements, and it is found in a course titled *The Fashion Industry*. The expectation reads as follows: students shall "demonstrate how various historical and cross-cultural influences are used in the creation of new fashion lines (e.g., Empire waistline; African, Chinese, Greek textile motifs)" (Ministry of Education and Training 2000b, 97). The entire English curriculum for Grades 9, 10, and 12 makes no reference to African-Canadians or Continental Africans, writers or scholars (Ministry of Education and Training 1999, 2003). Excluded along with the history of African-Canadians is the history of the accomplishments of Africans as a whole. The Ontario Ministry of Education learning expectations for Grade 12 philosophy make over 45 references to philosophers, only five of which are to non-Europeans, and none are to African thinkers (Public District School Board Writing Partnership

2002). The classical civilizations (Grade 12) course excludes Africans altogether from the broad designation inferred by the course's title. The course focuses entirely on ancient Greece and Rome, ignoring not only Afro-Asiatic contributions to these societies (despite the overwhelming evidence that such contributions are abundant) but also omitting African and Asian societies as a whole. The few mentions made refer to Asians (Persians) and Africans (Carthaginians) as the unworthy casualties of the Greek and Roman marches to civilization (Ministry of Education 2000a).

Taken as a whole, the silence is deafening. The curriculum confers illegitimacy upon those it excludes. For students schooled for privilege the message is clear: you, your history, your accomplishments, and your struggles matter. For racialized students, the opposite message is equally apparent: you are not the point. With a contestation of this very idea in mind, the following section begins a documentation of some of these marginalized histories, and provides a look at some of the literature and histories of African women in Canada in an attempt to formulate an African feminist Canadian history.

African-Canadian Women: A Transhistorical Understanding

Deep inside there is some colour stuff, but I really was not identifying with this when I was in Jamaica. I was "from Jamaica," that is how I knew myself—people in my village were mixed because during slavery there was a lot of mixing. They [the mixed people] considered themselves African too. Then I came here and all of a sudden I had to choose between being African, Jamaican, or Canadian. (Naoum)

The first record of an African person in Canada is that of Mathieu Da Costa in 1605. Although Da Costa was a free man, many Africans thereafter would come to this country, their bodies enslaved by Europeans (*Hymn to Freedom* 1994). Slavery in Canadian history constitutes a frightening historical blind spot. Institutionally, slavery provides an insight into the nature of oppression against African women specifically. Under slavery, African women were enslaved not only by their situations but also by their gender. The multiple jeopardies faced by African-Canadian women in the 1600s continue today. Although the institution of slavery as constructed in the time of Da Costa no longer exists, every African woman in Canada today faces race and gender oppression simultaneously. African-Canadian women also struggle along lines of sexuality, ethnicity, ability, and class. In the case of ethnicity and origin, African-Canadian women by no means constitute a homogeneous group. Although many African women trace their Canadian roots back 400 years, many African-Canadian women also trace their roots to the contemporary Caribbean, Africa, and the United States. The history of African-Canadian women unfolds before us and behind us to Jamaica, Trinidad, Haiti, Kenya, Ethiopia, and elsewhere. In order to understand our contemporary position within our history, we need to look beyond Canada's borders, currently and historically. The marginalization of African histories within Canada makes this task particularly necessary. With few historical accounts of African women, many people (of all races) have remained ignorant of the hardships endured by African-Canadian women here and abroad. No history exists in a vacuum and the case of African women in Canada powerfully demonstrates this point.

African-Canadian women can be (very) roughly understood as constituting two groups. The first is composed of people who have been here as long as the Europeans, in pockets from Nova Scotia to Montreal, to Southern Ontario, to the Prairies, and to British Columbia. The second group is those who came later to Canada from the Caribbean and Africa. As in many other societies that operate within racial hierarchies, Canadian citizenship does not make someone "Canadian." An informal but nonetheless powerful insider/outsider paradigm exists whereby Canadian = European, and immigrant = non-European. To return to the educational context once more, we see that Canadian history is European history, Canadian literature is European literature, and Canadians in history are Europeans in history. The divide, therefore, between African-Canadians who founded this nation and those who have arrived subsequently is thus moot; race trumps reality.

I am by no means advocating for a divide between new immigrant and non-immigrant bodies, but instead am pointing out the racialized nature of the process of Canadian identity construction. In this sense, the struggle for an African-centred Canadian history is a struggle against the way racial construction takes place in Canada—currently and historically. Thus, we have to unearth the past and re-centre the present and future.

Although the histories of all places from which African-Canadian women originate are relevant, they are too broad and varied to summarize here. A good place to start, however, is with some literature on Caribbean women's experiences, as Caribbean women have been in Canada from the beginning and are eternally positioned (despite their long histories here) as outsiders in the Canadian racial paradigm. Although such literature is scarce, among the existing works worth mentioning are Bridget Brereton's *Gendered Testimonies: Autobiographies, Diaries and Letters by Women as Sources for Caribbean History* (1998) and *Text, Testimony and Gender: An Examination of Some Texts by Women on the English-Speaking Caribbean from the 1770s to the 1920s* (1995). Providing further contextual analysis of the neglected contributions of women from the Caribbean is Hilary Beckles's *Historicizing Slavery in West Indian Feminisms* (1998).

For Brereton, diaries and private letters written in the nineteenth century by indigenous and European women have proved useful for capturing their situation, since few official documented materials of Caribbean women exist. Through their writings, the women provide a gendered insight into the setting and issues facing women of that period. It should be noted that the majority of letters reflect the educated European class as they had the opportunity to become learned and had access to writing materials. *Gendered Testimonies* reveals a society that was segregated along class and racial lines. African women who were enslaved recalled hardship and pain for their fellow women and witnessed many abuses at the hands of their European "masters" and "mistresses." Mary Prince, recalling her life as an enslaved person in Bermuda, witnessed "the murderous flogging of a pregnant fellow domestic, Hetty, followed by the birth of a dead infant and Hetty's own death" (Brereton 1998, 151). Slavery and its accompanying brutality are frequent topics in *Text, Testimony and Gender*. Excerpts from letters of three European women residing in the Caribbean point to the helplessness and defencelessness of being surrounded by a sea of African domestics. Maria Nugent, Elizabeth Fenwick, and Mrs A.C. Carmichael expressed similar accounts of African domestics, describing them as prone to "idleness," "pilfering," and "negligence" (Brereton 1995, 68–70). Unfortunately, Brereton's research reveals little about the ways enslaved women fought against their oppression.

Slavery in the West Indies has shaped the identities of African women (Beckles 1998). African enslaved women, as described by the European owners, were outside the bounds of feminine identity. Both their physical strength and their size belied masculine traits. Since African women were perceived as non-women and non-feminine, they could not "expect protection [or] support from European women, and had no line of defence against sexual assault" (Beckles 1998, 37). Some women of colour who were free opposed slavery and "developed sophisticated philosophical critiques of the slave system as representing a moral contradiction of humanist and Christian values" (Beckles 1998, 43). One such woman was Sarah Ann Gill, a Barbadian who campaigned against slavery, positing the incompatibility between slavery and Christian morality (Beckles 1998). Other contributors to the anti-slavery campaign

were two sisters, Anne and Elizabeth Hart, who lived in Antigua. During the 1820s, Elizabeth Hart demanded that enslaved people be given access to public education and be protected from any sexual predation from European men (Beckles 1998, 44). While these women fought for their enslaved counterparts, they were met with stubborn opposition from European slave-owners. If we accept the past as a terrain of struggle, we must necessarily emphasize the agentive elements of the history in question.

Adrienne Shadd (1994) examines the role of women working on both American and western Canada's soil during the period of the Underground Railroad in *The Lord Seemed to Say "Go": Women and the Underground Railroad Movement*. Shadd captures the neglected history of African women who participated in the Underground Railroad. These women, frequently overshadowed by the valour of Harriet Tubman, contributed to the freedom of female fugitives fleeing from the bonds of servitude. When the United States outlawed the overseas slave trade in 1807, the case to maintain enslaved African women became more pressing, as these women reproduced slave capital. The economic loss of an enslaved woman would be a blow for the enslaver/owner, for his future slave capital would disappear (Shadd 1994, 62). Women who risked their lives aiding enslaved Africans knew the dire consequences—imprisonment, torture, or worse, death—if caught.

In one heroic and daring incident that took place in Niagara, African women pinioned the sheriff and his men, stood fearlessly between the African and European men, and threw stones at the adversaries, all in an attempt to allow an enslaved African-American prisoner to escape from his jailors (Shadd 1994, 59–60). Hilary Beckles, Bridget Brereton, and Adrienne Shadd unearth the neglected deeds and perspectives of enslaved African women living in the diaspora. They provide the much-needed evidence of women who have endured danger, hardship, and suffering. These women provide a reference point from which lay people and academics alike can understand how historical experiences shatter the myths of Europeans as saviours and of enslaved people enjoying their enslavement.

Although dominant Canadian history tends to "forget" Canadian slavery while it so vehemently "remembers" its role in the Underground Railroad, most early African-Canadians did not arrive on this land as someone's property. So while it is important to understand that Canada, like the United States and Europe, is a product of the slave system and not the ingenuity or hard work of pioneering Europeans, we cannot read African-Canadian history as one of perpetual victimization. From coast to coast, African-Canadian settlements were established from the early 1800s onward. In all of these contexts, early African-Canadian women played integral roles in the sustenance and development of their people and their community. The areas around Halifax, Nova Scotia; Southern Ontario; Montreal, Quebec; and Victoria, British Columbia, were home to Canada's largest early settlements of African communities. While some were descended from enslaved ancestors in those areas and others were free or escaping from slavery in the United States, African communities arose in a climate of external friction and internal solidarity. Many Africans settled in Victoria, in response to mounting oppression in the United States as well as incentives from the local Canadian/British authorities. Years earlier, at the other end of the country, Africans freed from slavery in Jamaica were helping to create what is now Canada's oldest African settlement in Nova Scotia.

As Almeta Speaks (1994) demonstrates, these communities faced intense racism and oppression from the broader European community. We know that of the thousands of enslaved Africans who escaped from the United States into Canada during the relatively brief period (1833–1865) in which it was legal in the former but abolished in the latter, many returned to the United States after the Civil War brought slavery laws in line with international norms of the time. Further, we know that of the thousands of Maroons (formerly enslaved Africans from Jamaica who were freed and sent to Nova Scotia) many organized passage back to Africa (Speaks 1994). Such migration, back to the United States and to Africa, represents a considered response to Canadian racism and to the lack of opportunity for Africans in this newly emerging "land of opportunity." At the same time, Africans were faced with the task of community building internally. It is in this contextual duality between oppression and resistance that African-Canadian women emerged as community leaders and cultural custodians.

As far as community organizing, African women in Nova Scotia led their people through organizations like the Women's Institute of the African United Baptist Church, an organization still active today, which celebrates its elders and supports the community as a whole. In Montreal, the Coloured Women's Club (1902–present) sustained the African community during the Great Depression. The African immigrant community of Americans and West Indians sought and received the benevolence of the club, which, among other efforts, ran programs for the poor, coordinated an international relocation program, and was active in the advancement of women's rights. As far as resistance to external racial oppression, women in Ontario were central to the Underground Railroad and the ongoing struggles for the racial liberation of their people—a struggle that is still underway.

Conclusion

So, as we formulate a theory of African feminism in Canada, we do so in this historical and transhistorical context of our foremothers who remain at the centre of our communities. We can use the notions, or sites, of external and internal struggle and resistance to oppression in order to locate African feminism throughout our past and of course, within contemporary times. Externally, we resist by organizing, by writing, by fighting, by learning, by earning. Internally, we resist by rooting our families, by thinking, by loving our sisters and brothers, by mothering and other-mothering, by raising our youth and our community—at the same time, however, we struggle to define ourselves in a world all too happy to do that for us. We struggle, at the most fundamental levels, to be free in a society in which many people of African ancestry never asked to come to in the first place. We struggle and resist in a way that is unique to our oppression. We struggle, by the very way we are read as both female and non-European, in multiple ways. Without the historical accounts of black women, many would not know the stories of black women in Canada. This chapter has contributed to the scarcity of documentation in this area. More research is needed about the lives and histories of black people and black women in particular in Canada. Women of African ancestry must take up their pens and start documenting their stories.

Notes

1. In 2000, I introduced a course entitled *Black Feminist Thought*. Subsequently, I started searching for funds to carry out research in this area, more specifically, however, on black Canadian feminist thought. The aim of the study (funded by the Social Sciences and Humanities Research Council [SSHRC], 2005–2008) was to bring together the many strands of black feminist thought emerging across Canada by examining the historical, cultural, and ideological factors that have influenced black Canadian feminist theorizing. The study focuses on how personal, social, political, and economic experiences, cultural background, and other feminisms influence the basic principles of black Canadian feminist thought. In addition, the study examines what informs black Canadian feminist thought, how it is defined, lived, and named. The project provides an opportunity for black English-speaking women living in Canada to express their understanding of feminism according to their subjective and multiple realities.

2. Four hundred black Canadian women participated in my study from black communities in central, eastern, western Canada, and the Prairies. Three hundred filled out a questionnaire, while 40 women participated either in focus group discussions or in one-on-one interviews. The participants ranged in age from 25 to 68 years old and included community activists, academics, university and community college students, and women who work in unions, health care, education, social justice, social work, and politics, as well as homemakers. I interviewed women who were born in Canada as well as newcomers to Canada. In this chapter, pseudonyms are used for all the women who participated in this research.

3. The National Action Committee on the Status of Women (NAC) is the largest feminist organization in Canada. A coalition of more than 700 member groups, NAC has been fighting for women's equality for 27 years. NAC's membership is diverse and broadly based. Internationally, NAC has been participating in conferences and actions to promote international solidarity with women and advocating for women's equality rights globally. In 1996, Joan Grant Cummings, an African-Canadian woman, assumed leadership of the organization.

References

Atlantic Canadian History class assignments, Mount Allison University. 1991–93. www.ecf.toronto.edu/-shirley/african/timeline.html (accessed 8 March 2007).

Beckles, H.M. 1998. "Historicizing Slavery in West Indian Feminisms." *Feminist Review* 59, 1: 34–56.

Brereton, B. 1998. "Gendered Testimonies: Autobiographies, Diaries and Letters by Women as Sources for Caribbean History." *Feminist Review* 59, 1: 143–63.

Brereton, B. 1995. "Text, Testimony and Gender: An Examination of Some Texts by Women on the English-Speaking Caribbean from the 1770s to the 1920s." *Engendering History: Caribbean Women in Historical Perspective*. Kingston, Jamaica: Ian Randle, 63–93.

Bristow, P., D. Brand, L. Carty, A. Cooper, S. Hamilton, and A.L. Shadd, eds 1994. *"We're Rooted Here and They Can't Pull Us Up": Essays in African Canadian Women's History*. Toronto: University of Toronto Press.

Carty, L., ed. 1993. *And Still We Rise: Feminist Political Mobilizing in Contemporary Canada*. Toronto: Women's Press.

Collins, P. Hill. 2000. "The Social Construction of Black Feminist Thought." In *Black Feminist Thought: Knowledge, Consciousness and the Politics of Empowerment*. 2nd edn. New York: Routledge, 1–21.

Hull, G.T., and B. Smith. 1982. "Introduction: The Policies of Black Women's Studies." In G.T. Hull, P. Bell-Scott, and B. Smith, eds, *All the Women Are White, and All Blacks Are Men, but Some of Us Are Brave: Black Women's Studies*. Old Westbury, NY: Feminist Press, xvii-xxxii.

Hymn to Freedom. 1994. A. Speaks and S. Sweeney. Narr. Fil Fraser. Videocassette. Almeta Speaks Productions, Inc.

Kempf, A. 2008. "On the Souls of White Folks: Notes on the White *Crash* Conversation." In Philip Howard and George Sefa Dei, eds, *Crash Politics and Antiracism:*

Interrogations of Liberal Race Discourse. New York: Peter Lang, 91–109.

Ministry of Education and Training. 1999. *The Ontario Curriculum, Grades 9 and 10: English.* Toronto: Queen's Printer.

———. 2000a. *The Ontario Curriculum, Grades 11 and 12: Classical Studies and International Languages.* Toronto: Queen's Printer.

———. 2000b. *The Ontario Curriculum, Grades 11 and 12: Social Sciences and Humanities.* Toronto: Queen's Printer.

———. 2003. *The Ontario Secondary School Literacy Course (OSSLC), Grade 12.* Toronto: Queen's Press for Ontario.

———. 2004. *The Ontario Curriculum: Social Studies: Grades 1 to 6, History and Geography: Grades 7 and 8.* Toronto: Queen's Printer.

———. 2005a. *The Ontario Curriculum, Grades 9 and 10, Canadian and World Studies.* Toronto: Queen's Printer.

———. 2005b. *The Ontario Curriculum, Grades 11 and 12, Revised: Canadian and World Studies.* Toronto: Queen's Printer.

"Notable Dates in Canadian History." 1988. *The Canadian World Almanac and Book of Facts.* Toronto: Global Press, 21–27. www.ecf.toronto.edu/~shirley/african/timeline.html (accessed 8 March 2007).

Public District School Board Writing Partnership. 2002. *Course Profile, Philosophy: Questions and Theories,* *Grade 12, University Preparation.* Toronto: Queen's Printer for Ontario.

Shadd, A. 1994. "The Lord Seemed to Say 'Go': Women and the Underground Railroad Movement." In P. Bristow, D. Brand, L. Carty, A. Cooper, S. Hamilton, and A.L. Shadd. eds, *"We're Rooted Here and They Can't Pull Us Up": Essays in African Canadian Women's History.* Toronto: University of Toronto Press, 41–68.

Steady, F.C. 1987. "African Feminism: A Worldwide Perspective." In R. Terborg-Penn, S. Harley, A. B. Rushing, eds, *Women in Africa and the African Diaspora.* Washington, DC: Howard University Press, 2–34.

Wane, N.N. 2002. "Black Canadian Feminist Thought: Drawing from Experiences of My Sisters." In N.N. Wane, K. Deliovsky, and E. Lawson, eds, *Back to the Drawing Board: African Canadian Feminisms.* Toronto: Sumach Press, 29–53.

———. 2004. "Black Canadian Feminism Thought: Tensions and Possibilities." *Canadian Woman Studies/les cahiers de la femme* 23, 2: 145–154.

———. 2007. "Uncovering the Wells: Uncovering the Well: African Feminisms in Canada." Paper presented at the Indigenous Women's Conference, Trent University, Peterborough, ON, 17 March 2007.

Questions for Critical Thought

1. Why has there been a blank spot in the Canadian curriculum regarding the contribution of African and Caribbean women to Canadian history, according to Wane? Who is disadvantaged by this omission? Who benefits?

2. Why is it important that cultural groups learn about their ancestors? How can groups whose history has not been formally recorded gather information about their families and their cultural groups? How is this problem similar to what the First Nations people of Canada have experienced?

3. According to Wane, how has the black feminist movement sought to educate Canadians about the history of African and Caribbean women in Canadian history? Has it been successful? Can you think of examples of African and Caribbean women who have been the focus of attention in the Canadian school system curricula, the media, music, theatre, and/or the arts?

4. Wane contends that African and Caribbean women did not come to Canada as passive victims, but they have had a long history of resistance. What are some examples of this resistance? How can we incorporate this information into Canadian history both formally and informally?

5. Has the globalization of information in the world today due to the Internet and mass telecommunications systems made us more tolerant of and more knowledgeable about African and Caribbean women of various cultural, religious, and ethnic groups in Canada and in the world? Why or why not?

Conclusion

Although schooling assumes a level playing field for all participants, regardless of their gender, race, or class, schooling doesn't recognize inequalities of condition that affect students' prospects and opportunities. As a result, unequal outcomes are perpetuated. At this juncture, we can formulate some questions about merit. What if merit is based on a system that is unfair to begin with? What if it is awarded not on ostensibly objective measures but on the basis of access to opportunity, rewards, and resources? What if merit is inaccessible to those historically marginalized on the basis of gender, race, and class? What if merit just sounds fair yet sustains advantage for those already positioned to take up opportunity? Such questions challenge fundamental principles of our systems of education. The readings in this section have raised these questions and shown the consequences of conventional practices. The authors reveal the shortcomings of educating the individual without addressing the inequality of the collective.

Recommended Readings

Brenda Beaghan. 2001. "Micro Inequities and Everyday Inequalities: 'Race,' Gender, Sexuality, and Class in Medical School." *Canadian Journal of Sociology* 26, 4: 583–610.

- This 1990s study by Brenda Beaghan examines the microlevel and interactional informal practices of inclusion and exclusion used to convey messages to medical school students. Beaghan concludes that hierarchies of everyday inequality marginalize students according to their gender, race, class, and sexual orientation.

Agnes Calliste, and George Dei, eds, with Margarida Aguiar. 2001. *Critical Race and Gender Studies*. Halifax, NS: Fernwood.

- This collection examines how gendered and racially minoritized bodies negotiate and share identities across boundaries of time, culture, and space. The contributors examine the relational aspects of difference in a variety of social sites in an effort to enhance anti-racist feminist scholarship and practice.

Ratna Ghosh and Ali A. Abdi. 2013. *Education and the Politics of Difference*. Toronto: Canadian Scholars' Press.

- Ratna Ghosh and Ali A. Abdi examine the everyday reality of cultural minorities in the Canadian school system. Even though Canada is a multicultural country, educational policies and practices often marginalize and exclude racialized minorities and First Nations students from the political process of acquiring an education. Ghosh and Abdi use several case studies in order to study the implications that discriminatory practices that have emerged in the Canada school system, particularly in the post-9/11 world, have had on Canadian students. The authors envision a school system in the future that will embrace all students regardless of their gender, race, cultural, religious, or class background.

Anne Wagner, Sandra Acker, and Kimine Mayuzumi, eds 2009. *Whose University Is It Anyway? Power and Privilege on Gendered Terrain*. Halifax, NS: Fernwood.

- Even though universities have become more diverse over the past few decades, not all groups have achieved equality. This collection of 14 essays examines equity issues from various perspectives. The authors give examples of how the social location of an individual—for example, being a tenured professor, or a student, or a teaching assistant, or a part-time faculty member—is shaped by gender, race, age, and other forms of social inequality.

Terry Wotherspoon. 2014. *The Sociology of Education in Canada: Critical Perspectives*. 4th edn. Toronto: Oxford University Press.

- Terry Wotherspoon examines the Canadian school system and the political and social process of schooling. The author emphasizes the nature and the causes of social inequality in the Canadian education system, which he contends are due to systemic structural and cultural barriers that simultaneously silence some students while empowering others. Wotherspoon argues that issues such as bullying, new technologies in the classroom, and the biases of a "hidden curriculum" based on heteronormative and hegemonic racist discourses socially reproduce a pervasive class structure in Canadian society.

PART FOUR

....

Inequality and Health

I n this section, the general health of the Canadian population will be discussed using a critical sociological perspective. Each author proposes that women experience inequality through various forms of discrimination that are based on intersections of race and ethnicity, disability, size, sexuality, and class, and that are subsequently manifested individually and collectively in the health of the nation. This section examines, from a historical and comparative perspective, four major areas in the sociology of health and illness: the medicalization of women's bodies, formal and informal health care institutions, the role that health care personnel play in administering medical care to women with disabilities, and the political economy of the beauty industry. Public attitudes and current controversies about public health care policies reflect the narrow focus of the unifactorial model of disease characterizing modern medicine and deflect attention away from pertinent social issues. The authors address these controversies, and show how the social construction and the medicalization of women's bodies are important forms of social control.

The physical and emotional health of women who are disabled is the subject of Kari Krogh's reading on home care for women with disabilities. Krogh suggests that home care is a gendered issue, and that it is a site of oppression that is not experienced solely within the social structures of Canadian society. Instead, it is experienced through the physicality of the sometimes "invisible" chronic illnesses that women experience more frequently than men. In addition to being materially disadvantaged and caregivers themselves, many women who are disabled suffer from abuse by their home caregivers. Krogh suggests that home care programs that are self-directed, flexible, give the recipient choices, and allow women to act with agency will enable women with chronic health problems to become full citizens of the state.

The effect that culture and ethnicity have on immigrant women's health is the subject of Marian MacKinnon and Laura Lee Howard's reading. In their interviews with immigrant women, MacKinnon and Howard find that the Canadian medical care system erects barriers that prevent racialized women from receiving the health care to which they are entitled. Women's experiences with the medical system are complicated by their lack of language skills, cultural capital, and knowledge about the medical care system. In addition, health practitioners are not sensitive to many immigrant women's cultural, social, and alternative medical practices and needs, which may influence the health of immigrant women and their self-reporting behaviour. When women come to Canada, their morbidity rates increase and their health deteriorates due to the burdens that they must carry as immigrants, in addition to being caregivers and kin-keepers of their families. The problems that immigrant women typically experience—including underemployment; the loss of cultural, religious, and/or social identity; grief; loneliness; and social isolation—are stressors that subsequently affect their overall mental, social, and physical health.

The physical health of young women who are developing an "unfit identity" is the focus of the following reading, written by Carla Rice. She uses a feminist, poststructuralist analysis to examine the body narratives of diverse Canadian women who describe their social identity as one that is based on their size. Their identities are compounded by anti-fat messages from the media that not only suggest they are unhealthy and physically less capable, but also question their sexuality and their femininity. Rice concludes that women should deftly negotiate their identities and challenge anti-fat stereotypes that are socially and culturally constructed and transmitted by the media and other social institutions in Canadian society.

In the final reading in this section on health and inequality, Evelyn Nakano Glenn examines the role that the global media and the Internet have played in promoting the commodification of mercury-based skin-lightening products in printed ads, on the Internet, and in television commercials. She suggests that the ancient practice of colourism that was a form of social hierarchy based on gradations of skin colour has, despite the breakdown in traditional racial boundaries, escalated due to the globalization of transnational pharmaceutical and cosmetic corporations' campaigns. Light skin is regarded as a form of symbolic social capital, and young, upwardly mobile, darker-skinned women as well as aging, white-skinned women are consuming these unsafe products in order to enhance their attractiveness and desirability.

Redefining Home Care for Women with Disabilities: A Call for Citizenship

Kari Krogh

Introduction

For disabled women, home care is more than the provision of assistance that facilitates physical or emotional well-being—it is an essential pre-requisite for achieving full citizenship. Without formal and informal **home care**, women with disabilities cannot access the world and engage in their communities. Specifically, many women with long-term impairments require assistance with bathing, dressing, and eating before they can attend class, go to work, participate in a community event, or go out dancing with a friend.

In this chapter, I will explore ways that gender issues intersect with home care and home care policy to affect the lives of women with long-term impairments. I will focus on home care in the form of general personal assistance, personal hygiene or grooming, housework, meal preparation, errands, and informal health monitoring over the long term rather than medical and rehabilitative interventions or other therapies associated with post–acute care discharge from hospital. Many people with disabilities prefer to refer to such home care services as personal assistance or attendant care, emphasizing its location outside of the home, or home support to indicate its non-medical nature. For the purposes of this chapter I will use *home care* and *home support* interchangeably.

Home support can enable people with disabilities to move through various physical, social, economic, and political spaces to achieve their personal goals. For example, it might include assisting someone who has a mobility impairment in navigating within the home, neighbourhood, campus, and pool to achieve goals related to personal health, socialization, education, or employment.

I provide a definition of disability according to the central debates within the physical or mental impairment to the social, political, and economic forces that in effect create **disabling barriers**. I also recognize the value of a phenomenological description of the impairment experience in understanding issues such as fluctuations in levels of impairment and, consequently, care needs. Both these approaches can inform the ways that home support is understood in the lives of people with disabilities and ultimately assist in putting forward policy recommendations that would improve the lives of disabled women. I will draw on data I have collected as a researcher of home care from the perspectives of people with disabilities (e.g., Krogh 2001a, 2001b; Krogh, Johnson, and Bowman 2003; Krogh and the Home Support Action Group 2000). I will also incorporate what I have learned through my engagement with the disability community where the analysis is important but not always gendered. Finally, I will draw indirectly from my own experiences of providing and receiving care as a disabled woman.

Home care is a gendered issue (see, for example, Morris 2001), and disability, like other forms of disadvantage, adds an additional interwoven layer of complexity to the analysis. Women are more likely than men to need care and less likely to receive the level of assistance that they require (Roeher Institute 1995; Statistics Canada 2001a). Impairments related to mobility are more common in women as are chronic illnesses (Statistics Canada 2001b). Women frequently have their experiences dismissed and their need for assistance denied when they present less visible impairments such as pain and fatigue that are commonly associated with chronic conditions such as rheumatoid arthritis or fibromyalgia

(Council of Canadians with Disabilities 2002; Masuda 1998). Society's values are reflected in assessment procedures that not only act as part of a system of surveillance but also frequently render these women ineligible and unworthy of subsidized home care. Many women who live with long-term impairments also live with the effects of **gender socialization** and are expected to adopt and maintain caregiving roles even when these responsibilities clearly have a negative impact on their health (see, for example, Katz et al. 2000). With the exception of studies on older women and papers written by disabled women, an examination of the role of women with impairments in providing care is notably absent in the published literature.

Women with disabilities who require home care face inequities in society that may be complicated and reinforced by oppression based on, for example, economic status, sexual orientation, or race. They are underrepresented in the workforce (Fawcett 1996), and yet they are often not provided with the level of home care assistance that would enable them to receive an education, job training, or volunteer experience. Women with and without disabilities form a web of interactions and are affected by the powerful forces of globalization, privatization, and regional as well as national health and caregiving policy. It is critical that a feminist analysis of home care acknowledge and include a disability perspective. I propose that disability issues are ultimately women's issues. The category of "disabled" is frequently used to make us distinct, separate, and other. As a challenge to this, I invite women to recognize their current or future embodied connection to the terms "disabled," "care provider," and "care recipient."

One woman, whom I interviewed as part of a research study I coordinated on the impact of home care in the lives of people with disabilities, described how the meaning of home care differs for each person receiving care: "We are people who are still trying to live our lives, both before [and] even when we get to be seniors with disabilities . . . [We are] university students or professors or activists, we're television watchers, we're

people who want to run marathons. . . . I need people helping me . . . It took a lot of fight to get us out of institutions . . . to maintain our independence and freedom. . . . What is independence? What does it look like—it's different for everybody" (Krogh 2001a).

A Social Model of Disability

Defining the Social Model of Disability

The way society defines disability has profound implications for how health and home care issues, health policy, and policy participation are understood and approached. A social or sociopolitical model of disability has been presented by disability rights activists and academics within the emerging discipline of disability studies. It is presented here in an effort to locate home care for women with disabilities outside of a medical framework.

Barnes, Mercer, and Shakespeare (1999, 31) in their book, *Exploring Disability: A Sociological Introduction*, described the social model as follows:

> The social model focuses on the experience of disability, but not as something which exists purely at the level of individual psychology, or even interpersonal relations. Instead, it considers a wide range of social and material factors and conditions, such as family circumstances, income and financial support, education, employment, housing, transport and the built environment, and more besides. At the same time, the individual and collective conditions of disabled people are not fixed, and the experience of disability therefore also demonstrates an "emergent" and temporal character. This spans the individual's experience of disability, in the context of their overall biography, social relationships and life history, the wider circumstances of disabling barriers and attitudes in society,

and the impact of the state policies and welfare supports systems.

The social model of disability or the sociopolitical formulation of disability was characterized by Rioux (1997, 105) as follows:

1. disability is assumed not to be inherent to the individual independent of the social structure;
2. priority is given to the political, social, and built environment;
3. secondary rather than primary prevention is emphasized;
4. disability is recognized as difference rather than as an anomaly;
5. disability is viewed as the interaction of individuals with society;
6. inclusion of people with disabilities is seen as a public responsibility;
7. the unit of analysis is the social structure; and
8. the points of intervention are the social, environmental, and economic systems.

Transforming the Medical Model of Disability

This framework represents an important challenge to the medical model of disability which has dominated, and continues to dominate, the lives of disabled women and men by constructing them as clients or patients in need of improvement through treatment, surgery, rehabilitation, or remediation. The social model locates communities, institutions, and governments within society as sites where impairment (i.e., functional difference) is transformed into disability (i.e., oppression or barriers) and thus identifies society as the central place of intervention. Essential concepts within the home care debate are, in effect, transformed through this paradigmatic shift. Terms such as *care, control, expertise, professional dominance*, and *personal problem* are transformed into *rights, choice, experience, individual* and *collective responsibility*, and *social problem*. Within this model of disability, the focus becomes the

social pathology (e.g., structures) with an emphasis on elimination of systemic barriers (e.g., choice in care options) as well as the provision of political and social entitlements (e.g., reformulation of social policy; see Rioux 1997).

Researchers and government departments such as Human Resources Development Canada are increasingly recognizing the role of environment in the creation of disability. This is reflected to some extent, for example, in the Participation and Activity Limitation Survey that defines a person with disability as someone who reports difficulties with daily living activities, or who indicated that a physical or mental condition or health problem reduced the kind or amount of activities in which they could participate (Statistics Canada 2001b). The World Health Organization's (2001) new framework, the International Classification of Functioning, Disability and Health (ICF) examines the body, in addition to individual activities, social participation, and social environments, and recognizes the role of environmental factors in either facilitating functioning (body functions, activities, and participation) or raising barriers (see the Human Resources Development Canada's [2002] report, "Advancing the Inclusion of People with Disabilities").

A focus on impairment is problematic because it can be seen to emphasize a medical model of disability that focuses on the body while diverting attention away from political targets such as policy. Members of our society automatically assume a correlation between health and the perfect body. The discourse of the perfect body reveals and reinforces how society understands health in relation to disability. The differently abled or impaired body is assumed to be unhealthy when this would not necessarily be the case—there are, in fact, many people with impairments who experience good health in relation to their own standards or norms (Tighe 2001). While people with disabilities expect and desire good health care, they challenge the use of the medical model and notions of the perfect body in a discussion of home care.

This concern can be seen to be consistent with what Hooyman and Gonyea (1999, 165–6) present as a feminist model of health. In their opinion, "in a feminist model, health is not just an individual personal problem, but also the responsibility of community and government . . . [and] requires a strong public sector presence that takes leadership in defining policy directions to insure entitlement to health care based on rights of citizenship." This focus on citizenship is central to the disability analysis of home care policy. People who live with long-term impairments not only have insights related to their own bodies; they also have knowledge of ways to navigate through society to achieve their personal goals. Home support, when shaped by people with disabilities themselves, can enable full citizenship. However, this requires flexibility in service delivery, an acceptance of the active role of people with disabilities in society, and sufficient resources.

Making Space for Impairment and the Complexity of Chronic Illness

Phenomenology and the Social Model of Disability

Within the disability studies arena and the disability movement, there has been criticism that an emphasis on the social model has left little space for the phenomenological articulation of the experience of impairment. This is an issue of particular concern for women with disabilities, including those requiring home care, who wish to acknowledge and describe their bodily experience and not deny this as part of being fully human. In fact, women with chronic illness challenge the notion that oppression is experienced solely within social structures (and thus outside the body) when they describe the physicality of having their emotional and physical energy drained by particular interactions relating to evaluation of their home care eligibility.

There is a risk that descriptions of bodily pain may actually contribute to rather than challenge society's notions that equate disability with pain, sickness, and tragedy (Clare 1999; Wendell

2001). For women with long-term impairments, there is a concern that overmedicalization of their circumstances will cause the general public and health administrators to believe they need to reside in a long-term care institution when non-medical and community-based personal assistance is what they know they need (Snow 1992). Even worse, a focus on the experience of impairment could be misconstrued to justify acts of murder to end suffering as in the highly publicized instance of Tracy Latimer, the 12-year-old Canadian girl with cerebral palsy who was killed by her father (Malhotra 2001). Women with disabilities wish to be free to describe their bodily experiences and the challenges associated with the ongoing reassessment of the body within various social, physical, and political spaces. Women with disabilities also wish to be free to publicly celebrate their bodies and their lives as worth living. Disabled feminists such as Jenny Morris (2001) question why the social model cannot be adhered to while also making room for a description of the ways in which impairments affect women's lives. Women who live with impairments are calling for a reconsideration of disability in a manner that acknowledges the struggles within the impaired body enmeshed within a social world.

Women are more likely than men to be impaired by a chronic illness such as multiple sclerosis, rheumatoid arthritis, chronic fatigue immune dysfunction syndrome, depression, and fibromyalgia (Trypuc 1994; Wendell 2001). It is important that descriptions of living with these impairments are available to build an understanding of how women's daily tasks are or are not accomplished and supported through home care. The impairments that commonly accompany chronic illness include pain, fatigue, and memory difficulties. These forms of impairment last over six months and are less visible than other forms of impairment. Such conditions can also go into remission and then recur or fluctuate from day-to-day or change considerably over time, particularly if the condition is degenerative (Wendell 1996; 2001). Those who have multiple impairments including seasonal affective disorder may find that their need for personal supports follows a seasonal cycle. These types of impairments do not fit easily into home care "assessment instruments" and procedures—they are difficult to measure objectively and are impossible to separate from women's everyday bodily experience. Evaluators responsible for assessing eligibility for home care are often charged with the task of compartmentalizing symptoms within the body and rating impairment levels as if they are static.

Marginalization of Chronic Illness

Those who implement the assessment of need may lack knowledge of such conditions and question, "Why should you receive assistance? You certainly don't look disabled" (Rhonda Wiebe, a recipient of home care services, personal communication, 4 April 2003). Applying a Foucauldian analysis, the "**gaze**" of the home care assessor or administrator legitimizes the application of power over women with disabilities while excluding alternative interpretations (Foucault 1973; 1977). Women who face this form of discrimination would benefit from advocacy support from consumer-directed organizations. This is not always easy, given that chronic illness has been marginalized within the disability community. For example, Humphrey (2000) found that the propensity to consider only tangible impairments as evidence of a genuine disability clearly marginalizes those with non-apparent impairments while bolstering the claim of those with a visible impairment that they represent all disabled people. Further, women with these forms of impairment are frequently considered lazy, slackers, malingerers, uncooperative, hypochondriacs, or otherwise inadequate (Wendell 2001; Young 2000). Constructing women disabled by chronic illness in these ways functions to delegitimate their requests for assistance.

The value-laden gaze has increasingly been used to "scale bodies" against biological norms to determine social acceptability. Disability is ultimately a matter of degree—the bureaucratic and arbitrary line that is drawn between disabled and

not disabled enough in order to determine eligibility for service is based on what Young (2000, 170–1) and others have called a "politics of resentment" that motivates certain people, including health system administrators, to draw that line as far down the extreme end of the continuum as possible. This operates to build an expectation that people with disabilities will legally conform to certain socially constructed norms.

Embodiment and Home Care Assessment

Helen Meekosha (1999) reminded us that assuming a fixed disability status disadvantages women, who are more likely to have degenerative conditions such as multiple sclerosis and arthritis. Disabled women must "continually renegotiate the relationship between body, self and socially constructed disability" (175) in their day-to-day dealings with support systems. One example is chronic fatigue. Wendell (2001) described this as one of the most commonly misunderstood impairments associated with chronic illness. She explained how this particular form of fatigue is qualitatively different from healthy people's experience of fatigue in that it is more debilitating, lasts longer, and is less predictable. When she clearly articulates how every action requires energy, including thinking, watching, listening, speaking, and eating, the reader cannot help but understand the importance of personal assistance in the form of home support for people who experience this form of impairment, especially when it is recognized that "pushing oneself" can lead to risk of relapse, hospitalization, or permanent damage (25). Pain-related disability may also fluctuate over time. Pain impairment is more likely to be reported by women (11.4 per cent) than by men (8.8 per cent). In fact, young women with disabilities are much more likely to experience pain-related limitations (59.0 per cent) than their male counterparts (42.6 per cent) (Cossette and Duclos 2001). Like fatigue, descriptions of the embodied experience of pain can also inform us of the impact of this form of impairment on the need for support when undertaking activities of daily living.

Disputes between national and provincial medical bodies over their level of acceptance of a condition can also cause problems for individual women requesting assistance, especially when the province, responsible for administering home care, publicly denies that a condition such as fibromyalgia, for example, is legitimate. Current procedures for ensuring support discriminate against people, the majority of whom are women, who live with impairments related to conditions that are not always recognized by doctors or easily measured (Council of Canadians with Disabilities 2002). Even when conditions are recognized, they may be considered not sufficiently disabling to warrant service. Through a normalization of disability, society constructs and reinforces the notion that only those with particular impairments are legitimate and worthy of assistance. Professional discourses and texts of home care, including assessment tools and care provision guidelines, frequently operate to disregard women's experience of impairment. Dealing with challenges to their lived realities on an ongoing basis can take a heavy emotional and physical toll on the health of women with disabling chronic illness.

Home Care for Women with Disabilities

Women's Need for Care

Disability affects 12.4 per cent of the Canadian population residing within households. It affects more women (10.4 per cent) than men (9.4 per cent) between the ages of 15 and 64 years, and more women (42 per cent) than men (38 per cent) over 65 years of age. Overall, 13.3 per cent of women and 11.5 per cent of men report a disability (Human Resources Development Canada 2002). In terms of severity, in 2001, at least one in four persons with disabilities (26.9 per cent) experienced severe activity limitations, and 14.0 per cent reported having a very severe disability. A larger proportion of women with disabilities reported a severe level of activity limitation compared to men with disabilities (28.3 per cent vs. 25.1 per cent). Conversely, men (36.4 per cent) were more likely than women (32.2 per cent) to report a mild degree of limitation. In total, approximately 1,283,080 women reported having moderate to severe disabilities, whereas this level of impairment affected 971,780 men in 2001 (Human Resources Development Canada 2002).

In all age groups, women (12.2 per cent) are more likely to have mobility disabilities than men (8.6 per cent). During the working years (15–64 years of age), more women (8.3 per cent) than men (6.7 per cent) report that less visible pain-related impairment limited their activities. It is important to recognize that people frequently live with multiple impairments—only 18.2 per cent of people with disabilities report having a single form of impairment (Statistics Canada 2001b).

It is also worth noting that these statistics exclude the Yukon, Northwest Territories, and Nunavut, as well as First Nations reserves. The 2000–2001 Canadian Community Health Survey reported that overall rates of disability were significantly higher among Aboriginal peoples than other Canadians (31 per cent for those of working age and 53 per cent for seniors). Of those with disabilities identified in 1991, the Aboriginal Peoples Survey reported that 45 per cent had mobility impairments and 35 per cent had disabilities associated with agility (Human Resources Development Canada 2002).

Women and Men with Disabilities Receiving Care

More women with disabilities need support than men with disabilities. However, these women are less likely than their male counterparts to receive the level of care they need. The Participation and Activity Limitation Survey (1991) reported in "Advancing the Inclusion of Persons with Disabilities" that, while 1.1 million women with disabilities needed assistance, only 44 per cent of them received all the assistance they needed. In contrast, 700,000 men needed assistance and 50 per cent had all they needed (Human Resources Development Canada 2002).

The "Disability Supports: Patterns in Usage and Need among Adult Canadians with Disabilities" document prepared by the Roeher Institute (1995) reported that nearly two million adults with disabilities needed help with one or more everyday activities. Less than half of those (46.3 per cent) who needed help received all the assistance they needed, and 8 per cent needed help but received none. As stated earlier, women are less likely than men to have all the help they need. The same is true for:

- people outside the labour force who consider themselves completely prevented from working because of disability,
- people with low family incomes, people who are not receiving disability pensions/benefits,
- people with disability expenses that are not reimbursable by any plan,
- people living in rural communities,
- people with a severe level of disability, and
- older adults.

Major areas of unmet need for help with everyday activities include heavy household chores, regular housework, and grocery shopping, although there is also considerable need for help with meal preparation and personal finances. According to the Canadian Community Health Survey (2000–2001), 24 per cent of adults with disabilities stated that in the previous 12 months they did not receive all the health care they needed; in the 1994–1995 survey this statistic was 10 per cent (Human Resources Development Canada 2002; Statistics Canada 2001a).

Disability does not exist in isolation. It is important to recognize that women with disabilities experience "interlocking forms of oppression" related to class, race, sexual orientation, (dis)ability status, and form of impairment (see Razack 1999, 139). These factors affect one another and

function to maintain privilege for some and disadvantage for others. For example, women with disabilities experience high rates of unemployment and low or no literacy (Fawcett 1996). Literacy and employment exist within a set of care provision relations that operate to maintain an unjust position for women with disabilities in society. Women who survive on low incomes or who have limited education have greater levels of unmet need (Thomas 1996). Literacy plays a role in enabling people to navigate the health care bureaucracy (Canadian Centre on Disability Studies 2002). Without support to conduct activities of daily living, including engagement with informal and formal educational or job training settings, women with disabilities will continue to experience economic and social disadvantage.

Women who provide care are required to reorganize their lives in order to provide the care that their family members need, and women who receive care are forced to reshape personal relationships, such as the mother-daughter relationship, in order to have the care they require. Katz et al. (2000) found that older women with impairments received less informal care (15.7 hours) per week than men with impairments (21.2 hours). The disparity was even greater among married women with disabilities (14.8 hours) and married men with disabilities (26.2 hours). While 44.6 per cent of disabled women relied on their children for care, only 22.8 per cent of disabled men did. More than 80 per cent of these children were daughters, daughters-in-law, and granddaughters.

What often goes unrecognized is the fact that many disabled women also provide care to others. The research in this area is limited—probably influenced by the fact that researchers often equate disability with dependency and inadequacy by researchers (see Oliver 1992). However, 20 per cent of older disabled women with two or more impairments affecting their daily activities have been found to provide informal care to their spouses. This is a much greater proportion than the disabled male counterparts (8 per cent) who provide care to their spouses (Katz et al. 2000).

Disability and Care as Women's Issues

Gender, home care, impairment, and disability are interconnected, and yet there are, as Marika Morris (2001) pointed out, definite gaps in the literature as it pertains to women with disabilities. There are several ways in which women acquire disabilities more frequently than men. For example, women may acquire long-term impairments through domestic abuse and violence (Meekosha 1999). A number of studies have determined an association between care provision and deteriorating health in women (Canadian Study of Health and Aging 1994). For instance, Keating et al. (1999) found that almost one-third (27.5 per cent) of the female unpaid caregivers versus 10.6 per cent of male caregivers reported negative health effects resulting from their caregiving role. In fact, a recent study suggested that caregivers experiencing the strain of caregiving have 63 per cent higher mortality rates (Schultz and Beach 1999). Gender socialization is not only interwoven with issues of caring; it also plays a direct role in the mechanisms that cause impairment.

Enabling Citizenship for Women with Disabilities

Stereotypical images of citizenship are frequently associated with active and able-bodied white men. These notions need to be challenged. Women who live with disability, for example, are deserving of those conditions that would enable them to contribute fully to their communities, even if their means of engagement are unique.

It is important to consider the political, organizational, and interpersonal arrangements that affect the relationships intended to result in the provision of care. It is also critical that women's issues associated with both the provision and acceptance of support be considered. The Roeher Institute and Status of Women Canada (2001) produced a document entitled "Disability-Related Support Arrangements, Policy Options, and Implications for Women's Equality" in which

they proposed criteria for equality of well-being between women providing and receiving support, including: promotes self-determination, fosters mutual recognition, encourages respectful interdependence, ensures security, democratizes decision-making processes, and promotes citizenship. This report also stated that the promotion of the equality of women's well-being requires that attention be paid to entitlement to supports, assessment procedures, eligibility criteria, access, and the framework of benefits. Ultimately this requires "policy and program development that questions the current ideological basis of programs, and that is based on clear and consistent principles of human rights and criteria of equality of well-being" (88).

Caregiver–Receiver Relationship

The inclusion of the perspectives and voices of women who receive home care are essential to an analysis of home care, and issues that affect all women are inextricably linked to broader social and political factors. Globalization and privatization influence home care policies in ways that negatively impact women, both with and without disabilities, who provide and receive care. As a result of these forces, Canadians have witnessed the introduction of policies that shift care to the community without adequate resources. We have also seen a transfer of publicly administered home care services to privately operated and for-profit agencies and privatization that has resulted in the tendering of contracts to those agencies that cut costs by paying staff poorly and prohibiting unions. In addition, we have also witnessed processes that introduced new definitions of "disability" and "home care" in order to reduce the number of people eligible for service and the amount of service provided. All of these have an impact on the level and quality of care, and ultimately affect the provider and the recipient as well as their relationship.

Informal care provision transforms family life. The National Alliance for Care Giving and the American Association of Retired Persons (1997) found that 43 per cent of all caregivers report that their caregiving responsibilities have caused them to have less time for other family members than before and to forgo vacations, hobbies, and other personal activities (Bookwala and Schultz 2000).

In one focus group, women with disabilities stated that women with children should have enough government-subsidized home support to keep their families together and that their role as mother should not be devalued because of the acquisition or existence of impairment. The need for child care or child nurturing assistance has also been recognized within the disability community and yet only a couple of programs offer such a service—for example, the Centre for Independent Living in Toronto and the Centre for Independent Living in Winnipeg. Nurturing support is generally not considered a part of home care and tends only to be provided in extreme circumstances (Masuda 1998). Using home care services to meet child care needs is antithetical to a characterization of women with disabilities as asexual, passive, and dependent. In contrast to dominant notions of disability, sexuality, and parenting, O'Toole and Doe (2002) presented a discussion of the creative caregiving and innovative independence of disabled parents.

Institutional practices and the discourse of health care management in effect introduce and enforce new meanings for the act of caring, the care provider, and those receiving care. Women with impairments in need of assistance have their identity transformed through eligibility assessments that ignore complex, less visible impairments, emphasize inability, and assume passivity. Women informal care providers are expected to provide the majority of care with little or no financial compensation as part of their gendered role. The health care system regulates care, for example, by assessing and requiring informal supports before supplementing care formally within a community context. In these ways loving care becomes transformed into a relation of body maintenance.

Women's negotiation of providing and receiving care is complex. Stress arises in part because of the nature of the demands, and also because of apparent contradictions associated with multiple roles: for example, a young adult woman with a disability continues to depend upon a parent for her basic needs; a child is expected to provide daily personal care to her mother who has a disability; an older woman with memory, fatigue, and pain-related impairments continues to provide care to her husband even though she herself is in need of care. These are situations where government-subsidized home care can be introduced to protect full citizenship and opportunity for all women regardless of disability status or stage of life.

Dominant notions of a citizen as a white able-bodied male need to be challenged, as does the idea that worthy citizens are economically and physically independent taxpayers. In fact, the way we envision how citizenship is enacted—for example, as owning property—needs to be replaced by a much more inclusive and diverse vision. Home care is a prerequisite to full citizenship that is mediated through others—for women with disabilities, their rights, opportunities, and responsibilities may be achieved with the provision of formal or informal home support. The rights of the disabled care recipient have been given little attention when the rights of the provider have been emphasized (Walmsley 1993). Consider, for example, the introduction of unions and other forms of safeguards for workers but no equivalent for recipients. As women we need to recognize that these are important considerations for employees and we also need to acknowledge consumers' concern that governments typically find the resources by reducing services to people with disabilities (Mary Ennis, personal communication, 6 April 2003). Administrators who use economic arguments to present provider and receiver needs as mutually exclusive need to be challenged as part of a process of building linkages among disabled and able-bodied women. Canadian policy makers should address both sets of concerns in recognition of citizenship rights for all women.

The care relationship has been examined by disability scholars, and, while some will argue that all people are interdependent (Shakespeare 2000), others will emphasize that this form of relating is qualitatively distinct. There are important power relations to acknowledge. For example, Twig (2000) described inherently unequal relations within the dynamic of nakedness during bathing when one person is undressed in the presence of another who is fully clothed. In fact, Morris (2001, 13) claimed that "the more personal the task, the greater the potential for abuse of human rights—and the greater the potential for the 'caregiver' to protect and promote human rights." The care provider's role can be central to achieving full personhood for a woman with a disability. Thus, the protection of human rights must be placed at the forefront of our discussions of home care.

One woman with a disability involved in the study described home care and policy making in the following way: "It's hard enough trying to maintain a life but when you have to rely on other people to help you, you have to be so accommodating, so patient, but that doesn't mean you want to be accommodating and patient to government officials who think that our lives are less valuable" (Krogh 2001a). Members of society often think of patience as a descriptor for the care provider, but within this reciprocal relationship, both parties require patience and need to understand the sources of strain that originate outside the relationship. When government-subsidized home care is not provided at sufficient levels, it is not uncommon for recipients to consider this an attack on the value of their contribution as well as their ability and right to contribute economically, socially, and politically to their communities (Krogh 2001a).

When women in society are expected to care for others regardless of their own physical, emotional, intellectual, and spiritual needs, they become at risk of developing health problems that may interfere directly with the quality of care provision. In fact, as a result of such circumstances, women with disabilities who receive care may be at risk for neglect and abuse. Studies indicate that caregiving responsibilities result in personal and interpersonal loss and that the quality of the caregiver–care recipient relationship deteriorates with increasing care demands (Bookwala and Schultz 2000; Williamson, Shaffer, and Schultz 1998). It has also been found that caregiving wives rated their ongoing relationship with the care recipient to be poorer than did caregiving husbands (Bookwala and Schultz 2000). Among some female providers of care, there has been a demonstrated correlation between higher levels of physical and emotional strain (Bookwala and Schultz 1998) as well as greater depressive symptoms in the caregivers (Bookwala, Yee, and Schultz 2000), with perceived higher levels of "behaviour problems" in the care recipient. This transformation within the caring relationship could in part be related to the fact that the family becomes engulfed by a health care system that emphasizes, and in fact necessitates, a conceptualization of the care recipient as passive, needy, and dependent.

Abuse and Care

Abuse by personal assistance providers is a significant problem, especially for women with disabilities. In comparison to able-bodied women, women with disabilities have been found to be more likely to experience abuse by personal assistants and health providers, and they were more likely to experience abuse over a longer time period (Saxton et al. 2001). Sobsey and Doe (1991) also found that having a disability and receiving disability supports played a distinct role in making people vulnerable to abuse. In 44 per cent of cases they examined, the abuse took place within a relationship specifically related to the person's disability. In particular, 28 per cent of abusers were service providers such as personal care assistants. Less than half of the women reported the abuse because of their fear and their dependence on the abuser.

Abuse or harassment can be linked to multiple sites of discrimination related to, for example, gender, disability, or sexual orientation. One woman who relies on home care described the need for peer support for women who receive care and who want to live their lives fully and openly with dignity: "Home support, making people aware of the fact that we have the right to live in our own apartments, we have the right to live our own lives and to live our lives the way we choose, including being gay and living in that lifestyle and all that entails. To have safety around that, to teach people if you're being abused, it's okay to say something. Just because these people care for you doesn't mean they have the right to abuse you" (Krogh, Johnson, and Bowman 2003).

The form of the abuse must be understood within the unique life context of women with disabilities, including their need for care. For example, women with disabilities may experience neglect and abuse when, after an argument with their care provider, they are left undressed in the shower or on the toilet for long periods of time. Women with disabilities are vulnerable to the effects of a society that devalues them while placing care providers under high levels of personal, physical, emotional, and financial stress. In one study women with disabilities identified feeling "mistreated or disrespected by their case managers," "lost in bureaucracy," or being "unfairly rejected for services by agencies" as forms of abuse (Saxton et al. 2001, 406). When such abuse and neglect occurs, the ability of women with disabilities to participate in daily life activities is compromised as much as their personal emotional and physical health and safety.

High levels of violence, sexual abuse, and neglect exist among disabled women (Sobsey and Doe 1991). Given this situation, choice and control over who, when, and how care is provided are important considerations for women with disabilities. One woman who grew up in the government system of "care" spoke in her interview with me about the significance of being able to create a safe space for herself by receiving her care through a self-managed care system whereby she personally selected the people hired to provide her personal care:

Home to me means, a little bit different maybe than most people, my home here is the first home I ever had in my life, a space that's mine, a space where I can kind of recoup [sic] from the rest of the world and people that I can bring into my life that I choose to have in my life and feeling safe about it, because I've never had the traditional home life. With that comes working in the framework that I choose to work from as opposed to institutional living or institutional structure and I'm very particular about who I let into my home. (Krogh, 2001a)

Care as Control and Surveillance

Controlling forces in society construct people with disabilities. Limiting notions of disability are commonly reflected and reinforced by care systems and the interpersonal relationships they encompass (Krogh 2001a). When values that equate disability with dependence become codified within professional discourses, they function as forms of surveillance and discipline (see Foucault 1977) and are thus disabling. In effect, these disabling values can operate ideologically to obscure central issues for people with disabilities, namely social participation and full citizenship (Priestley 1999).

Independence for people with disabilities does not mean doing everything for oneself, but it does mean having personal control over how help is provided. A pervasive characteristic of policy making within the community-based care arena has been the construction of disability as dependency. A unidirectional and causal relationship between impairment and dependency is typically assumed and has been challenged by disability studies scholars such as Michael Oliver (see Oliver 1996). When people with disabilities are assumed to be dependent, they become objects of control.

The central focus should be on issues of citizenship and rights as well as notions of choice and control over care. As Jenny Morris (2001) clearly stated, "Whatever 'care' is—whether it is in the form of formal services, cash payments, or personal relationships—if it does not enable people 'to state an opinion,' 'to participate in decisions which affect their lives' and 'to share fully in the social life of their community,' then it will be unethical" (15). She concludes that society is in need of an ethic of care based on the principle that to deny the human rights of our fellow human beings is to undermine our own humanity. Home care provision should recognize that all people, regardless of the nature of their impairment, have the capacity to express preferences.

Even when services are supplied directly to the person with a disability, they are frequently not delivered in a way that enables people with disabilities to have control over their activities of daily living or community participation (Barnes, Mercer, and Shakespeare 1999). Disabled researchers have pointed out their concern that care providers are viewed to be in need of resources and support—it is implied that they are in a position to speak on behalf of those who require care (Morris 1993). Given these restrictions, community care has been described as "the most exploitative of all forms of so-called care delivered in our society today for it exploits both the person providing and receiving care and these are most likely to be women rather than men. It ruins relationships between people and results in thwarted life opportunities on both sides of the caring equation" (Brisenden 1989, 10).

The focus of care administration is not on how care can be provided to support individuals in meeting their self-identified needs within a framework of their immediate and longer term life priorities, but on monitoring what type of care service is provided—when, where, by whom, and at what level. Care management procedures and instruments function to control expenditures (Browne 2000). They are also products of a society that constructs and expects people with disabilities to be dependent, passive, and

eternally grateful (see, for example, Linton 1998 for a discussion of this construction of disability). Morgan's (1995) study results, based on a social service survey of 26,000 households, found that only 7 per cent of the households had long-term sick or disabled persons within them. Of these households, only 2 per cent reported any use of social services, challenging dominant notions of people with disabilities as a drain on the system.

Female bodies are more likely to be the objects of regulation and surveillance by a patriarchal state (Meekosha 1999). Disabled women, in greater numbers than disabled men, have been incarcerated in prisons, hospitals, nursing homes, and a multitude of institutions (Australian Institute of Health and Welfare 1993). Women are also overrepresented as social service recipients (Ferguson 2000). When women with disabilities attempt to access services such as government-subsidized home care, they must be expected to give up what Orme (2001) referred to as their right to freedom from interference and their right not to reveal details of their personal life.

In addition, people with disabilities effectively have their everyday lives dominated by a health care management system of assessment and surveillance that does not offer adequate access to appeal procedures or independent confidential complaint mechanisms. The Council of Canadians with Disabilities (CCD) stated that the most common reason why people with impairments seek medical appointments is to have their disability certified in order to receive benefits. CCD seriously questioned whether this form of surveillance is the best use of Canada's health resources (Council of Canadians with Disabilities 2002, 47). In a national study conducted by the DisAbled Women's Network (Masuda 1998), one participant described control in relation to a woman with a mental health disability who was cut off from benefits because she had not seen her doctor regularly. She stated, "You are required to make regular visits to your doctor, whether or not you need it, just to reaffirm that you are still disabled" (4). In general, the women with disabilities described how it was increasingly difficult to qualify for disability benefits. A woman in Nova Scotia stated, "It seems there is a fear that people may be pretending to be disabled and someone may actually get benefits that they don't deserve. When applying for benefits, women with mental health disabilities are always turned down unless they have strong advocacy support" (4). Similar circumstances exist for people who rely on benefits, including home care service associated with employee benefits programs after they acquire a long-term impairment.

Silencing the "Other"

Cultural imperialism involves the universalization of a dominant group's experience and culture resulting in its establishment as the norm (Bourdieu and Passeron 1977; Young 1990). Through this process people with disabilities are simultaneously made invisible through cultural norms and identified as visibly different, reinforced by stereotypes. Ultimately these function to "create and isolate the 'other.'" Proctor (2001) offers an important piece of work in which older people with memory impairments come to see themselves as unworthy of even an explanation of their care. One participant in Proctor's study stated, "I should have been given an explanation. Well, I shouldn't. They haven't got time to give everyone explanations" (369). This example illustrates how dominant norms or notions related to being a passive and grateful recipient of care can become internalized by women with disabilities. It also represents a form of symbolic violence (Bourdieu 1985).

To be successful in applying for home care, a person with a disability must often internalize assessment standards, clearly articulating and demonstrating her dependency. While this process can be viewed as an act of legitimating administrative surveillance (see Foucault 1977), it is also often experienced, at the immediate individual level, as a necessary act for survival. Emphasizing dependency creates an internal discord for many people who live with impairments, as it runs counter to many individuals' goals to

live and be portrayed as self-determining and independent or interdependent. The direct funding programs represent one way that notions of need for care and self-direction have attempted to be reconciled, but the outcome has been one of mixed results.

Self-Directed Care

Self-managed care programs are under provincial jurisdiction—and therefore differ among the provinces in terms of administrative structures and eligibility criteria (Keefe and Fancey 1998)—and are intended to increase choice and control by enabling care recipients to purchase and manage their own home care. Within this model, the consumer receives funds directly from the government or via a government-appointed non-profit agency such as an Independent Living Resource Centre. By way of a contract, the person with long-term impairments who requires assistance agrees to act as the employer and use the funds for purchasing services. In this way, the government attempts to no longer be responsible for employer responsibilities such as those associated with labour standards.

These programs have tremendous potential because of the increased levels of choice, control, and independence. However, in reality, there are several challenges that limit the realization of these ideals. The consumer is expected to assume the roles of personnel manager, financial administrator, and staff trainer without compensation. While it is clear that such a system saves money, it is frustrating for consumers who are not provided with enough funds to ensure reliable and quality care. Employees must often be willing to work at a lower wage with fewer benefits compared to most agency or government-administered care. As the coordinator of the Home Support Action Group in Victoria, BC, explained, "the fundamental flaw of these programs is that they are set up so that the potential for self-determination is the very last consideration" (Gordon Argyle, personal communication, 7 April 2003).

As stated previously, people who receive services may internalize the dominant societal norms reflected in home care policy, administration, and service. Interestingly, there has been some research on how people who use direct funding come to view themselves in relation to their impairment and society. Those who received services delivered through traditional means tended to view their own impairment and its effects on mobility as the cause of their problems. In contrast, those people who directed their own care were more likely to view barriers outside of the body in locations such as physical architecture and societal attitudes (Kvetoslava 1999). This shift corresponds with a move away from an internalization of an individualized medical model of disability to one that more holistically portrays disability within a sociopolitical context.

The personal control that can be associated with self-directed care provides a sense of safety for some women with disabilities. One female participant stated, "I fought so hard to get here, so hard to have independence and so hard to have safety.... If you give me the control, I have an element of safety but if somebody else has that control, I would be devastated" (Krogh 2001a).

Some research indicated that the majority of people with disabilities wish to have the option of receiving their care through a self-directed program rather than administered through an agency (Kestenbaum 1992). This research also found that such programs produce increased flexibility in terms of what types of services are provided and when. They are frequently perceived as empowering because recipients have a greater say in developing and monitoring their own support system and in leading their lives as they choose (Kestenbaum 1993a, 1993b; Morris 1993). From the funder's perspective, it has been viewed as a less costly option than government-administered community-based care or residential services (Hollander et al. 2002).

The role of disability organizations in providing peer support to those using self-directed care is critical given that oppression and exclusion result in fewer opportunities for people with disabilities

to develop their skills as managers. A central purpose of the care—namely, exercising citizenship rights for community participation—needs to be acknowledged. Without addressing these concerns, direct funding only provides women and men with disabilities with an opportunity to become more directly involved in a system that oppresses them.

Flexibility in relation to the nature and site of all home care service is required regardless of the system of administration. Home care, when it works well, can enable many people with disabilities to define themselves and their lifestyles in ways that might counter dominant societal norms. Referring to cuts in services and service options, one participant stated, "It will affect our freedom, our level of independence and what we classify as independence being stuck back in boxes as opposed to being able to choose, people imposing values and beliefs . . . of how it should be" (Krogh 2001a).

However, self-determination is only possible when adequate levels of resources are provided. As Priestley (1999) contended, those who do not have adequate levels of resources are placed in a position of "self-regulation and surveillance, forced to impose upon themselves the values of a welfare system which prioritizes treatment over social integration and participatory citizenship" (670).

Economics and Efficiency

Economics

Many studies have calculated the costs of care and projected economic comparisons between institutional and community-based care. For example, the total home care (all forms of home care including post-acute care) spending in Canada was $3.4 billion in the 2000–1 fiscal year. Of this amount, about $0.7 billion (20 per cent) came from private sources and the remaining $2.7 billion (80 per cent) from public sources (Coyte 2000). The rhetoric during the past decade espoused a need to manage uncontrolled health care spending. However, such concerns arose at the same time that those costs began to stabilize as a share of the Gross Domestic Product (Evans 1993), and by the mid-1990s governments at all levels had contained health care costs (Rachlis and Kushner 1994).

Costs and impacts of home care versus institutional care have been investigated in a series of 15 sub-studies coordinated by Neena Chappell and Marcus Hollander. One of these studies (Hollander et al. 2002), for example, included 580 individuals over 65 years of age in BC and Manitoba who require home or institutional care. It was found that home care costs to government were, on average, approximately 40 to 50 per cent of residential care costs. Interestingly, it was found that recipients of home care services and informal caregivers contributed approximately half of the care costs of the community clients and about one-third of the care costs of facility clients. This demonstrates how the shift away from hospital-based care to community-based care has been used to redirect and reduce costs for governments. They conclude their study with the question, "Is it reasonable for government to pay fully for short-term curative care provided by physicians and hospitals but not pay the same proportion for people with ongoing care needs?" (3).

Efficiency

As an ideology, efficiency is used to justify the erosion of the Canadian health care system (Burke 2000). Underlying the use of efficiency as a measure of public policy worth is the debate between the role of the state versus the role of the market. It also reflects an appreciation of independent, rather than collective or interdependent, notions of rights and responsibilities (Tuohy 1992). This has direct implications for people with disabilities who wish to live independently or interdependently. Canadian politics increasingly favours the market, decentralization, and individualism, which will continue to have a negative impact on women who provide and receive informal and formal care.

Efficiency is part of an atomizing, isolating, and individualizing discourse, and it operates to degrade social capital in the form of social organization, including networks, norms, and trust (Putnam 1993). Such social capital is crucial to social coordination and the organization of forms of resistance to change. Efficiency can thus be used to reduce social and political participation of citizens. Burke (2000) argued that ultimately the principles of quality, equity, and universality are being sacrificed to the narrow concerns of efficiency. As illustrated elsewhere in this chapter, this has been witnessed in relation to home care and, specifically, women.

Numerous researchers have pointed out that economic arguments for home care do not consider all of the true costs of care, particularly as they relate to the impacts upon women caregivers (Fast, Williamson, and Keating 1999). Disabled people are directed to rely largely on informal care providers, charities, and non-profit organizations for the support they need (Krogh, Johnson, and Bowman 2003; Krogh 2001a). For people with disabilities, relying on unskilled community volunteers to provide home care through charities is problematic for many reasons. Not least, it requires people with disabilities to assume the degrading role of objects of pity in order to get what they need. In response to the final recommendations report of the Romanow Commission on the Future of Health Care in Canada, the Council of Canadians with Disabilities wrote to the federal minister of health commending the recommended efforts to begin to address the home support needs of people with mental health disabilities. The council also clearly stated their overall concerns about the low priority given to home support for people with all forms of impairment. CCD wrote, "it is a grave disservice to a host of persons with disabilities across Canada that Mr. Romanow has decided that their home support needs are not on a par to those of other populations. It is especially alarming that Mr. Romanow has decided that our citizenship rights are too expensive to be maintained, therefore our needs are not a priority worthy of being addressed in a timely and appropriate fashion" (Council of Canadians with Disabilities, 22 January 2003).

When people with disabilities are required to approach charities for basic services such as baths, they are thus invited to participate in their own oppression by constructing themselves in terms of their personal failings and as objects of pity, rather than in terms of their abilities and valuable contributions to society, or as citizens deserving of a basic right to self-determination (Krogh, Johnson, and Bowman 2003). The option of going to a consumer-directed organization for peer support or care management training is seriously impeded when these non-profit community organizations have their core funding continually reduced or threatened (Boyce et al. 1999). Michael Hall and Paul Reed (1998) concluded that the second social net of voluntary organizations is too small and vulnerable to handle what governments expect of them when they cut funding to such organizations and their programs.

Efficiency necessitates the construction of care recipients as passive and dependent and does not make room for either notions of collaborative engagement in tasks or consumer prioritization of activities to support social and economic participation in society from the perspective of the person receiving home care. A self-determined process can take time—a person with an impairment affecting learning or cognition may need concepts presented in plain language supplemented with drawings, and if socialized to be passive, she may need access to peer support to review her options before making a decision. A person receiving information related to such a decision from a woman using an augmentative and alternative communication system will need to wait to receive information as each symbol or letter is pointed to in sequence.

Efficiency discourse poses several problems for people with disabilities. In terms of service and accomplishment of home care-related tasks, people with disabilities often accomplish their tasks differently from able-bodied people. For many it is centrally important that they participate as much as possible in directing and engaging in their activities of daily living, including services provided through home care, even if it takes longer. A service system that emphasizes time is inherently problematic, especially when this is done at the expense of self-determination and dignity for people who live with impairments.

The needs and desires of people with disabilities become secondary to the efficiency of the system. Referring to a reorganization of her home support after a home care contract tendering process in her region, an interviewee stated, "When they changed the system around, they changed those hours on me too which meant that I had to retrain my body to go to the bathroom at a slightly different timeframe . . . It took a while, and the stress of it was just [incredible], because I didn't know if I could do it. I had had those hours for about 14 years and overnight . . . like forget it" (Krogh 2001a).

Home Care and Full Citizenship

Disability and Citizenship

While there seems to be a general acknowledgement that people with disabilities in Canada need and deserve supports, many of the existing home care policies do not reflect this notion. For example, Canadian government reports such as "In Unison: A Canadian Approach to Disability Issues" reflect the notion that people with disabilities should receive support in their efforts to be active in their communities and society (Government of Canada 2000). However, people with disabilities in Canada clearly struggle to receive the home support they need (British Columbia Coalition of People with Disabilities, 2000). A woman who requires home support proposed some questions for policy makers to consider, based on her own life experience: "How would you feel if you were stuck in bed and couldn't get out? And all you could do was not get out the door, not get up to turn on the radio or you know, go to the fridge and get yourself a drink whenever you wanted to, even in your own home, that wouldn't be living—to live in your own bed is no life at all" (Krogh 2001a).

Home care for people with disabilities is a sociopolitical issue, not an individual medical problem. Conceptualizing home support in terms of medical procedures solely within the home acts to divert attention away from the rights for citizenship and the role of society in creating or addressing social, economic, and political issues that impose restrictions. The reification of social problems into individual medical concerns has been discussed in both feminist health literature (Pirie 1988; Wuest 1993) and disability studies literature (Morris 1993). The social model of disability with a recognition of the value of phenomenological descriptions of embodied experience forms a valuable basis for understanding the significance of home support in the lives of women with disabilities.

The ideologies of "caring" and "efficiency" in combination with the dominance of the individualistic medical model of disability within home care have operated to undermine the citizenship and civil rights of disabled people. Women with disabilities experience systemic discrimination in education, employment, and health care. State-assured citizenship protections and rights appear to have little application in the lives of many of these women. Feminist disability researcher Jenny Morris (2001) concluded that "in many situations the human and civil rights of disabled people cannot be promoted without particular action being taken, resources being made available, which would give us equal access. Specific entitlements (that is, different treatments) are necessary for equal access" (11).

After an extensive community consultation process, Prince Edward Island has introduced a disability supports program in which individual recipients are allowed choice in determining the type of support they need in order to achieve their personal goals. Since the introduction of the program, this approach has supported increasing numbers of people in returning to or entering

the workforce (Brian Bertelsen, Coordinator of Disability Supports and Services for Prince Edward Island, personal communication, 25 January 2003). However, it is important to note that monthly financial caps on services present significant barriers to achieving personal goals, including community living for those individuals who require relatively high levels of care.

People with disabilities receiving home support have had to fight to receive and maintain levels and types of support as new, more restrictive guidelines are introduced related to the type of services provided. For example, some regions have removed meal preparation or social participation supports (Health Canada 1999). Other regions no longer include housekeeping, reflecting a definition of health and home support that no longer includes household hygiene (Krogh, Johnson, and Bowman 2003; Krogh 2001a). Such a trend is of particular concern to women who live with compromised immune systems. Supports located outside of the home that facilitate community participation are increasingly being considered unnecessary. New and future users of home care are at particular risk of never receiving the level of care they need to enable them to engage in society as full citizens (Roeher Institute and Status of Women Canada 2001).

Home care is required by many disabled people for access to their communities and a full range of life opportunities. Independent living principles include flexibility, choice, and control as well as access to peer support. As Morris (1993) pointed out, when the philosophy and aims associated with the independent living movement are neither understood nor accepted, community care policy initiatives only result in institutionalization within the community. Flexibility, choice, and control within home and community settings are not only important social determinants of health; their presence or absence constitutes the distinction between institutional and community living (Priestley 1998, 1999). Choice in relation to the care provider has been associated with health outcomes, but studies have generally not examined the negative impact of having care imposed in ways that offer limited choice to the care receiver. For women with disabilities, choice might be in the form of the administration of care (direct care, agency care, supported living, or institutional care); the nature of the tasks involved (e.g., personal hygiene, house cleaning, accompanying a person doing their shopping, assisting a person with the physical act of organizing course papers while studying for an exam); or the organization of the delivery of care (sequence, priority activities, location).

Women, Disability, and Citizenship

Women with disabilities are frequently assumed to be dependent, passive, and needy, rather than interdependent and active contributors to their communities. Their exclusion from citizenship discussions may be further complicated when the nature of their contributions does not conform to society's expectations. Thus, as mentioned earlier, society's images of citizenship omit disability by reflecting and perpetuating hegemonic notions of normalcy (Meekosha and Dowse 1997). Disability challenges our use of simple binaries such as rights versus duties within citizenship debates because the assumption is that these are guided by people with able bodies who are free to accept assistance or not.

Within a feminist critique of citizenship, women need to become aware of those forms of citizenship that for some necessitate the categorization of women with disabilities as objects of caring work (Meekosha and Dowse 1997). We also need to recognize our interconnectedness within communities and focus on the development of strategies that acknowledge a full range of experiences and foster effective participation for all women.

One disabled woman in the study described the interpersonal relationship that enables citizenship through the provision of home support in the following way:

Everything that we want to do outside our own home and to be up and about in your own home, to have people in, you need home care in order to do that and the quality of home care is important because for a younger disabled adult, you need a person that is flexible and understands that you don't just live for a person walking into your house to get you up, get you dressed, give you a bath, you have a life outside your apartment and therefore they are just a small part of your life . . . but in another instance they are also the most important part of your life because you cannot do anything else if you can't get out of bed. (Krogh and the Home Support Action Group 2000)

Citizenship rights are located in both social and political arenas. Nira Yuval-Davis (1997) explained that without "enabling" social conditions, political rights are vacuous, and at the same time, citizenship rights without obligations also construct people as passive and dependent. She concluded that "the most important duty of citizens, therefore, is to exercise their political right and to participate in the determination of their collectivities', states', and societies' trajectories" (21–22).

Citizenship rights must be extended to provide opportunities for engagement to people with disabilities in the development of home care policy, programs, program evaluation, eligibility criteria, assessment tools, and procedures. Most importantly, all home care programs must incorporate an accessible appeal mechanism that includes representation from organizations that are consumer-directed: i.e., led by persons with disabilities, including disabled women's organizations. The importance of an arm's-length relationship of such an appeal board has been emphasized (Community Living Transition Steering Committee 2002). Particular attention should be paid to the various forms of impairment, gender issues, and the need for peer support and self-determination.

The full implications of citizenship need to be acknowledged by the women providing and receiving care, within the context of their relationship. Canada needs a set of national home care standards in order to establish expectations for the provinces.

The Need for a National Standard

Administration of home care is a provincial responsibility and several studies have documented that, without a national standard, there are significant differences among the provinces in terms of eligibility criteria, user fees, and range of service (see Health Canada 1999). Variations also exist in terms of how publicly funded home care is delivered: direct provision by public employees, competitive tendering by private agencies, partnership between government and non-profit providers, and self-managed care (Campbell et al. 2002).

The reworking of eligibility criteria appears to be designed to create ineligibility to reduce costs rather than to facilitate the exercising of rights. This has been seen, for example, through the redefining of terms used to regulate home care service including disability, eligibility criteria, and types of services. Consequently, Canadians who live with long-term impairments are at increasing risk of being arbitrarily reassessed as eligible for less or no care. Reassessment can be introduced in waves through particular regions or it can be initiated by such factors as an individual's move to a new region. This is a mobility rights issue because a move to a new region necessarily involves a reassessment. The Charter of Rights and Freedoms is intended for all Canadians, but the freedom of mobility rights as articulated by section 6(2)(a), which states that "every citizen of Canada and every person who has the status of a permanent resident of Canada has the right to move to and take up residence in any province," does not seem to apply to Canadians who rely on government-subsidized home care. People with disabilities who require home support are not free to move from one province to another, nor are they necessarily free to move within their own province. The Council of Canadians with

Disabilities now advises people with disabilities requiring home care to think very carefully before moving to a new region, province, or territory because the reassessment that such a move triggers is likely to result in fewer hours of home care (Laurie Beachell, personal communication, 24 January 2003).

A report entitled "Without Foundation" (Pollak and Cohen 2000) reviewed health care in BC and provided alerts to other regions in Canada undergoing health care restructuring. The authors concluded that inadequate funding has created a growing gap between health needs and the public services available. They went on to state that, rather than focusing on prevention and early intervention, health care services have become increasingly crisis oriented. They described the cuts to home support in BC as "drastic" and claim that they have created "an explosion of problems for patients, family members, care providers and health administrators" (6). Specifically, they referred to declining health due to poor nutrition, stress, and isolation; hospitalization; higher rates of injury among workers; and the denial of people's basic human right to live at home and participate in their community.

Social participation is critical to the efforts of all people with disabilities to achieve full citizenship. Yet some provinces do not consider this a legitimate rationale for accessing home care and other services. Disabled people will probably be kept alive in their rooms but will not be enabled to venture beyond the four walls of their bedrooms or homes (Krogh 2001a; Krogh and the Home Support Action Group 2000). Social participation supports health. As one woman with a disability who relies on home care stated, "the more we're involved in our community, the healthier we are—with our [physical] health, our mental health" (Krogh 2001a).

It is well recognized that people with disabilities experience a number of "disincentives" to work, including the cost of technology and the risks associated with losing medical coverage. Increasingly, women with disabilities who are offered employment must further assess the costs of becoming employed given that, in many provinces, they will be expected to pay user fees for their own home care once they start earning an income. The application of user fees and other factors considered in determining the amount of payment required—such as assets or cash in the bank—varies among the provinces and territories.

The disability community has been calling for National Standards for Home Care for several years (Council of Canadians with Disabilities 2002). Given the historical conflict between the federal and provincial governments, provinces appear unable to commit to a policy of consistent, quality standards of home care for disabled people. At this time, federal leadership is required to assure citizenship rights for all Canadians. Given the various service delivery methods—private, non-profit, government, and self-directed administration—it is unlikely that a single model can be mandated within all regions. A set of national principles or standards for home support put forward by the federal government can be achieved through a variety of means by provinces in order to qualify for federal dollars (Campbell et al. 2002). Cost-sharing between provincial and federal governments, as well as across those ministries responsible for health, employment, education, and social services could also be considered.

Concluding Comments

Canada requires a set of national home care standards that explicitly recognize the role of home support as a necessary service that mediates citizenship. A national standard would eliminate significant variations that currently exist among provinces and territories, and would thus not only assure a precondition for equal opportunities for citizen participation, but also represent a move to protect mobility rights as outlined in section 6(2)(a) and equality rights under section 15 of the Charter of Rights and Freedoms for people with disabilities. Modes of delivery could vary as long as sufficient funds are provided to deliver quality home care.

A direct-funding program option must be made available in all provinces and territories. It is crucial that this method of care delivery be accompanied by sufficient resources for both the service and consumer-directed organizations that can provide subcontracted assistance, training, and peer support. All regions of Canada need to have an impartial appeal mechanism that includes guiding principles related to promoting citizenship and equal opportunity as well as certain restrictions to limit the influence of economics in decision making. Flexible service in terms of the nature of tasks that are performed, and where and how they are organized within the context of the disabled woman's life is essential. National standards should include a range of services including meal preparation and house cleaning that are frequently required, yet increasingly being eliminated because they are not seen as medically necessary.

Definitions of disability, home support, and citizenship reflected in and reinforced through home support policy must be re-examined and challenged. In particular, the individualistic medical definition of disability needs to be replaced by a sociopolitical definition of disability that acknowledges phenomenological embodied and situated expertise; the notion of home support as merely a medical service needs to be greatly expanded to acknowledge that it is also a facilitator of citizen participation; and the idea must be discarded that those who live interdependently rather than independently are passive and less worthy members of society.

Home care and disability are gendered issues. For example, care recipients and providers are most likely to be women—poor working and living conditions for paid and unpaid care providers lead to increasing numbers of women becoming disabled through long-term injuries or the aggravation of a chronic condition—and disabled women must negotiate their various socially influenced roles, including parent and caregiver. Existing policies and programs differentially disadvantage women with disabilities in comparison to men with disabilities. In addition, they particularly discriminate against women with certain forms of impairments—for example, those related to non-visible chronic illness, developmental disability, and mental health impairment, as well as women who experience interlocking forms of discrimination related to, for instance, race, ethnicity, sexual orientation, poverty, or literacy. Programs must reflect a commitment to reduce the systemic social, economic, and political discrimination based on gender, class, race, ethnicity, and sexual orientation that women with disabilities experience. Disabled women who rely on home support deserve to be provided with assurances of safety and respect in ways that recognize their identities, expertise, priorities, and personhood. These points must be considered in policy making, program design, and the creation of meaningful and accessible opportunities for women with disabilities to participate in policy making, program design, implementation, evaluation, and appeal procedures.

Home care is ultimately about voice. When home care does not work well, women with disabilities live in isolation from their communities and in fear of arbitrary decisions made about eligibility for supports. Within Canadian society, we have seen a number of developments, such as more accessible municipal transit, that are intended to facilitate engagement in society for people with disabilities, but without home supports, many people with disabilities cannot get out of bed to access such services. Inadequate levels of home support and a limited choice about the nature of its provision in effect act to institutionalize people within the confines of their own homes. It is necessary to reconsider political processes and home support administrative systems and the values that underlie them in order to create opportunities for people, especially women with disabilities, from a range of social locations.

Representatives from disabled women's organizations, ethnocultural disability organizations, and cross-disability organizations must play a role in policy design, program implementation, and evaluation, and serve on appeal committees.

Finally, we must recognize that issues affecting all women are inextricably linked whether we consider care providers, care recipients, or both. Efforts to improve home support policy, programs, and services for care recipients must be advocated for alongside improved working conditions for women who provide the majority of formal and informal care. Together we can work to improve the social, political, and economic circumstances that directly influence the quality of the care relationship.

Disability activists have made it clear that home care for people with disabilities should be considered a right, not a luxury (British Columbia Coalition of People with Disabilities 2000; Council of Canadians with Disabilities 2002). The essence of home support as an essential component of life was made vivid when one woman with a disability in the study stated, "I can't plan ahead because tomorrow morning, they might cut my hours back . . . so what I've been doing for the last whatever number of years that I've been having these hours [threatened is] . . . I'm living day to day . . . and how would that impact your life if you couldn't plan for next week or next month or the summer? I mean, people don't plan day to day, they make a plan for the future. At this moment, I don't have any plans for the future because I don't know what the future will bring. If I can't get out of bed, there's no use planning anything" (Krogh 2001a).

The author would like to acknowledge personnel support and research grants from the Canadian Institutes of Health Research and the Social Sciences and Humanities Research Council.

References

Australian Institute of Health and Welfare. 1993. *Australia's Welfare 1993: Services and Assistance.* Canberra: Australian Government Publishing Service.

Barnes, C., G. Mercer, and T. Shakespeare. 1999. *Exploring Disability: A Sociological Introduction.* Malden, MA: Blackwell.

Bookwala, J., and R. Schultz. 1998. "The Role of Neuroticism and Mastery in Spouse Caregivers' Assessment of and Response to a Contextual Stressor." *Journal of Gerontology: Psychological Sciences* 53B: 155–64.

———. 2000. "A Comparison of Primary Stressors, Secondary Stressors, and Depressive Symptoms between Elderly Caregiving Husbands and Wives: The Caregiver Health Effects Study." *Psychology and Aging* 15: 607–16.

Bookwala, J., J.L. Yee, and R. Schultz. 2000. "Caregiving and Detrimental Mental and Physical Health Outcomes." In D.M. Williamson, P.A. Parmelee, and D.R. Shaffer, eds, *Physical Illness and Depression in Older Adults: A Handbook of Theory, Research and Practice*. New York: Plenum, 93–131.

Bourdieu, P. 1985. *Outline of a Theory of Practice*. Cambridge, UK: Cambridge University Press. (Original work published in 1972 as *Esquisse d'une theorie de la pratique*.)

Bourdieu, P., and J.C. Passeron. 1977. *Reproduction in Education, Society and Culture*. Beverly Hills, CA: Sage.

Boyce, W., K. Krogh, J. Kaufert, J. Hall, C. La France, and H. Enns. 1999, May. "How Consumer Organizations of People with Disabilities are Responding to Social, Economic and Political Change." In proceedings from conference entitled *Research to Action: Working Together for the Integration of Canadians with Disabilities*. Halifax, NS, 151–6.

Brisenden, S. 1989. *A Charter for Personal Care* (Progress 16). London: The Disablement Income Group.

British Columbia Coalition of People with Disabilities. 2000, July/August. "Home Support: The Quiet Crisis." (Special issue). *Transitions Magazine*.

Browne, P.L. 2000. *Unsafe Practices: Restructuring and Privatization in Ontario Health Care*. Ottawa: Canadian Centre for Policy Alternatives.

Burke, M. 2000. "Efficiency and the Erosion of Health Care in Canada." In M. Burke, C. Mooers, and J. Shields, eds, *Restructuring and Resistance: Canadian Public Policy in an Age of Global Capitalism*. Halifax, NS: Fernwood, 178–93.

Campbell, B., C. Blouin, J. Foster, R. Labonte, J. Lexchin, M. Sanger, S. Shrybman, and S. Sinclair. 2002. *Putting Health First: Canadian Health Care Reform, Trade Treaties and Foreign Policy*. Ottawa: Canadian Centre for Policy Alternatives.

Canadian Centre on Disability Studies. 2002. *Report of a Study of the Accessibility of Adult Literacy Programs for Individuals with Disabilities in Manitoba*. Winnipeg, MB.

Canadian Study of Health and Aging. 1994. "Patterns of Caring for People with Dementia in Canada." *Canadian Journal on Aging* 13: 470–87.

Clare, E. 1999. *Exile and Pride: Disability, Queerness and Liberation*. Cambridge, MA: South End Press.

Community Living Transition Steering Committee. 2002. *Recommendations Report, Ministry of Children and Family Development, BC*. Retrieved 6 May 2003, from www.cltsc.bc.ca/Final_Report.htm.

Cossette, L., and E. Duclos. 2001. *A Profile of Disability in Canada, 2001* (Report from Statistics Canada, Housing, Family and Social Statistics Division.) Ottawa: Government of Canada.

Council of Canadians with Disabilities. 2002. *Consumers with Disabilities Speak Out on Health Issues* (Submission to the Romanow Commission on the Future of Health Care in Canada.) Winnipeg, MB.

———. 2003, January 22. Letter to Federal Minister of Health Anne McLellan. Winnipeg, MB.

Coyte, P. 2000. "Home Care in Canada: Passing the Buck." *Canadian Journal of Nursing Research*.

Evans, R.G. 1993, July/August. "Health Care Reform: The Issue From Hell." *Policy Options* 14.

Fast, J., G.M. Williamson, and N. Keating. 1999. "The Hidden Costs of Informal Elder Care." *Journal of Family and Economic Issues* 20: 301–26.

Fawcett, G. 1996. *Living with Disability in Canada: An Economic Portrait*. Ottawa: Human Resources Development Canada, Office for Disability Issues.

Ferguson, S. 2000. "Beyond the Welfare State? Left Feminism and Global Capitalist Restructuring." In M. Burke, C. Mooers, and J. Shields, eds, *Restructuring and Resistance: Canadian Public Policy in an Age of Global Capitalism*. Halifax, NS: Fernwood.

Foucault, M. 1973. *The Birth of the Clinic: An Archaeology of Medical Perception*. Trans. A.M.S. Smith. New York: Vintage Books. (Originally published 1963 as *Naissance de La Clinique*.)

———. 1977. *Discipline and Punish: The Birth of the Prison*. Trans. A. Sheridan. New York: Random House. (Originally published 1975 as *Surveiller et Punir: Naissance de la Prison*.)

Government of Canada. 2000. *In Unison: People with Disabilities in Canada*. Retrieved 6 May 2003 from http://socialunion.gc.caIn_Unison2000.

Hall, M., and P. Reed. 1998. "Shifting the Burden: How Much Can Government Download to the Nonprofit Sector?" *Canadian Public Administration* 41 (1): 1–20.

Health Canada. 1999. *Provincial and Territorial Home Care Programs: A Synthesis for Canada* June. Retrieved 6 May 2003, from www.hc-sc.gc.ca.

Hollander, M.J., N. Chappell, B. Havens, C. McWilliam, and J.A. Miller. 2002. *Research Report for Substudy 5: Study of the Costs and Outcomes of Home Care and Residential Long-term Care Services* (Report for the Health Transitions Fund). Victoria, BC: University of Victoria and Hollander Analytic Services.

Hooyman, N.R., and J.G. Gonyea. 1999. "A Feminist Model of Family Care: Practice and Policy Directions." *Journal of Women and Aging* 11: 149–69.

Human Resources Development Canada. 2002. *Advancing the Inclusion of Persons with Disabilities*. Ottawa: Government of Canada. Retrieved 6 May 2003, from www.hrdc-drhc.gc.caIhrib/sdd-ddslodildocument-slAIPD/fdrOOO.shtml.

Humphrey, J.C. 2000. "Researching Disability Politics, or, Some Problems with the Social Model in Practice." *Disability and Society* 15:1, 63–85.

Katz, S.J., M. Kabeto, and K.M. Langa. 2000. "Gender Disparities in the Receipt of Home Care for Elderly People with Disability in the United States." *Journal of the American Medical Association* 284: 3022–7.

Keating, N., J. Fast, J. Frederick, K. Cranswick, and C. Perrier. 1999. *Eldercare in Canada: Context, Content and Consequences.* Ottawa: Statistics Canada.

Keefe, J.M., and P.J. Fancey. 1998. *Financial Compensation Versus Community Supports: An Analysis of the Effects on Caregivers and Care Receivers* (Final report for Health Canada). Halifax, NS: Mount Saint Vincent University, Department of Gerontology.

Kestenbaum, A. 1992. *Cash for Care.* Nottingham, UK: Independent Living Fund.

———. 1993a. *Making Community Care a Reality: The Independent Living Fund 1988–1993.* London, UK: Royal Association for Disability and Rehabilitation and the Disablement Income Group.

———. 1993b. *Taking Care in the Market: A Study of Agency Homecare.* London, UK: Royal Association for Disability and Rehabilitation and the Disablement Income Group.

Kitwood, T., and K. Bredin. 1992. "A New Approach to the Evaluation of Dementia Care." *Journal of Advances in Health and Nursing Care* 1 (5): 41–60.

Krogh, K. 2001a, April. *Beyond Four Walls: Impact of Home Support on Work, Health and Citizenship of People with Disabilities* (Multimedia research report distributed at the World Health Organization's Rethinking Care from the Perspectives of People with Disabilities: A Global Congress.) Retrieved 6 May 2003 from www.ryerson.cat-kkrogh.

———. 2001b. "Video Action Research: Possibilities as an Emancipatory Research Methodology and Reflections on a Health Policy Study for People with Disabilities." Paper presented at the Society of Disability Studies conference, June. Winnipeg, MB.

Krogh, K., and the Home Support Action Group. 2000. *Beyond Four Walls: Impact of Home Support on Health, Work and Citizenship for People with Disabilities* (Research-based video resulting from study funded by the Social Sciences and Humanities Research Council.) Victoria, BC: University of Victoria, Faculty of Human and Social Development.

Krogh, K., J. Johnson, and T. Bowman. 2003. "The Politics of Accountability: Home Support and Citizenship for People with Disabilities." Unpublished manuscript, Ryerson University, School of Disability Studies.

Kvetoslava, R. 1999. *Personal Assistance—A Key Toward Independence in the Life of People with Severe Disabilities in Slovakia* (Report of the Ministry of Labour, Social Affairs and Family of the Slovak Republic).

Lakey, J. 1994. *Caring About Independence: Disabled People and the Independent Living Fund.* London: Policy Studies Institute.

Linton, S. 1998. *Claiming Disability: Knowledge and Identity.* New York: New York University Press.

Malhotra, Ravi. 2001. "Tracy Latimer, Disability Rights and the Left." *Canadian Dimension* 35: 23–5.

Masuda, S. 1998. *The Impact of Block Funding on Women with Disabilities.* Ottawa: DisAbled Women's Network Canada.

Meekosha, H. 1999. "Body Battles: Bodies, Gender and Disability." In T. Shakespeare, ed., *The Disability Reader: Social Science Perspectives.* New York: Cassell, 163–97.

Meekosha, H., and L. Dowse. 1997. "Enabling Citizenship: Gender, Disability and Citizenship in Australia." *Feminist Review* Autumn 57: 49–72.

Morgan, C. 1995. *Family Resources Survey Great Britain 1993/94.* London: Department of Social Security.

Morris, J. 1993. *Independent Lives? Community Care and Disabled People.* Basingstoke, UK: Macmillan.

———. 2001. "Impairment and Disability: Constructing an Ethic of Care That Promotes Human Rights." *Hypatia* 16 (4): 1–16.

Morris, M. 2001. *Community Care and Caregiving Research: A Synthesis Paper.* Ottawa: Women's Health Bureau, Health Canada and the Home and Continuing Care Unit, Health Care Directorate, Health Canada, and the Status of Women Canada.

National Alliance for Care Giving and the American Association of Retired Persons. 1997. *Family Care Giving in the U.S.: Findings from a National Survey* (Final Report). Bethesda, MD: National Alliance for Care Giving.

Oliver, M. 1992. "Changing the Social Relations of Research Production?" *Disability, Handicap and Society* 7: 101–14.

———. 1996. *Understanding Disability: From Theory to Practice.* Basingstoke, UK: Macmillan.

Orme, J. 2001. *Gender and Community Care: Social Work and Social Care Perspectives.* Basingstoke, UK: Palgrave.

O'Toole, C.J., and T. Doe. 2002. "Sexuality and Disabled Parents with Disabled Children." *Sexuality and Disability* 30: 1, 89–101.

Pirie, M. 1988. "Women and Illness Role: Rethinking Feminist Theory." *Canadian Review of Sociology and Anthropology* 25: 628–48.

Pollak, N., and M. Cohen, eds 2000. *Without Foundation* (Report produced by Canadian Centre for Policy Alternatives–BC Office, British Columbia Government and Service Employees' Union, British Columbia Nurses' Union and Hospital Employees' Union.) Vancouver, BC: Canadian Centre for Policy Alternatives.

Priestley, M. 1998. "Discourse and Resistance in Care Assessment: Integrated Living and Community Care." *British Journal of Social Work* 28: 659–73.

———. 1999. *Disability Politics and Community Care.* Philadelphia: Jessica Kingsley.

Proctor, G. 2001. "Listening to Older Women with Dementia: Relationships, Voices and Power." *Disability and Society* 16 (3): 361–76.

Putnam, R.D. 1993. "The Prosperous Community: Social Capital and Public Life." *The American Prospect* 4 (13). Retrieved 6 May 2003 from www.prospect.org/printIV4/13/putnam-r.html.

Rachlis, M., and C. Kushner. 1994. *Strong Medicine: How to Save Canada's Health Care System.* Toronto: HarperCollins.

Razack, S. 1999. *Looking White People in the Eye: Gender, Race and Culture in the Courtrooms and Classrooms.* Toronto: University of Toronto Press.

Rioux, M.H. 1997. "Disability: The Place of Judgment in a World of Fact." *Journal of Intellectual Disability Research* 41 (Part 2): 101–11.

Roeher Institute. 1995. *Disability Supports: Patterns in Usage and Need Among Adult Canadians with Disabilities* (Report). Toronto.

Roeher Institute and Status of Women Canada. 2001, February. *Disability-Related Support Arrangements, Policy Options, and Implications for Women's Equality* (Report prepared by the Roeher Institute for Status of Women Canada.) Retrieved 6 May 2003 from www .swc-cfc.gc.ca/pubs/0662653238/2oo102_066265323 8_e.html.

Saxton, M., M.A. Curry, L.E. Powers, S. Maley, K. Eckels, and J. Gross. 2001. "'Bring My Scooter So I Can Leave You': A Study of Disabled Women Handling Abuse by Personal Assistance Providers." *Violence against Women* 7: 393–417.

Schultz, R., and S.R. Beach. 1999. "Caregiving as a Risk Factor for Mortality: The Caregiver Health Effects Study." *Journal of the American Medical Association* 282: 2215–9.

Shakespeare, T. 2000. *Help.* Birmingham: Venture Press.

Snow, J. 1992. "Living at Home." In D. Driedger and S. Gray, eds, *Imprinting our Image: An International Anthology by Women with Disabilities.* Charlottetown, Prince Edward Island: Gynergy Books.

Sobsey, D., and T. Doe. 1991. "Patterns of Sexual Abuse and Assault." *Disability and Sexuality* 9: 243–59.

Statistics Canada. 2001a. *Canadian Community Health Survey, 2000–2001.* Ottawa: Health Statistics Division, Government of Canada.

———. 2001b. *Participation and Activity Limitation Survey, 2001: A Profile of Disability in Canada.* Ottawa: Government of Canada.

Thomas, P.G. 1996. "Visions Versus Resources in the Federal Program Review." In A. Armit and J. Bourgault, eds, *Hard Choices or no Choices: Assessing Program Review.* Toronto: Institute of Public Administration of Canada, 39–46.

Tighe, C.A. 2001. "Working at Disability: A Qualitative Study of the Meaning of Health and Disability for Women with Physical Impairments." *Disability and Society* 16: 511–29.

Trypuc, J.M. 1994. "Gender Based Mortality and Morbidity Patterns and Health Risks." In B. Singh Bolaria and R. Bolaria, eds, *Women, Medicine, and Health.* Halifax, NS: Fernwood.

Tuohy, C.J. 1992. *Policy and Politics in Canada: Institutionalized Ambivalence.* Philadelphia: Temple University Press.

Twig, J. 2000. *Bathing: The Body and Community Care.* London: Routledge.

Walmsley, J. 1993. "Talking to Top People: Some Issues Related to the Citizenship of People with Learning Disabilities." In J. Swain, V. Finkelstein, S. French, and M. Oliver, eds, *Disabling Barriers: Enabling Environments.* London: Sage in association with Open University, 257–66.

Wendell, S. 1996. *The Rejected Body: Feminist Philosophical Reflections on Disability.* New York: Routledge.

———. 2001. "Unhealthy Disabled: Treating Chronic Illnesses as Disabilities." *Hypatia* 16 (4): 17–33.

Williamson, G.M., D.R. Shaffer, and R. Schultz. 1998. "Activity Restriction and Prior Relationship History as Contributors to Mental Health Outcomes among Middle-aged and Older Spouse Caregivers." *Health Psychology* 17: 152–62.

World Health Organization. 2001. *International Classification of Functioning, Disability and Health (ICF).* Retrieved 6 May 2003 from http://www3.who.int/icf/ icftemplate.cfm.

Wuest, J. 1993. "Institutionalizing Women's Oppression: The Inherent Risk in Health Policy that Fosters Community Participation." *Health Care for Women International* 14: 407–14.

Young, I.M. 1990. *Justice and the Politics of Difference.* Princeton, NJ: Princeton University Press.

———. 2000. "Disability and the Definition of Work." In L. Francis and A. Silvers, eds, *Americans with Disabilities: Exploring Implications of the Law for Individuals and Institutions.* New York: Routledge.

Yuval-Davis, N. 1997. "Women, Citizenship, and Difference." *Feminist Review* 57: 4–27.

Questions for Critical Thought

1. Why does Krogh claim that home care is a gendered issue? How are women socialized into this role? How is the idea of home care culturally and socially specific?

2. Why are women more often than men affected by less visible degenerative conditions that require home care? What are examples of these conditions, and why is it difficult for women to obtain home care support? Have you ever provided home care for a relative or a friend? How did the role of being a caregiver change your life? How did this role change your relationship with the person that you were caring for?

3. Should the state play a more active role in accessing and supporting women with

disabilities? How can the state reduce the interlocking oppressions that especially elderly women experience?

4. Krogh reports that home care workers can be abusive towards their clients. How can home care workers be effectively monitored to ensure that especially their elderly and mentally challenged clients are treated with dignity and respect?

5. What measures can we take in our families and in our communities to remove barriers and to protect the human rights and citizenship rights of disabled women?

Affirming Immigrant Women's Health: Building Inclusive Health Policy

.... *Marian MacKinnon and Laura Lee Howard*

Introduction

Societies throughout the world have become more culturally diverse as the number of immigrants and refugees increases worldwide. Canadian society is no exception.[1] Many authors have commented on the effect of culture and ethnicity on the health and health beliefs held by immigrant women, as well as on family and professional relationships (Anderson 1990; Majumdar and Carpio 1988). Some authors have observed that immigrant women of all ages have encountered significant difficulty in adapting to the beliefs, values, and bureaucratic structures of a new culture (Barney 1991; Die and Seelbach 1988; Driedger and Chappell 1987; Lipson and Meleis 1985).

Lack of language skills and uprootedness have been found to be the two issues that cause the most emotional distress (Coombs 1986). Immigrant women often feel torn from the familiar and placed in a setting for which they feel unprepared emotionally and culturally. In this new context, established patterns no longer work (Stevens, Hall, and Meleis 1992). In addition, lack of transportation and consequent physical isolation has been flagged as a significant cause of distress (Rathbone-McCuan and Hashimi 1982).

Violence in the home also impacts the health of immigrant women. Beleaguered with daily problems, the women struggle with difficulties that undermine their ability or desire to report domestic violence. In addition, mental health resources are limited and frequently culturally insensitive.

The health of immigrant women has been found to be at risk because of the many responsibilities they carry, the work and energy required to try to make sense of two different cultures, the effort needed to make their values understood and accepted, the loss of their social life, the language difficulties they frequently encounter, and the difficulties caused by differences in symbolic meanings. Their life trajectory has been altered dramatically from the expected. Finally, immigrant women often have to face the stress of feeling subordinate in their host society (Aroian 1990; Lipson 1992; Meleis 1991).

Not surprisingly, social support has been identified by researchers as a major variable providing protection from mental and physical illness, especially during such stressful life events as immigration, whether chosen or forced. Loss of such support is believed to predispose the individual to feelings of vulnerability and to eventual illness (MacKinnon 1993). During the transition period of immigration, there is often a loss of social support until new systems are established (Meleis et al. 1998). During this period, the health of immigrant women may be compromised (Meleis et al. 1998).

Grief represents another risk factor for the health of immigrant women. Anderson (1991) described a theme of persistent grief that influences everything in the life of immigrant women. Disman (1983) noted that "an immigrant's grief is for the loss of almost everything that once was familiar." She further reported that accounts by immigrants of their feelings after arrival in the new country reflect a unified theme of a loss-related transition.

Current knowledge about the effects of immigration adds support to Shareski's (1992) observation that in order to provide culturally sensitive care to immigrant women, "diet, language and communication processes, religion, art and history, family life processes, social group interactive patterns, value orientations, and healing beliefs and perceptions" must be understood. This author further notes that the most important step toward providing culturally sensitive and competent health care is an increased awareness of our own cultural beliefs and practices, especially an increased awareness that each of us *has* a culture and cultural traditions. In the end, culturally sensitive health care is "a matter of respect for the client's viewpoint of health" (Shareski 1992).

Most of the research on immigrant women's health has focused on the problems that immigrant women face in the new country; in some cases investigators have examined the effects of those problems on the individual's health. Few if any of the studies, however, address what health means to these women; what, if anything, they did before they immigrated to maintain their health; and whether they are able to continue those practices in the new country. No studies were found that asked immigrant women what *they* believe influences their health or what *their* experiences are with the health care system of their new country.

This research project sought to address that gap through interviews with 22 women aged 20 to 70 from 15 countries. All had arrived in PEI within the past 20 years, with the average period of residence being just over nine years. The average family income of those who responded to this item was $29,000 per annum. The majority of the women—13 out of 22—worked outside the home or wished to, most in positions that required less than their educational preparation and experience. Five others wanted paid employment outside the home but were unemployed. The interviews were conducted in English using an interpreter where necessary, and no distinction was made between immigrant and refugee women. Interviews were one and a half to three hours in length and followed a semi-structured interview guide (developed with the assistance of a group of immigrant women and health care professionals educated in other cultures), which provided opportunities to explore topics raised by the respondents. A personal data questionnaire was used to collect demographic and other background information. Once analyzed and collated, the data were returned to the target group, who confirmed that the findings represented the message they had sought to convey.

Research Questions, Goals, and Objectives

Research Questions

- How do immigrant women define health?
- What factors do immigrant women perceive as influencing their health?
- Is culture/gender-sensitive health care available to immigrant women?

Goals

- To increase cultural awareness among health care providers about the health beliefs, health maintenance, and health use patterns of immigrant and refugee women in PEI;

- To improve the accessibility of health care services to immigrant women in PEI; and
- To influence health care policy towards inclusion of the cultural needs and patterns of immigrant women in PEI.

Objectives

- To determine what health means to immigrant women and to discover their perceptions of factors influencing their health;
- To explore the health maintenance patterns of immigrant women;
- To explore the experiences (positive and negative) of immigrant women in using professional health care services, focusing on the significance of gender, language, and culture; and
- To provide guidelines to policy-makers with regard to the health, health care delivery, and health service needs of immigrant and refugee women.

Methodology

Design of the Study

Given the nature of the research questions under investigation, this qualitative research study used an exploratory descriptive design. Prior to the development of a semi-structured interview guide, a focus group meeting took place with seven immigrant women to gather their ideas and suggestions regarding the topics to address and how best to frame the questions. Telephone interviews were then carried out with five individual health care professionals educated in other cultures to gain their input regarding questions for the interview guide. Once a draft of the guide was developed, further input was sought from the Research Advisory Committee (RAC), the members of which represented individual immigrant women, the University of PEI (UPEI), and relevant government and non-government agencies. The

information gained was applied in developing the study's interview guide (Appendix).

The study used three interpreters. While they were not professionally trained, one had worked with immigrants at the Association of Newcomers to Canada (ANC), and another had been interviewed herself. Hence, two of them were familiar with the interview schedule. The third was given the opportunity to look at the interview schedule before the interview. Familiarity with the interview guide gave them the opportunity to identify any questions they may have had and to become comfortable with translation of the content. The research assistant was available to answer their questions.

The Population

Twenty-two women from 15 countries—Bangladesh, Bosnia, Burma, Croatia, China, Cuba, Egypt, Germany, Guatemala, Macau, Morocco, Nigeria, Pakistan, the Philippines, and Syria—were interviewed. Criteria for inclusion in the study included being 20 to 80 years of age and older and having lived in PEI for 20 years or less. Potential respondents were identified mainly through the PEI ANC and the InterCultural Health Assembly of PEI.

The Sample

The sample was a non-probability, convenience sample selected from the accessible population of both immigrant and refugee women in PEI. Data saturation and accessibility were the main factors determining sample size.

The women interviewed were between the ages of 21 and 70, and had arrived in PEI within the past 20 years. Two of the women were between the ages of 21 and 30, 10 were between the ages of 31 and 40, four were aged 41 to 50, four were between the ages of 51 and 60, and two were aged 61 to 70. Eighteen of the women were married, one was single with a child, two were widowed, and one was separated. The length of time they had lived in PEI varied from 14 months to

20 years, with the average length of time lived in PEI being nine years, two months. Five women chose not to answer the question about income. The average family income for those who answered the question was $29,000 per annum.

Two respondents were full-time students in career-oriented programs at the local college, and one was taking a short program at the college. Seven women were working full-time in paid positions outside the home, six were working part-time in paid positions outside the home, and one did not want paid work outside the home at this time. Five wanted paid work but were unemployed. Of those who worked outside the home in paid positions, almost half were not working in their area of educational preparation and experience. Most were working in positions that required less than their level of education. One woman, for example, was an accountant working as a waitress. Another woman, a nurse who had achieved a managerial position in her country of origin, was able to attain a position as a staff nurse in PEI.

Data Collection

Data were obtained by means of one-to-one audiotaped interviews in the homes of the women interviewed; the interviews were one and a half to three hours in length. The interview guide was intended to ensure that the same questions were asked in each interview. Open-ended questions were used to help focus the respondents' thoughts and to allow freedom of expression, while probes were used to encourage greater depth in the exploration of topics raised by the respondents. The interviews were conducted in English and translated, where necessary, by an interpreter. The audiotapes were transcribed word for word in their entirety by a typist. Data collection took place over a period of approximately four months. The researchers used a personal data questionnaire to collect demographic and other background data. The principal investigator worked closely with the research assistant who conducted the interviews. From the date of receiving funding at the end of March 1998, to the writing of the final report (May 2000), the study spanned a period of roughly two years.

Data Analysis

Content analysis and the constant comparative method (Glaser and Strauss 1967) were used to analyze the data and the research assistant's notes. The two analytic procedures of making comparisons and asking questions were used to isolate emerging concepts into categories and themes (Strauss and Corbin 1990). The data analysis was completed by the principal investigator in consultation with the co-principal investigator and the research assistant.

No differentiation was made between immigrant and refugee women during data collection or analysis, and throughout this report the phrase "immigrant women" refers to both immigrant and refugee women.

Credibility

The researchers used several measures to maintain the credibility and dependability (Polit and Hungler 1996) of the study. The criterion of prolonged engagement was met through in-depth exploration of the topics with each woman over a period of one and a half to three hours. Credibility was further strengthened through data source and investigator triangulation. In addition, the research assistant had considerable experience as a researcher; she had lived and worked in several different countries and cultures, and had worked with immigrant groups in PEI.

The credibility criterion of persistent observation (Polit and Hungler 1996) could have been better addressed in two areas. All questions were not addressed in each interview, and topics raised spontaneously by the respondents were not consistently followed through. These two omissions may have weakened the depth and scope of the data obtained in some areas. However, the criterion of persistent observation was strengthened through peer debriefing sessions with the research assistant, who kept brief notes describing and interpreting her own experiences and behaviours and those of the respondents during the interviews. These notes were intended to provide a measure of her ability to be objective. The content of the notes were discussed in debriefing sessions with the principal and co-principal investigators.

The credibility of the data was further upheld when the data were returned to the target group and confirmed by them as representing the message they had hoped to convey. After reviewing the findings, the response of one member of the target group was: "I don't see what I said, but everything put together is the feeling of most immigrant women."

Discussions were held with the interpreters prior to the interview to confirm their understanding of the questions and to standardize approaches and translations to be used in each interview. In addition, every attempt was made to maintain privacy.

Ethical Considerations

The proposed study and semi-structured interview guide were reviewed and approved by the UPEI Senate Research Ethics Committee. RAC also reviewed the proposal for ethical considerations.

At the beginning of each interview, the focus of the study was explained to each respondent. Prior to the interviews, verbal consent was obtained, using an interpreter if necessary. Permission to audiotape the interview was obtained. All respondents were verbally reassured that the information would be kept confidential and that they would not be identified in any way in the final written report or in other venues where the data might be presented.

In addition, each respondent was informed in plain language that participation in the study was fully voluntary and that they had the right to terminate their participation at any time without jeopardizing present or future health care for themselves or their families. Respondents were further informed that they could refuse to answer any question with which they did not feel comfortable, and they were encouraged to request clarification at any time on issues related to the study.

Findings and Discussion: Major Health Issues and Themes

Meleis et al. (1998) identified four health care issues for immigrant women. Three of the issues identified will be used as a framework for discussion of the health concerns and health care needs disclosed in this study:

- immigrant women are unrecognized resources,
- vulnerability to health risks, and
- barriers to health care.

Along with the three major health issues, several themes that correspond to some of the determinants of health emerged during data analysis. Several authors have described the determinants of health in slightly different ways. Those used to discuss the findings of this study are based on an adaptation of the determinants identified by the UPEI School of Nursing (Munro et al. 2000). Those determinants are:

- social support networks,
- income and social status,
- education,
- employment and working conditions,
- physical environment,
- **biopsychological endowment** and genetics,
- personal health practices and coping,
- early childhood development, and
- health services.

The five determinants that emerged as themes in this study are:

- biopsychological endowment,
- personal health practices,
- social support networks,
- socio-economic factors, and
- health services.

Health Issue I: Immigrant Women Are Unrecognized Resources

Immigrant women have not been involved in studies about—and have not been recognized as resources for—their own health care (Meleis et al. 1998). By contrast, immigrant women were involved in this study and had input into the questions addressed. Their voices were heard in the collection of data, and they had the opportunity to respond to the findings.

The following two sections discuss immigrant women's beliefs about health and health maintenance practices. The two themes that emerged in this category relate to two determinants of health: biopsychological endowment and personal health practices.

Theme 1: Biopsychological endowment

Biopsychological endowment refers to the "interrelationship between biological, psychological, social, and environmental factors affecting health, human behaviour, and physical development" (Munro et al. 2000). The responses the women in this study gave in answer to the question about what health means to them seem to describe this interrelationship.

One woman described the meaning of health as follows:

Able to do all things physically that you can and that you want to. Feel joyful. Can do many things, feel energetic, don't feel tired, feel happy, enjoy what I am doing. Can do all the things I have to do with my family, my father and my children. Walk, think, work. When you are healthy, you can do anything you want.

When asked what she was able to do when she felt healthy, another woman emphasized the value of health with her answer:

I can work perfect, I can talk better, I can have [better] relationship with people, I can dance, I can do everything. Everything is positive in my mind when I am healthy.

Strong threads that emerged in the women's answers to the question about the meaning of health were the ability to do what they want to do—fulfill their responsibilities at work and at home, be involved in their interests, and look after their own health and that of their families.

They reported that health means being able to do the things expected of them—to work hard, go to school, go to work, do housework, and take care of family.

Many of the women described mental health as feeling happy, being able to handle stress, and to have good interpersonal relationships. A quotation from one of the women demonstrates this:

Mental health very important, translates outward to whatever you do and how you relate to people. Affects your thinking and everything.

Mental health was also described as being able to live on one's own, being able to work, have hope, aspirations, ambition, and a feeling of belonging to family and community. A comment that supports this view:

Think, the ability to handle stress, to face all of what affects you in your life . . . I think mentally healthy people can treat things more objectively, so they can come over [overcome] the difficult times and they can still continue with their life. It means being able to adjust yourself to your environment. Be flexible to all changes. Like I was thinking, mentally healthy people can handle those things a little better than others.

Spiritual health was described as feeling comfortable, happy, confident, and safe. They further described spiritual health as feeling kind and helpful toward others, more patient, more composed, and able to enjoy simple things. Those who believe in a divinity said that part of spiritual health was feeling close to God. For one woman, being healthy in a spiritual way means that

I am happy with myself, and if I am happy with myself, I feel fine. I feel comfortable, I will be able to transmit that to other people. If [I] feel spiritually healthy you can transmit that to your mind and then you can show physical[ly] that you are healthy.

Another woman described spiritual health as follows:

Contact with God, helping people, being honest, go [to] church. If spiritually aware of the good things and bad things, then we won't give each other trouble, kill them, beat them, rob them.

The women described a variety of ways they nurture their spiritual health. Some read, others listen to music, still others said they found spiritual comfort in nature. One woman found that reviewing her day each evening—thinking about what made her happy or unhappy—helped to support her spiritual health.

All of the women interviewed believed that physical, mental, and spiritual health are closely related, that health in one area affects health in the other two areas. All stated that when they were physically healthy their psychological state was more positive, they were able to think about the future and make plans, they had hope, felt relaxed, and did not feel homesick. They indicated that when they were physically healthy they felt satisfied and very capable and were inspired to engage in social and leisure activities, their self-esteem was improved, they felt full of energy and more motivated to take care of their own health.

They reported that when they were not healthy, they felt tired, depressed, and lacking in energy. They said they were not able to care for family members and were not motivated to care for their own health. Further, they tended to isolate themselves and to avoid social and leisure activities. Some said they felt depressed and cried. However, they also said they tried to force themselves to go to work or school, and to continue taking care of their families even when they felt sick.

In summary, the immigrant women in this study appear to recognize the importance of health to their ability to take care of themselves and their families, to relate to other people in positive ways and to financially support themselves or go to school. This underscores the need for health care providers to create environments that support the physical, mental, and spiritual well-being of immigrant women. It suggests the need to recognize the women as resources for their own health, and to empower them through appropriate policies and programs to achieve control over their own health (Meleis et al. 1998; Munro et al. 2000). "To empower is to value, to eliminate stereotyping, to decrease isolation and alienation, to develop partnerships, to enhance involvement, to support collectivity, and to provide support, options, and choices" (Shields 1995).

Theme 2: Personal health practices and coping

The second theme in the category of immigrant women as unrecognized resources in their own health care is personal health practices. It refers to behaviours that individuals engage in for the purpose of maintaining or improving their health. These practices often include physical activity, a healthy diet, social activities aimed at promoting relaxation and reducing stress, and building positive interpersonal relationships (Munro et al. 2000; Pender 1996).

The immigrant women in this study reported that health is "the most important thing," and they were very conscious of the need to engage in activities to maintain their health. The activities included eating well, sleeping well, exercising, and keeping active and busy ("lots of hard work," "walking," "aerobics," and "swimming"). When asked what she does to maintain her health, one woman answered this way:

> Have a good way of eating, it is easier in my country, we can eat all the vegetable[s], they are no expensive like here. Vegetables, fruits and many things are really, really nutritious. To stay healthy, eat right, walk, exercise.

Food was identified by all of the women as important, not only to maintaining physical health, but also to maintaining mental and spiritual health. One woman emphasized its importance when she said,

> They don't realize how important it is to have the foods. . . . The public don't aware, don't aware, don't realize.

Another woman voiced her concern about the importance of good food and seemed to miss former rituals around food preparation and family meals. She also may have been expressing some concern about acculturation when she declared,

> My son use[d] to Canadian food, fries, oh my god, the fries, the hamburger! But I use[d] to cook everyday to cook. We use[d] to cook everyday and everything fresh, not frozen. We don't cook anything here, everything frozen . . . .

Obtaining what they believe to be healthy food was reported to be a problem. One woman said,

> Can hardly stay healthy. Too much dependence on cars. Need more physical activity, have gained 22 pounds and still gaining.

Many women commented on the cost of fresh fruit and vegetables. They claimed such items were less available here and that most of the food in Canada and PEI is prepared (frozen) and therefore less healthy. They seemed to be influenced by

what they see on TV and tended to believe that all Canadians eat either frozen or fast food. All of the women who were asked the question about whether the food in PEI is different answered an adamant "yes!"

Having social and leisure activities was also noted to be important. Some women reported that before coming to Canada, they belonged to a choir, played the flute, or went dancing. Others described engaging in more physical activities, such as going to the gym, playing basketball, and swimming. Several of the women mentioned walking, and the importance of getting out into the outdoors.

In addition, use of herbal medicines was described as part of their personal health practices. More than half of the women said they could not find the same herbs here, and therefore had family send them from their country of origin. For less serious illnesses they treated themselves with herbal medications. For more serious illnesses that did not respond to self-treatment, or when they did not know what was wrong with them and when a child was ill, they went to a doctor. Usually, however, they used traditional or herbal remedies before going to a doctor. One woman said,

> I don't take medicines unless I need a specific medicine. Those kind of medicine not really good at the same time, so that's why I try to take those medicines just when I am really bad, you know.

Another woman shared a memory from her country of origin:

> When I have a headache, my mom go out in garden and just pick some leaves and put on my head.

Some examples of herbal remedies included a mixture of cloves and rosewater placed on the back of the neck for headache, taking a mixture of lemon and banana for sunstroke, and a hot honey and lemon drink for a cough and cold.

This group of women asserted that seeing a physician was not part of maintaining their health, but was important to return to health if sickness occurred. The majority of the women said they would not go to a doctor for an emotional condition, such as depression, and indicated they would treat themselves. Several of the women reported they would feel embarrassed or ashamed to go to a doctor for sadness or depression and said they dealt with such problems by talking to friends and/or family; through physical activity such as long walks; or through distraction, such as playing with the children or working hard.

Some of the women openly stated they felt a doctor would not be able to help with such a problem. Comments included:

It is my problem, I would solve it.

Best to fight that by yourself or with the help of family, friends or with herbal medicines.

Another said she would not go to a doctor for sadness or loneliness, adding, "*You think he is going to help me?*" Yet another woman, discussing how her culture deals with emotional problems, explained why going to the doctor was not a viable option for her:

If we have problem, in our culture they say you only supposed to talk to family, like you shouldn't talk outside the family because you always want the family looks good. So, most . . . people is pretty shy talk about their personal life, even [if] have problem.

Four women said they *would* go to a doctor for treatment of depression, and one had already done so.

All of the women included visiting with family and friends as activities that help to maintain their health. One woman described her family this way: "everybody reaching out and watching out for one another." She included extended family in her description of family. Another woman expressed the importance of family this way:

My own experience for my family, we have a very healthy food and also our relation for my family is really unite[d]—we really unite[d], relations [relatives] and family and we farm lot of hard working, so that keep us full of energy and healthy too. We work the farm, and we work fishing.

More than half of the women who were asked the question said they were not able to do the same things here to maintain their health as they did in their country of origin. Those who had engaged in physical activity said it was more difficult to do so in PEI. Others who participated in social and leisure activities, such as music or dance, also felt unable to continue with those activities in PEI.

In summary, the findings presented in this section seem to support the view that immigrant women should be recognized as a resource for their own health. They convey strong beliefs about health and how to maintain it. They treat themselves before going to a doctor, and they treat emotional illness and distress through talking with friends or family or by distracting themselves with activity. However, many report they are not able to continue their health maintenance practices in PEI. Language limitations, absence of social support (for companionship and/or child minding), non-availability of traditional foods and herbal remedies, as well as transportation problems and lack of familiarity with their new community all seem to interfere with their ability to continue with their former health maintenance patterns. The fact that they are unable to continue with their health maintenance patterns increases their vulnerability to health risks.

Health Issue II: Vulnerability to Health Risks

Immigrant women are believed to be at greater risk for illness than their non-immigrant counterparts. Immigration itself is associated with increased morbidity. A number of other factors, singly or in combination, also increase their risk for illness. These factors include language difficulties, multiple responsibilities, financial and employment **stressors**, lack of acceptance by their host communities, culture conflict, and a perceived lack of social support.

As a result of these stressors, they also may be at risk of developing stress-related physical symptoms and mental health problems (Meleis et al. 1998). Immigrant women's health is at risk because they do not have access to culturally appropriate health promotion material in their language. In addition, physicians are often unaware of illnesses that are more common to members of their cultural and ethnic background.

Theme 1: Social support

Social support refers to having ongoing access to a social network, such as family and friends. Integration into a social support network contributes to the positive experiences of feeling loved and valued. It includes emotional support, instrumental assistance, advice and information, and affirmation (Munro et al. 2000; Pender 1996).

All the women in this study identified social support (the ability to visit family, having a good family environment and support from family, and the ability to visit friends) as an important factor influencing their health. In terms of how social support helps to maintain health and reduce health risks, two interviewees had these explanations:

Family. Miss them a lot and when I think too much about them, I get depressed. [That] affects my health (pause) miss my country. I can live without my country, but without my family is more difficult.

Well, in my country I was always healthy, yeah. Not having family and being home too much, depressed here, you know, feel you are alone. We don't have any relatives . . . always have a headache and tired, being with family makes you always happy. So since I move

here, I always have headache, tired all the time, bored.

A single mother in the study emphasized the importance of social support from family and friends when she said,

I worry because I want family and friends. [I feel] safer or something like that, like, I am just my son and I (pause). Sometimes I thought I don't have anybody else. Feel all alone.

Two other women accentuated the importance of friends to maintaining health when they said,

"Friends very important to be able to talk," and another remarked, "to stay healthy it's really difficult because when you are get over still think about your friends and you got [get] depressed and still it's empty."

These findings are important demonstrations of the significance of social support from family and friends to the health of immigrant women. Social support is believed to reduce the influence of stressors by providing a sense of stability, predictability, and acceptance (Stewart 2000). Social support was found by Meleis et al. (1998) to provide protection from mental and physical illness especially during stressful life events, such as chosen or forced immigration. Loss of such support is believed to increase health risk and predispose the individual to illness (MacKinnon 1993; Pender 1996). Social support is thought to influence health by "promoting healthy behaviours, by providing information, or by providing tangible resources" such as child care (Pender 1996).

Theme 2: Socio-economic factors

The socio-economic factors discussed in this section include language ability, employment, and social status (acceptance by the community). These topics were raised by the women in this study as important elements affecting their health.

The majority of the women interviewed identified language as a major factor influencing their health. Some comments from the women may best demonstrate this point:

Language stresses out. Not being able to communicate.

[Language] big problem, because you can't say anything you want to say. When you know the language is easy to do anything fast.

You want to talk to somebody, just to talk. Without language you can't, you feel frustrated.

Referring to the inability to completely express herself, one woman said, "language alone does not describe this fully." Immigrant women are frequently frustrated in their attempts to fully communicate feelings and symbolic meanings. They need time to express themselves and to tell their story. They are not accustomed to the North American "communication style based on short answers to short questions" (Meleis et al. 1998).

Analysis of the demographic data raised the issue of underemployment and low status jobs. Almost half the women who were employed were not employed in their area of educational preparation and expertise, and most were in low paying, low status jobs. Boyd (1984) also found that immigrant women tend to have low status jobs such as domestic work or fast food service. In addition, they were found to have family responsibilities and consequently to do double, if not triple shifts.

In addition, immigrant women frequently have to deal with the feeling that they are not fully accepted and tend to be viewed as subordinate to the dominant culture. One woman, indicating a need for greater acceptance, described the feeling of not fitting in:

We are living in the community but it's just like water and oil, you shake the bottle, they mix together, you cannot tell the difference and I say, "Hello Joe, how are you?" and then the bottle settles down, oil and water separates. We don't feel we are really mixed with the neighbours, with the community.

Hattar-Pollara and Meleis (1995) asserted that "immigrant women often have to deal with unfriendly neighbourhoods and outright hostility in the communities where they live. Many are frustrated and saddened by the frequent reminders that they do not belong and this makes their integration into the mainstream even more difficult." Their accents or appearance often set them apart, and they may be treated with disrespect or outright prejudice (Lalonde, Taylor, and Moghaddam 1992).

Health Issue III: Barriers to Health Care

Immigrant women may have fewer problems accessing health care in Canada than they might have elsewhere. In Canada, they are able to access basic health services free of charge. However, few have extra health insurance coverage, and in spite of the advantage of "free" health care, they still have to face the complexity of learning how to access health care services, and they must endure the problem of language.

In spite of some difficulties, such as those identified above, 18 of the 22 women indicated they like Canada's health care system in general. There were several very positive comments. One woman stated,

I don't know anyone have a problem for Medicare or support from the government. I don't know, but all the immigrants I know, I have never heard a complaint.

An additional comment included this:

I like it because you get sick, you don't need to worry tonight, you can go to the hospital right away. You don't have to wait until you have money.

Language was identified as a major barrier by almost all (20 of 22) of the women in this study. In addition, all who were asked the question (13 of 13) conveyed the need for trained professional interpreters. One woman expressed the need this way:

You don't feel comfortable when some other people is [interpreting] especially the special exams that women have to have.

Researchers have noted that inadequate English may interfere with identifying appropriate sources for care, making appointments, describing problems, and understanding verbal and written instructions (Lipson and Omidian 1997). Often the women are expected to find their own interpreter and this in itself is daunting. Finding a friend or family member who has the time and the language skills to interpret is difficult, and in addition, there is the privacy issue (Lipson and Omidian 1997). As articulated by the women in this study, they are likely to go for medical or hospital care only when they or their children are very ill, or in an emergency.

More than half the women said their visits to a doctor in Canada were similar to visits to a doctor in their country of origin and that the questions asked were similar. Some comments about Canadian doctors, however, indicate that the women may have encountered barriers to obtaining the kind of health care they value. The following comments demonstrate their concerns:

Doctors [here] don't really listen. If I go to the doctor, I want help, I do not want to be told I will get over it. I want to be taken seriously. I feel angry and frustrated. Take Tylenol, I get that a lot.

They just do a physical check-up from head to toe. They don't use, I find, like a holistic view to assess your, like, physical and mental problems. I guess they don't have time, and like, they never have time to ask me how I feel.

Doctors here full of theory. They are really knowledgeable persons, but I never get the help I was expecting. In my country, they don't know so much, but they help me.

[Doctors] don't give you enough time. They want that you say them [tell them] so fast, what do you want or what do you feel and when you go with children, it is really difficult.

The finding that immigrant women don't feel they receive adequate care from physicians in Canada is supported in the literature by the findings of Meleis et al. (1998), who claim that immigrant women need to talk and need time to tell their story in their own way. If this does not happen, the women often feel their concerns have not been heard, they have not been given good care, and quite possibly they have been misunderstood. They are not accustomed to Canada's customary and brief 10-minute appointment.

Another barrier, for more than half the group (13 of 22), was the preference for a female doctor, especially for gynecological examinations and any situation where they had to remove their clothing. One woman said, "If there is no female doctor, I would not get a gynecological exam." The remainder of the women said it did not matter whether the doctor was male or female: "what matters is how they do their work." Because of the shortage of doctors in PEI, the women who preferred to go to a female doctor had difficulty doing so.

Cultural sensitivity was perceived as a barrier for almost half (10 of 22) the group. Three of those surveyed had this to say about cultural sensitivity in health care:

I think it is a good one. They are quite helpful, [but] not sensitive to your culture.

It's really, really good. But strange to me.

Doctor doesn't know about tropical medicine or health problems from other countries and isn't open to learning about them.

Notably, the women identified cultural insensitivity (rudeness) among doctors' receptionists as a barrier to health care. Two quotes demonstrate this:

No, they don't try and sometimes they are really, really easy words, that they are really easy to understand, but . . . you feel sometimes worse because you are trying hard to do the best that you can, but in that time that they say that or they look at you in that way, you in that moment, you like come back [withdraw] and you don't want to talk . . . or you don't want to ask more.

The receptionists are so, so rude, especially when they see you are not from here. You try hard, but they really can't understand you; they don't try.

Approximately half the women (10 of 22) found the long waits for appointments with doctors and the long waits in doctors' offices to be frustrating. One said,

[It is] not convenient to see a doctor. You have to wait two weeks to get an appointment, then wait two to three hours in a clinic. I rather stay home if I have a problem.

She acknowledged that this is an issue for everyone and does not indicate discrimination against immigrant women.

Referral to a specialist was also perceived to be an issue by almost all (19 of 22) of the women. They asserted that they were accustomed to going directly to a specialist and were frustrated with the delays in being referred. They stated that it is "hard to get past the family doctor." All felt that they should be able to go directly to a specialist without being referred by the family doctor. One comment was:

Have to wait three months for specialist. In pain the whole time, no family doctor, don't know the system, don't know who to ask.

All of the women who were asked (10 of 10) identified the need for information about the health care system. All felt that it was very necessary to have information upon arrival rather than three to four years later when they became Canadian citizens. They also said they need to know about Canadian laws and women's rights and other relevant issues. Unfortunately, because of inconsistencies in following the interview guide, 12 women were not asked this question.

In summary, factors described as barriers to getting the health care they need included: language and the need for interpreters; long waits for doctors' appointments, and availability of doctors; inappropriate and/or culturally insensitive care; the sense that doctors don't listen, don't discuss, and don't give enough time; and reluctance on behalf of family doctors to refer to a specialist.

A small number of women identified transportation as a problem, and an additional few identified no health plan, lack of coverage for medication and dental services and for alternative health care services such as masseuses and chiropractors, as interfering with getting the health care they need.

Summary of the Outcomes

This research illuminated the perspectives of immigrant women on their health, their health maintenance practices, and their needs and experiences in relation to the health care system in PEI. The findings indicate that some of the determinants of health play a significant role in the health of immigrant women. This finding has implications for further research in the area of immigrant women's health and the determinants of health. The results of this research also indicate a need for language programs, employment programs, health promotion programs in several languages, a community outreach program, and the need for professional cultural and language interpreters in health care, along with training programs for them. The findings indicate the need to promote culturally sensitive care in hospitals, clinics, and in the community. The study reveals a need for cultural content to be included in education programs for nurses and physicians, and for an information booklet on Canada's health care system.

Note

1. In Canada the largest number of immigrants and refugees can be found in Quebec, Ontario, Manitoba, Alberta, and British Columbia (Statistics Canada 1996). However, other provinces also receive a steady flow of people from different parts of the world and Prince Edward Island (PEI) is no exception. Approximately 150 immigrants arrive in PEI every year and a total of 4,380 immigrants live on the island. Consistent with the national statistics on gender, slightly more than half of them (2,230) are women (Statistics Canada 1998). While this is not a large number compared to those in some other provinces in Canada, the immigrants who come to PEI face similar problems, and they may also face somewhat different problems, such as cultural isolation. Because they are fewer in number, there are sometimes fewer cultural supports and services available to them.

References

Anderson, J.M. 1985. "Perspectives on the Health of Immigrant Women: A Feminist Analysis." *Advances in Nursing Science* 8, 1: 61–76.

———. 1990. "Health Care across Cultures." *Nursing Outlook* 38, 3: 136–9.

———. 1991. "Immigrant Women Speak of Chronic Illness: The Social Construction of the Devalued Self." *Journal of Advanced Nursing* 16: 710–17.

Aroian, K.J. 1990. "A Model of Psychological Adaptation to Migration and Resettlement." *Nursing Research* 39: 5–10.

Barney, K.F. 1991. "From Ellis Island to Assisted Living: Meeting the Needs of Older Ethnic Adults from Diverse Cultures." *The American Journal of Occupational Therapy* 45, 7: 586–93.

Boyd, M. 1984. "At a Disadvantage: The Occupational Attainments of Foreign Born Women in Canada." *International Migration Review* 18: 1091–119.

Coombs, S. 1986. *Understanding Seniors and Culture: Multicultural Guide 3*. Edmonton: Alberta Culture; Cultural Heritage Division.

Die, A.H., and W.C. Seelbach. 1988. "Problems, Sources of Assistance, and Knowledge of Services Among Elderly Vietnamese Immigrants." *The Gerontologist* 28, 4: 448–52.

Disman, M. 1983. "Immigrants and Other Grieving People: Insights for Counseling Practices and Policy Issues." *Canadian Ethnic Studies* 5, 3: 106–18.

Driedger, L. and N.L. Chappell. 1987. *Aging and Ethnicity: Toward an Interface*. Toronto: Butterworths.

Flaskerud, J.H. 1990. "Matching Client and Therapist Ethnicity, Language, and Gender: A Review of the Research." *Issues in Mental Health Nursing* 11, 4: 321–36.

Glaser, B.G. and A.L. Strauss. 1967. *The Discovery of Grounded Theory Strategies for Qualitative Research*. New York: Aldine De Gruter.

Hattar-Pollara, M. and A.I. Meleis. 1995. "Stress of Immigration and the Daily Lived Experiences of Jordanian Women in the United States." *Western Journal of Nursing Research* 17: 521–38.

Kaufert, J.M. and R.W. Putsch. 1997. "Communication Through Interpreters in Healthcare: Ethical Dilemmas Arising from Differences in Class, Culture, Language, and Power." *The Journal of Clinical Ethics* 8, 1: 71–87.

Lalonde, R.N., D.M. Taylor, and F.M. Moghaddan. 1992. "The Process of Social Identification for Visible Immigrant Women in a Multicultural Context." *Journal of Cross-Cultural Psychology* 23: 25–39.

Lipson, J.G. 1992. "Iranian Immigrants: Health and Adjustment." *Western Journal of Nursing Research* 14: 10–29.

Lipson, J.G., and A.I. Meleis. 1985. "Culturally Appropriate Care: The Case of Immigrants." *Topics in Clinical Nursing* 7: 48–56.

Lipson, J.G., and P. Omidian. 1997. "Afghan Refugee Issues in the US Social Environment." *Western Journal of Nursing Research* 19: 110–26.

MacKinnon, M. 1993. *Towards Meeting the Health Care Needs of the Chinese Elderly: Meaning and Potential Health Consequences Associated with Care Receiving for the Chinese Elderly*. Unpublished Master's thesis, Memorial University of Newfoundland, St John's.

Majumdar, B., and B. Carpio. 1988. "Concept of Health as Viewed by Selected Ethnic Canadian Populations." *Canadian Journal of Public Health* 79, 12: 430–4.

Meleis, A.I. 1991. "Between Two Cultures: Identity, Roles, and Health." *Health Care for Women International* 12, 4: 365–77.

Meleis, A. I., J.G. Lipson, M.A. Muecke, and G.R. Smith. 1998. *Immigrant Women and Their Health: An Olive Paper.* Indianapolis, IN: Center for Nursing Press, Sigma Theta Tau.

Munro, M., M. Gallant, M. MacKinnon, G. Dell, R. Herbert, G. MacNutt, M. McCarthy, D. Murnaghan, and K. Robertson. 2000. *The Prince Edward Island Conceptual Model for Nursing: A Nursing Perspective of Primary Health Care.*

Pender, N.J. 1996. *Health Promotion in Nursing Practice.* 3rd edn. Stamford, CT: Appleton-Lange.

Polit, D.F. and B.P. Hungler. 1996. *Essentials of Nursing Research: Methods, Appraisal, and Utilization.* 4th edn. Philadelphia: Lippincott.

Rathbone-McCuan, E., and J. Hashimi. 1982. *Isolated Elders.* Rockville, MD: Aspen.

Shareski, D. 1992. "Beyond Boundaries: Cross-Cultural Care." *Nursing BC* 24, 5: 10–12.

Shields, L. 1995. "Women's Experiences of the Meaning of Empowerment." *Qualitative Health Research* 5: 15–35.

Statistics Canada. 1996. *Profile of Divisions and Subdivisions in Newfoundland.* Catalogue no. 95-182-XPB. Ottawa: Statistics Canada.

———. 1998. *1996 Census, The Nation Series: Immigration and Citizenship.* Catalogue no. 93F0023XDB96000. Ottawa: Statistics Canada.

Stevens, P.E., J.M. Hall, and A.I. Meleis. 1992. "Examining Vulnerability of Women Clerical Workers from Five Ethnic/Racial Groups." *Western Journal of Nursing Research* 14: 754–74.

Stewart, M. 2000. "Social Support, Coping, and Self-care as Public Participation Mechanisms." In M.J. Stewart, ed., *Community Nursing: Promoting Canadians' Health*, 2nd edn. Toronto: Saunders, 83–104.

Strauss, A., and J. Corbin. 1990. *Basics of Qualitative Research: Grounded Theory Procedures and Techniques.* Newbury, CA: Sage Publications.

Then, K.L. 1996. "Research Rounds: Focus Group Research." *Canadian Journal of Cardiovascular Nursing* 7, 4: 31.

Questions for Critical Thought

1. Why do the authors ensure that the voices and concerns of immigrant women themselves are the focus of their project?

2. In what ways is the medical system "culturally insensitive" to immigrant women? What forms does this insensitivity take? Who benefits from cultural insensitivity? Should there be mandatory courses in medical schools that address this issue? Do you think that people who work as translators and caregivers for immigrant women should also have special training? What would you emphasize in a program that would focus on the needs of immigrant women?

3. Why did these women continue to use herbal and traditional medicines rather than make greater use of the public health care system, which they purported to value? Do you think that homeopathic medicines and traditional practices from other cultures should be supported by the medical care system in Canada? Why or why not?

4. The authors found a lack of familiarity with English to be an important factor in the inequality of health care services among racialized women. More specifically, they assert that North American communication emphasizes "short answers to short questions" in contrast with some groups who express themselves through "story." What is your response to these claims? Are "story" forms of communication common among immigrant groups? Does adaptation to Canadian society threaten traditional languages and forms of communication?

5. Of the several recommendations the authors make to improve access and remove barriers to health care services for immigrant women, what would you argue is of highest priority? Why? What would be easiest to achieve? What would be the most difficult?

Appendix

ID Code #:

Date:

Location of Interview:

Time to Complete:

Audiotaped: Yes_____ No _____ #:

Guidelines

Questions are asked in an open-ended manner that requires more than a "Yes" or "No" answer and in a way that allows the respondent to determine the direction of the answer.

Questions are very broad and open-ended to begin with and then move to specifics, using probes of the respondent's responses to obtain more information, if needed.

A probe might be: "Could you talk a little more about that . . . about how employment affects your health?"

Use of reflection would be paraphrasing what the respondent has said and then waiting for them to elaborate. For example, " . . . health is . . . (pause) good mental and physical health . . . (pause)"?

Both probes and reflection can be used for each question to obtain depth of meaning (both the broad and the specific) about the topic in question.

Semi-Structured Interview Guide

1. What does health mean to you? If someone tells you they are healthy, what do you think they mean?
   Probes: Is mental well-being a part of it? Does a spiritual life or spirituality play a part?
2. Talk a little about the relationship between physical health, mental health, and spiritual health.
3. What are some of the ways you feel when you are healthy?
   Probe: What kinds of feelings and thoughts are part of being healthy?
4. Talk a little about some of the things you are able to do when you are healthy.
   Probe: What kinds of activities are a part of being healthy?
5. Tell me about some of the things you are *not* able to do when you are *not healthy* or when you are ill?
   Probe: Family obligations, work?
6. Compare what you do here to stay healthy with what you did in your country.
   Probes: Traditional medicines, herbal treatments, dietary practices, exercise. Do you have hot and cold conditions? What are some of the treatments you use for them?
7. Can you think of some general kinds of things in your life that affect your health?
   Probes: Would money or having a job be some of the things that affect your health? Employment? Family and friends? Language or the availability of language classes? Interpreters?

8. How do they affect the things you do to stay healthy?
9. What are some of the things that you like about Canada's health care [system]? What are some of the things you don't like about it?
10. Describe some of your experiences going to the clinic, the hospital, or a doctor.
11. When you first came, what would have helped you meet your health care needs?
12. How important is a doctor to maintaining your health?
13. How important are other professionals besides your doctor to maintaining your health?
    Probes: Social worker? Employment counsellor? Interpreters? Pharmacist? Religious leader? Dentist?
14. Can you describe for me some of the reasons you would go to your doctor? Here? In your own country? Are the reasons for the visit the same?
    Probes: Would you go to a doctor if you felt sad? Lonely? Why or why not? If you were having family problems, such as not getting along with your husband or having difficulties with a teenage child? Why or why not?
15. Describe your visits to your doctor in your own country . . . and your visits to your doctor here . . . what were they like . . . (pause)?
    Probes: What kinds of questions did your doctor ask? What kinds of questions did you ask? What kinds of topics did you raise?
16. Does it matter to you whether the doctor is male or female?
    Probes: Tell me how it matters. What are some things that make it matter? How comfortable are you talking to a male doctor about female health concerns? How comfortable are you being examined by a male doctor?
17. What, if anything, would stop you from going for health care when you need it? (Interfere or prevent).
    Probes: Are you able to make your own decision about going for health care? Does your husband play a role?
18. What else or what other things are needed in Canada's health care system in order to meet your health needs?
    Probe: Qualified interpreters?
19. Is there anything else you would like to say or talk about?
    Probe: Anything you would like to tell me about . . . ?

Becoming "The Fat Girl": Acquisition of an Unfit Identity

.... *Carla Rice*

I want my point made public. Sometimes I just want to hold a press conference and tell everybody off. [Laughs] I've always been lonely, the odd person out. . . . I'm a fantastic person, but nobody could see past the fat. It angers me more than it hurts me. But it hurts. (Leila)

In North American society, there are many disparaging depictions and few positive portrayals of girls and women perceived as fat. Despite growing dialogue about body acceptance, overweight and obesity increasingly are interpreted as unattractive, downwardly mobile, not physically or emotionally healthy, and lacking in body and self-control (Bordo 1993; LeBesco 2004). Within global and national public health discourses, obesity currently is conceptualized as an **epidemic** as well as an illness or disease (Fairburn and Brownell 2002; Raine 2004). Throughout feminist and social scientific accounts, fat is seen as a disease of the social and the biological body, shaped by gender, class, race, and other inequalities (Beauboeuf-LaFondant 2003; Lovejoy 2001; Orbach 1979). Amid escalating anti-fat attitudes over the past 30 years, weight has emerged as a major marker of social status in Western countries. Consequences of body size standards and stereotypes are especially exacting and far-reaching for girls and women, who encounter frequent evaluation of physical appearance and difference as part of their social experience of gender.

Post-structuralist and feminist perspectives emphasize how bodies and identities are shaped and experienced through cultural representations and social relations. Unfinished at birth, bodies are moulded and modified over the course of a life through the intermingling of biology with culture and society. For some contemporary theorists, physiology, psyche, and society all play a part in the body's dynamic process of "becoming" (Birke 2000; Grosz 1994). From a **feminist post-structuralist** vantage point, cultural meanings given to bodies also become a basis of identity in social relations (Brah 2001; Woodward 1997). People construct a sense of their bodily self from messages, spoken and unspoken, that they receive from popular images and people they encounter throughout their lives (Jenkins 1996). This occurs when they grasp how others perceive their bodies and understand the personal and social significance of these perceptions to their sense of identity and possibility (Rice et al. 2005).

In our society, one location that may be more generative of identity than other social spaces is school, a place where perceptions of appearance and difference shape children's sense of belonging and standing (Rice 2003). When they enter school, children for the first time are grouped together under the authoritative presence of adults. The organization of student bodies by age and grade heightens children's consciousness of physical differences and encourages body conformity as a condition of belonging (James 2000). For girls especially, association of idealized face and body features with popularity and social power teaches them that an attractive appearance is a cultural requirement of gender (Currie 1999; Thorne 1999). Children who diverge from cultural standards often experience devaluation of physical differences as a result of stereotyping and stigma. This includes fat girls, who may be marginalized by cultural messages about the abject fat female body interwoven throughout their everyday interactions.

Origins of anti-fat attitudes are found in the cultural and social milieu. Anxieties about fat also are intensified through dominant health discourses concerning the occurrence, causes, and consequences of obesity and overweight. Within current social theory, implications of cultural and medical assertions and assumptions with regards to overweight are being critically examined. For example, research in social psychology is starting to investigate consequences of size stereotypes for the body and self-images of people perceived as fat, especially kids[1] (Eisenberg, Neumark-Sztainer, and Story 2003; Neumark-Sztainer, Story, and Faibisch 1998; Pesa, Syre, and Jones 2000; Vessey et al. 2003; Young-Hyman et al. 2003). Critical studies in sociology, physical education, and health also are questioning the impetus and implications of conceptualizations of obesity as a disease caused by overeating and physical inactivity (Campos 2004; Cogan and Ernsberger 1999; Gard and Wright 2005; Sobal and Maurer 1999a, 1999b). For example, some studies suggest that size stereotypes have many negative consequences for individuals' bodily self-images; in addition, defining overweight or obesity as a disease caused by personal health practices may foster fat people's adoption of harmful habits, increase stigma against size differences, and deflect attention away from structural roots of health problems associated with fat. Yet the ways in which cultural and medical assertions about weight, activity, appetite, and health might affect girls' bodies and behaviours, including eating and exercise, remain unexplored. Also unknown are consequences of negative messages for fat girls' emerging social identities, especially gender.

In response to these gaps, this article offers a feminist post-structuralist theory of fat based on body narratives of diverse women who retrospectively recount experiences of becoming the "fat girl" within a Canadian context. Through examining cultural messages concerning fatness and fitness conveyed to contributors within their childhood social worlds, I analyze the intersections of their personal body histories with broader social and political histories. I use critical social and feminist theory to uncover relationships in the narratives that are currently unmapped within the conventional literature on childhood obesity: connections between negative perceptions of size differences and the emergence of fat girls' "unfit" bodies and identities. Stories of participants trace how harmful consequences of weight stereotyping crystallize in fat girls' greater susceptibility to engage in problem eating and to avoid physical activity. Furthermore, persistent negative perceptions of fatness create a difficult double bind for participants by blocking opportunities for claiming credible feminine or tomboy identities. While anti-fat attitudes compromise their physical abilities and identity choices, contributors also show creativity and courage at self-making, by mediating attributions of difference with improvisational identities as a constant and dynamic process. In light of recent warnings raised throughout media coverage, epidemiological research, and government reports about the apparent obesity epidemic among kids, this analysis concludes with discussion of the study's implications for future feminist research and praxis.

Methodology and Interpretation

This analysis emerges from a qualitative research project I undertook several years ago to understand women's diverse experiences of their bodies across the life span. I became interested in women's body image formation through my 20 years' experience as an activist and clinician working with women with a range of body image struggles. Because most body image research focuses on

white, middle-class, and non-disabled women's weight problems, I decided to interview diverse women to learn more about similarities and differences in their body experiences. This research asks: *How do women negotiate cultural meanings given to bodies and use these interpretations to shape their identities, subjectivities, and sense of life possibilities?* The research traces the role of the body in women's identity acquisition in the timeframe from early childhood to late adolescence; it follows their creation of body images and initiation into body modification projects as attempts to give symbolic and material form to preferred accounts of themselves.

When I began this study, I combined inductive methods of **grounded theory**—to uncover and build theory from informants' accounts—and **phenomenology**—to unearth participants' experiential knowledges of their lived bodies in the social world (Creswell 1998). While inductive methods offered an ethical starting point for suspending my own theoretical commitments, I found that the research questions I asked and the stories participants told were inevitably value-based. With this realization, I turned to feminist post-structuralist methodology to understand epistemological positions that influenced my implementation of methods and interpretation of findings (Naples 2003). Methodological and interpretive approaches evolved over time to encompass four guiding principles: (1) use of a hybrid "inductive-deductive" approach to integrate methodology and interpretation; (2) emphasis on contradiction, complexity, and theoretical plurality; (3) privileging of participants' experiential knowledges, agency, and creativity; and (4) attending to experiences of difference throughout interviewing and theory building.

Data Collection and Coding Methods

To obtain body histories of 81 diverse women, I combined snowball and strategic sampling (Strauss and Corbin 1998). Written and word-of-mouth advertising through community organizations, universities, and media outlets was purposely planned to facilitate greater inclusion of women from under- and misrepresented groups. I crafted an open-ended, semi-structured interview guide to capture contributors' experiences of their bodies in narrative time and in diverse social spaces.[2] In my initial conversations with those marginalized by mainstream research on body image, many expressed an ethical commitment to telling their stories as a way of revisioning conventional accounts and enriching understanding about implications of differences. Following detailed discussion about the scope and aims of the project, I carried out in-depth individual interviews spanning one, two, or three sessions at my office, home, or the homes of contributors. I applied a constant comparative method to discover common themes that emerged through distinguishing among events told by the women. These I emphasized in proportion to their significance to the women themselves, as determined by frequency and prominence in the narratives.

Transcripts were coded separately by myself and by a research assistant; as coding progressed, we met periodically to discuss commonalities and discrepancies in developing categories. Coding with a collaborator helped to increase "**construct validity**"[3] by guarding against my possible imposition of oppressive conceptual frameworks onto participants' lives (Lather 1991). To check "face validity" of emerging analyses with groups under investigation (Lather 1991), I conducted public talks in diverse community settings as well as private consultations with selected interviewees having "insider knowledges" of themes discussed in this article (White 2002). Audience and interviewee responses to analyses were of immeasurable value in enriching knowledge generated in the research.

Participant Profiles

The research draws on body narratives told by women between the ages of 20 and 45, with an average age of 30 (see Table 1: Selected participant profiles). Importantly, most participants (90 per cent) came to see themselves as over- or underweight, and 25 per cent formed a "fat" identity by the end of childhood. Contributors were equally composed of racialized and non-racialized women,[4] including Northern European (28 per cent), African-Caribbean (20 per cent), South Asian (14 per cent), Southern and Eastern European (13 per cent), and Asian (10 per cent) Canadian women. Percentages of participants roughly reflected the ethnoracial makeup of the Canadian city where the study was conducted.[5] Contributors' mobility and sensory disabilities included cerebral palsy and blindness (11 per cent); their facial and physical differences consisted of craniofacial conditions and scoliosis (9 per cent); and their chronic illnesses ranged from rheumatoid arthritis to reproductive disorders (23 per cent). While women evenly described growing up in middle- (43 per cent) and working- or welfare-class households (40 per cent), at the time of the interview a majority (61 per cent) reported that their income situation was "limited" (under $30,000).

These statistics provide a partial snapshot of participants' identities, yet they also collapse multifaceted differences into pre-defined categories. Complex and contradictory meanings of differences given in interactions had implications for women's bodies and lives that were not easily predicted by conventional groupings. However, concerns and issues regarding body and self-image emerged as a common thread among those with differences in size. Accounts of 18 women who formed a fat identity by the end of childhood and/or who witnessed effects of anti-fat attitudes on other kids are analyzed throughout this article. Emphasized in the following theoretical framework are cultural representations and social relations productive of fatness that underpin participants' personal accounts.

Competing Frames of Fatness

I wasn't what a girl should be. I was going to be a big kid. I wasn't necessarily going to be fat, though. It became a self-perpetuating cycle

TABLE 1   Selected participant profiles

Participant name	Size identity	Cultural/ethnic background	Country of birth	Disability, physical difference, or chronic illness	Class background	Current income (limited under $30,000)/occupation	Age
Anjula	Worried about weight since 4th grade	South Asian, Hindu	Canada		Immigrant, middle class	Limited, student	21
Aurora	Has identified as too thin since high school	Ecuadorian	Ecuador	Scoliosis in early adolescence	Immigrant, working class	Limited, student	26
Catherine	Fat identity from age 8	White Protestant	Canada		Working to middle class	Middle, teacher	37
Erum	Fluctuates, identified as overweight since age 10 or 11	South Asian, African, Middle Eastern, Muslim	Canada	Polycystic ovarian syndrome	Immigrant, working class	Limited, student	22
Gayle	Identified as fat since 3rd or 4th grade	Welsh, English, Scottish, Métis	Canada		Middle class	Limited, student	26
Gina	Identified as overweight since 2nd grade	Estonian	Canada	Cerebral palsy	Working class	Working to middle class, office worker	36
Isobel	Fluctuates, identified as fat since age 10	African, Brazilian, Celtic	Brazil	Psychiatric diagnosis	Immigrant, working class	Disability benefits, the arts	31
Iris	Fluctuates, identified as fat since age 7 or 8	English	Canada	Auto-immune deficiency (thyroid)	Middle class	Limited, unemployed academic	32
Katerina	Average	German, Austrian	Canada	Psychiatric diagnosis	Immigrant, working class	Limited, bank clerk	32
Leigh	Fluctuates, identified as fat from 2nd grade	Chinese, Trinidadian (2nd generation) Canadian (first generation)			Immigrant, working class	Middle, urban planner	24
Leila	Identified as overweight since 4th or 5th grade	Scottish	Canada	Spinal problems from birth	Working class	Limited, office	34

(Continued)

TABLE 1 *Continued*

Participant name	Size identity	Cultural/ethnic background	Country of birth	Disability, physical difference, or chronic illness	Class background	Current income (limited under $30,000)/occupation	Age
Marianne	Identified as overweight since age 9	Cultural – European, Ethnic – African-American	Canada	Middle class		Limited, public relations	33
Maude	Fluctuates, identified as fat since 2nd grade	White Canadian	Canada	Blind from adolescence	Working class	Limited, Massage therapist	27
Rose	Fluctuates, identified as too thin in childhood and as too fat from age 15	Korean-born, Canadian-raised	Korea		Immigrant, working class		24
Salima	Fluctuates, identified as fat from 5th grade	South Asian, Indian	England		Immigrant, working class	Working class, day care worker	30
Sharon	Identified as fat since age 7 or 8	West Indian	England		Immigrant, working to middle class	Middle, policy analyst	31
Sylvie	Identified as fat since 3rd grade	Italian, Scottish	Canada		Working class	Middle, manager	38
Yolanda	Identified as overweight since 4th or 5th grade	Dutch, Indonesian	Canada		Middle class	Middle, editor	23

Note: Of 81 women participating in the study, the table includes profiles only of those quoted in this article.

of eating to feed myself emotionally because I didn't fit. I think I became fat because of circumstance. Like, cultural environment shaped my size. (Sylvie)

In North American societies, two competing frames shape current dialogue on obesity and overweight: obesity as an "epidemic" versus as a "myth" (Campos 2004; Gard and Wright 2005). The first frame—the epidemic of obesity—dominates public discussion and debate. Fear of a **pandemic** of fat people has made obesity a "hot topic" in many Western countries. Global and national public health institutions have fuelled this fear by interpreting obesity as an escalating epidemic that threatens the health and fitness of Western populations and nations. The World Health Organization (WHO) has even referred to the global spread of obesity as "globesity" (WHO 2000, 2003). The apparent increase in overweight and obesity among Canadians over the past 25 years is deemed in many federal and provincial public health reports to constitute a "Canadian epidemic" (Basrur 2004; Raine 2004). Obesity epidemic discourses have become so prominent and pervasive throughout Canada and other Western countries that they often have invalidated alternative views.

As recently as the 1980s, there was active dialogue and debate within North America about the concepts, causes, and consequences of obesity and overweight. In text and talk, academics, activists, and medical experts argued whether obesity was a body type or disease type; debated dangers of dieting; and acknowledged that weight prejudice was an increasingly intolerable aspect of everyday experiences of fat people, especially women (Bennett and Gurin 1983; Ciliska 1990; Ernsberger 1987). Feminist theorists in particular provided alternative positions to conventional medical accounts, by situating experiences of diversely embodied women within patriarchal social relations (Millman 1980; Orbach 1979). In economically privileged, media-driven parts of the world where women are identified socially with their bodies, feminists showed how pervasive cultural messages about valued or devalued female body

sizes, shapes, and capacities had especially serious consequences. Although alternative feminist, sociological, and scientific perspectives entered mainstream media stories throughout the 1980s, these increasingly were marginalized by obesity epidemic rhetoric. Initially adopted by the United States government, Canadian institutions also embraced this conceptualization and commissioned mounting reports that framed fatness as a disease of Westernized societies. Media coverage of reports generated much public discussion and galvanized many politicians in ways that further framed debate, confirming the emerging consensus that obesity was an epidemic (Gard and Wright 2001; Lawrence 2004).

Critical analysis of obesity discourses shifts emphasis from stemming the epidemic of fat folk to examining the emergence of a cultural idea—obesity as a dangerous disease—that has captured the cultural imagination (Barthes 1972). Throughout Western history, body size has been a signifier for the health, fitness, welfare, and status of individuals, groups, and nations. Social historians confirm that celebration and **stigmatization** of fat has fluctuated at different times among different social groups (Schwartz 1986; Stearns 1997). While concerns about medical and moral risks of fatness circulated in pre-modern times, morally laden interpretations of overweight as symbolic of wealth and waste have intensified over the last century (Stearns 1997). These negative meanings have gained momentum within a visual culture profuse with size stereotypes (Braziel and LeBesco 2001), as well as amid growth of a multi-billion-dollar weight loss and pharmaceutical industry that profits from size prejudice (Fraser 1998). They find credence in a moral climate censorious of effortless lifestyles and excessive consumption seen to signify social decline (Gard and Wright 2005). Finally, they gain acceptance in a political economy more invested in changing bodies of fat people than in shifting structural roots of health problems associated with fat. Erasure of uncertainty and complexity about causes of overweight is accomplished through appeals to personal responsibility that place burden and blame for one's weight solely on the individual (Crawford 2004; Evans, Rich, and Holroyd 2004). Within rhetoric privileging personal responsibility, overweight folks facing contextual constraints are viewed as lacking knowledge, skills, or ethics to take healthy actions.

Throughout Western countries, present day dominance of obesity discourses was preceded and made possible by earlier government efforts to improve the health and fitness of citizens. From the late 1960s onwards, state promotion of physical activity as a method of population health improvement gained prominence, in Canada and elsewhere (Bauman et al. 2004; Rootman and Edwards 2004). In response to growing concerns about excessive consumption and sedentary lifestyles of Western populations (Gard and Wright 2001), governments initiated public education campaigns that called for more physical activity to prevent fatness and promote fitness in citizens. Through a chain of binaries and signifiers, messages that associated firm active bodies with national strength also linked a flabby sedentary citizenry with stagnation of the state. Signifying the future health and prosperity of Western nations, children typically were targeted as a group needing special attention (Gard and Wright 2005).

Importantly, the efficacy of such interventions has never been established. Studies show fat children and youth are less likely to be physically active and more likely to engage in problem eating. *Yet research has not revealed whether overeating and under-exercising increase overweight or whether being fat increases their susceptibility to problem eating and inactivity* (Boutelle et al. 2002; Duncan et al. 2002; Mellin et al. 2002). Some physical education scholars speculate that demanding physical education practices introduced in the 1970s actually may have dissuaded many overweight students from participating in physical activity (Gard and Wright 2005). Moreover, fitness promotion campaigns inadvertently may have reinforced stereotypes and stigma, which current studies confirm have harmful consequences for children's body and self-images (Barker and Galambos 2003; Burrows, Wright, and Jungersen-Smith 2002; Holt and

Ricciardelli 2002; Krahnstoever Davison and Birch 2002; O'Dea and Caputi 2001; Van den Berg et al. 2002; Vander Wal 2004). Charting effects of anti-fat attitudes on a previous generation may be critically important for assessing implications of obesity epidemic rhetoric on a current cohort of fat kids.

In the past 40 years, feminist scholarship has provided alternative conceptions of size that challenge conventional medical accounts. Writers concerned with understanding women's bodily oppression in patriarchal society have centred experiences of embodied subjects as feminism's theoretical touchstone (Brownmiller 1984; Greer 1971; Kruks 2001). Concern of feminist activists and clinicians with cultural messages about the ideal and abject female body mounted throughout the 1980s and 1990s, when increased prevalence of eating and body image problems led many to focus attention on the profound consequences of gendered body standards, especially for girls and young women (Orbach 1979; Schoenfielder and Wieser 1983; Székely 1988). With the turn to post-structuralism, theorists moved away from probing constraints placed on female bodies in patriarchal structures toward exploring ways that bodily selves are shaped through social discourses (Butler 1990; Smith 1993). To understand individual investment in body alteration, feminists interrogated how meanings about female bodies that are produced through language and imagery contour women's desires to embody a particular image (De Lauretis 1987; Ussher 1997). By situating individual body struggles within a broader context, feminist scholarship has made a major contribution in bringing to light harmful consequences of cultural images and social interactions that instruct women that their bodies are unacceptable and in need of alteration for them to be viewed as worthy people (Bordo 1993). Through synthesizing first-person with post-structuralist accounts, feminists further have revealed the pivotal role of restrictive representations and others' evaluative responses in women's body image, identity, and self-making (Davis 1995; Mama 1995).

Feminist and post-structuralist perspectives emphasize how cultural meanings that contour bodily experiences also intervene in biology to shape physiology (Fausto-Sterling 2000; Grosz 1994; Marshall 1996). New emphasis on the inter-activity of physiology, psyche, and society in the body's becoming has important implications for feminist analyses of fat. Such a perspective posits that neither genetics nor health habits alone determine size; instead, individuals' weights may develop differently depending on the relationships of sized bodies with psyches and surrounding worlds. Theorizing the physiology of weight as an interactive process calls into question mechanistic or moralistic scientific and cultural claims that faulty genes or bad habits cause fat. It raises important ethical questions about discourses that advocate individual interventions based on the erroneous belief that personal behaviour alone causes overweight. Finally, it challenges approaches that sanction stigmatization of overweight and obesity based on the misguided conviction that fat women have not taken correct action to ensure a socially or medically acceptable size. Drawing on feminist insights about the body's becoming, this article argues that size is a social form produced at the intersection of biology, psychology, and culture. *Women's coming-of-age body histories show how the unfit fat body is made from interactions of large bodies, cultural representations, and social practices that shape bodies of size.*

Acquiring an Unfit Identity

My mom would ask me to go down the store. I had so much anxiety about that . . . . I think it was because of being overweight and people commenting even though that's not what I thought consciously. All I knew then was that it was uncomfortable to go outside. (Salima)

Women with differences in size recount how they were rendered as physically and also as socially unfit through the ongoing dialogue of their social relations. This included the symbolic systems, physical environments, spatial arrangements, and visual, verbal, and even physically violent exchanges, which taught them that they transgressed the culturally normal body. For most participants, negative perceptions of fatness became increasingly commonplace as they moved through childhood, occurring at home, on the street, and especially at school. Stereotypes concerning size also were cumulative, recurring in relationships with parents, peers, teachers, health providers, strangers, and others. According to women's narratives, memorable anti-fat attitudes received through cultural representations gained meaning and momentum in everyday interactions. When images and messages resonated across situations, they had significant implications for participants' developing sense of body and self.

Learning Size Differences

Participants tell how critical comparisons and comments were the most memorable sources of cultural knowledge about body size binaries. For most women, including Aurora, parents and family members first imparted the significance of size differences through body-based comparisons with sisters, cousins, and female friends: "My sister is chubbier. They'd always make that distinction. I was 'la flaca.' and she was 'la gorda.' Together, we make the perfect ten. It was terrible. They're lavishing on me and disregarding her."

As a result of body-based comparisons, a majority of women acquired consciousness of unequal values given to different sizes. Stories of Catherine, Gayle, and many others further suggest that gendered power relations operating in encounters with fathers, brothers, and other boys frequently opened up big girl bodies to a particularly critical gaze.

My brother started to give me the nickname Moose or Cow. Those names hurt. But I wasn't aware of it and it [being big] wasn't negative until people started to comment. (Catherine)

In Grade 4, Thomas Lum, yelled out at me, "Fat." I tried to run after him and catch him, but I'm not built to run. I thought, "My God, I am fat." That was the first time I can remember it really impacting on me. From that point on, things went downhill with my attitude with my body. (Gayle)

Through greater power given to their harsh and harassing comments, boys and men dictated anti-fat attitudes that informed women's body and self-perceptions. For many, designation of their bodies as "fat" laid the foundation for their forced accommodation to an unfit identity, imbued with incapacities associated with female fatness that negatively affected and shaped their embodied being.

State-Sponsored Fitness Promotion Campaigns Heighten Consciousness of Size

Within Canada, memorable messages for many women interviewed were state-sponsored fitness tests delivered through school physical education curricula and public service announcements (PSAs) disseminated through television and print media. In one PSA entitled "FitFat" that ran throughout major Canadian media in the late 1970s, an ungainly, chubby "a" cartoon character was contrasted with an able, slimmed down "i" figure (Lagarde 2004). By visually and vocally linking fitness with thinness, this clip reproduced positive cultural meanings associated with thin and replayed negative meanings given to fat. The images and messages, in positioning fat as opposite to fit, also conveyed that fatness and fitness could *not* coincide within the same body. Importantly, few women in this study could even vaguely recall contents of messages. Yet as Maude's story illustrates, they vividly recount consequences

of them, which included instilling a nascent sense that their bodies were in some way bad or wrong:

I remember this feeling of dread when the ads came on TV. Once my father and I were watching, I remember a man's voice saying, "This year fat's not where it's at." This made me so self-conscious because I was already feeling bad about my body. (Maude)

Negative Perceptions of Fatness Produce Physical Unfitness

For women in this study, body standards and stereotypes were communicated everywhere at school. These were conveyed through school furniture and dress codes, playground and classroom interactions, popular physical education pedagogies such as fitness tests and team selection, as well as classroom organizing practices of seating arrangements, lineups, and student placement in class pictures. Entering school environments for the first time, women recall being grouped together by age, grade, and physical traits under the authoritative presence of adults (James 1995, 2000). As a result, all developed increased consciousness of their own and other kids' proximity to norms in height, weight, and physical ability. Because women-as-girls had little access to alternative frameworks with which to question meanings associated with assigned or implied differences, they were especially susceptible to incorporating others' attributions into their developing body and self-images. Subjected to an evaluative gaze in gendered interactions at school (Currie 1999; Thorne 1999), those perceived as fat frequently faced greater censure for failure to conform to body standards. Contributors tell how being positioned around certain notions of standard bodies was a common occurrence that began before school age. Yet classroom and schoolyard practices of categorizing students according to perceived similarities and differences in age, size, height, gender, and athletic abilities had implications for participants' sense of physical identity and possibility throughout the school years.

A majority of women in this study enjoyed participation in physical education. Once identified as "the fat girl," however, many describe how their continual **framing** according to the attribution of fat rather than by their actual and potential range of abilities eroded their physical agency. When teachers and students rooted assessments of fat girls' abilities in stereotypical notions concerning their size, as Iris explains, they produced girls' presumed lack of strength, coordination, and skill:

> Once I was a fat kid, there's limitations on your abilities. You're unfit basically . . . NO, I lost confidence in that. I didn't like sports or gym. Not because I couldn't actually perform the sports. It's because I didn't like being taunted. (Iris)

Within recent feminist research, experiences of gender, race, and weight-related harassment emerge as a major obstacle to girls' participation in physical activity at school (Bauer, Yang, and Austin 2004; Cockburn and Clarke 2002; Larkin and Rice 2005). For many respondents in this study, routines and requirements of physical education such as fitness testing, public performance, weight measurements, and revealing clothes also increased their exposure to the evaluative gaze of others.

> My teacher commented on how I was gaining weight, when I was about 10. He said that I had poor eating habits. When we had to run in the gym, he said I had problems running . . . . It didn't feel very good. I felt upset in front of everybody. (Isabel)

> My body became a source of torment. This is why I HATE my grade 5 teacher: he had the practice of letting kids divide up teams for sports. My best friend and I were always picked last. (Gayle)

According to women's narratives, pedagogical practices that undermined fat girls' sense of physical ability often dissuaded them from participation in school physical activities. By exposing big girls' bodies to others' critical gaze, school design of dress codes and open change rooms further instilled a negative sense of physical appearance, giving rise to stressful strategies to conceal size difference.

> When I was younger, we had a school uniform and the gym uniform was shorts and a T-shirt. Maybe they thought, "They are little kids. What do they have to hide?" But sweatshirts or sweatpants weren't even an option. So I hated gym because we had to wear shorts and I hated my thighs. Whenever I could, even if I hadn't forgotten my shorts, I would leave them in my gym locker. I would tell my gym teacher I had forgotten my shorts and could I wear my tracks? . . . I did it so frequently. (Anjula)

> I loved school, but I hated the students and I hated the interaction. I hated gym class. I hated changing in the change rooms. I didn't want them to see my body. (Yolanda)

For participants of diverse sizes, stresses of size and gender differences resulted from compulsory participation in a state-sponsored physical education curriculum called the "Canada Fitness Awards." Designed to improve Canadian children's fitness levels, the program awarded gold, silver, or bronze "badges" (designed to reflect the Olympic medals system) based on student completion of chin-up, push-up, and long jump competitions. Some, including Rose, recall how challenges involved in public evaluation of physical performance were intensified by gender and size biases built into the tests:

> I hated Canada Fitness because my friend was athletically gifted and she always got the red excellent badge. I always got the bronze. It was horrible to test kids in front of other

kids. How many chin ups you could do . . . .
Women generally can't do as many because
of upper body strength. If you have long legs
it is easier to do the hurdles or the long jump.
(Rose)

Weighted in favour of children with long legs
and upper body strength and against those who
lacked height or well-developed arm muscles,
women describe how fitness tests tended to privilege boy over girl bodies as well as tall over short
ones. Yolanda further describes how compulsory
fitness tests heightened consciousness of her
appearance and ability differences, and diminished confidence in her physical abilities:

I wasn't doing very well in ParticipACTION or
Fitness Canada. I didn't like running around
in shorts and I always wore track pants . . . .
But I was active in my own way. I biked to
school, I walked to school. I was active everyday. (Yolanda)

Because masculine ability norms required in
sport contradict feminine appearance ideals
obliged by culture (Cockburn and Clarke 2002;
Kirk and Tinning 1994; Krane et al. 2004; Oliver
and Lalik 2004), interviewees encountered critical
looks and comments for failing to meet standards
of the athletic boy or measure up to images of the
attractive girl. Participants of all sizes and shapes
avoided physical activity to evade others' judgements. Yet the consequences of such marginalization were especially marked for fat girls. Seen as
commensurate with cultural standards of passive
femininity, physical inability also is viewed as productive of fatness. As a result, fat women tell how
they frequently faced exclusion for having a body
that failed to qualify as fit *and* confronted social
disapproval for their ensuing disengagement from
physical activities.

As many feminist sociologists have noted, girls
and women in sport commonly confront the cultural contradiction of an active female body (Krane
et al. 2004; Lenskyj 1994; Malcom 2003). Because
female athletes often are evaluated according to

skilful execution of sport as much as convincing
performance of femininity, they may have to meet
and manage conflicting expectations of athleticism and attractiveness to be successful in sport.
For participants perceived as fat, this contradiction was especially difficult to navigate. Seen as
contravening a male athletic and female attractive body, fat athletes tell how they encountered
deeply disparaging assessments of their physical
performance in sport despite their display of skill.

I rode and I show-jumped. In my first big
horse show . . . I remember being given a fifth
place ribbon and the judge walking up to
me and saying, "Actually you should've been
first. But your job was to sit there and look
pretty and frankly you need to lose weight."
First, I remember feeling mad because . . . it
wasn't my horse's fault the way I looked, she'd
done her job beautifully. I should by all rights
have been first. And he was denying it to me
on my appearance. That's when things really
sort of hit home that these things were very
important. (Iris)

Fatness Signifies Personal and Social Unfitness

In a culture that equates merit and morality with
body size conformity, women's narratives imply
that fatness becomes a physical marker of personal disorder as well as a bodily sign of social
unfitness. This is especially evident in narratives
of women who attended schools for kids with disabilities. At Gina's school, for example, officials
separated and regulated the eating of students
perceived as fat. Segregation of fat kids with disabilities created an identifiable group of "others"
who were doubly disabled by the perception that
they were incapable of maintaining control over
their eating and weight.

They had definite ideas about kids with disabilities, it was this institutional attitude.
They stuck any kids that they perceived

to be too big or too fat on the diet table in the cafeteria, right? For years, myself and a number of my friends were on this diet table. Nothing reinforces that more because then your peers are on this side of the wall, you're on that side of the wall and they're telling you that you are being segregated . . . . That was very damaging because it was at public school and everybody was young and peer pressure [was intense]. (Gina)

For women with disabilities, cultural messages about the disabled body, such as bodily fragility, vulnerability, and dependency (Rogers and Swadener 2001), intersected with messages about the fat form, including incapacity, overindulgence, and lack of restraint or willpower (Bordo 1993; LeBesco 2004). Although both bodily differences were interpreted as impairments that needed fixing, cultural treatment of disability as an inherent attribute contrasted sharply with framing of fatness as an intentional act. Fat disabled kids were regulated because their fatness was seen as a deliberate action that further impaired an unfit form. Fatness signified surrender of the disabled child's self to excessive appetites that could be restrained only through greater control of the already incapacitated body.

According to contributors, being a big girl was not the equivalent of being a fat girl. Significantly, women's bigness became fatness within environments that produced girls' social and physical unfitness and led to exercise habits typically associated with fat. Fat became a problem for participants because it emerged out of a disordered relationship between big girls' bodies and social relations that refused to see female physical and social fitness as embodied by anything but a thin, able form.

Other-Gendering Fat Girls

The boys would say "you're fat" and the girls would say "that fat girl." Guys would call girls fat more than girls would call girls fat. "You're fat. Get away from me." (Erum)

Fat Becomes a Dominating Identity

For most participants, fat became a major marker of place and power in girlhood and, for many, a dominating identity they have carried throughout their lives. Framed first as "unfit" fat kids and only secondarily as girls with other identities, characteristics, abilities, and aspirations, they learned, like Marianne, "to collapse people's negative reactions into my size." Gina, too, describes how she was haunted by negative perceptions of her physical differences, which caused her to become confused about whether "I'm unattractive because I'm overweight, disabled, or because I'm disabled and overweight." Throughout their accounts, size intermingled with and/or overrode other devalued differences inscribed on women's bodies, becoming a defining characteristic thought to express something essentially faulty or flawed about them (Degher and Hughes 1999). For example, combined racial, disability, and weight-related harassment made it difficult for racialized women and those with disabilities to distinguish which physical differences were being devalued within interactions. Yet when fatness was framed as a personal flaw or moral failure at home and school, as Leigh testifies, it became a recurring source of shame.

I was the only Chinese kid in class. So I didn't know: "Are they picking on me because I'm Chinese or are they picking on me because I'm bigger than they are?" Of course it's obvious by the name they are calling you when they are picking on you but sometimes it is not that easy to differentiate . . . . More from my family that I was given all these comments and made to feel bad about myself. People talk about overweight people being shamed into losing the weight. I don't know how they ever thought that shame would work. But I guess that's what my mom thought that she would do. What my mom taunted me with was also heard by my siblings. I guess that's what bothered me the most, that they learned this from my mother. (Leigh)

Anti-Fat Prejudice Obstructs Efforts at Establishing Credible Feminine and Tomboy Identities

Women's narratives illustrate how gender became a core definition of the self in childhood. Rather than being a cohesive identity, the salience of gender shifted in social situations and in intermingling with other identities (Thorne 1999). While gender fluidity was a significant feature of their childhood accounts, gender identities frequently became fixed in a negative direction by devaluation of women's size differences. Fat women tell how they were perceived to possess a body that "other-gendered" them within interactions as "improper," "odd," or "not" girls. Gayle, for instance, describes how peer perceptions of fat positioned her as other than a feminine girl:

It wasn't big breasts that made me feel like an improper female, but it was fat, fat, fat . . . . So because of my fat . . . I was made to feel like an improper female if I showed any signs of femininity. In grade 3, I liked a boy. There was nothing remotely sexual. He had the best sense of humour and I really liked him: "Look, he's your boyfriend!" "Oooh, you like him!" That was a total shock to me, having to watch your actions so that they can't be construed as you like someone . . . . I was having enough dealings with being "fat ol' Gayle, fat stupid Gayle." My "fat, ugly" label stuck and I was pretty much a loser, weird Gayle. (Gayle)

For women in this study, failing at becoming a feminine girl often opened up other possibilities for gender. The in-between status of "tomboy" enabled many to express attributes that the feminine girl discourse disallowed, such as athleticism, competitiveness, curiosity, and strength (Davies 2002; Thorne 1997). Once given the attribution of "fat," however, women found their status

as tomboy was difficult to sustain. When cultural meanings of boy bodies as wiry, gutsy, and strong conflicted with interpretations of fat bodies as inert, inept, and weak, participants perceived as fat frequently faced disqualification from tomboy identities through exclusion from tomboy pursuits. As Sylvie's narrative suggests, exclusion often occurred through boys' aggressive challenges to big girls' physical abilities and strength:

I remember my "fall from grace" from being one of the boys. When I was a kid I was stronger than they were. I used to beat the shit out of half of them. I didn't throw like a girl, I didn't run like a girl. I didn't fight like a girl. So no one picked on me. And no one treated me like a girl . . . . I can remember in grade five when the boys started to become stronger than me. They would gang up on me so I couldn't beat them up any more. So I got banished . . . . I became the classic fat kid. I was teased. The boys hated me. I could no longer beat them up. I went from being a powerful kid to totally despised, despicable. (Sylvie)

While many study contributors continued to express athleticism and/or aggression in interactions as kids, girls' designation as tomboy meant such activities now belonged to the boys' domain. As a result, participants of all sizes encountered increased pressure to relinquish boy-coded activities and tomboy identities as they approached adolescence to avoid renouncing femaleness and heterosexuality (Barden 2001).

Size Intermingling with other Differences Disqualifies Gender

Black and other racialized women indicate that images of an attractive female body spanned a broader range of sizes and shapes in their communities than in mainstream contexts. However, those in this cohort grew up during a time when communities of colour comprised less than 5 per cent of the Canadian population (Statistics

Canada 2003). For this reason, most contributors recall being one of only a few children within their communities and schools identified as an ethnoracial minority. Coming of age at a time prior to the existence of segmented television channels, black and other racialized women in this study also had little access to an alternative cultural imaginary in which to revision beauty. Subjected to **racial othering** and to racial isolation within social and cultural landscapes of childhood, many lacked a cultural or community context in which to develop a critical consciousness about racist beauty ideals or to imagine an alternative body aesthetic (Poran 2002). As a result, many, including Sharon, tell how negative perceptions of their colour combined with negative perceptions of their size to disqualify their gender:

> I didn't feel like a girl. Do girl things. I was not a girl, not a boy, just someone existing. Then compound that with being a black female. It's even worse 'cause you feel, Jesus, I'm nowhere. Cause it's bad enough being a white little girl and you're fat. But when you're fat and you're black, it's like holy fuck. That's like the lowest. The worst thing you could ever be. (Sharon)

Black feminists have analyzed how black women are seen as more masculine, aggressive, and athletic within dominant discourses of femininity (Hammonds 1999; Collins 2004). Overweight African-Caribbean Canadian women suggest that meanings of female blackness as more masculine may intermingle with meanings of fatness as less vital and less active, and position them as neither boys nor girls.

Compliance with Culturally Feminine Bodies Is Secured through Surveillance and Violence

Women further reveal how surveillance and control of big girls' bodies caused many to develop problem eating practices, including dieting,

bingeing, and starving behaviours. When those perceived as fat failed to "qualify" as girls, doctors, mothers, and others encouraged and enforced dieting routines as a strategy for remaking their bodies to fit gendered size norms. While others justified dieting using discourses of "healthy weights," concern over health masked deeper anxieties regarding girls' adherence to a culturally feminine body. Pressures to comply with cultural constructions of the feminine girl were closely connected to pressures to adapt to cultural weight norms (McKinley 1999). As Sharon illustrates, messages about healthy weights augmented messages about femininity to enforce adherence to both imperatives.

> I was 8 or 9, and my doctor said, "You should try and lose some weight. Don't you want to go to your high school prom?" He said that boys don't go out with fat girls. So I fucked off with that doctor. I told my mother I'm not going to him. 'Cause my mother was there when he said this. She sat there quietly. She had brought me to him to try and help me to lose weight . . . . They put me on pills. They just made me sleep. I didn't lose weight . . . . I liked food, too. So don't tell a kid, okay she's a little big, but Jesus Christ, she wants to eat. That was when I started to hide the food. (Sharon)

For most participants in this study, regulation of weight through enforced dieting routines resulted in lifelong struggles with food and eating. Some women developed compulsive, binge, and secretive eating practices as a direct response to adult interventions. Others took up extreme dieting, anorexic, and bulimic practices in the transition to womanhood when they faced increased pressure to look and appear as desirable. Because it was considered a failure, default, or rebellion against cultural notions of female attractiveness, fatness in girls—as Katerina vividly illustrates—was treated as a very significant, symbolic, and threatening state of embodied being (Millman 1980).

I'll never forget this, she [a girl perceived as fat in Katerina's grade school class] was walking home.... A bunch of boys got together and they spit all over her. Her jacket was covered in spit. That's when her mother complained. 'Cause that was . . . abuse. To this day I can't believe that they did that to her. Her mother brought the jacket to school and said, "Look at this. This is what they did to my daughter." (Katerina)

Many social commentators starting with Foucault have argued that power in modern society operates indirectly through creating desire within people for conformity to a "normal" body (Foucault 1980, 2003). Women in this study testify that girls' compliance with gendered size norms also is secured through direct, repressive, and often violent control of their bodies and appetites. Women-as-girls recount how negative perceptions of size intersecting with other differences positioned them as "other" prior to adolescence. For many, the process of becoming fat that adversely affected their body images and eating practices predated adolescence, a period that many feminist psychologists and theorists argue is fraught with dangers to girls' bodies and psyches.

Contesting Negative Meanings

Before I was overweight I was a fairly confident kid. But once I was overweight, the children's chants . . . I got beaten up quite often . . . . It took a long time for my confidence to be beaten down, I am still fairly outgoing and trying to do well in school. I was very creative. (Iris)

Women-as-Girls Mediate Attributions of Difference to Improvise Identities

Women's stories reveal that they possessed limited power and resources in girlhood to challenge the intense emotions of contempt and fear that

female fatness aroused. In childhood, participants had few options for intervening in broader physical, social, and symbolic environments. Yet they still found creative strategies to contest received meanings and improvise unique identities. Some took on a comedic role to ameliorate peers' disparaging perceptions. Many focused on developing intellectually or artistically as a method of divesting themselves from the devalued trait. A few, including Leila, asserted their physical abilities despite stereotypic perceptions of unfitness, by reversing the cliché of the fat girl being chosen last:

If I wasn't the team captain, I was chosen last. Most of the time I was the team captain, I made sure of that. My momma didn't raise no fool. [Laughs] But I always tried to be the team captain so I wouldn't have the rejection of being last. (Leila)

Exploiting cultural associations of size with aggression and masculinity, some fat women resorted to violence to resist negative attributions. Boys responded to fat girls' aggression with vengeance because girls' use of physical violence flaunted the power of fat female bodies, challenging the lowly place of fat girls on the social landscape as they understood it.

I was fighting this boy, who I knew I could beat up. But he was one of the popular boys and the other kids knew that, and so all the boys got in a circle. We're having a fight in the schoolyard and I started winning and the boy started to get really angry. He stopped fighting and another boy took his place. Then when the other boy got tired, another boy took his place. So all of them fought me and after a while, you're going to get tired, because you can't fight everybody, and I got exhausted. Then they all started pounding me. So they were putting me in my place. (Sylvie)

The narratives show that women perceived as fat creatively and continually resisted forced reconciliation to an unfit identity. All attempted to preserve a positive sense of themselves despite devaluation of body differences. Yet women also describe how others' regulation and retaliation undermined their capacities for action. Negative consequences of social perceptions were especially marked in the transition to womanhood, when participants faced greater pressure to assert credible gender and sexual identities to "qualify" as women (Rice 2003). While all confronted increased censure as they navigated social relations of adolescence, their continued agentic actions underscore the abilities of girls marginalized by bodily differences to craft a self in the context of disparaging images and daily intrusions. Women's stories indicate that fat has become a major marker of difference for many girls growing up in the West. Size has joined sex, disability, and race as a powerful visual symbol of devalued identity that positions girls as deficiently different and undermines their sense of identity and possibility as they make their way in our increasingly body-centred world.

Conclusion

Over the past three decades, obesity and overweight have been reframed. Once seen as an uncertain condition that increased individuals' susceptibility to future chronic illness, obesity now is interpreted as a disease of epidemic proportions. Yet the designation of obesity as a dangerous disease may have serious costs and consequences for the bodies and lives of people perceived as fat, especially girls. According to women in this study, anti-fat attitudes make possible and permissible combined gender, race, and weight-related harassment that undermines fat girls' bodily self-images. Such attitudes also are supported by pedagogical practices of weight measures, fitness tests, revealing clothes, and team selection in physical education that encourage and enforce body hierarchies at school. From the perspectives of

participants, negative perceptions and practices are likely to do little to promote physical fitness in girls. Instead, by framing them as unfit, anti-fat discourses may produce fat girls' presumed lack of physical ability, strength, and skill. Finally, fear of bodily difference that fuels adult imposition of dieting routines typically results in big girls' development of problem eating, including bingeing, yo-yo dieting, bulimia, and anorexia. Ironically, women's experiences indicate that anti-fat perceptions and practices may be productive of the very behaviours and bodies that they are attempting to prevent!

Within contemporary discourses, causes and cures of obesity span from the individual realm of biology and behaviour to the social realm of the environment (Lawrence 2004). Individualized frameworks that limit causes of obesity to bodies and behaviours confine solutions to information or interventions intended to alter people's weights through changing their eating and exercise habits. In shifting burden and blame for fat from unhealthy individuals to unhealthy environments, systemic frameworks emphasize changing social conditions that cause fat (Fairburn and Brownell 2002; Lawrence 2004). Yet women's body histories reveal how size is a social form produced at the intersection of biology and culture, where the unfit fat body is made from interactions of large bodies, cultural representations, and social practices that shape body sizes. Broadening the focus beyond personal to social responsibility is an important step in identifying social factors that may be productive of health problems associated with fat (Brownell and Horgen 2004). However, in reframing obesity as a disease or disturbance of the social body (Lovejoy 2001), systemic approaches do little to disrupt cultural devaluation of fat. Instead, fatness remains a powerful cultural signifier of body otherness through conflation of body size with health status.

Women in this study suggest that fitness promotion programs commonplace in the 1970s and

1980s contributed to their problem eating and exercise practices. Framing fat as unhealthy and unfit within physical and social environments of home, clinic, and school caused contributors to avoid physical activities, to engage in secretive eating, and eventually to gain weight. As women so eloquently explain, these messages also had significant implications for their sense of well-being, belonging, and self. Their narratives show how designating obesity as a dangerous disease supports morally laden health discourses and pedagogical practices that fix fat bodies as unfit. With a renewed focus on fatness prevention through fitness promotion, today's obesity epidemic proponents likewise may be leading a new cohort of large kids to adopt problem eating and exercise practices, possibly contributing to their greater struggles and increased overweight. Rather than endorsing perspectives with such potentially harmful effects, a preferred approach may be to intervene in aspects of physical, social, and cultural environments that obstruct girls' efforts at engaging in good eating and exercise habits. For example, a "body equity" approach that advocates greater acceptance of diverse bodies in school settings (and elsewhere) could enhance girls' body images, expand their opportunities to explore enjoyable physical activities, and increase their capacities to make good food choices (Rice and Russell 2002; Larkin and Rice 2005).

The present study is an opening conversation about the ways in which cultural messages adversely affect the bodies and lives of girls and women perceived as fat. More research is needed to understand implications of size stigma for diverse groups, especially fat girls coming of age in a cultural milieu that is ever more rejecting of fat. Insights that emerge from contributors' accounts suggest that feminist and post-structuralist perspectives may illuminate the role of cultural meanings in making fat bodies. To expand lines of inquiry into fat from medical and scientific domains to the social and cultural terrain (LeBesco 2004), critical fat studies may be needed. Critical fat studies would explore the emergence and operations of size differences within cultural representations and social relations. They would investigate how fat intersects with gender, disability, class, race, and nation to affect the bodies and lives of diverse individuals and groups. Such scholarship also could engage critically with medical and scientific knowledges and encourage more respectful responses to fat bodies. Finally, critical fat studies would open up space for thinking about other ways to approach the relationship of fatness to fitness and health. This might involve moving away from cultural practices of enforcing body norms and toward more creative endeavours of exploring physical abilities and possibilities unique to different bodies. In a social world that is as generative as it is dismissive of fat, such a stance might go a long way in remaking devalued size differences into inhabitable identities.

Acknowledgements

I want to thank the women who generously agreed to participate in this research project, from whom I have learned so much. I also wish to acknowledge and thank my colleagues Claire Carter, Margaret Hobbs, Colleen O'Manique, Lorna Renooy, and Hilde Zitzelsberger as well as Natalie Beausoleil, Jan Wright, Eithne Luibheid, and the anonymous reviewers whose perceptive comments contributed to strengthening ideas developed in this article.

Notes

1. I use the North American colloquial "kid" in this article to reference common spoken language that children (including women-as-girls in this study) use to describe themselves and their social group.

2. The *Body Image Across the Life Span Interview Guide* developed for this research is available by contacting me at carlar@uoguelph.ca.

3. Lather (1991) defines "construct validity" as a self-reflective process of interrogating conceptual frameworks to guard against researcher imposition of theoretical preconceptions onto participants' experiences. She uses the term "face validity" to mean checking emerging analyses with communities under investigation to ensure they reflect the realities of respondents' lives while taking into account people's possible investment in "ideologies that do not serve their best interests" (Lather 1991, 63).

4. In this article, the term *racialization* refers to others' reading of women's perceived phenotypic bodily features according to preconceived racial categories and privileging these differences within everyday interactions (Rice 2003). Racialized women in this study frequently became conscious of negative cultural meanings given to differences in face and body features as

a result of racial stereotyping and stigma when they entered school. While a majority of white women could not recall acquiring a racial identity because they were never categorized as racially different, Eastern and Southern European, European-Caribbean, and Jewish women related experiences of being marginalized as "other than white."

5. The "visible minority" population in Canada has grown in the past 25 years from an estimated 5 per cent of the population in 1981 to 13.4 per cent in 2001, mainly due to changes in racist immigration policies (Boyd and Vickers 2000, 9–10; Chard and Renaud 1999, 22–23; Statistics Canada 2003). In 2001, South Asian, Asian, and African Canadians comprised the largest racialized groups in Canada, and were concentrated in metropolitan areas of Toronto, Vancouver, and Montreal (Chard and Renaud 1999; Statistics Canada 2003). While most racialized women in this study grew up in major urban centres, many came of age before the cultural and racial landscapes of cities changed. As with those who inhabited small cities or towns, they recall being one of only a few children within their ethnic communities and schools identified as an ethnoracial minority.

References

Barden, Nicola. 2001. "The Development of Gender Identity." In Susannah Izzard and Nicola Barden, eds, *Rethinking Gender and Therapy: The Changing Realities of Women*, 6–29. Philadelphia: Open University.

Barker, Erin and Nancy Galambos. 2003. "Body Dissatisfaction of Adolescent Girls and Boys: Risk and Resources Factors." *Journal of Early Adolescence* 23, 2: 141–65.

Barthes, Roland. 1972. *Mythologies*. Trans. A. Lavers. New York: Hill and Wang.

Basrur, Sheela. 2004. *Healthy Weights, Healthy Lives. A Report of the Chief Medical Officer of Health*. Toronto: Ontario Ministry of Health and Long-Term Care.

Bauer, Katherine, Wendy Yang, and Bryn Austin. 2004. "How Can We Stay Healthy When You're Throwing all of This in Front of Us?" Findings from focus groups and interviews in middle schools on environmental influences on nutrition and physical activity. *Health Education and Behaviour* 31, 1: 36–46.

Bauman, Adrian, Judith Madill, Cora Craig, and Art Salmon. 2004. "ParticipACTION: This Mouse Roared, but Did It Get the Cheese?" *Canadian Journal of Public Health* 95, S2: S14–19.

Beauboeuf-LaFondant, Tamara. 2003. "Strong and Large Black Women? Exploring Relationships between Deviant Womanhood and Weight." *Gender and Society* 17, 1: 111–21.

Bennett, William, and Joel Gurin. 1983. *The Dieter's Dilemma: Eating Less and Weighing More*. New York: Basic Books.

Birke, Lynda. 2000. *Feminism and the Biological Body*. New Brunswick, NJ: Rutgers University Press.

Bordo, Susan. 1993. *Unbearable Weight: Feminism, Western Culture and the Body*. Los Angeles: University of California Press.

Boutelle, Kerri, Dianne Neumark-Sztainer, Mary Story, and Michael Resnick. 2002. "Weight Control Behaviours among Obese, Overweight, and Nonoverweight Adolescents." *Journal of Pediatric Psychology* 27, 6: 531–40.

Boyd, Monica, and Michael Vickers. 2000. "100 Years of Immigration in Canada." *Canadian Social Trends* 58, 2–12 (Statistics Canada Catalogue No. 11-008).

Brah, Arvar. 2001. "Difference, Diversity, Differentiation." In Kum-Kum Bhavnani, ed., *Feminism and "Race*," 456–78. New York: Oxford University Press.

Braziel, Jana, and Kathleen LeBesco, eds 2001. *Bodies Out of Bounds: Fatness and Transgression*. Berkeley: University of California Press.

Brownell, Kelly, and Katherine Horgen. 2004. *Food Fight*. New York: Contemporary Books.

Brownmiller, Susan. 1984. *Femininity*. New York: Linden Press/Simon and Schuster.

Burrows, Lisette, Jan Wright, and Justine Jungersen-Smith. 2002. "'Measure Your Belly': New Zealand Children's Construction of Health and Fitness." *Journal of Teaching in Physical Education* 22, 39–48.

Butler, Judith. 1990. *Gender Trouble: Feminism and the Subversion of Identity.* New York: Routledge.

Campos, Paul. 2004. *The Obesity Myth.* New York: Gotham Books.

Chard, Jennifer, and Viviane Renaud. 1999. "Visible Minorities in Toronto, Vancouver, and Montreal." *Canadian Social Trends* 54, 20–5 (Statistics Canada Catalogue No. 11-008).

Ciliska, Donna. 1990. *Beyond Dieting: Psychoeducational Interventions for Chronically Obese Women.* New York: Brunner/Mazel.

Cockburn, Claudia, and Gill Clarke. 2002. "'Everybody's Looking at You!': Girls Negotiating the 'Femininity Deficit' They Incur in Physical Education." *Women's Studies International Forum* 25, 6: 651–65.

Cogan, Jeanine, and Paul Ernsberger. 1999. "Dieting, Weight, and Health: Reconceptualizing Research and Policy." *Journal of Social Issues* 55, 2: 187–205.

Collins, Patricia Hill. 2004. *Black Sexual Politics: African Americans, Gender and the New Racism.* New York: Routledge.

Crawford, Robert. 2004. "Risk Ritual and the Management of Control and Anxiety in Medical Culture." *Health: An Interdisciplinary Journal for the Study of Health, Illness and Medicine* 8, 4: 505–28.

Creswell, John. 1998. *Qualitative Inquiry and Research Design: Choosing among Five Traditions.* Thousand Oaks, CA: Sage.

Currie, Dawn. 1999. *Girl Talk: Adolescent Magazines and Their Readers.* Toronto: University of Toronto Press.

Davies, Bronwyn. 2002. "Becoming Male or Female." In Stevi Jackson and Sue Scott, eds, *Gender: A Sociological Reader,* 280–90. New York: Routledge.

Davis, Kathy. 1995. *Reshaping the Female Body: The Dilemma of Cosmetic Surgery.* New York: Routledge.

De Lauretis, Teresa. 1987. *Technologies of Gender: Essays on Theory, Film, and Fiction.* Bloomington: Indiana University Press.

Degher, Douglas, and Gerald Hughes. 1999. "The Adoption and Management of a "Fat" Identity." In Jeffery Sobal and Donna Maurer, eds, *Interpreting Weight: The Social Management of Fatness and Thinness,* 11–27. New York: Aldine de Gruyter.

Duncan, Michael, Lorayne Woodfield, Stephen O'Neill, and Yahya Al-Nakeeb. 2002. "Relationship between Body Image and Percent Body Fat among British School Children." *Perceptual and Motor Skills* 94, 1: 197–203.

Eisenberg, Marla, Dianne Neumark-Sztainer, and Mary Story. 2003. "Associations of Weight-Based Teasing and Emotional Well-Being among Adolescents." *Archives of Pediatrics and Adolescent Medicine* 157, 8: 733–8.

Ernsberger, Paul. 1987. "NIH Conference on Obesity: By Whom and for What." *Journal of Nutrition* 11, 7: 1164–71.

Ernsberger, Paul, and Richard Koletsky. 1999. "Biomedical Rationale for a Wellness Approach to Obesity: An Alternative to a Focus on Weight Loss." *Journal of Social Issues* 55, 2: 221–59.

Evans, John, Emma Rich, and Rachel Holroyd. 2004. "Disordered Eating and Disordered Schooling: What Schools Do to Middle-Class Girls." *British Journal of Sociology of Education* 25, 2: 123–42.

Fairburn, Christopher, and Kelly Brownell, eds 2002. *Eating Disorders and Obesity: A Comprehensive Handbook.* 2nd edn. New York: Guilford Press.

Fausto-Sterling, Anne. 2000. *Sexing the Body: Gender Politics and the Construction of Sexuality.* New York: Perseus Books.

Foucault, Michel. 1980. *Power/Knowledge: Selected Interviews and Other Writings, 1972–1977.* Trans. C. Gordon. New York: Pantheon Books.

———. 2003. In V. Marchetti and A. Solomoni, eds, *Abnormal: Lectures at the College de France, 1974–1975.* Trans. G. Burchell. New York: Picador.

Fraser, Laura. 1998. *Losing It: False Hopes and Fat Profits in the Diet Industry.* New York: Plume Books.

Gard, Michael, and Jan Wright. 2001. "Managing Uncertainty: Obesity Discourses and Physical Education in a Risk Society." *Studies in Philosophy and Education* 20, 535–49.

———. 2005. *Obesity Epidemic: Science, Morality and Ideology.* New York: Taylor and Francis.

Greer, Germaine. 1971. *The Female Eunuch.* St. Albans, UK: Paladin.

Grosz, Elizabeth. 1994. *Volatile Bodies: Toward a Corporeal Feminism.* Bloomington: Indiana University Press.

Hammonds, Evelynn. 1999. "Toward a Genealogy of Black Female Sexuality: The Problematic of Silence." In Janet Price and Margrit Shildrick, eds, *Feminist Theory and the Body,* 93–104. New York: Routledge.

Holt, Kate, and Lina Ricciardelli. 2002. "Social Comparisons and Negative Affect as Indicators of Problem Eating and Muscle Preoccupation among Children." *Journal of Applied Developmental Psychology* 23, 3: 285–304.

James, Allison. 1995. "On Being a Child: The Self, the Group, and the Category." In Anthony Cohen and Nigel Rapport, eds, *Questions of Consciousness,* 60–76. London: Routledge.

———. 2000. "Embodied Being(s): Understanding the Self and the Body in Childhood." In Alan Prout, ed., *The Body, Childhood, and Society,* 19–37. New York: Palgrave Macmillan.

Jenkins, Richard. 1996. *Social Identity.* New York: Routledge.

Kirk, David, and Richard Tinning. 1994. "Embodied Self-Identity, Healthy Lifestyles and School Physical Education." *Sociology of Health and Illness* 16, 5: 600–25.

Krahnstoever Davison, Kirsten, and Leann Lipps Birch. 2002. "Processes Linking Weight Status and Self-Concept among Girls from Ages 5 to 7 Years." *Developmental Psychology* 38, 5: 735–48.

Krane, Vicki, Precilla Choi, Shannon Baird, Christine Aimar, and Kerri Kauer. 2004. "Living the Paradox: Female

Athletes Negotiate Femininity and Muscularity." *Sex Roles* 50, 5/6: 315–29.

Kruks, Sonia. 2001. *Retrieving Experience: Subjectivity and Recognition in Feminist Politics*. Ithaca, NY: Cornell University Press.

Lagarde, Francois. 2004. "The Mouse under the Microscope: Keys to ParticipACTION's Success." *Canadian Journal of Public Health* 95, S2: S20–6.

Larkin, June and Carla Rice. 2005. "Beyond 'Healthy Eating' and 'Healthy Weights': Harassment and the Health Curriculum in Middle Schools." *Body Image* 2, 3: 219–32.

Lather, Patti. 1991. *Getting Smart: Feminist Research and Pedagogy with/in the Postmodern*. New York: Routledge.

Lawrence, Regina. 2004. "Reframing Obesity: The Evolution of News Discourse on a Public Health Issue." *Harvard International Journal of Press-Politics* 9, 3: 56–75.

LeBesco, Kathleen. 2004. *Revolting Bodies? The Struggle to Redefine Fat Identity*. Boston: University of Massachusetts Press.

Lenskyj, Helen. 1994. "Sexuality and Femininity in Sport Context: Issues and Alternatives." *Journal of Sport and Social Issues* 18, 356–76.

Lovejoy, Meg. 2001. "Disturbances in the Social Body: Differences in Body Image and Eating Problems among African American and White Women." *Gender and Society* 15, 2: 239–61.

McKinley, Nita. 1999. "Ideal Weight/Ideal Women: Society Constructs the Female." In Jeffery Sobal and Donna Maurer, eds, *Weighty Issues: Fatness and Thinness as Social Problems*, 97–105. New York: Aldine De Gruyter.

Malcom, Nancy. 2003. "Constructing Female Athleticism: A Study of Girls' Recreational Softball." *American Behavioral Scientist* 46, 10: 1387–404.

Mama, Amina. 1995. *Beyond the Masks: Race, Gender and Subjectivity*. London: Routledge.

Marshall, Helen. 1996. "Our Bodies Ourselves: Why We Should Add Old Fashioned Empirical Phenomenology to the New Theories of the Body." *Women's Studies International Forum* 19, 3: 253–65.

Mellin, Alison, Dianne Neumark-Sztainer, Mary Story, Marjorie Ireland, and Michael Resnick. 2002. "Unhealthy Behaviours and Psycho-Social Difficulties among Overweight Adolescents: The Potential Impact of Familial Factors." *Journal of Adolescent Health* 31, 2: 145–53.

Miller, Wayne. 1999. "Fitness and Fatness in Relation to Health: Implications for a Paradigm Shift." *Journal of Social Issues* 55, 2: 207–19.

Millman, Marcia. 1980. *Such a Pretty Face: Being Fat in America*. New York: W.W. Norton.

Naples, Nancy. 2003. *Feminism and Method: Ethnography, Discourse Analysis, and Activist Research*. New York: Routledge.

Neumark-Sztainer, Dianne, Mary Story, and Loren Faibisch. 1998. "Perceived Stigmatization among Overweight African–American and Caucasian Adolescent Girls." *Journal of Adolescent Health* 23, 5: 264–70.

O'Dea, Jennifer, and Peter Caputi. 2001. "Association between Socioeconomic Status, Weight, Age and Gender, and the Body Image and Weight Control Practices of 6- to 19-Year-Old Children and Adolescents." *Health Education Research* 16, 5: 521–32.

Oliver, Kimberly, and Rosary Lalik. 2004. "Critical Inquiry on the Body in Girls' Physical Education Classes: A Critical Post-Structural Perspective." *Journal of Teaching Physical Education* 23, 162–95.

Orbach, Susie. 1979. *Fat is a Feminist Issue: The Anti-diet Guide to Permanent Weight Loss*. New York: Berkley Books.

Pesa, Jacqueline, Thomas Syre, and Elizabeth Jones. 2000. "Psychosocial Differences Associated with Body Weight among Female Adolescents: The Importance of Body Image." *Journal of Adolescent Health* 26, 5: 330–37.

Poran, Maya. 2002. "Denying Diversity: Perceptions of Beauty and Social Comparison Processes among Latino, Black and White Women." *Sex Roles* 47, 1/2: 65–81.

Raine, Kim. 2004. *Overweight and Obesity in Canada: A Population Health Perspective*. Ottawa: Canadian Institute for Health Information.

Rice, Carla. 2003. "Becoming Women: Body Image, Identity, and Difference in the Passage to Womanhood." Unpublished doctoral dissertation, York University, Toronto.

Rice, Carla, and Vanessa Russell. 2002. *Embodying Equity: Body Image as an Equity Issue*. Toronto: Green Dragon Press.

Rice, Carla, Hilde Zitzelsberger, Wendy Porch, and Esther Ignagni. 2005. "Creating Communities across Disability and Difference." *Canadian Woman Studies* 24, 1: 187–93.

Rogers, Linda, and Beth Blue Swadener, eds 2001. *Semiotics and Dis/ability: Interrogating Categories of Difference*. Albany, NY: State University of New York Press.

Rootman, Irving, and Peggy Edwards. 2004. "The Best Laid Schemes of Mice and Men . . . ParticipACTION's Legacy and the Future of Physical Activity Promotion in Canada." *Canadian Journal of Public Health* 95, S2: S37–44.

Ross, Bruce. 2005. "Fat or Fiction: Weighing the Obesity Epidemic." In Michael Gard and Jan Wright, eds, *Obesity Epidemic: Science, Morality and Ideology*, 86–106. New York: Taylor and Francis.

Schoenfielder, Lisa, and Barb Wieser, eds 1983. *Shadow on a Tightrope: Writings by Women on Fat Oppression*. Iowa City, IA: Aunt Lute Book Company.

Schwartz, Hillel. 1986. *Never Satisfied: A Cultural History of Diets, Fantasies, and Fat*. New York: The Free Press.

Smith, Dorothy. 1993. *Texts, Facts, and Femininity: Exploring the Relations of Ruling*. Toronto: Routledge.

Sobal, Jeffery, and Donna Maurer, eds 1999a. *Interpreting Weight: The Social Management of Fatness and Thinness*. New York: Walter de Gruyter.

——. eds 1999b. *Weighty Issues: Fatness and Thinness as Social Problems*. New York: Walter de Gruyter.

Statistics Canada. 21 January 2003. Visible Minority Groups and Sex for Population, for Canada, Provinces, Territories, Census Metropolitan Areas and Census Agglomerations, 2001 Census (Statistics Canada Catalogue No. 97F0010XIE2001002). Retrieved 12 May 2006 from www.statcan.ca/bsolc/english/bsolc?catno=97F0010X2001002.

Stearns, Peter. 1997. *Fat History: Bodies and Beauty in the Modern West.* New York: New York University Press.

Strauss, Anselm, and Juliet Corbin. 1998. *Basics of Qualitative Research: Techniques and Procedures for Developing Grounded Theory.* Thousand Oaks, CA: Sage.

Székely, Eva. 1988. *Never Too Thin.* Toronto: The Women's Press.

Thorne, Barrie. 1997. "Children and Gender: Constructions of Difference." In Mary Gergen and Sara Davis, eds, *Toward a New Psychology of Gender: A Reader,* 185–201. New York: Routledge.

———. 1999. *Gender Play: Girls and Boys in School.* New Brunswick, NJ: Rutgers University Press.

Ussher, Jane. 1997. *Fantasies of Femininity: Reframing the Boundaries of "Sex."* New York: Rutgers.

Van den Berg, Patricia, Eleanor Wertheim, Kevin Thompson, and Susan Paxton. 2002. "Development of Body Image, Eating Disturbance, and General Psychological Functioning in Adolescent Females: A Replication Using Covariance Structure Modeling in an Australian Sample." *International Journal of Eating Disorders* 32, 1: 46–51.

Vander Wal, Jillon. 2004. "Eating and Body Image Concerns among Average-Weight and Obese African American and Hispanic Girls." *Eating Behaviors* 5: 181–87.

Vessey, Judith, Mary Duffy, Patricia O'Sullivan, and Margo Swanson. 2003. "Assessing Teasing in School-Age Youth." *Issues in Comprehensive Pediatric Nursing* 26, 1: 1–11.

White, Michael. 21–25 October 2002. Intensive Training in Narrative Therapy. Toronto: Brief Therapy Training Centres, Gail Appel Institute.

Woodward, Kathleen, ed. 1997. *Identity and Difference.* Thousand Oaks, CA: Sage/The Open University.

World Health Organization. 2000. *Obesity: Preventing and Managing the Global Epidemic.* Geneva, Switzerland: Author.

———. 2003. *Controlling the Global Obesity Epidemic.* Geneva, Switzerland: Author. Retrieved 30 April 2006 from www.who.int/nutrition/topics/obesity/en/index.html.

Young-Hyman, Deborah, David Schlundt, Leanna Herman-Wenderoth, and Khristine Bozylinski. 2003. "Obesity, Appearance, and Psychosocial Adaptation in Young African American Children." *Journal of Pediatric Psychology* 28, 7: 463–72.

Questions for Critical Thought

1. How is stigma against size differences socially constructed in Canadian society? What roles do the family, the school, and the media play in reinforcing this form of inequality?

2. What are the social, political, and economic implications of what the World Health Organization has described as "globesity" among Western countries?

3. What historical, economic, and political conditions explain why certain social groupings celebrate "fat" while others stigmatize "fat"? What role have cultural and religious values played in either celebrating or stigmatizing "fat"?

4. How has feminist scholarship sought to understand women's bodily oppressions in patriarchal societies? Has it been successful in raising our awareness about body size and eating disorders such as anorexia nervosa, bulimia, and binge eating disorder? Should information about eating disorders be addressed in the elementary school system curriculum? Why or why not?

5. How has "framing fatness" created an intersection of inequality that disadvantages women, especially in the form of **other-gendering**? How do the intersections of body size and race affect women's sexual identities?

Yearning for Lightness: Transnational Circuits in the Marketing and Consumption of Skin Lighteners

.... *Evelyn Nakano Glenn*

With the breakdown of traditional racial boundaries in many areas of the world, widespread and growing consumption of skin-lightening products testifies to increasing significance of **colourism**—social hierarchy based on gradations of skin within and between racial/ethnic groups. Light skin operates as a form of **symbolic capital**, one that is especially critical for women because of the connection between skin tone attractiveness and desirability. Far from being an outmoded practice or legacy of colonialism, the use of **skin lighteners** is growing fastest among young, urban, educated women in the global South. Although global in scope, the skin-lightening market is highly segmented by nation, culture, race, and class. This article examines the "yearning for lightness" and skin-lightening practices in various societies and communities and the role of **transnational** pharmaceutical and cosmetic corporations in fuelling the desire for light skin through print, Internet, and television ads that link light skin with modernity, mobility, and youth.

Colourism remains a persistent frontier of intergroup and intragroup relations in the twenty-first century. Sociologists and anthropologists have documented discrimination against darker-skinned persons and correlations between skin tone and socio-economic status and achievement in Brazil and the United States (Hunter 2005; Sheriff 2001; Telles 2004). Other researchers have revealed that people's judgements about other people are literally coloured by skin tone, so that darker-skinned individuals are viewed as less intelligent, trustworthy, and attractive than their lighter-skinned counterparts (Herring, Keith, and Horton 2003; Hunter 2005; Maddox 2004).

One way of conceptualizing skin colour, then, is as a form of symbolic capital that affects, if not determines, one's life chances. The relation between skin colour and judgements about attractiveness affects women most acutely, since women's worth is judged heavily on the basis of appearance. For example, men who have wealth, education, and other forms of human capital are considered "good catches," while women who are physically attractive may be considered desirable despite the lack of other capital. Although skin tone is usually seen as a form of fixed or unchangeable capital, in fact, men and women may attempt to acquire light-skinned privilege. Sometimes this search takes the form of seeking light-skinned marital partners to raise one's status and to achieve intergenerational mobility by increasing the likelihood of having light-skinned children. Often, especially for women, this search takes the form of using cosmetics or other treatments to change the appearance of one's skin to make it look lighter.

This article focuses on the practice of skin lightening, the marketing of skin lighteners in various societies around the world, and the multinational corporations that are involved in the global skin-lightening trade. An analysis of this complex topic calls for a multi-level approach. First, we need to place the production, marketing, and consumption of skin lighteners into a global political-economic context. I ask: How is skin lightening interwoven into the world economic system and its transnational circuits of products, capital, culture, and people? Second, we need to examine the mediating entities and processes by which skin lighteners reach specific national/

ethnic/racial/class consumers. I ask: What are the media and messages, cultural themes and symbols used to create the desire for skin-lightening products among particular groups? Finally, we need to examine the meaning and significance of skin colour for consumers of skin lighteners. I ask: How do consumers learn about, test, and compare skin-lightening products, and what do they seek to achieve through their use?

The issue of skin lightening may seem trivial at first glance. However, it is my contention that a close examination of the global circuits of skin lightening provides a unique lens through which to view the workings of the Western-dominated global system as it simultaneously promulgates a "white is right" ideology while also promoting the desire for and consumption of Western culture and products.

Skin Lightening and Global Capital

Skin lightening has long been practised in many parts of the world. Women concocted their own treatments or purchased products from self-styled beauty experts offering special creams, soaps, or lotions, which were either ineffective sham products or else effective but containing highly toxic materials, such as mercury or lead. From the perspective of the supposedly enlightened present, skin lightening might be viewed as a form of vanity or a misguided and dangerous relic of the past.

However, at the beginning of the twenty-first century, the search for light skin, free of imperfections such as freckles and age spots, has actually accelerated, and the market for skin-lightening products has mushroomed in all parts of the world. The production and marketing of products that offer the prospect of lighter, brighter, whiter skin has become a multi-billion-dollar global industry. Skin lightening has been incorporated into transnational flows of capital, goods, people, and culture. It is implicated in both the formal global economy and various informal economies.

It is integrated into both legal and extralegal transnational circuits of goods. Certain large multinational corporations have become major players, spending vast sums on research and development and on advertising and marketing to reach both mass and specialized markets. Simultaneously, actors in informal or underground economies, including smugglers, transnational migrants, and petty traders, are finding unprecedented opportunities in producing, transporting, and selling unregulated lightening products.

One reason for this complex multi-faceted structure is that the market for skin lighteners, although global in scope, is also highly decentralized and segmented along socio-economic, age, national, ethnic, racial, and cultural lines. Whether the manufacturers are multi-billion-dollar corporations or small entrepreneurs, they make separate product lines and use distinct marketing strategies to reach specific segments of consumers. Ethnic companies and entrepreneurs may be best positioned to draw on local cultural themes, but large multinationals can draw on local experts to tailor advertising images and messages to appeal to particular audiences.

The Internet has become a major tool/highway/engine for the globalized, segmented, lightening market. It is the site where all of the players in the global lightening market meet. Large multinationals, small local firms, individual entrepreneurs, skin doctors, direct sales merchants, and even eBay sellers use the Internet to disseminate the ideal of light skin and to advertise and sell their products. Consumers go on the Internet to do research on products and shop. Some also participate in Internet message boards and forums to seek advice and to discuss, debate, and rate skin lighteners. There are many such forums, often as part of transnational ethnic websites. For example, IndiaParenting.com and sukh-dukh .com, designed for South Asians in India and other parts of the world, have chat rooms on skin care and lightening, and Rexinteractive.com, a Filipino site, and Candymag.com, a site sponsored by a magazine for Filipina teens, have extensive forums on skin lightening. The discussions on these forums provide a window through which to view the meaning of skin colour to consumers, their desires and anxieties, doubts and aspirations. The Internet is thus an important site from which one can gain a multi-level perspective on skin lightening.

Consumer Groups and Market Niches

Africa and African Diaspora

In Southern Africa, colourism is just one of the negative inheritances of European colonialism. The ideology of white supremacy that European colonists brought included the association of blackness with primitiveness, lack of civilization, unrestrained sexuality, pollution, and dirt. The association of blackness with dirt can be seen in a 1930 French advertising poster for Dirtoff. The poster shows a drawing of a dark African man washing his hands, which have become white, as he declares, *"Le Savon Dirtoff me blanchit!"* The soap was designed not for use by Africans but, as the poster notes, *pour mechanciens automobilises et menagers*—French auto mechanics and housewives. Such images showing black people "dramatically losing their pigmentation as a result of the cleansing process" were common in late nineteenth- and early twentieth-century soap advertisements, according to art historian Jean Michel Massing (1995, 180).

Some historians and anthropologists have argued that pre-colonial African conceptions of female beauty favoured women with light brown, yellow, or reddish tints. If so, the racial hierarchies established in areas colonized by Europeans cemented and generalized the privilege attached to light skin (Burke 1996; Ribane 2006, 12). In both South Africa and Rhodesia/Zimbabwe, an intermediate category of those considered to be racially mixed was classified as "coloured" and subjected to fewer legislative restrictions than those classified as "native." Assignment to the coloured category was based on ill-defined criteria, and on arrival in urban areas, people found themselves classified as native or coloured on the basis of skin tone and other phenotypic characteristics. Indians arriving in Rhodesia from Goa, for example, were variously classified as "Portuguese Mulatto" or coloured. The multiplication of discriminatory laws targeting natives led to a growing number of blacks claiming to be coloured in both societies (Muzondidya 2005, 23–4).

The use of skin lighteners has a long history in Southern Africa, which is described by Lynn Thomas and which I will not recount here (2008). Rather, I will discuss the current picture, which shows both a rise in the consumption of skin-lightening products and concerted efforts to curtail the trade of such products. Despite bans on the importation of skin lighteners, the widespread use of these products currently constitutes a serious health issue in Southern Africa because the products often contain mercury, corticosteroids, or high doses of **hydroquinone**. Mercury of course is highly toxic, and sustained exposure can lead to neurological damage and kidney disease. Hydroquinone (originally an industrial chemical) is effective in suppressing melanin production, but exposure to the sun—hard to avoid in Africa—damages skin that has been treated. Furthermore, in dark-skinned people, long-term hydroquinone use can lead to **ochronosis**, a disfiguring condition involving gray and blue-black discolouration of the skin (Mahe, Ly, and Dangou 2003). The overuse of topical steroids can lead to contact eczema, bacterial and fungal infection, **Cushing's syndrome**, and **skin atrophy** (Margulies n.d.; Ntambwe 2004).

Perhaps the most disturbing fact is that mercury soaps used by Africans are manufactured in the **European Union (EU)**, with Ireland and Italy leading in the production of mercury soap. One company that has been the target of activists is Killarney Enterprises, Ltd., in County Wicklow, Ireland. Formerly known as W&E Products and located in Lancashire, England, the company was forced to close following out-of-court settlements of suits filed by two former employees who had given birth to stillborn or severely malformed infants due to exposure to mercury. However,

W&E Products then secured a 750,000-pound grant from the Irish Industrial Development Authority to relocate to Ireland, where it changed its name to Killarney Enterprises, Ltd. The company remained in business until 17 April 2007, producing soaps under the popular names Tura, Arut, Swan, Sukisa Bango, Meriko, and Jeraboo. (The latter contained up to 3 per cent mercuric iodide.) Distribution of mercury soap has been illegal in the EU since 1989, but its manufacture has remained legal as long as the product is exported (Chadwick 2001; Earth Summit 2002, 13–14). These soaps are labelled for use as antiseptics and to prevent body odour; however, they are understood to be and are used as skin bleaches. To complete the circuit, EU-manufactured mercury soaps are smuggled back into the EU to sell in shops catering to African immigrant communities. An Irish journalist noted that the very same brands made by Killarney Enterprises, including Meriko and Tura (banned in both the EU and South Africa) could easily be found in African shops in Dublin (De Faoite 2001; O'Farrell 2002).

As a result of the serious health effects, medical researchers have conducted interview studies to determine how prevalent the practice of skin lightening is among African women. They estimate that 25 per cent of women in Bamaki, Mali; 35 per cent in Pretoria, South Africa; and 52 per cent in Dakar, Senegal, use skin lighteners, as do an astonishing 77 per cent of women traders in Lagos, Nigeria (Adebajo 2002; del Guidice and Yves 2002; Mahe, Ly, and Dangou 2003; Malangu and Ogubanjo 2006).

There have been local and transnational campaigns to stop the manufacture of products containing mercury in the EU and efforts to inform African consumers of the dangers of their use and to foster the idea of black pride. Governments in South Africa, Zimbabwe, Nigeria, and Kenya have banned the import and sale of mercury and hydroquinone products, but they continue to be smuggled in from other African nations (Dooley 2001; Thomas 2004).

Despite these efforts, the use of skin lighteners has been increasing among modernized and cosmopolitan African women. A South African newspaper reported that whereas in the 1970s, typical skin lightener users in South Africa were rural and poor, currently, it is upwardly mobile black women, those with technical diplomas or university degrees and well-paid jobs, who are driving the market in skin lighteners. A recent study by Mictert Marketing Research found that 1 in 13 upwardly mobile black women aged 25 to 35 used skin lighteners. It is possible that this is an underestimation, since there is some shame attached to admitting to using skin lighteners (Ntshingila 2005).

These upwardly mobile women turn to expensive imported products from India and Europe rather than cheaper, locally made products. They also go to doctors to get prescriptions for imported lighteners containing corticosteroids, which are intended for short-term use to treat blemishes. They continue using them for long periods beyond the prescribed duration, thus risking damage (Ntshingila 2005). This recent rise in the use of skin lighteners cannot be seen as simply a legacy of colonialism but rather is a consequence of the penetration of multinational capital and Western consumer culture. The practice therefore is likely to continue to increase as the influence of these forces grows.

African America

Colour consciousness in the African-American community has generally been viewed as a legacy of slavery, under which mulattos, the offspring of white men and slave women, were accorded better treatment than "pure" Africans. While slave owners considered dark-skinned Africans suited to fieldwork, lighter-skinned mulattos were thought to be more intelligent and better suited for indoor work as servants and artisans. Mulattos were also more likely to receive at least rudimentary education and to be manumitted. They went on to form the nucleus of many nineteenth-century free black communities. After the civil war, light-skinned mulattos tried to distance themselves from their darker-skinned brothers and sisters, forming exclusive civic and cultural organizations, fraternities, sororities, schools, and universities (Russell, Wilson, and Hall 1992, 24–40). According to Audrey Elisa Kerr (2005), common folklore in the African-American community holds that elite African-Americans used a "paper bag" test to screen guests at social events and to determine eligibility for membership in their organizations: anyone whose skin was darker than the colour of the bag was excluded. Although perhaps apocryphal, the widespread acceptance of the story as historical fact is significant. It has been credible to African-Americans because it was consonant with their observations of the skin tone of elite African-American society (Kerr 2005).

The preference and desire for light skin can also be detected in the long time practice of skin lightening. References to African-American women using powders and skin bleaches appeared in the black press as early as the 1850s, according to historian Kathy Peiss (1998). She notes that *American* magazine criticized African-Americans who tried to emulate white beauty standards: "Beautiful black and brown faces by application of rouge and lily white are made to assume unnatural tints, like the vivid hue of painted corpses" (Peiss 1998, 41). How common such practices were is unknown. However, by the 1880s and 1890s, dealers in skin bleaches were widely advertising their wares in the African American press. A Crane and Company ad in *Coloured American* magazine (1903) promised that use of the company's "wonderful Face Bleach" would result in a "peach-like complexion" and "turn the skin of a black or brown person five or six shades lighter and of a mulatto person perfectly white" (Peiss 1998, 41–2).

Throughout the twentieth century, many African-American leaders spoke out against **skin bleaching**, as well as hair straightening, and the African-American press published articles decrying these practices. However, such articles were far outnumbered by advertisements for skin bleaches in prominent outlets such as the *Crusader*, *Negro World*, and the *Chicago Defender*.

An estimated 30 to 40 per cent of advertisements in these outlets were for cosmetics and toiletries, including skin bleaches. Many of the advertised lighteners were produced by white manufacturers; for example, Black and White Cream was made by Plough Chemicals (which later became Plough Shearing), and Nadolina was made by the National Toilet Company. A chemical analysis of Nadolina Bleach conducted in 1930 found it contained 10 per cent ammoniated mercury, a concentration high enough to pose a serious health risk. Both brands are still marketed in African-American outlets, although with changed ingredients (Peiss 1998, 210, 212).[1]

The manufacture and marketing of black beauty products, including skin lighteners, provided opportunities for black entrepreneurs. Annie Turnbo Malone, who founded the Poro brand, and Sara Breedlove, later known as Madam C.J. Walker, who formulated and marketed the Wonder Hair Grower, were two of the most successful black entrepreneurs of the late nineteenth and early twentieth centuries. Malone and Walker championed African-American causes and were benefactors of various institutions (Peiss 1998, 67–70; see also Bundles 2001). Significantly, both refused to sell skin bleaches or to describe their hair care products as hair straighteners. After Walker died in 1919, her successor, F.B. Ransom, introduced Tan-Off, which became one of the company's bestsellers in the 1920s and 1930s. Other black-owned companies, such as Kashmir (which produced Nile Queen), Poro, Overton, and Dr Palmer, advertised and sold skin lighteners. Unlike some white-produced products, they did not contain mercury but relied on such ingredients as borax and hydrogen peroxide (Peiss 1998, 205, 212, 213).

Currently, a plethora of brands is marketed especially to African-Americans, including Black and White Cream, Nadolina (without mercury), Ambi, Palmer's, Dr Daggett and Remsdell (fade cream and facial brightening cream), Swiss Whitening Pills, Ultra Glow, Skin Success, Avre (which produces the Pallid Skin Lightening System and B-Lite Fade Cream), and Clear Essence (which targets women of colour more generally). Some of these products contain hydroquinone, while others claim to use natural ingredients.

Discussions of skin lightening on African American Internet forums indicate that the participants seek not white skin but "light" skin like that of African-American celebrities such as film actress Halle Berry and singer Beyonce Knowles. Most women say they want to be two or three shades lighter or to get rid of dark spots and freckles to even out their skin tones, something that many skin lighteners claim to do. Some of the writers believe that Halle Berry and other African-American celebrities have achieved their luminescent appearance through skin bleaching, skilful use of cosmetics, and artful lighting. Thus, some skin-lightening products, such as the Pallid Skin Lightening System, purport to offer the "secret" of the stars. A website for Swiss Lightening Pills claims that "for many years Hollywood has been keeping the secret of whitening pills" and asks, rhetorically, "Have you wondered why early childhood photos of many top celebs show a much darker skin colour than they have now?"[2]

India and Indian Diaspora

As in the case of Africa, the origins of colourism in India are obscure, and the issue of whether there was a privileging of light skin in pre-colonial Indian societies is far from settled. Colonial-era and postcolonial Indian writings on the issue may themselves have been influenced by European notions of caste, culture, and race. Many of these writings expound on a racial distinction between lighter-skinned Aryans, who migrated into India from the North, and darker-skinned "indigenous" Dravidians of the South. The wide range of skin colour from North to South and the variation in skin tone within castes make it hard to correlate light skin with high caste. The most direct connection between skin colour and social status could be found in the paler hue of those whose position and wealth enabled them to spend their lives sheltered indoors, compared to the darker hue of those who toiled outdoors in the sun (Khan 2008).

British racial concepts evolved over the course of its colonial history as colonial administrators and settlers attempted to make sense of the variety of cultural and language groups and to justify British rule in India. British observers attributed group differences variously to culture, language, climate, or biological race. However, they viewed the English as representing the highest culture and embodying the optimum physical type; they made invidious comparisons between lighter-skinned groups, whose men they viewed as more intelligent and marital and whose women they considered more attractive, and darker-skinned groups, whose men they viewed as lacking intelligence and masculinity, and whose women they considered to be lacking in beauty (Arnold 2004).

Regardless of the origins of colour consciousness in India, the preference for light skin seems almost universal today, and in terms of sheer numbers, India and Indian diasporic communities around the world constitute the largest market for skin lighteners. The major consumers of these products in South Asian communities are women between the ages of 16 and 35. On transnational South Asian blog sites, women describing themselves as "dark" or "wheatish" in colour state a desire to be "fair." Somewhat older women seek to reclaim their youthful skin colour, describing themselves as having gotten darker over time. Younger women tend to be concerned about looking light to make a good marital match or to appear lighter for large family events, including their own weddings. These women recognize the reality that light skin constitutes valuable symbolic capital in the marriage market (Views on Article n.d.).

Contemporary notions of feminine beauty are shaped by the Indian mass media. Since the 1970s, beauty pageants such as Miss World–India have been exceedingly popular viewer spectacles; they are a source of nationalist pride since India has been highly successful in international pageants such as Miss World. As might be expected, the competitors, although varying in skin tone, tend to be lighter than average. The other main avatars of feminine allure are Bollywood actresses, such as Isha Koppikar and Aishwarya Rai, who also tend to be light-skinned or, if slightly darker, green-eyed.

Many Indian women use traditional homemade preparations made of plant and fruit products. On various blog sites for Indians both in South Asia and diasporic communities in North America, the Caribbean, and the United Kingdom, women seek advice about "natural" preparations and trade recipes. Many commercial products are made by Indian companies and marketed to Indians around the globe under names as "fairness cream," "herbal bleach cream," "whitening cream," and "fairness cold cream." Many of these products claim to be based on ayurvedic medicine and contain herbal and fruit extracts such as saffron, papaya, almonds, and lentils (Runkle 2004).

With economic liberalization in 1991, the number of products available on the Indian market, including cosmetics and skin care products, has mushroomed. Whereas prior to 1991, Indian consumers had the choice of two brands of cold cream and moisturizers, today, they have scores of products from which to select. With deregulation of imports, the rise of the Indian economy, and growth of the urban middle class, multinational companies see India as a prime target for expansion, especially in the area of personal care products. The multinationals, through regional subsidiaries, have developed many whitening product lines in various price ranges that target markets ranging from rural villagers to white-collar urban dwellers and affluent professionals and managers (Runkle 2005).

Southeast Asia: The Philippines

Because of its history as a colonial dependency first of Spain and then of the United States, the Philippines has been particularly affected by Western ideology and culture, both of which valorize whiteness. Moreover, frequent intermarriage among indigenous populations, Spanish colonists, and Chinese settlers has resulted in a substantially mestizo population that ranges widely on the skin colour spectrum. The business and political elites have tended to be disproportionately light-skinned with visible Hispanic and/or Chinese appearance. In the contemporary period, economic integration has led to the collapse of traditional means of livelihood, resulting in large-scale emigration by both working-class and middle-class Filipinos to seek better-paying jobs in the Middle East, Asia, Europe, and North America. An estimated 10 million Filipinos were working abroad as of 2004, with more than a million departing each year. Because of the demand for domestic workers, nannies, and care workers in the global North, women make up more than half of those working abroad (Tabbada 2006). Many, if not most, of these migrants remit money and send Western consumer goods to their families in the Philippines. They also maintain transnational ties with their families at home and across the diaspora through print media, phone, and the Internet. All of these factors contribute to an interest in and fascination with Western consumer culture, including fashion and cosmetics in the Philippines and in Filipino diasporic communities (Parrenas 2001).

Perhaps not surprising, interest in skin lightening seems to be huge and growing in the Philippines, especially among younger urban women. Synovate, a market research firm, reported that in 2004, 50 per cent of respondents in the Philippines reported currently using skin lighteners (Synovate 2004). Young Filipinas participate in several Internet sites seeking advice on lightening products. They seek not only to lighten their skin overall but also to deal with dark underarms, elbows, and knees. Judging by their entries in Internet discussion sites, many teens are quite obsessed with finding "the secret" to lighter skin and have purchased and tried scores of different brands of creams and pills. They are disappointed to find that these products may have some temporary effects but do not lead to permanent change. They discuss products made in the Philippines but are most interested in products made by large European and American multinational cosmetic firms and Japanese and Korean companies. Clearly, these young Filipinas associate light skin with modernity and social mobility. Interesting to note, the young Filipinas do not refer to Americans or Europeans as having the most desirable skin colour. They are more apt to look to Japanese and Koreans or to Spanish- or Chinese-appearing (and light-skinned) Filipina celebrities, such Michelle Rodriguez, Sharon Cuneta, or Claudine Barretto, as their ideals.[3]

The notion that Japanese and Korean women represent ideal Asian beauty has fostered a brisk market in skin lighteners that are formulated by Korean and Japanese companies. Asian White Skin and its sister company, Yumei Misei, headquartered in Korea, sell Japanese and Korean skin care products in the Philippines both in retail outlets and online. Products include Asianwhiteskin Underarm Whitening Kit, Japanese Whitening Cream Enzyme Q-10, Japan Whitening Fruit Cream, Kang Tian Sheep Placenta Whitening Capsules, and Kyusoku Bhaku Lightening Pills.

East Asia: Japan, China, and Korea

East Asian societies have historically idealized light or even white skin for women. Intage (2001), a market research firm in Japan, puts it, "Japan has long idolized ivory-like skin that is 'like a boiled egg'—soft, white, and smooth on the surface." Indeed, prior to the Meiji Period (starting in the 1860s), men and women of the higher classes wore white-lead powder makeup (along with blackened teeth and shaved eyebrows). With modernization, according to Mikiko Ashikari, men completely abandoned makeup, but middle- and upper-class women continued to wear traditional white-lead powder when dressed in formal kimonos for ceremonial occasions, such as marriages, and adopted light-coloured modern face powder to wear with Western clothes. Ashikari (2003) found through observations of 777 women at several sites in Osaka during 1996–7 that 97.4 per cent of women in public wore what she calls

"white face," that is, makeup that "makes their faces look whiter than they really are" (3).

Intage (2001) reports that skin care products, moisturizers, face masks, and skin lighteners account for 66 per cent of the cosmetics market in Japan. A perusal of displays of Japanese cosmetics and skin care products shows that most, even those not explicitly stated to be whitening products, carry names that contain the word "white," for example, facial masks labelled "Clear Turn White" or "Pure White." In addition, numerous products are marketed specifically as whiteners. All of the leading Japanese firms in the cosmetics field—Shiseido, Kosa, Kanebo, and Pola—offer multi-product skin-whitening lines, with names such as "White Lucent" and "Whitissimo." Fytokem, a Canadian company that produces ingredients used in skin-whitening products, reports that Japan's market in skin lighteners topped $5 billion in 1999 (Saskatchewan Business Unlimited 2005). With deregulation of imports, leading multinational firms, such as L'Oréal, have also made large inroads in the Japanese market. French products have a special cachet (Exhibitor Info 2006).

While the Japanese market has been the largest, its growth rate is much lower than those of Korea and China. Korea's cosmetic market has been growing by 10 per cent per year while that of China has been growing by 20 per cent. Fytokem estimates that the market for skin whiteners in China was worth $1 billion in 2002 and was projected to grow tremendously. A 2007 Nielsen global survey found that 46 per cent of Chinese, 47 per cent of people in Hong Kong, 46 per cent of Taiwanese, 29 per cent of Koreans, and 24 per cent of Japanese had used a skin lightener in the past year. As to regular users, 30 per cent of Chinese, 20 per cent of Taiwanese, 18 per cent of Japanese and Hong Kongers, and 8 per cent of Koreans used them weekly or daily. However, if money were no object 52 per cent of Koreans said they would spend more on skin lightening, compared to 26 per cent of Chinese, 23 per cent of Hong

Kongers and Taiwanese, and 23 per cent of Japanese (Nielsen 2007).

Latin America: Mexico and the Mexican Diaspora

Throughout Latin America, skin tone is a major marker of status and a form of symbolic capital, despite national ideologies of racial democracy. In some countries, such as Brazil, where there was African chattel slavery and extensive miscegenation, there is considerable colour consciousness, along with an elaborate vocabulary to refer to varying shades of skin. In other countries, such as Mexico, the main intermixture was between Spanish colonists and indigenous peoples, along with an unacknowledged admixture with African slaves. *Mestizaje* is the official national ideal. The Mexican concept of *mestizaje* meant that through racial and ethnic mixture, Mexico would gradually be peopled by a whiter "cosmic race" that surpassed its initial ingredients. Nonetheless, skin tone, along with other phenotypical traits, is a significant marker of social status, with lightness signifying purity and beauty, and darkness signifying contamination and ugliness (Stepan 1991, 135). The elite has remained overwhelmingly light-skinned and European-appearing while rural poor are predominantly dark-skinned and Indigenous-appearing.

Ethnographic studies of Mexican communities in Mexico City and Michoacan found residents to be highly colour conscious, with darker-skinned family members likely to be ridiculed or teased. The first question that a relative often poses about a newborn is about his or her colour (Farr 2006, chapter 5; Guttman 1996, 40; Martinez 2001). Thus, it should not be a surprise that individuals pursue various strategies to attain light-skinned identity and privileges. Migration from rural areas to the city or to the United States has been one route to transformation from an Indian to a mestizo identity or from a mestizo to a more cosmopolitan urban identity; another strategy has been lightening one's family line through marriage with a lighter-skinned partner. A third strategy has been to use lighteners to change the appearance of one's skin (Winders, Jones, and Higgins 2005, 77–8).

In one of the few references to skin whitening in Mexico, Alan Knight (1990) claims that it was "an ancient practice . . . reinforced by film, television, and advertising stereotypes" (100). As in Africa, consumers seeking low-cost lighteners can easily purchase mercury-laden creams that are still manufactured and used in parts of Latin America (e.g., Recetas de la Farmacia-Crema Blanqueadora, manufactured in the Dominican Republic contains 6,000 ppm of mercury; NYC Health Dept 2005). The use of these products has come to public attention because of their use by Latino immigrants in the United States. Outbreaks of mercury poisoning have been reported in Texas, New Mexico, Arizona, and California among immigrants who used Mexican-manufactured creams such as Crema de Belleza-Manning. The cream is manufactured in Mexico by Laboratories Vide Natural SA de Cv., Tampico, Tamaulipas, and is distributed primarily in Mexico. However, it has been found for sale in shops and flea markets in the United States in areas located along the US–Mexican border in Arizona, California, New Mexico, and Texas. The label lists the ingredient calomel, which is mercurous chloride (a salt of mercury). Product samples have been found to contain 6 to 10 per cent mercury by weight (Centers for Disease Control 1996; US Food and Drug Administration 1996).

For high-end products, hydroquinone is the chemical of choice. White Secret is one of the most visible products since it is advertised in a 30-minute, late-night television infomercial that is broadcast nationally almost nightly.[4] Jamie Winders and colleagues (2005), who analyze the commercial, note that the commercial continually stresses that White Secret is "una formula Americana." According to Winders, Jones, and Higgins, the American pedigree and English-language name endow White Secret with a cosmopolitan cachet and "a first worldliness." The infomercial follows the daily lives of several young urban women, one of whom narrates and explains how White Secret cream forms a barrier against the darkening rays of the sun while a sister product transforms the colour of the skin itself. The infomercial conjures the power of science, showing cross-sections of skin cells. By showing women applying White Secret in modern, well-lit bathrooms, relaxing in well-appointed apartments, and protected from damaging effects of the sun while walking around the city, the program connects skin lightening with cleanliness, modernity, and mobility (Winders, Jones, and Higgins 2005, 80–4).

Large multinational firms are expanding the marketing of skin care products, including skin lighteners, in Mexico and other parts of Latin America. For example, Stiefel Laboratories, the world's largest privately held pharmaceutical company, which specializes in dermatology products, targets Latin America for skin-lightening products. Six of its 28 wholly owned subsidiaries are located in Latin America. It offers Clariderm, an over-the-counter hydroquinone cream and gel (2 per cent), in Brazil, as well as Clasifel, a prescription-strength hydroquinone cream (4 per cent), in Mexico, Peru, Bolivia, Venezuela, and other Latin American countries. It also sells Claripel, a 4 per cent hydroquinone cream, in the United States.[5]

Middle-Aged and Older White Women in North America and Europe

Historically, at least in the United States, the vast majority of skin lightener users have been so-called white women. Throughout the nineteenth and early twentieth centuries, European-American women, especially those of Southern and Eastern European origins, sought to achieve whiter and brighter skin through use of the many whitening powders and bleaches on the market. In 1930, J. Walter Thomson conducted a survey and found 232 brands of skin lighteners and bleaches for sale. Advertisements for these products appealed to the association of white skin with gentility, social mobility, Anglo-Saxon

superiority, and youth. In large cities, such as New York and Chicago, some Jewish women used skin lighteners and hair straighteners produced by black companies and frequented black beauty parlours (Peiss 1998, 85, 149, 224).

By the mid-1920s, tanning became acceptable for white women, and in the 1930s and 1940s, it became a craze. A year-round tan came to symbolize high social status, since it indicated that a person could afford to travel and spend time at tropical resorts and beaches. In addition, there was a fad for "exotic" Mediterranean and Latin types, with cosmetics designed to enhance "olive" complexions and brunette hair (Peiss 1998, 150–1, 148–9).

However, in the 1980s, as the damaging effects of overexposure to sunrays became known, skin lightening among whites re-emerged as a major growth market. Part of this growth was fuelled by the aging baby boom generation determined to stave off signs of aging. Many sought not only toned bodies and uplifted faces but also youthful skin—that is, smooth, unblemished, glowing skin without telltale age spots. Age spots are a form of hyperpigmentation that results from exposure to the sun over many years. The treatment is the same as that for overall dark skin: hydroquinone, along with skin peeling, exfoliants, and sunscreen.[6]

Multinational Cosmetic and Pharmaceutical Firms and Their Targeting Strategies

Although there are many small local manufacturers and merchants involved in the skin-lightening game, I want to focus on the giant multinationals, which are fuelling the desire for light skin through their advertisement and marketing strategies. The accounts of the skin-lightening markets have shown that the desire for lighter skin and the use of skin bleaches is accelerating in places where modernization and the influence of Western capitalism and culture are most prominent. Multinational biotechnology, cosmetic, and pharmaceutical corporations have coalesced through mergers and acquisitions to create and market personal care products that blur the lines between cosmetics and pharmaceuticals. They have jumped into the field of skin lighteners and correctors, developing many product lines to advertise and sell in Europe, North America, South Asia, East and Southeast Asia, and the Middle East (Wong 2004).

Three of the largest corporations involved in developing the skin-lightening market are L'Oréal, Shiseido, and Unilever. The French-based L'Oréal, with $15.8 billion in sales in 2006, is the largest cosmetics company in the world. It consists of 21 major subsidiaries including Lancôme; Vichy Laboratories; La Roche-Posay Laboratoire Pharmaceutique; Biotherm; Garnier; Giorgio Armani Perfumes; Maybelline, New York; Ralph Lauren Fragrances; Skinceuticals, Shu Uemura; Matrix; Redken; and SoftSheen Carlson. L'Oréal is also a 20 per cent shareholder of Sanofi-Synthélabo, a major France-based pharmaceutical firm. Three L'Oréal subsidiaries produce the best-known skin-lightening lines marketed around the world (which are especially big in Asia): Lancôme Blanc Expert with Melo-No Complex, LaRoche-Posay Mela-D White skin lightening daily lotion with a triple-action formula, and Vichy Biwhite, containing procystein and vitamin C.

A second major player in the skin-lightening market is Shiseido, the largest and best-known Japanese cosmetics firm, with net sales of $5.7 billion. Shiseido cosmetics are marketed in 65 countries and regions, and it operates factories in Europe, the Americas, and other Asian countries. The Shiseido Group, including affiliates, employs approximately 25,200 people around the globe. Its two main luxury lightening lines are White Lucent (for whitening) and White Lucency (for spots/aging). Each product line consists of seven or eight components, which the consumer is supposed to use as part of a complicated regimen involving applications of specific products several times a day.[7]

The third multinational corporation is Unilever, a diversified Anglo-Dutch company with an annual turnover of more than $40 billion and net profits of €5 billion in 2006 (Unilever 2006). It specializes in so-called fast-moving consumer goods in three areas: food (many familiar brands, including Hellman's Mayonnaise and Lipton Tea), home care (laundry detergents, etc.), and personal care, including deodorants, hair care, oral care, and skin care. Its most famous brand in the skin care line is Ponds, which sells cold creams in Europe and North America and whitening creams in Asia, the Middle East, and Latin America.

Through its Indian subsidiary, Hindustan Lever Limited, Unilever patented Fair & Lovely in 1971 following the patenting of niacinamide, a melanin suppressor, which is its main active ingredient. Test-marketed in South India in 1975, it became available throughout India in 1978. Fair & Lovely has become the largest-selling skin cream in India, accounting for 80 per cent of the fairness cream market. According to anthropologist Susan Runkle (2005), "Fair & Lovely has an estimated sixty million consumers throughout the Indian subcontinent and exports to thirty-four countries in Southeast and Central Asia as well as the Middle East."

Fair & Lovely ads claim that "with regular daily use, you will be able to unveil your natural radiant fairness in just 6 weeks!" As with other successful brands, Fair & Lovely has periodically added new lines to appeal to special markets. In 2003, it introduced Fair & Lovely, Ayurvedic, which claims to be formulated according to a 4,500-year-old Indian medical system. In 2004, it introduced Fair & Lovely Oil-Control Gel and Fair & Lovely Anti-Marks. In 2004, Fair & Lovely also announced the "unveiling" of a premium line, Perfect Radiance, "a complete range of 12 premium skin care solutions" containing "international formulations from Unilever's Global Skin Technology Center, combined with ingredients best suited for Indian skin types and climates." Its ads say, "Experience Perfect Radiance from Fair & Lovely. Unveil Perfect Skin." Intended to compete with expensive European brands, Perfect Radiance is sold only in select stores in major cities, including Delhi, Mumbai, Chennai, and Bangalore.[8]

Unilever is known for promoting its brands by being active and visible in the locales where they are marketed. In India, Ponds sponsors the Femina Miss India pageant, in which aspiring contestants are urged to "be as beautiful as you can be." Judging by photos of past winners, being as beautiful as you can be means being as light as you can be. In 2003, partly in response to criticism by the All India Democratic Women's Association of "racist" advertisement of fairness products, Hindustani Lever launched the Fair and Lovely Foundation, whose mission is to "encourage economic empowerment of women across India" through educational and guidance programs, training courses, and scholarships.[9]

Unilever heavily promotes both Ponds and Fair & Lovely with television and print ads tailored to local cultures. In one commercial shown in India, a young, dark-skinned woman's father laments that he has no son to provide for him and his daughter's salary is not high enough. The suggestion is that she could neither get a better job nor marry because of her dark skin. The young woman then uses Fair & Lovely, becomes fairer, and lands a job as an airline hostess, making her father happy. A Malaysian television spot shows a college student who is dejected because she cannot get the attention of a classmate at the next desk. After using Pond's lightening moisturizer, she appears in class brightly lit and several shades lighter, and the boy says, "Why didn't I notice her before?" (BBC 2003).

Such advertisements can be seen as not simply responding to a pre-existing need but actually creating a need by depicting having dark skin as a painful and depressing experience. Before "unveiling" their fairness, dark-skinned women are shown as unhappy, suffering from low self-esteem, ignored by young men, and denigrated by their parents. By using Fair & Lovely or Ponds, a woman undergoes a transformation of not only her complexion but also her personality and her fate. In short, dark skin becomes a burden and handicap that can be overcome only by using the product being advertised.

Conclusion

The yearning for lightness evident in the widespread and growing use of skin bleaching around the globe can rightfully be seen as a legacy of colonialism, a manifestation of "false consciousness," and the internalization of "white is right" values by people of colour, especially women. Thus, one often-proposed solution to the problem is re-education that stresses the diversity of types of beauty and desirability and that valorizes darker skin shades, so that lightness/whiteness is dislodged as the dominant standard.

While such efforts are needed, focusing only on individual consciousness and motives distracts attention from the very powerful economic forces that help to create the yearning for lightness and that offer to fulfill the yearning at a steep price. The manufacturing, advertising, and selling of skin lightening is no longer a marginal, underground economic activity. It has become a major growth market for giant multinational corporations with their sophisticated means of creating and manipulating needs.

The multinationals produce separate product lines that appeal to different target audiences. For some lines of products, the corporations harness the prestige of science by showing cross-sectional diagrams of skin cells and by displaying images of doctors in white coats. Dark skin or dark spots become a disease for which skin lighteners offer a cure. For other lines, designed to appeal to those who respond to appeals to naturalness, corporations call up nature by emphasizing the use of plant extracts and by displaying images of light-skinned women against a background of blue skies and fields of flowers. Dark skin becomes a veil that hides one's natural luminescence, which natural skin lighteners will uncover. For all products, dark skin is associated with pain, rejection, and limited options; achieving light skin is seen as necessary to being youthful, attractive, modern, and affluent—in short, to being "all that you can be."

Notes

1. Under pressure from African-American critics, Nadolina reduced the concentration to 6 per cent in 1937 and 1.5 per cent in 1941.
2. Discussions on Bright Skin Forum, Skin Lightening Board, are at http://excoboard.com/exco/forum.php?forumid=65288. Pallid Skin Lightening system information is at www.avreskincare.com/skin/pallid/index.html. Advertisement for Swiss Whitening Pills is at www.skinbleaching.net.
3. Skin whitening forums are at www.candmag.com/teen-talk/index.php/topic,131753.0.html, and www.rexinter-active.com/forum/topic.asp?TOPIC_ID=41.
4. Discussion of the ingredients in White Secret is found at www.vsantivirus.com/hoax-white-secret.htm.
5. I say that Stiefel targets Latin America because it markets other dermatology products, but not skin lighteners, in the competitive Asian, Middle Eastern, African, and European countries. Information about Stiefel products is at its corporate website, www.stiefel.com.
6. Many of the products used by older white and Asian women to deal with age spots are physician-prescribed pharmaceuticals, including prescription-strength hydroquinone formulas. See information on one widely used system, Obagi, at www.obagi.com.
7. *Shiseido Annual Report 2006*, 34, was downloaded from www.shiseido.co.jp/e/annual/html/index.htm.

Data on European, American, and Japanese markets are at www.shiseido.co.jp/e/story/html/sto40200.htm. World employment figures are also at this site. White Lucent information is at www.shiseido.co.jp/e/whitelucent_us/products/product5.htm. White Lucency information is at www.shiseido.co.jp/e/whitelucency/ (all accessed 6 May 2007).

8. "Fair & Lovely Launches Oil-Control Fairness Gel" (Press Release, 27 April 2004) is found at www.hul.co.in/mediacentre/release .asp?fl==2004/PR_HLL_042704.htm (accessed 6 May 2007). "Fair & Lovely Unveils Premium Range" (Press Release, 25 May 2004) is available at www.hul.co.in/mediacentre/release.asp?fl=2004/PR_HLL_052104_2.htm (accessed on 6 May 2007).
9. The Pond's Femina Miss World site is http://femina-missindia.indiatimes.com/articleshow/137504l.cms. The All India Democratic Women's Association objects to skin lightening ad is at www.aidwaonline.com/content/issues_of_concern/women_and_media.php. Reference to Fair & Lovely campaign is at www.aidwa.org/content/issues_of_concern/women_and_media.php. "Fair & Lovely Launches Foundation to Promote Economic Empowerment of Women" (Press Release, 11 March 2003) is found at http://hul.co.in/mediacentre/release.asp?fl=2003/PR_HLL_031103.htm (all accessed 2 December 2006).

References

Adebajo, S.B. 2002. "An Epidemiological Survey of the Use of Cosmetic Skin Lightening Cosmetics among Traders in Lagos, Nigeria." *West African Journal of Medicine* 21, 1: 51–5.

Arnold, David. 2004. "Race, Place and Bodily Difference in Early Nineteenth Century India." *Historical Research* 77: 162.

Ashikari, Makiko. 2003. "Urban Middle-Class Japanese Women and Their White Faces: Gender, Ideology, and Representation." *Ethos* 31, 1: 3, 3–4, 9–11.

BBC. 2003, July 24. "India Debates 'Racist' Skin Cream Ads." *BBC News World Edition*. http://news.bbc.co.uk/hi/south_asia/308945.htm (accessed 8 May 2007).

Bundles, A'Lelia. 2001. *On Her Own Ground: The Life and Times of Madam C.J. Walker*. New York: Scribner.

Burke, Timothy. 1996. *Lifebuoy Men, Lux Women: Commodification, Consumption, and Cleanliness in Modern Zimbabwe*. Durham, NC: Duke University Press.

Centers for Disease Control and Prevention. 1996. *FDA Warns Consumers Not to Use Crema De Belleza*. FDA statement. Rockville, MD: US Food and Drug Administration.

Chadwick, Julia. 2001, June. "Arklow's Toxic Soap Factory." *Wicklow Today*. www.wicklowtoday.com/features/mercurysoap.htm (accessed 18 April 2007).

De Faoite, Dara. 2001, May 27. "Investigation into the Sale of Dangerous Mercury Soaps in Ethnic Shops." *The Observer*. http://observer.guardian.co.uk/uk_news/story/0,6903,497227,00.html (accessed 1 May 2007).

del Guidice, P., and P. Yves. 2002. "The Widespread Use of Skin Lightening Creams in Senegal: A Persistent Public Health Problem in West Africa." *International Journal of Dermatology* 41: 69–72.

Dooley, Erin. 2001, October. "Food Research Bears Fruit" *Environmental Health Perspectives*. 109, 10: A469.

Earth Summit. 2002. *Telling It Like It Is: 10 Years of Unsustainable Development in Ireland*. Dublin, Ireland: Earth Summit.

Exhibitor Info. 2006. www.beautyworldjapan.com/en/efirst.html (accessed 8 May 2007).

Farr, Marcia. 2006. *Rancheros in Chicagoacan: Language and Identity in a Transnational Community*. Austin: University of Texas Press.

Guttman, Matthew E. 1996. *The Meanings of Macho: Being a Man in Mexico City*. Berkeley: University of California Press.

Herring, Cedric, Verna M. Keith, and Hayward Derrick Horton, eds 2003. *Skin Deep: How Race and Complexion Matter in the "Colour Blind" Era*. Chicago: Institute for Research on Race and Public Policy.

Hunter, Margaret. 2005. *Race, Gender, and the Politics of Skin Tone*. New York: Routledge.

Intage. 2001. "Intelligence on the Cosmetic Market in Japan." www.intage.co.jp/expess/0l_08/market/indexl.html (accessed November 2005).

Kerr, Audrey Elisa. 2005. "The Paper Bag Principle: The Myth and the Motion of Colourism." *Journal of American Folklore* 118: 271–89.

Khan, Aisha. 2008. "'Caucasian,' 'Coolie,' 'Black,' or 'White'? Colour and Race in the Indo-Caribbean Diaspora." Unpublished paper.

Knight, Alan. 1990. "Racism, Revolution, and Indigenismo: Mexico, 1910-1940." In *The Idea of Race in Latin America, 1870-1940*, edited by Richard Graham Austin: University of Texas Press.

Maddox, Keith B. 2004. "Perspectives on Racial Phenotypicality Bias." *Personality and Social Psychology Review* 8: 383–401.

Mahe, Antoine, Fatimata Ly, and Jean-Marie Dangou. 2003. "Skin Diseases Associated with the Cosmetic Use of Bleaching Products in Women from Dakar, Senegal." *British Journal of Dermatology* 148, 3: 493–500.

Malangu, N., and G.A. Ogubanjo. 2006. "Predictors of Tropical Steroid Misuse among Patrons of Pharmacies in Pretoria." *South African Family Practices* 48, 1: 14.

Margulies, Paul. n.d. "Cushing's Syndrome: The Facts You Need to Know." www.nadf.us/diseases/cushings.htm (accessed 1 May 2007).

Martinez, Ruben. 2001. *Crossing Over: A Mexican Family on the Migrant Trail*. New York: Henry Holt.

Massing, Jean Michel. 1995. "From Greek Proverb to Soap Advert: Washing the Ethiopian." *Journal of the Warburg and Courtauld Institutes* 58: 180.

Muzondidya, James. 2005. *Walking a Tightrope, towards a Social History of the Coloured Community of Zimbabwe*. Trenton, NJ: Africa World Press.

Nielsen. 2007. "Prairie Plants Take Root." In *Health, Beauty and Personal Grooming: A Global Nielsen Consumer Report*. www.acnielsen.co.in/news/20070402.shtml (accessed 3 May 2007).

Ntambwe, Malangu. 2004, March. "Mirror Mirror on the Wall, Who is the Fairest of Them All?" *Science in Africa, Africa's First On-Line Science Magazine*. www.scienceinafrica.co.za/2004/march/skinlightening.htm (accessed 1 May 2007).

Ntshingila, Futhi. 2005, November 27. "Female Buppies Using Harmful Skin Lighteners." *Sunday Times*, South Africa. www.sundaytimes.co.za.

NYC Health Dept. 2005. "NYC Health Dept Warns against Use of 'Skin Lightening' Creams Containing Mercury or Similar Products Which Do Not List Ingredients." www.nyc.gov/html/doh/html/pr/pr008-05.shtm (accessed 7 May 2007).

O'Farrell, Michael. 2002, August 26. "Pressure Mounts to Have Soap Plant Shut Down." *Irish Examiner*. http://archives.tcm.ie/irishexaminer/2002/08/26story510455503.asp.

Parrenas, Rhacel. 2001. *Servants of Globalization: Women, Migration, and Domestic Work*. Palo Alto, CA: Stanford University Press.

Peiss, Kathy. 1998. *Hope in a Jar: The Making of America's Beauty Culture*. New York: Metropolitan Books.

Ribane, Nakedi. 2006. *Beauty: A Black Perspective*. Durban, South Africa: University of KwaZulu-Natal Press.

Runkle, Susan. 2004. "Making 'Miss India': Constructing Gender, Power and Nation." *South Asian Popular Culture* 2, 2: 145–59.

———. 2005, February. "The Beauty Obsession." *Manushi* 145. www.indiatogether.org/manushi/issue145/lovely.htm.

Russell, Kathy, Midge Wilson, and Ronald Hall. 1992. *The Colour Complex: The Politics of Skin Colour among African Americans*. New York: Harcourt Brace Jankovich.

Saskatchewan Business Unlimited. 2005. "Prairie Plants Take Root in Cosmetics Industry." *Saskatchewan Business Unlimited* 10, 1: 1–2.

Sheriff, Robin E. 2001. *Dreaming Equality: Colour, Race and Racism in Urban Brazil*. New Brunswick. NJ: Rutgers University Press.

Stepan, Nancy Ley. 1991. *The Hour of Eugenics: Race, Gender, and Nation in Latin America*. Ithaca, NY: Cornell University Press.

Synovate. 2004. "In:fact." www.synovate.com/insights/infact/issues/200406/ (accessed 21 March 2007).

Tabbada, Reyna Mae L. 2006, September 20. "Trouble in Paradise." Press release. www.bulatlat.com/news/6-33/6-33-trouble.htm.

Telles, Edward E. 2004. *Race in Another America: The Significance of Skin Colour in Brazil*. Princeton, NJ: Princeton University Press.

Thomas, Iyamide. 2004. "'Yellow Fever': The Disease That is Skin Bleaching." *Mano Vision* 33 (October): 32–3. www.manovision.com/ISSUES/ISSUE33/33skin.pdf.

Thomas, Lynn M. 2008. "Skin Lighteners in South Africa: Transnational Entanglements and Technologies of the Self." In *Shades of Difference: Why Skin Colour Matters*, edited by Evelyn Nakano Glenn. Stanford, CA: Stanford University Press.

Unilever. 2006. Annual report. www.unilever.com/ourcompany/investorcentre/annual_reports/archives.asp (accessed 6 May 2007).

US Food and Drug Administration. 1996. *FDA Warns Consumers Not to Use Crema De Belleza*. FDA statement, 23 July. Rockville, MD: US Food and Drug Administration.

Views on Article-Complexion. n.d. www.indiaparenting.com/beauty/beauty041book.shtml (accessed November 2005).

Winders, Jamie, John Paul Jones III, and Michael James Higgins. 2005. "Making Gueras: Selling White Identities on Late-Night Mexican Television." *Gender, Place and Culture* 12, 1: 71–93.

Wong, Stephanie. 2004. "Whitening Cream Sales Soar as Asia's Skin-Deep Beauties Shun Western Suntans." *Manila Bulletin*. www.mb.com.ph/issues/2004/08/24/SCTY 2004082416969.html# (accessed 24 March 2007).

Questions for Critical Thought

1. What is colourism? What is its social and political origin? What role has colonialism played in establishing and reinforcing racial hierarchies?
2. How has the global market of the Western world contributed to the increase in the use of skin lighteners? Which transnational corporations are involved in the production of skin lightening agents? Do you know anyone who has used a skin-lightening agent? How has the use of it affected their appearance, their behaviour, and their health?
3. Compare and contrast the reasons that skin-lightening products are used by Indian, Filipina, and Japanese women, according to Glenn. Why has a new market in skin lighteners emerged in North America? What other cultural groups in the world use skin lighteners?
4. What role does patriarchy play in supporting the acquisition of skin-lightening products by upwardly mobile women? How has the consumption of skin lighteners contributed to the acquisition of symbolic capital in the marriage market in India and other countries in the world?
5. How has the globalization of the practice of skin lightening affected the overall health and welfare of women of the world? How can unsafe practices of skin lightening and other forms of bodywork that women engage in be challenged?

Conclusion

How and why the male-dominated, allopathic medical professions seek to identify, problematize, and medicalize changes in the natural life cycle of women is the dominant theme throughout the chapters in this section. From an early age, women are socialized to engage in bodywork and to aspire to culturally dictated anti-fat standards of health and beauty that are part of the patriarchal "gaze" of society. In addition, all women's bodies, but especially racialized women's bodies, are subject to the policing practices of the state and health care professionals. Racialized women and disabled women from lower socio-economic backgrounds are more likely to underuse the medical care system, but when they do use it, they are confronted by systemic racism and caregivers who are insensitive to their cultural, linguistic, and social needs. Conversely, racialized women who are upwardly mobile are more likely to engage in the use of dangerous skin-lightening products to acquire light-skinned privileges. The degree of inequality that women experience is highly correlated with poor health, and it is intensified by the aging process and the intersections of class, size, sexuality, race, and ethnicity.

Recommended Readings

Pat Armstrong, Madeline Boscoe, Barbara Clow, Karen Grant, Margaret Haworth-Brockman, Beth Jackson, Ann Pederson, and Morgan Seeley, eds 2009. *A Place to Call Home: Long Term Health Care in Canada*. Halifax, NS: Fernwood.

- In this edited volume the authors look at what they call "the invisible side" of long-term care in the home. The gendering of long-term care, among both caregivers and care recipients, is examined. The authors propose that policies and actions that empower women and raise social awareness about the long-term care of the elderly, the chronically ill, and physically or mentally challenged are essential in order to reduce this form of social inequality.

B. Singh Bolaria. 2002. "Income Inequality, Poverty, Food Banks and Health." In *Health, Illness and Health Care in Canada*, 3rd edn. Eds B. Singh Bolaria and Harley D. Dickinson. Toronto: Nelson.

- Since the 1980s, more Canadians have become dependent on food banks, which, Singh Bolaria explains, is due to the links between the feminization of poverty, food security, health, and nutrition. Bolaria proposes that a dependency on food banks exacerbates the debilitating life conditions that dependent populations experience.

Tania Das Gupta. 2009. *Real Nurses and Others: Racism in Nursing*. Halifax, NS: Fernwood.

- Drawing on her research with nurses and other health care workers who face racial harassment in the workplace, Das Gupta examines the political economy of the health care industry using an intersectional theoretical framework. Systemic racism continues in the health care system, and there is, according to Das Gupta, a general lack of support by the management that makes it difficult for those who experience racism in the workplace to contest it.

Diane Driedger and Michelle Owen, eds 2008. *Dissonant Disabilities: Women With Chronic Illnesses Explore Their Lives*. Toronto: Canadian Scholars' Press.

- This collection of essays examines how women who live with chronic illnesses deal with the complications of everyday life. Framed by a critical disability perspective, the text examines such issues as how women cope with workplace alienation and how they maintain a balance between their public and private lives.

Carmen H. Logie, Llana James, Wangari Tharo, and Mona R. Loutfy, 2011. "HIV, Gender, Race, Sexual Orientation, and Sex Work: A Qualitative Study of Intersectional Stigma Experienced by HIV-Positive Women in Ontario, Canada." *PLoS Medicine* 8, 11. doi:10.1371/journal.pmed.1001124.

- This community-based qualitative investigation analyzes data that measures the impact that the stigmatization of being HIV-positive has on marginalized women. The study, which is based on 15 focus groups in five Ontario cities, discusses the strategies that the women use to cope with the intersections of sexism, racism, homophobia, and transphobia that they experience on a daily basis. As HIV-positive rates increase among marginalized women and sex workers in Ontario, the authors argue that there are various factors that are simultaneously taking place on micro, meso, and macro levels creating barriers to women's health and well-being.

PART FIVE

Inequality and Social Justice

S cholarship on inequality in Canada has evolved from early research on the integration of ethnic groups to more complex inquiries into the intersections of gender,
race, class, and other axes of social organization. These categories have themselves
undergone theoretical transformation. No longer discrete attributes of identity, sexism, racism, and classism are now understood as interlocking systems of oppression.
Canadian social theorists have come to understand that the process of domination and
power relations must be studied before inequality as a relational social problem can be
fully understood. There is no inequality without domination; no oppression without
power; no resistance without change.

One arena in which the social relations of inequality play out is that of the justice system. Yet the term "justice" has multiple, even contradictory, meanings, as some of the
writers here assert. How is this so? As a formal institution, the justice system is conceptualized both as the cause and the remedy for justice. It serves to protect the rights and
property of individuals, and, certainly, it is intended to uphold the principles of equality
and to protect individuals and groups against discrimination. However, critical analyses have shown that formal justice and social justice do not necessarily converge in the
legal system. Indeed, patterns of inequality emerge, following the contours of gender,
race, and class. The procedures and discourse of the justice system can legitimize the
inequality that results from discriminatory treatment in the system and across social
systems.

In Part Five we broaden the formal discourse of "justice" by considering issues of
"social justice" as well. In this way, we can discover connections between the principles
guiding the system and their contradictory effects on marginalized groups. In overlooking these effects, reforms to the justice system may reinforce inequalities by, for
example, encouraging the overrepresentation of Aboriginal peoples in the system (see
Monture-Angus) or ignoring the effects in peoples' lives of social factors such as racism,
welfare, the labour market, and child care (see Duffy and Mandell, and Nelson).

The intersections of inequality are clearly in evidence in this section. Ann Duffy and
Nancy Mandell explain how economic inequality, or poverty, was established through
historical processes and is maintained through contemporary social policy and structures. These include the nature of the labour market for women, traditional women's
roles, and diminished welfare state programs, in addition to ideological antagonisms

toward the poor. An overemphasis on the measurement of poverty diverts attention away from the stigmatization of poverty and the culture of poverty that are experienced by a growing number of Canadians. Solutions to economic inequality must acknowledge the many factors that create and perpetuate poverty, as well as its myriad effects upon those marginalized by gender, race, age, disability, and class.

Patricia Monture-Angus writes on the overrepresentation of Aboriginal peoples in the criminal justice system. She posits that programs intended to alleviate inequitable treatment of Aboriginal offenders are flawed in trying to change the victims of the system rather than the system itself, which is responsible for reproducing inequities. Monture-Angus argues against individualistic analyses of crime. Instead, she stresses that looking at structural factors, such as legislation and the legal system, as well as at broader historical processes, primarily colonialism, is essential to understanding the problem. Monture-Angus maintains that the social problems that give rise to the overrepresentation of Aboriginal peoples in the criminal justice system are not caused by factors inherent to Native cultures, but are the result of unequal power relations and unjust distribution of power and resources.

The issue of justice is broadened in Jennifer Nelson's reading on the erasure of Africville, a historical black neighbourhood within the environs of Halifax. In her analysis of the social organization of place, Nelson describes a systematic "eviction, suppression, and denial" of the community. Africville's eradication was accomplished through the racism, neglect, and exclusion from municipal services that cast the neighbourhood as a "blight" in the industrializing urban centre. Echoing a theme from other readings in this section, Nelson shows how "improvement" (here, relocation and urban development) was undertaken in the spirit of reconciliation, thus avoiding accountability for racist practices. The dominant group maintained their innocence by silencing the experience of those marginalized on the basis of colonial attitudes about race and class.

The residues of colonialism are the focus of Sarah Hunt's chapter on decolonizing sex work. Hunt is a mixed-blood Kwakwaka'wakw woman, who writes about the overrepresentation of Indigenous women in the sex trade. Hunt proposes that the social origins of violence and sex are intertwined in the policies of colonialism and the Canadian Indian Act. Poverty, unsettled land claims, and racist and sexist stereotypes about Indigenous peoples have resulted in chronic unemployment and underemployment, which have subsequently forced Indigenous women with few life choices into the sex work industry. She addresses the controversial problem of missing and murdered Aboriginal women who were sex workers in Vancouver's Downtown Eastside. Hunt concludes by proposing the following eight approaches to decolonizing sex work: embracing sex workers as members of Indigenous communities, meeting sex workers' basic needs, recognizing a multiplicity of Indigenous cultural practices and beliefs, supporting a rights-based approach, acknowledging agency and voice, supporting freedom of mobility, allowing women to control their own bodies, and promoting community change, beyond legal response.

While the Indigenous peoples of Canada live in both rural and urban centres, foreign-born Canadians usually live in large cities. According to the 2011 census data, 46.0 per cent of Toronto's population is foreign-born, with most of the city's immigrants coming from Middle Eastern countries and China (Statistics Canada 2014). The rise in the number of practising Muslims living in Toronto since 2000 has caused some tension in the city. In 2003 the Islamic Institution of Civil Justice announced that it would begin offering arbitration in family disputes, which, according to Anna Korteweg's research on the Canadian media, resulted in a two-year debate in the mainstream media about whether Sharia law should be introduced in Ontario. In this reading, Korteweg examines the debate in the context of religion, gender, immigration, and ethnicity. She argues that acting with agency may be defined as overtly resisting domination or it may also take the form of an "embedded agency" where Muslim women may act as agentic religious subjects.

Women acting with agency is the main focus of the final reading in this section on social justice. Wangari Esther Tharao and Linda Cornwell document the work of the Women's Health in Women's Hands (WHIWH) feminist organization in Toronto. The WHIWH centre seeks to identify and to promote methods to prevent the continuation of female genital mutilation (FGM) in Canada. Feminist discourse links FGM to the economic and social oppression of women, and it is considered to be a component of the broader matrix of domination and violence against women. Tharao and Cornwell describe the WHIWH, a non-governmental organization (NGO), as an inclusive, multicultural, multilingual, community health centre that plays a leadership role in serving, empowering, and enabling women from FGM-practising communities to fulfill their life aspirations and to promote the eradication of FGM in Canada.

Reference

Statistics Canada. 2014. *Immigration and Ethnocultural Diversity in Canada.* Accessed 14 July 2014. http://www12.statcan.ca/nhs-enm/2011/as-sa/99-010-x/99-010-x2011001-eng.cfm#a2.

The Growth of Poverty and Social Inequality: Losing Faith in Social Justice

....*Ann Duffy and Nancy Mandell*

Poverty in Canada Today

The economic upheaval of 2008 promises to change, at least for several years, Canadians' perceptions and experiences of poverty. Not only are enormous numbers of Canadians facing lay-offs and growing unemployment rates, but also many have seen their savings and pension funds dramatically reduced. In this process, poverty has edged ominously closer, and the comforting line presumed to separate the safe and the marginalized has been increasingly blurred.

Poverty is one of the great unresolved and often overlooked social issues confronting Canadians. Although Canada numbers among the wealthiest countries in the world, many of its citizens, especially children, the disabled, and single mothers are unable to escape the debilitating effects of impoverishment. Despite periods of strong economic growth, many sectors of the population have been left behind, and now, as food and energy prices soar, their economic marginalization is likely to become even more harrowing.

Evidence of the poverty problem is everywhere. In virtually every small town and city, the persistent appeals from food banks speak to the hunger in our midst. In March 2008, 704,414 Canadians used a food bank at least once, and fully one-third of food banks report difficulty meeting the demand for their services (Food Banks Canada 2008; Pasma 2008). Since 1997, when comparable data on food bank use were first collected, food bank use has increased by 6 per cent. Considered at their inception in the 1980s as a short-term, stop-gap form of assistance, they have become a permanent fixture in our communities, and harsh economic times only underscore their significance (Food Banks Canada 2008). For example,

as Ontario shed thousands of manufacturing jobs throughout 2008, food bank use increased by an unprecedented 13 per cent from 2007. Based on this rate of increase, by March 2009, 350,000 Ontarians will be turning to food banks at least once a month (Findlay 2008).

Not surprisingly, food bank clients represent a cross-section of the population—students, seniors, families, workers, and welfare recipients. In 2008, 230 Ryerson University students were using the university's food bank each week, up 30 per cent from the preceding year (Wallace 2008; McGrath 1998). One in seven (14.5 per cent) of those using food banks in Canada had paid employment, but their wages were too low to be stretched to cover their living expenses. More than one in three food bank clients (37 per cent) are children. Not surprisingly, fully half of food bank users are relying on social assistance to live—a fact that underscores the inadequacies of welfare payments to meet numerous families' basic requirements (Food Banks Canada 2008).

Equally grim reminders of poverty can be found during any walk through the inner core of our major cities. There, huddled on hot air gratings or squatting in bus shelters, it is easy to find some of the estimated 200,000 to 300,000 Canadians who each year struggle with homelessness, and the 150,000 who are chronically under-housed (CBC News 2007). In 2007, there were an estimated 1,020 shelters providing a total of 26,872 beds on a regular basis (up 22 per cent from 2006) (Wellesley Institute 2008; Human Resources and Skills Development Canada [HRSDC] 2008b). Needless to say, these statistics only hint at the dimensions of the problem. In Vancouver between April and December of 2007, homeless shelters turned away people more than 40,000 times (Bula 2008).

These are the individuals pushed to the periphery of our society—by mental illness, addictions, and other misfortunes. A recent Toronto survey reported that more than one-third of its homeless population had suffered a severe brain injury prior to ending up homeless (Alphonso 2008, A11). Of course, the homeless are amongst the most visible symptoms of Canada's poverty. Behind closed doors are hundreds of thousands more poor Canadians—some relying on social assistance or disability income, some depending on minimum wage employment, and all struggling to keep going in a society that too often ignores their plight.

Despite extensive evidence, it is difficult for some well-to-do Canadians to appreciate the extent of poverty in Canada. While it is easy to see that hordes of homeless, starving children in nineteenth-century Montreal (or modern Somalia) were (or are) poor, it may be more difficult to identify those contemporary Canadians who have too little to get by, who need to choose between paying the rent or feeding the kids, and who are unable to participate in any meaningful fashion in the social, political, educational, and spiritual life of the nation. While these individuals are not necessarily starving or homeless, they are deeply deprived.

It is not, of course, necessarily easy to draw a line between the poor and the non-poor. After all, polls suggest that as many as half of Canadians fear they would fall into poverty if they missed one or two paycheques (CBC News 2007), and between 2002 and 2006 more than one in five Canadians (18 to 60 years old) experienced low income for at least one year (HRSDC 2008a, 27). To sort out the murkiness surrounding poverty, government agencies, social researchers, and advocacy groups have proposed a number of definitions of poverty. To date, despite these efforts, Canada has not arrived at an "official" designation of poverty and the definitional debate continues to rage (Sarlo 2008; Smith 2008; Broadbent 2005; Fellegi 1997). Clearly the definition of poverty or homelessness that a researcher or policy group embraces has broad implications. Employing a stricter or more lenient definition to count the poor may, at the stroke of a pen, dramatically reduce or increase the number of poor. For governments who are seeking to respond painlessly and inexpensively to pressures for social reform, "reduction by redefinition" is a tempting alternative.

Keeping in mind these ongoing definitional debates, the best-known and most widely used poverty measure in Canada is the Statistics Canada definition (adopted in 1973; reset in 1992). It establishes income cut-offs below which people are considered to live in "straitened circumstances." The cut-offs are based on the notion that poor families must spend 20 per cent more of their income than the average family of a similar size on the necessities of food, shelter, and clothing. Since the average Canadian family spent about 43 per cent of its after-tax income on food, clothing, and shelter in 1992, poor families are ones that must spend 63 per cent of their income for these necessities. Since 1992, the national Consumer Price Index has been used to index the income cut-offs for inflation. Today, the low-income after-tax cut-offs (LICOs-IAT) typically refer to income after taxes since taxes may significantly reduce available funds. These income cut-offs vary by household size and the population density in one's area of residence, resulting in 35 **low-income cut-offs**. For example, a single person living in Toronto in 2006 on less than $17,500 (after taxes) is considered "poor" by the Statistics Canada definition (1992 base), while a two-person family living on less than $13,989 (after taxes) in a rural area is deemed poor. The ultimate result is a gauge of "relative" poverty. If a family of three living in Vancouver earns $20,000 after taxes, they are considered poor relative to families of comparable size living in cities of comparable size; if the family was smaller or they were living in a rural area, they might not qualify as "poor" (HRSDC 2008a; Canadian Council on Social Development [CCSD] 2008a).

While the Statistics Canada poverty profile produced with the LICOs-IAT provides us with a revealing picture of poverty in Canada, it has serious limitations. First, these 35 categories do not include Aboriginal reserves, institutional inmates (homes for the aged, prisons), residents of the Yukon, the Northwest Territories, and Nunavut, and the homeless. Second, it tells us nothing about the duration of poverty, that is, how long any one individual is poor. Third, many analyses are dissatisfied with the adjustments by location. According to Statistics Canada, it is 31 per cent less expensive to live in rural areas. But while research suggests that shelter costs are lower in rural areas than in the city, transportation costs are higher. Furthermore, access to subsidized public services such as child care, health services, and education, as well as to competitively priced goods, is more challenging in many rural areas. In short, many analysts maintain that the adjustments by location are likely inaccurate. Fourth, the LICOs-IAT measure ignores differences in the actual level of need in particular households. For example, caring for a child with a severe disability and lacking access to subsidized services may significantly increase household economic needs (Canada and the World Backgrounder 2005a; Ross and Shillington 2000).

Not surprisingly, as a result of these criticisms, other approaches to poverty have been advanced. In particular, the Market Basket Measure (MBM), a measure based on the cost of a specific basket of goods and services, has been devised to provide an "absolute" measure of poverty. From this vantage point, if an individual or family, regardless of number of members or place of residence, does not have the monies to purchase these goods and services, they are considered to be "poor." This "absolute" measure is clearly much more sensitive to the regional variations in costs across Canada; if fuel or food is more expensive in Vancouver than Toronto, the MBM will capture such differences and their impact on family economies. For example, in 2006, according to the MBM definition 11.9 per cent of all Canadians were "poor," while the LICOs-IAT approach indicates that 10.5 per cent were impoverished (HRSDC 2008a). Not surprisingly, social researchers are urging that the MBM definition be employed as a necessary

supplement to the LICOs-IAT approach. Both of these measures present poverty as a static phenomenon when, of course, it is a fluid category. Each year between 2000 and 2006, about 1 million people entered low income, while about 1.1 million exited it (HRSDC 2008a, 9). Unemployment, illness, accident, marital breakup, or disability may, even in the course of a month, tip the balance. Similarly, in the course of a lifetime, a variety of factors (gender, age, marital status, and number of children) may trigger a slide into poverty. Given these patterns, the problem of poverty needs to be understood as encompassing a broad continuum of individuals and families both below and above the designated poverty line and influenced by powerful social and economic forces.

Even if it were possible to point out who is poor and who is not, the poor are far from a homogeneous group. In the first place, they do not consist solely of people on welfare. Many poor Canadians are employed, but their wages are so low that they do not exceed the LICOs-IAT levels. Nonetheless, with very few exceptions, if you were among the 1.7 million Canadians (including almost half a million children) relying on welfare in 2005, you were living in poverty and, in all likelihood, surviving on an income significantly below the LICOs-IAT (CCSD 2008c). Despite the "complicated, cumbersome and stigmatizing process" required to qualify for welfare, welfare payments typically mean poverty (National Council of Welfare 2008a). For example, in 2007, the total welfare income for a lone parent with one child living in Ontario was $16,439 per annum, while the LICOs-IAT for this individual would be $21,851. Since this family type is receiving 75 per cent of the poverty level, they are, in fact, doing quite well compared to many other welfare recipients. A couple with two children living on welfare in Quebec receives only 64 per cent of the poverty rate, and a single employable individual in New Brunswick receives a total welfare income of $3,574 or 19 per cent of the LICOs-IAT (National Council of Welfare 2008b, 44–5).

Not only do welfare payments not lift most recipients out of poverty, over the course of the past two decades, the dollar value of many welfare benefits has steadily declined because of legislated cuts in welfare benefits as well as the lack of annual cost-of-living adjustments. In Ontario between 1989 and 2007, welfare incomes (in constant 2007 dollars) for all categories of recipients declined—by 24 per cent for single employable individuals and by almost 12 per cent for single parents with one child; in contrast, welfare benefits improved for a few jurisdictions (Quebec, Newfoundland and Labrador, New Brunswick, Saskatchewan, and the Yukon) (National Council of Welfare 2008b, 76–7). Given these patterns, it is not surprising that so many food bank clients are welfare recipients.

In addition to the poor who rely solely on welfare, many other Canadians—the "working poor"—are poor because their earnings from work are below the poverty markers. Indeed, paid employment is common amongst the poor with 44 per cent of poor households having at least one working adult, and in Ontario in 2008, 70 per cent of children living in poverty had a parent who was working (Torjman 2008; Monsebraaten 2008a, A4). In some instances these people are also welfare recipients since they are often allowed, even encouraged, to improve their economic situation by taking paid employment. This encouragement takes the form of monthly "earnings exemptions," meaning that welfare recipients are allowed to keep a portion of their earned income. These exemption rules vary from province to province, by the overall employability of the individuals, and by the size of the family. In some provinces, they include work-related expenses such as child-care expenses. Although the provincial and territorial governments' stated intention is to reduce welfare rolls, despite the already low level of welfare support, some policies on earnings exemptions may make it difficult for welfare recipients to take on paid work. For example, in Ontario in 2007 a lone parent with one child was not allowed to keep any earned income during the first three months on welfare and after that may have retained only

50 per cent of gross earnings. In Alberta in 2007 a single employable individual was allowed to retain $115 and 25 per cent of any remaining net income (National Council of Welfare 2008b, 34–5).

In short, despite combining paid earnings with welfare or pension income, numerous Canadians still fall into the ranks of the poor. In addition, there are many, especially working-age individuals and families, who draw all their income from paid employment and yet cannot escape poverty. According to the 2006 census, 2,375,000 Canadians aged 18 to 64 earned an income that was below the LICOs-IAT (Statistics Canada 2008a, 87). Because this segment (11.3 per cent) of the paid labour force is poorly paid—often their jobs are short-term, part-time, seasonal, contract-based, and in low-wage segments of the economy such as the sales and service industries—they also live in poverty. In Ontario, for example, 42 per cent of poor families have at least one parent working and another 29 per cent include a parent who is working part-time or part-year (Monsebraaten 2008a, A4). If wages are low, even full-time employment cannot prevent poverty. In 2005, 2.2 million Canadians (almost 16 per cent of all workers aged 15 or older) had jobs that paid less than $10 per hour. In many instances these individuals were working at the provincial minimum wage rates, none of which exceeded $8.50 per hour even in 2007. As poverty activists point out, to live above the approximately $18,000 a year low-income cut-off, a single employable Ontarian or Albertan would have to earn $10 per hour and work full-time year-round (CCSD 2008a). In 2008, Ontario's minimum wage reached $8.75 and increased to $10.25 in 2010. On 1 June 2014, it was increased to $11.00 per hour. While almost two-thirds of minimum wage workers are young (under 25), almost one-third are adult workers aged 25 to 54, and the overwhelming majority (two-thirds) of all minimum wage workers are women (Sussman and Tabi 2004). This pattern helps explain the single mother who, despite her full-time employment, is living below the LICOs-IAT, or the two-income teen family that earns $27,000 a year—$5,000 below the poverty line in Ontario. Whenever the worker is a single parent, when only one parent in the family is employed, when the work is minimum wage, part-time, contract, short-term, irregular, or unskilled, and when there are dependent children in the home, employment frequently fails to provide an escape from poverty (Monsebraaten 2008a; Kazemipur and Halli 2000).

Taken as a whole, the portrait of poverty in Canada today is sobering. Despite the fact that economic growth has translated to improvements in poverty rates between 2000 and 2006, the 2006 census data reveal that about one in ten Canadians is poor in terms of the LICOs-IAT, and more than three-quarters of a million children and youth (760,000 Canadians under age 18) are poor. Some 32 per cent of lone-parent families headed by women are low-income, down from a high of 53 per cent in 1996. About 29 per cent of unattached individuals and 5.4 per cent of men and women aged 65 and older live below the income cut-offs (Statistics Canada 2008a, 87; Statistics Canada 2006c).

Specific segments of the population have particularly high incidence rates of low income: lone parents (with at least one child under age 18), especially lone mothers; Aboriginal Canadians living off-reserve; unattached individuals aged 45 to 64, especially with work-limiting disabilities; and recent immigrants. Using the MBM, HRSDC calculates that about 31 per cent of lone parents, 34 per cent of unattached individuals aged 45 to 64, one-quarter of recent immigrants, and 29 per cent of Aboriginal Canadians living off-reserve experience low income. Overall, low income rates for families whose main income recipient belongs to one of these high-risk groups are almost three times higher than for other economic families. Further, the rates of persistent poverty for members of these groups are over four times higher than for other families (HRSDC 2008a, 23–8). The uneven geographic distribution of some of these groups—for example, recent immigrants, who tend to concentrate in Montreal, Toronto, and Vancouver—likely contributes to a distinct regional dimension in Canadian poverty. For example, according to the 2006 census, low income rates for children averaged 11.3 per cent in Canada, but ranged from a high of 16.1 per cent in British Columbia to an estimated low of 4.0 per cent on Prince Edward Island (Statistics Canada 2008a, 87–108). Age is another critical determinant of poverty rates. Young families (couples with children) headed by people under the age of 25 are much more likely to be poor, as are single, widowed, and divorced women over the age of 64 (Canada and the World Backgrounder 2005c). Families and individuals with a low level of education are more likely to be poor, as are families with only one wage-earner.

Disability is another key determinant of impoverishment. According to the Council of Canadians with Disabilities (CCD), disabled Canadians living on social assistance receive at best about $12,000 a year and at worst less than $7,000. Many people with disabilities look forward to becoming senior citizens since their incomes will improve when they turn 65 (CCD 2008). Using the MBM of poverty, almost one-third of Canadians with a work-limiting disability were living on low income in 2006 (HRSDC 2008a, 23). Increasingly, recent immigrant status is also being recognized as an important factor in poverty rates. Regardless of the immigrant's age and educational background and despite an immigration policy that has strategically selected highly skilled immigrants, there is a growing poverty and earnings gap between immigrants and Canadians who are native-born (Picot 2004; Picot and Myles 2005, 20). In 2006, one in four recent immigrants was living on low income according to the MBM (HRSDC 2008a, 23). As with other groups at high risk for impoverishment, persons with disabilities and recent immigrants experienced an improvement in their poverty rates between 2000 and 2006, and yet their economic marginalization remains clear. With the dramatic downturn in the economy in 2008, this progress, however unsatisfactory, may be jeopardized.

The Feminization of Poverty

At certain ages and in certain life scenarios, Canadian women may also be particularly at risk of being poor. The "feminization of poverty" refers to the fact that women in many industrialized Western nations, as well as in developing countries, are more likely to be poor than men (Pearce 1978; Goldberg 1990; Nelson 2006). In recent years this pattern has continued for Canadian women as adults and as seniors. For example, in the 65 years and over category, 7.0 per cent of women fall below LICOs-IAT but only 3.4 per cent of comparable men (Statistics Canada 2008a, 87). Furthermore, adult women of all ages are at heightened risk for persistent poverty; between 1999 and 2004, more women (6.3 per cent) than men (4.6 per cent) lived below the poverty cut-offs for at least four of these six years (HRSDC 2008e). Nor is this a new problem. The ranks of the poor have long been populated by women who are deserted, widowed, or orphaned (Katz 1975, 60; Simmons 1986).

While the reasons behind women's impoverishment are complex, they have much to do with traditional gender ideology, inequities in the labour force, flaws in family law, and the way we respond to marriage breakdown as a society. For generations, women have been expected to devote their lives to their unpaid duties in marriage and motherhood. Although many wives and mothers also worked for pay, such work was generally restricted. Lower pay rates for women, rules against the employment of married women, and the peripheralization and stigmatization of "women's work" all reinforced the notion that women's place was in the home (Statistics Canada 2006c; Duffy and Pupo 1992, 13–40).

Throughout the twentieth century, however, these notions came under increasing attack. The women's movement, advanced education for women, and the reduction in family size, among other factors, undermined the traditional sexual division of labour. In particular, increasing numbers of Canadians have found that they cannot survive on the uncertain income of a single breadwinner. The failure of wages to keep pace with inflation, increases in taxation, high unemployment, skyrocketing housing costs, and the loss of high-paying industrial and resource-extraction jobs have made the male-breadwinner family increasingly anachronistic. By 2004, 65 per cent of women with children under the age of three were in the paid labour force (Statistics Canada 2006c, 105).

However, significant gender differences in work and family life persist. Many mothers continue to take time away from paid employment when their children are young and/or balance family and paid work with part-time or self-employed work (Cranford. Vosko, and Zukewich 2006). To the degree women live a more traditional life—that is, marry, have children, and assume primary responsibility for domestic and childcare work—they risk impoverishment. Even if they minimize their paid work interruptions or consistently maintain a presence in the part-time labour force (as currently over 20 per cent of adult Canadian women do), they run the risk of low income if their marriage ends in divorce or early widowhood (Statistics Canada 2006c, 109; 2006b). Being employed in traditionally low-paid women's occupations and taking time off to care for young children can result in economic disaster when a marriage ends in divorce, when women face long years of widowhood, or when women become single parents.

Single parenthood, typically the result of divorce, can have devastating effects on women's economic well-being. More than one in three (35 per cent) lone-parent mothers are poor (MBM 2006), in contrast to a poverty rate of 12 per cent for single-parent fathers. While both figures indicate a marked improvement from 2000 when the low-income rate for single fathers was 20 per cent and for single mothers 43 per cent, women continue to be disadvantaged (HRSDC 2008a, 31).

For many of these women, low income is a direct consequence of marriage breakup. In the first year after divorce (depending upon family size) women's household incomes drop by between 20 to 40 per cent while men's incomes decline much less. Three years post-divorce, women's incomes remain significantly below their incomes during the marriage and well below their ex-husbands' current incomes. Not surprisingly, ex-husbands tend to have generally higher incomes than ex-wives and women typically assume primary custody of the children. Further, despite numerous efforts, the enforcement of child support payments from non-custodial parents remains plagued with difficulties. Although increasingly both women and men will find it difficult to maintain a household without two income earners and many women have made considerable advances in the labour market, the dominant divorce patterns continue to contribute to the feminization of poverty (Ambert 2005).

Despite the neediness of single mothers, welfare policy has often done little to improve their situation. For example, in Ontario, single welfare mothers of school-age children are required to sign up for workfare, and these mothers, along with other welfare recipients, have faced dramatic reductions in the dollar value of their welfare benefits. (Workfare is the social policy that requires able-bodied recipients of social welfare benefits to take some form of state-orchestrated employment.) Similarly in Alberta, new regulations restrict both eligibility for support and the amount of welfare payments while also mandating that welfare recipients participate in job training programs. Unfortunately, these efforts have tended to inadequately address the particular problems of single mothers—notably, the need for reliable, low cost child care and the inadequacy of women's jobs in the low-wage, low-skill sector of the market economy (Breitkreuz 2005). To further compound their plight, single mothers must also confront the persistent tendency to stereotype mothers on welfare as somehow less worthy of social support than, for example, low-income two-parent families. Popular ideology stigmatizes single mothers who receive social assistance as promiscuous and irresponsible (Goar 2008).

Growing old provides no guarantee of relief for women. While policy initiatives in the 1980s and 1990s eased much of the poverty burden for the elderly, it has by no means been eliminated. Unattached women over the age of 64—typically widowed, divorced, or separated—face high rates of poverty. A recent study found that five years after a woman was widowed, her income had declined by more than 15 per cent; in contrast, a man who lost his spouse experienced a 5.8 per cent increase in income in those five years. Not surprisingly more women (8.7 per cent) than men (5.1 per cent) experienced poverty five years after they were widowed (Statistics Canada 2006b). Unattached women aged 75 and older experience even higher rates of impoverishment. Women are particularly at risk because they are less likely to receive income from occupational pension plans, the Canada/Quebec Pension Plan, and investments. The traditional gender pattern—work interruptions to take care of family responsibilities, work in low-paying jobs with poor benefits, and part-time and contractual work—contributes to high rates of female impoverishment whenever women find themselves without a spouse (Statistics Canada 2006c; McDonald 1997). These patterns also mean that women may not be able to access adequate government pension benefits to top up their income in old age and may not be able to save for their retirement through private savings plans (Gazso 2005, 59).

In short, traditional social structural parameters of women's lives put them at risk if they end up on their own. Yet they are likely to confront this fate. Based on current trends in marriage (including common-law marriage), motherhood, divorce, child custody arrangements, and life expectancy, most Canadian women can expect to spend a portion of their adult lives without a male breadwinner in the home—as pregnant teens, single mothers, divorced middle-aged workers, and/or elderly widows (Statistics Canada 2006c). Despite these pervasive social realities, many Canadian women still often do not plan their paid work and marital/relationship lives so that they achieve financial well-being and autonomy (Duffy, Mandell, and Pupo

1988). In a culture that perpetuates unrealistic notions of romantic love, marital life, and parenting, and in an economy premised on the peripheralized, low-wage, ghettoized work of women, too many women continue to be set up for poverty (McKeen 2004).

Predictably, certain groups of women—immigrant women, homeless women, the disabled, minority women, and Aboriginal Canadians—are at greater risk. Aboriginal women, for example, have lower than average labour force participation rates, higher rates of fertility, lower incomes, and substantially higher rates of unemployment (Statistics Canada 2006c, 181–209). Despite the facts that their families tend to be larger and lone parenthood is relatively more common, Aboriginal women aged 25 to 54 relied on a median income that was on average $8,000 less than that of non-Aboriginal women (National Council of Welfare 2007, 23). Visible-minority and immigrant women are similarly disadvantaged since they frequently find that racial and ethnic discrimination, along with language difficulties and inadequate government policy, translate into long hours of low-wage work, higher rates of unemployment, and increased rates of low income (Statistics Canada 2006c, 225, 228, 249, 252, 254). Age intensifies the inequality and foreign-born elderly women who are recent immigrants have lower average incomes than their Canadian-born counterparts as well as higher rates of reliance on government transfer payments (Statistics Canada 2006c, 211–38). Aboriginal and visible-minority women also appear to be overrepresented amongst homeless women. A recent Toronto survey found that more than one-quarter of homeless women identified as belonging to a racialized group and one in five identified as Aboriginal (Street Health Report 2007; Bacquie 2008).

Disability also takes a toll on many women's lives. Although most disabled adults live on low income, disabled women are generally worse off than their male counterparts. For example, women with mild and moderate disabilities have employment rates that are approximately 10 percentage points lower than those of comparable males (Statistics Canada 2006c, 294). This gendered pattern is also reflected in income levels with women aged 15 and over with disabilities averaging $17,200 while comparable men earned $26,900. Predictably, a larger percentage (26 per cent) of women than men with disabilities are living below low-income cut-offs (20 per cent). This gender difference in income and poverty rates is further amplified as women with disabilities become seniors (Statistics Canada 2006c, 296–7).

The Poverty of Children

Interwoven with the impoverishment of women and families is the poverty of children. Some 760,000 Canadian children, according to the 2006 census, are growing up in low-income families (Statistics Canada 2008a, 87). Despite a unanimous vote in the House of Commons in 1989 to eradicate child poverty by the year 2000, Canadian child poverty rates actually grew from 1989 to 1996. Although the number of Canadian children increased by 6 per cent between 1989 and 1997, the number of poor children rose by 37 per cent in the same period. While there has been some easing of child poverty rates in the last several years, the latest census figures reveal that the low-income rate for Canadians under age 18 is twice that of senior Canadians (Statistics Canada 2008a, 87). Clearly much remains to be done. Placed in an international context this record seems particularly bleak. Canada ranked nineteenth out of twenty-six developed countries in child poverty, better than the United States and Britain but worse than the Czech Republic, Hungary, and Poland (UNICEF 2005).

Part of the reason for persistent child poverty is the increase in single-parent families and the economic marginalization of immigrant families. For example, in British Columbia, which has experienced a dramatic rise in child poverty, almost two-thirds of children living in families headed by lone-parent mothers are poor in contrast to only 15 per cent of children in two-parent families (First Call: BC Child and Youth Advocacy Coalition 2005). These children are poor because their parents are poor and their parents' poverty often stems from unemployment, underemployment, inadequate minimum-wage levels, and reduced social welfare supports (First Call: BC Child and Youth Advocacy Coalition 2005).

Predictably, when children's parents are members of at-risk groups in Canada—Aboriginals, recent immigrants, or the disabled—the likelihood of poverty is greatly increased. For example, Aboriginal children and youth are more likely than other Canadians to live in the "deepest poverty" (National Council of Welfare 2007, 21). Poverty among children from two-parent recent immigrant families has grown dramatically— from 22 per cent in 1980 to 39 per cent in 2001 (CCSD 2003).

The Lost Generation: The Poverty of Young Adults

Children are also at greater economic peril if their parents are young. Young people who marry and have dependents are in a particularly difficult economic position. Between 1993 and 2005, one-fifth (21 per cent) of families of women who were teenage mothers lived below the income cut-offs compared with only 12 per cent of adult mothers (Statistics Canada 2008d). When the young form families, they are less likely to complete high school and post-secondary education. Without these qualifications, they are severely disadvantaged in the current economy. A generation ago they might have been able to find good-paying, secure employment in the manufacturing or resource extraction sectors, but today employment primarily is available in the service sector. As a result, young, poorly educated workers often find themselves trapped in part-time, dead-end, minimum-wage jobs (Jackson 2005). In light of the kinds of employment available to many young people, combined with declining earnings

for young Canadians, it is not surprising that median net worth of Canadian households where the major income recipient was between 15 and 34 years old was just $18,800, compared to $99,500 for those with an earner between 35 and 44 years old (Sauve 2002–3). Lacking the financial resources and economic security to launch an independent adult life, many young adults must choose between prolonged dependency (as reflected in rising numbers of young adults living with their parents) and struggling to survive on low income (Myles 2005).

The Changing Face of Poverty

Viewed from the vantage point of 2006, the latest census data, low-income patterns amongst Canadians have improved markedly between 1980 and 2006. In the past 10 years, market incomes for senior families as well as single-mother families have experienced significant gains. Recently, there have been increases in government transfer payments to unattached individuals—29 per cent of whom live below the low-income threshold—as well as to families with children—7 per cent of whom are below the LICOs-IAT. Even between 2005 and 2006, the additional income needed to enable low-income families to move above the low-income cut-offs shrank from $8,000 to $7,000 (Statistics Canada 2008b). The improvements for the poor, of course, were not matched by the dramatic income improvements experienced by the top one-fifth of income earners in Canada who, between 1995 and 2005, saw their after-tax incomes increase by 28 per cent relative to the incomes of the bottom one-fifth of Canadians. Indeed, despite the improvements for certain segments of the low-income population, the gap between the rich and poor in Canada has grown steadily larger since at least the late 1970s (HRSDC 2008c; HRSDC 2008a, i–ii; Statistics Canada 2007).

Over the last several decades the fortunes of the poor have fluctuated with the overall health of the economy. However, social policy has also made for significant change. Canada's seniors remain the outstanding success story, and improvements in their economic situation demonstrate that poverty is neither inevitable nor irreversible. In the 1960s, the plight of impoverished seniors—many of whom were elderly women—made headlines when reporters suggested that some seniors were being reduced to eating cat food in order to survive. Policy changes, including the creation of the federal Guaranteed Income Supplement in 1967 for low-income seniors, the creation of the Canada/Quebec Pension Plan in 1966, and the implementation of provincial supplements have meant a dramatic shift. In 1980, more than one in three seniors were living below the income cut-offs; by 2006 a relatively small percentage of seniors (5.4 per cent) were living below the LICOs-IAT (Statistics Canada 2008a, 87; CCSD 2003; National Council of Welfare 1999).

Policy initiatives have also helped respond to child poverty rates. The Canada Child Tax Benefit (1998) is an income supplementation program that helps low-income families with children across the country. In 2003, the plan added a Child Disability Benefit to help families with children with disabilities. While these programs have not necessarily lifted families out of poverty, they have reduced the depth of poverty for many (Torjman 2008, 14). In addition to these federal programs, individual provinces have tackled the problem. Quebec in 2004 became the first jurisdiction in Canada to embark on an official anti-poverty strategy and has succeeded in dramatically reducing its sizeable child poverty rates (Torjman 2008, 1). In recent months, the province of Ontario has promised to release a poverty plan that will reduce poverty rates, particularly amongst urban children (Talaga and Benzie 2008). However, the dramatic economic downturn of 2008 may jeopardize such initiatives. The recent announcement that the City of Toronto lacks budgeted resources to cover an increase in its welfare rolls hints at

the potential problems of a worsening economy (Moloney 2008).

Canadian Poverty in International Context

Canadians often take comfort in the fact that the pattern of social inequality in Canada is better than that in the United States (CCSD 2008b). In the United States, the top 1 per cent of Americans own 38 per cent of the nation's wealth and the bottom 40 per cent own 1 per cent. The bottom 20 per cent of US income earners not only have more debt than assets, their incomes have barely grown in real terms since the mid-1970s (Canada and the World Backgrounder 2004). Not surprisingly, these patterns are reflected in overall poverty rates. In 2002, when Canada's poverty rate was about 10 per cent, in the United States it reached 17 per cent. Furthermore, 31 per cent of the US poor were victims of persistent poverty (5 years or more) in contrast to 24 per cent of the Canadian poor (Statistics Canada 2005b). Similarly, the US child poverty rate was 7 per cent higher than the Canadian rate.

However, when we compare Canada to countries other than the United States, we find less reason for pride. According to recent statistics, Canada ranks 18th out of 30 industrialized countries in terms of income inequality—certainly well ahead of the United States at 27th place but behind France, Hungary, Germany, Australia, and South Korea (Monsebraaten 2008b). In Sweden, for example, only about 6 per cent of the population is poor—and less than 3 per cent of all children (Canada and the World Backgrounder 2005b). Finland and Belgium successfully reduced poverty among lone-parent families, and Germany and the United Kingdom have substantially reduced the percentage of persistently poor people (Picot and Myles 2005). In almost all of these success stories, the governments have allocated significant resources to addressing poverty.

Struggling with Poverty: The Personal Experience

Being poor has always meant much more than getting by at some arbitrary level of income, and understanding poverty demands more than a statistical overview (Burman 1988). Poverty often affects people's lives, their sense of self, and their most important relationships with others. Although the toll of poverty is most apparent in the lives of children, few adults survive impoverishment unscathed. For children and their families, poverty still generally translates into inadequate housing in unsafe areas (Statistics Canada 2006a). In Calgary, Edmonton, Vancouver, and Toronto as well as on remote reserves, poor children are likely to live with substandard heating, too little hot water, improper ventilation, generally unsafe conditions (exposed wiring and electrical outlets, and so on), and too little space in which to play and study. Even inadequate housing in large metropolitan areas may gobble up social assistance benefits, leaving little for other necessities, let alone for emergencies. Housing problems are frequently compounded by neighbourhoods plagued with high rates of crime and vandalism, inadequate play facilities, high levels of pollution, and hazardous traffic (Raphael 2007; McMurtry and Curling 2008; Goar 2008; Welsh 2008; Doolittle 2008; Baxter 1988, 1993).

Poor families also often lack the income to maintain a nutritious diet. High housing costs and the spectre of homelessness mean that food budgets are stretched to the limit. The end result may be ill health and frequent hospitalization, even among infants. While Canada's food banks and soup kitchens provide a stopgap solution for many families, numerous poor children clearly get by on too little food or food with high fat and sugar content (Statistics Canada 2008c). Not surprisingly, the poorest of the poor, the homeless, are frequently plagued by health problems, including malnourishment, chronic respiratory and ear infections, gastrointestinal disorders, and sexually transmitted disease, and chronic infections.

The psychological health of the poor also reflects the painful social and emotional environment in which they live. The pressure of poverty contributes to family breakdown and dislocation. Life often becomes unpredictable and insecure. Being poor means not knowing whether you will be able to continue living in your home, whether you will retain custody of your children, or whether your children will have to change schools and make new friends. In these and numerous other ways, the foundations of one's life may be shattered. Living with this profound uncertainty inevitably takes a toll on self-confidence and hopefulness (Neal 2004; Hurtig 1999). Evidence also suggests that poor families are more subject to family violence, including woman abuse as well as child abuse and neglect (Goar 2008; Statistics Canada 2005a; Gelles and Cornell 1990, 14–15). Growing up poor often means coping with a parent or parents who are struggling with fear, anger, frustration, isolation, and despair. The emotional and psychological realities of poverty are complex, and reactions to poverty reflect the particular personal circumstances and biography of each individual. Many poor adults and children cope with courage, resourcefulness, and a sense of humour, and many poor children grow up with positive adult role models and a strong sense of family loyalty. However, the adults in most poor children's lives are not only deeply troubled by their economic straits but also vulnerable to abuse and exploitation as a result. Poverty typically means more than doing without; it means feeling cut off from the mainstream of our consumer society. With few exceptions, the lives and experiences of the poor are not reflected sympathetically on television or in the movies; the advertisements in magazines and on subway trains underscore the insufficiencies of their lifestyle. Mothers must scramble to make sure that their children have the money to "fit in." As one mother said, "Another thing that comes out [of the monthly budget] that's very important is the children's milk money for school, and their pizza and hot dog money every week, because they won't be ostracized. I won't have other children saying they're too poor to get those." However, meeting these needs means that "sometimes I can afford [heating] oil, sometimes I can't" (Power 2005, 652).

Many of the poor, who must rely on social assistance for all or part of their income, report that dealing with the social work apparatus compounds feelings of stigmatization and vulnerability. Even when individual welfare workers are helpful and supportive, the relationship between worker and client is structured to erode the autonomy, power, and privacy of the poor. The negativity of some welfare workers exacerbates a bad situation. One single mother comments, "Every time I come back from there I cry. They make you feel so low, they make you feel like you're worthless, and they think they're God because of what they give you. And they give you nothing. They don't!" (Power 2005, 649). Another single mother adds, "They [social services] show up at your door unannounced. They're supposed to give you 24 hours notice if they're going to come to your home. . . . They'll degrade you; they'll sit there and they'll humiliate you in a room full of 30 people and think nothing of it" (McIntyre et al. 2003, 325; Blouin 1992). Home visits by welfare workers, personal questions from workers, and the constant fear of being "reported to welfare" for not following the rules tend to undermine clients' sense of personal power and self-confidence.

Problems with the welfare apparatus are complicated by the negative reactions of the general public to welfare recipients. Commonly, landlords will not rent to people on welfare, and women on welfare may find themselves labelled as desperate and available. Degradation becomes part of everyday experience: "And then the taxi driver is looking at you, 'Oh, not another charity case'" (McIntyre et al. 2003, 324). Most commonly, the social assistance recipient has to confront the still popular belief, held by much of the general public as well as many social assistance workers, that people on welfare cheat (Blackwell 2003, 107–8). Informed by the historical notions that many of the poor are not "deserving" or should be punished for their plight, popular attitudes toward the provision of adequate social assistance remain ambivalent and uninformed.

Despite the enormous pressure to "get back on your feet," there seem to be endless road blocks on the path to getting off welfare. For many single mothers, adequate child care support is a major obstacle to employment: "The day care she went to when she was a baby, every day they called. I had just started this job and every day, I swear, every day they were calling me that something was wrong with her. I'd come in, walk in at 9:00, by 10:00 she's got a rash, or pink eye or something and then I had to leave" (Mason 2003, 50). It may seem that every effort to move forward is being undermined. A Toronto single mother of three recounts her recent struggles. When her youngest child started grade 1, she took a part-time job to improve their economic situation. However, her "extra" income immediately caused her subsidized rent to double. After taxes and employment-related expenses, she found she had made no economic improvement in her family's situation—despite her paid work (Monsebraaten 2008a, A4).

What Is to Be Done about Poverty?

Several basic points are clear from the above discussion. Poverty, whether homelessness in Vancouver or a food bank at Ryerson University, is a significant social issue across Canada and, in all likelihood, it is about to become even more important. The victims of poverty include the most vulnerable Canadians, such as individuals with disabilities and children. Secondly, poverty is clearly rooted in the economic system. While we can see that some individuals—teenage mothers, high school drop-outs, and so on—may have made poor decisions, their impoverishment can be traced to the low rates of minimum wages across Canada, the decline in manufacturing and resource extraction work, the dramatic growth in precarious and non-standard employment in the service sector of the economy, and the weak response from federal, provincial, and municipal governments to the inequities in our midst. Finally, as evidenced by both Canadian experiences and international comparisons, it is not the case that "the poor are always with us." Innovative and generous social policies, in Canada and elsewhere around the world, have demonstrated that it is possible to reduce both the numbers of poor and the negative outcomes of poverty. This knowledge and the implied hopefulness will likely be increasingly significant in the next several years.

References

Alphonso, C. 2008. "For Many, Brain Injury at Root of Homelessness." *Globe and Mail* 8 October: A11.

Ambert, A. 2005. "Divorce: Facts, Causes and Consequences." Vanier Institute of the Family. www.vifamily.ca/library/cft/divorce_05.html.

Bacquie, S. 2008. "Homeless Women in Canada." *Section 15.ca.* http://section15.ca/features/news/2008/08/22/homelessness/.

Baxter, Sheila. 1993. *A Child Is Not a Toy: Voices of Children in Poverty.* Vancouver: New Star Books.

———. 1988. *No Way to Live: Poor Women Speak Out.* Vancouver: New Star Books.

Blackwell, J. 2003. "The Welfare State Rewards Laziness." In J. Blackwell, M. Smith, and J. Sorenson, eds, *The Culture of Prejudice.* Toronto: Broadview Press, 107–12.

Blouin, Barbara. 1992. "Welfare Workers and Clients: Problems of Sexism and Paternalism." *Canadian Woman Studies* 12, 3: 645.

Boyd, Monica. 1989. "Immigration and Income Security Policies in Canada: Implications for Elderly Immigrant Women." *Population Research and Policy Review* 8: 5–24.

Breitkreuz, Rhonda. 2005. "Engendering Citizenship? A Critical Feminist Analysis of Canadian Welfare-to-Work Policies and the Employment Experiences of Lone Mothers." *Journal of Sociology and Social Welfare* 32, 2: 147–65.

Broadbent, Ed. 2005. "Addressing Child Poverty." *Perception* 27, 3 & 4: 9.

Bula, F. 2008. "Shelters Turned Away Homeless 40,000 Times in Nine Months." *Vancouver Sun* 22 May. www.canada.com/vancouversun/news/story.html?id+0f7602e2-1444-4cb8-9fc5-343fcd803fef.

Burman, Patrick. 1988. *Killing Time, Losing Ground: Experiences of Unemployment.* Toronto: Wall & Thompson.

Canadian Council on Social Development (CCSD). 2003. "Census Shows Growing Polarization of Income in Canada." 16 May. www.ccsd.ca/pr/2003/censusincome.htm.

———. 2008a. *CCSD's Stats & Facts: Labour Market—Earnings.* www.ccsd.ca/.

———. 2008b. *Growing up in North America: The Economic Well-being of Children in Canada, the United States and Mexico.* www.ccsd.ca/.

———. 2008c. "Stats & Facts: Economic Security—Poverty." www.ccsd.ca/.

Canada and the World Backgrounder. 2004. "Survival of the Richest." 70, 1 (September): 17–23.

———. 2005a. "Deciding Where Poverty Starts." 70, 5 (March): 4–7.

———. 2005b. "Poor Families Equal Poor Children." 40, 5 (March): 23–7.

———. 2005c. "Putting a Face on Poverty." 70, 1 (March): 8–11.

CBC News. 2007. "Homelessness 'Chronic' in Canada: Study." 26 June. www.cbc.ca/canada/story/2007/06/26/shelter.html.

Council of Canadians with Disabilities. 2008. "Poverty and Disability: Senate Committee Hears from Canadians with Disabilities." www.ccdonline.ca/en/socialpolicy/poverty/senate-committee.

Cranford, C.J., L. Vosko, and N. Zukewich. 2006. "The Gender of Precarious Employment in Canada." In V. Shalla, ed., *Working in a Global Era: Canadian Perspectives.* Toronto: Canadian Scholars' Press, 99–119.

Doolittle, R. 2008. "Agencies Brace for Crime Wave." *Toronto Star* 27 December: A17.

Duffy, Ann, and Norene Pupo. 1992. *Part-Time Paradox: Connecting Gender, Work, and Family.* Toronto: McClelland & Stewart.

Duffy, Ann, Nancy Mandell, and Norene Pupo. 1988. *Few Choices: Women, Work and Family.* Toronto: Garamond Press.

Fellegi, I.P. 1997. "On Poverty and Low Income." Statistics Canada. www.statcan.gc.ca/pub/13f0027x/4053039-eng.htm.

Findlay, S. 2008. "Food Bank Use Soars 13%." *Sun Media* 3 December. http://cnews.canoe.ca/CNEWS/Canada/2008/12/03/pf-7615691.html.

First Call: BC Child and Youth Advocacy Coalition. 2005. Unpublished working document.

Food Banks Canada. 2008. *Hunger Count 2008: Food Bank Use in Canada.* Toronto: Food Banks Canada.

Gazso, Amber. 2005. "The Poverty of Unattached Senior Women and the Canadian Retirement Income System: A Matter of Blame or Contradiction?" *Journal of Sociology and Social Welfare* 32, 2 (June): 41–62.

Gelles, Richard J., and Claire P. Cornell. 1990. *Intimate Violence in Families.* 2nd edn. Newbury Park, CA: Sage.

Goar, C. 2008. "Abuse Follows in Poverty's Wake." *Toronto Star* 14 November: AA6.

Goldberg, Gertrude Schaffner. 1990. "Canada: Bordering on the Feminization of Poverty." In Gertrude Schaffner Goldberg and Eleanor Kremen, eds, *The Feminization of Poverty: Only in America?* New York: Praeger.

Human Resources and Social Development Canada (HRSDC). 2008a. *Low Income in Canada: 2000–2006 Using the Market Basket Measure—Final Report.* www.hrsdc.gc.ca/en/publications_resources/research/index.shtml.

———. 2008b. "Well-being in Canada: Housing—Homeless Shelters and Beds." www4.hrsdc.gc.ca/.

———. 2008c. "Well-being in Canada: Financial Security—Income Distribution." www4.hrsdc.gc.ca/.

———. 2008d. "Well-being in Canada: Financial Security—Low Income Incidence." www4.hrsdc.gc.ca/.

———. 2008e. "Well-being in Canada: Financial Security—Low Income Persistence." www4.hrsdc.gc.ca/.

Hurtig, Mel. 1999. *Pay the Rent or Feed the Kids: The Tragedy and Disgrace of Poverty in Canada.* Toronto: McClelland & Stewart.

Jackson, Andrew. 2005. *Work and Labour in Canada: Critical Issues.* Toronto: Canadian Scholars' Press.

Katz, Michael B. 1975. *The People of Hamilton, Canada West: Family and Class in a Mid-Nineteenth-Century City.* Cambridge, MA: Harvard University Press.

Kazemipur, A., and S.S. Halli. 2000. *The New Poverty in Canada: Ethnic Groups and Ghetto Neighbourhoods.* Toronto: Thompson Educational Publishing.

McDonald, Lynn. 1997. "The Invisible Poor: Canada's Retired Widows." *Canadian Journal of Aging* 16, 3: 553–83.

McGrath, Paul. 1998. "Food Banks Part of Life on Campus." *Toronto Star* 23 February: F1, F2.

McIntyre, Lynn, Suzanne Officer, and Lynne M. Robinson. 2003. "Feeling Poor: The Felt Experience of Low-Income Lone Mothers." *Affilia* 18, 3: 316–31.

McKeen, W. 2004. *Money in Their Own Name: The Feminist Voice in Poverty Debate in Canada, 1970–1995.* Toronto: University of Toronto Press.

McMurtry, R., and A. Curling. 2008. "Roots of Violence Grow in Toxic Soil of Social Exclusion." *Toronto Star* 15 November: AA6.

Mason, Robin. 2003. "Listening to Lone Mothers: Paid Work, Family Life, and Childcare in Canada." *Journal of Children and Poverty* 9, 1: 41–54.

Moloney, P. 2008. "Crisis Looms in Welfare Rolls." *Toronto Star* 29 November: A6.

Monsebraaten, L. 2008a. "Having a Job, but Losing Ground." *Toronto Star* 2 April: A4.

———. 2008b. "Income Gap Growing Wider." *Toronto Star* 21 October: A4.

Myles, John. 2005. "Postponed Adulthood: Dealing with the New Economic Inequality." Canadian Council on Social Development. www.ccsd.ca.

National Council of Welfare. 1999. *Poverty Profile 1997.* Ottawa: Minister of Public Works and Government Services Canada.

———. 2007. *First Nations, Metis and Inuit Children and Youth: Time to Act.* Ottawa: Ministry of Supply and Services.

———. 2008a. "New Report: Poverty Line is Being Cracked but Not Broken. Cross-Canada Action Needed as Economy Worsens, National Council of Welfare Says." www.ncwcnbes.net.

———. 2008b. *Welfare Incomes, 2006 and 2007.* Ottawa: National Council of Welfare.

Neal, Rusty. 2004. "Voices: Women, Poverty and Homelessness in Canada." The National Anti-Poverty Organization's Study on Homelessness. Ottawa.

Nelson, Adie. 2006. *Gender in Canada.* 3rd edn. Toronto: Pearson Prentice Hall.

Pasma, C. 2008. "Towards a Guaranteed Livable Income: A CPJ Backgrounder on GLI." Ottawa: Citizens for Public Justice.

Pearce, Diana. 1978. "The Feminization of Poverty: Women, Work and Welfare." *Urban and Social Change Review* 11 (February): 28–36.

Picot, Garnett. 2004. "The Deteriorating Economic Welfare of Canadian Immigrants." *The Canadian Journal of Urban Research* 13, 1: 25–45.

Picot, Garnett, and John Myles. 2005. "Income Inequality and Low Income in Canada: An International Perspective." Statistics Canada Catalogue no. 11F0019MIE. Ottawa: Minister of Industry.

Power, Elaine M. 2005. "The Unfreedom of Being Other: Canadian Lone Mothers' Experiences of Poverty and 'Life on the Cheque.'" *Sociology* 39, 4: 643–60.

Raphael, D. 2007. *Poverty and Policy in Canada.* Toronto: Canadian Scholars' Press.

Ross, David, and Richard Shillington. 2000. *The Canadian Fact Book on Poverty.* Ottawa: Canadian Council on Social Development.

Sarlo, C. 2008. "Measuring Poverty in Canada." *Fraser Foum.* Vancouver: Fraser Institute.

Sauve, Roger. 2002–3. "Rich Canadians, Poor Canadians and Everyone in Between." *Transition Magazine* 32, 4. www.vifamily.ca.

Simmons, Christina. 1986. "'Helping the Poorer Sisters': The Women of the Jost Mission, Halifax, 1905–1945." In Veronica Strong-Boag and Anita Clair Fellman, eds, *Rethinking Canada: The Promise of Women's History.* Toronto: Copp Clark Pitman.

Smith, J. 2008. "Definition of Poverty Stalls Federal Committee." *Toronto Star* 16 April. www.thestar.com/article/415057.

Statistics Canada. 2005a. "National Longitudinal Survey of Children and Youth: Home Environment, Income and

Child Behaviour." *The Daily* 21 February. www.statcan
.ca.gc.ca/daily/.

———. 2005b. "Study: Trends in Income Inequality in
Canada from an International Perspective." *The Daily*
10 February. www.statcan.gc.ca/daily/.

———. 2006a. "Study: Neighbourhood Characteristics
and the Distribution of Crime in Regina." *The Daily* 2
November. www.statcan.gc.ca/daily/.

———. 2006b. "Study: The Death of a Spouse and the
Impact on Income." *The Daily* 10 July. www.statcan.
gc.ca/daily/.

———. 2006c. *Women in Canada: A Gender-Based Statistical
Report*. 5th edn. Ottawa: Ministry of Supply and Services.

———. 2007. "Study: Income Inequality and Redistribution."
The Daily 11 May. www.statcan.gc.ca/daily/.

———. 2008a. *Income in Canada 2006*. Ottawa: Minister of
Industry. Catalogue no. 75-202-X.

———. 2008b. "Income of Canadians." *The Daily* 5 May.
www.statcan.gc.ca/daily/.

———. 2008c. "Study: Impact of Neighbourhood Income on
Child Obesity." *The Daily* 18 February. www.statcan.gc.ca/
daily/.

———. 2008d. "Study: Life after Teenage Motherhood." *The
Daily* 23 May. www.statcan.gc.ca/daily/.

Sussman, Deborah, and Martin Tabi. 2004. "Minimum
Wage Workers." *Perspectives on Labour and Income* 5,
3 (Summer).

Talaga, T., and R. Benzie. 2008. "Province to Release Poverty
Plan." *Toronto Star* 3 December: A22.

The Street Health Report. 2007. "Research Bulletin #2:
Women & Homelessness." Toronto: Ontario Women's
Health Network.

Torjman, S. 2008. *Poverty Policy*. Ottawa: Caledon Institute
of Social Policy.

UNICEF. 2005. *Child Poverty in Rich Countries 2005*. www
.unicef-irc.org.

Wallace, K. 2008. "Students Flood Food Bank." *Toronto Star*
19 November: A13.

Wellesley Institute. 2008. "Housing Insecurity at Record
Levels." Toronto: Wellesley Institute. http://wellesley-
institute.com/node/1601/.

Welsh, M. 2008. "Poorest Areas Also Most Polluted, Report
Shows." *Toronto Star* 27 November: A6.

Questions for Critical Thought

1. Since Duffy and Mandell argue that poverty is not an unsolvable problem but a product of particular social and political policies, what factors were involved in establishing the historical "roots" of poverty? What factors contribute to the growing gap between rich and poor in contemporary Canadian society? Do we have a social obligation to give economically disadvantaged members of our society social, psychological and economic aid? Why or why not?

2. What solutions are possible for the feminization of poverty? Why are the authors pessimistic about solutions to women's poverty in Canada? What can we do as individuals, as a community, and as a nation to reduce women's poverty in Canada? What can we do as individuals and as a nation to reduce women's poverty throughout the world?

3. How is the feminization of poverty affected by intersections of race, age, and class? Why are elderly women often called the "invisible poor"? How can we alleviate this social problem?

4. In what way is poverty a public issue, as Duffy and Mandell maintain? While the consequences of poverty for the poor are clear, what are the consequences of poverty for those with adequate or higher incomes?

5. How would you describe yourself in terms of economic advantage and disadvantage? To what do you attribute your position? How do you explain economic inequality? What is the difference between temporary and chronic poverty? Have you or members of your family experienced temporary or chronic poverty?

Lessons in Decolonization: Aboriginal Overrepresentation in Canadian Criminal Justice

....*Patricia A. Monture-Angus*[1]

And it was rare for Crees to commit any crimes against one another at that time, even though there were so many people of different tribes, they did not very often commit violent crimes against one another, they lived together peacefully.

—Peter Vandall, Cree Elder, Atahk-akop's Reserve, Sandy Lake, Saskatchewan (quoted in Ahenakew and Wolfart 1987)

Introduction

The loss of and interference with peaceful existence in many Aboriginal communities has been the subject of many reports, inquiries, academic studies, and research. Much of this work has been funded by government dollars. Unfortunately, the analysis of the "problem" in Aboriginal communities has generally had a distinct and overly narrow focus. The majority of our understanding has been developed without a serious regard for the pattern of colonialism that is clear and pronounced in Aboriginal communities and Aboriginal experiences, including the experience of the criminal justice system. This has serious consequences for Aboriginal peoples.[2]

In some jurisdictions, Aboriginal people account for over half the admissions to correctional institutions. The overrepresentation of Aboriginal people in the system of Canadian criminal justice is all too often seen as an Aboriginal problem—that is, a problem *with* Aboriginal people. In 1983, Don McCaskill observed,

The conventional explanation for this phenomenon views native offenders as members of a pathological community characterized by extensive social and personal problems. The focus is inevitably on the individual offenders. They are seen as simply being unable to adjust successfully to the rigors of contemporary society. They are part of a larger "Indian problem" for which various social service agencies have been created to help Indians meet the standards of the dominant society. The long-range goal is that, in time, with sufficient help, Indians will lose most of their culture, adopt the values of the larger society, become upwardly mobile, and be incorporated into mainstream society. In short, Indians will assimilate. (McCaskill 1983)

Professor McCaskill made this observation nearly two decades ago. Unfortunately, since then, these theoretical presumptions have changed very little, and the belief that Aboriginal people should change to fit the system is still implicit. It is important to question why a system that has so markedly failed Aboriginal peoples (and people) has been allowed to continue to operate in an unjust and colonial manner for so many years and through so many reports and inquiries. In fact, McCaskill's point was made before the majority of justice reports were commissioned.

This failure to take responsibility for the continued perpetuation of colonial relations in current criminal justice practices and policies has not escaped the gaze or understanding of Aboriginal people and our governments. It is a situation that magnifies the contempt that Aboriginal peoples have for a system that is neither fair and just nor responsible. My purpose in agreeing to add my voice to the others is simple. I choose to name and expose the colonialism present in both Canada's criminal justice system and in the literature about the overrepresentation of Aboriginal people in that system. By naming and exposing, I hope to narrow the gap that exists between the understanding of justice relations in Aboriginal communities and the research communities, including the university.[3]

At the outset, several myths must be exposed for what they are. It is curious to me that non-Aboriginal people always think that Aboriginal peoples have lost their culture. Having your culture interfered with (and even made illegal),[4] does not mean that your culture fails to exist. The response of non-Aboriginal people to Aboriginal people who are skilled at being bicultural (because our survival generally depends on this skill) is misinterpreted. Because I have learned to relate to you on terms that you have defined cannot lend itself to a reasonable construction of Aboriginal culturelessness. Because I can understand non-Aboriginal ways does not necessarily mean I can no longer understand or, worse yet, that I reject Aboriginal ways of doing, thinking, and being. All that can be concluded is that non-Aboriginal people have not been as successful (as a group) at understanding Aboriginal culture as some Aboriginal people have been successful at understanding Canadian culture and ways. This does not mean that Aboriginal people have chosen to assimilate. For the most part, we have not.

The second myth is a component of the larger myth that "Indians were savages." As the opening quote indicates, there were few problems of crime and disorder among Aboriginal populations at the time of contact and for some years after. This reality is well-documented but infrequently given the respect or position in the discourse that it deserves.[5] Any curious mind considering this fact can easily conclude that Aboriginal people had systems to maintain order in our communities. This is true despite the fact that we did not have prisons, punishment, and all the trappings that Canadians recognize as the characteristics of an organized and institutionalized justice system. The crux of the problem is Canada's failure (that is, non-Aboriginal people including policy makers, researchers, prison administrators, politicians,

lawyers, and so on) to own and address the fact that Aboriginal overrepresentation in the justice system is not necessarily the individual failure of particular Aboriginal people but also the impact and vestige of colonialism.

Colonialism is not a difficult concept to understand. It is easily conceptualized:

> Colonialism involves a relationship which leaves one side dependent on the other to define the world. At the individual level, colonialism involves a situation where one individual is forced to relate to another on terms unilaterally defined by the other. The justice system becomes a central institution with which to impose the way of life of the dominant society. (McCaskill 1983)

Recognizing colonialism as a central explanation—if not *the* central explanation—for Aboriginal overrepresentation in the justice system is essential. At the same time, we must recognize that the process of colonization requires colonizers, not just the colonized (Freire 1996). The process of decolonization is not just an Aboriginal responsibility but must also involve the colonizer learning new ways of relating to enclaved peoples. It is very difficult to honour my commitment to live in a decolonized way when I survive in an environment where others (Aboriginal and not) continue to remain committed to the entrenchment of the colonizers' ways. So far my efforts to decolonize my own life and mind have proven to be part of a long and difficult process.

The Many Justice Reports

The situation of Aboriginal people and Canada's criminal justice systems has been studied by commissions, inquiries, and task forces since 1967. In 1990, the Alberta Cawsey Commission noted,

> The real proliferation in reports began in the mid-1980s. . . . Seventeen of the twenty-two reports were released between 1984 and

1990 (and note that this does not include the anticipated Blood and Manitoba Inquiry Reports). In 1988 and 1989, alone, 11 reports were published. This suggests that, in the last five to six years, something has occurred to make all levels of Government acutely aware and concerned with Native involvement in the Criminal Justice System. Considering the repetition of recommendations it could be speculated that this "something" is an awareness that earlier recommendations were not implemented, or that current strategies are not effective (but perhaps with a hope that more of the same might be). (Alberta 1991)

Since 1991, in addition to the reports that were expected, the Royal Commission on Aboriginal Peoples has published a volume of collected justice papers (RCAP 1993) and the Law Reform Commission of Canada studied and reported on the impact of the criminal sanction on Aboriginal Peoples (LRCC 1991). Correctional Service Canada released two reports that considered the situation of Aboriginal people in federal prisons. In 1996, the Royal Commission on Aboriginal Peoples released the report *Bridging the Cultural Divide: A Report on Aboriginal People and Criminal Justice in Canada* (1996a). This report is largely a discussion of the previous justice reports and offers little that is new to the discussion. Obviously the Royal Commissioners felt that "more of the same" might just work! Later in the year, the Royal Commission released its six-volume final report.

The final report of the Royal Commission on Aboriginal Peoples offers little to no discussion of justice issues given the fact that a separate report on justice was issued earlier in the same year. This is unfortunate, as it misconstrues the centrality that justice issues occupy within Aboriginal communities. Justice issues overlap with most if not all issues that Aboriginal communities face, including self-government. Justice, therefore, should have been a central and integrated focus in the final report as well. The commissioners noted that there are four important dimensions of social change in Aboriginal lives and

communities: **healing**, economic opportunity, human resources, and institutional development. Matters of criminal justice have a significant relationship with at least two of the four dimensions— healing and institutional development. Prior to 1996 and the release of this report, at least one healing lodge had already been constructed for federally sentenced women. This healing lodge is an institution under the authority of Correctional Service Canada.

In defining healing, the commissioners state,

Healing is a term used often by Aboriginal people to signify the restoration of physical, social, emotional and spiritual vitality in individuals and social systems. It implies the revitalization of their confidence in themselves, their communities and cultures, confidence that must be grounded in their daily lives.

Healing also has an intercultural meaning. Learning about and acknowledging the errors of the past, making restitution where possible, and correcting distortions of history are essential first steps in the process of healing between Aboriginal and non-Aboriginal people. In Volume 1, we recommended remedies for past injustices and neglect in *residential schools, relocation policies, and the treatment of veterans*. (RCAP 1996c, emphasis added)

Given the rates of **overrepresentation of Aboriginal persons in the Canadian criminal justice system**, and particularly the rates that demonstrate over-incarceration, I find the exclusion from this last list of matters of criminal justice to be particularly disturbing.

There is a haunting repetition throughout the two decades of reports and the corresponding 1,500 recommendations.[6] The Cawsey Commission makes these comments on the trends in the recommendations:

Despite the patterns of recommendations, there have been changes in the type of recommendations made over the years. The Reports between 1967 and 1978 made wide-ranging recommendations that put the Criminal Justice System in a wider societal context. These recommendations included alcohol treatment, diversion, economic development and recreation as crime prevention strategies.

Of the later reports, only *Policing in a Pluralistic Society* (1989) includes such recommendations. Later reports tend to be very Criminal Justice System–specific and frequently focus on only one component, such as the Police (especially the Police), the Courts, or corrections. It should be noted that: (1) only one report deals with Native victims of crime; and (2) recommendations dealing with specific services are concentrated in certain reports (e.g., the policing studies). In addition to these reports there have been an increasing number of reports on discrimination, education, and socio-economic conditions, which may account for the decrease in contextual recommendations in the Criminal Justice reports. (Alberta 1991)

The work of the Cawsey Commission has been the only attempt to rigorously analyze the existing recommendations.[7] The overall conclusion is obvious: the problem cannot be characterized as one of *not* knowing what is happening to Aboriginal people in the justice system, as pointed out clearly in 1991 by the Alberta study.

Of greater concern than the failure to do much in practical or analytical terms with existing recommendations is the pattern in the kinds of recommendations put forward in the studies. As the Cawsey Commission notes, recommendations become more specific over time. The more specific the recommendations become, the more Aboriginal involvement in the criminal justice system as a result of colonial relations is disguised. This shifts the fault to Aboriginal people and nations at the same time as it shifts responsibility away from the system. If in fact colonialism,

racism, and discrimination cause the present rates of Aboriginal overrepresentation, as concluded by the Aboriginal Justice Inquiry of Manitoba, then this trend in the recommendations to become more specific (and individualized) conceals the real problem and leaves little hope for real change in the near future.

This is not the only concern that arises from an analysis of the commissioned reviews. In 1993, the Royal Commission on Aboriginal Peoples reviewed eight of the major justice reports and noted that "the extent to which recommendations have been implemented is a matter for concern; certainly the release of an inquiry report has not necessarily signified the beginning of change and amelioration of the problem" (Blackburn 1993). The realization that few reports have been substantially implemented raises a series of questions. This is an area where systematic research of government responses would benefit our understanding.[8] It is not Aboriginal communities that need to be further studied. There are two sides to the justice problems Aboriginal people face, and the truth is that very little is known about why the knowledge we have has not been fully implemented. Rather, our communities need to be resourced so that crime and justice projects can begin or be strengthened. After all, one of the things we do know is that, in the words of Justice Cawsey, "Everything that has worked for natives has come from natives" (RCAP 1993). The most important realization is that Aboriginal people's struggle with the criminal law sanction is not manifest only in our overrepresentation. Aboriginal struggles with the criminal law sanction in Canada are also not a new phenomenon. They did not begin in 1967 when Canadians began to study the issue as well as label it as a problem; it is a historic relationship that finds its origins in the time of contact (see Kly 1991; Schuh 1979; Stonechild 1986). The historical understanding that is accessible concerning the relationship between Aboriginal peoples and the criminal justice system is at best rudimentary, a result of the fact that the "problem" has been studied from only one location.

Most frequently, discussion about Aboriginal people and the Canadian criminal justice system focuses on two issues—over- and underrepresentation. With these two issues as the focus, there is little hope that systemic change will occur within the system. Remedies to overrepresentation look at individualized ways of decreasing the number of Aboriginal people involved with the system. Diversion programs, fine options, and sentencing circles are three examples of such initiatives. The underrepresentation of Aboriginal people with authority within the system is addressed by equity hiring, which is hoped to increase the numbers of Aboriginal people employed by the system. Both of these kinds of "quick fixes" also rely on cross-cultural education to enhance their successes. All of the energy devoted to these kinds of activities actually diverts attention from the larger structural problems within the system. For example, Aboriginal people have had their internal power to address problems of law and order within their communities directly interfered with by instruments such as the Indian Act. The Royal Commission on Aboriginal Peoples, in one of the small references to justice in the final report, addresses this concern:

> Effective enforcement of *Indian Act* by-laws and the most common criminal offences involves not only laying charges against offenders, but also prosecution, adjudication and sentencing. The current situation with outside police forces refusing to enforce by-laws, the limited criminal justice jurisdiction of *Indian Act* justices of the peace, the forced reliance on provincially and territorially administered courts, and the absence of any authority for bands to correct these anomalies means jurisdiction gaps, confusion over procedures and policies, and the continuing inability of bands to provide effectively for the safety and security of their own members.
>
> Paradoxically, most bands have moved from a position of extremely heavy judicial control of reserve law and order matters to

a situation of almost no control, except by outside forces on a sporadic basis. From a position of too much enforcement, they have arrived at one of not enough. This is just one of the legacies of the past, but it is one that has profoundly serious consequences for daily life in most reserve communities. (RCAP 1996b)

Criminal justice experts (who tend to be non-Aboriginal people) minimize the historic relations between Aboriginal people and the state as a source of the problems that Aboriginal people presently face in the existing criminal justice system. This is a significant difference that continues to separate Aboriginal and non-Aboriginal understandings of the problem. As an Aboriginal woman who struggles to understand decolonization, I am aware of the impact of the history of my people in this country. I know that the Royal Canadian Mounted Police (formerly known as the North West Mounted Police) were actively involved in suppressing our traditional forms of government and insisting that we follow the Indian Act model of non-democratic elected rule. These facts ground my response to the criminal sanction in such a way that I cannot view the Canadian system as a just one.

The Contours of Overrepresentation within Institutions of Criminal Justice

The overrepresentation of Aboriginal people in the Canadian criminal justice system has been the starting place of every Canadian justice inquiry mandated in the last three decades. In keeping with this well-established preoccupation with documenting the current situation, this paper also considers the statistics. Truly the picture revealed is bleak. No commission or inquiry has managed to fully move beyond this fixation with numbers—even the Royal Commission on Aboriginal Peoples formed almost their entire research agenda on this numerical documentation preoccupation. We all admit there is a problem, but this preoccupation with documentation is a trend that must not continue, as it ensures that no meaningful change can occur. This paper adds the theory of decolonization to the statistical picture that is overwhelmingly available.

It is still difficult to rely on existing data to provide a clear and complete picture of Aboriginal involvement and experience of the justice system.[9] Data collection methods are inconsistent across various components of the justice system. The federal/provincial sharing of criminal jurisdiction also complicates the problem by adding a further level of data inconsistency. National police statistics were abolished three decades ago. In police data, only gender is specified; age, race, and other socio-demographic data are not consistently available (Johnson and Rodgers 1993). In the 1980s Statistics Canada abandoned efforts to collect national court data (Johnson and Rodgers 1993). All of this raises concerns about the reliability of the statistical pictures we have all been insistently drawing. In 1967, the authors of the report *Indians and the Law* experienced difficulties in data collection that they described as follows:

> Since collection of such data by the provincial agencies required special report forms not ordinarily used, the information was difficult to obtain. Indeed, serious difficulties were encountered in practically all agencies because very few differentiate between Indians and non-Indians when recording arrests, court appearances or sentences. Consequently, the statistics are not as complete as would be desirable although they do indicate trends that cannot be ignored. (Laing and Monture 1967)

After almost three decades of looking at the problem of Aboriginal overrepresentation, the statistical picture remains incomplete. Perhaps this is one of the reasons that researchers remain preoccupied with examining the statistical backdrop. Nonetheless, either situation is a barrier to meaningful change in the experiences of Aboriginal people in Canada's justice system.

It is helpful to understand the patterns that emerge when statistical information is examined. These patterns help us understand the shape of the discrimination that Aboriginal people are exposed to in their current experiences of criminal justice. We know more about federal offenders than we do about provincial offenders or young offenders. It is difficult to make inter-provincial comparisons of young offenders and provincial offenders because of differences in record-keeping practices across the provinces. It must be understood that the statistical picture is incomplete and perhaps inaccurate. What is absolute is that Aboriginal people are clearly and dramatically overrepresented in the Canadian justice system. This alone is sufficient evidence to question the justness of that system. Aboriginal overrepresentation is only a window through which the existing system can begin to be examined and understood.

The overrepresentation of Aboriginal people in Canadian prisons is a well-acknowledged fact. In Manitoba, Aboriginal people account for only 12 per cent of the population but represent half of the admissions to correction institutions (Manitoba 1991). The overrepresentation of Aboriginal offenders in the federal system is most pronounced in the Prairie region (Alberta, Saskatchewan, and Manitoba). As of November of 1994, Aboriginal inmates accounted for 75 per cent of the individuals incarcerated federally in the Prairie region.[10] In the fiscal year 1989–90, the overrepresentation was greatest in the province of Saskatchewan (Correctional Service Canada 1994a). Correctional Service Canada noted in 1998, "While the proportion of Aboriginal offenders has increased from 10.4 per cent in March 1993 to 12.4 per cent in March 1997, the percentage of Aboriginal employees for this same period has only increased from 2.4 per cent to 3.2 per cent." In and of itself, the overrepresentation is a disturbing fact. It is, however, a superficial and incomplete portrait of the reality that faces Aboriginal people caught by the Canadian criminal justice system.[11]

The data provided by the Aboriginal Justice Inquiry of Manitoba are an informative place to start looking in detail at the experience of Aboriginal people in the justice system. Data for the other western provinces are not unlike that of Manitoba. The Manitoba report notes in 1989 that 40 per cent of the population at Stoney Mountain prison were Aboriginal men.[12] This figure has steadily increased since 1965, when it was noted that Aboriginal men accounted for 22 per cent of the federal admissions at the same prison (Manitoba 1991).[13] Despite attempts in the last two decades to address the problem of overrepresentation, there has been no meaningful decrease in the rate of overrepresentation. In fact, the situation has steadily worsened in this federal prison.

In Saskatchewan, the situation is even worse. Aboriginal prisoners account for 55 per cent of the population at Saskatchewan Penitentiary. There is reason to question the accuracy of this statistic as "some managers suggest that the official figures … underestimate the number of Aboriginal inmates in their Institutions" (Correctional Service Canada 1994a). Compare this with the realization that in the 1920s, only 5 per cent of all provincial inmates in Saskatchewan were Aboriginal (School of Human Justice 1991). This is despite a number of well-intentioned attempts to address Aboriginal overrepresentation. The reforms attempted have not been successful if the standard is a decrease in overrepresentation. Reforms may have changed, perhaps even improved, the individual experience of Aboriginal offenders. Improving the individualized experience of Aboriginal offenders (that is, the amount of cultural distance they experience while in the system) does not amount to challenging the structural barriers that are the cause of the overall rates of overrepresentation. The failure of past reforms must be taken seriously and form a basis for the conclusion that a new direction in correctional reform is required.

The statistical evidence that is available clearly indicates that the situation is not going to improve in the next decade. The overrepresentation of Aboriginal youth in Manitoba's provincial institutions is more pronounced than in the federal population. In 1990, "64 per cent of the Manitoba Youth Centre population and 78 per cent of Agassiz's population were Aboriginal youth" (Manitoba 1991). Provincial offenders in Manitoba are also overrepresented. In 1989, 47 per cent of the admissions to Headingley Institution were Aboriginal. The same pattern of increasing disproportional representation in youth and provincial offender populations over the decade must be noted. The many attempts at amelioration have been failures if the reduction in overrepresentation is the measure of meaningful change.

Those involved in corrections understand that there is a pattern in the progression of individuals from youth to provincial to federal institutions. Since the overrepresentation of Aboriginal people is most pronounced in youth offender populations, and more pronounced in provincial than in federal institutions, there is no relief to be seen from the disproportional representation of Aboriginal people in custodial institutions in the next few years. If youth overrepresentation was notably lower than provincial and federal overrepresentation, there would be some immediate hope for a decrease in overrepresentation in provincial and federal inmate populations in the future. The concern is deepened when it is noted that the portion of the Aboriginal population between the ages of 15 and 24 is greater than that found in the Canadian population. This further evidence predicts that we will see a continued increase in the overrepresentation of Aboriginal people in Canadian prisons, jails, and youth facilities—that is, unless something radically different is done to combat the continued increase in rates of incarceration for Aboriginal people.

The figures presented thus far in the paper largely involve only the overrepresentation of Aboriginal men. Men account for a greater percentage of all adult offenders. On any given day the head count in federal prisons tallies around 18,400 men (Correctional Service Canada 1994c); women number only 500.[14] The number of individual lives of women *directly* affected by incarceration is far lower than for men. However, the rate of overrepresentation of Aboriginal people in the criminal justice system is most noted among Aboriginal women. In a decade-old Saskatchewan study, it was found that a treaty Indian woman is 131 times more likely, and a Métis woman 28 times more likely, to be incarcerated than a non-Aboriginal woman (Jackson 1988). As these figures are now a decade old and the overrepresentation of Aboriginal women in the Canadian criminal justice system has continued to increase, these figures will now be higher. This is true for both provincially and federally sentenced women, particularly in the Prairie region. In Manitoba, 67 per cent of the 1989 admissions to the Portage jail for women were Aboriginal women (Manitoba 1991). In the 1996 Arbour Inquiry, the commissioner notes in her report,

> As of September, 1995, Aboriginal women comprised just over 13 per cent of federally sentenced women overall. However, they comprised 19 per cent of the population of federally sentenced women in prison, and only 7 per cent of federally sentenced women in the community. Seventy-three per cent of federally sentenced Aboriginal women were in prison, while only 49 per cent of the non-Aboriginal federally sentenced women were in prison. (Solicitor General 1996)

The impact of incarceration on Aboriginal people must thus include a gendered analysis.

The impact of incarceration on Aboriginal women must be understood through an analysis of the development of correctional policy in Canada. The system was created to house prisoners, the vast majority of whom were and remain men.[15] Until 1934 when the federal Prison for Women was opened in Kingston, women were housed in prisons alongside men. Women's incarceration was an afterthought in corrections. The system of incarceration in Canada is a system designed and developed for men, by men, and about male crime. Just as women were an afterthought in corrections, so were Aboriginal people. It is equally true that the system of corrections in Canada was designed and developed for white men by white men. Aboriginal

women are, therefore, an afterthought within an afterthought (Correctional Service Canada 1990). This situation must be seen to be unacceptable. The Task Force on Federally Sentenced Women, mandated in 1989, was the first to be charged with examining the situation of women in federal prisons. Because of a strong Aboriginal women's lobby, our views were included in this work. The task force report, *Creating Choices* (1990), did not examine the overall situation of women in conflict with the law, but it examined only the situation of women sentenced to federal terms of imprisonment. In this way, the report is narrowly focused and no clear national picture is available on the way that women experience the full range of criminal justice sanctions.

The figures that document the drastic overrepresentation of Aboriginal people in the Canadian criminal justice system measure only the experience of those who have come into direct contact with the penal system. This particular focus can diminish the overall impact that the criminal justice sanction has on Aboriginal people and our communities. For example, it is known that men are more likely to be federal prisoners (at more than a ratio of 20:1). It is a serious error to conclude that the problem of overrepresentation is borne by our men. Those men are brothers, fathers, husbands, and sons of Aboriginal women. Statistics indicate that in one urban centre, Winnipeg, 43 per cent of Aboriginal families are headed by single women compared with 10 per cent of non-Aboriginal families (Manitoba 1991). It is unnecessary to wonder where *all* of these men have gone. We know, logically, that some of them are incarcerated. Aboriginal women may not be directly affected by the criminal justice system as frequently as men, but the impact the system has on our lives is equally extreme.

It is not just the fact of overrepresentation and the repercussions felt in our families and communities that must be publicly noted and must evoke concern—the depth of the disparity in the treatment of Aboriginal and non-Aboriginal offenders must also be noted. The Aboriginal Justice Inquiry of Manitoba concluded that every aspect of the criminal justice system is problematic for Aboriginal people (Manitoba 1991). The inquiry conducted a survey and reviewed provincial court records and came to some startling observations. Aboriginal people are more likely to be charged by police for multiple offences. Twenty-two per cent of Aboriginal people appearing in court face four or more charges, while for non-Aboriginal people this happens in 13 per cent of the cases. Once arrested, Aboriginal people are 1.34 times more likely to be held in jail prior to their court appearances. Once in pretrial custody, Aboriginal people spend 1.5 times longer in custody before their trials. When preparing for court appearances, Aboriginal people see their lawyers less frequently and for less time than do non-Aboriginal people: "Forty-eight per cent of Aboriginal people spent less than an hour with their lawyers compared to 46 per cent of non-Aboriginal inmates who saw their lawyers for more than 3 hours" (Manitoba 1991).[16] These 1991 findings have been reached by other reviews since then. Although statistics from one jurisdiction cannot be assumed to apply to other areas, there is no information that suggests that the same kinds of difficulties do not face the majority of Aboriginal offenders in other parts of the country. Furthermore, the overrepresentation of Aboriginal people in correctional institutions is clearly and obviously linked to these factors.

In the Manitoba courts, the disparity in treatment of Aboriginal people is also remarkable. Sixty per cent of Aboriginal people entered guilty pleas, while only 50 per cent of non-Aboriginal people did the same. Aboriginal people received jail terms in 25 per cent of the cases, while non-Aboriginal people were jailed in 10 per cent of the cases. Aboriginal people receive longer sentences and receive absolute or conditional discharges less frequently (Manitoba 1991). These statistics also enhance our understanding of the patterns of and reasons behind the grave overrepresentation of Aboriginal people in Canadian prisons. There are important systemic patterns within the justice system that contribute to Aboriginal overrepresentation in prisoner populations. Furthermore, Aboriginal

overrepresentation is not properly explained by theories of individual Aboriginal pathology.

After documenting the pattern of overrepresentation of Aboriginal people in Canadian prisons, courts, and police contacts, the commissioners of the Aboriginal Justice Inquiry came to this poignant conclusion: "These statistics are dramatic. There is something inherently wrong with a system which takes such harsh measures against an identifiable minority. It is also improbable that **systemic discrimination** has not played a major role in bringing this state of affairs into being" (Manitoba 1991). The recognition that the problem of criminal justice and corrections is in fact systemic has yet to be fully incorporated into the thinking of those with the power to change correctional relations. An analysis of the reforms to date indicates that the vast majority of reforms have expected Aboriginal people to change to fit into the system—that is to say, that most efforts at reform have been individualized as opposed to systemic. Reforms such as provincial court workers and legal education projects have been established to assist Aboriginal people in understanding the foreign system of Canadian laws and justice relations. Why is it that Aboriginal people are expected to change to accommodate the system rather than the system changing in such a way that Aboriginal people are fundamentally respected by that system? A system of justice that is capable of singling out any identifiable group to receive special and more excessive contact cannot be seen to be just and fair. However, this situation has not only existed in Canada since at least 1967, the situation has continued to worsen.

Once incarcerated, Aboriginal offenders continue to receive unequal treatment. The Aboriginal Justice Inquiry of Manitoba again provides an interesting window to the shape of the problems within correctional institutions. The inquiry surveyed 258 inmates, 60 Aboriginal and 198 non-Aboriginal. The Aboriginal inmates reported that they felt Aboriginal spirituality was not respected in their institution (81 per cent). Fewer than five per cent of these inmates indicated that they had regular access to spiritual activities (Manitoba 1991). In fact, the commissioners of the inquiry concluded that Aboriginal spirituality is not being encouraged in institutions but instead is actively discouraged (Manitoba 1991). Although Correctional Service Canada has made efforts in the last decade to improve cultural and spiritual services, they still lag behind the need. In a 1997 research report commissioned by the Correctional Service, 67.9 per cent of inmates surveyed indicated that they did not have enough access to cultural activities (Correctional Service Canada 1997). In the same report, 40.7 per cent of the inmates surveyed that their spiritual needs were not being met (Correctional Service Canada 1997).

Aboriginal inmates also report that programming in the institutions is not acceptable. In most cases appropriate programming that addresses their needs is not available.[17] "Yet, if they do not participate in the programs that are offered, that fact appears on their record and harms their chances for parole" (Manitoba 1991). Aboriginal offenders are forced to engage in programs that have little personal (cultural) worth if they wish to have any opportunity to secure a parole. The statistics available on parole indicate that Aboriginal people are less likely to be granted parole. There is a relationship between the services available in prison to Aboriginal inmates that are culturally sensitive and the rate of paroles granted to them. In 1998, in its review of the Corrections and Conditional Release Act, Correctional Service Canada summarizes its findings:

> Findings revealed that proportionately, Aboriginal offenders were more likely to be serving their sentence in institutions than in the community on supervision. Aboriginal offenders were also less likely to be released on full parole, more likely to be released on statutory release, and significantly more likely to be referred for detention. When granted parole, they received it later in their sentence and were more likely to be returned to imprisonment for a technical violation of

> supervision conditions. (Correctional Service Canada 1998)

In 1994, 60 per cent of non-Aboriginal offenders were granted parole, while only 44.5 per cent of Aboriginal offenders were granted parole. These release rates are an improvement over the 1980 figures, but there is still a long way to go. For several years now, and particularly in the Prairie region, Aboriginal inmates have been able to have elder-assisted parole hearings. Studies indicate that this has not significantly improved the rate of granting of parole to Aboriginal offenders, but parole board members report that these types of hearings have provided Aboriginal inmates with the opportunity to have "hearings that are more relaxed and informal which many find is conducive to openness and sincerity" (Correctional Service Canada 1994b). It is not documented whether Aboriginal offenders agree with this conclusion.

As equally remarkable as the overrepresentation of Aboriginal people as clients in the criminal justice system is the exclusion or underrepresentation of Aboriginal people from any place of authority in the criminal justice system (Manitoba 1991). There are very few Aboriginal lawyers, police officers, court personnel, corrections workers, or parole officers. There is usually no one in our communities employed in the system to turn to if we are confused about what is happening to us in that system. As a result, Aboriginal people view the justice system as a system that belongs to Canada and not to Aboriginal people. We understand that as the clients of that system, we "support" it; in fact, the system is built on the backs of many Aboriginal offenders and their families. Aboriginal people see little if any benefit accruing to our communities from this system. We do not earn our livelihood by involvement in that system—instead, we pay fines and we see dollars and people going out of our communities and know that the benefit goes to the government and Canadians in general (Manitoba 1991). It is little wonder that Aboriginal people have little respect for the Canadian criminal justice system.

The overrepresentation of Aboriginal people in penal institutions, their disparate treatment in prisons, and their chronic underrepresentation in positions of employment within the justice area are merely glimpses of the way in which justice relations have a negative impact on Aboriginal people. Although it would be unfair to stereotype reserves as all having high crime rates, there is a greater statistical likelihood that an individual living on reserve will be victimized by crime.[18] The national crime rate is 92.7 criminal acts per 1,000 population. The Department of Indian Affairs reports that the crime rate on reserves is 165.6 per 1,000 population—1.8 times the national average (Manitoba 1991). Even more troubling is the fact that the rate of violent crime is greater on Indian reserves—3.67 times the national rate (Manitoba 1991). Indian people are more likely to be victims of crime, and the "opportunity" to be a victim of violent crime is even greater. The need to address the difficulties in Canadian criminal justice as it is applied to Aboriginal people is a concern that is much broader than the mere jailing of our citizens. It is a reflection of the life experiences of Aboriginal people and has a negative impact on the quality of life in our communities. The impact of the Canadian criminal justice system and its failure to provide meaningful correctional and criminal justice services to Aboriginal offenders also creates additional burdens on our communities and on victims.

Understanding the Colonial Impact of Canadian Justice Institutions

The situation of over- and underrepresentation must be understood to create the situation where Aboriginal people can have no respect for Canada's system of criminal law and corrections. This is not the fault[19] of Aboriginal people, but must be seen to be a systemic problem that is the responsibility of the Canadian justice system and those who support it.

Canadians must also come to understand colonization and, more importantly, decolonization. It is very difficult for Aboriginal people to live in a decolonized manner when the practice of colonialism is still alive and well in Canada. Since 1967 and the release of the report of the Canadian Corrections Association, social scientists, often in partnership with government departments, have searched for the cause of Aboriginal criminality. In the 1967 report, the discussion concluded with a realization "that much of whatever trouble these people were having with the law could be understood only in light of economic conditions, culture patterns, minority group status and other underlying factors" (Laing and Monture 1967). Since the release of the Donald Marshall Inquiry report in 1989, the factors analyzed to produce an understanding of Aboriginal criminality became individualized. This is troubling. Economic disadvantage, underemployment, substance abuse, and other factors that are used to explain Aboriginal over-involvement are not the sources of the problem but symptoms of the problems of a society that is structured on discriminatory values, beliefs, and practices that are then applied without consent to Aboriginal nations. The outcome of the individualized analysis of Aboriginal patterns of crime conceals the true relationship.

Commissioners Hamilton and Sinclair note in the *Report of the Aboriginal Justice Inquiry of Manitoba* two immediate answers to the reasons for the shocking overrepresentation of Aboriginal people in the criminal justice system. Either Aboriginal people commit disproportionately more crimes than do non-Aboriginal people, or Aboriginal people are the victims of a discriminatory justice system. They further add,

We believe that both answers are correct, but not in the simplistic sense that some people might interpret them. We do not believe, for instance, that there is anything about Aboriginal people or their culture that predisposes them to criminal behaviour. Instead, we believe that the causes of Aboriginal criminal behaviour are rooted in a long history of discrimination and social inequality that has impoverished Aboriginal people and consigned them to the margins of Manitoban society. (Manitoba 1991)

In particular, discrimination in the justice system cannot be simply understood. Discrimination comes in many forms: Aboriginal people experience discrimination in the courts and in jails; in our communities, we have a greater statistical likelihood of being victimized; and we recognize familiar patterns of exclusion in the lack of opportunity to be employed within the justice system. The two causes of Aboriginal overrepresentation expressed by the Manitoba commissioners lead to several logical conclusions about reforming the justice system.

I have never been an advocate of reform of the existing system as being a full and complete remedy. This became a hardened opinion during my years as a volunteer in the Kingston area penitentiaries.[20] This lesson is reaffirmed every time I consider the government-sponsored justice reports. It saddens me to think that it is even a necessary remedy, but it is. Reform of the existing system is most necessary. Many Aboriginal prisoners are currently serving sentences in Canada's prisons and jails. These are relatives and friends on whom I cannot turn my back. I am very much convinced that even if the existing system was reformed in such a way that Aboriginal people were proportionately represented and received equal treatment, Aboriginal people would still continue to report that they perceive the Canadian criminal justice system as unfair.

Another factor affects the perception of Aboriginal people that they are treated unfairly by the existing system, a factor that has largely been ignored in the academic literature and multiple reports but that I have heard mentioned by many Aboriginal people. This forgotten factor is history. There is a long history of

the criminal law sanction being used to control, oppress, and force the assimilation of Aboriginal peoples. This is carefully remembered by some Aboriginal people. There are a number of examples of the problematic nature of the historical relationship.

Examining the introduction of alcohol to Aboriginal populations provides an important example of the way that an understanding of historical relations must complement present-day understandings. The abuse of alcohol has been demonstrated to influence the participation in criminal activity. This is true across most categories of offences and is particularly true for Aboriginal offenders. Alcohol was introduced into Aboriginal nations by European traders who learned they could accumulate great profits when they relied on alcohol as a trade commodity. For the Cypress Hills area (southern Saskatchewan) it has been reported that "the trading of whiskey could boost a trader's profits substantially. In 1854 a clear profit of 45 per cent could be made on trading a $9.67 gun for $416.00 worth of buffalo robes. Proof alcohol cost the trader $3.25 to $6.00 a gallon—diluted and spiced up it could bring up to $50.00 in hides. In one rate of exchange, two robes were traded for one large glass of 'rot-gut' whiskey" (Hildebrandt and Hubner 1994).[21] Today, the history of Aboriginal peoples' introduction to alcohol consumption is forgotten. It is within this relationship that one of the seeds of Aboriginal overrepresentation in the criminal justice system is firmly rooted.

The Aboriginal Justice Inquiry of Manitoba was the first Canadian report to develop a consistent focus on the effect of racism, individual and systemic, in the overrepresentation of Aboriginal people within the criminal justice system. This focus on racism and criminal sanction extends back in time to the period of contact. In their own words, the commissioners explain,

Historically, the justice system has discriminated against Aboriginal people by providing legal sanction for their oppression. This oppression of previous generations forced Aboriginal people into their current state of social and economic distress. Now, a seemingly neutral justice system discriminates against current generations of Aboriginal people by applying laws which have an adverse impact on people of lower socio-economic status. This is no less racial discrimination; it is merely "laundered" racial discrimination. It is untenable to say that discrimination which builds upon the effects of racial discrimination is not racial discrimination itself. Past injustices cannot be ignored or built upon. (Manitoba 1991)

The work of the Aboriginal Justice Inquiry introduced a new level of analysis to an old question. The question of Aboriginal over-involvement in all relations of criminal justice in Canada is analyzed at a systemic level. Racism is understood to be the central factor.

Racism is in fact an incomplete explanation of what is happening in the Canadian criminal justice system. Racism does not emphasize enough the historical relationships that appear when the overrepresentation of Aboriginal people in Canadian jails is placed in context. In fact, colonialism is also a necessary component of the explanation. The Canadian justice system is now the central institution that reinforces colonial relationships with Aboriginal people. In many ways, the system of incarceration has taken the place that residential schools once occupied. This fact must influence the way that any reformation of Canadian criminal justice systems proceeds.

Beyond the individual and systemic discrimination that can be measured by disproportional rates of over- and underrepresentation, beyond the context that is exposed when history is remembered, is the shocking fact that the branches of the criminal justice system in Canada continue to this day to operate in a way that oppresses the mechanisms and practices of social control in Aboriginal communities. This third factor obviously continues to create the situation where rates of Aboriginal overrepresentation will continue to increase. And yet, it is barely noted in the literature. It has not been the topic of any extensive research program.

Walking toward the Future

When I think about reforming the Canadian criminal justice system, I often find myself reflecting on my experiences of the struggle that individuals have faced to keep out of prison. Learning to walk on this side of the prison wall has been difficult for many people with whom I have shared small parts of this experience. Little in the way of programming within the prison system has prepared them for the journey that they face outside. Little is known in a scholarly sense about what works in the "aftercare" field. I know of no rigorous studies of this issue. Few resources are devoted to providing post-incarceration services and programs.

I am not totally dismayed by the situation of Aboriginal people in the Canadian criminal justice system, as there are sources of hope on the horizon. Perhaps the most promising, other than the faith I have in my people, are the new provisions of the Corrections and Conditions Release Act. Section 81 of this legislation allows for the release of an Aboriginal offender to the Aboriginal community. Both Aboriginal offender and Aboriginal community are broadly defined. This section allows for the possibility that Aboriginal communities can gain "care and custody" of Aboriginal prisoners prior to their parole release dates. Subject to the minister's approval and adequate levels of both funding and support, Aboriginal communities can now step forward creatively to bring our people home. This is a broad section that does not step on the hope that things will someday change. Unfortunately, more could be done with this section to speed up the realization of the potential it holds.

The question of how we keep our people out of the justice system has become central in my thoughts on criminal justice and Aboriginal peoples. Intuitively I know the answer. Caring and connection keeps people out. This does not surprise me, because I understand that the vast majority of Aboriginal law is nothing more than rules about kinship and caring. Aboriginal law is relational-based. The question of how we keep our people out is the question I wish to leave you with.

Notes

1. Mohawk Nation, Grand River Territory, currently residing at the Thunderchild First Nation, Saskatchewan. Associate Professor, Department of Native Studies, University of Saskatchewan. This article is written for my brothers and sisters in iron cages. It is written with prayer that meaningful change is not far away.

2. In recent articles I have chosen to adopt constitutionally prescribed language. "Aboriginal peoples" include the Indian (status and not), Inuit, and Métis. I intend this language to include all Indigenous peoples of the territory now known as Canada.

3. In the refereeing process that is part of the standard practice of academic scholarship, I received some feedback from "colleagues" that I can only describe as hateful. This situation nearly caused me to withdraw this chapter from this text. It has resulted in the withdrawal of one section of the paper. [This note refers to Monture-Angus's experiences when this article was first published in *Visions of the Heart: Canadian Aboriginal Experiences* (2000).]

   In writing this paper and in choosing to distinguish between Aboriginal and non-Aboriginal researchers, policy makers, scholars, and so on, I meant no disrespect to "white" people. However, the truth of the matter is that if we cannot even acknowledge that there are differences in Indigenous and "white" knowledge systems and practices, then it will remain impossible to overcome colonialism. Colonial relations cannot be addressed until we all understand the detail of this situation for both the colonized and the colonizer. This is the primary reason why this paper distinguishes between Aboriginal and non-Aboriginal people.

   For now, I am unwilling to share the preliminary analysis of several scholars' work as examples of the way non-Aboriginal scholars disappear the colonial legacy embedded in Aboriginal overrepresentation and the manner in which one scholar has bastardized and fundamentally misunderstood the sacred ways of Aboriginal people (at least as I was taught). There will again come a time when I carry the strength to speak fully to these issues. In this publication, because of the complicity of those involved in the publishing process, I choose silence.

4. For example, in 1886, section 114 of the Indian Act provided for a term of imprisonment not to exceed six months (and not less than two months) for anyone engaging in the "festival" known as the Potlatch or the dance known as the Tamanawas. A similar provision existed in subsequent Indian Acts until the 1951

amendments. Since it was first enacted, the section was broadened to include many other Indian ceremonies and dances.

5. See the work of William B. Newell (Ta-io-wah-ron-ha-gai), *Crime and Justice among the Iroquois Nations* (1965) and L.F.S. Upton, *Micmacs and Colonists: Indian-White Relations in the Maritimes, 1713–1867* (1979).

6. No systematic and detailed analysis of these recommendations has ever been undertaken and made accessible. The Royal Commission on Aboriginal Peoples disappointingly did not attempt such a project, even though it was well within their mandate and their resources. Rather, every study commissioned replicates the ones that came before. Part of this is a problem of the multiple jurisdictions involved in criminal justice matters and the fragmentation of services, from prevention to policing to corrections.

7. The Cawsey Commission notes that the top 10 recommendations are (in no particular order): "cross-cultural training for non-Native staff; employ more Native staff; have more community-based programs in corrections; have more community-based alternatives in sentencing; have more special assistance to Native offenders; have more Native community involvement in planning, decision-making, and service delivery; have more Native advisory groups at all levels; have more recognition of Native culture and law in Criminal Justice System service delivery; emphasize crime prevention programs; and, self-determination must be considered in planning and operation of the Criminal Justice System" (4–7). This report also notes that there "has been very little focus at the front-end of the system." Little attention has been paid to victim services and prevention.

8. A recent paper by Professor Russel Barsh (1996), "Anthropology and Indian Hating," discusses this very problem with the preoccupation with studying Aboriginal people to the exclusion of those who did (and do) the colonizing. An important collateral issue, how do "white" scholars situate themselves in their work, is discussed by Professor Denise McConney in "Dear Wynonah (First Daughter)" (1996).

9. The most complete picture available is found in the Aboriginal Justice Inquiry of Manitoba, which focuses on justice relations and experiences in the province of Manitoba only. No comprehensive national picture is available.

10. As of 31 March 1997, Correctional Service Canada reports this figure to be 64 per cent in the Prairie region

(Correctional Service Canada 1998), a decrease of 11 per cent from the 1994 figures cited. The report does not note this decrease, nor is any explanation put forward. It seems appropriate to note the problems with relying on self-report data that were mentioned earlier in this chapter.

11. I believe justice to be a much larger relation than just one involving the criminal law sanction. This paper will, however, focus on the consequences of Aboriginal over-representation in the existing justice system. Discussions of the broader meaning of justice can be found in Patricia A. Monture-Okanee, "Aboriginal Peoples and Canadian Criminal Justice: Myths and Revolution" (1994) and "The Roles and Responsibilities of Aboriginal Women: Reclaiming Justice" (1992).

12. Stoney Mountain is a federal penitentiary operated by Correctional Service Canada. It houses prisoners who are serving sentences of longer than two years. Provincial prisons (discussed in the next paragraph of the text) are prisoners who are serving sentences of less than two years. Youth offenders are under the age of 18.

13. It must be noted that these statistics are subject to criticism. Part of the increase in the overrepresentation may be due to the fact that it has become more acceptable to admit Aboriginal ancestry. Federal data rely solely on self-report figures.

14. These numbers were provided to the members of the Task Force on Federally Sentenced Women. Also note that between the years 1989–90 and 1994–95, the fed-

eral prison population has grown quickly, increasing by 22 per cent. This figure is twice the historic average (Canada 1996).

15. For fuller discussions on the situation of women in conflict with the law, see Elizabeth Comack, *Women in Trouble* (1996) and Karlene Faith, *Unruly Women* (1993).

16. Part of this phenomenon may be explained by the greater number of guilty pleas that Aboriginal people enter.

17. The Aboriginal inmates indicated what kinds of programs they would like to see in the Manitoba institutions. The most desired program was educational or vocational (43 per cent). The next most desired were programs involving spirituality and culture (29 per cent). Also in demand were life-skills programs (14 per cent) and "alcohol and drug dependency, stress management, crafts, parenting, marital counselling and Native languages" (Manitoba 1991).

18. Figures such as these are available for registered Indians only.

19. I do not believe that assigning blame is necessarily part of the solution to the problems that exist in the justice system.

20. I lived in the Kingston area from 1983 to 1988. I was actively involved in the prisons during those years and have maintained many of the friendships I made there after I left the area. My involvement with the Task Force on Federally Sentenced Women also reinforced this view.

21. Similar figures and the tale of a trader can be found in Mary Weekes, *The Last Buffalo Hunter* (1994).

References

Ahenakew, Freda, and H.C. Wolfart, eds 1987. *Waskahikaniwiyiniw—Acimowina* (Stories of the House People). Winnipeg: University of Manitoba Press.

Alberta. 1991. *Report of the Task Force on the Criminal Justice System and Its Impact on the Indian and Métis People of Alberta*. Vol. 3. *Working Papers and Bibliography*. Edmonton: Solicitor General.

Barsh, Russel. 1996. "Anthropology and Indian Hating." *Native Studies Review* 11, 2: 3–22.

Blackburn, Carole. 1993. "Aboriginal Justice Inquiries, Task Forces and Commissions: An Update." In *Aboriginal Peoples and the Justice System*, Royal Commission on Aboriginal Peoples. Ottawa: Supply and Services, 15–41.

Canada. 1996. *Corrections Population Growth*. Report for the Federal/Provincial/Territorial Ministers Responsible for Justice. Ottawa: Supply and Services.

Comack, Elizabeth. 1996. *Women in Trouble: Connecting Women's Law Violations to Their Histories of Abuse*. Halifax, NS: Fernwood.

Correctional Service Canada. 1990. *Creating Choices: The Report of the Task Force on Federally Sentenced Women*. Ottawa: Correctional Service Canada.

——. 1994a. "Aboriginal Issues." Internal CSC Newsletter.

——. 1994b. *Care and Custody of Aboriginal Offenders*. Ottawa: Solicitor General.

——. 1994c. *Inmate Profile*, 29 June. Ottawa: Correctional Service Canada.

——. 1997. *Aboriginal Offender Survey: Case Files and Interview Sample*. Ottawa: Correctional Service Canada.

——. 1998. *CCRA 5-Year Review: Aboriginal Offenders*. Working Group on the Review of the Corrections and Conditional Release Act. Ottawa: Supply and Services.

Faith, Karlene. 1993. *Unruly Women: The Politics of Confinement and Resistance*. Vancouver: Press Gang.

Freire, Paulo. 1996. *Pedagogy of the Oppressed*, trans. Myra Bergman Ramos. New York: Continuum.

Gosse, Richard, James Youngblood Henderson, and Roger Carter, eds 1994. *Continuing Poundmaker and Riel's Quest: Presentations Made at a Conference on Aboriginal Peoples and Justice*. Saskatoon: Purich Publishing.

Hildebrandt, Walter, and Brian Hubner. 1994. *The Cypress Hills: The Land and Its People*. Saskatoon: Purich Publishing.

Jackson, Michael. 1988. *Locking up Natives in Canada: Report of the Canadian Bar Association Committee on Imprisonment and Release*. Toronto: Canadian Bar Association.

Johnson, Holly, and Karen Rodgers. 1993. "Statistical Overview of Women and Crime in Canada." In Ellen

Adelburg and Claudia Currie, eds, *In Conflict with the Law: Women and the Canadian Justice System.* Vancouver: Press Gang, 85–116.

Kly, Yussuf. 1991. "Aboriginal Canadians, the Anti-Social Contract, and Higher Crime Rates." On Les Samuelson and Bernard Schissel, eds, *Criminal Justice: Sentencing Issues and Reform.* Toronto: Garamond Press, 81–94.

Laing, Arthur, and Gilbert C. Monture. 1967. *Indians and the Law.* Ottawa: Canadian Corrections Association.

LaPrairie, Carol. 1995. "Seen but Not Heard: Native People in Four Canadian Inner Cities." *Journal of Human Justice* 6, 2: 30–45.

Law Reform Commission of Canada (LRCC). 1991. *Aboriginal Peoples and Criminal Justice.* Report 34. Ottawa: LRCC.

McCaskill, Don. 1983. "Native People and the Justice System." In Ian A.L. Getty and Antoine S. Lussier, eds, *As Long as the Sun Shines and Water Flows: A Reader in Canadian Native Studies.* Vancouver: University of British Columbia Press, 288–98.

McConney, Denise. 1996. "Dear Wynonah (First Daughter)." *Native Studies Review* 11, 2: 116–24.

Manitoba. 1991. *Report of the Aboriginal Justice Inquiry of Manitoba: The Justice System and Aboriginal People.* Vol. 1. A.C. Hamilton and C.M. Sinclair, Commissioners. Winnipeg: Queen's Printer.

Monture-Angus, Patricia. 1995. *Thunder in My Soul: A Mohawk Woman Speaks.* Halifax, NS: Fernwood.

Monture-Okanee, Patricia. 1992. "The Roles and Responsibilities of Aboriginal Women: Reclaiming Justice." *Saskatchewan Law Review* 56, 2: 237–66.

———. 1994. "Aboriginal Peoples and Canadian Criminal Justice: Myths and Revolution." In Richard Gosse, James Youngblood Henderson, and Roger Carter, eds, *Continuing Poundmaker and Riel's Quest: Presentations Made at a Conference on Aboriginal Peoples and Justice.* Saskatoon: Purich Publishing, 222–32.

Newell, William B. (Ta-io-wah-ron-ha-gai). 1995. *Crime and Justice among the Iroquois Nations.* Montreal: Caughnawaga Historical Society.

Royal Commission on Aboriginal Peoples (RCAP). 1993. *Aboriginal Peoples and the Justice System: Report of the National Round Table on Aboriginal Justice Issues.* Ottawa: RCAP.

———. 1996a. *Bridging the Cultural Divide: A Report on Aboriginal People and Criminal Justice in Canada.* Ottawa: Supply and Services.

———. 1996b. *Report of the Royal Commission on Aboriginal Peoples.* Vol. 1. *Looking Forward, Looking Back.* Ottawa: RCAP.

———. 1996c. *Report of the Royal Commission on Aboriginal Peoples.* Vol. 5. *Renewal: A Twenty-Year Commitment.* Ottawa: RCAP.

School of Human Justice, University of Regina. 1991. Brief submitted to the Saskatchewan Indian and Métis Justice Review Committee.

Schuh, Cornelia. 1979. "Justice on the Northern Frontier: Early Murder Trials of Native Accused." *Criminal Law Quarterly* 22: 74–111.

Solicitor General. 1996. *Report of the Commission of Inquiry into Certain Events at the Prison for Women in Kingston.* The Honourable Louise Arbour, Commissioner. Ottawa: Public Works and Government Services Canada.

Stonechild, Blair. 1986. "The Uprising of 1885: Its Impacts on Federal/Indian Relations in Western Canada." *Saskatchewan Indian Federated College Journal* 2, 2: 81–96.

Upton, L.F.S. 1979. *Micmacs and Colonists: Indian–White Relations in the Maritimes, 1713–1867.* Vancouver: University of British Columbia Press.

Weekes, Mary. 1994. *The Last Buffalo Hunter.* Saskatoon: Fifth House Publishers.

Questions for Critical Thought

1. Why does Monture-Angus argue that understanding colonialism is key to explaining the overrepresentation of Aboriginal peoples in the criminal justice system? Do you believe that racial profiling of Aboriginal men is a social problem in Canada? Why or why not?

2. How have common responses to Aboriginal crime reproduced their oppression? Monture-Angus asserts that the Canadian criminal justice system is a "mechanism of social control in Aboriginal communities." How is this manifest? Who benefits from this mechanism of social control?

3. Do you think that the social class and gender of Aboriginal peoples affect their experiences in the criminal justice system?

4. Why does Monture-Angus criticize reforms to the criminal justice system that are intended to improve the problem of overrepresentation of Aboriginal peoples in this system? What solutions to the problem of overrepresentation does she recommend?

The Space of Africville: Creating, Regulating, and Remembering the Urban "Slum"

Jennifer J. Nelson

There is a little frequented part of the City, overlooking Bedford Basin, which presents an unusual problem for any community to face. In what may be described as an encampment, or shack town, there live some seventy negro families. . . .

The citizens of Africville live a life apart. On a sunny, summer day, the small children roam at will in a spacious area and swim in what amounts to their private lagoon. In winter, life is far from idyllic. In terms of the physical condition of buildings and sanitation, the story is deplorable. Shallow wells and cesspools, in close proximity, are scattered about the slopes between the shacks.

There are no accurate records of conditions in Africville. There are only two things to be said. The families will have to be rehoused in the near future. The land that they now occupy will be required for the further development of the City.[1]

This chapter traces a series of events that demonstrate how the space of Africville, Nova Scotia, was legally regulated by the City of Halifax throughout its existence. This space remains a contested site—a reminder to the city that burial of past injustice requires diligent maintenance. Through exploration of several events over time, it becomes clearer that the notion of a united black community, which exists on its own terms and is subject to the same rights and freedoms as the greater white community, was and remains inconceivable. The dislocation of Africville residents from their land and community was more than an isolated, finite project; on the contrary, the process has been one of ongoing eviction, suppression, and denial.

The role of a spatial analysis becomes clear in three ways throughout the discussion. First, the legal regulation of space governs what can and cannot happen within it, in ways that may not be obviously defined as racist in law itself, nor perhaps to a community not directly and negatively affected by such regulation. Second, the regulation and limitation of spaces of resistance are easily masked as a necessary measure to protect the public, a reasonable and equitable measure that applies equally to all citizens, rather than targeting any specific group. Third, the violence inherent in the regulation of racialized space is rendered invisible when law is conceived as being a product of consensus of liberal social values. The inequities can only be heard when the differing stories of those involved are allowed to emerge. Thus, this chapter makes an argument for context-specific considerations of wrong doing that go beyond an assumed consensus of "fairness" to a series of legal actions that were planned and carried out by one group against another.

While there are many elements to the Africville story that tell a tale of spatial and racial discrimination, for the purposes of length and poignancy, I have selected a few key moments from a broader and ongoing struggle to demonstrate the inconceivability to a racist society of an enduring communal black presence.

As a white writer, I believe it is important to make clear my choices in directing the study's conceptual bent towards whiteness-as-dominance, rather than attempting to replicate "the black experience" of Africville, a story which is not mine to tell. While not intended to alienate or exclude, I acknowledge that this form of analysis and the conclusions I make embody a critique directed to the white community, which people of colour may not find to be "new" or illuminating. Further, I do not mean to suggest at any stage of analysis that resistance and opposition were absent among Africville residents themselves. Certainly, organization against the city's plans took place at the time of Africville's forced dislocation, and various events and projects that seek justice, encourage remembrance, and celebrate resistance have been underway ever since. I am merely choosing here to focus on the dominant players whose governance made resistance insufficient to save Africville. It is the practices of the dominant group that we must critically examine if we seek to educate for change among a white community that is accountable for things done to black communities.

A Story of Un/settlement

Consideration of this or any other urban development must recognize the significance of its prior occupancy and revisit the colonial past to retell some of the histories of initial dispossession of the land involved. . . . The issue is not only one of initial invasion, but of ongoing dislocation and exclusion.[2]

To "begin at the beginning" draws one into a complex history of black settlement in Nova Scotia in the eighteenth century, a history too detailed to fully discuss here. Briefly, the means by which black residents of the province came to form the community of Africville must be regarded in the context of a history of the displacement and enslavement of black people by whites in North America, of hostile reception upon settlement in Nova Scotia, complete with a world view that demanded their containment and denial, and of a young nation struggling to form its identity through the predominantly British colonial enterprise.

Although slavery was never legally instituted in Nova Scotia, some whites held slaves at the time the City of Halifax was founded in 1749 and throughout the next 50 years. The practice failed to reach the proportions of American plantation cultures, due more to a paucity of arable farmland

than to widespread public opposition. The number of slaves following the arrival of slave-holding Loyalists is thought to be around 1,500. While officially frowned upon by the courts at a relatively early date, Nova Scotia's "slave culture" was undermined as the labour of incoming free black and white Loyalists could be had for little more than the price of keeping slaves.

Soon-to-be Africville residents were among the wave of refugee blacks who arrived after the War of 1812 and who were allotted space in rural regions, particularly present-day Preston, where rocky, inadequate soil made survival off the land impossible. The Africville site on the shores of Bedford Basin, not far from today's city centre, held the hope of diminished isolation, better employment and living conditions, and other economic opportunities. Having purchased the properties in the 1840s from white merchants, founders William Brown and William Arnold established the boundaries within which Africville would develop. Along with other early families, they established a church congregation and elementary school, a postal office, and a few small stores. Although land conditions for farming were no better than on their former plots, a few head of livestock were kept, the Bedford Basin offered a steady supply of fish, and the new location held the increased chance of obtaining waged labour in the city.[3]

Throughout the community's approximately 120-year history, Halifax's development, particularly in the industrial and disease- and waste-management sectors, encroached on Africville land. In addition to the construction of railway lines, which required the destruction of several Africville buildings, an oil plant storage facility, a bone mill, and a slaughterhouse were built. Encircling these establishments were a leather tanning plant, a tar factory, another slaughterhouse, and a foundry. Shortly after the settlement of Africville, the city established Rockhead Prison on the overlooking hillside; about twenty years later, the city's infectious diseases hospital was placed on this hill, and the open city dump was located about one-and-a-half miles away. Additional construction of railway lines to different factories dislocated more Africville families. Destruction of many surrounding industries following the Halifax Explosion of 1917 resulted in new facilities being built in their places. For decades, this waterfront region was the target of much discussion regarding expropriation for industrial expansion by the City of Halifax, a plan which became solidified in the 1947 rezoning of the city. In the early 1950s, the city dump was moved directly onto Africville land—350 feet from the westernmost home—and two years later, the city placed an incinerator only fifty yards beyond its south border.

Throughout Africville's existence, building permits to improve homes were increasingly difficult to obtain from the city government. Requests for water lines and sewers, which would bring sanitation and quality of life closer to the standards for the rest of the city, were refused. Police and fire protection and garbage collection on par with such services received by the rest of Halifax were denied. Living conditions were ironically described by city officials as intolerable and unsanitary—in short, as justification for the inevitable dismantling of the community and eviction of its 400 residents. Discussion of the dismantling continued, until finally, in the 1960s, the threat became a more serious reality. By the end of the decade, despite avid resistance and organization on the part of Africville residents themselves and in concert with other community groups, Africville was expropriated by the City of Halifax for the purposes of industrial development, as well as for the alleged benefits of "slum clearance" and "relocation" of the residents.[4]

Due to an informal system of handing down properties and housing within families and between in-laws over the years, many residents were unable to prove legal title to their land; thus, they had little recourse when faced with the proposition to sell or be evicted. Due to historical, social, and economic conditions, residents had no formal community leadership that would be seen as legitimate political representation and little access to the legal and bureaucratic bargaining tools of the municipality. Most were forced to

accept the city's small compensation, or to settle for low prices offered for homes they had not been permitted to maintain and improve, located in what was defined as "the slum by the garbage dump."[5] In a seeming mockery, when moving companies refused to be hired, city garbage trucks, which had never serviced Africville, were sent to carry away the residents' belongings.

The last Africville home was bulldozed in 1970. Most of the former residents had to adjust to living in public housing facilities, struggling to pay rent for the first time in their lives, while those who owned their own homes would suffer financial difficulties in the near future. Separated from friends, family, and their strong sense of community, many Africvilleans were left with the insufficiency of welfare dollars and the meagre $500 compensation they had received—defined as a "moral claim"—from the benevolent city.

Stage 1: Inducing Illness

Of particular interest to a critical geographical race analysis is the manner in which the control of space and the control of bodies through control of space become tools for defining a community's physical and metaphorical boundaries, its character, and how individuals or groups will be determined through such understandings and associations. David Goldberg writes,

> The slum is by definition filthy, foul smelling, wretched, rancorous, uncultivated, and lacking care. The racial slum is doubly determined, for the metaphorical stigma of a black blotch on the cityscape bears the added connotations of moral degeneracy, natural inferiority, and repulsiveness . . . the slum locates the lower class, the racial slum the underclass.[6]

In denying the community of Africville essential services that would facilitate its health and its development within the larger metro area, the city produced the community, in the "outside" public mind, as a place of dirt, odour, disease, and waste. These associations, which came to be manifested as the conflation of Africville with degeneracy, filth, and "the slum," justified the further denial of essential services on the basis of how Africville had come to be known. Working from a basic assumption that the use and characterization of space is socially determined, and that the ideologies surrounding race are socially produced, it is possible to speak of a socio-spatial dialectic wherein "space and the political organization of space express social relationships but also react back upon them."[7]

In the formation of Africville, and its regulation over time, we see an extension of this dialectic in the relationship between power-dominance and the creation of the slum. Particular race relations in this context produced certain space as repository for all that the dominant group wanted to contain and distance itself from. In the **self-fulfilling prophecy**—that is, Africville becoming exactly what it was set up to become in the eyes of the outer white community—the slum legitimates dominance by offering a concrete example of filthy, intolerable conditions, a notion of helplessness, and a lack of self-determination that are seen as inherent to its inhabitants. The origins of the conditions in question and the absence of choice for the residents must be conveniently forgotten, and this forgetting is accomplished most easily when the dominant group can achieve an axiomatic yet unspoken association of blackness with inevitable demise. As Barnor Hesse discusses in terms of "diasporic outside/inside," the internal Other, as opposed to the colonial Other overseas, poses a particular problem in Western societies: "Temporal nativization of the 'other,' outside/inside the West is accompanied by a spatial nativization in which people are compressed into prefabricated landscapes, the ghetto, the shanty town, and undergo a process of 'representational essentializing' . . . in which one part or aspect of people's lives comes to epitomize them as a whole."[8]

At the same time that we see that observable concrete realities of poverty and deprivation exist,

we see in the creation of the racial slum a set of knowledge-making practices that serve to legitimate all that we must believe about Africville in order to dominate it. As Henri Lefebvre writes,

> Space is not a scientific object removed from ideology and politics; it has always been political and strategic. If space has an air of neutrality and indifference with regard to its contents and thus seems to be "purely" formal . . . it is precisely because it has been occupied and used, and has already been the focus of past processes whose traces are not always evident on the landscape. Space has been shaped and moulded from historical and natural elements, but this has always been a political process. . . . It is a product literally filled with ideologies.[9]

The ideologies produced in the making of Africville-as-slum involve narratives about raced bodies that are tied to, but must not be conflated with, the spaces they inhabit. Take, for instance, the moving of the dump into Africville: this act was received by Africvilleans in the only way they saw possible—to make use of it, to salvage the things that others threw away, repair or clean them, and go on with life:

> We try to make the dump work for us. . . . There's all kinds of scrap metal in there that you can collect and sell. . . . There's ways of tellin' good stuff from bad. . . . We got fellas here who can get [car] parts off the dump and make the worst lookin' wreck in the world run like new. . . . You know what really gets up folks' behinds out here? When those newspapers talk about us "scavenging" food and clothes off the dump. People read that stuff and think we're runnin' around diggin' week-old tomatoes and nasty rags out of that messy dump. Any fool knows you get stuff off the trucks *before* they throw it on the dump . . . by the time the ladies out here get through workin' on second-hand clothes with their needle and thread, you'd never

know they were bound for the dump. Some folks say the dump was put here to try to drive us out. If that's true, things kind of backfired, didn't they?[10]

The dump, although smelly and distasteful, becomes incorporated into social practice as a means of survival. At the same time, from "outside," Africville becomes characterized more strongly than ever as a space of garbage, of the waste of the white community. The use of the dump can be viewed as proof that the black community is indeed comfortable being associated with dirt, that it is natural for them to live off the waste of others. Spaces are manufactured in ways that dictate what sorts of activities can and will take place in them. Life practice, then, determines both insider and outsider perceptions of identity: from within, perhaps, emerges a sense that the community can survive against unfair odds. Black identity in the outside white public discourse becomes intimately bound up with space/place in a negative sense—they are no longer simply people who live near the dump; they are "scavengers."

To see Others as recipients of your garbage, as *desiring* your waste, constitutes a very particular kind of relation and belief system about their place, their culture, their "peoplehood," on a dramatic level (as well as, very intimately, a belief system about your own place, culture, personhood). Dominant group members are not required to see how these relations are formed; on the contrary, "common-sense" views engender and support a sense that they are natural, that some people simply live "this way."

Many space theorists have described the way in which both marginalized groups and peripheral space signal an existence "beyond" society, apart from civilized norms, and as separate space in which undesirable activities could take place in order to preserve the purity of dominant, ruling space.[11] Essentializing the people and the space of Africville becomes apparent in the notion of the community as a site "outside" the rest of society, metaphorically, and spatially. As Peter Marcuse makes clear in his concept of

the *residual city*, racial minority spaces frequently come to house the wastes of society, be they pollutants from industrial manufacturing, sewer systems, and garbage disposal areas, or houses for others deemed undesirable, such as AIDS victims or the homeless.[12] This means that undesirable places and practices are located across a boundary that is rarely crossed, or crossed for specific purposes, that are "outside" the purity of the white middle-class home—for instance, the treatment of disease or exploring the red light district.[13] Specific to Africville would be the acts of buying liquor illegally[14] or disposing of waste. (Garbage, by definition, is material that is useless, has been thrown out. It is not a legitimate part of your space. It *must* be taken away from where you live, to another place.)

David Sibley's research on gypsy communities has been influential in pulling together many factors, discourses, and social sanctions that enable the construction of a marginal community as "separate," inferior, and slum-like. He speaks of the problematic of perceived "disorder," particularly in travelling communities, whose borders are never clear and require strict regulation.[15] Despite its more than 100-year history and long line of founding families, Africville residents were frequently thought of as a group of transients. In her essay on "the homeless body," Samira Kawash explores how the absence of place, while socially constituted, is seen as highly problematic and in need of legal and social systems of order-making and containment.[16] Although the Africville population was not seen in quite the same light as the homeless, their image as being outside society, undeserving of "place," and as threats to the place of the rest of the community, I believe, form some similar conceptions in the dominant public mind. Narratives of disorder become clear as well through references that are made in news reports and in the original relocation study to the community's criminal element, its potential for disease, and to the possibility that its population was composed mainly of squatters.

Goldberg discusses the making of the slum as **periphrastic space**, characterized by "dislocation, displacement, and division" from the rest of society. He concludes that this is "the primary mode by which the space of racial marginality has been articulated and reproduced."[17] At the same time, he notes that periphrastic space is not physically marginal to the urban centre, but, quite the contrary, is usually central, promoting a constant surveillance of its inhabitants and conditions. He refers to Vancouver's Chinatown and other similarly positioned communities, as functions of "that set of historical categories constituting the idea of the project: idealized racial typifications tied to notions of slumliness, physical and ideological pollution of the body politic, sanitation and health syndromes, lawlessness, addiction, and prostitution."[18]

These notions help to fuel an anachronistic sense of Africville's Otherness in time and space. Consider, for instance, the quotation at the beginning of this chapter from the provincially commissioned Stephenson Report: imposing on land coveted for "development of the city" and threatening the city's borders (even though it was there first), Africville becomes *not* part of the city. The representation of an "encampment" connotes an axiomatic impermanence, antithetical to progress and development of "society," which is already understood to be *not*-Africville. The abrupt solution proposed does not take into account the desires or needs of the residents themselves from their own perspectives. His sweeping disregard for any possibility of the community's survival is achieved in one brief and conclusive paragraph in a lengthy report that devotes detailed analysis to the upgrading of many other areas of Halifax, some of which are identified as exhibiting "the worst" conditions in the city.[19]

The depiction of Africville as "an unusual problem for any community to face"[20] suggests who is considered to be—*and not to be*—"the community." One might also question what, exactly, was "unusual" about a peripheral, underprivileged, and neglected black population in a North American urban centre with a dominant white majority. To see the situation as an isolated case sidesteps a critical interrogation of the systemic causes of racial oppression. In any case, Africville's "life apart" begs the question, "Apart from *what*?" The answer can only mean some combination of society-community-nation-progress-time-space-history. Indeed, this view must be fundamental to the description of a place as "little frequented," although 400 people were living there.

Interestingly, as the City of Halifax justified its forced dislocation of Africville residents through reference to land use and the need for industrial development, Sibley points out how outsider societies are understood to be contrary to, even the antithesis of, "development."[21] The wild and untamed lifestyle connoted in Africville's "private lagoon" was easily imagined as an outdated freedom, as an intolerable privilege of inhabiting valuable harbourfront space. Space that had to be made white.

Stage 2: Euthanasia

We knew all about segregation. But we didn't look at ourselves as a segregated community. We just looked at ourselves as a community. And when the people from the Progressive Club and others like them held out integration like some kind of Holy Grail, we told them we weren't sure exactly what integration could do for us as a community.

And the fact that we would raise doubts about it—well, that kind of shocked 'em.[22]

To solidify the ideologies produced around the space of Africville, the project of racial desegregation enabled an appearance, to many whites, of good intent that relied on a mode of imposed euthanasia—that is, the necessity of putting the community out of its misery.[23] When suffering is seen as "obvious" and incurable, destruction can be looked on as a form of rescue. Investments in the inevitability of this solution are so strong that it is extremely common for white people to ask, upon hearing of this issue, what Roger Simon might call the obscene question, "Why wouldn't they just leave?"[24] This question relies on a learned arrogance that assumes the solution being offered, in this case, to live among white people, is superior, and that the notion of free choice based on a common understanding of the experience exists. The many outsider narratives surrounding the slum construct a background against which implicit and explicit understandings of the (invisibly white) self and community as legitimately dominant are formed. The logic of the slum is productive in its own death, making common-sense knowledge of the fact of its dependence and inevitable need of an outside solution.

What, then, are we to make of the role of law in carrying out the solution in question? Not surprisingly, there was little space for Africville residents to contextualize their claims within a history of poverty, racism, and colonialism inflicted upon them by the same dominant group enacting the current violence. I have struggled with the problematic of identifying the precise legal (illegal?) moves made by the city—in all the accounts I have read the destruction of the community was simply "carried out." There are no references made to specific legal rulings or principles in the historical accounts, other than the mention of a more recent law passed to prevent certain forms of public protest. Nowhere in city reports from the time of relocation have I found expressions of doubt that Africville *could* be removed. Nor does there seem to exist a concern with justifying the removal through official channels. Instead, a common-sense logic prevails, composed of interwoven themes of understandings to which "we," as rational, race-neutral beings, are assumed to adhere. I soon felt forced to realize that it may be precisely the legality of the process that is so strikingly violent. This violence of the legal process is an integral thread in the common-sense discourse of relocation that, from a relatively privileged perspective, is easy to miss. In his discussion of liberal discourses of desegregation, as applied in various contexts, Goldberg summarizes well what I felt to be the imprecision of the legal process:

Law's necessary commitment to general principles, to abstract universal rules, to develop objective laws through universalization, is at once exclusive of subjectivities, identities and particularities. . . . So when law in its application and interpretation invokes history the reading is likely to be very partial, the more so the more politicized the process becomes. And race, I am insisting, necessarily politicizes the processes it brackets and colors.[25]

I have seen no legal opening for demonstrating, for example, that to be black, poor, displaced, and faced with the threat of physical removal from your home, in a segregated city in Nova Scotia, is not the same thing as to be white, professional, and arguing that the new mall's parking lot should not be placed in your backyard. There is little framework in place within which to claim that "relocating" in this context is different from simply "moving to a new house," hoping you'll soon get to know the neighbours. Such assumed neutrality of experience in the eyes of the law is extremely imprecise and misleading, while attempts to understand injustice are made difficult when context does not come into play. As Sherene Razack demonstrates in her analysis of the murder of an Aboriginal woman working as a prostitute in the Canadian West, any attempt to suggest a context in which race, gender, white male violence or discourses around the bodies inhabiting racialized, degenerate zones, is seen to bias the case. She illustrates how this renders particular identities invisible: "Since bodies had no race, class or gender, the constructs that ruled the day, heavily inflected with these social relations, coded rather than revealed them explicitly."[26] More than a matter of having "the wrong information," which can then be corrected, the discourses that define what white individuals in positions of power can hear about the subordinate group allow a self-concept of innocence to continue. Elsewhere, Razack writes, "Storytelling as a methodology in the context of law runs up against the problem of the dominant group's refusal to examine its own complicity in oppressing others. The power of law's positivism and the legal rules that underpin it are willing accomplices in this denial of accountability."[27]

To acknowledge complicity in histories of oppression and violence would be to give up an individual and collective sense of self and place. To ensure that this toehold is intact, the appearance of accountability can be manufactured through such venues as the $500 "moral claim" given to those residents who could not prove title to their homes. Take for instance the 1994 letter from R.J. Britton, the Halifax director of Social Planning, to City Council, reviewing the options that were perceived to be available at the time: "The City can use its statutory powers to remove the blight and at the same time, temper justice with compassion in matters of compensation to families affected."[28] Britton goes on to pronounce the "official story" that is to be known about Africville in public consciousness. This includes clauses assuring city officials that the aggressive bulldozer approach taken in the 1960s was simply the accepted method of "relocation" at the time, that the utmost compassion was given at various stages of negotiation, and that, since the actual cost of relocation was in the end approximately nine times the estimated cost, they can be assured of their benevolence. (On the contrary, it could be seen as their mistake and as evidence that rehabilitating the community might have been possible after all.) Compensation is cited as "at least very fair and perhaps generous." In this telling of the official story, historical distance excuses what are seen as minor glitches in the project of "relocation," and officials are permitted to feel good about their current perspectives and their predecessors' conduct. Moreover, as the "official story" ends, these leaders move beyond compassion to a sense of friendship and celebration: "The City of Halifax does need to recognize the reality of Africville in its history, celebrate the contributions the Africville people made to the City, and to continue to seek and help in their full participation in the life of the City."[29]

It is clear that within the governmental discourses surrounding Africville, officials define their innocence based on the absence of a legal structure that would hold them accountable in any way. What is perhaps most astounding is the absolute investment in legality as a moral foundation. This investment and the uninterrogated belief in its epistemic assumptions strike one as almost childlike in their simplicity: "If something is illegal, it is *wrong*; if something is legal, it is *correct*; if something is not our legal obligation but we offer it anyway, this makes us *good*." Not only are questions of accountability erased, they are made to seem unequivocally absurd when dominant subjects can believe they have kindly gone "above and beyond" their responsibilities. What is forgotten is that Africville's residents had no part in defining what would constitute these moral parameters, nor in constructing what was a legal or moral way of thought that made racism invisible.

What are the theoretical tools that might interpret the city's intended "slum clearance" or "industrial development" as processes that had, and continue to have, consequences for a poor black community? It is clear that straightforward *evidence* of racism, or even of what is definable as harm, will not be forthcoming. Richard Thompson Ford offers a detailed study of the manner in which segregation upholds itself even when legislative policy seeks to disband it. Were racial segregation banned, he posits, the structures in place to maintain people's links to specific areas, networks, services, and survival mechanisms devised by various communities, regardless of their differing socio-economic statuses, would see that desegregation remained extremely difficult at best.[30] Similarly, Goldberg traces the discriminatory and regulatory consequences of seemingly race-neutral legal rulings. He cites examples from South African **apartheid**, under which landlords could refuse to rent property to families with more than a certain number of children.[31] It so happened that black families tended to have larger than average numbers of children, thus the areas in which they were permitted to live could be "raced" without having to name this intent.

As Africville residents were moved, some were targeted by similar policies, having to give away some of their children or break apart families, forming household structures that differed from those they had known for generations. In some cases, single mothers were required to marry the fathers of their children in order to qualify for the new housing projects,[32] thus removing their power of choice to live as they pleased and implementing a value system based on the centrality of the nuclear family, rather than on Africville's sense of community and co-operation among extended relatives and friends. There are lawful ways in which to invoke "universal" values to bolster regulatory measures, as Goldberg points out:

> That the State in the name of its citizenry insists on overseeing—*policing*—the precise and detailed forms that housing must take for the poor and racialized suggests that we really are committed to the kinds of disciplinary culture that inform current practice. The principle of agent autonomy so deeply cherished at the core should not, it seems, extend to the periphery; the racially marginalized should not be encouraged to exercise independence (least of all with public monies).[33]

In "relocating" them to their new homes, the municipality hoped, perhaps assumed, that Africville residents would melt into their new neighbourhoods, establishing the appearance of a desegregated city regardless of the hostility they might experience from white neighbours and regardless of the great psychic expense they might suffer—an expense that would make it only too apparent "why they wouldn't just leave."

Stage 3: Burial

Drawing on Heidegger and on architectural theory, David Harvey theorizes the *genius loci*. Taken from the Roman, *genius* refers to a "guardian spirit" that determines the essence of one's identity. Harvey expands this to explore the essence of identity and community as it is associated with specific central locations. He speaks of how buildings and places absorb relations that occur within them, that these variant relations—to environment, history, physiology, sociality, psychology—become embodied in meanings that are projected onto the *genius loci*. In part, this reading practice begs the distinction of space from "place." As I intend it, *space* is the more general term, referring to any conceptual or actual space, including place. Place depicts a space upon which identity is founded. While either may be political, I see place as automatically so, referring to and incorporating notions of "home," collective history, and social location in reference to an identified group or individual. Place is the more precise term, encompassing the particular meanings embedded in spaces that are of significance to those who occupy them.

Harvey describes place as having a quality of "permanence." He studies a wealthy, walled community, which insulates itself against the outside world's perceived danger and degeneracy, as an example of place-making. His "place," and that of Heidegger whose work he engages, is intimately bound up with identity, roots, belonging, continuity, and readings onto space of particular memories.[34] I do not believe that *genius loci* is limited to a connotation of positive or negative meaning-making, but that, depending on how it is used, it can incorporate the violences, inequities, or comforts of how we come to understand our "place" in the world. Harvey's walled community shifts focus to the way in which dominant subjects make their place in the world through rigid boundary-maintenance designed to keep degeneracy at bay.

In a similar vein, Kathleen Kirby examines the mapping of space as fundamental to the formation of the "Cartesian subject."[35] Speaking of the necessity of establishing identity through the mastery of unknown places, she notes how space, for the privileged newcomer, is studied and "known" while space itself is not actively permitted to "know," to act back upon, the dominant subject. When this relationship shifts, such disorder is profoundly disturbing to the privileged (usually) white male subject who "explores" and, through mapping, conquers and reformulates space into something felt to be his own. It is in the project of this expropriation, with its concomitant distancing from the environment, that dominant subjects come to know themselves. While Kirby's theory is set out among "New World" explorer narratives, a greatly similar mechanism is at work in Africville, where white panic over the possibility of an enduring black presence is played out in a continual project of re-examining, rezoning, and reformulating the environment, making it clear who is in control and who may not achieve this subjugation of space.

A new stage in this project began in the 1980s when the city established Seaview Memorial Park on Africville's former site. Named after Seaview Church, which was destroyed before the rest of Africville, the park lies under a major bridge between the cities of Halifax and Dartmouth and winds for several acres along a stretch of waterfront. Landscaped as a gently rolling green space, the park provides benches overlooking the water and gravelly walking trails. A paved parking lot has replaced the oily dirt roads former residents have described. When the park was opened in 1985, the city's mayor announced plans to build a swimming pool there—on this site where Africville had been denied the installation of water lines throughout its existence.[36] A reunion with several hundred former Africville residents or descendants and their families takes place there each summer. In 1988, a monument was built near the park's entrance, engraved with the names of the area's first black settlers. This monument is the only visible evidence that Africville once existed, and even its tribute does not tell the story of the destruction of this community.

Standing in the park attempting to feel some semblance of connection to my project, I was struck by the manufactured ignorance and erasure available to someone like myself—born after Africville's destruction, white, never having been taught this element of my province's history. Attempting to map the images in photographs and stories onto the site was futile. The land is not the same shape; it is not the same colour; its contours have been altered. It could easily be seen as a park where Halifax proudly honours a founding black family and a community that happened to blend silently into the city's past. Unless one knows, nothing in sight speaks to the history of this space.

To read the park as *genius loci*, I believe, helps to situate it as a site of evidence with multiple meanings that can be read onto it, or onto the monument itself, depending on the histories and awarenesses people bring to it. As much as the monument shapes memory and dictates how we are to remember the story it depicts, it is important to remember that socially made preconceptions interact with our interpretation of what is being presented. Obviously, those who enter Seaview Memorial Park as their "place," or as a grounded symbol of continued resistance, will define this locale differently from those who remember driving to Africville to dump their garbage. Different still are the definitions of those who have never been to the city before, who visit as tourists or newcomers and "receive" a history that has been laid out for them, even as they bring specific conceptual tools to its interpretation. For them, the space says nothing of the violence that has been enacted upon it. It is in this act of burying the true story and dramatic transformation of the land that forms a poignant link in the chain of events that evicted Africville from its own space.

In the compression of time and space embodied in the monument and in the park, what might prevent us from seeing space as possessed of a history, of seeing the land we stand on as intimately problematic? What is *buried* beneath this symbol of remembering, or what truths does it hold down? It seems that the emptiness of space, here, is another form of *genius loci* for the Cartesian subject, who is complicit or silent in Africville's dislocation. In hiding the evidence where the community once stood, the city continued to produce an ongoing regulation of space to serve the purpose of memory-making. It predetermined how the space was to be received—as recreational land, a "neutral" green space open to "anyone." As non-black outsiders, we can imagine little more than a mythic existence of a black community, either romantic or slum-like, well in the past. In knowing ourselves through its reclamation and subjugation, we return to our "place" and know that it is *not* that place, which existed only as a site of intolerable disarray awaiting our inevitable intervention and organization.

The monument and park may foster a collective white belief in a sense of innocence or, in what Jane Jacobs has called reconciliation. Tracing the effect of "Aboriginal walking tours," which display Aboriginal cultural artworks alongside traditional colonial monuments in the urban space of Melbourne, Australia, Jacobs explores the narrative of reconciliation that underpins this public positioning of histories. In its attempt to unite historically colonized and colonizing groups under a common national identity, reconciliation "attempts to bring the nation into contact with the 'truth' of colonization—and this includes the attendant emotional 'truths' of guilt, anger, regret and hurt—in order that there might be a certain 'healing.'"[37] The anxieties this discourse raises among non-Aboriginals as to their understandings of their past and their place in the nation's history are, in Jacobs's view, rekindling a more overt racism imbued with a sense that Aborigines now possess too much power and privilege.

Would this sort of defensive hostility result from attempts to retell the truth of Africville's history in the public forum? Do the monument and park, along with more recent acceptance of memorials in the form of plays, music, and art displays, incur a sense of reconciliation among white Halifax residents, a sense that they have gone far enough in paying tribute to "unfortunate" events of the past? Informally expressed regret, combined with the more common-sense notion that Africvilleans are "still bitter" and should "put the past in the past," fail to expose personal and collective complicity, much less to ignite a strong public legal move towards material compensation. Further, they allow a sense of personal achievement in having come to a point of understanding, of believing we relate to what happened, that we regret

what those before us did, while remaining distinct from the whole mess. As in the Australian case Jacobs describes, we have seen heightened resentment against Africville residents who are making demands at the government level, while many white residents assert that the city has been generous and compassionate where there was no racism to begin with.

How might the way in which the Africville story is "told" enable a dominant, privileged audience to receive a message of complicity and responsibility? As Lefebvre writes, "Monumental space offered each member of a society an image of that membership, an image of his or her social visage."[38] To usefully explore the social visage of a community that forced the dislocation of others, it is crucial to understand the way we remember or forget, but we also must look further to determine the historical understandings and memories we bring to the Africville monument. When these remembrances are disconnected from the actual space, as they are in most white public consumption of the story, the story may retain a mythic quality, like an entertaining but "unreal" war narrative from ancient history. The potential of a physically grounded analysis, in which we can hear the story from the perspectives of former residents and connect it to their space, is lost.

Silencing the Ghosts

In 1994, there was a resurgence of municipal panic when two brothers, former Africville residents, occupied Seaview Memorial Park. They were protesting the lack of compensation and demanding renewed claims on Africville land. The Carvery brothers, teenagers when they left Africville, set up camp in Seaview on the site of their former home for over a year, getting through a cold winter with only a tent and a few survival implements. The authorities failed in their repeated threats and attempts to evict them, which included locking the park's only public washroom.[39] Their protest took place at the same time that the city was preparing to host the G7 summit. To allow the ghosts of Africville (though in reality very much alive) to seep through the carefully managed fabric of a well-tended burial would cause Halifax worldwide embarrassment—whether over a failure to manage "its blacks" or over leaked knowledge of its injustices is not clear.

News reports during this time reflect a daily concern with the presence of the Carvery brothers in the park and cite complaints from Halifax residents who claimed the Carverys' protest "took away from their enjoyment of the park."[40] A few months before the summit, despite widespread protest from the black community, a law was passed that forbade citizens to camp in public parks overnight. Mayor Fitzgerald, who earlier claimed his government had "bent over backwards" in attempt to negotiate with Africville protesters, cited the new ordinance as falling under the Protection of Property Act. In contrast to two days earlier, when the city had had no legal recourse against those sleeping overnight in a city park, he was able to announce that "people are in the park illegally and we want them off."[41] The Carverys eventually moved their protest just outside the park's border, to an area that did not fall under municipal jurisdiction. As the city alone could not evict them without provincial and federal consent, they maintained their campsite for several more years.[42]

The city's destruction of Africville was the culmination of a moral panic at the possibility of an independent, sovereign blackness. The nation makes itself not through exclusionary practice alone, but, to borrow Sibley's term, through "geographies of exclusion."[43] Through the desecration of space as black, the appropriation of space as white, the suppression of the story of this violence and the denial of accountability, the life of Africville is grounded upon a geography of racism and its discursive organization. Like the proverbial lie, once told, the story necessitates the telling of a chain of "maintenance fictions," complete with the management of space in such a way that the fictions prevail intact and that oppositional stories remain buried. For the purposes of demonstrable racist harm, it will never suffice

to engage in a strictly information-based investigation, for it can never be proven within such a paradigm that Africville was destroyed because a black presence was disdained.

The legal, social, and historical logic of "relocation" tells us that the city's actions were unfortunate but necessary, humanitarian, compassionate, non-racist, integrative, progressive, and, perhaps above all, innocent. A conceptual analysis of the regulation of space over time helps us look beyond this, perhaps because it asks as many questions as it answers: Why was industrial development not carried out? Why was "empty" recreational space created instead? Why didn't this take place in a white neighbourhood? Why is there no dump in the city's prosperous south end? Why does the city still speak of "black areas" in derogatory ways? For it appears that the discourse of integration, never realized, is more a discourse of erasure from sight and site.

Africville's story does not begin in 1962; it does not even begin in 1862. It begins in slavery, in Preston, in the founding of Halifax and the nation, in the hunting of the Mi'kmaq by British settlers.[44] In short, our perceptions of what functions as "evidence" must shift to allow the building of a context of ongoing oppression that may inform the way such issues are approached in law, to re-examine common key assumptions about fairness and equity which, by design, will serve the case badly. Our framework must shift from one of innocence or pity to one of justice.

Legal decision making follows social histories that include poverty and racism. Such histories rely upon complex narratives of blackness that operate in the making of the slum. In turn, legal policy is producing further histories that perpetuate racist practice. These phenomena operate as threads knotted together; to remove any one would make the story of Africville qualitatively different. To discuss any one in isolation is to belittle and betray any attempt at truth or justice. In drawing continuities along a chain of evictions, burials, denials, and complicities through time, their logical sequence becomes evident: depriving the community of essential services;

defining the community as slum-like based on the conditions this deprivation promotes; dislocating both persons and space, claiming the inevitability of destruction; altering the space and redefining its purpose and use by opening a park; installing a monument to suggest a sense of reconciliation; suppressing the true story when it resurfaces, and legislating restrictions on protesters who resurrect it.

As I have tried to demonstrate, the legal moves inherent in Africville's history as a degenerate site become clearer when a spatial analysis is permitted to trace and broaden the scope of what are considered to be regulatory measures. If we want to resist the official story, we must insist that history be alive and visible, and look at Africville's destruction not as a segment of the past but as fabric in the history of the present.

Notes

1. G. Stephenson, *A Redevelopment Study of Halifax, Nova Scotia* (Halifax: Corporation of the City of Halifax, 1957), 27–8.
2. L. Johnson, "Occupying the Suburban Frontier: Accommodating Difference on Melbourne's Urban Fringe," in A. Blunt and G. Rose, eds, *Writing Women and Space: Colonial and Postcolonial Geographies* (New York: Guilford Press, 1994), 146.
3. For early historical information, I have relied on: Africville Genealogical Society, eds, *The Spirit of Africville* (Halifax: Formac, 1992); D.H. Clairmont and D.W. Magill, *Africville Relocation Report* (Halifax: Institute of Public Affairs, Dalhousie University, 1971); D.H. Clairmont and D.W. Magill, *Africville: The Life and Death of a Canadian Black Community*, 1st and 3rd edn (Toronto: McClelland and Stewart, 1974, 1999); F. Henry, *Forgotten Canadians: The Blacks of Nova Scotia* (Don Mills, ON: Longman Canada Limited, 1973).
4. For documentation of relocation, see Clairmont and Magill, *Africville*, and the Africville Genealogical Society, eds, *The Spirit of Africville*.
5. The letter of R.J. Britton, Director of Social Planning for the City of Halifax, to Halifax City Council can be found in "Letter to Halifax City: Re: Africville Genealogy Society," in the Halifax Public Library: Africville File, 28 October 1994. Housing purchase prices are listed in this letter. The amounts city council claims to have paid are seen as inaccurate by some Africville activists with whom I have spoken. There have been accusations of bribery, in which city officials are alleged to have offered residents suitcases of cash in exchange for their eviction. See J. Robson, "Last Africville Resident," *The Mail Star* (Halifax) 12 January 1970, 5.
6. David Goldberg, *Racist Culture* (Oxford: Blackwell, 1993), 191–2.
7. Henri Lefebvre, "The Production of Space (Extracts)," in N. Leach, ed., *Rethinking Architecture: A Reader in Cultural Theory* (London: Routledge, 1997), 140.
8. Barnor Hesse, "Black to Front and Black Again," in M. Keith and S. Pile, *Place and the Politics of Identity* (London: Routledge, 1993), 175.
9. Henri Lefebvre, "Reflections on the Politics of Space," *Antipode* 8 (1976): 31.
10. C.R. Saunders et al., "A Visit to Africville," in Africville Genealogical Society, eds, *The Spirit of Africville*, 33.
11. See Goldberg, *Racist Culture*, 7; David Sibley, "Racism and Settlement Policy: The State's Response to a Semi-Nomadic Minority," in P. Jackson, ed., *Race and Racism: Essays in Social Geography* (London: Allen and Unwin, 1987), 74; David Sibley, *Geographies of Exclusion* (London: Routledge, 1995); P. Stallybrass and A. White, *The Politics and Poetics of Transgression* (Ithaca: Cornell University Press, 1986); E. Said, *Culture and Imperialism* (New York: Vintage, 1993).
12. P. Marcuse, "Not Chaos, but Walls: Postmodernism and the Partitioned City," in S. Watson and K. Gibson, eds, *Postmodern Cities and Spaces* (Cambridge: Blackwell, 1995), 243.
13. Sherene Razack, "Race, Space and Prostitution," *Canadian Journal of Women and the Law* 10, 2 (1998): 338.
14. Reports of some bootlegging in Africville are cited in Clairmont and Magill, *Africville Relocation Report*.
15. David Sibley, *Outsiders in Urban Societies* (Oxford: Blackwell, 1981).
16. Samira Kawash, "The Homeless Body," *Public Culture*, 10 (1998), 319.
17. Goldberg, *Racist Culture*, 190.
18. Ibid., 198. See also K. Anderson, *Vancouver's Chinatown: Racial Discourse in Canada, 1875–1980* (Montreal: McGill-Queen's University Press, 1991).
19. Stephenson, *A Redevelopment Study of Halifax, Nova Scotia*. The Stephenson Report focuses most intensely on the downtown region of Halifax and what might be done about the poor and overcrowded living conditions of its residents, the majority of whom would have been white.
20. Ibid.
21. Sibley, *Outsiders in Urban Societies*.
22. C.R. Saunders, "Relocation and Its Aftermath: A Journey Behind the Headlines," in Africville Genealogical Society et al., eds., *Africville: A Spirit that Lives On* (Halifax: The Art Gallery, Mount Saint Vincent University, 1989), 17.
23. Many references to the city's intended desegregation are cited in Clairmont and Magill, *Africville Relocation Report*, and Clairmont and Magill, *Africville: The Life and Death of a Canadian Black Community*; see also Britton,

"Letter to Halifax City: Re: Africville Genealogy Society," note 5 above.

24. R. Simon, "The Touch of the Past: The Pedagogical Significance of a Transactional Sphere of Public Memory," in P. Trifonas, ed., *Revolutionary Pedagogies: Cultural Politics, Education, and the Discourse of Theory* (New York: Routledge, 2000), 61.

25. Goldberg, *Racist Culture*, 204.

26. Sherene Razack, "Gendered Racial Violence and Spatialized Justice: The Murder of Pamela George," in Sherene Razack, ed., *Race, Space, and the Law: Unmapping a White Settler Society* (Toronto: Between the Lines, 2002).

27. Sherene Razack, *Looking White People in the Eye: Gender, Race and Culture in Courtrooms and Classrooms* (Toronto: University of Toronto Press, 1998), 40.

28. Britton, "Letter to Halifax City: Re: Africville Genealogy Society," note 5 above.

29. Ibid.

30. R. Thompson Ford, "The Boundaries of Race: Political Geography in Legal Analysis," *Harvard Law Review* 107 (1994), 1843.

31. Goldberg, *Racist Culture*.

32. Clairmont and Magill, *Africville Relocation Report*.

33. Goldberg, *Racist Culture*, 204–5.

34. D. Harvey, *Justice, Nature and the Geography of Difference* (Cambridge: Blackwell, 1996).

35. Kathleen Kirby, "Re: Mapping Subjectivity: Cartographic Vision and the Limits of Politics," in N. Duncan, ed., *Bodyspace: Destabilizing Geographies of Gender and Sexuality* (London: Routledge, 1996), 45.

36. L. MacLean, "Seaview Officially Opens," *The Mail Star* (Halifax), 24 June 1985, 1.

37. Jane Jacobs, "Resisting Reconciliation: The Secret Geographies of (Post)colonial Australia," in S. Pile. and M. Keith, eds, *Geographies of Resistance* (London: Routledge, 1997), 206–8.

38. Lefebvre, "The Production of Space Extracts," 140.

39. M. Lightstone, "Africville Showdown Brewing," *The Halifax Daily News*, 12 February 1995.

40. C. MacKeen, "City Responds to Protest over Seaview Park Land," *The Halifax Chronicle-Herald*, 12 May 1995.

41. T.L. Paynter, "City Gives Carverys the Boot," *North End News*, 24 March 1995; M. Lightstone, "Mayor: 'No Racism in This,'" *The Halifax Daily News*, 25 March 1995; C. McKeen, "Get Out, Protesters Warned," *The Halifax Chronicle-Herald*, 17 May 1995, A1.

42. Charles Saunders, "Scenes from Africville Reunion," *Halifax Daily News*, 8 August 1999, 20.

43. Sibley, *Geographies of Exclusion*.

44. See Bonita Lawrence, "'Real' Indians and Others: Mixed-Race Urban Native People, the Indian Act, and the Rebuilding of Indigenous Nations" (PhD diss., Ontario Institute of Studies in Education, University of Toronto, 1999).

Questions for Critical Thought

1. How was the "ongoing eviction, suppression and denial" of Africville in Halifax legitimized by the dominant white society? How did the members of this group avoid an admission of racism? Who benefited from this "innocence"?

2. Why does Nelson argue that the 1988 monument and park at the former Africville site was simply a gesture of "reconciliation"? Why is she critical of this gesture? What do you think the Canadian and Nova Scotian governments should do to commemorate this community?

3. Why were the personal experiences of exclusion and injustice of the residents of Africville never heard during the destruction of their homes and neighbourhood? What do you predict would have happened to Africville if the black residents there had been able to express their views?

4. The razing of Africville is not an isolated event in Canadian history. Are you aware of similar events that have occurred in your local communities? How have these events been commemorated? If they have not been commemorated, can you explain why not?

Decolonizing Sex Work: Developing an Intersectional Indigenous Approach

Sarah Hunt

In the early 1990s, I attended my first Valentine's Day Memorial March for women who had gone missing from, or been murdered in, Vancouver's Downtown Eastside. There, violence had come to be expected, and police were slow to respond to the deaths and disappearances of female residents (Cameron 2010). The community's proud history as the home of vibrant immigrant populations and the site of diverse social justice and arts movements is often overshadowed by its current concentration of visible street-level drug use, poverty, and sex work. As a young mixed-blood **Kwakwaka'wakw** woman, I was familiar with the struggle to get attention from police and the media about the violence in our communities. This was not unique to the Downtown Eastside but was prevalent, in rural and urban on-reserve and **off-reserve First Nations communities**. In my late teens, my passion for breaking the silence about intergenerational violence and abuse was fuelled by the writing of **Indigenous** women that I had been introduced to in university women's studies classes (Campbell 1973; Chrystos 1988, 1995; Allen 1992; Brant 1994; Acoose 1995; Dumont 1996; Maracle 1996).[1] But that Memorial March made the silences even clearer for me.

Before the march began, as I listened to elders and families speak about their lost loved ones, I scanned the lists of names that lined the painted banners. I stopped when I read the name Sheila Hunt. Until then, the missing women had been members of a broader community, both Indigenous and non-Indigenous—women who were marked as "outsider" by a society that shuns sex workers, substance users, the poor, and the homeless, among many others. But this stopped my heart. It suddenly

occurred to me that if I were related to this woman, or any of the other missing women, I might never hear about her life because of the shame and silence in our communities. Women and girls who leave smaller communities to go to the city and end up on the streets of the Downtown Eastside are often not talked about. They, like those of us who break the silence about abuse or who dare to leave a violent relationship, are often pushed away rather than being supported. At times, it feels that the shame has deeper roots than the love. From that day on, this added layer of silence informed my work and became the measuring stick for my ethics and accountability.

Soon after the march that year, I began looking for research on the overrepresentation of Indigenous women in the sex trade. Surprisingly, I found that very little work had been done in Canada, at least the sort of work that made it into written form, such as research, scholarly writing, or community publications. Due to this lack of research and publication, I became inspired to write my honours thesis about the colonial stereotypes of Indigenous women that were integral to the colonial project. The same stereotypes that were used to justify keeping us confined to reserves, that barred us from cities, prohibited our spiritual practices, and took away our children, were alive and well in this ongoing invisibility in the Downtown Eastside. Since that time, I have been involved in community-based research, program development, and education on violence, sexual exploitation, and a range of other issues in Indigenous communities across British Columbia. And, since then, both nothing and everything have changed.

In recent years, increasing recognition has been given to the reality that large numbers of Indigenous women have gone missing from, or been found murdered in, communities across Canada. A national study reported that over 500 Indigenous women have been identified as missing or murdered, their cases largely remaining unsolved (NWAC 2010). Awareness about the national scale of this issue emerged only after the police identified a serial killer in Vancouver's Downtown Eastside and pressed charges for the deaths of 26 of the 67 women officially identified as missing from that community. The first trial focused on six of the cases, and the offender was convicted of second-degree murder. Today, many Canadians are aware of the missing women from Vancouver and the horrors some of them experienced at the hands of a serial killer. Although we know that not all were Indigenous, 39 of the 67 were (Pratt 2005). It has become commonplace for the image of the missing women to be invoked whenever violence against Indigenous women is mentioned, thus muddling the complexity of their lives. After years of community advocacy, the police have finally been forced to sit up and pay attention as the world looks on. But that's usually where the story ends: the missing women. What about the women who are still working in the sex trade today, right now, in cities and towns, on highways and street corners, in communities across Canada? And what is the relationship between violence targeted at **sex workers** in the Downtown Eastside and the broader racialized violence experienced by Indigenous women at a national level?

In order to have a view to the present and the future, as well as of the injustices of the past, this chapter argues for a shift in the way that sex work is talked about in Indigenous communities. It is based on the available literature and the insights I've gained from my work in this area, and it recommends a series of approaches that I believe provide a strong foundation for **decolonizing** our views about sex work; these include centring the voices, agency, freedom, and mobility of Indigenous sex workers.

Colonialism in Canada: Situating Sex Work in Relation to Colonial Violence

Diverse and distinct Indigenous groups have lived in what is now called North America since time immemorial. The cultural and political practices of Indigenous peoples prior to contact with Europeans, and their experiences since colonialism began, vary widely. Thus, there is no single history of **colonialism** in Canada—each Indigenous nation has its own cultural identity and set of practices, and its own engagement with the Canadian and provincial governments. However, some common colonial ideologies and practices have been imposed on Indigenous peoples through the formation of the Canadian state and its continued relationship with them.

The country of Canada officially formed in 1867, formalizing the claims that European settlers had been slowly making over the vast territories of Canada since first arriving in the fifteenth century. **Confederation** signalled the formal dismissal of Indigenous sovereignty and governance, which pre-dated contact with Europeans and continue to be practised in diverse ways to this day. In 1876, the federal government instituted the **Indian Act**, which established Canada as the paternal figure to Indigenous people, with the power to decide how the lives of "Indians" were to be lived (RCAP 1996). All aspects of their lives were covered in this act, including governance of Indian reserves and details of daily life in these communities, which were to be mediated by agents of the federal Department of Indian Affairs (Moss and Gardner-O'Toole 1991).

Although the Indian Act has been changed many times since then, it remains in effect today, shaping Indian bands, Indian status, and reserves. Other significant legal documents work in complex relationship with the Indian Act, including section 35(I) of the **1982 Constitution Act**, which recognizes and affirms the rights of Indigenous peoples as pre-existing the formation of Canada (see Borrows 2010). Indigenous people continue to navigate the relationship between Canadian and Indigenous law in broader efforts toward sovereignty and self-determination. However, as Coulthard (2007) has argued, Indigenous struggles to gain recognition and justice under Canadian law serve to reinforce the power of the colonial state, as the terms of recognition are always set by the state rather than within the terms of Indigenous nations. Thus, given that Canadian law provides the primary avenue for seeking justice for Indigenous people, some argue that this approach will always have limitations because of the colonial relationship between the state and Indigenous peoples. Although the **Assembly of First Nations** and some individual Indigenous leaders continue to work closely with the Canadian government, many Indigenous people are looking to self-affirmation, assertions of Indigenous sovereignty, and the resurgence of Indigenous legal and cultural traditions alongside (or instead of) greater recognition in Canadian law (Alfred 2005; Coulthard 2007; Corntassel 2008) under models of legal pluralism (Borrows 2010).

The Indian Act comprises colonial ideas about Indians, including racist and sexist stereotypes and ideologies, beginning with the beliefs that Indigenous people are inferior to Europeans and that women are inferior to men. For example, it legislated that only male **band members** could vote or hold office in band governance, which limited women's power in band politics until revisions were made to the act in 1951 (Peters 1998). Further, until 1985, when the act was again modified, Indian women lost their status if they married non-status men, whereas non-Indian women gained **Indian status** by marrying status men (*Indian Act, ss.* 20, 109–13). The repercussions are still felt today as many women and their children continue to be denied status due to administrative and legislative issues.

Ideas about Indigenous people, including Indigenous women's sexuality, existed in the colonial imagination prior to contact between Europeans and Indigenous people in Canada. Colonial agents in Europe imagined a world available for seizure, settlement, and development,

envisioning Indigenous people as savages who were in need of being saved from their heathen ways, either by force or surrender (Williams 1990). As Said (1978) has shown in his analysis of Orientalism, the European or dominant identity has been fabricated in relation to representations of racialized Others in order to construct **essentialized** difference between dominant and marginalized groups.[2] In the colonial imagination, Indigenous women were portrayed as sexually licentious savages or beasts of burden and were conflated with an imagined colonial landscape, which signified that it was open for settlement (Acoose 1995). Imagining Indigenous people as savage rendered them less than human, allowing settlers and colonizers to deny them rights and their humanity. Though colonial strategies changed over time and space, Indigenous people were often portrayed as inferior Others in need of being saved for their own good (Francis 1992).

At a material level, colonial ideologies in Canada came to be rendered real through law, violent acts of dispossession, and grounded and embodied colonialism. The Indian Act is one way that colonial ideologies became, quite literally, the law of the land. Colonial measures were justified partially through depicting Indigenous women as lewd and licentious, as colonial agents worked to legitimize the constraints placed on their activities and movements (Carter 1993). In some areas, this included a pass system in which Indigenous women must obtain permission from Indian Agents (federal employees) to leave their reserves (RCAP 1996). This 1885 measure, which kept Indigenous women away from cities, was justified by fears of white settlers and government agents that they would bring their supposed immorality to virtuous white women or end up working as prostitutes. The confinement of First Nations on Canadian reserves remained until about the 1950s, when Indigenous people began moving to urban areas in efforts to access resources and opportunities. The connection between First Nations people and reserves is determined by the Indian Act, which funnels resources and rights through bands and their reserve lands.

Violence and sex were also intertwined through colonialism and the Indian Act, as is evident in the widespread sexual and physical abuse in church-run **residential schools**.[3] Indeed, as Smith (2005, 12) writes, "The extent to which Native peoples are not seen as 'real' people in the larger colonial discourse indicates the success of sexual violence, among other racist and colonialist forces, in destroying the perceived humanity of Native peoples." In the early days of Canadian colonialism and settlement, Indigenous women were partners of white men, fulfilling a reproductive and familial role until the arrival of European women. However, the sexual availability of Indigenous women became seen as a threat when greater numbers of European women immigrated to Canada, and in 1921, the **House of Commons** considered a Criminal Code amendment that would make it an offence for any white man to have an "illicit connection" with an Indigenous woman (Carter 1993). Thus, ideas about Indigenous women were linked to the powerful technologies of the law, as "officials propagated an image of Aboriginal women as dissolute, as the bearers of sinister influences, to deflect criticism from government agents and policies" (ibid., 150).

The legacy of colonialism lives on, as poverty and unsettled land claims shape the lives of Indigenous people to this day, with First Nations band governance defined and overseen by Ottawa. Interpersonal violence is just one of the ongoing manifestations of Canada's colonial relationship with Indigenous people. Although they cannot replace experiential knowledge, statistics do shed light on these violent realities. In the 2004 **General Social Survey on Victimization**, 4 in 10 self-identified Aboriginal people aged 15 and over reported that they were victimized at least once in the past year (Brzozowski et al., 2006).[4] This proportion was well above the level of 2.8 out of 10 for non-Indigenous Canadians. In the same study, Aboriginal people were three times more likely than other Canadians to be victims of violent crime, specifically sexual assault, robbery, and physical assault; this trend was highest among people aged 15 to 34, which was 2.5 times higher than for other age groups. The 2009 General Social Survey found that Aboriginal women were three times more likely to be victims of violence than non-Indigenous women (Brennan 2011), with 13 per cent of Indigenous women reporting violence in the previous year. The mortality rate due to violence is three times higher for Indigenous women than for non-Indigenous women, a rate that rises to five times higher for the 25- to 44-year-old age group (Health Canada 2000).

Indigenous people have responded to the racist and sexist stereotypes and the realities of violence in our communities through writing, art, advocacy, and other acts of resistance. A number of Indigenous women writers have spoken back to the stereotypes of squaw, Indian princess, and sexually available brown woman, as well as the violence justified by these images of us (see Acoose 1995; Dumont 1996; Maracle 1996).

But has Indigenous women's refusal of these sexual stereotypes resulted in simultaneously distancing ourselves from women who are working in the sex trade? We need to examine the moralistic stance against sex work, and the connation of sex work with exploitation, to see how we have internalized both this stereotype and its opposite. Although resistance to degrading and dehumanizing stereotypes of Indigenous people is important, it is simultaneously essential to look at how our responses affect—or fail to affect—the material reality of violence. In discussions about colonial violence, Indigenous sex workers are often invoked as nameless, voiceless, placeless victims, in memory of past injustices. The remembering and calls for justice are important, but the conversation must not stop there. We need to move away from positioning ourselves as advocates for, and saviours of, some disempowered sister-Other and instead facilitate a process that centres the voices of sex workers themselves. Otherwise we risk reproducing the discourses of colonialism that constitute Indigenous women as without agency.

Bringing Them to Light: Emergence of a Discourse Related to the Missing Women

Jiwani and Young (2006) argue that historically entrenched stereotypes about women, indigeneity, and sex trade work confer multiple degenerate statuses to the missing women from Vancouver's Downtown Eastside and continue to situate them at the margins. They suggest that media representations of the missing women serve to naturalize particular women's susceptibility to violence, blaming the women themselves for the violence they encounter. Pratt (2005) similarly states that Indigenous women are rendered as outside the public life of cities and outside the realm of law and rights. Despite Indigenous people's overrepresentation among the missing women, the issue of indigeneity remained a sidenote in media coverage (Jiwani and Young 2006). As England (2004) contends, representations of Indigenous women in the Downtown Eastside oscillated between invisibility and hypervisibility: invisible as victims of violence and hypervisible as deviant bodies. In recent years, violence against Indigenous women has become more visible in mainstream media, yet little has changed. It can be argued that the violence itself has become hypervisible, but that it does not count as real violence, because Indigenous women are seen as less than human, as unworthy of response; violence is normalized and assumed to be part of the everydayness of Indigenous spaces. The violent reconstruction of Indigenous identities as inherently savage—more than racialized and sexualized, but categorically Other, within the broad discourse of Western identity—is rendered invisible through its naturalization.

Of course, violence against Indigenous sex workers is not unique to the Downtown Eastside of Vancouver. Indigenous women working in the sex trade have been murdered in Edmonton, Winnipeg, and other cities across Canada. The roots of this violence can be seen in Canadian newspapers from the nineteenth century, which indicate a widespread conflation of Indigenous woman and prostitute, and an accompanying belief that when Indigenous women encountered violence, they got what they deserved and were not worthy of police intervention (Carter 1993). These attitudes are alive today. As noted by the commissioner in the inquiry into the murder of Helen Betty Osbourne in The Pas, Manitoba, the violence of the offenders was justified by their assumptions that Aboriginal women are promiscuous and have no human value beyond the sexual gratification of men (Razack 2000). Razack contends that such assumptions also appear to be operating when police fail to respond to the disappearance of Aboriginal women, as their presumed involvement in prostitution is reason enough for inaction. Harris (1991) further notes that representations of Indigenous women are marked by strategic silences, which strip them of their agency and silence them as victims. Indeed, old colonial stereotypes are alive and well in the images of Indigenous women we see in the media and mainstream Canadian culture.

Knowledge of Sex Work Involvement: Gaps, Invisibility, and Silence

The hypervisibility of violent acts and the invisibility of sex workers themselves go hand in hand, contributing to the lack of sustained efforts to improve the quality of life for Indigenous people engaged in sex work. The lives and voices of Indigenous sex workers are obscured by discourses of victimization that, on the surface, aim to draw attention to marginalization and colonial violence but fail to provide a space for Indigenous sex workers to speak for themselves and define their own struggles.

Despite the increased awareness about violence against sex workers, we know little about the lives of Indigenous sex workers, which begs important questions: What does it mean that Indigenous people are overrepresented in the sex trade? What might a decolonizing analysis bring to discussions of sex work in Canada, beyond the polarization of debates around decriminalization and prohibition?

Anecdotal evidence from service providers and outreach workers indicates that Indigenous women are highly overrepresented in the street-level sex trade.[5] Although there are few studies on the topic, those that exist similarly indicate a high rate of Indigenous women's involvement. For example, Farley and Lynne (2005)—who take a **prohibitionist** stance against sex work—interviewed 100 street-based sex workers in Vancouver, a city where 1.7 per cent of the population is Indigenous, and found that 52 per cent of their participants were Indigenous. Another Vancouver study (Currie 2000) estimated that 70 per cent of street-level sex workers in the Downtown Eastside were Indigenous women. What is not clear, however, is how many Indigenous women work in other sectors of the trade, including the indoor industry.

Another significant gap in the research and literature is regarding sex work in rural areas, including reserve communities and smaller towns and cities. Research conducted in five rural communities in British Columbia found that formal and informal sex work was happening in private homes, cars, outside, and in motels, through exchanges of sex for transportation and accommodation, drugs and alcohol, and clothing and money (Justice Institute of British Columbia 2006). Study participants, who were mainly service providers, adults with a history of involvement in sex work, and youth, stated that the primary barrier to addressing the health and safety needs of sex workers was the inability of community leaders and politicians to admit that sex work was occurring in their communities.

Conflating Issues: Youth, Sexual Exploitation, and Human Trafficking

As I have argued elsewhere (Hunt 2010), Indigenous sex work has been conflated with sexual exploitation, domestic trafficking, intergenerational violence, and the disappearance or abduction of Indigenous girls and women. Interestingly, and problematically, girls and women are talked about together, as though they are a single category, which echoes colonial views of Indigenous people as children in need of paternalistic surveillance and control. Although some research, such as that by Kingsley and Mark (2000), themselves Indigenous women who identify as having been sexually exploited, has provided some insight into the needs of Indigenous young people who have been exploited, the same has not been done with adult sex workers. Many adult sex workers first became involved as youth, which undoubtedly has implications for their adult sex-working experiences; however, a nuanced exploration of this issue has yet to be initiated. Instead, children, youth, and women are conjoined as victims, and their varying degrees of agency and choice remain unexamined.

Many Indigenous women experience sexual violence, among other forms of violence, on a daily basis. Yet efforts to raise awareness about sexual violence have conflated sex work with other forms of victimization. As previously mentioned, my own work on this issue emerged from an awareness of the normalized violence faced by Indigenous children, youth, and adults, as well as the shame and silence associated with sexual abuse. Sex work is indeed situated within the broader context of colonial violence, but in the conflation of sexual violence and sex work, critical and nuanced discussions have been neglected.

In recent years, "**human trafficking**" has become a growing discourse among academics and other experts concerned with Indigenous girls and women (Sethi, 2007; Sikka 2009). In 2009, the Assembly of Manitoba Chiefs, which represents First Nations people in the province, initiated a human trafficking campaign focused on stopping the sexual exploitation of First Nations people. The campaign material indicates that approximately 400 children and youth are being sexually exploited on the streets of Winnipeg each year. Although the campaign groups women and children together as potential victims of trafficking, no information is provided regarding the context of adult sex work in Winnipeg generally or regarding the distinctions between situations for youth and adults specifically.

Supporting Sex Workers: Responses from Indigenous Organizations

Given the overrepresentation of Indigenous women in sex work, it is surprising that sex work remains a largely unexplored issue within Indigenous communities. It is also surprising that sex workers' rights organizations include little Indigenous representation. In both sex work advocacy and Indigenous movements, the voices and diverse experiences of Indigenous sex workers too often go unheard. Of the few Indigenous voices to have taken up the issue of Indigenous sex work, the ones most often listened to are those who position all sex workers as victims of colonial violence. For example, the Aboriginal Women's Action Network (AWAN) in Vancouver has taken a prohibitionist position, arguing that sex work is inherently violent and that greater legislation is needed to stop sexual demand for women's and children's bodies (Aboriginal Women's Action Network 2007). Further, it claims to speak on behalf of indigenous women from both urban and reserve communities across the country.

Across the country in Toronto, and in opposition to AWAN's prohibitionist stance, the Native Youth Sexual Health Network (NYSHN) and Maggie's: Toronto Sex Workers Action Project, Canada's oldest sex-worker-run organization, have partnered in an effort to support Indigenous sex workers through an Aboriginal Sex Worker Outreach and Education Project (see www.nativeyouthsexualhealth.com and http://maggiestoronto.ca). This is Canada's first program by and for Indigenous people that centres on a harm-reduction and sex workers' rights framework and is located in the broader struggle for Indigenous rights, self-determination, and

sovereignty (Maynard 2010; van der Meulen, Yee, and Durisin 2010). Indigenous organizations like the NYSHN are beginning the important work of centralizing the voices of Indigenous people in talking about issues of sexuality, sex work, and decolonizing our bodies. Sex workers are particularly vulnerable members of our communities, and we must act as allies by working with and alongside them, listening to their voices and responding to their needs. We must also assume that we, meaning Indigenous people and communities, necessarily comprise past and present sex workers, rather than furthering the gap between a perceived "us" and "them."

At a national level, the Native Women's Association of Canada (NWAC) has argued for decriminalizing sex workers themselves and criminalizing, instead, those who profit from their work, including johns and pimps, while taking a stance that prostitution is inherently exploitative—evidenced by their use of the term "sexual exploitation" rather than "sex work" or "prostitution" in a statement released during 2011 (Women's Coalition for the Abolition of Prostitution 2011). However, in 2011, NWAC passed a resolution at its annual general meeting in support of harm-reduction approaches that both support sex workers where they are at and recognize that violence is a result of **stigma** and discrimination rather than inherent to sex work itself, demonstrating a possible shift in its position (NWAC 2011). The final report from NWAC's Sisters in Spirit Initiative, a national study of more than a hundred pages focusing on the lives of missing and murdered Indigenous women and girls, dedicated only half a page to the issue of sex work, claiming that it was not a factor in these women's disappearances (NWAC 2010). The Assembly of First Nations (AFN)—the body that represents First Nations people at a national level, including constitutional issues with the federal government—has not concerned itself with sex work. Although this may be due, in part, to the issue of gendered disparity within the organization, as only one woman is presently serving on the 11-member AFN executive committee, even the AFN's Council of Women does not include sex work in the list of key issues that it addresses. It is important to note that efforts to address sex work generally assume that all sex workers are female and that those who "exploit" or profit from them are male, failing to deal with the involvement of Indigenous men, boys, **two-spirit**, and **transgender** people in the trade. As an Indigenous person, I argue that we need to examine what lies at the heart of our inability to support our community members engaged in sex work. Further, we must strengthen our capacity to include this issue among all the other issues of marginalization in our communities.

The rights of Indigenous sex workers will become visible only if we decolonize dominant conceptualizations of sex work and Indigenous women's position within its various sectors. As Indigenous people, we have long experienced being spoken for, misrepresented, and silenced by dominant discourses about Indians and Others. Why, then, are we continuing to reproduce these conceptualizations in our own communities? We must advance new frameworks for addressing violence, while at the same time we must undo colonial notions that Indigenous women lack the ability to make decisions for themselves. Further, we must reconcile the reality that Indigenous people continue to engage in sex work within the context of colonial violence in Canada. As a result of our inability to tackle these issues, Indigenous sex workers, their voices, and their humanity are rendered silent. The hypervisibility of the stereotypical sexualized and racialized victim stands in stark contrast to the invisibility and silence around sex work itself.

Decolonizing Sex Work: Recommended Approaches

In order to address the current and ongoing needs of Indigenous people in the sex trade, I suggest that we must begin by humanizing sex workers as part of the broader Indigenous movements of regeneration and reclamation of our rights. To this end, I recommend the following approaches, which draw on broad efforts to strengthen Indigenous communities rather than situating the struggle purely within discourses on violence against women. These approaches are intended as a starting place, as each community must develop its own specific strategies to deal with unique issues faced by sex workers local to that context.

Embracing Sex Workers as Members of Our Indigenous Communities

Yee (2009) argues that reducing stigma and humanizing sex workers must start within Indigenous communities. Focusing on traditional teachings, such as respect, acceptance, and the principle "all our relations," will begin to increase inclusion of sex workers in broader community healing and cultural practice. Indigenous leaders and organizations must look at their role in marginalizing the voices of sex workers and seriously consider the ways in which they can be embraced rather than shamed and silenced. Many Indigenous people have internalized the attitudes about our sexuality taught to us through residential schools and generations of dehumanization under the Indian Act. Indeed, it is difficult to untangle ideas about sexuality that have been, and continue to be, projected onto us from those that we ourselves believe. However, this deconstruction is a necessary part of decolonization. Movements to reclaim and remake Indigenous practices must include examinations of sexuality on both individual and collective levels. Talking openly about sexuality and instilling a sense of pride and empowerment in ourselves and our children are integral to decolonizing the bodies of all Indigenous people, including sex workers of all genders. The inclusion of sex workers in broader **Indigenous revitalization** and self-determination movements is integral to the recommendations that follow.

Meeting Sex Workers' Basic Needs

Many Indigenous sex workers are concentrated in street-level work where they may have fewer resources and lower quality of life than their counterparts in other sectors. Poverty, homelessness, addiction, violence, intergenerational abuse, and other vulnerabilities that are rooted in our colonialist history must be addressed in an effort to improve the lives of Indigenous sex workers. Poor quality of life is prevalent in many Indigenous communities, which can contribute to the level of choice Indigenous people can exercise about whether or not to engage in sex work. This is not only an urban reality. For example, people in northern and isolated communities who lack transportation may exchange sex for a ride into a nearby town. Some argue that these conditions have led Indigenous women—as well as men and transgender people—to enter sex work without a "real choice." Although we must focus on the inequities that put Indigenous women in positions where trading sex becomes one of only a few options, we must simultaneously acknowledge the agency of Indigenous people. Indeed, addressing the basic needs of sex workers, and all Indigenous people, must be at the centre of any approach to decolonizing sex work.

Multiplicity of Indigenous Cultural Practices and Beliefs

Looking to Indigenous teachings, we must work within our own communities to determine the best ways to support people in the sex trade. This means accepting a multiplicity of approaches based on relationships among people, communities, and traditions rather than creating one "right" way forward.

Indigenous people have always had their own unique traditions and localized strategies, which have been more effective and meaningful in speaking to local inequities than mainstream or government-imposed strategies. The challenge here is that some Indigenous people find their community leaders to be disapproving of efforts to support sex workers. Shifting the power in our communities might mean not including official leadership (such as the chief and council) in the dialogue and, instead, starting a dialogue among unpaid supporters, natural helpers, elders, and others. This work entails identifying individuals who are willing to listen to the needs and experiences of sex workers and who can act as their allies and advocates. If possible, distinct cultural teachings and principles should be identified by elders and healers to guide local efforts to discuss sex work in a meaningful and respectful way. We can strive to be guided by our own intellectual traditions, which are embedded in Indigenous oral traditions: "Understanding who we are as Indigenous peoples, and the ways of thinking that make us Indigenous, ought to provide the foundation for how we learn to navigate our way in the dominant culture" (Turner 2004, 66).

Supporting a Rights-Based Approach

Indigenous people have a complex relationship to international human rights discourses because these have been defined and determined by powerful state actors rather than being based on Indigenous world views and principles. However, international human rights provide broad standards that are useful in advocating for a baseline set of conditions to which each individual is entitled. These basic human rights include the right to be free from violence, forced labour, and child abuse, as well as the right to freedom of mobility. This means that individuals who are forced into sex work have the right to protection and assistance in exiting from it. It also means that those who choose sex work have the right to protection from violence. These state-guaranteed protections are clearly not being upheld in many jurisdictions. Indigenous communities may also have their own concept of rights, which can be incorporated into broader developments of a **rights-based approach**.

Acknowledging Agency and Voice

Currently, depictions of Indigenous sex workers as helpless victims contribute to a social context in which many of them are denied agency and voice, yet agency and voice are imperative in rehumanizing people who work in the sex trade. Agency involves the ability to make decisions for yourself, to be considered as a person with choices rather than having those choices determined for you by another individual or state actor. Indigenous views of agency can be quite different from European or Canadian concepts. For example, some Indigenous traditions recognize that all living things have an inherent agentic ability, including rocks, the land, trees, and animals. These Indigenous conceptions of agency are being fostered in revitalization movements and must include recognition of the agency of all members of our communities, including sex workers. Listening to the voices, experiences, and needs of sex workers requires allies to step back and unlearn the stereotypes and assumptions we carry. The voices of sex workers must be at the centre of efforts to improve safety, increase choice and agency, and humanize their experiences within the context of our communities and families.

Supporting Freedom of Mobility

In an effort to reduce violence against women in broader society as well as in Indigenous communities, women are often told to stay home, not wear provocative clothing, keep out of trouble, and not put themselves in dangerous positions (Lonsway and Fitzgerald 1994; Canadian Resource Centre for Victims of Crime 2009; Patterson 2011). This rhetoric serves to blame women for the violence they endure. Restricting Indigenous people's mobility has also been a central component of colonialism, through the creation of reserves,

mandatory residential schools, and efforts to restrict land and resource use. The rights of Indigenous peoples have been depicted as fixed in the past, at the point of contact with settlers, and any changes in our traditions have been seen as moves toward inauthenticity. **Anishinabek** legal scholar Borrows (2009) argues that mobility is a fundamental aspect of asserting our rights as Indigenous people. Portrayals of Indigenous peoples as nomadic or less attached to land and territory (due to their concepts of property ownership and land use) have been part of denying their rights to their lands. Recognition of the right to mobility includes individual and collective rights to resist forced relocation, such as has been the case for some First Nations in Canada, as well as the right to move freely. It is in this spirit of asserting Indigenous mobility that sex workers must be encouraged and supported in moving between and within community spaces. This may include efforts to ensure equal access to health care, ceremonial spaces, and family gatherings in urban and rural areas, as well as safe movement between and among rural and urban communities.

Controlling Our Own Bodies

As discussed above, Indigenous women's bodies have been violated through colonization. This has involved the control of our bodies by the state and by a number of other powerful decision makers who think they know what is best for us. The Canadian government has used various means to control Indigenous bodies, including forced sterilization for some residential school students (Haig-Brown 1988; Chrisjohn, Young, and Maraun 2006). Those who want to prohibit and outlaw sex work are part of a movement to control the bodies of sex workers, which I see as a continuation of our colonial legacy. As with all Indigenous people, sex workers must be free to make decisions about their own bodies, including making money through sexual acts.

Community Change, beyond Legal Response

Indigenous people know that we cannot rely on the Canadian legal system to protect our communities and ourselves. The Canadian nation-state was accomplished through the establishment of the Canadian legal system, which wholeheartedly ignored Indigenous law and sovereignty. Law, regarded by the West as an instrument of civilization, was also the West's most vital and effective instrument of empire during its colonization of Indigenous peoples (Williams 1990). Fighting for recognition and protection solely through Canadian law is inherently limited given the colonial history and ongoing power of law. Debates around decriminalization and prohibition are focused on a legal system that is inherently oppressive to Indigenous people, as the dismissal of Indigenous sovereignty and Indigenous law depends upon the perpetuation of "the myth of inferiority" (Borrows 2010, 17) of Indigenous peoples and their failure to count as legitimate subjects. Laws against murder and violence fail to prevent the death and violation of Indigenous people of all ages and genders because we are not valued within the dominant culture that created and maintains the legal system. Although decriminalization may have an impact on the ability of sex workers to seek police protection, Indigenous women's relationship with Canadian law will continue to frame their relationship to justice. Therefore, decolonizing sex work must go beyond debates about decriminalization, as legal responses can go only so far in providing justice and safety for Indigenous sex workers.

Conclusion

My motivation and inspiration for this work is twofold: first, the steadfast resistance and memory of the determination of my ancestors, who have gone before me; and second, the strength, health, and brilliance of the generations yet to come. We need to look forward and back simultaneously, walking and speaking in both memory and anticipation of the lives yet to be lived. The voices of sex workers must be heard in efforts to improve their safety and reduce their vulnerability. Both Indigenous and non-Indigenous allies must look into their own hearts and ask themselves how their views and experiences might affect their feelings about sex work and their ability to be effective allies.

Twenty years ago, when I attended that Women's Memorial March on Valentine's Day in Vancouver's Downtown Eastside, community members were struggling to get the media, justice officials, and the general public to acknowledge systemic violence against women. And though today the dominant image of the Downtown Eastside is that of an Indigenous sex worker, current media and police attention has not translated into changes in the lives of Indigenous people in the sex trade.

Indeed, Indigenous sex workers' lives remain largely invisible, and many issues remain underexplored: sex work in rural communities and on reserves must be acknowledged and better understood; the role of reserve geographies and power relations inherent in band governance should be considered in connection with sex work in these communities; and efforts should be made to assess the ability of service providers to meet Indigenous sex workers' needs and to better integrate Indigenous perspectives and analyses of colonialism in front-line organizations. Further, intergenerational involvement in sex work will affect our future generations, and we must consider the implications for all aspects of community growth and revitalization. On a broad level, we must seek to better understand how issues of housing, poverty, trauma, and systematic racism/sexism/**homophobia**/colonialism shape the choices facing sex workers and their ability to assert individual agency. Measures must be taken to improve safety for all Indigenous people, but particularly those who are at heightened risk of violence, such as sex workers, children, youth, women, and two-spirit people. The links between interpersonal violence and systemic colonial violence, both ideological and material, must be examined in relation to sex work. Additionally, the voices and experiences of sex workers must be recognized along with their particular histories, which could include victimization (such as childhood sexual abuse), while respecting their decisions, agency, and resilience. We have a long way to go in reconfiguring approaches that increase safety in the lives of Indigenous sex workers. Let's make sure to put the voices, needs, and rights of sex workers themselves at the centre of this movement.

Notes

1. From first contact with Europeans to the present day, the English language has contained many ever-changing names for us, including Indigenous, Aboriginal, Native, First Nations, and Indian. In recent years, critical Indigenous scholars in Canada and abroad have begun using the term *Indigenous* rather than *Aboriginal* when referring to the broad grouping of First Nations (government-designated status Indians), non-status, Métis, and Inuit peoples of Canada, as well as for first peoples internationally. The use of *Aboriginal* and *Indian*, neither of which were created by Indigenous people ourselves, was perpetuated by the state. As a Kwakwaka'wakw scholar, I align my work with that of other Indigenous people who wish to link the local experiences of first peoples in Canada with others around the world, asserting the shared primacy of our relationship to the lands of our ancestors as well as the international quality of our political movements. I primarily use the term *Indigenous* in this chapter but also employ *First Nations* to talk specifically about federally recognized Indian bands and status Indians.

2. Said critiques Orientalism as a constellation of false assumptions underlying Western attitudes toward racialized Others, particularly Eastern peoples. He argues that racist images of Others are rooted in Eurocentric prejudice and have served as an implicit justification for European imperialism and colonialism.

3. Attendance at these federally mandated schools was optional at first, but a 1920 revision to the Indian Act made it a requirement for all status Indian children. The purpose of the schools was to assimilate Indigenous children into white society, in efforts to get rid of "the Indian problem" (Haig-Brown 1988).

4. *Aboriginal* is the term used in this government research, meaning individuals who self-identify as having First Nations, Métis, or Inuit ancestry.

5. Indigenous men, transgender, and two-spirit people are also present in street-level work, but, again, the numbers are unclear, and little research has been done in this area.

References

Aboriginal Women's Action Network. 2007. Statement opposing legalized prostitution and total decriminalization of prostitution. 6 December.

Acoose, J. 1995. *Iskwewak-Kah 'Ki Yaw Ni Wahkomakanak: Neither Indian princesses nor easy squaws.* Toronto: Women's Press.

Alfred, T. 2005. *Wasáse: Indigenous Pathways of Action and Freedom.* Peterborough, ON: Broadview Press.

Allen, P.G. 1992. *Sacred Hoop: Recovering the Feminine in American Indian Traditions.* 2nd edn. Boston: Beacon Press.

Borrows, J. 2009. "Physical Philosophy: Mobility and the Future of Indigenous Rights." In *Indigenous Peoples and the Law: Comparative and Critical Perspectives,* ed. B. Richardson, I. Shin, and K. McNeil, 403–20. Portland: Hart.

———. 2010. *Canada's Indigenous Constitution.* Toronto: University of Toronto Press.

Brant, B. 1994. *Writing as Witness: Essays and Talk.* Toronto: Women's Press.

Brennan, S. 2011. Violent Victimization of Aboriginal Women in the Canadian Provinces, 2009. *Juristat* (Statistics Canada, Canadian Centre for Justice Statistics) 85-002-X (17 May). www.statcan.gc.ca/pub/85-002-x/2011001/article/11439-eng.pdf.

Brzozowski, J.A., A. Taylor-Butts, and S. Johnson. 2006. Victimization and Offending among the Aboriginal Population in Canada. *Juristat* (Statistics Canada, Canadian Centre for Justice Statistics) 85-002-XIE 26, 3.

Cameron, S. 2010. *On the Farm: Robert William Pickton and the Tragic Story of Vancouver's Missing Women.* Toronto: Knopf Canada.

Campbell, M. 1973. *Half-breed.* Toronto: McClelland and Stewart.

Canadian Resource Centre for Victims of Crime. 2009. *Victim Blaming.* Canadian Resource Centre for Victims of Crime, Ottawa. http://crcvc.ca/docs/victim_blaming.pdf.

Carter, S. 1993. "Categories and Terrains of Exclusion: Constructing the 'Indian Woman' in the Early

Settlement Era in Western Canada." *Great Plains Quarterly* 13: 147–61.

Chrisjohn, R.D., S.L. Young, and M. Maraun. 2006. *The Circle Game: Shadows and Substance in the Indian Residential School Experience In Canada.* Penticton: Theytus Books.

Chrystos. 1988. *Not Vanishing.* Vancouver: Press Gang.

———. 1995. *Fire Power.* Vancouver: Press Gang.

Corntassel, J. 2008. "Toward Sustainable Self-Determination: Rethinking the Contemporary Indigenous-Rights Discourse." *Alternatives* 33: 105–32.

Coulthard, G. 2007. "Subjects of Empire: Indigenous Peoples and the 'Politics of Recognition' in Canada." *Contemporary Political Theory* 6, 4: 437–60.

Currie, S. 2000. *Assessing the Violence against Street Involved Women in the Downtown Eastside/Strathcona Community.* Report for the Ministry of Women's Equality, Province of British Columbia.

Dumont, M. 1996. *A Really Good Brown Girl.* London: Brick Books.

England, J. 2004. "Disciplining Subjectivity and Space: Representation, Film and Its Material Effects." *Antipode* 36, 2: 295–321.

Farley, M., and J. Lynne. 2005. "Prostitution of Indigenous Women: Sex Inequality and the Colonization of Canada's First Nations Women." *Fourth World Journal* 6, 1: 1–29.

Francis, D. 1992. *The Imaginary Indian: The Image of the Indian in Canadian Culture.* Vancouver: Arsenal Pulp Press.

Haig-Brown, C. 1988. *Resistance and Renewal: Surviving the Indian Residential School.* Vancouver: Tillicum Library.

Harris, D.W. 1991. "Colonizing Mohawk Women: Representations of Women in the Mainstream Media." *Resources for Feminist Research* 20, 1–2: 15–20.

Health Canada, 2000. *The Health of Aboriginal Women.* Ottawa: Health Canada, Women's Health Bureau.

Hunt, S. 2010. "Colonial Roots, Contemporary Risk Factors: A Cautionary Exploration of the Domestic Trafficking of Aboriginal Women and Girls in British Columbia, Canada." *Alliance News* 33: 27–31.

Indian Act [Repealed], R.S.C. 1985, c. 32 (1st Supp.), ss. 20, 109–13.

Jiwani, Y., and M.L. Young. 2006. "Missing and Murdered Women: Reproducing Marginality in News Discourse." *Canadian Journal of Communication* 31, 4: 895–917.

Justice Institute of British Columbia. 2006. *Violence in the Lives of Sexually Exploited Youth and Adult Sex Workers in BC: Research Report.* New Westminster: Justice Institute of BC, Centre for Leadership and Community Learning.

Kingsley, C., and M. Mark. 2000. *Sacred Lives: Canadian Aboriginal Children and Youth Speak Out about Sexual Exploitation.* Vancouver: Save the Children Canada.

Lonsway, K.A., and L.F. Fitzgerald. 1994. "Rape Myths: In Review." *Psychology of Women Quarterly* 18: 133–64.

Maracle, L. 1996. *I Am Woman: A Native Perspective on Sociology and Feminism.* Vancouver: Press Gang.

Maynard, R. 2010. "Sex Work, Migration and Anti-Trafficking: Interviews with Nandita Sharma and Jessica Yee." *Briar Patch* 39, 4: 28–31.

Moss, W., and E. Gardner-O'Toole. 1991. *Aboriginal People: History of Discriminatory Laws.* BP-175E. Ottawa: Parliamentary Research Branch, Library of Parliament.

Native Women's Association of Canada (NWAC). 2010. *What Their Stories Tell Us: Research Findings from the Sisters in Spirit Initiative.* Ottawa: Native Women's Association of Canada.

———. 2011. AGM sex trade resolution "In support of Aboriginal Sex Workers Harm Reduction," 08-05-2011. E-mailed statement.

Patterson, J. 2011. "Sex Assault Still Somehow Women's Fault." *Victoria Times Colonist* 1 April. www2.canada .com/victoriatimecolonist/.

Peters, E.J. 1998. "Subversive Spaces: First Nations Women and the City." *Environment and Planning D: Society and Space* 16: 665–85.

Pratt, G. 2005. "Abandoned Women and Spaces of the Exception." *Antipode* 37, 5: 1053–78.

Razack, S. 2000. "Gendered Racial Violence and Specialized Justice: The Murder of Pamela George." *Canadian Journal of Law and Society* 15, 2: 91–130.

Royal Commission on Aboriginal Peoples (RCAP). 1996. *Report of the Royal Commission on Aboriginal Peoples.* Vol. 4, *Perspectives and Realities.* Ottawa: Canada Communication Group.

Said, E. 1978. *Orientalism.* New York: Vintage Books.

Sethi, A. 2007. "Domestic Sex Trafficking of Aboriginal Girls in Canada: Issues and implications." *First Peoples Child and Family Review* 3, 3: 57–71.

Sikka, A. 2009. *Trafficking of Aboriginal Women and Girls in Canada.* Aboriginal Policy Research Series. Institute on Governance.

Smith, A. 2005. *Conquest: Sexual Violence and American Indian Genocide.* Cambridge: South End Press.

Turner, D. 2004. "Perceiving the World Differently." In *Intercultural Dispute Resolution in Aboriginal Contexts,* ed. C. Bell and D. Kahane, 57–69. Vancouver: UBC Press.

van der Meulen, E., J. Yee, and E. Durisin. 2010. "Violence against Indigenous Sex Workers: Combatting the Effects of Criminalization and Colonialism in Canada." *Research for Sex Work* 12: 35–37.

Williams, R. 1990. *The American Indian in Western Legal Thought: The Discourses of Conquest.* New York: Oxford University Press.

Women's Coalition for the Abolition of Prostitution. 2011. "Prostitution Poses a Fundamental Threat to Women's Security. The Solution: Decriminalize Women and Criminalize the Demand." News release. Toronto, 16 June. http://vancouver.mediacoop.ca/.

Yee, J. 2009. "Supporting Aboriginal Sex Workers' Struggles." *Canadian Dimension* 43, 1: 45–47.

Questions for Critical Thought

1. What is colonialism? How has this form of colonization affected former and cur-
    rent generations of Canadians' political, social, and cultural attitudes about the
    First Nations people of Canada?
2. What role(s) has patriarchy played in promoting and discouraging women from
    working in the sex trade industry? What political and social positions do different
    feminist groups take on sex work?
3. What is the "stigma" that is associated with women and men who are sex workers?
    How does this stigma reproduce social inequality in Canadian society?
4. Why is it important that the voices of Indigenous women such as Sarah Hunt are
    acknowledged by various sectors of Canadian society? What are the eight ways
    that she proposes to decolonize sex work?
5. How can non-Indigenous people contest the politics of exclusion that marginalize
    Indigenous women and men? How can we raise awareness in our communities
    about the lack of information about missing and murdered Aboriginal women?

The Sharia Debate in Ontario: Gender, Islam, and Representations of Muslim Women's Agency

....*Anna Korteweg*

In late 2003 the Canadian media reported that the Islamic Institute of Civil Justice would start offering arbitration in family disputes in accordance with both Islamic legal principles and Ontario's Arbitration Act of 1991. A vociferous two-year debate ensued on the introduction of **"Sharia law"** in Ontario. This article analyzes representations of Muslim women's agency that came to the fore in this debate by examining reports in three Canadian newspapers. The debate demonstrated two notions of agency. The predominant perspective conceptualized Muslim women's agency as their ability to resist domination, tying secularization to agency. A second strain of the debate portrayed agency as embedded in intersecting social forces of domination and subordination. The first perspective homogenized diverse Muslim communities, fostering the **gendered racialization** of these communities. Understanding agency as embedded, by contrast, enabled conceptualizations of Muslim women as agentic religious subjects.

In late 2003, a small Muslim organization in Ontario, Canada, proposed to offer arbitration for private business and family matters in accordance with Islamic legal principles and provincial and federal law. An intense debate on the introduction of Sharia law in Ontario erupted. The debate ended in early 2006, when the provincial premier amended the Ontario Arbitration Act to disallow all forms of religious arbitration. This article analyzes divergent perceptions of immigrant Muslim women's agency that were brought to light during the debate.

Feminist critiques of Western understandings of women's agency focus on false universalisms and the damage their unthinking application can do to the political struggles of women in the global

South (Bulbeck 1998; Mohanty 2003; Tripp 2006). Similar universalisms structure public debates on gender equality that occur in the context of large scale immigration from the global South to the global North, particularly in relationship to Muslim immigrants (Abu-Lughod 2002; Korteweg 2006; Okin 1999). What are often conceptualized as geographically distinct cultural practices coincide as people from across the globe become neighbours in cities like Toronto, where, in 2006, 45.7 per cent of the population was foreign-born, most coming from Asia.[1] In such cities, the north/south divide, conditioned by unequal global capitalist development in a context of spatial separation, is transposed onto experientially far more intimate social-political contestations within what are now local communities of divergent origins, ethnicities, and migration statuses (Mohanty 2003). In these contexts, assumptions about agency rooted in Christian, but ostensibly secular, traditions (Mack 2003) are put into question.

The debate on Sharia-based arbitration reflected two divergent representations of agency. Dominant discourses saw Muslim (immigrant) women's agency as contingent upon their resistance to Islam. An alternate framing represented agency as embedded in religious (and other) contexts. As the theory of **embedded agency** would suggest, this latter framing facilitated more nuanced representations of Muslim women as both agentic and religious subjects. By contrast, seeing agency solely as resistance to gendered religious practices homogenized religious Muslims as a group. This homogenization enabled the gendered racialization of the very diverse Canadian Muslim immigrant communities and discounted the notion that Muslim women's capacity to act could be informed by religion.[2]

"Sharia in Ontario": Outline of a Debate

In late 2003, Syed Mumtaz Ali, a retired lawyer and scholar of Islamic jurisprudence, announced in the media that the Islamic Institute of Civil Justice (IICJ) would offer arbitration in family and business disputes in accordance with both Islamic legal principles and Ontario's Arbitration Act, 1991, which became law in 1992 (Boyd 2004, 4). Established in part to diminish a backlog in the courts, the Ontario Arbitration Act of 1991 allowed for religious, as well as non-religious, arbitration in private matters.[3] After the law came into effect in 1992, Jewish and Christian groups set up arbitration boards that ruled in accordance with their religious principles. All of these arbitrations were legally binding, as long as they did not violate existing Canadian law.

Within Islam, the term *Sharia* covers the general set of principles and moral obligations that structure religious Muslims' lives (Abou el Fadl 2004, 30–1; Rohe 2004). Sharia includes, but is not limited to, a set of laws that govern family matters, including custody, inheritance, and divorce. Islamic jurisprudence, or *fiqh*, is considered to be in the realm of people and is open to interpretation and change to some extent (Abou el Fadl 2004, 31). Historically, there are different schools of Islamic jurisprudence that can come to different conclusions on how family matters should be resolved (see also Emon 2006; Wadud 2005). Such variations were largely obscured in the debate that ensued upon IIJC's announcement; instead, the debate focused almost entirely on Muslim women's ability to safeguard their interests.

In response to the IIJC's announcement, Ontario Premier McGuinty asked Attorney General Michael Bryant and Sandra Pupatello, the minister responsible for women's issues, to investigate the issue. In June of 2004, they commissioned former Attorney General Marion Boyd to conduct a study on the feasibility of continuing to allow religious arbitration under the Arbitration Act of 1991. In her report, various interest groups expressed the fear that Muslim arbitration boards could undo the "many years of hard work, which have entrenched equality rights in Canada . . . to the detriment of women, children and other vulnerable people" (Boyd 2004, 3). These interest groups construed Muslim women's capacities as severely limited by Islam, and Islamic legal rules regarding family matters as inherently gender unequal (Boyd 2004). Nonetheless, in her report, Boyd argued that religious arbitration based on what she called "Islamic legal principles" was permitted under the Arbitration Act, and should continue to be allowed. At the same time, Boyd appealed to a society-wide obligation to ensure that women would be able to address unfair decisions in any type of arbitration. Her proposed amendments to the Arbitration Act focused on institutionalized oversight and education on the principles of religious arbitration and Canadian family law. Courts were directed to look at arbitral decisions in the aggregate to identify whether rulings contravened existing Canadian law. The education measures were to ensure that people would understand the legal ramifications of their decision to arbitrate, know their rights to appeal if they did not agree with the arbitral decision, and comprehend the relationship between religious law and Canadian law.

Rejecting Boyd's recommendations, McGuinty announced on Sunday, 11 September 2005, that he would put forth an amendment to ban all religious arbitration, including Christian and Jewish arbitration, under the Arbitration Act, to ensure that there would be "one law for all Ontarians." McGuinty's decision implied that only such a legal context could safeguard Muslim immigrant women's capacity to act.

Understanding Muslim Women's Agency

From a theoretical perspective, agency requires an underlying sense of self, as well as an ability to assess the impact of one's actions on future outcomes and the impact that past actions have had on present conditions (Emirbayer and Mische 1998; McNay 2000). The debates surrounding Sharia law did not address these facets of agency, but rather questioned Muslim immigrant women's capacity to act in a self-interested way. The notion of self-interested action calls

forth two understandings of agency: as a reaction against forces of domination, or as embedded in particular historic cultural, social, and economic contexts (Bulbeck 1998; see also Ahearn 2000; Mahmood 2001; McNay 2000).

In bringing the concept of embedded agency to feminist sociology, I draw on work by a number of feminist theorists from outside the field who argue that women's capacity to act is obscured when read only from their resistance to forces of domination (Ahearn 2000; Mack 2003; Mahmood 2001; McNay 2000; Mihelich and Storrs 2003; Ortner 1996, 2001). Agency is, of course, always informed by social contexts. The distinction here is between seeing agency solely as resistance, which captures actions that explicitly aim to undermine hegemony, and embedded agency, which captures practices that do not have this explicit aim, yet still reflect active engagement in shaping one's life. The notion of embedded agency allows for a richer sense of how practices of domination and subordination, such as those associated with religion, structure the subjectivity underlying the capacity to act (Mihelich and Storrs 2003). By seeing agency as potentially embedded in social forces like religion, which are typically construed as limiting agentic behaviour, the capacity to act is not contingent on adopting liberal "free will" and "free choice" approaches to subjectivity (see also Ahearn 2000; Mihelich and Storrs 2003; Ortner 2001).

Many of the debates on the integration of Muslim immigrants in the nation-states of the global North have focused on the ability of Muslim women to resist forces of domination and avoid the gendered subordination often seen as inherent in Islam. For instance, the continuing debates on the **hijab** often construe the wearing of the veil as a sign of limited agency and of the incompatibility between Islamic and Western values (Ahmed 1992; Alvi, Hoodfar, and McDonough 2003; Atasoy 2006; Bartkowski and Read 2003; Bloul 1998; Fournier and Yurdakul 2006; Killian 2003; MacLeod 1992). Discussions of forced marriage and **honour killing** similarly reinforce that Muslim women's capacity to act is severely constrained by their religion

(Kogacioglu 2004; Korteweg and Yurdakul 2008; Razack 2004). Public debates often frame these issues as indications of the ways in which Islam coincides with a particular form of patriarchy that severely circumscribes Muslim women's capacity to act (Abu-Lughod 2002; Razack 2004). In this process, Muslims also become ethnically "other" and often actors both within and outside Muslim communities ethnicize religion through appeals to women's proper role in the family, their bodily comportment, and so on (Bloul 1998; Korteweg 2006). By positioning women as objects, this process of **ethnicization** also supports notions of Muslim women's limited agency.

Yet the agency of religious Muslim women can also be understood in dramatically different ways. In her work on the Egyptian Islamic revival movement, Saba Mahmood (2001) argues that liberal theories of freedom are the result of locally specific historic trajectories, rather than the universal set of norms and values they purport to be. Mahmood argues against feminist theories, such as those articulated by Judith Butler (1993), in which agency is understood as the capacity to resist dominant understandings of right action. Approaches like Butler's link agency to resistance and liberal subjectivity to freedom or autonomy (see also Ahearn 2000; McNay 2000; Ortner 2001). Such a framework, Mahmood argues, can only understand women's active participation in an Islamic revival movement that seems to reinforce gender difference and attendant gender inequalities as either delusional or as somehow materially self-interested (Mahmood 2001; see also MacLeod 1992). Mahmood (2001) proposes a different reading in which women involved in this religious movement actively shape their desire through embodied practices linked to piety under Islam (veiling, modesty in clothing, the practice of shyness, etc.). She concludes that for these women, agency does not flow from freedom (or those parts of our lives in which we are free from constraints by others), but rather is formed in direct relationship to structures of subordination.

These embedding contexts extend beyond religious ones. For example, Rachel Bloul (1998, 1)

shows that the lives of Maghrebi immigrant women were informed by discourses of "engendering ethnicity" practised by both French and Maghrebi men, in which the wearing of the veil became a way to draw ethnic boundaries between majority French and minority Maghrebi society. Yet these processes also had an impact on Muslim women's agency; the capacity of Muslim men to influence the local political economy of their neighbourhoods increased women's labour force participation and extended the sphere in which (veiled) women could move (Bloul 1998). Similarly, North African women's responses to the French public debate regarding the headscarf show that these women occupied a variety of subject positions regarding when to wear the veil and that they interpreted the veil differently depending on the strength of their connection to majority French society (Killian 2003). Such findings imply that Muslim women's agency is shaped by local and national social, cultural, and political struggles that intersect with, but also move beyond, religion per se (see also Fournier and Yurdakul 2006). Furthermore, this agency is not (solely) informed by resistance, but directly shaped by these intersecting forces.

In sum, the literature implies the importance of identifying which conceptualizations of agency are mobilized in debates like those considered here. As I noted above, the legal arbitration process presupposes a capacity to act in one's self-interest, and the concerns voiced by various community groups centred on whether Muslim women had the **agentic capacity** to resist forces of domination that many believed inherent in Islamic legal practice. In what follows, I analyze newspaper articles to see whether this conceptualization of agency dominated in the debate and to what extent a conceptualization of agency as embedded held sway. To see how these conceptualizations in turn structure the contexts of women's agency, I pay attention to how divergent conceptualizations of agency fostered calls for different kinds of state intervention. Furthermore, I examine how conceptualizations of agency promoted visions of social groups as more or less different from majority society along ethnic and racial lines.

Methodology

To analyze how Muslim women's agency was conceptualized in the context of Canadian press coverage, I looked at three newspapers: the *Globe and Mail*, the *National Post*, and the *Toronto Star*. The *Globe and Mail* and the *National Post* are Canada's two nationally distributed papers. The *Globe and Mail* generally reflects the political centre of Canadian politics, while the *National Post* is a more neo-conservative paper. The *Toronto Star* is Toronto's leading local paper. It has the largest distribution of any paper in Canada, the Greater Toronto Area having the greatest population density in Canada. Reflecting the position of Toronto in Canadian politics, the *Star* tends to be politically to the left of the two national papers.

With the help of my research assistants, I created a database of articles by searching for the word "Sharia" and filtering out the articles that concerned foreign countries. The three newspapers published between 21 and 45 articles each in the period beginning in December 2003 with Syed Mumtaz Ali's announcement that he would introduce Islamic arbitration and ending with the cessation of religious arbitration altogether in February 2006, for a total of 108 articles. Roughly half of the articles are op-eds, editorials, comments, and opinion pieces. National, or sometimes international, news comprise the remainder (see Table 1).

Newspapers construct social problems as they selectively report on certain issues and not others and as they highlight some aspects of these issues and not others (Best 2002; Critcher 2003; Ferree 2003; McCarthy, McPhail, and Smith 1996; Smith et al. 2001; Spector and Kitsuse 1977). Recognizing this, I approached the data analysis in ways designed to uncover representations of agency reflected in arguments regarding the advisability of instituting Sharia-based tribunals. I quickly realized that a select group of people was treated as sources of authority on the topic in both news and opinion pieces. The debate was quite polarized, and members of the various Muslim communities were called on to comment on either the "for" or "against" side. I identified the actors who were quoted in more than one article or op-ed by coding both the news and editorial pieces and marking each article that contained a meaningful quote by a particular person, noting whether they argued for or against the institutionalization of Sharia-based tribunals (see Table 2). I also focused on the op-eds and editorials as another place where the issue was strategically framed and again counted how many writers or editorial boards made arguments for and against (see Table 3).

I then conducted a qualitative discourse analysis of the portrayals of Muslim women's agency that drove these arguments. In my presentation of these findings, I hone in on the voices of Muslim women and men who participated in the debate. Their assertions reflected the overall discursive representations of Muslim women's agency that structured the debate. Furthermore, the participation of Muslim women and men in the debate could itself be read as particular representations of agency, thus adding a layer of complexity to the analysis.

TABLE 1   Article distribution by newspaper

	Globe and Mail	National Post	Toronto Star	Total
News	25 (60%)	9 (43%)	22 (49%)	56 (52%)
Editorials	17 (40%)	12 (57%)	23 (51%)	52 (48%)
Total	**42 (100%)**	**21 (100%)**	**45 (100%)**	**108 (100%)**

TABLE 2   People quoted in The *Globe and Mail*, the *National Post*, and the *Toronto Star*

Quoted for	Number of articles	Quoted against	Number of articles
1. Syed Mumtaz Ali	16	1. Homa Arjomand	22
2. Mohammed Elmasry	7	2. Tarek Fatah	14
3. Mubin Shaikh	6	3. Alia Hogben	14
4. Anver Emon	4	4. June Callwood	7
5. Katherine Bullock	3	5. Fatima Houda-Pepin	4
6. Riad Saloojee	2	6. Sally Armstrong	3
7. Ali Hindy	2	7. Marilou McPhedran	3
8. Wahida Valiante	2	8. Ayaan Hirsi Ali	3
		9. Soheib Bencheikh	2
Total	**41**		**72**

TABLE 3   Editorials and opinion pieces for and against in the *Globe and Mail* (*GM*), the *National Post* (*NP*), and the *Toronto Star* (*TS*)

Editorials for	Number of editorials	Editorials against	Number of editorials
Editorial Board *GM*	5	3 regular columnists *GM*	6
3 guest columnists *GM*	3	Open letter to McGuinty *GM*	1
TS Editorial Board	4	5 regular columnists *TS*	6
1 regular columnist *TS*	5	5 guest columnists *TS*	5
2 guest columnists *TS*	2	4 regular columnists *NP*	4
Editorial Board *NP*	2	3 guest columnists *NP*	2
2 guest columnists *TS*	2		
Total	**23**		**24**

Representing Muslim Women's Agency

As in many debates about Islam and Western liberal values, gender (in)equality and presumptions of Muslim women's limited agency became a flashpoint for arguments against public recognition of Muslim religious practices (Abu-Lughod 2002; see also Okin 1999). Authors like Bloul (1998) show that both majority and minority men constitute ethnic difference by positioning Muslim women as objects. In the case of the Ontario Sharia debate, both self-identified secular and self-identified religious Muslim women, as well as men, actively participated in the debate. These participants both represented and articulated divergent understandings of agency.

The arguments against, put forth by Muslim women and men, were widely shared among the participants in the debate. The tabulations of Table 2 and Table 3 show that largely secular Muslim voices arguing against Sharia-based tribunals were joined by those from members of majority society, most of whom were women, and that these voices, quoted in a total of 72 articles, dominated in the debate. The voices arguing for the institution (with state oversight) of Sharia-based arbitration were less well represented in 42 articles and more narrowly confined to the Canadian religious Muslim communities, though the editorial boards of all three newspapers shared their views.

Privileging Agency of Resistance

Secular Muslim women, such as Homa Arjomand, Fatima Houda-Pepin, and Ayaan Hirsi Ali, occupied a prominent place in the debate (see Table 2). These three women contributed almost half of all quotations against the adoption of Sharia-based tribunals. Their participation in the debate could be read as an example of agency through resistance—they were often portrayed in the newspapers as Muslim women who, through their own experience, came to understand Islam as inhibiting agency. Newspaper accounts juxtaposed their active engagement in the public sphere with quotes in which these women highlighted the detrimental effects of Islam on Muslim women's capacity to act.

Often the newspaper articles that quoted them started with a portrayal of Islamic law as riddled with injustice and (gendered) oppression. This line of argument took on multiple guises. For example, Fatima Houda-Pepin, a representative for the Liberal Party in Quebec's provincial parliament and a Muslim immigrant from Morocco, argued,

We've seen the sharia at work in Iran. . . . We've seen it at work in Afghanistan, with the odious Taliban regime, we've seen it in Sudan where the hands of hundreds of innocent people were cut off. We've seen it in Nigeria with attempts of stoning. . . . The list is very long. Is that what we want to import to Canada? (*NP* 11 March 2005)

This equation of Sharia-based tribunals with the worst examples of justice enacted under the guise of Islam was widespread among the arguments against arbitration. Opponents framed immigrants from non-Western societies as bringing practices that contravene the dominant norms of majority society. In such quotations, Houda-Pepin represented Muslim immigrants who rejected the importation of the norms and practices associated with Islam in non-Western countries. In so doing, Houda-Pepin exercised agency expressed through resistance to Islamic law and practice.

The link between gendered practices and Muslim women's agency came to the fore in discussions of how Sharia-based tribunals might work within Canada. Homa Arjomand, the most quoted person in the opposition, was one of the prime movers against the IICJ's proposal. The newspapers described Arjomand as a refugee from Iran who worked on women's rights issues there and saw her friends killed one by one. After a harrowing trip across the mountains from Iran into Turkey in the late 1980s, she ended up a refugee in Canada. When the Sharia proposal hit the newspapers, she started the International Campaign Against Sharia Law in Canada. In one article, Arjomand described how

she has counselled many Muslim women whose rights were abused during informal arbitration by Muslim leaders. In the case of one family who turned to their Markham, Ont., mosque for resolution of a dispute, the results were not positive for the wife and adolescent daughter. The woman of Pakistani origin, and her 15-year-old daughter were "returned" to Pakistan against their will, Ms. Arjomand said, and the daughter was placed in the custody of an uncle and preparations were made for an arranged marriage.

The father then married a 19-year-old woman and brought her to Canada. "Was the mother forced to leave the country? We don't know what really happened here," said Ms Arjomand. (*GM* 9 September 2004)

Arjomand's agency was here linked to her resistance, first to the Islamic regime in Iran, then to attempts to bring Islamic jurisprudence into the Canadian legal sphere. The juxtaposition between the descriptions of Arjomand and the Markham mother and daughter reinforced the link between Islam and limited agency, foreclosing representations of embedded agency.

Descriptions of abuses of power in Canadian Muslim communities' interpretations of Islamic jurisprudence became the bases for arguments that connected Islam directly to the oppression of women. In the resulting representation of women's relationship with Islam, the conceptualization of Muslim women's agency was implicitly or explicitly tied to secularism, privileging the modern but deeply Western subject whose agency is expressed through resistance (Bulbeck 1998; Mack 2003; Mahmood 2001). The most extreme version of the idea that agency depends on women's resistance to all expressions of religion appeared in a number of op-ed pieces by Margaret Wente, a regular columnist for the *Globe and Mail*. Wente often recounted arguments made by Muslim women. For example, when Ayaan Hirsi Ali (a Somali-born woman who at the time was a member of the Dutch parliament and who now works for the American Enterprise Institute in the United States) visited Toronto in the summer of 2005 to help Arjomand's campaign, Wente wrote a full-page article based on this visit in which she interspersed her analysis with quotes from Hirsi Ali:

> "Canadian law," [Ayaan Hirsi Ali] says, "is now offering some Canadian men the opportunity to oppress us." She believes in the strict separation of religion and state. She believes that the religious law of any faith—Muslim, Christian, Jewish—invariably oppresses women. And she believes that the promised safeguards, such as the right to appeal any decision to a secular court, are a load of hooey for women who live, as many Muslim women do, in a closed society. "What is freedom of choice when you depend on your family and clan for everything?" (*GM* 20 August 2005)

Again, such arguments predicated the agency of Muslim women on their resistance to religiously informed family and community practices. Secularization became the way to create the conditions within which Muslim women had the capacity to act; without secularization, family relationships structured by Islam could not be penetrated by the more liberal ways of the host society in which immigrants found themselves.

Representations of Embedded Agency

A conceptualization of agency as embedded takes seriously that women's subjectivity is informed by their religious practices in ways that directly shape their agentic behaviour (Mahmood 2001). Marion Boyd's report on the advisability of Sharia-based tribunals recognized this link between subjectivity and agency and argued for continuing to allow arbitration based on Islamic principles, contingent upon institutionalizing oversight measures (Boyd 2004). The participation of self-identified religious Muslim women and men in the debate further showed that agency could be embedded in religion (and its intersection with gender, immigration, and ethnicity).

Religious Muslim participants in the debate constructed the link between agency and Islam in three ways that reflected conceptualizations of embedded agency. First, proponents of Sharia-based arbitration made claims against the state from a perspective in which Muslim women's agency was embedded in religious and other contexts. After Ontario Premier McGuinty announced that he was going to end all religiously based arbitration, proponents emphasized that religious immigrant Muslim women needed state protection, claiming that religious arbitration would continue but now without the oversight of Canadian legal institutions. For example, in one of her editorials for the *Globe and Mail*, regular columnist Seema Khan argued that women suffered under informal Islamic jurisprudential practices and she claimed that women could be protected only through institutionalized state oversight:

> Too many unqualified, ignorant imams [make] back-alley pronouncements on the lives of women, men and children. The practice will continue without any regulation, oversight or accountability . . . We have missed a golden opportunity to shine light on abuses masquerading as faith, and to ensure that rulings don't contradict the Charter of Rights and Freedoms. (*GM* 15 September 2005)

Khan, in her participation in Canadian society as a self-identified religious woman, illustrated the possibility of embedded agency, or a capacity to act informed by religiosity. In her columns on Sharia-based arbitration, she extended this capacity to all religious Muslim women. However, given the clear possibility of abuse in unmonitored, informal arbitration processes, this agency could not solely be embedded in religious contexts, but also needed to be safeguarded by the Canadian state. Thus, Khan and others who argued for the institution of Sharia-based tribunals nuanced the negative link between Islam and agency put forth by secular Muslim women (and others) by pointing the finger at poorly trained imams and a lack of transparency in decision making, rather than at Islam in general. In claiming that Sharia-based arbitration needed to be institutionalized, proponents argued that Islamic jurisprudence does not necessarily contradict Canadian standards of gender equality and, by extension, does not solely curtail women's agency. Rather than making agency contingent on resistance, these women and men promoted the intersection of religion with state oversight, or a strengthening of some of the social forces in which agency was embedded to increase the possibility of gender equality in Sharia-based decision making.

A second line of argument put forth by religiously identified Muslim women also nuanced the dominant understanding of Islam as always limiting women's agency. Alia Hogben, the president of the Canadian Council for Muslim Women, was, like Khan, a self-described religious woman. In an op-ed piece written for the *Toronto Star*, Hogben, the second most cited person against Sharia-based arbitration, argued that it was impossible for Muslims to be against Sharia as the term "metaphorically describes the way Muslims are to live" (*TS* 1 June 2004; see also Raza *TS* 24 December 2004). Yet she was against Sharia-based tribunals because she believed that allowing them would negatively affect a group of religious Muslim women within Canadian society.

One of Hogben's primary concerns was that the use of the term *Sharia* would lead religious Muslim women to believe they were mandated to go to Sharia-based tribunals rather than the secular court system to negotiate issues surrounding family dissolution and inheritance. According to Hogben, Canadian law was already "congruent with the principles of Islam," and Sharia-based tribunals were simply unnecessary except to make rulings that are detrimental to women (*TS* 1 June 2004). In other words, even though their agency was embedded in religious contexts, religious Muslim women might act in ways that were detrimental to their self-interest. Thus, Hogben differed from Khan in arguing that institutionalized recognition of Islamic jurisprudential practice would amount to public recognition of those aspects of Islam that would always curtail women's agency. For Hogben, women's agency could be informed by Islam as private practice, but also needed to be embedded in a secular public sphere. Taken jointly, Khan and Hogben's participation in the debate showed that being embedded in a religious context created more nuanced representations of the ways religion could inform agency than the outright rejection of such a possibility that dominated in approaches that construed Muslim women's agency as resistance to religion.

A third link between agency and religiosity was articulated by the person who started the debate, Syed Mumtaz Ali. He was the most quoted proponent of Sharia-based arbitration and the only one to voice a perspective in which the agency associated with using Sharia-based tribunals was unproblematically embedded in religion; for Mumtaz Ali, there simply was no tension between the strictures of religion and religious Muslim women's agency. Early on in the debate, the *Globe and Mail* stated that Mumtaz Ali "hopes some of the arbitrators will be women" (13 December 2003). However, from his religious perspective, women's attendant capacity for agency was based on a particular understanding of the relationship between women and men within Islam:

> [Mr Mumtaz Ali] also acknowledged that inheritance and divorce rulings under Islamic law tend to favour men, for historical reasons. "Brothers and sons always get more. But it is because under the Islamic system, the man has the duty and responsibility to look after the woman," he said.
>
> Women may use the tribunal to negotiate prenuptial agreements that allow them to initiate divorce proceedings without the permission of their husbands: "They are in the driver's seat before they marry," Mr Mumtaz Ali said. (*GM* 11 December 2003)

This argument represented devout Muslim women's agency as embedded. They had the capacity to act as religious women; they could be arbitrators and negotiate an equal right to divorce prior to their marriage. In Mumtaz Ali's interpretation, Islam renders women and men unequal, but this inequality, in Mumtaz Ali's perception at least, is erased by differences in obligation. Yet conceptualizations of embedded agency are about recognizing that agency can be differently informed by historically, culturally, and socially specific interacting social forces. Mumtaz Ali's assertions were clearly problematic in that, unlike the arguments put forth by religious Muslim women like Khan and Hogben, his did not recognize how these contexts contained complex forces of resistance and domination.

Mumtaz Ali notwithstanding, the vast majority of the arguments, whether for or against the institution of Sharia-based tribunals, reflected widespread agreement across the Muslim communities in Canada that Sharia-based tribunals risked constraining devout Muslim women's agency, either by definition or because of abusive practices by imams in a context of limited state oversight. Religious Muslim women, particularly recent immigrants, according to the arguments, would not be able to act in their own self-interest given the pressures of their family and community and given existing experiences with the treatment of women within informal Islamic jurisprudential practices.

These possibilities were assessed differently depending on whether agency was (implicitly) recognized as embedded or as solely expressed through resistance. The dominant representations of agency as resistance to religious strictures led to arguments against state recognition of Sharia-based tribunals. These arguments rooted agency in secularism and positioned the state as the guardian of the secular public sphere. The less dominant representations of agency as embedded in religion more often led to calls for state oversight of Sharia-based tribunals to reduce the potential for abuse and strengthen the aspects of Islamic jurisprudence that support women's capacity to act in their own interests. In these representations, the state facilitated the agency of devout Muslim women.

Implications: The Problem of Racialization

A failure to recognize that Muslim women's agency can be embedded in religion is problematic, not only because it narrows public debate, but also because it risks a narrowing of possible policy responses to concerns of immigrants from the global South to the North. An expanding literature explores the ways portrayals of gender inequality within the Muslim world, whether that world is situated in the global South or in immigrant communities within the global North, are rooted in orientalist discourses that strategically justify Western actors' interventions in these communities (Abu-Lughod 2002; Falah 2005; Kogacioglu 2004; Razack 2004, 2007). These discourses reify monolithic portrayals of the impact of religion on Muslim women. A similar reification occurred in representations of Muslim women's agency as resistance that dominated in the Canadian Sharia debate.

Some participants in the debate, mostly proponents, but also opponents to Sharia-based arbitration, highlighted the potential racialization of Muslim immigrants in the dominant portrayals of Muslim women's agency. Racialization refers to the process of imputing innate group differences that distinguish subordinate groups from majority society. Where Bloul (1998) discusses the engendering of ethnicity in French discourses on the veil, participants in the Canadian Sharia debate saw a process of racialization that was clearly gendered. For example, Tarek Fatah, communications director for the Muslim Canadian Congress, an organization that advocates against bringing religion into the public sphere, saw such racialization intersecting with Muslims' immigrant status. In an editorial, Fatah wrote,

> If implemented, this law will also cut along class and race lines: a publicly funded, accountable legal system run by experienced judges for mainstream Canadian society, and cheap, private-sector, part-time arbitrators for the already marginalized and recently arrived Muslim community. For groups like the Muslim Canadian Congress, there is no such thing as a monolithic "Muslim family/ personal law," which is just a euphemistic, racist way of saying we will apply the equivalent of "Christian law" or "Asian law" or "African law." (*TS* 22 June 2005)

The first part of the quote echoed arguments that recent immigrants should have the same rights and privileges as long-time Canadians, which informed discourses that saw agency solely in resistance. However, the second part indicated how the dominant discursive portrayals of Islam fostering this understanding of Muslim women's

agency could also be read as a form of racialization. This racialization occurred through the homogenization of "the" Muslim community and the drawing of stark boundaries between that community and the rest of Canadian society facilitated by discourses that linked Muslim women's agency to resistance to Islam.

Faisal Kutty, general counsel for the Canadian-Muslim Civil Liberties Association, which supported the institutionalization of Sharia-based tribunals, implicitly argued that the racialization of Muslims within the debate prevented (state) recognition of the ways all women's agency was embedded:

> [I] can appreciate that many are concerned about the exploitation of Muslim women. However, the discourse is now bordering on being racist. For instance, critics contend that true consent cannot be ascertained, as Muslim women will be forced to cave in to social pressure and accept unfair decisions. The concern is valid but is not restricted to Muslims and can be partly addressed by imposing duties on arbitrators. (*NP* 4 January 2005)

Kutty accepted that women's agency was embedded in social contexts, and that such social contexts could lead to curtailing women's agency (like Khan, he advocated for institutional oversight of Sharia-based arbitration). However, he also asserted that in the public debate, gender inequality was recognized when it was situated within the Muslim community, but not in majority society. As Kutty argued, the debate singled out Islam, rather than addressing systemic expressions of gender domination that, according to some, structured all overtly gender-neutral arbitration processes (see also Bakht 2004). By associating gender inequality with Muslim communities, gender equality was discursively linked to majority society. In doing so, the debate positioned Canadian Muslims as racialized others. This racialization became gendered through the associations between gender inequality and Islam that flowed from linking agency solely to resistance.

Conclusion

The concept of embedded agency draws our attention to the way forces like religion have multiple effects on women's agency. By approaching agency as embedded in such forces, public debates can move away from associating liberty and freedom with pulling women out of the contexts that shape agency and ultimately subjectivity. In the case of the debate on Sharia-based arbitration, the relative absence of such an approach to agency led to the homogenization of Islam and diverse Canadian Muslim communities to the point of "being racist," in the words of one of the participants in the debate. Furthermore, the privileging of agency as resistance to religion and its concomitant emphasis on secularism as that which can safeguard women's capacity to act seems to have informed the Ontario government's decision to halt all religious arbitration in the province. This decision constituted a failure to recognize the possibility that religious women might want to be able to enact certain religious practices, but that they might need government assistance in securing a fair interpretation of Islamic jurisprudence.

Many of the tensions surrounding the integration of immigrants in Western Europe, and to a lesser degree in Canada, centre on the presumed incompatibility between Western and Muslim religious values. These debates often focus on issues of gender inequality and the treatment of women within Islam. Conceptualizing Muslim women's agency as embedded enables an analysis that does not predicate women's capacity to act on liberal freedom, but rather carefully situates agency in the contexts that inform it. As Tripp (2006) illustrates in her analysis of Western feminists interventions in the case of Amina Lawai, the Nigerian woman sentenced to death by stoning for adultery, misrecognizing the forces that inform women's agency can hinder, rather than facilitate, their capacity to act.

To investigate the broader implications of the findings reported in this article, two further avenues of research should be pursued. First, the newspaper debates discussed in here tell us little of what happens in the daily lives of Muslim women who do not actively participate in public debate. Further research needs to examine the ways devout Muslim women negotiate their lives in the intersections of Canadian (and other states') legal practices and their (communities') interpretations of religious dictates. This research should seek out these women to understand their perspectives and desires with respect to living a life in accordance with religious practice within multidimensional social and political contexts. Here, understanding religion and other social forces as intersecting in dynamic ways will help us move towards a fuller understanding of how agency is embedded in religious and other contexts. Such research can and should occur in any immigrant-receiving nation-states that grapple with religious and other culturally informed differences.

Second, we need to see how policy (mis)recognition of women's agency, as reflected, for example, in policy approaches to wearing the veil, arranged marriages, and honour-related violence, affects women's capacity to act. These issues all come up repeatedly in debates on Muslim women's integration in the global North. Knowing the various ways Muslim women relate to these practices and how their religiosity intersects with gender, class, migration status, ethnicity, and race can provide the basis for an analysis, which assesses whether (proposed) policies impede or facilitate women's agency. Such assessments require us to understand agency as embedded in multiple social forces, rather than flowing solely from liberal, secular practices. This research would further our understanding of how various state institutions can work to support rather than undermine women's varied expressions of agency.

Ultimately, the concept of embedded agency is applicable in any inquiry into what shapes women's (and men's) capacity to act. Representations of agency rooted in the Western, liberal tradition do not produce socially untethered free-floating subjects. As the portrayals of the secular Muslim women's arguments in the Sharia debate show, they produce an agentic subject embedded in its own particular political-philosophical tradition. In our globalizing world, these traditions increasingly stand in tension with other conceptualizations of the forces that shape agency.

Notes

1. See Statistics Canada, *2006 Census: Immigration in Canada: A Portrait of the Foreign-Born Population, 2006 Census: Findings*, accessed 29 January 2008, www12.statcan.ca/english/census06/analysis/immcit/toronto.cfm.

2. A caveat about terminology—in 2006, an estimated 700,000 Muslims resided in Canada, the majority in the Greater Toronto Area and the province of Ontario. Taken together, Muslim communities constitute the largest religious minority in Canada. However, the Muslim world stretches across the globe, and Canadian Muslims reflect the resulting cultural, ethnic, and linguistic diversity, as well as diverse interpretations of Islam. I use the terms *Muslim women* and

Muslim men throughout this article to identify people who are situated as Muslims within public debate, sometimes adding the modifiers *secular* and *religious*, or *devout*. By *secular Muslim women*, I mean those who in their self-descriptions, as published in the newspapers, adhere to the ideal of a secular public sphere, but who might (or might not) practise their religion in private. When I discuss women who self-identify or who were presented as religious, I use the modifiers *devout* or *religious*.

3. The Arbitration Act covers a wide range of private legal issues, but I focus on arbitration of family matters because this took centre stage in the debate.

References

Abou El Fadl, K. 2004. *Islam and the Challenge of Democracy: A* Boston Review *Book*. Edited by Joshua Cohen and Deborah Chasman. Princeton: Princeton University Press.

Abu-Lughod, Lila. 2002. "Do Muslim Women Really Need Saving? Anthropological Reflections on Cultural Relativism and Its Others." *American Anthropologist* 104, 3: 783–90.

Ahearn, Laura M. 2000. "Language and Agency." *Annual Review of Anthropology* 30: 109–37.

Ahmed, Leila. 1992. *Women and Gender in Islam: Historical Roots of a Modern Debate*. New Haven: Yale University Press.

Alvi, Sajida Sultana, Homa Hoodfar, and Sheila McDonough. 2003. *The Muslim Veil in North America: Issues and Debates*. Toronto: Women's Press.

Atasoy, Yildiz. 2006. "Governing Women's Morality: A Study of Islamic Veiling in Canada." *European Journal of Cultural Studies* 9, 2: 203–21.

Bakht, Natasha. 2004. "Family Arbitration Using Sharia Law: Examining Ontario's *Arbitration Act* and Its Impact on Women." *Muslim World Journal of Human Rights* 1, 1: 1–24.

Bartkowski, John P., and Jen'nan Ghazal Read. 2003. "Veiled Submission: Gender, Power, and Identity among Evangelical and Muslim Women in the United States." *Qualitative Sociology* 26, 1: 71–92.

Best, Joel. 2002. "Review: Constructing the Sociology of Social Problems: Spector and Kitsuse Twenty-Five Years Later." Reviewed Work(s): *Constructing Social Problems* by Malcolm Spector and John I. Kitsuse. *Sociological Forum* 17, 4: 699–706.

Bloul, Rachel. 1998. "Engendering Muslim Identities: Deterritorialization and the Ethnicization Process in France." Published by Women Living Under Muslim Law. www.wluml.org/english/pubsfulltxt.shtml?cmd[87]=i-8268 (accessed 31 October 2007).

Boyd, Marion. 2004. "Dispute Resolution in Family Law: Protecting Choice, Promoting Inclusion." www

.attorneygeneral.jus.gov.on.ca/english/about/pubs/boyd/ (accessed 12 September 2005).

Bulbeck, Chilla. 1998. *Re-Orienting Western Feminism: Women's Diversity in a Postcolonial World*. Cambridge: Cambridge University Press.

Butler, Judith. 1993. *Bodies That Matter: On the Discursive Limits of "Sex."* New York: Routledge.

Critcher, Chas. 2003. *Moral Panics and the Media*. Buckingham: Open University Press.

Emirbayer, Mustafa, and Ann Mische. 1998. "What is Agency?" *American Journal of Sociology* 103, 4: 962–1023.

Emon, Anver. 2006. "Conceiving Islamic Law in a Pluralist Society: History, Politics and Multicultural Jurisprudence." *Singapore Journal of Legal Studies* (Dec.): 331–55.

Falah, Ghazi-Walid. 2005. "The Visual Representation of Muslim/Arab Women in Daily Newspapers in the United States." In Ghazi-Walid Falah and Caroline Nagel, eds, *Geographies of Muslim Women: Gender, Religion, and Space*. New York: Guildford Press.

Ferree, Myra Marx. 2003. Resonance and Radicalism: Feminist Framing in the Abortion Debates of the United States and Germany. *American Journal of Sociology* 109, 2: 301–44.

Fournier, Pascale, and Gökçe Yurdakul. 2006. "Unveiling Distribution: Muslim Women with Headscarves in France and Germany." In Y. Michal Bodemann and Gökçe Yurdakul, eds, *Migration, Citizenship, Ethnos*. New York: Palgrave Macmillan.

Killian, Caitlin. 2003. "The Other Side of the Veil: North African Women in France Respond to the Headscarf Affair." *Gender & Society* 17, 4: 567–90.

Kogacioglu, Dicle. 2004. "The Tradition Effect: Framing Honor Crimes in Turkey." *Differences: A Journal of Feminist Cultural Studies* 15, 2: 118–52.

Korteweg, Anna C. 2006. "The Murder of Theo Van Gogh: Gender, Religion and the Struggle over Immigrant Integration in the Netherlands." In

Y. Michal Bodemann and Gökçe Yurdakul, eds, *Migration, Citizenship, Ethnos*. New York: Palgrave Macmillan.

Korteweg, Anna C., and Gökçe Yurdakul. 2008. "Islam, Gender, and Immigrant Integration: Boundary Drawing in Discourses on Honour Killing in the Netherlands and Germany." *Ethnic and Racial Studies* 32, 2: 218–38.

McCarthy, John D., Clark McPhail, and Jackie Smith. 1996. "Images of Protest: Dimensions of Selection Bias in Media Coverage of Washington Demonstrations, 1982 and 1991." *American Sociological Review* 61 (June): 478–99.

Mack, Phyllis. 2003. "Religion, Feminism, and the Problem of Agency: Reflections on Eighteenth-Century Quakerism." *Signs: Journal of Women in Culture and Society* 29, 1: 149–77.

MacLeod, Arlene Elowe. 1992. "Hegemonic Relations and Gender Resistance: The New Veiling as Accommodating Protest in Cairo." *Signs: Journal of Women in Culture and Society* 17, 3: 533–57.

McNay, Lois. 2000. *Gender and Agency: Reconfiguring the Subject in Feminist and Social Theory*. Cambridge: Polity Press.

Mahmood, Saba. 2001. "Feminist Theory, Embodiment, and the Docile Agent: Some Reflections on the Egyptian Islamic Revival." *Cultural Anthropology* 16, 2: 202–36.

Mihelich, John, and Debbie Storrs. 2003. "Higher Education and the Negotiated Process of Hegemony: Embedded Resistance among Mormon Women." *Gender & Society* 17, 3: 404–22.

Mohanty, Chandra Talpade. 2003. "'Under Western Eyes' Revisited: Feminist Solidarity through Anticapitalist Struggles." In *Feminism without Borders: Decolonizing Theory, Practicing Solidarity*. Durham, NC: Duke University Press.

Okin, Susan Moller. 1999. "Is Multiculturalism Bad for Women?" In Joshua Cohen, Matthew Howard, and Martha C. Nussbaum, eds, *Is Multiculturalism Bad for Women?* Princeton: Princeton University Press.

Ortner, Sherri. 1996. *Making Gender: The Politics and Erotics of Culture*. Boston: Beacon Press.

———. 2001. "Specifying Agency: The Comaroffs and Their Critics." *Interventions* 3, 1: 76–84.

Razack, Sherene. 2004. "Imperilled Muslim Women, Dangerous Muslim Men, and Civilized Europeans: Legal and Social Responses to Forced Marriages." *Feminist Legal Studies* 12: 129–74.

———. 2007. "The 'Sharia Law Debate' in Ontario: The Modernity/Premodernity Distinction in Legal Efforts to Protect Women from Culture." *Feminist Legal Studies* 15: 3–32.

Rohe, Matthias. 2004. "Application of Sharia Rules in Europe—Scope and Limits." *Die Welt des Islams* 44, 3: 323–50.

Smith, Jackie, John D. McCarthy, Clark McPhail, and B. Augustyn. 2001. "From Protest to Agenda Building: Description Bias in Media Coverage of Protest Events in Washington, DC." *Social Forces* 79, 4: 1397–423.

Spector, Malcolm, and John I. Kitsuse. 1977. *Constructing Social Problems*. Menlo Park, CA: Cummings.

Tripp, Aili Mari. 2006. "Challenges in Transnational Feminist Mobilization." In Myra Marx Ferree and Aili Mari Tripp, eds, *Global Feminism: Transnational Women's Activism, Organizing, and Human Rights*. New York: New York University Press.

Wadud, Amina. 2005. "Citizenship and Faith." In Marilyn Friedman, ed., *Women and Citizenship*. Oxford: Oxford University Press.

Questions for Critical Thought

1. What does Korteweg mean by the term *embedded agency*? Why does she consider the term *agency* problematic when discussing Muslim women?

2. Korteweg gives an example of engendering ethnicity that was carried out by French and Maghrebi men. What forms of engendering ethnicity take place in Canadian society? What forms of engendering ethnicity take place in other countries in the world?

3. What are Sharia-based tribunals and why are feminist groups opposed to their implementation in Ontario? In which countries in the world are Sharia-based tribunals used?

4. According to Korteweg's research, which groups or individuals in Canadian Muslim society are most likely to support religious arbitration? Which groups or individuals in the Muslim community do not?

5. What is agentic agency, according to the author? Who is most likely to act with agentic agency in Muslim society? Can you think of other examples of agentic agency that might be carried out in Canadian Muslim society?

Feminist Leadership and Female Genital Mutilation in Canada: A Community Health Centre's Advocacy and FGM Eradication Efforts

.... *Wangari Esther Tharao and Linda Cornwell*

... And now, hear my appeal!
I appeal for dreams broken,
I appeal for my right to live as a whole human being,
I appeal to you and all peace-loving people.
Protect, support and give a hand
To innocent little girls who do no harm,
Trusting and obedient to their parents, their elders
And they know only smiles.

Initiate them to the world of love,
Not to the world of feminine sorrow.
—Dahabo Elmi Muse[1]

Female genital mutilation (FGM),[2] also known as "female circumcision," is an old, deeply rooted tradition that was originally practised mainly in Africa and several Middle Eastern countries but has recently become a matter of global concern. The term *female genital mutilation* has been highly debated by both opponents and proponents of the FGM debate, and although not universally acceptable, has now been adopted by the World Health Organization (WHO) (1997) as the appropriate terminology to describe the procedure. To many activists involved in the fight to eliminate the practice, the alternative terminology, *female circumcision*, is incorrect since it does not effectively capture or explain the extent of the damage done to women (Hedley and Dorkenoo 1992). *Mutilation* is a powerful word that implies pain and suffering as well as permanent crippling, deformity, and disfigurement, hence revealing a degree of tissue destruction so severe that it can be fatal. Consequently, female genital mutilation is the term adopted by

Women's Health in Women's Hands (WHIWH), a pro-choice, feminist, anti-racist, anti-oppression women's organization in Toronto, Canada, whose leadership and feminist organizing laid the groundwork for FGM eradication efforts in Canada. The efforts and the organizing strategies employed by WHIWH to work effectively with women of the South living in the North to support their efforts in the fight against FGM practices will be highlighted.

Female genital mutilation became a matter of international concern in the 1970s and 1980s when it was brought to the forefront by Western feminists, who described it as a "barbaric practice" and a human and reproductive rights abuse against women and girl children (Momoh 1999). This early debate portrayed women from FGM-practising communities as passive, helpless, lacking power to advocate for themselves, and in need of being "rescued" from their "barbaric" practices. The debate pitted Western feminists against women from FGM-practising communities who were the supposed beneficiaries of the efforts being made on their behalf. FGM, as a violation of women's human and reproductive rights, generated unprecedented reactions of outrage, even from women who might have been considered "victims" of the practice, creating a divide between activists fighting to end the practice and communities opposed to its abolition (Akale 1999). The issue was further complicated by differences in opinion among those who actively opposed it. Western feminists had a different opinion from feminists and activists from practising communities/countries who saw the practice as retrograde and cruel and who, with great bravery, opposed it publicly. Western feminists tended to deal with FGM in isolation, ignoring its links to the general economic and social oppression of all women everywhere and the oppression of women both in developed and developing countries (El Sadaawi 1980). On the other hand, many feminists and activists (particularly those from FGM-practising communities living in the North) wanted FGM to be considered within a broader matrix of other types of violence against women. It has been argued that violence against women, whether perpetrated by men on women, or by women on women, has no political, social, or cultural barriers. Whether it is in the form of rape at home or in refugee camps, assault, wife battering, and sexual harassment in the North, infanticide and dowry deaths in India, trafficking or prostitution in the Philippines and Thailand, violence negatively affects women's health, drains their energies, and undermines their efforts to further their own and their communities' development (Akale 1999; Massaquoi 2005). Locating FGM in this wider **matrix of violence** tended to eliminate the attitude of Western cultural superiority with which many FGM advocates from the North had originally approached FGM eradication efforts. The acknowledgement that Western countries have also developed ways of abusing women, of violating their rights, and of exercising power over them, forced Western women to recognize the universality of the oppression of women and allowed for a more culturally sensitive approach to FGM. This more global understanding shifted the debate about FGM from being an isolated issue of "those women" to an issue that can be incorporated into broader efforts to eliminate gender-based violence. It also supported women's advocacy efforts in their fight to have the practice of FGM criminalized by including it amongst other types of violence that had already been legislated as crimes against women.

Migration of women from the South to the North has also brought the issue of FGM closer to home. Driven by forces of globalization, war, poverty, gender violence, economic imperatives, and so on, migration has resulted in the movement of large numbers of immigrants from FGM-practising communities in the South to industrialized countries of the global North, including Europe, Australia, and North America, making a practice that was viewed by many Western feminists as "affecting those poor women over there" (Retlaff 1999) an issue of global concern. Women from FGM-practising communities, mainly African women, have immigrated to and made Canada their home for several decades, but it was only in the early 1990s that FGM became an issue of concern for many professionals, particularly those involved in health care provision, when they began caring for increasing numbers of Somali women. The outbreak of the civil war in Somalia led many Somali women, who undergo the most extreme form of FGM (infibulation),[3] to flee for their lives and seek refuge in developed countries such as Canada.

Before the arrival of Somali women into Canada, few Canadians, including health care professionals, were aware of the existence of FGM. Although a small number of studies had been conducted by health professionals with reference to Somali women (WHIWH 1993), many health care providers responsible for the health and well-being of all Canadian residents, had no comprehension of FGM, nor did they have any understanding of its effects on the health of affected women in their care. As the numbers of infibulated women seeking health care increased, particularly in Toronto, which served as the final destination for most of the Somalis seeking refugee status in Canada, FGM came to the attention of Ontario's health institutions (WHIWH 1993) and the Canadian public.

In addition to barriers of language and culturally insensitive services, infibulated women also faced racist attitudes by service providers. According to Esther Tharao and Notisha Massaquoi (2001), an infibulated woman had the following to say about prenatal care and child delivery services that were available for women affected by FGM:

Having my first child in Canada was a very scary thing. I didn't speak the language and did not have any family here. When I went for my first prenatal examination the doctor gasped and said "Oh my God." He had never examined anybody who had undergone Female Genital Mutilation. I felt humiliated and very exposed.... When I went to the hospital to deliver my baby, the doctor called all his colleagues to come and look at me without my permission. This is not a humane way to treat people. (76–7)

The racist undertones with which the Canadian press informed the public about FGM were mirrored in the attitudes of those who were providing care, and the impact on the affected communities was profoundly negative. Any article discussing FGM inevitably included the words "barbaric," "primitive," "crude," "cruel," and "abhorrent," thereby exposing the writer's racist attitudes towards the "Other" as well as her or his ignorance of what has passed for normal medical practices in the West for hundreds of years. A most unfortunate consequence of these racist attitudes was the silencing of women from affected communities, which further limited their access to appropriate health services. The racist undertones of the public discourse on FGM are highlighted in an article entitled "There Is No Place Here for Barbarism," published by the *Niagara Falls Review* (1992). According to the article,

Canadians are tolerant people, some would say too much so. But on this matter there is no middle ground. We will not permit the immigration of female mutilation, any more than we would permit an Arab's hands to be severed if such a person was caught shoplifting.

We are more civilized than that . . . and isn't that one of Canada's redeeming qualities that attract new citizens?

The discourse around FGM is tied to racism and colonial ideologies. It is a narrative that is easy to understand since it ties into the Western perception of Third World women as passive "victims" of tradition and patriarchal systems from which they need to be rescued. This discourse fails to recognize that throughout history, and in all cultures, women have been bound by definitions of beauty, as seen through the male gaze, and have

been subjected to extreme modifications to the female body such as foot binding in China, the excessive corseting of the Victorian woman to achieve an hourglass figure, and the wrapping and flattening of the breasts to achieve the boyish figure so desired in the 1920s. In Europe and North America, clitoridectomies were prescribed as a treatment for female hysteria, nymphomania, and intractable masturbation. Included were "'disorderly women' whom one doctor identified as every woman from women's rightists, bloomer-wearers to midwives. . . . Included too were lesbians, anyone suspected of lesbian inclinations and those with an aversion to men" (Gunning 1992). The last known case of clitoridectomy in the United States was performed on a child of five, as a cure for masturbation, in 1948 (Ehrenreich and English 1978).

We have only recently learned of the continuing female genital modifications of any female child born in the West with what is considered to be genital abnormalities (e.g., a clitoris longer that an inch), genital mutilations that have caused much suffering and trauma. Especially distressing is the recent development and popularity of cosmetic genital surgeries in the West such as labia majora and minora remodelling, pubic **liposuction**, vaginal reconstruction, vaginal rejuvenation, and clitoral reduction—all forms of female genital mutilation. In the mass media, accounts of these operations are presented as trends with beneficial outcomes when it comes to aesthetics and sexuality (Essen and Johnsdotter 2004). In this context, it must be acknowledged that cosmetic surgery, seen from a perspective of beauty, is one of the reasons FGM is performed in practising communities. A Somali woman activist we spoke to in 1998 stated, "When we see ourselves, that area is neat and smooth just like the palm of my hand with nothing dangling down. This is how we were taught it should be, not exposed and ugly." While in the West, the **"husband's stitch"** (i.e., the tightening of the vagina after delivery) is considered normal, a similar request from a Somali woman would be a cultural practice that has been banned and criminalized. Any initiatives for the eradication of FGM must be informed by a global and historical understanding of the mutilation and modification of the female body. To avoid implications of cultural racism, North American women activists involved in the struggle to eradicate FGM must view the genital surgeries performed in Western countries with the same lens as those performed in Africa.

What types of strategies would be effective in working with a community that had already been alienated, shamed, and traumatized by insensitive and racist service providers and by a hostile public that had already been influenced by the media? Although Western feminists and advocates were perceived by the community as having little understanding of the issue, they appeared to be attempting to assume leadership without involving or giving any credit to the efforts of many African activists who had been involved in the fight to eliminate the procedure at the grassroots level in their own countries long before FGM had become an international issue.

Women's Health in Women's Hands (WHIWH),[4] a community health centre mandated to provide services from an inclusive feminist, pro-choice, anti-racist, anti-oppression, and multilingual participatory framework to women from the Caribbean, African, Latin American, and South Asian communities, was uniquely positioned to take a leadership role. In partnership with women from FGM-practising communities, WHIWH set out to pave the way for FGM eradication efforts in Canada. Its unique position was based on several factors. First, it had a workforce and board of directors that reflected the women it was mandated to serve, including African women from FGM-practising communities. This meant that the lead organization was one with whom women were familiar and had developed a trusting relationship, and had appropriate philosophical principles and ideals. Second, based on the model of empowerment that the centre used in its efforts to support women dealing with health-related issues, women from FGM-affected communities advocating for the elimination of the practice would take the lead and would be provided with the necessary skills to move the issue forward in partnership with the centre. Allowing affected women to take the lead role in FGM eradication efforts as "cultural insiders" with an in-depth understanding of the reasons why the practice continued, even amid calls for its elimination, would help bridge the divide that had been created between Western feminists and African feminists and advocates involved in efforts to eliminate the practice. Third, from its inception, the centre adopted the World Health Organization's 1985 definition of health. It viewed women's health as a state of complete physical, mental, and social well-being, and not merely the absence of illness or infirmity. In its efforts to work effectively with the women in its priority populations to improve their health and well-being, WHIWH employed strategies that incorporated the physical, psychological, socio-economic, cultural, political, and spiritual dimensions of women's lives. Health was seen as the ability to fulfill one's aspirations, dreams, and hopes in a new, always challenging, and often hostile environment. With this definition of health in mind, WHIWH set out to pave the way for FGM eradication efforts locally, provincially, and nationally. This required leadership and community development through education and training, awareness raising, networking and information sharing, advocacy, provision of care and support, resource development, and research.

By the early 1990s, FGM had been identified as an issue that violated the basic human rights of girls and women, their reproductive health, physical and mental integrity. It was considered a form of violence against women and girls by several international conventions, including the Convention on the Elimination of All Forms of Discrimination (CEDAW) (1981), the Vienna Declaration and Plan for Action (1993), and the Center for Reproductive Law and Policy and Rainbo (2000). Some Western countries, particularly France and the United Kingdom, had already criminalized the practice of FGM and had developed strategies to raise awareness, train health professionals to deal effectively with the issue, and work proactively with affected communities to eradicate the practice in their new countries of residence (WHO 1992). Something similar needed to happen in Canada. Individuals and organizations with the necessary leadership would need to take on an issue that involved fighting for the rights of affected women. Feminists from different geographic, racial, religious, cultural, and class backgrounds had organized for years to improve the status of women (Bunch 1997), and this was an issue that required effective feminist leadership to ensure social transformation. Being a feminist organization, WHIWH had already developed the framework to deal with and move forward issues of concern for immigrant and refugee women of colour.

The early stages of FGM eradication efforts required the employment of various strategies targeting various stakeholders to ensure that health programs and services delivered to women were appropriate, culturally sensitive, and were meeting their specific needs. A clear and comprehensive understanding of the implications of FGM, as a health and human rights issue for affected women, was essential as were resources, both human and financial. If FGM were ever to be eradicated, changes in policy and legislation were also essential. Linkages and partnerships needed to be developed, maintained, and/or strengthened between affected communities and those working with them, the government, and other affiliated bodies.

The strategies used, activities undertaken, results obtained, organizations involved, and the roles played by all parties involved in FGM eradication efforts will be highlighted in this article. We hope to illustrate a road map paved by many hands over the past 14 years and mark the major milestones along the pathway.

The Beginnings: Leadership Development during the Early Years

To address FGM effectively required that WHIWH strengthen its own internal capacities in preparation for working with women from affected communities. The goal was to ensure that WHIWH was in a position to provide culturally appropriate, sensitive, and linguistically accessible services. The centre organized education and training workshops on issues related to FGM for its diverse workforce. Training included the epidemiology and history of FGM, reasons why it is practised, and its health and social implications—all within a broader framework of violence and abuse of women's human and reproductive rights. This groundwork helped ensure that health care providers were well informed and had the necessary skills to deal with the complexity of FGM. It also ensured that staff had the necessary skills to facilitate the integration of FGM-related health concerns within the broader health programs the centre was providing to ensure that FGM was not treated as a separate issue. Having strengthened its own capacities, the centre was now in a position to work with others.

In 1990, the Canadian Centre for Victims of Torture, a centre in Toronto working with immigrants and refugees from war-torn areas, was also seeing a growing number of Somali women and was providing settlement services as well as counselling to deal with postwar trauma. In conjunction with the Toronto Department of Public Health and several members of the Somali community, a Somali Women Advocacy Group for community development, with the issue of FGM as a central focus, was established. WHIWH was invited to become part of the group, to provide expertise through advocacy, political lobbying, and health care for infibulated women (WHIWH 1993). The group identified FGM as a serious health concern requiring immediate attention. This led to the establishment of a broader FGM committee, with membership from affected communities (including men), WHIWH, the Canadian Centre for Victims of Torture, and Toronto Public Health. The committee's main objective was to develop recommendations for public health on how to deal with the issues of FGM effectively and in a culturally appropriate manner.

Expansion of the Circle of Care

The committee soon realized that if any substantial progress was to be made in the implementation of recommendations that required changes to medical practices and health care delivery, the College of Physicians and Surgeons of Ontario (CPSO) needed to be involved. In 1991, WHIWH lobbied the College by making a submission on the needs of women affected by FGM to the CPSO Task Force on Sexual Abuse of Patients. The WHIWH submission, together with that of the Toronto Medical Officer of Health, in 1992 led to the CPSO policy banning physicians from practicing FGM (WHIWH 1993). On 27 January 1992, the Council of the CPSO announced that female circumcision, excision, and infibulation were banned, and that the performance of any of these procedures by a physician licensed in Ontario would be considered professional misconduct (CPSO 1992). The College also made it illegal to re-infibulate women after delivery.

Protection of young girls at risk of being mutilated was also seen as paramount and any recommendations from the FGM Committee on the protection of the girl child required the support of Children's Aid Societies (CAS). This led to the involvement of the Ontario Association of Children's Aid Societies. WHIWH, assisted by three Somali women facilitators, conducted a one-day training and child protection strategy discussion workshop for front-line workers from CAS. In 1992, the Ontario Association of Children's Aid Societies issued a statement asserting that FGM constituted a form of child abuse under the Child and Family Services Act of 1984 (WHIWH 1996b).

Also in 1992, the Ontario Ministry of Community and Social Services coordinated consultations with various agencies, including WHIWH, Ministry of Health and Long Term Care, Women's Health Bureau, Ontario Women's Directorate, Ontario Association of Children Societies, Toronto Public Health, Canadian Centre for Victims of Torture, College of Physicians and Surgeons of Ontario, Family Services Centre of Ottawa-Carleton, and Minister of Solicitor General. This was an indication that the Government of Ontario was hearing the voices of those involved in highlighting the issue of FGM.

All these changes required a mechanism to ensure through education that both affected communities and health care providers were aware of the legal repercussions and the impact of FGM on the physical, psychological, sexual, and reproductive well-being of women. The development of culturally sensitive materials tailored to the needs of both professionals and affected communities was also necessary.

Community Education and Training of Service Providers

In 1992, WHIWH received funding from the Women's Health Bureau, Ontario Ministry of Health, for the first FGM-related project in Canada whose goal was to develop and deliver a workshop on FGM for health care professionals and to develop educational materials for health care professionals, educators, and affected communities. Hawa Mohammed, a Somali woman who had already established an international reputation as a tireless advocate for the elimination of FGM, was hired to coordinate the project. Hawa was instrumental in integrating the many elements required for the success of the project. In the WHIWH *Final Report on Female Genital Mutilation* (1993), Hawa wrote,

> It is difficult to give a straightforward report of all that has been entailed in implementing this project. So many elements were involved; so many people; so many constituents had to be brought together and so many political/social alliances had to be forged. The amount of time that I and many other Somali women have put into this project is immeasurable. The organization has grown so much because of our work with Somali women. (20)

As this project required a philosophical and methodological approach that would lead to social transformation, the need for leadership development and self-empowerment for Somali women was fundamental. Consequently, women from the affected communities were substantive partners in the process as advocates, community outreach strategists, and storytellers who would present their personal case history narratives for use during the training sessions. The project was also sensitive to the importance of providing training for health care professionals that was culturally competent and facilitated through a process of mutual respect between the health care professionals and the community.

According to the WHIWH Final Report on FGM (1993), the following activities were undertaken: a literature review conducted at the initial stages of the project resulted in the establishment of background information for the project, as well as a collection of research works, books, conference proceedings, and videos that were kept by the centre for reference and for use by others searching for information on FGM. The project also used the first four months to facilitate self-help support groups for women for self-empowerment and leadership development. The support groups provided an avenue to assess the women's and their community's knowledge of human biology, particularly the reproductive health system and health complications of FGM. A pre-test questionnaire was also administered to obstetricians/gynecologists and family physicians who had infibulated/excised women as clients or who had knowledge of FGM. Information from the two sources was used to develop and tailor the curriculum that would be used in the workshops planned for health care professionals, and for awareness and education of affected women and their communities. A seven-member advisory board was established to guide the project.

A Somali Women's Facilitator Group was also established and included women from the earlier Somali Women Advocacy Group that was being run by the Canadian Centre for Victims of Torture. The Facilitator Group was comprised of 12 women, including doctors, nurses, educators, lawyers, social scientists, and community women leaders. All of these women had been subjected to FGM and hence had a first-hand, in-depth understanding of the issues. WHIWH provided leadership training to this core group to prepare them for their role as community activists in the fight for the elimination of FGM. They were educated on the immediate and long-term health and psychological effects of FGM, its effects on marriage and relationships, as well as its human rights and legal implications. They also received training to build individual and group facilitation skills. They were expected to go into the community and facilitate education to raise awareness about FGM based on the information provided to them during their training. The group worked closely with the project coordinator on a volunteer basis and played a direct role in the implementation, delivery, and evaluation of project activities. As community members, they provided direct links in the community. These 12 women helped organize a forum that brought 58 women from affected communities together to discuss the consequences of FGM. Because they had established strong linkages within their communities, they excelled at outreach. Also, as they had been transformed from being custodians of a harmful cultural practice into advocates for the elimination of a harmful practice, they were ideally situated to articulate the negative effects of FGM to their peers and community leaders. Topics discussed at the forum included FGM and its effects on the health and well-being of women, FGM and religion, and FGM and child abuse laws in Canada. Surveys on the positions of religion and the law vis-à-vis FGM were delivered, and orientation workshops and forums on FGM and religion for both men and women were organized (WHIWH 1993). The Somali women facilitators knew that it was essential to include men in the process in order to achieve community transformation.

Informal and open discussion groups, designed to encourage the free expression of opinions, individual emotions, sentiments, and beliefs, were delivered to Somali women at various sites, including English as a Second Language classes. The issue of FGM as child abuse was an important part of the dialogue because mothers found it difficult to believe that they were abusing their daughters by raising them within cultural norms. To ensure that the women truly understood the legal position of FGM in Canada, legal literature on the subject was translated into Somali and distributed to Somali women through the support groups, women volunteers, and facilitators.

Workshops for health care professionals were delivered in 1992. The resource people included representatives from government, CPSO, legal and medical professions, women leaders from the affected communities, as well as WHIWH staff. Fourteen women leaders facilitated the four workshops set for the day that dealt with the following topics: clinical health, psychological health, legal/social implications, and child protection. There was a consensus that the provision of health and social services for women affected by FGM was inadequate in terms of quality. Particularly problematic was the Canadian medical system's almost total reliance on Caesarian delivery even in cases where women wished to deliver vaginally as was their normal practice (WHIWH 1993).

To deal with the shortcomings in services, the following recommendations were made, as drafted in the WHIWH *Final Report on FGM* (1993).

Formation of an Inter-Ministerial Task Force on FGM

It was recommended that a task force be established with representatives from all ministries, groups, and institutions providing health, legal, educational, and other social services to the communities affected by FGM. Affected communities also needed to have a voice on the task force. The task force's mandate, membership, and specific tasks were to be decided by WHIWH and the Ontario Women's Directorate with information from the workshop as background for its activities.

Education and Training of Providers and Communities

To better understand and care for patients who were infibulated/excised, service providers needed to be trained and educated about FGM and the special needs of affected women. Training workshops, seminars, and discussion panels needed to be organized for health and social service providers to raise awareness about FGM, its origin, history, geography, demography, myths, and misconceptions. Education and training materials tailored to the needs of the different stakeholders, such as individuals, institutions, and groups, including doctors, nurses, teachers, child protection workers, social workers, and other service providers, were needed to increase the effectiveness of such training programs. Literature on FGM needed to be translated into the languages spoken by the communities where FGM was practised and disseminated within each community. It was also recommended that WHIWH establish a resource/reference library containing available literature on FGM.

Legal

To eradicate FGM in Canada and to protect children at risk in all the provinces, legislation needed to be passed by the Parliament of Canada prohibiting the practice of FGM. Specific reference to FGM needed to be included in the Criminal Code. FGM needed to be recognized as a human rights issue—a form of torture and violence against women and children. In this context, it was important that FGM not be confused with the community's right to the protection of its culture. Institutions for child protection needed to recognize FGM as child abuse. It was recommended that Canada follow the example of other Western countries such as the United Kingdom, France, and Sweden, which had specifically prohibited the practice of FGM.

Health

Health professionals needed to demonstrate cultural and emotional sensitivity, as well as moral integrity when attending to patients affected by FGM. Special care was needed when examining or assisting infibulated/excised women in childbirth and delivery. Doctors (family physicians, gynecologists, and obstetricians) and nurses required training to understand the permanent physical and psychological trauma that women affected by FGM have suffered since childhood. Health professionals needed to be made aware of their responsibilities to inform the parents of children at risk of being genitally mutilated that FGM is illegal in Canada.

Research and Information

More studies were needed to determine the kinds of trauma that women affected by FGM suffer—not only the physical damage, but also the psychological and social effects of FGM. This would require a research program, jointly coordinated by WHIWH and the Ontario Women's Directorate, with contributions being sought from hospitals and various service agencies providing care and/or assistance to women affected by FGM.

Financing and Funding

No program, however well conceived, could have any long-term effective impact unless it had both human and financial resources allocated to it. Therefore, permanent funding was required to ensure continuation of the work already started in Ontario and across Canada. To secure adequate funding, ministries and agencies of social, health, and legal services needed to contribute to the program for the eradication of FGM, provincially and nationally.

Provincial, National, and International Collaborative Efforts

Since immigrant populations from communities where FGM is practised lived in major metropolitan areas across Canada, institutions needed to cooperate at the municipal, provincial, and national levels in order to pool efforts, information,

and activities in a coordinated response to FGM. International agreements that had already identified FGM as an abuse of women's human rights and as violence against women and the girl child needed to be adopted in Canada.

Affected Communities

Communities affected by FGM needed education and training about Canadian laws on child abuse, violence against women, and the protection of children. To implement such a program, cultural interpreters, community workers, and professionals from the community itself were to be used. They needed to be encouraged to participate in the whole process. Women's support groups, youth groups, parents, and professionals needed to be provided with incentives, opportunities, and moral and financial support in order to organize themselves as both facilitators and beneficiaries of the transformation processes. Community participation was seen as the most important determinant of the eradication of FGM.

Implementation of the Recommendations

The recommendations of the training workshop provided a platform from which organizations, governments, and women leaders could continue the social transformation process, individually or collectively. WHIWH lobbied the Ontario Ministry of Health and Long Term Care and received funding for a core position to hire a Community Health Educator (FGM Eradication Program) in order to enable the centre to continue the efforts started in the first FGM project. This program included the implementation of, and follow-up on, the recommendations made in the professional training workshop, as well as those made by all the affected women who participated in project activities throughout its life cycle.

Ongoing support groups were set up for affected women that incorporated FGM at their core but dealt with other issues of importance to the women. It was noted at the beginning of the process that FGM was not the women's main priority. Settlement issues (including housing, family reunification, the immigration/refugee process, employment, child care, and language) were much more vital to the women's health and well-being (WHIWH 1995a). A young women's forum on FGM was organized and delivered in 1993, which helped bring the issue of young women to the forefront. Ongoing training and leadership development for professionals and affected communities became an integral part of the core program offered at WHIWH. The centre also continued to lobby at the provincial and federal levels of government for policy and legislation changes, and funding for education.

As there was a lack of educational materials for professionals and community workers as well as for affected communities, the Ontario Women's Directorate provided Women's Health in Women's Hands with funding for the development of two booklets:

- *Pre- and Postnatal Care of the Patient*—a resource targeted to the health care professionals providing pre- and postnatal care for pregnant women, which explained the different types of FGM and provided step-by-step instructions on how to perform a vaginal delivery for infibulated women, as well as information on the postnatal care required after defibulation (WHIWH 1995c).

- *Information for Educators and Service Providers to Support the Student and her Family*—a resource developed for teachers working with young girls and service providers working with affected women that provided information to enable effective support of young girls, women, and their families. The issues of absence from school and many or prolonged trips to the bathroom were some examples of the effects of FGM on the lives of young girls. Teachers needed to have a clear understanding of the impact of FGM in order to provide appropriate support for their students (WHIWH 1995b).

Advocacy to Influence Policy and Legislative Changes

Women's Health in Women's Hands (1996b) also played a pivotal role in persuading provincial and national organizations to adopt anti-FGM resolutions. The centre used its influence to propose resolutions on FGM to organizations such as the National Action Committee on the Status of Women and the Association of Ontario Health Centres. WHIWH also lobbied the Canadian Council for Refugees, the Ontario Coalition of Agencies Serving Immigrants, and the Ontario Public Health Association to ensure that they also adopted resolutions on FGM, thereby strengthening the ground to lobby both the provincial and federal governments to take a stand on the issue.

Provincial Government

Lobbying the Ontario government led to the establishment in 1994 of a Provincial Interministerial Task Force on FGM under the direction of the Ontario Women's Directorate (WHIWH 1996b). Membership included community representatives, WHIWH service providers, the College of Physicians and Surgeons, the Children's Aid Society, Toronto Public Health, the Ontario Women's Directorate, the Ministry of Health and Long Term Care, the Ministry of the Attorney General, the Ministry of Citizenship, the Ministry of Education and Training, the Ministry of Community and Social Services, the Ontario Human Rights Commission, and the Ministry of the Solicitor General and Correctional Services. The federal government was represented ex-officio by Justice Canada, Health Canada, Status of Women Canada, and the Canadian Advisory Committee on the Status of Women.

The mandate of the task force was to develop and recommend strategies and policies designed to provide support for girls and women who have undergone FGM, to prevent FGM, and to support community development work by and for women affected by FGM (Ontario FGM Prevention Task Force 1995).

Federal Governmental Involvement

On 8 March 1994, the Canadian Advisory Council on the Status of Women called on the federal government and other organizations to eradicate FGM. The same year, due to intense lobbying by WHIWH, its partner agencies, and others involved in the fight to eradicate FGM in Canada, the federal minister of justice issued an official statement that FGM was an act included in the Criminal Code. Although the statement was inadequate (the Honourable Alan Rock, the incumbent minister of justice, did not see the need to introduce legislation dealing specifically with the practice of FGM), it was seen as a small step in the right direction (Memorandum on FGM from Assistant Deputy Attorney General, 12 October 1994).

Though unwilling to introduce new legislation, Canada's firm stand on an issue that violated women's rights, as well as their physical, sexual and reproductive health integrity, was highlighted in 1994 when a Somali woman who had fled Somalia to avoid the mutilation of her daughter was granted asylum on the basis that the right to personal security would be grossly infringed upon if she were forced to return to Somalia. Canada had taken its first monumental step in recognizing FGM as a gender issue and a human rights violation. The two-member immigration panel was satisfied that, if returned to Somalia, the authorities would not protect the claimant's daughter from the physical and emotional ravages of FGM, given the evidence of its widespread practice in that country (Farnsworth 1994).

This was followed by the establishment of a Federal Interdepartmental Working Group on Female Genital Mutilation (1994), which was chaired by Health Canada, with representatives from the Ministry of Justice, the Privy Council Office, Status of Women Canada, Heritage Canada, and Citizenship and Immigration Canada. The group's mandate was to identify and promote methods to prevent the continuation of FGM by affected communities living in Canada.

Due to the central role WHIWH was playing in Canada in relation to FGM prevention and advocacy, it was chosen as one of the lead NGOs to present women's health issues at United Nations' Fourth World Conference on Women held in Beijing, China, in 1995. The Beijing Conference recognized that FGM was "a form of violence against women, equated with battering, rape, sexual abuse and forced prostitution"—a definitional framework WHIWH had always used to move forward the issue of FGM. Canada signed and ratified the declaration and the Fourth World Conference on Women Platform for Action developed at the conference, giving Canadian advocates ammunition to continue fighting for changes in legislation.

FGM Legislation and Law Review: Amendment of Bill C-27 (1)

CEDAW and the Beijing Platform for Action designated FGM as an issue of violence against women and thus a human rights issue. Having ratified the two conventions, as well as other United Nations' conventions that classified FGM as a human and women's rights issue, Canada needed to change its legislation to conform to this framework. Due to intense lobbying based on the above conventions, the Government of Canada proposed changes in legislation to criminalize FGM through the provisions of Bill C-27, an Act to Amend the Criminal Code (Child Prostitution, Child Sex Tourism, Criminal Harassment, and Female Genital Mutilation), Section 268 (3 and 4).

In 1996, WHIWH convened a legal working group consisting of a consultative and an advisory body comprised of legal experts and women from the countries most affected by FGM. The committee formed a small community working group to work on the proposed amendments to Bill C-27. Two consultants were hired to help the group with legal issues such as interpreting the bill and preparing a legal brief. A legal education workshop was organized to provide the group with a good working knowledge of the Canadian legal system. The women wrote a proposal outlining necessary amendments that was presented by the Legal Committee to the House of Commons Standing Committee on Justice and Legal Affairs on 26 November 1996 (WHIWH 1996a).

According to the committee, the bill as it stood allowed for misinterpretation due to its unclear language:

- The definition of female genital mutilation did not include all types of FGM.

- The bill stated that women under 18 years of age could not be operated on, with or without consent, leaving the question of what would happen to women over 18 unanswered.

- The bill implicitly medicalized FGM by stating that there are times when operations on the female genitalia are medically approved. The committee believed that this could provide a loophole for supporters of the practice by placing FGM and legitimate surgical procedures into the same category.

- Fairness in sentencing for practitioners and accomplices was also an issue. Practitioners needed to be given longer sentences than accomplices who would likely be parents or guardians.

After three readings and debates in the House of Commons, followed by three readings before the Senate, Bill C-27 was amended with respect to the definition of FGM and rules about the prosecution of FGM practitioners. The bill, which now included the suggested amendments, was put into effect on 26 May 1997. This was a triumphant moment for organizations such as WHIWH, who had lobbied for this legislative change for years. From then on, energy and resources could be devoted to community and leadership development for transformation.

However, the issue faded into silence in the federal arena after the FGM legislation was passed. The Federal Interdepartmental Working Group on Female Genital Mutilation lay dormant, without

any activities for several years, until the late 1990s when it commissioned key informant research across Canada to examine the health care issues for women affected by FGM and to identify some prevention strategies, resulting in a report entitled *FGM and Health Care: An Exploration of the Needs and Roles of Affected Communities and Health Care Professionals in Canada* (Huston 1999). This report led to several recommendations to the federal government, one of which included the formation of a national FGM network whose main goal would be to move forward the issue of FGM in Canada (Huston 1999). The network held its first teleconference on 30 November 2000. In the fall of 2000, the FGM Working Group released its second report, *Female Genital Mutilation and Health Care, Current Situation and Legal Status, Recommendations to Improve the Health of Affected Women* (Huston 2000). The Federal Interdepartmental Working Group on Female Genital Mutilation appears to have been disbanded in 2001, following the release of this report.

Unifying the voices of FGM eradication advocates requires a discursive framework that locates FGM on the continuum of violence against women—a continuum that bridges the gap between "us" and "them," making it possible to join forces and move forward gender-based violence issues.

The journey and milestones in the fight to eradicate female genital mutilation in Canada is a tribute to the dedication and leadership provided by Hawa Mohammed, to courageous women who have worked side by side with WHIWH staff, and to all the stakeholders involved in the process. Women's Health in Women's Hands created a safe space for affected women, providing them with training and leadership development for community transformation. They stood up for their rights and confronted a patriarchal cultural system that had oppressed, abused, and violated their human rights and their physical, sexual, and reproductive health integrity for centuries. Although the process has been challenging and the struggle to eradicate FGM continues, this has been a positive start.

WHIWH has effectively integrated FGM education and advocacy into its core programs and continues to provide ongoing leadership development and training, support for service providers and medical, nursing, and social work students in universities and colleges, as well as support and care for affected women. Leadership development and empowerment of women and communities affected by FGM has been the most effective way to promote the eradication of female genital mutilation.

Notes

1. Lines from a poem by Dahabo Elmi Muse that won the First Prize in the Poetry Competition for Female Poets of Benadir and was recited during the closing ceremony of the International Seminar on the Eradication of Female Genital Mutilation held in Mogadishu, Somalia, in 1988.
2. FGM is defined as all procedures involving partial or total removal of the external female genitalia or any other injury to the female genital organs for cultural or other non-therapeutic reasons (WHO 1997).
3. Infibulation, also known as pharaonic mutilation, involves the removal of the clitoris, labia minora, parts of the labia majora, and the stitching together of the vulva to obliterate the urethra and the vaginal orifice except for a small opening. This obstruction may lead to urinary and menstrual flow retention, dysmenorrhea, and infections of the reproductive and urinary systems.
4. Women's Health in Women's Hands is a community health centre that provides community, mental, and clinical health promotion support from an inclusive, feminist, pro-choice, anti-racist, anti-oppression, and multilingual participatory framework for women from African, Caribbean, Latin American, and South Asian communities living in Toronto.

References

African Women Development and Communication Network. *Report of the Regional Seminar on NGO Governance and Management for African Women NGOs, AMWA, FEMNET/WILDAF, 21–27 November 1998.* Akina Mama wa Afrika (Organization), Afrika Office, Nyanga, Zimbabwe.

Akale, M.C. 1999 20–26 June. "Who Has the Right to Name Female Genital Mutilation a Crime?" Paper presented at the Women's Worlds 7th International Interdisciplinary Congress on Women, Tromso, Norway.

Akwi-Ogojo, A. Report of the First African Women's Leadership Institute. Thematic discussions and working groups, *Taking the African Women's Movement into 21st Century,* 22 February–14 March 1997, Akina Mama wa Afrika [Organization], Afrika Office, Kampala, Uganda.

Bill C-27, An Act to Amend the Criminal Code (Child Prostitution, Child Sex Tourism, Criminal Harassment, and Female Genital Mutilation). House of Commons, Second Session, Thirty-fifth Parliament, 45 Elizabeth II.

Bunch, C. 1997, 22 February–March. "African Women Leadership Institute Lecture 2: Women's Human Rights." African Women Leadership Institute, Compilation of Background Working Papers and Lectures Prepared for the First African Women's Leadership Institute, Entebbe, Uganda.

Center for Reproductive Law and Policy and Rainbo. 2000. *Legislation on Female Circumcision/Female Genital Mutilation in the United States.* New York. www.reproductiverights.org/pub_bojgmhandbook.html.

Clarke, N., Cornwell L., Gibson, F., Keyi V., Mohamed H., and S. Telfer. 1993. *Female Genital Mutilation: Information for Educators and Service Providers to Support the Student and Her Family.* Toronto: Women's Health in Women's Hands.

College of Physicians and Surgeons of Ontario. 1992, March. *New Policy: Female Circumcision, Excision, and Infibulation.* Toronto: College of Physicians and Surgeons of Ontario.

Ehrenreich, B., and D. English. 1978. *For Her Own Good.* Garden City: Anchor Press/Doubleday.

El Saadawi, N. 1980. *The Hidden Face of Eve: Women in the Arab World,* Edited and Translated by Sherif Hetata, London: Zed Press.

Essen, B., and S. Johnsdotter. 2004. "Female Genital Mutilation in the West: Traditional Circumcision Versus Genital Cosmetic Surgery." *Acta Obstetricia et Gynecologica Scandinavica* 83: 611–13.

Farnsworth, H.C. 1994. "Canada Gives a Somali Woman Refuge from Genital Rite." *New York Times* 21 July, A5.

Gunning, I. 1992. "Arrogant Perception, World-Travelling and Multicultural Feminism: The Case of Female Genital Surgeries." *Columbia Human Rights* 23: 189–248.

Hedley, R., and E. Dorkenoo. 1992. *Child Protection and Female Genital Mutilation.* London: Foundation for Women's Health Research and Development.

Huston, P. 1999. *Recommendations to the Federal Interdepartmental Working Group on Female Genital Mutilation (FGM): A National Consultation on the Report on FGM and Health Care.* Ottawa: Scientific Communications International Inc.

———. 2000. *Female Genital Mutilation and Health Care, Current Situation and Legal Status, Recommendations to Improve the Health of Affected Women.* Ottawa: Women's Health Bureau, Health Canada.

Massaquoi, N. 2005. "Think Globally Act Appropriately: A Community Health Centre's Response to Violence against Women." In *Surviving in the Hour of Darkness: A Look at Women of Colour, Indigenous Women and Healing.* Edited by G. Sophie Harding. Calgary: University of Calgary Press.

Momoh, C. 1999. "Female Genital Mutilation: The Struggle Continues." *Practice Nursing* 10, 2: 31–3.

"No Place Here for Barbarism." 1994. *Niagara Falls Review* 24 March.

Ontario Association of Children's Aid Society (CAS). 1995. Policy on Female Genital Mutilation, 19 May (amended draft). Toronto: Children's Aid Society.

Ontario FGM Prevention Task Force. 1995, June. *Female Genital Mutilation Prevention/Eradication Strategies, Draft Paper.* Report for Ontario Women's Directorate, Violence Against Women Prevention Unit.

Retlaff, C. 1999. "Female Genital Mutilation: Not Just 'Over There.'" *Journal of International Association of Physicians in AIDS Care* (May) 5, 5.

Tharao, E., and N. Massaquoi. 2001. "Black Women and HIV/AIDS: Contextualizing Their Realities, Their Silence and Proposing Solutions." *Canadian Women Studies/les cahiers de la femme* 21, 2: 72–80.

United Nations Fourth World Conference on Women. 1995. "Platform for Action." www.un.org/womenwatch/daw/beijing/platform/index.html.

UN Women. "Convention on the Elimination of All Forms of Discrimination against Women (CEDAW)." Accessed 2 March 2015. www.un.org/womenwatch/daw/cedaw.

United Nations. 1993, 25 June. "The Vienna Declaration and Program Action." World Conference on Human Rights. 22 Plenary Session. United Nations Publication. DPI/1394/39399.

Women's Health in Women's Hands (WHIWH). 1993. *Final Report, Female Genital Mutilation Project April 1992–March 1993.* Toronto: Women's Health in Women's Hands.

———. 1995a. "Community-Based Approach" Model.

———. 1995c. *Female Genital Mutilation: Pre- and Post Natal Care of the Patient.*

———. 1996a. *Brief submitted to the House of Commons Justice Committee on Bill C-27* (FGM), 26 November.

———. 1996b. *Quarterly Report, Female Genital Mutilation Eradication Program.*

World Health Organization (WHO). 1992. *Female Genital Mutilation: Integrating the Prevention and Management of the Health Complications into the Curricula of Nursing and Midwifery, A Teacher's Guide.* Geneva, Switzerland: Department of Gender and Women's Health Department of Reproductive Health and Research, Family and Community Health, World Health Organization.

———. 1993. "Female Genital Mutilation—World Health Organization Calls for the Elimination of Harmful Traditional Practices." 46th World Health Assembly press release, 12 May.

———. 1997. "What is Female Genital Mutilation?" WHO Report. Geneva, Switzerland, 3–7.

Questions for Critical Thought

1. What is the matrix of violence against women? How does female genital mutilation (FGM) fit into this matrix?

2. What role do the authors claim patriarchy and the male gaze play in perpetuating the practice of FGM in Somalia? What roles do cultural traditions, marriage patterns, and religious values play in reinforcing the practice of FGM in Somalia and in other countries in the world?

3. According to Tharao and Cornwell, why have feminists who come from countries where FGM is practised challenged the attitudes of Western feminists on this topic? What has been the result of this challenge? What strategies do Tharao and Cornwell recommend should be followed to raise social awareness about this issue in Canada?

4. What problems has the non-governmental organization Women's Health in Women's Hands (WHIWH) had in providing culturally appropriate, sensitive, and accessible services to women?

5. How have Canadian organizations contributed to raising public awareness about this issue? What other strategies can we develop to educate Canadians about FGM and other forms of violence against women?

Conclusion

The readings in Part Five describe processes of domination, which are also stories of struggle, resistance, and success. In narratives of the unemployed, Aboriginal peoples and other racialized people, refugees, and poor women, we hear challenges to the shift away from equality as entitlement to equality as privilege that is taking place in the policy and practice of law. In listening to these narratives, we may hear a way forward toward the "broad-based theoretical and political project" Stasiulis refers to in our introductory section.

Recommended Readings

Wendy Chan and Kiran Mirchandani, eds 2002. *Crimes of Colour: Racialization and the Criminal Justice System in Canada.* Peterborough, ON: Broadview Press.

• The essays in this book examine racialization and criminalization in Canada. The authors document the history of the treatment of racialized peoples such as First Nations groups, immigrants, and racialized minorities, and analyze how government policy racialized these individuals and groups.

Kristen Gilchrist. 2010. "Newsworthy Victims?: Exploring Differences in Canadian Press Coverage of Missing/Murdered Aboriginal and White Women," *Feminist Media Studies* 10, 5: 373–90.

• Five hundred and eighty-two Aboriginal women have been missing or murdered since the 1980s, according to the Native Women's Association of Canada. Sixty-seven per cent of the women were murdered, 20 per cent are missing, 4 per cent of the cases are suspicious deaths, and 9 per cent are cases where it is unclear whether the woman was murdered or is missing. Aboriginal women are three times more likely to experience violence than white women in Canada. Kristen Gilchrist examines the mainstream media's coverage of the deaths of three Indigenous and three white women. In this content analysis, she considers the length of each article, the frequency of articles on each case, whether the story is front-page news or not, and the personal details about the women's lives that are reported in each article. She concludes that sympathetic and detailed reports were written about the white women, and the articles about the Aboriginal women reflect a broad matrix of domination. Gilchrist draws our attention to the lack of information in the mainstream media about the cases of missing and murdered Aboriginal women.

Elya M. Durisin, Emily van der Meulen, and Victoria Love. 2013. *Selling Sex: Experience, Advocacy and Research on Sex Work in Canada.* Vancouver: University of British Columbia Press.

- This groundbreaking book on sex work brings together a broad spectrum of perspectives on a form of labour that has rarely been viewed as a legitimate form of work. This edited volume is unique in that it brings together the ideas of researchers, academics, advocates, and sex workers who are from different age groups, genders, and social backgrounds. Topics addressed include human trafficking, police violence, the social stigma of sex work, anti-prostitution feminism, and initiatives to organize sex workers. The authors challenge mainstream narratives about sex workers and the sex work industry.

Carmela Patrias and Ruth A. Frager. 2001. "'This is Our Country, These Are Our Rights: Minorities and the Origins of Ontario's Human Rights Campaigns.'" *Canadian Historical Review* 82, 1: 1–35.

- This article explains how human rights activists in the post–Second World War era helped to reform the nature of Canadian society by making it more responsible to and reflective of its diverse population. Carmela Patrias and Ruth Frager discuss the important role that racialized minorities played in changing Ontario legislation, which would eventually outlaw discrimination on the basis of gender, race, religion, ancestry, and national origin.

Sherene Razack, ed. 2002. *Race, Space, and the Law: Unmapping a White Settler Society.* Toronto: Between the Lines Press.

- The authors in this book reject the premise that space and the arrangement of people in space emerges naturally over time. Instead, they critically examine the role that the law has in shaping and supporting the hierarchies that produce oppressive spatial categories.

PART SIX

Canada and Global Inequality

D ue to economic restructuring, not only on a national but also on a global scale, the Canadian labour market has shifted from a goods-producing to a service-producing sector since the mid-1990s. Currently, nearly three-quarters of the Canadian workforce is employed in the service sector, which comprises a broad range of industries and disparate wage levels, and includes much part-time employment and many jobs with limited security. Contractual labour arrangements that are monitored by government regulations and restrictions are described as the primary labour market; however, there is a large secondary labour market that includes household and domestic labour, the homeworker industries, and cottage industry economies. The sociology of labour focuses on trends in wage distribution among different populations, as well as labour relations, occupational issues such as the de-skilling debate surrounding the transition to a post-industrial society, and structural changes in the demographic composition of labour markets. In addition to these important issues, authors in this section examine why racialized and gendered men and women have fewer opportunities to excel in the world of sport and are overrepresented in jobs often characterized by low wages, unstable and unsafe working conditions, little job security, no pensions, and no social security benefits.

Today there is a worldwide movement of people seeking to improve their lives by escaping political, religious, and gender persecution, civil wars, and poverty. In the first reading in this section Nira Yuval-Davis uses an intersectional analysis to examine the transnational effects that an interconnected global economy has had on the politics of citizenship and "belonging." Yuval-Davis argues that due to the neo-liberal polices of globalization and glocalization during an "age of migration," various sites of oppression have been experienced by immigrants throughout the world. Yuval-Davis contends that securitization, economic and political globalization have not raised international labour standards, nor have human rights on a universal level improved. Instead, she proposes that the result of global neo-liberalist policies and practices is the gendering of global restructuring that has manifested itself in the feminization of migration, which has subsequently produced high rates of social dislocation, poverty, and limited life chances and choices for women and their families.

As more women enter the labour force to support their families, child-care and domestic workers are more readily sought by Canadians. Sedef Arat-Koç proposes that a form of transnational mothering in Canada is provided by migrant workers who are the domestic service "solution" to housework and child-care problems. Arat-Koç argues that while women have increasingly taken on greater workloads in the labour force, this has not been counterbalanced by men taking on a greater role in domestic responsibilities and the state offering more substantial support in the form of child-care leaves, inclusive benefits, and work-based child-care programs. Ironically, as the need for domestic labourers has increased, their working conditions have deteriorated, Arat-Koç points out. Domestic workers have to deal with not only inadequate working conditions, but also the social-psychological dimensions of coping with prolonged periods of separation from their own families. In addition to social isolation, loneliness, and depression, there are no guarantees that these women will eventually be granted landed immigrant status and that their children will be allowed to come to live with them in Canada. Arat-Koç concludes that a system of stratified transnational reproductive work has emerged that is based on hierarchies of class, gender, race and ethnicity, and place.

Hierarchies based on intersections of class, gender, race, ethnicity, and sexual orientation are examined by Helen Jefferson Lenskyj. In this chapter on social inequality in the athletic world, Jefferson Lenskyj focuses on the roles that colonialism, performative regulation, and white femininity have played during the Olympic Games. Jefferson Lenskyj argues that the bodies of skaters and swimmers have undergone special scrutiny as debates about their appearance, attire, and behaviour have generated a gendered, raced, and sexualized "gaze" by the media and general public. She suggests that the Gay Games has provided a "compelling case study of a counter-hegemonic sporting event" that reveals some of the contradictions within the swimming and skating events at the Olympic Games.

In the final chapter of this book, we move from social inequality in the world of sports to a chapter on the political economy of food production. Deborah Barndt presents us with a penetrating analysis of globalization from, as she puts it, the bottom up *and* the top down. Tracing the movement of the "corporate tomato" from its cultivation in the fields and greenhouses of Mexico to the supermarket and fast-food chains of Canada, Barndt reveals the impact of globalization on the interlocking systems of gender, race, and class (among other factors such as age, marital status, and rural/urban residence). An exploited female workforce is characteristic of the tomato export trade at both "ends" of the system. Inequities occur not only in wages, type, and status of work, but in the outcomes of production as well. Whether in Mexico or Canada, women are adversely affected by consumption patterns created by agribusiness, and by its harmful effects to biodiversity, cultural diversity, and health. The workplace is a site of restructuring for women workers through market forces stressing flexibility, competitiveness, and efficiency. In her integration of the social, cultural, and political workings of globalization and women's work on the "tomato trail," Barndt describes their tangled roots (and routes).

The Politics of Belonging: Framing the Questions

.... *Niral Yuval-Davis*

In the aftermath of the 7/7 bombings in London during the summer of 2005, one question seems to have bothered many of the journalists who wrote about the event: How is it possible that "British" people were able to carry out such atrocities in Britain? The reasons why these particular people became suicide bombers are no doubt complex and could be found in their individual biographies as well as in some more general micro- and macro-social and political factors. The theoretical question at the heart of this chapter concerns the assumptions that led these journalists—and so many others in the general public in Britain and outside it—to feel that carrying a British passport, or even being born and educated in Britain, should have automatically made them belong with other British citizens and "immune" from taking part in such an attack. In other words, why would people's nationality be more important to them than their religious and political beliefs, and why should they feel more loyal to the British nation than to other political and religious collectivities? Are nationalist politics of belonging still the hegemonic model of belonging at the beginning of the twenty-first century? And if so, what kind of nationalism is this? And if not, what other political projects of belonging are now competing with nationalism? Mohammad Sidique Khan, one of the 7/7 bombers who made a videotape that was shown by Al Jazeera (1 September 2005), talks about "my people" in his statement, but he meant Muslims all over the world, and definitely not the British people.

The questions of belonging and the politics of belonging constitute some of the most difficult issues confronting all of us these days, and this chapter hopes to contribute to the understanding of some of them. In these post-9/11 (and 7/7) times, "strangers" are seen not only as a threat to the cohesion of the political and cultural community but also as potential terrorists, especially the younger men among them. The question of who is "a stranger" and who "does not belong," however, is also continuously being modified and contested, with growing ethnic, cultural, and religious tensions within as well as between societies and states. Politics of belonging have come to occupy the heart of the political agenda almost everywhere in the world, even when reified assumptions about **"the clash of civilizations"** (Huntington 1993) are not necessarily applied. As Francis B. Nyamnjoh (2005, 18) notes, "in Africa, as elsewhere, there is a growing obsession with belonging, along with new questions concerning conventional assumptions about nationality and citizenship." Ulf Hedetoff and Mette Hjort (2002, x) point out that "today belonging constitutes a political and cultural field of global contestation, anywhere: between ascriptions of belonging and self-constructed definitions of new spaces of culture, freedom and identity."

The aim of this chapter is to frame, both theoretically and contextually, the main debates that have emerged both in academia and in the political arena around various major political projects of belonging. Alongside the **hegemonic** forms of citizenship and nationalism that have tended to dominate the twentieth-century constructions and contestations of multiculturalism, indigenous and diasporic political projects of belonging and multi-faithism constitute only some of these debates. The effects of **globalization**, mass migration, the rise of both fundamentalist and human rights movements on the politics of belonging, with its radicalized and gendered dimensions, will also be investigated.

The chapter uses an intersectional analytical perspective to deconstruct simplistic notions of national and ethnic collectivities and their boundaries and to interrogate some of the differential effects that various political projects of belonging have on members of these collectivities, who are differently located socially, economically, and politically. Thus, the first part of this chapter examines the notion of intersectionality. After this theoretical framework has been clarified, the chapter introduces the notions of belonging and the politics of belonging, and social locations, identifications, and values. The chapter then outlines some of the general features of the contemporary globalization context, within which the various intersectional political projects of belonging operate. It discusses globalization, how states have been reconfigured under neo-liberal globalization, and the ways in which mass migration and the discourse of **securitization** can affect and are affected by these processes.

Intersectionality

Lesley McCall (2005, 1771) and others argue that intersectionality is "the most important theoretical contribution that women's studies, in conjunction with related fields, has made so far." Indeed, the imprint of intersectional analysis can be easily traced to innovations in equality legislation, human rights, and development discourses. Amazingly enough, however, in spite of the term's "brilliant career" (Lutz 2002), intersectionality hardly appears in sociological stratification theories (a notable exception is Anthias 2005; see also Yuval-Davis 2011). So what is intersectionality?

Epistemologically, intersectionality can be described as a development of feminist **standpoint theory**, which claims that it is vital to account for the social positioning of the social agent and challenge "the god-trick of seeing everything from nowhere" (Haraway 1991, 189) as a cover for and a legitimization of a hegemonic masculinist "positivistic" positioning. **Situated gaze**, situated knowledge, and situated imagination (Stoetzler and Yuval-Davis 2002) construct how we see the world in different ways. However, intersectionality theory is even more interested in how the situatedness of different social agents

shapes the ways they affect and are affected by different social, economic, and political projects. In this way it can no doubt be considered as one of the outcomes of the mobilization and proliferation of different identity groups' struggles for recognition (Taylor 1992; Fraser 1995).

The history of what is currently called "intersectional thinking" is long. Many pinpoint the famous speech of the emancipated slave Sojourner Truth (Brah and Phoenix 2004) during the first wave of feminism as one early illustration of the concept. Speaking at an abolitionist convention, Sojourner Truth argued that, although she worked hard and carried heavy loads, she was not less of a woman or a mother than privileged women, who were constructed as weak and in need of constant help and protection as a result of what society considered to be "feminine" ways.

Before intersectional analysis became mainstream, it was carried out for many years by mainly black and other racialized women who, from their situated gaze, perceived attempts by feminists and others since the start of the second wave of feminism to homogenize women's situation, and especially to find it analogous to that of black people, misleading and absurd. As bell hooks, who chose Truth's **crie du coeur** "Ain't I a Woman?" as the title of her first book (hooks 1981), mockingly remarked in the introduction to that book, "This implies that all women are White and all Blacks are men."

As Avtar Brah and Anne Phoenix (2004, 80) point out, other black feminists fulfilled significant roles in the development of intersectional analysis. As early as 1977, the Combahee River Collective, a black lesbian feminist organization from Boston, for example, identified the need to develop an integrated analysis and practice based upon the fact that the major systems of oppression were interlocking. Angela Davis, who, for many, has come to symbolize the spirit of revolutionary black feminism, published her book *Women, Race and Class* in 1981. The term *intersectionality* was itself, however, introduced in 1989 by another American black feminist, the legal and critical race theorist Kimberlé Crenshaw, when she discussed the issues surrounding black women's employment in the United States and the intersection of gender, race, and class in black women's exploitation and exclusion. Intersectional analysis was developed roughly at the same time by several European and post-colonial feminists as well (e.g., Bryan, Dadzie, and Scafe 1985; James 1986; Essed 1991; Lutz 1991). Examining the parallel development of feminist standpoint theory, Sandra Harding (1997, 389) wrote, "feminist standpoint theory was evidently an idea whose time had come, since most of these authors worked independently and were unaware of each other's work." Thus, feminist standpoint theory and intersectional theorizing are now recognized on a global scale.

Intersectionality is a metaphorical term meant to evoke images of a traffic intersection with an indeterminate or contested number of intersecting roads, depending on the various users of the terms and how many social divisions are considered in the particular intersectional analysis. As will be discussed below, the number of intersections can change considerably from two to infinity. In a 2008 lecture, Kum-Kum Bhavnani used the term *configurations* as an alternative metaphor to emphasize the flowing, interweaving threads that constitute intersectionality, which she found a much too rigid and fixed metaphor. Davina Cooper (2004, 12) also explains that she used the term *social dynamics* rather than *intersectionality* because she wants her terminology to trace the shifting ways relations of inequality become attached to various aspects of social life. While I agree with all these explanations, which are important for the theorization of intersectionality in this book, I retain the term intersectionality because, being so widespread, it evokes an intuitive understanding of the subject matter.

Three main positions in relation to the intersectionality approach used in this chapter need to be clarified here. The first relates to the division McCall (2005) makes between those approaches to intersectionality that she calls "inter-categorical" and "intra-categorical"; the second relates to the

relationships that should be understood as existing between the various intersectional categories; and the third relates to the boundaries of the intersectional approach and thus the number of and which social categories should be included in intersectional analysis inter- or intra-categories.

According to McCall, intersectional studies either use an inter- or intra-categorical approach. By an inter-categorical approach she means that the work focuses on the way the intersection of different social categories, such as race, gender, class, and so on affects particular social behaviours or the distribution of resources. Intra-categorical studies, on the other hand, are less occupied with the relationships among various social categories and instead problematize the meaning and boundaries of the categories themselves, such as whether black women were included in the category "women" or the shifting boundaries of who is considered to be "black" in a particular place and time. Unlike McCall, I do not see these two approaches as mutually exclusive. Instead, I would ask for intersectional thinking that combines the sensitivity and dynamism of the intra-categorical approach with the more macro socio-economic perspective of the inter-categorical approach.

As will be elaborated below, I consider as crucial the analytical differentiation between different facets of social analysis—that of people's positionings along socio-economic grids of power, that of people's experiential and identificatory perspectives of where they belong, and that of their normative value systems. These different facets[1] are related to each other but are also irreducible to each other. Moreover, although I consider intersectional analysis to be a development of feminist standpoint theory, I would also argue that there is no direct causal relationship between the situatedness of people's gaze and their cognitive, emotional, and moral perspectives on life. People born into the same families and/or the same time and social environment can have different identifications and political views. For this reason alone, it is not enough to construct inter-categorical tabulations in order to predict and, even more so, to understand people's positions and attitudes to life.

The Boundaries of Intersectional Analysis and Intersectional Categories

Kimberlé Crenshaw (1989, 139) defines intersectionality as "the multidimensionality of marginalized subjects' lived experiences." Other black feminists (e.g., Dill 1983; Bryan, Dadzie, and Scafe 1985) also remain within the triad boundaries of race, class, and gender. Philomena Essed (1991) even limits intersectionality to the two dimensions of "gendered racisms" and "racist genderisms." Others have added the specific categories they were interested in, such as age (e.g., Bradley 1996), disability (e.g., Oliver 1996; Meekosha and Dowse 1997), **sedentarism** (e.g., Lentin 1999), or sexuality (e.g., Kitzinger 1987). In other works, however, feminists have attempted to develop complete lists of cateogories of difference, which include much higher numbers. For example, Helma Lutz (2002) discusses 14 categories while Charlotte Bunch (2001) lists 16. Floya Anthias and I (1983, 1992; see also Yuval-Davis 2006, 2011) strongly argue that intersectional analysis should not be limited only to those who are on the multiple margins of society, but rather that the boundaries of intersectional analysis should encompass all members of society, and thus intersectionality should be seen as the right theoretical framework for analyzing social stratification. There is a parallel here with the struggle that many of us witnessed during the 1970s and 1980s to point out (what these days seems much more obvious) that everybody, not just racialilzed minorities, have "ethnicities" and that members, especially men in hegemonic majorities, are not just "human beings" but are also gendered, classed, ethnocized, etc.

In *Gender Trouble*, Judith Butler (1990) mocks the "etc." that often appears at the end of long (and different) lists of the social divisions mentioned by feminists. She sees it as an embarrassed admission of a "sign of exhaustion as well as of the illimitable process of signification itself" (1990, 143). Nevertheless, the question remains of whether there are, or are not, in any particular historical condition, specific and limited numbers of social divisions that will construct the grid of power relations within which the different members of the society are located.

I have two different answers to this question, which are not mutually exclusive. The first one is that, while in specific historical situations and in relation to the daily lives of specific people, there are some social divisions that are more important than others in constructing people's specific positionings relative to others around them, there are some social divisions—such as gender, age, ethnicity, and class—that will tend to shape most people's lives in most social locations, while other social divisions—such as those relating to disability, caste, or status as indigenous or refugee—will tend to affect fewer people globally. At the same time, for those people who are affected by these and other social divisions not mentioned here in particular historical contexts, such social divisions are crucial, and thus rendering them visible needs to be fought for. This is a case where recognition—of the social power axes, not of social identities—is of vital political importance.

My second answer relates to what Cornelius Castoriadis called the "creative imagination" (1987; see also Marcel Stoetzler and Yuval-Davis 2002) that underlies any linguistic and other social categories of signification. Although certain social conditions may facilitate the creative imagination, the construction of categories of signification is a product of human creative freedom and autonomy. Without specific social agents who will construct and point to certain analytical and political features, the rest of us would not be able to distinguish between analytical and political features. Rainbows include the whole spectrum of different colours, but how many of these colours we distinguish will depend on our specific social and linguistic milieu. Thus, struggles for recognition will always also include an element of construction. Moreover, understanding the relationships between positionings, identities, and political values, which I view as central to the study of belonging, is crucial (and impossible if these are all reduced to the same ontological level).

So, what are belonging and the politics of belonging?

Belonging and the Politics of Belonging

It is important to differentiate between belonging and the politics of belonging. Belonging is about an emotional (or even **ontological**) attachment, about feeling "at home." As Ghassan Hage (1997, 103) points out, however, "home is an on-going project entailing a sense of hope for the future" (see also Taylor 2009). Part of this feeling of hope relates to home as a "safe" space (Ignatieff 2001). In the daily reality of the early twenty-first century, in so many places on the globe, this emphasis on safety acquires a new poignancy. At the same time, it is important to emphasize that feeling "at home" does not necessarily only generate positive and warm feelings. It also allows the emotional engagement to be, at times, angry, resentful, ashamed, indignant (Hessel 2010).

Belonging tends to be naturalized and to be part of everyday practices (Fenster 2004a, 2004b). It becomes articulated, formally structured, and politicized only when it is threatened in some way. The politics of belonging comprise specific political projects aimed at constructing belonging to particular collectivity or collectivities, which are themselves constructed in these projects in very specific ways and with very specific boundaries (e.g., whether or not, according to specific political projects of belonging, Jews can be considered to be German, or whether abortion advocates can be considered Catholic). As Marco Antonsich (2010) points out, however, these boundaries are often spatial and relate to a specific locality/territoriality and not just to constructions of social collectivities. Of course, according to Doreen Massey (2005), space in itself is but an embodiment of social networks. However, as Carrillo Rowe (2005,

21) writes, "belongings are conditioned by our bodies and where they are placed on the globe." Nevertheless, diasporic and transnational belongings, especially those that use the virtual realities of the Internet can, at least partially, transcend these limits of physical geography. Also bell hooks (1990) talks about "homespace" as something that transcends the domestic. As Ulf Hannerz (2002) claims, home is essentially a contrastive concept, linked to some notion of what it means to be away from home. It can involve a sense of rootedness in a socio-geographic site or be constructed as an intensely imagined affiliation with a distant locale where self-realization can occur.

Belonging and the politics of belonging have been some of the major themes around which both classic psychology and sociology emerged. Countless psychological, and even more psychoanalytical, works have been dedicated to writings about the fears of separation of babies and children from the womb, from the mother, from the familiar, as well as the devastating—often pathological—effects on them when they cannot take belonging for granted (for more elaborate accounts of this, see, for example Rank 1973 [1929]; Bowlby 1969, 1973). Similarly, much of social psychology literature has been dedicated to people's need to conform to the groups they belong to for fear of exclusion and inferiorization and the ways people's interpersonal relationships are deeply affected by their membership or lack of membership of particular groups—as well as their positions in these groups (e.g. Lewin 1948; Billig 1976; Tajfel 1982).

In sociological theory, since its establishment, many writings have been focused on the differential ways people belong to collectivities and states—as well as the social, economic, and political effects of instances of displacement of such belonging/s as a result of industrialization and/or migration. Some basic classical examples are Tonnies's distinction between **Gemeinschaft** and **Gesellschaft** (1940 [1935]), Durkheim's division of **mechanical and organic solidarity** (1893) or Marx's notion of alienation (1975 [1844]). Anthony Giddens (1991) has argued that during modernity people's sense of belonging becomes reflexive, and Manuel Castells (1996–98) has claimed that contemporary society has become the **"network society"** in which effective belonging has moved away from civil societies of nations and states into reconstructed defensive identity communities.

Belonging

People can "belong" in many different ways and to many different objects of attachment. These can vary from a particular person to the whole of humanity, in a concrete or abstract way, by self or other identification, in a stable, contested or transient way. Even in its most stable **"primordial"** forms, however, belonging is always a dynamic process, not a reified fixity—the latter is only a naturalized construction of a particular hegemonic form of power relations. Belonging is usually multi-layered and, to use geographical jargon, multi-scale (Antonsich 2010) or multi-territorial (Hannerz 2002).

To clarify our understanding of the notion of social and political belonging, it would be useful to differentiate between three major analytical facets in which belonging is constructed.[2] The first facet concerns social locations; the second relates to people's identifications and emotional attachments to various collectivities and groupings; and the third relates to ethical and political value systems with which people judge their own and others' belonging. These different facets are interrelated, but cannot be reduced to each other.

Social Locations

When it is said that people belong to a particular sex, race, class, or nation, that they belong to a particular age group, kinship group, or a certain profession, we are talking about people's social and economic locations, which at each historical moment would tend to carry with them particular weights in the grids of power relations operating in their society. Being a man or a woman, black or white, working-class or middle-class, a member of

a European or an African nation, people are not just different categories of social location, with different contextual meanings; they also tend to have certain positionalities along axes of power that are higher or lower than other such categories. Such positionalities, however, would tend to be different in different historical contexts and are also often fluid and contested. Sometimes, however, as Sandra Harding (1991) and Nancy Fraser (in Fraser and Honneth 1998) have commented, certain differences would not necessarily have differential power positionings but are only the markers for different locations. This, again, can only be related to specific differences in particular historical moments and contexts.

Social locations, however, even in their most stable format, are virtually never constructed along one power vector of difference, although official statistics—as well as identity politics—would often tend to construct them in this way. This is why the intersectional approach to social locations is so vitally important.

Marxists and other sociologists have traditionally tended to prioritize class, even when recognizing other axes of social location, while feminists have tended to prioritize gender, and those who are focused on issues of race and ethnicity have tended to prioritize people's locations according to these categories. Indeed, in different historical moments, different systems of stratification tend to give differential weight to different intersectional categories of location and axes of power and they might operate in many different ways—hence the need for case studies using an intra-categorical research approach to complement more macro inter-categorical ones. Much depends on people's ability to move up those grids of power and the extent to which locations ascribed at birth can be transcended, either by moving from one category of location to another, such as becoming "middle class" while being originally "working class," or, even more dramatically, being **transgender** or becoming assimilated into a different national, ethnic, or even racial collectivity. Different locations along social and economic axes are often marked by different embodied signifiers, such as colour of skin, accent, clothing, and mode of behaviour. However, these should not be collapsed and automatically equated with subjective identifications and social attachments.

Identifications and Emotional Attachments

Identities are narratives, stories people tell themselves and others about who they are (and who they are not) (Martin 1995; see also Kaptani and Yuval-Davis 2008; Yuval-Davis 2010). Not all of these stories are about belonging to particular groupings and collectivities—they can be, for instance, about individual attributes, body images, vocational aspirations, or sexual prowess. However, even these stories will often relate, directly or indirectly, to self and/or others' perceptions of what being a member of such a grouping or collectivity (ethnic, racial, national, cultural, religious) might mean. Identity narratives can be individual or they can be collective, with the latter often acting as a resource for the former. Although they can be reproduced from generation to generation, it is always in a selective way: they can shift and change, be contested and multiple. These identity narratives can relate to the past, to a myth of origin; they can be aimed to explain the present and probably; above all, they function as a projection of future trajectory.

Identity narratives can be verbal, but can also be constructed as specific forms of practices (Fortier 2000). Narratives of identities can be more or less stable in different social contexts, more or less coherent, more or less authorized and/or contested by the self and others, depending on specific situational factors, and can reflect routinized constructions of everyday life or those of significant moments of crisis and transformation. They include both cognitive and emotional dimensions with varying degrees of attachment: "individuals and groups are caught within wanting to belong, wanting to become, a process that is fuelled by yearning rather than positing of identity as a stable state." (Probyn 1996, 19).

Of course not every belonging is important to people in the same way and to the same extent, and emotions, as perceptions, shift in different times and situations and are more or less reflective. As a rule, the emotional components of people's constructions of themselves and their identities become more central, the more threatened and less secure they become. In the more extreme cases people would be willing to sacrifice their lives—and the lives of others—for the narrative of their identities and the objects of their identifications and attachments to continue to exist. After a terrorist attack, or after a declaration of war, people will often seek to return to a place of less "objective" safety, as long as it means they can be close to their nearest and dearest, and share their fate.

Ethical and Political Values

Belonging is not just about social locations and constructions of individual and collective identities and attachments. It is also concerned with the ways these are assessed and valued by the self and others, and this can be done in many different ways by people with similar social locations who might identify themselves as belonging to the same community or grouping. These can vary not only in how important these locations and collectivities seem to be in one's life and that of others, but also in whether they consider this to be a good or a bad thing. Closely related to this are specific attitudes and ideologies concerning where and how identity and categorical boundaries are being/should be drawn, in more or less permeable ways, as different ideological perspectives and discourses construct them as more or less inclusive. It is in the arena of the contestations around these issues where we move from the realm of belonging into that of the politics of belonging.

The Politics of Belonging

The politics of belonging involves not only constructions of boundaries but also the inclusion or exclusion of particular people, social categories, and groupings within these boundaries by those who have the power to do this. But what are these kind/s of power?

Politics involves the exercise of power and different hegemonic political projects of belonging represent different symbolic power orders. In recent years, the sociological understanding of power has been enriched by the theoretical contributions of Michel Foucault (1979, 1991) and Pierre Bourdieu (1984, 1990). Traditionally, power was understood and measured by the effects those with power had on others. However, feminists and other grassroots activists, following Paulo Freire's *Pedagogy of the Oppressed* (1970), promoted a notion of "**empowerment**" in which people would gain "power of" rather than "power over." While this approach has been used too often to cover intra-communal power relations and the feminist "tyranny of structurelessness" with which Jo Freeman (1970) described the dynamics of feminist politics, the notion of empowerment fits with alternative theoretical approaches to power which focus on symbolic power.

Symbolic powers are of crucial importance when we deal with political projects of belonging, although more often than not, they are the focus for contestations and resistance. Adrian Favell (1999) defined the politics of belonging as "the dirty work of boundary maintenance." The boundaries the politics of belonging are concerned with are the boundaries of the political community of belonging, the boundaries that, sometimes physically, but always symbolically, separate the world population into "us" and "them." The question of the boundaries of belonging, the boundaries of Benedict Anderson's (1991 [1983]) "imagined communities" is central in all the political projects of belonging. The politics of belonging involve not only the maintenance and reproduction of the boundaries of the community of belonging by the hegemonic political powers (within and outside the community), but also their contestation, challenge, and resistance by other political agents. It is important to recognize, however, that such political agents would struggle both for the promotion of their specific position on the construction of collectivities and their boundaries as well as using these ideologies and positions in order to promote their own power positions within and outside the collectivities.

The politics of belonging also include struggles around the determination of what is involved in belonging, in being a member of such a community. As such, it is dialogical (Yuval-Davis and Werbner 1999) and encompasses contestations both in relation to the participatory dimension of citizenship as well as in relation to issues related to the status and entitlements such membership entails. In order to understand some of the contestations involved in different constructions of belonging promoted by different political projects of belonging, we need to look at what is required from a specific person in order for her/him to be entitled to belong, to be considered as belonging, to the collectivity. Common descent (or rather the myth of common descent) might be demanded in some cases, while in others it might be a common culture, religion, and/or language.

Loyalty and solidarity, based on common values and a projected myth of common destiny, tend to become requisites for belonging in pluralist societies. In other words, in different projects of the politics of belonging, the different facets of belonging—social locations, identities, and ethical and political values—can become the requisites of belonging and the delineation of boundaries.

Requisites of belonging that relate to "ascriptive" social locations—origin, "race," place of birth—would be the most racialized and the least permeable. Language, culture, and sometimes religion are more open to a voluntary, often assimilatory, identification with particular collectivities. Using a common set of values, such as "democracy" or "human rights," as the signifiers of belonging can be seen as having the most permeable boundaries of all.

However, these different discourses of belonging can be collapsed together or reduced down to each other in specific historical cases. Moreover, some political projects of belonging can present themselves as promoting more open boundaries than they actually do. Contested political projects exist virtually everywhere. For example, in India, there is contestation between it being a pluralist secular society, in which belonging is defined by being born in the country, or a Hindutva nation; in Australia, there is debate about whether Aboriginals can be part of an Australian nation or need their own self-determination as a "first nation"; and in the South African context, the issue is whether Afrikaners can be considered "indigenous" people rather than "settlers."

Globalization and Glocalization

Globalization and, as discussed below, glocalization need to be seen as the context within which contemporary contesting political projects of belonging are taking place. However, they are in themselves ongoing contesting and shifting processes, which are continuously being modified by various internal and external factors in which political projects of belonging play significant roles.

Globalization, especially in its neo-liberal format, has become increasingly visible in the post–Cold War period, with the fall of the Soviet Union and the rule of Ronald Reagan in the United States and Margaret Thatcher in the UK. As Jan Aart Scholte (2005) claims, however, **harbingers** of globality can be traced back hundreds, if not thousands, of years. Christopher Colombus was definitely not the first "foreigner" to "discover" America, even if we do not accept Gavin Menzies's controversial (2002) thesis that a huge Chinese fleet had visited America already in 1421. Raiders, and before them traders, have continuously advanced routes of (often unequal) exchange and communication across different parts of the globe. Notable transworld connectedness existed from the middle of the nineteenth century. However, the greatest expansion of transplanetary relations has transpired since the middle of the twentieth century and the **Bretton Woods** agreements that established the **World Bank** and the **International Monetary Fund (IMF)**. Saskia Sassen (2006, 17) points out that internal transformations in nation-states, which enabled globalization "proper," started in the late 1970s. She sees globalization as "an epochal transformation, one as yet young but already showing its muscle" (2006, 1).

There is only loose agreement about what actually constitutes globalization. Part of the confusion relates to different theories defining or emphasizing different elements as characterizing globalization as well as its connections with neo-liberalism. Immanuel Wallerstein (1976, 1980, 1989), who first put forward the model of the "world system," described it basically in terms of the development of a world economy in which unequal relationships existed between the centre and periphery. Other models of globalization (e.g, Meyer 1980; Robertson 1992; and Beyer 1994) have added to this model aspects of a global polity, global culture, and global society.

Scholte (2005), however, claims that most of the characteristics that are usually counted to typify globalization—such as internalization, liberalization, universalization, and Westernization—have existed previously. Only the "**respatialization** with the spread of transplanetary social connections" (Scholte 2005, 3) is distinctive and key to contemporary historical development (although, no doubt, the sense of respatialization occurred in each age in which major new transport and communication technologies have been introduced). This time/space compression, the specific respatialization of the present globalization, has been possible as a result of the micro-chip revolution, revolutionary changes in speed and the cost of global transport (Dicken 2003; Rodrigue 2006), and even more so in global communication, especially the Internet (Block 2004), creating what Castells calls "information societies": "social organization in which information generation, processing and transmission become fundamental sources of production and power because of new technological conditions emerging in this historical period" (Castells 2000 [1998], 21). These developments—and the differential access to them by different populations and segments of a population—have been crucial in shaping and structuring some of the central characteristics of contemporary politics of belonging.

It is not only descriptions but also explanations of the phenomenon that vary. In some ways there is collusion between Marxist and liberal economic theories, which see in globalization a natural continuation of the development of the logic of capitalism and the market economy since the nineteenth century. The Soviet Union, the Cold War, and the resultant welfare social democratic states are seen, from this perspective, as a temporary aberration that camouflaged, interrupted, and distorted this development until the global political balance of power shifted towards the time of the fall of the Soviet Union. For others, the post–Second World War period prepared the grounds for globalization with the development of various regulatory[3] apparatuses that were provided through a host of state, suprastate, and private governance mechanisms that have since brought about these new epochal changes, enhanced by the changing political context and the scientific and technological developments that changed basic relations and the mode of production.

As Saskia Sassen (2006) argues, the capabilities required for globalization developed within the context of (Western) nation-states and reached tipping points in which they were transformed by and became part of the new assemblage of the global economic and political order. Globalization reshaped and expanded capitalism (i.e., the economy), which is centred on surplus accumulation. The growth of transworld spaces has encouraged major extensions of capitalist production, including in the areas of information, communications, and finance biotechnology. Notable shifts occurred in the ways that processes of surplus accumulation operate—e.g., offshore arrangements and transworld corporate alliances—towards what Sassen calls "**hypercapitalism**."

Hypercapitalism, or neo-liberalism, however, is driven by the same impulses that drove nineteenth-century imperial capitalism, and it has found new fields for the "primitive accumulation of capital" with the appropriation of capital and goods from the public sector—spectacularly, in the post-communist countries but also in the spreading control of neo-liberal market norms in more and more sectors of the state, both in the so-called developing world as well as in the West.

The notion of the "global" is usually constructed as opposite to that of the "local." Local communities can have different relationships with the globalization process. They can, to a certain extent at least, still exist outside the globalization processes; they can coexist with the global environment/influence; and they can also be constituted as a reaction to the processes of globalization and become a site of resistance to it. As Erik Swyngedouw (1997) argues, **glocalization** relates to transformations in the international political economy and urban geography—the parallel shifts towards global and local scales of political relationships, such as the rising influence of the EU and G8 on the one hand, and the proliferation of local economic partnerships and initiatives on the other. There is an important role here for metropolises in connecting the local, the national, and the international.

However, we should not necessarily assume that naturalized and harmonized relationships always exist between the local and the global. The complex connection/relation between them does not necessarily imply mirroring but can also produce conflict and resistance. Graziella Moraes Dias da Silva and Luisa Farah Schwartzman (2006), for instance, discuss the different and contradictory ways in which affirmative action policies were received in Brazil. Rather than being perceived as anti-discrimination policies based on human rights, they were seen by many as the cultural imperialism of the United States, which threatened, under the different conditions in which affirmative action policies were carried in Brazil, certain constructions of "local essence."

It is for this reason that Roland Robertson (1995), who developed the notion of glocalization, argued that successful glocalization does not simply produce or reproduce random forms of **cultural heterogeneity**. It also registers the "standardization of locality" so that various localities may possess very similar structures, reference points, and symbolic textures or contents. The local becomes globally institutionalized. This will be crucial when we examine the glocal nature of various contemporary political projects of belonging.

Nevertheless, this does not mean that globalization equals homogenization. Jan Pieterse (1995) points out that globalization is instead developed more by the fluid and critical engagement of local social actors and results more in the processes of **creolization** and **hybridization**. Talal Asad (1986) has introduced within that context the important notion of "translation," which is much wider than the linguistic one. Even McDonald's, which has been used by Benjamin Barber (1995) and others to illustrate the impact of the commodification and standardization of globalization, in spite of the universal golden arches, conducts local market surveys and adapts its menus to local demands. Moreover, the local meaning of McDonald's can vary hugely, given its specific historical context. While in Moscow the arrival of McDonald's in 1990 was hailed as a welcome signifier of the opening of the Soviet Union to the big wide world, there was for quite some years a fierce local resistance to establishing a McDonald's in Paris.

Resistance to (as well as incorporation into) Western-dominated, neo-liberal globalization has been conducted on different levels, both by states, such as the Chinese state-controlled economic globalization or the Latin American globalizing economic anti-imperialism led by leaders such as Hugo Chavez and Evo Morales, and by non-statist movements, networks, and organizations, such as the **World Social Forum** (which started as an **anti-Davos** event) and the anti-globalization movement as a whole. Other movements of resistance have been the fundamentalist Islamist groups and organizations loosely coordinated by the Al-Qaeda network.

States and Neo-Liberal Globalization

The transformation of state apparatuses under neo-liberal globalization is usually constructed as their "**modernization**." States, in various forms and scales, from cities to empires, have existed since ancient times in different parts of the world. Since the French Revolution, although empires have continued to exist and grow (including, at certain times, the French empire), states have come to be seen as "nation-states" in which, to use Max Weber's classical definition (1948 [1947], 78), "a human community (successfully) claims the monopoly of the legitimate use of physical force within a given territory." This definition assumes a particular "human community," the nation, with particular boundaries, that is living in a particular territory, the "homeland," with particular borders, that is governed by a state that assumes a monopoly of the legitimate use of physical force to police that state within and fight its enemies without. The 1648 Treaty of Westphalia assumed this to be the basic legitimate form of geopolitical organization and it was hegemonic in international relations, at least in Europe itself, until the late twentieth century (Brenner et al. 2003).

This "holy trinity" of people, territory, and state was always more fiction than fact, as both collectivity boundaries and territorial borders have been continuously contested by both state and non-state agencies, and there have been more often than not blurred edges to what passed as the monopoly of legitimate use of physical force by the state.

With the growing hegemony of neo-liberal ideologies and policies and the strengthening of neo-liberal global market forces, more and more agencies and apparatus of the state, in more and more countries, have been privatized partially or fully (Panitch 1994; Jessop 2002; McBride 2005). This raises the same old question of what constitutes the specific sphere of "the state" to differentiate it from the sphere of "civil society" (which itself needs to be subdivided into economic, social, and domestic spheres). In one pole of the debate we have the classical Weberian definition in which the state has a monopoly on the legitimate use of physical power (1948 [1947]), and on the other we have the Foucauldian perspective (1979, 1991), according to which no such specific powers can be seen universally as the exclusive property of the state.

Part of the difference between these two perspectives stems from their different theorizations of the meaning of power. However, part of the difference between the two, is also, I believe, a result of the different historical times in which Weber and Foucault wrote their theorizations of the state. As Foucault pointed out (1991), late modernity brought with it new technologies of governance, a "governmentality" in which much of the work was done within the subjectivities of the citizens, rather than by the state exercising the external powers in its disposal. Given the number of civil wars throughout the globe, in which the military and other power sources of the state are used against particular sections of the population, such a Foucauldian portrayal of contemporary states seems, however, to lean much too heavily on the liberal fiction of the individual relationship between an abstract non-embodied citizen and the state.

A sense of belonging, as was argued above, is about feeling "at home," feeling "safe," and if not necessarily feeling in control, at least feeling able enough generally to predict expectations and rules of behaviour. It is not surprising, therefore, that when people feel that their entitlements as citizens who belong and live within a country or state are under threat, or their rights are being taken away from them, they will react. The discourses in which these frustrations are being expressed can follow very different directions. Various constructions of contemporary citizenship have grown as a result of and in resistance to these developments. Mass international migration, in addition to the growing pressure on citizens as a result of the reconfiguration of the state and citizens' social rights, has affected and changed people's politics of belonging, whether they choose to migrate or stay in their countries of origin.

International Migration

The relationship between citizens and their states is constructed as a permanent if not a static one. However, such an image is currently being challenged and technologies of governance have to be reinvented when in various states large numbers of people move in or out for a variety of economic, political, social, and ecological reasons. In their now classic book, *The Age of Migration* (2003), Stephen Castles and Mark J. Miller claim that the contemporary era is the **"age of migration."** They argue that as a result of the transport and communication revolutions, the deregulation of the neo-liberal global market, as well as the growing numbers of local wars and natural disasters, there are unprecedented numbers of people who are searching for a better future for themselves and their children, both as economic migrants and as asylum seekers. Some would be settling in other countries, some would be returning to their homes and/or their countries of origin after several years, and many would be developing transnational identities and lifestyles by carrying on travelling between the different locations. On the other hand, there are those, like Hein De Haas (2005), who would argue that the above picture is a myth—that these days, the percentage of international migrants in the total world population is almost on the same level as it was a century ago (about 2.5 per cent to 3 per cent).

This statistical picture, however, covers over a much more complex reality. First, given the huge growth of the global population during the last century, the actual number of people moving these days is much larger—about 150 million[4]—even if the percentage has remained more or less the same. Second, and even more importantly, while the percentage of migrants has largely remained static, the direction of migration has largely changed. A century ago, most of the migration was directed towards "the New World": colonies and settler societies and countries dominated by the West in America, Australia, Africa, and to a lesser extent Asia, in which a growing economy, as well as other social, political, and military factors, depended on more immigration. "Populate or perish" was a popular slogan in the Australia of these days. However, this slogan was also accompanied at the same time by what is known as white Australia immigration legislation, guided by the principle that the immigrant population had to be of "the right kind." For example, the **"yellow peril"** from the Pacific rim countries was kept away by force for many years until both the economic demands and a lack of alternative migrant power, as well as the rise of international anti-discrimination human rights legislation, have now changed the formal rules dominating Australian as well as other Western racialized immigration legislation into these becoming a bit more open, at least on the surface (De Lepervanche, 1980). Today, most of the migration is not from northern to southern countries but the other way around (with the exception of **"tiger economies"** like India or the Gulf oil countries), unless it is to the "near abroad" countries, as is the case with most of those who are fleeing war and famine (UN 2008;[5] Athukorala and Manning 2009).

In Western countries like Britain and France, although the popular slogan among anti-immigration restriction campaigners is that "we are here because you were there" is much too over-simplistic, the interdependencies that have developed between European powers and their ex-colonies have played important parts in the development of new ethnic communities. Similar phenomena also happened in other European and industrial countries in which migrant workers were brought in to fulfil specific economic needs in post–Second World War Europe and were never envisaged to become permanent parts of the society. Many arrived under visas that constructed them as "guest workers," which entitled them to work for a specific time in specific places and then go back to their countries of origin. However, the reality has been that many of these people have remained "permanently temporary"—some getting local citizenships, many bringing in other family members, and many establishing a transnational lifestyle of movement between countries, as long as the political and economic situation has allowed it.

Many others arrived under refugee and **asylum-seeking legislation**. While in many countries there has been a long tradition of giving sanctuary and refuge to persecuted minorities (Marfleet 2011), the formal international protection of refugees was produced in the post–Second World War period but was heavily constructed in the West, and especially in Germany, towards accepting refugees from the Eastern Bloc. With the growing number of asylum seekers from the South, especially in the post–Cold War period, we can see paradoxically that, on the one hand, the Refugees and Asylum Act becomes part of domestic legislation in Europe in the 1990s, but on the other hand, more and more regulations were passed that were making applications for refugee status increasingly difficult. In the post-9/11 era, when often anyone resisting their government was constructed as a potential terrorist, the legal status of a refugee has become more and more difficult to achieve (Fekete 2009).

It is important to point out, however, that the legal dichotomy that is so often made in the literature and official statistics between economic and asylum types of migration is based on a falsehood. The drive for migration, which is never taken lightheartedly, is most often spurred on by a generic aspiration to have a better chance of the good life, especially for children. To a great extent this upward mobility of aspirations works, especially relative to those in the South who have not migrated, even when, in terms of local class structure in the North, these immigrants and refugees remain at the bottom of the scale, given the average income gap between North and South. Moreover, in order to be able to migrate to the West, rather than just to camps in the "near abroad," there is usually a need for migrants to have extra personal—or familial—economic resources that would enable them to arrange transportation to the West—often in indirect and illicit ways, and involving a lot of personal hardship. Therefore, rather than a bipolar typology, voluntary and forced migration need to be seen as two extremes of the one long continuum.

Similarly, it is difficult to draw a clear line between legal and illegal migration. With the tightening up of both asylum legislation as well as that of work permits, it has become much more difficult to immigrate by legal means. On the other hand, in the **deregulated neo-liberal economic markets**, a lot of the leisure industry, from waiters to sex workers, as well as other unskilled branches of the economy, have come to depend on illegal migrants who are prepared to work for under the minimum wage and in extremely exploitative conditions (EWCO 2007).

One also cannot often differentiate easily between countries of immigration and countries of emigration. In all European countries, for example, there is, on the one hand, the immigration of both unskilled workers as well as professionals, especially in the high-tech and service and care industries for Europe's aging population. On the other hand, there is emigration of **"ex-pat"** experts, the retired, and other people who are attracted by the chance to live in other warmer and cheaper countries in Europe and outside it (Knowles and Harper 2010). The BBC quotes a 2006 study that stated that more than 5.5 million Brits,[6] 4 million Americans,[7] and 2 million French were living abroad.[8]

One of the characteristics of "the age of migration" that Castles and Miller (2003) talk about is "the **feminization of migration**." The International Organization for Migration website says, "Women account for 49.6 per cent of global migrants," quoting the United Nations' *Trends in Total Migrant Stock, the 2005 Revision*.[9] This includes women who migrated as family dependents—either with their husbands or following them—as well as the growing number of women who migrated on their own, whether they were leaving behind them families of their own in their countries of origin or not. Again, the dichotomy between women workers and family dependents, which has existed in official statistics, is fictitious, as so many of the women who migrate as family dependents both want and need to work. The situation is similar concerning women asylum seekers and refugees. Often both husband and wife

have been politically active, but only the husband receives the status of refugee. As a result there have been many cases in Britain, for instance, when the husband had died and the legal protection of the refugee status has been taken away from the family whose immigration status then becomes precarious (Bhabha and Shutter 1994). The whole question of the rights of family members to immigrate when one of them is granted such a right has been central in many debates concerning migration and reflects contesting ideologies about the importance of the family: For example, is it always the duty of the wife to follow the husband or also the other way around? Most importantly, what is the family and what are its boundaries? This also covers whether elderly parents could be allowed to accompany their adult children, whether extended family are also family for the sake of migration, whether common-law families have such rights, and, of course, whether partners of the same sex can be constructed as a family in migration legislation. All these questions have been paradoxically affected by, on the one hand, the tightening rules and regulations of migration and, on the other hand, the growing hegemony of formal anti-discrimination legislation.

With the growing trend of "people on the move" and the economic and social interdependencies on migration, there is an increasing blurring of the line for "insiders–outsiders," those who are considered "indigenous" citizens, those who are naturalized, those who are on work permits, those who are applying for asylum, those who receive "exceptional leave to remain," those who are on temporary contracts of work, which may or may not be open for extension, as well as the many who enter a country on a tourist visa and do not leave afterwards, remaining in the country after their asylum application has been rejected, etc. Probably one of the most confusing and problematic ways of dealing with migrants who want to stay permanently has been the recent British proposal of "earned Citizenship." As British Prime Minister Gordon Brown stated in his speech when announcing a further tightening of immigration controls in the UK, the case for managed and controlled migration is not "an issue for fringe parties nor a taboo subject" but about "what it means to be British" (Mulholland 2009).

"Earned citizenship" is but one extreme technology among many others that have developed in recent years in numerous countries in order to maintain some stability and control of the citizenship boundaries of belonging. Part of the reason for this—especially in the case of welfare states—is the state duty to provide various public services to migrants, from housing to health to education, as well as to monitor their incomes for tax purposes. Part of the reason for this development, however, has been as a result of a nationalist and racist **autochthonic** anti-immigration discourse. In Israel, for example, the extreme right has co-opted the discourse of some on the left who have been calling for a one-state solution in which both Jews and Palestinians would have equal rights, but are also demanding that the Palestinians would not only swear allegiance to the state but would have to wait for up to 20 years to prove their loyalty and good citizenship.[10]

Moreover, with the growing number of migrants, the changing nature of economy and society, and especially after 9/11, technologies for regulating migration have become part of the growing discourse of "securitization," in which (some) people's belonging to their state of residence and even citizenship has become more and more contingent (Bigo 2002; Huysmans 2002).

The "Securitization" Discourse

During the late 1980s and 1990s, the privatization of many branches of states started to take place. This happened as a result of conservative governments' decisions, the conditions of the structural adjustment policies imposed by the World Bank and the IMF, and the dismantling of the post-communist states after the fall of the Soviet Union. During that period, as part of the "dividends of peace," military budgets were reduced all over the globe. Various military and policing agencies in Western states tried during that period to find themselves a new *raison d'etre*. This was the time when the securitization of international borders against undocumented migrants started to intensify and the notion of environmental security was also born.

"**Terrorism**" is a strategy for radical groupings all over the world and of various persuasions, from extreme right to extreme left, secular and religious. It has been used throughout the world, including in the West, well before 9/11 (even if we discard its popularity in Russia in the nineteenth century), during anti-colonial struggles, and by Irish and Palestinian resistance movements, as well as various others, including Al Qaeda. It was also used by extreme right organizations, like those behind the 1995 Oklahoma bombing in the United States or the Tokyo subway train attack by a member of the Aum Shinrikyo (Supreme Truth Sect) in the same year. However, the scale of the hit and the targeting of the US Pentagon and the twin towers of the World Trade Center in 9/11, and especially the timing, given the political needs of the US administration and other Western governments at the time, have legitimized the rise of securitization as a primary political discourse both locally and globally and pushed some alternative official political discourses which developed in the post–Cold War political reality (including that of "human security") aside. The military-industrial complex has found a much more lucrative outlet. While no doubt Shimshom Bichler and Jonathan Nitzan (2010) are right in claiming that much, if not most, of the profits during this era have been the result of an indirect manipulation of the market, the domination of the White House by the extreme **neo-cons** has opened up the arena to a whole new field of privatization, one that touches—and threatens—the heart of contemporary politics of belonging in the West, as well as in the rest of the world.

Naomi Klein (2007) and others have drawn attention to the growth in private militias and "armed security contractors" at an unprecedented scale during the conflicts in Iraq and Afghanistan, although their role had expanded in importance even before that in other conflict areas such as in Africa. Mercenaries are nothing new in inter- as well as intra-military conflicts. In some ways, since the end of the citizen-soldier in many Western countries in the post–Vietnam War period, most of the soldiers in regular armies are not there because of their national citizenship duty but because of the pay and other "career opportunities." The main difference between state-controlled professional armies on the one hand and individual mercenaries who volunteer to fight for a particular state (as in the case of the Foreign Legion in France) or for particular leadership contenders (such as the failed coup which involved Mark Thatcher, the son of the ex-British prime minister in Equatorial Guinea in Africa) on the other hand, is that today mercenaries mostly work for companies that are run along the lines of other corporations, with shareholders and annual profits. As with many other new corporations that appeared as a result of states **"out-sourcing"** their services in particular areas, states (especially the United States in the case of Blackwater USA, for instance) have helped the extreme profitability of such companies not only by buying their services in bulk but also by subsidizing the building of their infrastructure. This applies not only to military conflicts. Blackwater USA, for instance, was centrally involved with the emergency and security services after hurricane Katrina in New Orleans.[11]

However, much of the profitability of this sector is not necessarily in providing privatized human power but in the mass development of security devices. As Klein (2007) pointed out, the securitization discourse has created a massive new market for various surveillance devices. She highlights the leadership role Israel has had in the industry and how the Palestinian occupied territories have become a global laboratory for technological innovations of this kind, especially in various surveillance technologies, which are also used more widely in civic areas of our lives, from border checks to public transportation to poor housing estates.

Barack Obama's entry into the White House and the global economic crisis, which has saddled Western governments with unprecedented levels of debt, might somewhat curtail t the continuation of the mass expansion of this market (as has been hinted at by Obama's decision to cut the "Star Wars" programme). Nevertheless, it seems that in other areas of militarization, relating to the war in Afghanistan and NATO's expansion in the south of Europe towards Iran and the Middle East, Obama's rule in the White House has perhaps intensified this expansion rather than reduced it (Chomsky 2009).

Overall, however, if globalization has been characterized by huge movements of goods, capital, and people across the globe, it is the movement of people that has been constructed as one of the major security risks for which so many technological devices have been produced and marketed. The effects of international migration on states' *modus operandi* and contemporary constructions of citizenship go far beyond the securitization of borders and affect the construction of citizenship and belonging of all residents of the state, especially its racialized minorities, who might or might not have legal citizenship.

The technology for profiling the population, from school age upwards, for instance in terms of "potential home grown terrorists," cannot but affect the differential sense of belonging of citizens. At the same time, there are growing sentiments of anxiety and resentment among members of the hegemonic majority, especially among the relatively less well off, that they "don't count" any more. This leads to them feeling more alien and less attached to the state and other sections of civil society.

While part of the explanation of the growing disenchantment with the state and political parties relates to the centrality in these societies of "the multicultural question" (Hall with

Yuval-Davis 2004) and the growing **ethnicization** of states, part of this change can also be seen as a result of internal shifts within the state apparatus and the relative power of various branches of the state which affects the relationship between citizens and the state and their sense of accessibility and claim on it, as well as the contestations which arise out of the presence of contesting political projects of belonging among various members of the same society.

There are many contemporary political projects of belonging; clusters of such projects that focus (often in a non-mutually exhaustive fashion)

around notions of citizenship, nationalism, religion and cosmopolitanism, constitute the heart of the political projects of belonging agendas in the contemporary world.

I leave the task of discussing others—such as, for example, political projects of belonging constructed around issues of youth, sexuality, ecology, work and consuming cultures—to others. However, as a feminist, I am interested in particular in the feminist political projects of belonging and the ethics of care, which many would argue is the feminist political project of belonging.

Notes

1. In my previous work (e.g., Yuval-Davis 2006) I related to these different analytical facets as different analytical levels. Cass Balchin drew my attention to the fact that the term *levels* assumes a hierarchy. And indeed I do believe that the term is a remnant of the old Marxist infra- and super-structural levels. As I do not want to assume a presupposed hierarchy here I'm using the term *facets*.

2. As will become clearer further on in the chapter, these facets can be reconstructed and reconfigured in many different ways by different political projects of belonging.

3. These regulatory apparatuses and the mechanisms, while enabling the progressive growth of neo-liberal globalization, were not strong enough to contain and prevent the systemic crisis within the global economic system. The extent to which they would be able, in the long term, to facilitate overcoming that crisis has still to be seen, as is the differential effects this crisis would have on different localities, different states, and societies and people who are differentially located, socially, economically, and politically.

4. BBC News, "Global Migration Reaches Record High," 2 November 2000, http://news.bbc.co.uk/1/hi/world/europe/1003324.stm.

5. United Nations Population Division, International Migrant Stock, The 2008 Revision Population, http://esa.un.org/migration.

6. Finlo Rohrer, "So What is the Right Stuff?" *BBC News Magazine*, 23 April 2008, http://news.bbc.co.uk/1/h1/uk/6210358.stm.

7. "Record Numbers of Americans Living Abroad," April 2005, www.shelteroffshore.com/index.php/living/more/americans_living_abroad/.

8. "The French Also Live Abroad," 18 August 2009, *French-Property.com*, www.french-property.com/news/french_life/french_living_abroad.

9. UNICEF, "Children, Youth and Migration," 24 February 2005, http://eva.un.org/migration.

10. Ami Isseroff, "Israel-Palestine: The Jewish One-State Solution—Are they Serious?" *Middle East Web Log*, 19 July 2010, www.mideastweb.org/log/archives/00000783.htm.

11. http://blog.mises.org/archives/004852.asp.9. However, with the growing complexity and risk of the operations in Iraq and Afghanistan, Blackwater changed its name to Xe, and shifted its business focus to training facilities (see Dana Hedgpeth, "Blackwater Sheds Name, Shifts Focus," *Washington Post*, 14 February 2009, www.washingtonpost.com/wp-dyn/content/article/2009/02/13/AR2009021303149_pf.html).

References

Anderson, B. 1991. [1983]. *Imagined Communities: Reflections on the Origins and Spread of Nationalism.* London: Verso.

Anthias, F. 2005. "Social Stratification and Social Inequality: Models of Intersectionality and Identity." On F. Devine, M. Savage, J. Scott, and R. Crompton, eds, *Rethinking Class: Culture, Identities and Lifestyles.* New York: Palgrave Macmillan.

Anthias, F., and N. Yuval-Davis. 1983. "Contextualising Feminism: Gender, Ethnic and Class Divisions." *Feminist Review* 15 (November): 62–75.

———. 1992. *Racialized Boundaries: Race, Nation, Gender, Colour and Class and the Anti-Racist Struggle.* London: Routledge.

Antonsich, M. 2010. "Searching for Belonging—An Analytical Framework." *Geography Compass* 4 (6): 644–59.

Asad, T. 1966. *The Idea of an Anthropology of Islam.* Washington, DC: Center for Contemporary Arab Studies.

Athukorala, P.C., and C. Manning. 2009. *Structural Change and International Migration in East Asia: Adjusting to Labour Society.* Melbourne: Oxford University Press.

Barber, B.R. 1995. *Jihad vs McWorld: How Globalism and Tribalism are Shaping the World.* New York: Times Books.

Beyer, P. 1994. *Religion and Globalisation.* London: Sage.

Bhabha, J., and S. Shutter. 1994. *Women's Movement: Women under Immigration, Nationality and Refugee Law.* Stoke-on-Trent: Trentham Books.

Bichler, S., and J. Nitzan. 2010, May 6. "Capital as Power: Toward a New Cosmology of Capitalism." *Dissident Voice.* (Newsletter). http://dissidentvoice.org/2010/05/capital-as-power/.

Bigo, D. 2002. "Security and Immigration: Toward a Critique of the Governmentality of Unease." *Alternatives: Global, Local, Political* 27 (1): 63–92.

Billig, M. 1976. *Social Psychology and Intergroup Relations.* New York: Academic Press.

Block, D. 2004. "Globalization, Transnational Communication and the Internet." *International Journal on Multicultural Societies* 6 (1): 13–28.

Bourdieu, P. 1984. *Distinction: A Social Critique of the Judgement of Taste.* Trans Richard Nice. London: Routledge & Kegan Paul.

——. 1990. *The Logic of Practice.* Cambridge: Polity Press.

Bowlby, J. 1969. *Attachment.* Vol. 1 of *Attachment and Loss.* London and New York: Basic Books.

——. 1973. *Separation: Anxiety and Anger.* Vol. 2 of *Attachment and Loss.* London and New York: Basic Books.

Bradley, H. 1996. *Fractured Identities: The Changing Patterns of Inequality.* Cambridge: Polity Press.

Brah, A., and A. Phoenix. 2004. "Ain't I a Woman? Revisiting Intersectionality." *Journal of International Women's Studies* 5 (3): 75–86.

Brenner, N., B. Jessop, M. Jones, and G. MacLeod. 2003. *State/Space: A Reader.* Maldern, MA: Blackwell.

Bryan, B., S. Dadzie, and S. Scafe. 1985. *The Heart of the Race: Black Women's Lives in Britain.* London: Virago.

Bunch, C. 2001. "Women's Human Rights: The Challenges of Global Feminism and Diversity." In M. DeKoven ed., *Feminist Locations: Global and Local, Theory and Practice.* New Brunswick, NJ: Rutgers University Press, 129–46.

Butler, J. 1990. *Gender Trouble: Feminism and the Subversion of Identity.* New York: Routledge.

Castells, M. 1996–98. *The Information Age: Economy, Society, Culture.* Oxford: Blackwell.

——. 2000. (1998). *End of Millenium.* Oxford: Blackwell.

Castles, S., and M.J. Miller. 2003. *The Age of Migration.* London: Macmillam.

Castoriadis, C. 1987. *The Imaginary Institution of Society.* Cambridge: Polity Press.

Chomsky, N. 2009, October 27. "Crises and Unipolar Moment." *The Globalisation Lectures.* School of Oriental and African Studies, London, www.soas.ac.uk/events/event52739.html.

Cooper, D. 2004. *Challenging Diversity: Rethinking Equality and the Value of Difference.* Cambridge: Cambridge University Press.

Crenshaw, K. 1989. *Demarginalizing the Intersection of Race and Sex.* Chicago: University of Chicago.

De Haas, H. 2005. "International Migration, Remittances and Development: Myths and Facts." *Third World Quarterly* 26 (8): 1269–84.

De Lepervanche, M. 1980. "From Race to Ethnicity." *Australian and New Zealand Journal of Sociology* 16 (1): 24–32.

Dicken, P. 2003. *Global Shift: Reshaping the Global Economic Map in the 21st Century.* Thousand Oaks, CA: Sage.

Dill, T.B. 1983. "Race, Class, and Gender: Prospects for an All-Inclusive Sisterhood." *Feminist Studies* 9 (1): 131–50.

Durkheim, E. 1965. (1893). *The Divisions of Labour in Society.* Trans. G. Simpson. New York: Free Press.

Essed, P. 1991. *Understanding Everyday Racism: An Interdisciplinary Theory.* Newbury Park, CA: Sage.

European Migrant Workers Observatory (EWCO). 2007. "Employment and Working Conditions of Migrant Workers." www.eurofound.europa.eu/ewco/studies/tn0701038s.htm.

Favell, A. 1999. "To Belong or Not to Belong: The Postnational Question." In A. Geddes and A. Favell, eds *The Politics of Belonging: Migrants and Minorities in Contemporary Europe.* Aldershot, UK: Ashgate, 209–27.

Fekete, L. 2009. *A Suitable Enemy: Racism, Migration and Islamophobia in Europe.* London: Pluto.

Fenster, T. 2004a. "Belonging, Memory and the Politics of Planning in Israel." *Social and Cultural Geography* 5: 403–17.

——. 2004b. *The Global City and the Holy City: Narratives of Planning, Knowledge and Diversity.* Upper Saddle River, NJ: Pearson/Prentice Hall.

Fortier, A.-M. 2000. *Migrant Belongings: Memory, Space, Identities.* Oxford: Berg.

Foucault, M. 1979. *Discipline and Punish: The Birth of the Prison.* Harmondsworth: Penguin.

——. 1991. "Governmentality." In G. Burchell, C. Gordon, and P. Miller, eds *The Foucault Effect: Studies in Governmentality.* Hemel Hempstead: Harvester Wheatsheaf, 87–104.

Fraser, N. 1995. "From Redistribution to Recognition? Dilemmas of Justice in a 'Post-Socialist' Age." *New Left Review* 212: 68–93.

Fraser, N., and A. Honneth. 1998. *Redistribution or Recognition? A Philosophical Exchange.* London: Verno.

Freeman, J. 1970. "The Tyranny of Structurelessness." *Berkeley Journal of Sociology.* http://flag.Blackened.net/revolt/hist_texts/structurelessness.html.

Freire, P. 1970. *Pedagogy of the Oppressed.* Trans. M. Bergman Ramos. New York: Continuum.

Giddens, A. 1991. *Modernity and Self Identity.* Cambridge: Polity Press.

Hage, G. 1997. "At Home in the Entrails of the West: Multiculturalism, 'Ethnic Food' and Migrant Home Building." In H. Grace, G. Hage, L. Johnson, J. Langeworth, and M. Symonds, eds, *Home/World Space, Community and Marginality in Sydney's West*. Western Sydney: Pluto Press.

Hall, S., with N. Yuval-Davis. 2004, August. "Rethinking the Multicultural Question." Video conversation with Nira Yuval-Davis at the ISA RC05 and RC32 interim conference on Racisms, Sexisms and Contemporary Politics of Belonging, London.

Hannerz, U. 2002. "Where Are We and Who We Want To Be." In U. Hedetoft and M. Hjort, eds, *The Post National Self: Belonging and Identity*. Minneapolis: University of Minnesota Press.

Haraway, D. 1991. *Simians, Cyborgs and Women: The Reinvention of Women*. London: Free Association Press.

Harding, S. 1997. "Comment on Hekman's 'Truth and Method: Feminism Standpoint Theory Revisited': Whose Standpoint Needs Regimes of Truth and Reality?" *Signs: Journal of Women in Culture and Society* 22 (2): 382–91.

Hedetoft, U., and M. Hjort. 2002. *The Postnational Self: Belonging and Identity*. Minneapolis: University of Minnesota Press.

hooks, b. 1981. *Ain't I a Woman: Black Women and Feminism*. Cambridge, MA: Sound End Press.

———. 1989. *Talking Back: Thinking Feminist, Thinking Black*. Toronto: Between the Lines.

———. 1990. *Yearning: Race, Gender and Cultural Politics*, Cambridge, MA: South End Press.

Huntington, S. 1993. "The Clash of Civilizations." *Foreign Affairs* 72 (3): 22–50.

Huysmans, J. 2002. "Defining Social Constructivism in Security Studies: The Normative Dilemma of Writing Security." *Alternatives: Global, Local, Political* 27 (1): 41–62.

Ignatieff, M. 2001. *Human Rights as Politics and Idolatry*. Princeton, NJ: Princeton University Press.

James, S. 1986. *Sex, Race and Class*. London: Housewives in Dialogue.

Jessop, B. 2002. "Liberalism, Neo-Liberalism, Urban Governance and the State: A Theoretical Perspective." *Antipode* 34, 452–72.

Kaptani, E., and N. Yuval-Davis. 2008. "Participatory Theatre as a Research Methodology." *Sociological Research Online* 13 (5). www.socresonline.org.uk/13/5/2.

Kitzinger, C. 1987. *The Social Construction of Lesbianism*. London: Sage.

Klein, N. 2007. *The Shock Doctrine*. New York: Metropolitan Books.

Knowles, C., and D. Harper. 2010. *Hong Kong: Migrant Lives: Landscapes and Journeys*. Chicago: University of Chicago Press.

Lentin, R. 1999. "Constitutionally Excluded: Citizenship and (Some) Irish Women." In N. Yuval-Davis and P. Werbner, eds, *Women, Citizenship and Difference*. London: Zed Books, 130–45.

Lewin, K. 1948. *Resolving Social Conflicts: Selected Papers on Group Dynamics*. New York: Harper & Row.

Lutz, H. 1991. *Migrant Women of Islamic Background*. Amsterdam: Middle East Research Association.

———. 2002, July. "Intersectional Analysis: A Way Out of Multiple Dilemmas?" Paper presented at the International Sociological Association conference, Brisbane.

McBride, S. 2005. *Paradigm Shift: Globalization and the Canadian State*. Halifax, NS: Fernwood.

McCall, L. 2005. "The Complexity of Intersectionality." *Signs: Journal of Women in Culture and Society* 30 (3): 771–800.

Marfleet, P. 2011. "Understanding 'Sanctuary': Faith and Traditions of Asylum." *Journal of Refugee Studies*. Special Issue on Faith-Based Humanitarianism in Contexts of Forced Displacement. 24 (3): 440–55.

Martin, D.C. 1995. "The Choices of Identity." *Social Identities* 1 (1): 5–16.

Marx, K. 1975. (1844). *Early Writings*. Harmmondsworth: Penguin.

Massey, D. 2005. *For Space*. London: Sage.

Meekosha, H., and L. Dowse. 1997. "Enabling Citizenship: Gender, Disability and Citizenship in Autstralia." *Feminist Review* 57: 49–72.

Menzies, G. 2002. *1421: The Year China Discovered the World*. London: Bantam.

Meyer, J.W. 1980. "The World Polity and the Authority of the Nation-state." In A.J. Bergesen, ed., *Studies of the Modern World-System*. New York: Academic Press.

Mulholland, H. 2009. "Gordon Brown Unveils Tougher Immigration Rules." *The Guardian* November 12. www.guardian.co.uk/politics/2009/nov/12/gordon-brown-announces-new-immigration-rules.

Nyamnjoh, F.B. 2005. *Africa's Media: Democracy and the Politics of Belonging*. London: Zed Books.

Oliver, M. 1996. *Understanding Disability: From Theory to Practice*. London: Macmillan.

Panitch, L. 1994. "Globalisation and the State." *Socialist Register* 30: 60–93.

Pieterse, J.N. 1995. "Global Systems, Globalization and the Parameters of Modernity." In M. Featherstone, S. Lash, and R. Robertson, eds, *Global Modernities*. London: Sage.

Probyn, E. 1996. *Outside Belongings*. London: Routledge.

Rank, O. 1973. (1929). *The Trauma of Birth*. London: Routledge & Kegan Paul.

Robertson, R. 1992. *Globalization: Social Theory and Global Culture*. London: Sage.

———. 1995. "Glocalization: Time-Space and Homogeneity–Heterogeneity." In M. Featherstone, S. Lash, and R. Robertson, eds, *Global Modernities*. London: Sage.

Rodrigue, J.-P. 2006. "Transportation and the Geographical and Functional Integration of Global Production Networks." *Growth and Change* 37 (4): 510–25.

Rowe, A.C. 2005. "Be Longing: Towards a Feminist Politics of Relation." *NWSA Journal* 17 (2): 15–46.

Sassen, S. 2006. *Territory, Authority, Rights: From Medieval to Global Assemblages*. Princeton, NJ: Princeton University Press.

Scholte, J.A. 2005. *Globalization: A Critical Introduction.* 2nd edn. New York: Macmillan.

Silva, G.M.D., and L.F. Schwartzman. 2006, July. "Discourses of Difference and Equality in an Affirmative Action Context in Brazil: the Local, the National, the Global." Paper presented at the XIV International Sociological Association World Congress in Sociology. Durban, South Africa.

Stoetzler, M., and N. Yuval-Davis. 2002. "Standpoint Theory, Situated Knowledge and the Situated Imagination." *Feminist Theory* 3 (3): 315–34.

Swyngedouw, E. 1997. "Neither Global nor Local: 'Glocalization' and the Politics of Scale." In D. Cox, ed., *Spaces of Globalization.* New York: Guilford Press, 137–66.

Tajfel, H. 1982. "Social Psychology of Intergroup Relations." *Annual Review of Psychology* 33: 1–39.

Taylor, C. 1992. *Multiculturalism and the Politics of Recognition: An Essay by Charles Taylor.* Edited by Amy Gutmann. Princeton, NJ: Princeton University Press.

Taylor, H. 2009. "Landscapes of Belonging: The Meaning of Home for Cypriot Refugees in London." PhD thesis, School of Humanities and Social Sciences, University of East London.

Tonnies, F. 1940. (1935). *Fundamental Concepts of Sociology (Gemeinschaft und Gesellschaft).* English translation. New York: American Book Company.

UN. 2008. "International Migrant Stock: The 2008 Revision." http://esa.un.org/migration/.

Wallerstein, I. 1976. *The Modern World-System: 1. Capitalist Agriculture and the Origins of the European World-Economy in the Sixteenth Century.* New York: Academic Press.

——. 1980. *The Modern World-System: 2. Mercantilism and the Consolidation of the European World-Economy in the Sixteenth Century.* New York: Academic Press.

——. 1989. *The Modern World-System: 3. The Second Era of Great Expansion of the Capitalist World-Economy.* New York: Academic Press.

Weber, M. 1948. (1947). *Essays in Sociology.* Trans H.H. Gerth. London: Kegan Paul, Trench, Trubner & Co.

Yuval-Davis, N. 2006. "Intersectionality and Feminist Politics." *European Journal of Women's Studies.* Special issue on Intersectionality. 13 (3): 193–209.

——. 2010. "Theorizing Identity: Beyond the 'Self' and 'Other' Dichotomy." *Patterns of Prejudice* 44, 261–80.

——. 2011. "Beyond the Recognition and Re-distribution Dichotomy: Intersectionality and Stratification." In H. Lutz, M.T.H. Vivar, and L. Supik, eds, *Framing Intersectionality: Debates on a Multi-faceted Concept in Gender Studies.* Aldershot, UK: Ashgate.

Yuval-Davis, N., and P. Werbner, eds 1999. *Women, Citizenship and Difference.* London: Zed Books.

Questions For Critical Thought

1. What important role did black feminists play in the development of intersectional theorizing, according to Yuval-Davis? What is feminist standpoint theory?

2. What does the term *situated gaze* mean? Can you think of three examples of situated gaze that are used to oppress and/or to empower certain groups of people?

3. Yuval-Davis states that "belonging" is an emotional or ontological attachment about feeling "at home." What does feeling "at home" mean to you, your family, and your friends? When and why does belonging and the politics of belonging become more important to you, your family, your friends, your neighbours, and to all Canadian citizens?

4. Define the term *glocalization*. How does this concept differ from the term *globalization*? Can you provide three examples of glocalization that are taking place in Canada today?

5. According to Castles and Miller we are currently experiencing "the age of migration." Why are people on the move in the twenty-first century? How have global migration patterns and the feminization of migration policies generated social inequality in Canada and in other countries in the world today?

Whose Social Reproduction? Transnational Motherhood and Challenges to Feminist Political Economy

Sedef Arat-Koç

The phrase *vagabond capitalist* pits the vagrancy and dereliction where it belongs—on capitalism, that unsettled, dissolute, irresponsible stalker of the world. It also suggests a threat at the heart of capitalism's vagrancy: that an increasingly global production can shuck many of its particular commitments to place, most centrally those associated with social reproduction, which is almost always less mobile than production. . . . Insisting on the necessity of social reproduction provides a critical arena, as yet undertheorized, within which many of the problems associated with the globalization of capitalist production can be confronted. (Katz 2001, 709–10)

One of the greatest achievements of **feminist political economy** has been to talk about **social reproduction**, to make visible and to problematize what would otherwise be invisible or seemingly trivial to the economy, to society, and even to (liberal) feminist theory. One of the purposes of this chapter will be to explore another layer of invisibility, to uncover the cases and the ways in which social reproduction takes place transnationally.

Feminist political economy studies social reproduction in the family-market-state nexus. Most theory assumes that this relationship takes place at the nation-state level. However, we are living in a world where social reproduction is increasingly taking place at a transnational level. Although there are many ways in which such transnationalization of social reproduction occurs, one of the most glaring examples is the experience of trans-border, transnational families.

This chapter focuses on the experiences of migrant **domestic workers** in Canada with transnational mothering to see how their experiences

of social reproduction can inform feminist political economy. To understand social reproduction, it is necessary that one go beyond the individual worker and her conditions here and now in Canada and look into her family relations transnationally.

In some ways, social reproduction occurring in a trans-regional, transnational scale is nothing new. Hontagneu-Sotelo and Avila (2000) suggest that contemporary "transnational motherhood" continues a long and dirty legacy of people of colour being admitted to some countries only through coercive systems of labour that do not recognize family rights. These systems have historical roots and close parallels in slavery, contract labour, and migrant labour systems such as those in South Africa under apartheid and in the US South involving Mexican workers, which were all "organized to maximize economic productivity and offered few supports to sustain family life" (Hontagneu-Sotelo and Avila 2000, 292). In Canada we have the precedents of Chinese families that were separated for 30 years or longer—between 1918 and 1947, when the Chinese Immigration Act completely banned all Chinese immigration, including those involving family reunification—and the residential school system, which systematically disabled First Nations people from providing nurture and culture for their children.

What *is* new and of growing significance for recent history, however, is the size and nature of the migrant labour force. There are currently 175 million people in the world who reside outside their country of birth (United Nations 2002). Many of these people do not have citizenship status and rights in the country of residence. In fact, there is evidence that with accelerating globalization of the economy, which creates a "push" factor in migration, there is also a tightening of borders in most advanced industrialized countries. In Saskia Sassen's frequently cited words, economic globalization is *"denationaliz(ing) national economics,"* whereas immigration is *"renationalizing* politics" (Sassen 1996, 59; emphasis mine). As a result, much recent migration is undocumented. What is interesting is that despite the tightening, even militarization, of borders and anti-immigration measures introduced in many countries, the number of migrants continues to climb rapidly. It is estimated by the US Census Bureau, for example, that the number of undocumented migrants in the United States increased from 3.5 million in 1980 to 8.7 million in 2000, despite the fact that around 2.7 million foreigners were legalized in 1987–88 (Adams and Liu 2001).

In recent decades we have witnessed a "feminization" of international labour migration. Men predominated in labour migration in the immediate post–Second World War period, but now half the world's legal and undocumented migrants and refugees are believed to be women (Ehrenreich and Hochschild 2003, 5). An International Labour Organization (ILO) report published in 1996 described the feminization of international labour migration as "one of the most striking economic and social phenomena of recent times." Making this phenomenon especially notable has been migration out of Asian countries that involves women migrating alone, as "autonomous, economic agents" in their own right (cited in Kempadoo 2004, 471).

Women migrants from several countries outnumber men. In Third World countries that rely on export-oriented development, female, as opposed to male, workers are especially encouraged to migrate, as women are thought to be more reliable than men in sending remittances, rather than spending their money on themselves (Ehrenreich and Hochschild 2003, 7). Female migrant workers, who typically send from half to nearly all of what they earn, not only ensure social reproduction for their families but also finance the specific economic development regimes of their countries. In 1994, remittances

from foreign domestic workers were the third largest source of foreign exchange for Sri Lanka. In that year, 84 per cent of Sri Lankan workers in the Middle East were women. They saved over 90 per cent of their earnings and remitted almost all these savings home (Samarasinghe, cited in Momsen 1999, 9).

Many women who are part of recent international migration are migrating precisely to fulfill reproductive roles for the "host" society. Whether they work as maids, nannies, caregivers for the elderly or the disabled, or sex workers, they are doing "women's work." The irony is that among those involved in transnational migration, it is specifically those who migrate to provide reproductive labour who are unable to care for their own children since they arrive as either temporary or undocumented workers. In both situations they lack rights to bring their children with them. "The ties of transnational motherhood suggest simultaneously the relative permeability of borders as witnessed by the maintenance of family ties and the new meanings of motherhood, and the impermeability of nation-state borders" (Hontagneu-Sotelo and Avila 2000, 292).

In some cases, states not only deny family rights but also are explicit in their denial of reproductive rights to migrant domestic workers. In Singapore, for example, Filipina domestic workers are required by the government to take pregnancy tests every few months. If a women is found to be pregnant, her work permit is deemed null, and she is required to return home (Human Rights Internet 2003).

In the first part of this chapter, I summarize research results from migrant domestic workers' experiences with transnational mothering in Toronto, Canada. In the second section, I raise some questions and make some analytical observations about what insights we might gain about social reproduction from the transnational mothering of some women. In the final section, I discuss the possible contributions a transnational perspective can provide to feminist political economy.

Transnational Motherhood for Migrant Domestic Workers in Canada: Research Results

In 2000 Fely Villasin and I did research among domestic workers in Toronto. This involved questionnaires, individual and group interviews with domestic workers and immigrant service providers, and archival research at a Toronto organization promoting domestic workers' rights, INTERCEDE. I reviewed case files and telephone logs of INTERCEDE from 1992 to 2000.

Canada, which receives significant numbers of immigrants every year, has created a multi-tier system for different groups of immigrants. Whereas business people and professionals can enter as "independent class" immigrants and enjoy many of the rights and freedoms of citizenship, except the franchise, some groups of workers, including domestic workers, are denied significant rights and liberties, including the right to live with their families and the freedom to choose their jobs and employers. Canada uses a point system to determine who can qualify to enter the country in the first tier of the immigration process. The official justification given for the denial of entry to domestic workers in this category has to do with the low number of points given their work (as well as the education and the work experience of the worker) under the system. The history of the temporary worker programs for domestic workers, however, reveals that the reasons may have a lot to do with the political will to create a flexible and vulnerable group of workers doing reproductive work.

The Live-in Caregiver Program (LCP), like all the previous immigration programs for domestic workers since 1970, is built on the premise that foreign domestic workers who arrive in Canada are—or should live as—single people. In reality, a significant proportion of domestic workers have children. Fifty-two per cent of respondents to our survey in 2000 admitted to having children.

The status of foreign domestic workers as single, unattached individuals is ensured through the treatment of domestic workers as temporary labour—as opposed to immigrants—as well as through the live-in requirement. Canada, along with western European countries and the United States, refuses to sign the International Convention on the Protection of the Rights of All Migrant Workers and Members of Their Families, adopted by the UN General Assembly in 1990. Canadian immigration regulations, as well as individual employers, assume that there is an incompatibility between this type of employment and the workers' parenting responsibilities. During the interviews a domestic worker explained that her employer did not allow her visiting daughter to stay in her house and the employer warned, "Don't forget you are working." Sometimes the worker herself internalizes the notion of incompatibility between worker status and parenting imposed by the state and the employer. One of the respondents to our questionnaire replied to the question "If you have children, did they come to Canada with you?" in the negative, explaining that she "did not come to Canada as an immigrant but as a worker" (in Arat-Koç with Villasin 2001, 21, 22).

The LCP allows domestic workers to apply for permanent resident status after two to three years of live-in service under temporary work permits. However, from the time of their arrival in Canada, it takes, on average, three to five years and often longer for domestic workers to sponsor their families. For many domestic workers, Canada is not necessarily the first country they go to on a temporary work permit. When several years of work abroad is combined with an average of three to five, sometimes up to seven, years of waiting in Canada, the experience and the impact of separation are profound for domestic workers and for their families.

Both in the societies that foreign domestic workers come from and in Canada, there are powerful ideologies surrounding motherhood that often glorify it and strongly emphasize maternal responsibility for children and even criminalize maternal neglect. In recent years, fundamentalist discourses prevalent in many societies and

neo-liberalism in state policies have increased the emphasis on maternal responsibility, both ideologically and practically. In some cases, migrant female workers have come from countries where they are exposed to contradictory messages. In the Philippines, for example, migrant workers are hailed by the state as "national heroes" (Rodriguez 2002) for their contributions through remittances; at the same time they are cast as negligent mothers by media that sensationalize the suffering of children in transnational families (Parrenas 2003). In addition to the experience of separation, therefore, the social, cultural, and ideological meanings attached to the mother–child relationship affected migrant workers.

In our research we found that it was not just powerful feelings of responsibility and guilt that made family separation painful for migrant domestic workers. It was also deprivation of their own needs for intimacy and support. One of the respondents to the questionnaire expressed with eloquence what being with her family meant to her: "One of the sweetest things in life is to be near or close to your loved ones . . . to share with them whatever life could bring in today and in the future" (in Arat-Koç with Villasin 2001, 24).

While domestic workers who were in bad or abusive relationships felt liberated when they left their countries, others mourned the loss of intimate ties. The impact of being deprived of close relations, if these are working, supportive relationships, can be devastating for anybody. The impact can be even more significant for immigrants who are in the process of adapting to working and living in a new country. During interviews, Edna regretted being separated from her common-law spouse as a feeling of "emptiness in the sense that [there is] no one who would comfort you when you have a problem or giving reassurance when you are down" (in Arat-Koç with Villasin 2001, 29).

For most migrant domestic workers, the decision to leave their children was an extremely painful one. In addition to handling practical questions regarding whom to leave their children with and whether the children would be safe, well-cared for, happy, and healthy, domestic workers had to deal with the heart-wrenching feelings during separation from their children. During her interview one domestic worker, Amor, described the time she bid her children goodbye and boarded the bus to Manila: "I could not walk up the bus, the driver had to carry me up. I was so weak and faint—leaving my kids and not knowing how long it would be before we could be together again." When she took her seat on the plane and was struck by the by the reality of separation, she "cried, and laughed and wailed like a madwoman" (in Arat-Koç with Villasin 2001, 26).

Even though migrant workers were very aware of the significance of their remittances for their children's upkeep and future, they experienced a profound sense of guilt, anxiety over the well-being of the children, and a sense of sadness, loss, and loneliness: "My life will not be complete. A part of me will always be missing, wondering about how my children are doing" (in Arat-Koç with Villasin 2001, 26). These mothers constantly worry about their children. They tended to blame themselves when the children were maltreated, got into trouble, or did badly in school. Even when there were no apparent problems, they felt anxiety about the unknown. One domestic worker said that her biggest regret was that she would "not know what is going on inside" her children and that she could not share "their troubles and triumphs" (in Arat-Koç with Villasin 2001, 27). Most mothers tried to maintain a good long-distance relationship with their children by spending large amounts of time on the telephone.

Our surveys and our interviews with domestic workers, as well as with professionals dealing with immigrants' health, revealed serious physical and mental health problems associated with separation from family. Complaints ranged from chronic stomach pain, muscle tension (specifically the neck and shoulders), sleep problems, and frequent headaches to severe anxiety and depression. Describing the effects of separation on herself, one of the respondents to the questionnaire wrote about "a gap, depression, frustration and loneliness." Another domestic worker dealt with similar feelings by "always wanting to keep [herself] busy because [she] always felt sad if [she was] not doing something" (in Arat-Koç with Villasin 2001, 27).

Mothers often assumed that the separation affected the children negatively, that they "felt as orphans," deprived of love of their parents. "The effect of separation on my children was overwhelming. [They] felt insecure and unprotected while I was away. The trust on me as a parent was totally diminished by the time we got together in Canada" (in Arat-Koç with Villasin 2001, 28). Some children were too young when the mothers left to know or remember them. Older children might be angry and resentful toward the mother, who, they thought, had betrayed them. Some children appreciated the economic necessity and the sacrifice but had deep feelings of longing and sadness. Other studies confirm this pattern. Rhacel Salazar Parrenas, who interviewed children of migrant domestic workers in the Philippines, reports on the profound sense of loss. When she asked Ellen, who was 10 when her mother left, how she felt about the children in her mother's care in New York, the girl responded,

Very jealous. I am very, very jealous. There was even a time when she told the children she was caring for that they are very lucky that she was taking care of them, while her children back in the Philippines do not even have a mom to take care of them. It's pathetic, but it's true. We were left alone by ourselves and we had to be responsible at a very young age without a mother. Can you imagine? (Parrenas 2003, 42)

Even as she experiences a sense of loss, Ellen was not unaware of her mother's dedication and commitment:

I realize that my mother loves us very much. Even if she is far away, she would send us her love. She would make us feel like she really loved us. She would do this by always being there. She would just assure us that whenever we have problems to just call her and tell

her ... And so I know that it has been more difficult for her than other mothers. She has to do extra work because she is so far away from us. (Parrenas 2003, 43)

Parrenas's research makes it clear that the children of transnational mothers who had positive surrogate parental figures and open, regular communication with their mothers were able to resolve the emotional challenges and focus on school. Even the well-adjusted, though, suffered the loss of family intimacy (Parrenas 2003). It was not unusual for some children to deal with feelings of loss and longing by emotionally withdrawing from the mother. Two of the respondents to our questionnaire who were still separated from their children said, "I think they do not miss me anymore or I don't exist. They don't care if I call or write to them." And, "They hardly know me.... Even in my vacation in the Philippines, I could feel the gap between us" (in Arat-Koç with Villasin 2001, 29).

Parrenas's interviews of children at the other end of the transnational family relationship reveal the psychology of emotional withdrawal. Eighteen-year-old Theresa said,

Telephone calls. That's not enough. You can't hug her, kiss her, feel her, everything. You can't feel her presence. It's just words that you have. What I want is to have my mother close to me, to see her grow older, and when she is sick, you are the one taking care of her and when you are sick, she is the one taking care of you. (Parrenas 2003, 50)

Jeek was eight when his parents left for New York. More than eight years later, he was still unable to join them. The distance of the relationship made him cynical about the benefits of sharing problems and emotions:

I talk to my mother once in a while. But what happens, whenever she asks how I am doing, I just say okay. It's not like I am really going to tell her that I have problems here.... It's not like she can do anything about my problems if I told her about them. Financial problem, yes she can help. But not other problems.... She will try to give advice, but I am not very interested to talk to her about things like that. (Parrenas 2003, 45)

Providing for and improving the life chances of their children was the main factor behind the decision of transnational mothers to leave, but they wanted to parent their children in more ways than just financially. During the interviews, some migrant workers expressed feelings of hurt that their children had started seeing them merely as providers (in Arat-Koç with Villasin 2001, 29).

It is not only women with children or married partners who have suffered family separation as a result of immigration regulations for domestic workers. Most people have close and meaningful relationships with people they see and are attached to as "family," such as parents, siblings, other relatives, same-sex partners, or intimate friends. As several participants in our research argued, one of the major problems with the Canadian immigration department's approach to family reunification has been the fact that the concept of "family" it uses imposes a narrow, Eurocentric, and heterosexist definition of the nuclear family that fails to resonate with definitions in the migrant worker's personal life, society, or culture.

Problems did not end if or when families were reunited. When children met their mothers in Canada, they often met strangers. Most mothers found it very hard to help their children get over feelings of abandonment. They also found it difficult to undo the distance that had developed between themselves and their children: "The children I take care of give me a hug as soon as I come to work, and hug me goodbye when I leave. They are much more affectionate than my own children who have joined me" (in Arat-Koç with Villasin 2001, 33–34).

In addition to problems in establishing trust, love, and intimacy, mothers found it difficult to establish authority over their children. As

mothers tried to fulfill their new maternal role, some children resented, resisted, and rejected this, questioning where their mother had been all these years and what right she had to control their lives (in Arat-Koç with Villasin 2001, 34).

The difficulties in re-establishing parent–child ties sometimes lasted many years, sometimes never ended. In addition to the challenges of re-establishing authority, intimacy, and trust, mothers were confronted with the anger of children who were having difficulties adjusting to life in a new country. Feeling powerless about imposed emigration, the children tended to blame their difficulties on the person who seemed to be responsible for making this decision. One domestic worker related a moving story of how her kids were "brainwashed" against her and how she has often "fe[lt] alone against the world," despite all the efforts she put into providing for them and sponsoring them to Canada. It took five years before her children even "began to understand" her. Still, she admitted, "It is really hard for us to get reunited with them after a long time of separation" (in Arat-Koç with Villasin 2001, 34).

As a result of the difficulties during the separation, as well as the challenges faced after reunification, most migrant domestic workers in our research experienced forced family separations as a form of abuse that emotionally scarred those involved for a long time, if not permanently.

Analytical Questions and Observations

What do the experiences of migrant domestic workers as transnational mothers teach us about relations of social reproduction? What additional insights does a transnational perspective on social reproduction provide us that we would not have with analyses at the level of nation-state?

One of the greatest theoretical advantages of socialist feminist over liberal feminist theory has been to show the ways in which women (and men) are not abstract, rational, and atomistic individuals but embodied beings constituted through social relations of power based on gender, class, and race. The question we may pose in relation to transnational motherhood is whether an analytical framework that assumes embodiment by gender, race, and class is enough.

In a different context, Gayatri Spivak pointed out the shortcomings of "focusing on the migrant as an effectively historyless object of intellectual and political activism" (Spivak 2000, 354). She argued that one could not simply treat the postcolonial migrant as a "blank slate," pretending that she could be analyzed simply within a class-gender-race calculus that begins and ends in the First World metropolis. The theoretical challenge at this juncture is to see the migrants as a historied subject and in her connectedness to her history, family, and home country, while avoiding essential conceptualizations of these forms of connectedness.

As early as the 1970s, political economists explored questions of how migrant labour benefits capital as well as the welfare state in receiving countries and how it also may serve to divide working-class struggle. They demonstrated how denial of social citizenship to migrant workers and their separation from family creates the possibility of paying only for the daily reproduction of workers as they actively worked, while transferring the responsibility and costs of their families' as well as their own upkeep during times of unemployment, sickness, disability, and old age on to the home country (Burawoy 1980; Castles and Kosack 1973; Gorz 1970).

The literature on the political economy of migrant labour can teach us a lot about social reproduction. To make sense of transnational motherhood, however, we may need additional theoretical insights and tools, as most of the women involved are doing reproductive and, specifically, care work. The implications of transfer of social reproduction in this case cannot simply be measured economically, in terms of its implications for capital and the welfare state.

Some writers mention the emergence of a "care deficit" in advanced industrialized countries when the accelerated movement of women into the labour force since the 1960s was followed with the failure of governments to provide public child care, on the one hand, and further cuts to public services and programs, on the other (Enrenreich and Hochschild 2003). While Third World countries respond to this "deficit," they do not do so because of a surplus of care. Rather, what the families, the communities, and the countries experience is a "care drain" (Hochschild 2003; Parrenas 2003).

A feminist political economy of transnational motherhood needs to clarify where it stands on motherhood. Feminists, socialists or not, do not believe motherhood and parenthood to be natural relationships. We do not glorify motherhood or assume mothers are the only or the best caregivers for children. As socialist feminists, we further believe that child care should not be a private responsibility of the mother or of the family, but that society and the state should at least share in the work, cost, and responsibility of raising children.

If socialist feminist theory (like most other feminist theories) denaturalizes motherhood and emphasizes collective responsibility for children, how do we articulate a critical position in relation to the forced imposition of transnational motherhood? The answer depends on how the position is framed—in essentialist glorification of motherhood or every mother's right to choose her own parenting arrangements.

> While demanding the right for women workers to live with their children may provoke critiques of sentimentality, essentialism, and the glorification of motherhood, demanding the right for women workers to choose their own motherhood arrangements would be the beginning of truly just family and work policies, policies that address not only inequalities of gender but also inequalities of race, class, and citizenship status. (Hontagneu-Sotelo and Avila 2000, 292)

Theory concerned with inequalities of race, class, and citizenship status, as well as gender, cannot go in the direction of *naturalizing* forced separation, while it *denaturalizes* motherhood. This, however, might be precisely what liberal feminist theory does through its notion of the atomistic individual and its fetishization of "choice" in contract relationships. In contrast, socialist feminists interrogate the relationships of inequality, power, and force involved in "choices" made in contract.

Shellee Colen's concept of "stratified reproduction" is useful in demonstrating and making sense of inequalities in social relations of reproduction. Stratified reproduction is a concept that shows how "reproductive labour—physical, mental, and emotional—of bearing, raising, and socializing children and of creating and maintaining households and people (from infancy to old age) is differentially *experienced, valued, and rewarded*" (Colen 1995, 78; emphasis mine). Colen talks about how "physical and social reproductive tasks are accomplished differentially according to inequalities that are based on hierarchies of class, race, ethnicity, gender, place in a global economy, and migration status" (78). The concept is useful in helping us to ask who is normatively entitled to be a parent, a caretaker, or to refuse child-bearing or rearing, to have others give care for her children. It also helps us to ask who can "give nurture or give culture (or both)." "Stratified reproduction" describes the "power relations by which some categories of people are empowered to nurture and reproduce, while others are disempowered." The concept helps us to identify "the arrangements by which some reproductive futures are valued while others are despised" (Ginsburg and Rapp 1995).

The concept of stratified reproduction can help to highlight not just the economic obstacles but also the various social, political, and policy systems that disable transnational mothers as well as other groups of women, such as poor single mothers or Aboriginal mothers separated from children by residential schools or child welfare agencies, from nurturing their children. It demonstrates not only how some mothers are unsupported and underserved by the state but also how they may also be over-regulated as mothers. The concept of stratified reproduction helps feminists to articulate demands, not of only women but also of their children, for equality and a decent life.

It is important to remember that any application of the concept of stratified reproduction to transnational mothers—or any other group—needs to employ the concept not just as one of inequality but also in *relational* terms, focusing on what production and reproduction of one form of stratification means for others. Employment of domestic workers, often as caregivers, brings together women who, despite the significant class differences, share a common condition: they both experience their paid work as incompatible with their reproductive roles and responsibilities. For both, social reproduction has to be hidden (either at home or in the country of origin) as a condition to secure and keep present employment.

Despite significant increases in women's participation in the labour force, there have been hardly any changes in organization of paid work and expectations of the workplace in most countries that accommodate this reality. According to ILO reports, people in the United States worked much longer hours in the 1990s than in the 1970s (Ehrenreich and Hochschild 2003, 8). For the employers of domestic workers, it is often the neo-liberal ethics and expectations of the contemporary workplace for many professionals, while for the domestic worker/caregiver, it is the requirements of live-in arrangements and immigration restrictions associated with temporary or undocumented status, that force both groups of women to tuck their maternal roles neatly away, out of sight and out of mind, from the market and the society they are living in.

Another common condition for both groups of women is that they have to raise their children in societies where child care is seen as an individual parental responsibility and where the state refuses any substantial role in social reproduction. For both the employer and the employee, the employment arrangement is a private solution to a private problem. For the domestic worker, it is a private solution to the problem of poverty and economic underdevelopment. For the employer, it is a private solution to care and domestic needs.

While both the employer and the employee are likely to be citizens of states that do not accept substantial public responsibility for social reproduction, employers who are citizens in receiving countries can at least theoretically make demands and claims on the welfare state, whether they are listened to or not. Migrant workers, on the other hand, are stateless in terms of their (in)ability to make claims on either state. Even though sending countries can, at least theoretically, negotiate basic rights for their citizens living in other countries, they are often reluctant to do so for fear of losing trade or risking remittances from the receiving countries (Pettman 1996, 191).

We can say that migrant domestic workers, who often lack citizenship rights, are the ideal subjects of a neo-liberal state since they are workers whose social reproduction is not just privatized in the home but can be totally hidden with the economic, social, and psychic costs transferred to a different location and state. With their lower wages, longer working hours, and lesser ability than citizen workers to negotiate working conditions, they are also the perfect workers who can help to conceal their employers' social reproductive needs.

Migrant domestic workers can be considered the ideal subjects of a neo-liberal state for concealing not just their own reproduction but also the needs and dependency of their employer. In many liberal societies, middle-class women's exercise of citizenship rights, their access to the public sphere as men's equals, has been achieved only on the condition that their labour-market participation resembles that of men. "In order to participate *like men* women must have workers who will provide the same flexibility as wives, in particular working long hours and combining care and domestic chores" (Anderson 2000, 190).

What makes a female employer of a migrant worker appear manlike and "independent"—that is, of family responsibilities—in her own workplace is precisely her dependency on an invisible worker. Migrant workers are ideally suited to support this type of labour-market participation,

since they can be (made to be) more flexible than citizen workers. Such flexibility is made possible by the vulnerability of the migrant or undocumented–non-citizenship status, often associated with a lack or near impossibility of asserting labour rights. "The fact that employers are citizens and the workers are not citizens formalizes their unequal power relations—even outside of the employment relationship, workers and their employers are not equal before the law" (Anderson 2000, 193).

Flexibility is also made possible by the "extra time" that migrant workers, with no family rights of their own in the country of immigration, can spare for their employers. Employers show a preference for workers with such legal status precisely because "migrant care workers can give the best possible care for their employers' families when they are free of care-giving responsibilities to their own families" (Parrenas 2003, 54). In Canada since the 1970s, the expectation of such flexibility and availability has been formalized through immigration programs that require migrant domestic workers to live with their employers.

Reliance on such flexible domestic help enables some women to participate equally in the labour market without any significant pressure being put on them to fight for a transformation of gender relations in the home and of the relations in the larger society between production and social reproduction, the state and civil society, and public and private spheres. Instead of being transformed, those relationships are merely reproduced with only some changes in the cast.

> Not only do migrant domestic workers, documented or undocumented, contribute to the state, they are also providing the welfare that is the social right of citizens, but to which many of these workers, however necessitous, have no right. By providing welfare, one of the crucial social rights of the citizen, they are helping to give meaning to the notion of citizenship status, while themselves being denied any of its rights. (Anderson 2000, 191)

Earlier I said that both the employer and the employee in a paid domestic labour relationship often have to hide their reproductive responsibilities to secure or keep their respective employment arrangements. While both the employer and the employee may share this condition, their relationship to each other is one that clearly emphasizes the social reproduction needs of one and denies those of the other.

The weakness of the welfare state and the absence or inadequacy of socialized child care explains much about the choice for some women to employ domestic workers, but this choice is also based on some class privileges that employers can enjoy by hiring vulnerable, underpaid, and flexible migrant workers. In addition to the advantages of flexible time, such workers provide luxuries to employers that would otherwise be well beyond their reach. As Bridget Anderson (2001) points out, domestic work is not only about "caring," which is socially necessary work. It "is also concerned with the reproduction of lifestyle, and crucially, of status." Domestic work reproduces not just people but also class subjects. While "we need to accommodate the raising of children, the distribution and preparation of food, basic cleanliness and hygiene ... nobody has to have stripped pine floorboards, handwash only silk shirts, dust gathering ornaments" (Anderson 2001, 6).

The choice to hire domestic workers rather than use child-care centres is also connected to middle-class assumptions about children's needs. As some sociologists have pointed out, there is a recent cultural obsession with security in many countries, especially in the United States, predating fears that resulted from the attacks of 11 September 2001. A sense of insecurity is displayed with everything from "nanny cams" and child monitors to the widespread use of security cameras in all types of public spaces (Furedi 2002; Katz 2001).

We accept the reality of transnational motherhood precisely in an environment of obsession with security, an increased sense of the vulnerability of children, and greater emphasis on the needs of "the child" in social and public policy. The irony of the obsession with security, as with social reproduction, is that it is often the relatively most secure whose needs for security, as well as quality social reproduction, become most visible and most clearly articulated. Clearly, response to risk, insecurity, and vulnerability are determined by class, race, and global inequalities. As the state downloads more and more responsibility on parents, as responsibility for social reproduction is more and more privatized, the sense of risk and insecurity in society increases.

Notes Toward a Feminist, Anti-Racist, Transnational Political Economy

Globalization corresponds to specific restructurings of social reproduction. Feminist political economy demonstrates the havoc caused in people's lives by such restructuring through neoliberalism in advanced industrial countries and structural adjustment policies in the Third World. Feminist research in Canada has documented the various social consequences of economic restructuring and the neo-liberal restructuring of the welfare state: increased economic insecurity for the vast majority of the people; loss of or diminished access to social assistance on the part of the working class and the poor; forced movement into workfare or into the labour force by single mothers with no corresponding support in the form of socialized child care; losses of public sector jobs for women—where they were highly represented; increased privatization of responsibility and increased domestic work for women with cuts and/or closings in education, health care, and care of the elderly and disabled. This documentation amounts to no less than a powerful demonstration of the *unsustainability* of neo-liberalism.

While studies at the level of the nation-state are valuable in advancing a critique of neo-liberalism, I would argue that a transnational perspective would not only add new insights to this critique but also raise further productive questions regarding the unsustainability of the global order we are living in. The case of transnational motherhood demonstrates the increased **racialization** and transnationalization of reproductive work. The case stands as an extreme example of the inequalities and injustices of *stratified reproduction*, of *who* is reproduced *how*. At the same time, however, the case is also useful as it exposes the myths of independence and "self-sufficiency" on which neo-liberalism heavily relies. Stories of transnational mothers lay bare and crystallize the relations of *dependence* that both the individual employers of migrant workers and First World states are involved in.

Canada, as an imperialist and settler society and one that, like the United States and Australia, continues to rely on immigration, has never been self-sufficient in social reproduction. For Canada, immigration has historically been essential to meet labour-market needs—for capital to reproduce itself. In addition, it has recently been defined as essential to sustaining the welfare state. With demographic realities of a low birth rate and a rapidly aging population, immigration is seen as "fresh blood" that would enable and improve the capacity of the Canadian welfare state to continue to offer social security.

There are several potential political implications of introducing a transnational perspective in political economy. Acknowledgement of the dependency of advanced capitalist nations on the rest of the world—for not only reproduction of capital but also social reproduction—urges us to ask whether the question of rights and entitlements can be limited to the level of the nation-state. There are proposals that encourage a post-national reconceptualization of rights.

Rethinking social reproduction in transnational dimensions helps to crystallize the inhumanity of capitalist reproduction on a global level. As Cindi Katz argues, it is by looking at social reproduction, especially in its global connections, that we

can most effectively expose "the vagrancy and dereliction" of capitalism as an "unsettled, dissolute, irresponsible stalker of the world" (Katz 2001, 709).

In its invisibility, transnational motherhood can help to hide the problems of the organization of the family, the economy, and the state under neo-liberalism. By making it visible, feminist political economy can help to force a rethinking and re-envisioning of the relations between/among the family, the economy, the community, the state, and the world. We may contemplate what is wrong with a world in which we talk about "care deficits" or unaffordability of social programs in the midst of levels of wealth unprecedented in human history; a world that creates "care deficits" in countries both importing and exporting migrant workers; where the paid caregivers are people who are themselves denied caring for and being cared for by their own families; where "independence" and "self-reliance" are fetishized as social possibilities and qualities of ideal workers and citizens as long as they involve the absence of demands on the workplace, the community, and the state, but can hide dependence on the invisible work of gendered, racialized others. We may contemplate the *possibility* and *desirability* of long-term survival in such a world. Through such contemplation, we may be compelled to envision new relations in, between, and among the family, economy, community, state, and world.

There are signs that such envisioning is already taking place. As Alice de Wolff (2003) demonstrates, in the 1990s and early 2000s Canadian public sector unions have developed and struggled for positive strategies in response to the growing tensions between paid employment and other life responsibilities. Campaigns for reduced work time, leaves for caring work, more inclusive benefits, and workplace-based child-care programs have helped to address work-life tensions, educate the larger public, and provide some concrete solutions. De Wolff argues that the gains are limited, both because the benefits do not reach beyond union membership and because they have taken place in a context of reduced govern-ment social spending and economic restructur-ing. Despite their limitations, however, these campaigns have been politically significant as

they have offered healthy collective alternatives to the individual solutions to work-life tensions that neo-liberalism forces.

References

Adams, Tamara, and Xijan Liu. 2001, October 11. ESCAP II: Evaluation of Lack of Balance and Geographic Errors Affecting Person Estimates. Executive Steering Committee for ACE Policy II, Report 2. Washington: US Census Bureau. www.census.gov/dmd/www/ ReportRec2.htm.

Anderson, Bridget. 2000. Doing the Dirty Work? The Global Politics of Domestic Labour. London and New York: Zed Books.

———. 2001. "Reproductive Labour and Migration." In Ali Rogers, ed., Transnational Communities Programme Working Paper Series. www.transcomm.ox.ac.uk/ working_papers.htm.

Arat-Koç, Sedef, with Fely Villasin. 2001. Caregivers Break the Silence: A Participatory-Action Research on the Abuse and Violence, Including the Impact of Family Separation, Experienced by Women in the Live-in Caregiver Program. Toronto: INTERCEDE.

Burawoy, Michael. 1980. "Migrant Labour in South Africa and the United States." In Theo Nichols, ed., Capital and Labour: Studies in the Capitalist Labour Process. London: Athlone.

Castles, Stephen, and Godula Kosack. 1973. Immigrant Workers and Class Structure in Western Europe. London: Oxford University Press.

Colen, Shellee. 1995. "'Like a Mother to Them': Stratified Reproduction and West Indian Childcare Workers and Employers in New York." In Faye D. Ginsburg and Rayna Rapp, eds, Conceiving the New World Order: The Global Politics of Reproduction, p. 78–102. Berkeley: University of California Press.

de Wolff, Alice. 2003. Bargaining for Work and Life. Toronto: Ontario Federation of Labour.

Ehrenreich, Barbara, and Arlie Russell Hochschild. 2003. Introduction to Global Woman: Nannies, Maids, and Sex Workers in the New Economy, p. 1–14. New York: Metropolitan Books.

Furedi, Frank. 2002. Culture of Fear. London and New York: Continuum.

Ginsburg, Faye D., and Rayna Rapp, eds 1995. Introduction to Conceiving the New World Order: The Global Politics of Reproduction, p. 1–18. Berkeley: University of California Press.

Gorz, André. 1970. "Immigrant Labour." New Left Review, May–June: 28–31.

Hochschild, Arlie Russell. 2003. "Love and Gold" In Barbara Ehrenreich and Arlie Russell Hochschild, eds, Global Woman: Nannies, Maids, and Sex Workers in the New Economy, p. 15–30. New York: Metropolitan Books.

Hontagneu-Sotelo, Pierrette, and Ernestine Avila. 2000. "'I'm Here, but I'm There': The Meanings of Latina Transnational Motherhood." In Maxine B. Zinn, Pierrette Hontagneu-Sotelo, and Michael A. Messner, eds, Gender Through the Prism of Difference, 2nd edn. Boston: Allyn and Bacon.

Human Rights Internet. 2003. "Singapore: Thematic Reports." www.hri.ca/fortherecord2003.

Katz, Cindi. 2001. "Vagabond Capitalism and the Necessity of Social Reproduction." Antipode 33 (4): 709–28.

Kempadoo, Kamala. 2004. "Globalizing Sex Workers' Rights." In Margaret L. Andersen and Patricia Hill Collins, eds, Race, Class and Gender: An Anthology, 5th edn, p. 465–73. Belmont, CA: Wadsworth Thomson.

Momsen, Janet Henshall. 1999. "Maids on the Move: Victim or Victor." In J.H. Momsen, ed., Gender, Migration and Domestic Service, p. 1–20. New York: Routledge.

Parrenas, Rhacel Salazar. 2003. "The Care Crisis in the Philippines: Children and Transnational Families in the New Global Economy." In Barbara Ehrenreich and Arlie Russell Hochschild, eds, Nannies, Maids, and Sex Workers in the New Global Economy, p. 39–45. New York: Metropolitan Books.

Pettman, Jan Jindy. 1996. Worlding Women: A Feminist International Politics. London and New York: Routledge.

Rodriguez, Robyn M. 2002. "Migrant Heroes: Nationalism, Citizenship and the Politics of Filipino Migrant Labor." Citizenship Studies 6 (3): 341–56.

Sassen, Saskia. 1996. Losing Control? Sovereignty in an Age of Globalization. New York: Columbia University Press.

Spivak, Gayatri. 2000. "Thinking Cultural Questions in 'Pure' Literary Terms." In Paul Gilroy, L. Grossberg, and A. McRobbie, eds, Without Guarantees: In Honour of Stuart Hall, p. 335–57. London and New York: Verso.

United Nations. 2002, October 28. "Number of World's Migrants Reaches 175 Million Mark." Press release. www.un.org/News/Press/docs/2002/pop844.doc. htm.

Questions for Critical Thought

1. What is transnational motherhood, according to Arat-Koç? How have immigration policies in the last 30 years contributed to this social injustice?
2. Why have changes in the global economy resulted in the feminization of international labour migration? Why has there been an increase in the demand for domestic care workers in Canada? How have other Western countries dealt with domestic care issues? Why (and how) have domestic workers been coerced into taking on jobs that are controlled by human traffickers and mafia groups in countries around the world?
3. What is the double bind of motherhood that Arat-Koç describes in her research? How can this social inequity be resolved? What has the Canadian government done to alleviate this serious social problem?
4. What is stratified reproduction? How does this concept explain, for example, the position of migrant domestic workers and Aboriginal women in Canada? What other social hierarchies may be explained by using this term?
5. What does Arat-Koç suggest that the Canadian state do to reduce the racialization and transnationalization of reproductive work in Canada? What can be done on a global scale to reduce this social problem?

In the Pool, on the Ice: Contested Terrain

.... *Helen Jefferson Lenskyj*

In this chapter, I focus on two spaces, the swimming pool and the ice rink, that are well suited to an analysis of gender politics and the Olympic industry. Beginning with an historical overview, I look at the ways in which skaters and swimmers were gendered, raced, and sexualized, with media coverage playing a key role in these processes. Debates about appearance, attire, and comportment are central to questions of identity construction and the swimming and skating body. Finally, the Gay Games provide a compelling case study of a counter-hegemonic sporting event, and reveal some of the contradictions that abound in these sports.

In the Pool

From Sidestroke to Crawl

Developments in swimming strokes provide an illuminating example of colonialism. In the nineteenth and early twentieth centuries, sidestroke was the dominant swimming style in Europe, England, Canada, and the United States. At an 1844 exhibition in London, spectators were shocked by the "grotesque" style of two **Ojibway** men who swam using a version of what is now known as the crawl: "totally unEuropean" was one commentator's damning description.[1]

In 1873, John Trudgen, a British swimmer, introduced an overarm stroke that he had learned from Indigenous people of South America, later termed the "Indian stroke." Although this stroke proved superior to the more "refined" European and English styles that male swimmers adopted— "graceful and elegant movements, with a minimum of splashing," as swimming historian Cecil Colwin described them—the overarm or crawl stroke did not gain widespread popularity for several decades.[2]

In the early 1900s, Dick Cavill, an Australian swimmer, raced a very fast Samoan woman who used an overarm style but did not kick. He subsequently adopted a straight-leg kick that a Pacific Islander swimmer had learned from Native people in Ceylon (now Sri Lanka). After further experimentation, he developed the so-called Australian crawl, which, given its origins, should more accurately be called the "*Indigenous peoples'* crawl." Australian swimmer Fanny Durack switched from the **Trudgen** to a version of the crawl in 1911, and proceeded to win every race over Australian opponent Mina Wylie, who until that time had beaten her.

Modest Attire for the Ladies

The question of appropriate swimwear for women commanded public and media attention through the twentieth century. Until the early 1900s, it was customary in most Western countries for women to swim in a swimming dress, only slightly shorter than street clothes of the day, with stockings and shoes. In other words, they swam fully clothed. When wet, the outfit weighed up to 22 pounds.[3] Heavy, neck-to-knee woollen suits with a modesty "skirt" (an extra layer of fabric across the front) were followed in the 1920s by a similar style in cotton knit (yet another fabric that sagged when wet) that was developed by Speedo, at that time an Australian company.

From 1916 on, American and Australian knitting mills capitalized on the popularity of women's swimming, changing their original mundane company names to catchier ones such as Speedo, Cole of California, Catalina, and Jantzen ("The Suit that Changed Bathing to Swimming").[4] Further developments in nylon and elasticized fabrics led to more streamlined suits that reduced drag, culminating in the full-length body suits that the International Swimming Federation (FINA) approved for swimmers at the Sydney 2000 Olympics. These suits were banned in 2009 following debates over the validity of records achieved by swimmers who wore them. Almost 100 years earlier, Australian professional swimmer Annette

Kellerman had been advocating for women's right to wear a form-fitting, full-length bodysuit with short sleeves, a style remarkably similar to the high-tech version of 2000, and equally controversial. Interestingly, between 2000 and 2009, the bodysuit had an unintended positive consequence for the women of Pakistan's national swim team, since it satisfied the Islamic dress requirement that women's bodies should be covered.[5]

Australian swimmer Mina Wylie wore a light-weight, sleeveless swimsuit made of silk and imported from England; its less restrictive style probably gave her an advantage over other swimmers.[6] Photographs of Wylie and Fanny Durack in 1912 posing proudly for the camera in their wet swimsuits bring to mind the title of a 2010 article, "How to Look Good (Nearly) Naked."[7] On the basis of her research on UK swimmers completed in 2009, Susie Scott introduced the concept of "**performative regulation**" in relation to the swimmers' individual and social bodies. As she demonstrated, "The near-naked state of the swimmer's body presents a potential threat to the interaction order, insofar as social encounters may be misconstrued as sexual, and so rituals are enacted to create a 'civilized' definition of the situation."[8] In the very different social context of the early 1900s, similar rituals may have smoothed the way for female swimmers. For example, at the 1912 Stockholm Olympics, Durack and Wylie wore green caps and green cloaks over their swimming costumes until they began their races, thereby conforming to the new official dress code for female swimmers.[9] In a photograph of the 1912 Australasian (combined Australian and New Zealand) Olympic team, the two women are shown wearing bulky bathrobe-style pants bearing the team logo, as well as long white dresses, while the men wore regular attire with team jackets.[10] Until at least the 1920s, female tennis players at Wimbledon and the Olympics attracted criticism when they wore dresses with short sleeves that revealed bare forearms (although they retained the prerequisite white stockings), while female swimmers pioneered functional swimsuit styles that eventually became more widely accepted.

Weighing in on women's Olympic sport in 1936, Finnish runner Paavo Nurmi pronounced swimming acceptable, but called for events such as javelin and high jump to be "forbidden" on the grounds that he "could not bear to watch [women] . . . contorting [and] convulsing" their bodies. He went on to explain that he admired the Dutch women swimmers, because "such contests do not prevent women from remaining ladies."[11]

By the 1980s, however, the evolution of high performance sport had led to specialized training programmes and a selection process based on optimal body types, producing female swimmers who would not have satisfied this conservative view of "ladies." Nor did female swimmers' bodies meet contemporary definitions of femininity in Western society. Former Olympic swimmer Nikki Dryden recalled how she saw herself in high school: "I knew I wasn't looking the same way as other young girls . . . [so] I became punk, dyed my hair, cut it short, I took it to extremes . . . away from femininity."[12]

It is possible, of course, that male authorities' constant references to the "beauty and grace" of the "ladies" in the pool concealed men's underlying interest in admiring female bodies wearing considerably less clothing than most women of the day—thereby confirming Allen Guttmann's theories on the eros/sport connection. As noted earlier, the women in sport administration who objected to male audiences certainly believed that voyeurism was men's prime motive. In the same vein, they wanted girls and women to have female coaches and trainers, a difficult goal to achieve in a period when career paths for women in sport were limited.

That situation had not changed significantly by the end of the twentieth century, largely on account of structural barriers. Competing at the national and internationals level in the 1990s, Dryden pointed out that almost all the coaches and support staff were men, with the possible exception of a female manager and "mother figure."[13] She noted that there were more female coaches in the National Collegiate Athletic Association (NCAA), and that these women,

successful swimmers themselves, could coach at the college level rather than start off in age-group coaching (children and adolescents), a job that required travelling and working on weekends and thus presented obstacles for many women, especially those with children.

The Swimmer's Body: Inappropriate Touching

Until the late 1980s, sexual harassment and sexual abuse in sport were rarely recognized or documented, and sport scholars were just beginning to address these issues.[14] The perpetrators were mostly male coaches, and their targets were mostly girls and young women, and sometimes boys. How widespread the problems were before Western feminist activists raised public awareness of abuse issues outside sport, and eventually within sport, is impossible to calculate. For many decades, there were reports of various kinds of physical abuse of young athletes in former Eastern Bloc countries, with the East German state-ordered **doping policy**, discussed below, representing the most serious example. As recently as 2004, reports from China, where an estimated two-thirds of the country's professional athletes were children, documented "inhumane" training methods and sexual abuse.[15] This is not to suggest that sporting practices in Western countries always hold to higher ethical standards in relation to child athletes.[16]

A widespread problem in Western countries as well as Eastern Europe was the kind of psychological abuse by male coaches that produced eating disorders—anorexia and bulimia. This abuse included daily public weigh-ins in an era when "it was okay to call girls fat," as Dryden explained. The problem was first recognized in the 1980s and was well documented among girls and women in sports such as gymnastics, where thinness was seen as contributing to winning performances, but less thoroughly investigated in other sports. By the end of the 1990s in Western countries, more effective measures were in place to train coaches and monitor coaching practices in order to prevent eating disorders, but other problems in coach–athlete relationships remained.

Swimming presents specific opportunities for both appropriate and inappropriate touching because of the nature of the sport, coaching styles, and the exposed body of the swimmer. A 2003 controversy in Australian high performance swimming circles uncovered the common and largely unquestioned coaching behaviours of the 1980s. Two female swimmers accused their male coaches, Scott Volkers and Greg Hodge, of sexual misconduct. Charges were dropped against Volkers; the Hodge case went to court, the swimmer lost, and Hodge successfully sued for damages on the grounds of defamation. The mainstream media's attempts at investigative journalism demonstrate their power to shape the discourse.

By 2003, both Volkers and Hodge were coaching national teams, and the 2004 Athens Olympics were less than a year away—not a convenient time for Australia to lose its top coaches. Since the accusations referred back to events of the 1980s and 1990s, journalists sought out retired female swimmers and coaches in a transparent attempt to support the position that "everyone was doing it" back in the day. That is, all the male coaches were giving full-body massages ("rub-downs") to young female and male swimmers because, at this time, teams did not have massage therapists—and it was "innocent." In Canada, too, Dryden recalled some "touchy-feely" swim coaches in the 1990s, and, again, "everybody knew." She also noted that going to the coach's hotel room "to talk about race strategy" was a routine practice.

Former Australian national coach Don Talbot admitted that "a lot of people" were uncomfortable with the "rub-down" practice—the young swimmers, male and female, the coaches, and the parents. He also acknowledged that the practice gave abusers "a foot in the door" by legitimizing touching of swimmers' bodies. However, former swimmers lined up to support Hodge and Volkers, and to validate the coaching practices of the 1980s and 1990s. Significantly, there was little if any support for the two women who

made the allegations, or for other victims who had remained silent. "I never, never found it was crossing the line of touchy-feely type things," said Michelle Ford, while Tracey Wickham, another 1980s champion, claimed that all coaches did what Hodge did: "fixing straps up, giving them a hug or kiss . . . patting them on the back," thereby skirting the real issue of sexual touching. Several swimmers and coaches expressed more concern about the "damage" to the sport and the coaching profession, claiming that male coaches were leaving swimming because of worries about false accusations.[17]

A few recommended "common sense," noting that coaches needed to be more aware of boundaries, and to adhere to the Australian swimming code of conduct, which specifically named "inappropriate intimacy" between coach and athlete as "sexual misconduct." Another provision stated that no person should "touch anyone in a way that makes them feel uncomfortable," thereby putting the responsibility for defining "uncomfortable" on the (child or adolescent) athlete rather than the (adult) coach.[18] Furthermore, coaching methods in sports such as gymnastics, swimming, and diving typically involve hands-on demonstrations and/or spotting, and cultural differences between coaches and athletes shape perceptions of appropriate and inappropriate touching. Viewing television coverage of Olympic events, one can see cultural differences played out in the range of interactions between coaches and athletes following successful or unsuccessful performances. The "different culture" excuse does not, of course, justify unethical behaviour on the part of coaches.

A scene that has remained with me for many years took place during women's gymnastics at the 1996 Atlanta Olympics: after one gymnast had performed poorly and was walking back to the bench, Márta Károlyi, wife of Romanian coach Béla Károlyi, both of whom were at that time coaching the US women's team, put her hand on the back of the girl's neck in what appeared to be a comforting gesture, then squeezed her neck and gave her a slight push. Since this took place in front of dozens of television cameras and millions of viewers, it raised serious questions about coaching practices behind closed doors. Observers have wondered if this "comforting gesture" was in fact a mild form of the physically and/or sexually abusive behaviour that young athletes are subjected to when they are outside of the public eye.

On the issue of sexual harassment, Dryden identified another underrecognized problem that she experienced as a member of the Canadian national team in the 1990s: sexual harassment at the hands of male peers. Unlike club teams, the national team included several very young female swimmers—she was 14, while most of her male teammates were in their late teens, "very sexually active" and, on occasion, sexually aggressive. Further adding to the dangers of this situation, after the competition, "everyone was drinking and partying," including underage swimmers and their coaches, and "no one ever talked about it, or warned you." These practices ended abruptly after 1992 when six swimmers on the national team were kicked out of the Olympic Village following "high jinks." A new rule applied to swimmers in the 1996 Olympics: "No sex, no drugs, no alcohol."

Doping and Swimming

Between 1972 and 1989, the German Democratic Republic implemented a policy of administering performance-enhancing drugs to athletes in government-sponsored elite sport schools. Of the thousands of athletes involved, most were under the age of 16 and were not told the purpose of the drugs, while those over 18 had to sign an oath of secrecy. Coaches and doctors were brought to trial in 1998, found guilty of bodily harm and administering drugs to minors, and given relatively small fines and/or suspended sentences. Hundreds of these young athletes subsequently developed physical and mental health problems, and some sought compensation in the courts.

German women, unrivalled swimming champions for more than 25 years, were the best-known products of the state doping policy. Some of these women testified against their coaches and subsequently told their stories to the media. In addition

to the **virilizing** effects of steroids, there were serious health outcomes, including liver cancer and infertility, and some of these women had children with birth defects.[19]

Chinese swimmers, almost all female, made dramatic improvements between the 1988 and 1996 Olympics, and their performances, as well as their impressive muscularity, prompted coaches to pressure FINA to introduce a more thorough and effective drug-testing programme. By 2000, 38 Chinese swimmers had tested positive for drugs, well ahead of the next country, Russia (USSR) with 8.[20]

Obstacles: Class and Race

The benefits of swimming, generally framed in terms of health and social control, have been widely recognized since the late 1800s. Opportunities for working-class families expanded over the course of the twentieth century as European workers' sport organizations and YWCAs, YMCAs, and YWHAs around the world offered classes to all ages in indoor pools. Single-sex organizations avoided potential problems involving appropriate apparel, but boys and young men continued to have more freedom and hence more opportunities for swimming outdoors—in rivers, lakes, and the ocean—than girls and women.

As the sport developed at the high performance level, the demands of training presented obstacles for working-class and ethnic minority swimmers in Western countries. **Systemic racism** in the United States, combined with social-economic inequalities, produced often insurmountable barriers for African American families. Before the changes brought about by the 1960s civil rights movement, public pools barred the entry of black swimmers, and they were unlikely to be able to afford fees for expensive country clubs, if indeed they were accepted as members. Even after the 1960s, inner city neighbourhoods where working-class black families lived were unlikely to have well-maintained public pools, nor did their local high schools. And, as author Philip Hoose pointed out, "the private club is the foundation of American competitive swimming."[21] These factors, as well as all the other expenses associated with meets, makes swimming out of reach for working-class families.

As a five-year-old in 1948, Chris Silva, who later became the first black swimmer on the US national team, experienced the racism of that era when he was the only black child taking part in a swimming clinic in Long Beach. His mother recalled that he was treated as an oddity because of his skin colour and his hair. A white man at the pool announced to everyone present (inaccurately, since Silva was an excellent swimmer) that the "heavy bones" of black people meant that they were unable to swim.[22]

Numerous other myths abounded concerning the black body's alleged inability to swim or float, for the most part based on racist, pseudo-scientific hearsay involving bone density, fast- and slow-twitch muscle ratio and so on. This kind of misinformation about black swimmers continues, to a lesser extent, today, in reference not only to African Americans but to black populations throughout the world. A Google search for the phrase "why no black swimmers in Olympics," generated countless results, with references to alleged physiological differences and deficits still surfacing in some of these sources. Significantly, the question does not appear to have generated the volume of racist research that was prompted by the success of black athletes, presumably because white scientists and the white sport world are more interested in black winners than black "losers." The fact that increasing numbers of black athletes are competing in swimming at the international level reveals the flaws in physiology-based explanations.

From Water Ballet to Synchronized Swimming

Australian professional swimmer Annette Kellerman, famed for her English Channel swims in the early 1900s, has sometimes been credited as the originator of water ballet, later called synchronized swimming, although American Esther Williams is more universally recognized as the pioneer, no doubt because of her high profile in film.

While it shares many features with ballet and figure skating, where men and women perform together, synchronized swimming is, strangely, a predominantly female sport, having women's pairs and team events, although there is greater participation and acceptance of male synchro swimmers in Europe than in other Western countries. The Gay Games, of course, include competitions for men as well as women, but no men, gay or straight, have that opportunity in the Olympics. In 2000, FINA accepted male/female pairs in international competition, but the federation did not push for mixed pairs' inclusion in the 2004 Olympic programme, and it has remained excluded.

The few American men who have competed in synchro swimming since 2000 continue to attract widespread media and public attention, both positive and negative, with Bill May and Kenyon Smith among the best-known male representatives of the sport. Ironically, much of the coverage echoes themes that were central in earlier decades when women began participating in non-traditional (male) sports. Journalists routinely ask these men how they got interested, what attracted them to the sport, and whether they have experienced any negative reactions. Many say they belonged to swim clubs as children, had sisters in synchro, watched them practising and then became interested themselves. Some were harassed as children, and some experienced occasional audience hostility as adults; others no doubt dropped out because of harassment.

The most salient problem that they identified was the "**gay stigma,**" and their most common reaction was remarkably similar to the "female apologetic" of the 1970s in women's sport: repeated affirmations of their heterosexual identity. Smith was quoted in a newspaper article as saying, "I'm the one who gets to hang out with a group of girls in bikinis everyday," but he assured readers that he did not date the women on his team, adding nobly, "I've had to break some hearts, unfortunately."[23] Bill May, presenting more of a **metrosexual image**, was reported to enjoy gourmet cooking.

When Bill May and female partner Kristina Lum competed in the pairs competition at the Goodwill Games in 1998, one commentator praised their "steamy, ground-breaking performance to Ravel's 'Bolero'" in which they appeared to be channelling British ice dancers Torvill and Dean. As Lum explained, "we really tried to play off the passion between a man and a woman."[24]

Commenting on the interest shown by Chinese officials after seeing the pair at the Goodwill Games, their coach, Chris Carver, expressed her admiration for the Chinese approach to sport: "They don't have the cultural roadblocks we do," she said. "They'll just take all the little boys out of villages and *make them do it*—kind of like they do with diving" (emphasis added).[25] This attitude on the part of an American coach (or indeed any coach) is disturbing, although those who have been acculturated into the world of Olympic sport may disagree. Indeed, officials in high performance sport institutes in liberal-democratic countries, including Canada, the United States, and Australia, select children and adolescents with athletic potential and often take them out of their homes for intense training, all in the name of Olympic medals and national pride.

Gina Arnold, one of the journalists who interviewed Carver and May, elaborated on the gay stigma. In a telling example of the social construction of heterosexuality, she explained, "In America, the idea of men doing synchronised swimming seems positively gay—but in fact, strictly speaking, it is the opposite of gay. The sight of May and Lum performing to Ravel's 'Bolero' is, frankly, a lot more *natural-looking* than the sight of two women mirroring one another's movements" (emphasis added).[26] Yet the relatively new Olympic event of synchronized diving—for men and for women— has similar components without necessarily attracting the homophobic "unnatural" stigma or assumptions that male (or female) divers are gay (although some are).

On the subject of male divers, an incident during the 2008 Beijing Olympics demonstrated some change in attitudes. When NBC reported on Australian Matthew Mitcham's gold medal win (remarkable in that he was the only non-Chinese diver, male or female, to win a gold medal at these Olympics), they failed to mention that he was gay and had a partner. When challenged about this omission, NBC went on at length about time limitations, privacy concerns, and so on, although their website had included the information that Mitcham was openly gay. The network eventually issued an apology for missing "the opportunity to tell Matthew Mitcham's story. We apologize for this unintentional omission."[27] As some critics noted, the heterosexuality of Olympic athletes—Michael Phelps, for example—was clearly revealed during NBC interviews; hence their initial claim that they did not discuss athletes' sexual orientation was untrue.[28] That this remained a blind spot for NBC in 2008 was disturbing, but the fact that there was any controversy at all about NBC's omission reflects some positive change in media practices as there is now a more open discourse taking place about LGBT issues, which seems to be the result of decades of LGBT activism.

Hegemonic or normative concepts of femininity and masculinity are also at play in the perception of synchronized swimming. Journalist Gina Arnold claimed that the "plastic grin" on the face of a female swimmer is readily accepted, while on a male swimmer it would look "phony." Presumably a smiling woman (even with nose clips and Vaselined hair) symbolizes hegemonic femininity. After all, the managed smile has come to be expected of women who provide entertainment and services for men—from flight attendants to sex trade workers.

In displays that are more ironic than serious, the men who compete in synchro in the Gay Games have the prerequisite smiles, along with the sequins and shaved legs. Illustrating the arbitrariness of body grooming behaviours, competitive male cyclists and swimmers also shave their legs, but when male synchro swimmers do so for image rather than functional reasons, the same result is read as effeminate. And when newspaper photographs of East German swimmer Cornelia

Ender at the 1976 Montreal Olympics showed that she had underarm hair as well as large quads, that "masculine" image alone implied steroid use.[29]

Further musing on the inclusion of men in synchro, Arnold predicted that athleticism would become more prominent and that the sport would "start getting respect." It seems more likely that men's participation will add more obvious **heteronormative** content to the routines rather than downplaying appearance and promoting athleticism. In the 1980s, when some women tried to persuade synchro officials to allow them to wear regular swimsuits and caps, they were unsuccessful.

Carver, the synchro coach, went on to say, "There's a whole new aspect with males . . . It's a lot like the pairs in figure skating. There's a lot of interplay, a lot of high lifts that are not there with the (women-only) duets. It's all very exciting." One might ask why, if the women's pairs appear so "unnatural," so lacking in interplay, athleticism, and excitement, the women-only sport is so popular. The fact that May received the US Synchronized Swimming Athlete of the Year award in 1998 suggests that different criteria were applied to males and females because his part of the routine, as in figure skating or ballet, was quite different from a woman's: he did the high lifts, for example.

On the Ice

Men, Women, and Skates

Female figure skaters have outnumbered men on the ice, and outperformed them in terms of sponsorships, since the 1930s. Before that time, it was a predominantly male activity, particularly in England and Europe but with significant differences in style. European influences eventually prevailed, and, as Mary Louise Adams explained in her comprehensive history of the sport, "To prove their mettle, English skaters had to temper their manly reserve, adopt a more expressive style, and skate like 'effete' Continentals."[30] This was probably the same "manly reserve" that caused British spectators to be shocked by the swimming performances of two Native North American men described earlier. By the 1980s, the notion of "effete" had taken on homophobic dimensions, as the lyric styles and fancy costumes of male figure skaters came to be interpreted as gay.

Sonja Henie popularized the sport for women following her performances at the Olympics in 1928, 1932, and 1936, and, of course, her Hollywood career. However, unlike men's figure skating, which has evolved in a range of ways—from lyrical to macho and back—in different countries and different historical periods, women's figure skating continues to reflect the legacy of Henie's **ultra-feminine** style. As Adams concluded, "figure skating continues to support and reward only a limited range of intransigently traditional femininities, none which foreground women's strength and power . . . Female figure skaters are almost always positioned as elegant princesses, bubbly pixies, or alluring vixens."[31] Of course, this positioning is the result of a complex system, as choreographers and coaches shape female skaters whose technical and artistic skills will win points, and whose image will entertain audiences and attract sponsorships, and the dominant image is that of **white femininity**. As a *Ms.* magazine journalist observed in 1994, the sport is "puritanical" and the women "have to be clean-cut, wholesome and virginal." At that time, American Tonya Harding was the only married woman who had performed singles skating in the Olympics.[32]

The Whiteness of Ice and Snow Sports

Only a small minority of Olympic figure skaters, male or female, are black, Hispanic, or South Asian. As with swimming, tennis, golf, and similar sports, this is largely an outcome of the combined effects of racism and **classism**. To rise to top levels in these sports requires membership in private clubs and considerable investments in time and money, which poses barriers to children in most working-class, black, Hispanic, and immigrant families.

Furthermore, winter sports have long been a predominantly white preserve as a result of systemic barriers as well as racist assumptions that "geography is destiny." Analyzing this aspect of the Winter Olympics, I found a favourite rationale for these sports' **whiteness** was geography: athletes from warm or temperate climates, it is claimed, are at a geographic disadvantage because they don't have access to year-round ice and snow. But no one argues that athletes from cold climates, lacking year-round access to outdoor fields, tracks, roads, mountains, or beaches, suffer a geographic disadvantage.[33] If geography were the key factor, Northern European athletes, for example, would be expected not to have much success in summer sports. But, in fact, athletes from Western countries, warm and cold, have had high medal counts in Summer and Winter Olympics throughout most of the twentieth century, and athletes from colder countries have outperformed those from warmer countries even in sports of the Summer Games, a trend that is in large part attributable to economic and political determinants.[34] In short, geography is not a barrier in countries that have the financial resources to compensate for any disadvantages posed by climate or in countries that have the greatest political investment in producing medal-winning performances every two years to gain sporting ascendancy on the world stage.

Sexism and Homophobia on Ice

Although men's individual figure skating allows for, perhaps encourages, the kind of flamboyancy often associated with gay male celebrities, the choreography of the pairs figure skating and ice dancing programmes counters this trend, as does the ruling against same-sex pairs competitions in international ice skating (with the notable exception of the Gay Games). In pairs figure skating and ice dancing, **heteronormativity** is announced in every move, with sexual attraction and tension between the two partners playing a key role in their performance, as synchro swimmer Kristina Lum pointed out. This posed a challenge for the

many brother-and-sister pairs who competed in international figure skating competition, particularly when they performed the unequivocally heterosexy tango, which became a compulsory component of ice dancing in 1976. Some brother–sister pairs avoided the problem by performing nonsexual, humorous routines, but most simply recognized that they needed to act the part, and seemed to assume that the audience would forget that they were siblings and focus on their performance.[35]

Both male and female figure skaters face a range of sexist and homophobic stereotypes: the women are expected to be graceful and beautiful, while the men are assumed to be gay—and in this context, gay is not good. In 2009, Skate Canada identified a problem of decreasing numbers of boys taking up the sport. They urged coaches and athletes to promote a more "masculine" skating style and to work at attracting more of "an ice hockey crowd"[36]—a curious goal in view of the sanctioned, crowd-pleasing violence of the National Hockey League in the United States and Canada.

Canadian Elvis Stojko had pioneered a more **"butch"** style of men's figure skating and costuming in the 1990s, to counter the so-called effeminacy trend. A Toronto journalist's commentary on his 1997 televised special, *Elvis Incognito*, gives some indication of his challenge to the "sequins-and-glitter" image of male figure skaters: "a multifaceted character who unveils himself during the show . . . having Elvis drive a motorcycle, lip synch an arena rock anthem . . . and hold forth cryptically on the benefits of martial arts."[37]

Just before the 2010 Vancouver Winter Olympics, Stojko called for greater emphasis on "masculinity, strength and power" in men's skating. "People in the gay community have to realize they've got to take themselves out of it," he added—not because he was "against anybody," but because, he claimed, people couldn't identify with "effeminate" performances, and the future of the sport was under threat. Like the Australian swimming coaches discussed earlier, Stojko expressed greater feeling and sensitivity towards "the sport" than towards the men, women, and children who constitute it. This kind of discourse, common in the world of high performance sport, obliterates the human element as it reifies the institution.

Apart from the obvious offensiveness of his statement, Stojko seems to have overlooked the longstanding presence of (mostly closeted) gay men in figure skating, as coaches, choreographers, and judges as well as skaters, and the fact that their performances had boosted its popularity significantly since the 1980s. In 1997, for example, the televised Canadian national championships attracted almost two million viewers over seven hours of prime-time coverage.[38] This is not to suggest that the sport of figure skating provided a welcoming climate for gay men or boys. After Canadian Brian Orser was outed through a **palimony suit** in 1998, he received public support, but no other skater came out as gay in solidarity with him.[39]

Rudy Galindo was the only figure skater to come out during his competitive career. Gay, working-class, Mexican American (and later HIV positive), he took a considerable risk doing so as he had already attracted negative attention from judges and audiences with his long hair, makeup, and "feminine" costumes. In 1996, he was left off Skate America's team, and, as he wrote in his autobiography, his coach was convinced that the US Figure Skating Association (USFSA) "didn't want an effeminate gay man representing the United States at Skate America," the most prestigious international competition held in the United States.[40] Discussing his Hispanic identity in a 2002 interview, Galindo said, "I think I was discriminated against my whole life in skating, practically. I had to work twice as hard and just make sure those judges had no excuse not to give me first or place me, at nationals or internationals."[41]

"Skating's Tragic Secret"

A chapter called "Skating's Tragic Secret" in American sportswriter Christine Brennan's 1997 book, *Inside Edge*, discussed the dramatic impact of the **AIDS crisis** on everyone involved in figure skating at the national and international levels,

including athletes, their partners and families, coaches, choreographers, and judges. The "secret" referred to the silence surrounding AIDS deaths in the figure skating world of the 1980s and into the 1990s; a 1992 report estimated that the number of deaths among American and Canada skaters and coaches was at least 40. Yet, as Brennan explained, the USFSA was slow to respond because it saw this as a potential public relations disaster: "AIDS means homosexuality . . . How does the organization say it has lost more athletes to AIDS than any other sport in the country?"[42] To acknowledge the presence of gay men in figure skating would jeopardize sponsorships and TV ratings, and raise fears among parents. In addition to the Americans, the high-profile figure skaters who died of AIDS included John Curry from the UK, Ondrej Nepela from Czechoslovakia, and Rob McCall, Brian Pockar, Dennis Coi, and Shaun McGill from Canada. The USFSA eventually held discussions and educational sessions on AIDS prevention for skaters and coaches.

"Bad Examples" of Masculinity?

In 2010, American Johnny Weir, whose **gender-bending** style made him a media magnet following the 2006 Torino Olympics, came out as gay, to no one's surprise, after having spent several years avoiding questions about his sexuality. During the 2010 Vancouver Olympics, two announcers on a Canadian sports channel made homophobic comments about Weir, claiming that he was a "bad example" for boys. Their so-called jokes included the suggestions that "We should make him pass a gender test" or "compete in the women's competition." Following a public outcry, the announcers and the television station issued apologies.[43] On a more positive note, when Weir married his partner in 2011, the mainstream media treated the event in much the same way that it treated heterosexual sport celebrities' marriages.

The year 1994 marked the first time that two men competed in the Gay Games figure skating pairs, in a routine that had the traditional lifts of opposite-sex pairs. Canadian skaters Jean-Pierre

Martin and Mark Hird had first practised together in the Bell Amphitheatre in Montreal, where Martin worked as a consultant and ice-show producer. When his boss objected, the pair started practising at a suburban Montreal rink, again sparking "a flood of complaints from parents scandalised by Mr. Martin lifting and spinning Mr. Hird," as reported by journalist Andre Picard, who went on to identify the arbitrary standards that make ice hockey masculine: "When 12 men skate together on the Montreal Forum ice, chasing a piece of hard black rubber and whacking each other for good measure, that's manly . . . But when Mr. Martin and Mr. Hird . . . spin and leap on the ice of the Bell Amphitheatre, the reaction is still decidedly cool, the recognition of their art . . . distant."[44] When Martin and Hird invited CBC television cameras to follow their experiences, culminating in the documentary titled *Breaking Barriers*, the Bell people reversed their decision and offered them free training time. One account of these events noted that objections had been made on the grounds that the two men had been seen kissing, which they said was untrue. Furthermore, there were two mentions of the fact that Martin and Hird "were friends but not lovers."[45] The reason for this commentator's emphasis on their relationship status is unclear. After all, the homophobic response reflected moral outrage that two gay men would dare to perform a routine reserved for a heterosexual couple, and their relationship to each other was a side issue.

As in men's synchro swimming, there has long been a pattern in American and Canadian men's figure skating circles of "coming out straight" in the media—that is, repeated assertions of heterosexuality through references to wives, girlfriends, and children. Given the gay stigma that the sport attracts, there appears to be no place for the metrosexual man in figure skating. Conversely, in sports where all the men are assumed to be straight—basketball, baseball, football, and ice hockey, for example—there is more scope for, and less threat to, players who fit the metrosexual image. These are men who devote an unusual (for a man) amount of attention to clothing, jewellery, personal appearance, and each other's bodies—in the locker room, in the nude. John Amaechi, a black basketball player and the first to come out as gay following his retirement from the National Basketball Association, discussed these practices in his 2007 autobiography *Man in the Middle*. As he explained, these exchanges, which included flaunting their "perfect bodies," reflected "an intense kind of camaraderie that felt completely natural to them but was a little too close for my comfort . . . and I'm the gay one."[46] Amaechi reported an interesting cultural twist in gay stereotypes. Growing up in England, he had a British accent, and whenever there were questions about his (hetero)sexuality, "people would quip, 'Oh, he's just English. Leave him alone.'"[47]

At elite levels in women's sport, however, a different set of norms prevailed in many locker rooms. As Nikki Dryden observed, the majority of swimmers covered up their bodies, in and out of the showers, while some soccer players even showered in their sports bras. This is a pattern I've also observed for the past 20 years among women on the university's swim team. Nudity seems to be taboo, perhaps as a kind of defence against rumours of lesbianism. In the 1990s, when Dryden was competing, she faced homophobic accusations because of her short hair and her close friendship with a female swimmer with whom she trained. The rumours, started by male peers, ruined their friendship, an outcome that she continues to find upsetting. And, like other young women trying to find their identity, she found that "the only way to be feminine was to have sex" with these boys.

Conclusion

Throughout the history of the Olympics, the politics of sex, gender, and sexuality have been played out in the pool and on the ice, as the arbitrary inclusions and exclusions of the Olympic programme reflected and reinforced gender binaries and heteronormativity. Unlike most male sports, men's figure skating displayed a level of "beauty and grace" traditionally reserved for female athletes, but this trend did not go unnoticed or unchallenged, as seen in recent moves to "masculinize" the sport. For their part, female figure skaters and synchro swimmers have had limited success in promoting athleticism and challenging

hegemonic femininity. An alternative sporting festival, the Gay Games, has successfully countered some of these trends. It will be interesting to observe whether the Gay Games will continue to be a separate sporting event or if it will be assimilated into the Olympic Games in the years to come.

Notes

1. Cited in C. Colwin, *Breakthrough Swimming* (Champaign, IL: Human Kinetics, 2002), 14; see also P. Hoose, *Necessities: Racial Barriers in American Sports* (New York: Random House, 1989), 70.
2. Colwin, *Breakthrough Swimming*, 3.
3. National Geographic, *Swimsuits: A Hundred Years of Pictures* (Washington, DC: National Geographic Society, 2000).
4. "Vintage Swimwear Timeline: Historical Timeline on the History of Swimwear," *GlamourSurf*, www.glamoursurf.com/swimwear_timeline.html (accessed 13 February 2015).
5. Nikki Dryden, former Canadian Olympian, interview with the author, Toronto, 14 May 2012.
6. Randwick City Council historical exhibit, *Come in for a Swim: Mila Wylie*, Bowen Library, Maroubra, New South Wales, May–October 2012.
7. S. Scott, "How to Look Good (Nearly) Naked: Regulation of the Swimmer's Body," *Body & Society* 16, 2 (2010): 143–68.
8. Ibid., 143.
9. M. Stell, *Half the Race: A History of Australian Women in Sport* (North Ryde, NSW: HarperCollins, 1992), 159; *Come in for a Swim*.
10. Australasian Olympic team 1912 photograph, New South Wales State Library, in *Come in for a Swim*.
11. Nurmi quoted in Stell, *Half the Race*, 108.
12. Nikki Dryden interview.
13. Ibid.
14. When I began researching these issues in 1990, there were very few sources. The most important was Donald Lackey's study of sexual harassment experienced by female athletes at the hands of male coaches in American college and university sport; see D. Lackey, "Sexual Harassment in Sports," *Physical Education* 47, 2 (1990), 22–6.
15. F. Hong, "Innocence Lost: Child Athletes in China," *Sport in Society* 7:3 (2004), 342.
16. C. Breckenridge, *Spoilsports* (London: Routledge, 2001).
17. "Swimming's Touchy Issue," *Sydney Morning Herald*, 20 September 2003; S. Meacham, "Too Close for Comfort," *Sydney Morning Herald*, 18 October 2003, 36; R. Yallop, "Intimacy and Betrayal," *The Australian*, 23 October 2003.
18. "Swimming's Touchy Issue."
19. K. Volkwein, "Sport and Ethics in Unified Germany—A Critical Analysis," in R. Barney and K. Meier (eds), *Proceedings of the First International Symposium for Olympic Research* (London, ON: University of Western Ontario, 1992), 55–66; Colwin, *Breakthrough Swimming*.
20. Colwin, *Breakthrough Swimming*, 215.
21. Hoose, Necessities, 77.
22. Ibid., 74.
23. K. Melloy, "No Olympic Glory for Male Synchronized Swimmers," *Edge Boston*, 30 July 2008, www.edgeboston.com/index.php?ch=news&sc=glht&sc2=news&sc3=&id=78177.
24. T. Ziemer, "Out of Sync: Male Synchro Swimmer Banned from Olympics," *ABC News*, 1 September 2008, www.tracyziemcr.com/ABC-NEWS-out-of-sync.htm.
25. G. Arnold, "Synch Different," *Metroactive*, 10–16 September 1998, www.metroactive.com/papers/metro/09.10.98/cover/synchroswim-9836.html.
26. Ibid.
27. "NBC Apologizes for Mitcham Gay Snub," *OutSports* 27 September 2008, www.outsports.com/2008/8/27/3860722/nbc-apologizes-for-mitcham-gay-snub.
28. "NBC Defends Not Saying Mitcham Is Gay," *OutSports* 25 September 2008, www.outsports.com/2008/8/25/3860718/nbc-defends-not-saying-mitcham-is-gay.
29. D. Morrow, "Olympic Masculinity," in K. Wamsley, R.K. Barney, and S.G. Martyn (eds), *The Global Nexus Engaged, Proceedings of the Sixth international Symposium for Olympic Research* (London, ON: University of Western Ontario, 2002), 126.
30. M.L. Adams, *Artistic Impressions: Figure Skating, Masculinity, and the Limits of Sport* (Toronto: University of Toronto Press, 2011), 104.
31. Ibid., 199.
32. K. Rounds, "Ice: Reflections on a Sport Out of Whack," *Ms*, May/June 1994, 27. Harding was better known for her involvement in the attack on Nancy Kerrigan, in an attempt to eliminate her rival from upcoming competitions.
33. See H. Lenskyj, "The Winter Olympics: Geography Is Destiny?" in H. Lenskyj and S. Wagg (eds), *Handbook of Olympic Studies* (Basingstoke, UK: Palgrave Macmillan, 2012), 88–102.
34. D. Wallechinsky, *Complete Book of the Olympics* (Harmondsworth, UK: Penguin, 1984); D. Johnson and A. Ali, "A Tale of Two Seasons," *Social Science Quarterly* 85, 4 (2004): 974–93.
35. S. James, "Brother–Sister Skating Pairs, Too Close for Comfort," *ABC News*, 19 February 2010, http://abcnews.go.com/Health/Olympics/olympic-brother-sister-skating-pairs-close-vancouver-ice/story?id=988749.

36.   T. Rogers. "Can Figure Skating Go Butch?" *Salon .com*, 15 February 2010, www.salon.com/2010/02/15/ elvis_stojko_interview/.

37.   D. Bell, "Figure Skating: The Never-Ending Story," *Globe and Mail*, 8 February 1997, D9.

38.   Ibid.

39.   Adams, *Artistic Impressions*, 58.

40.   R. Galindo, with E. Marcus, *Icebreaker* (New York: Pocket Books, 1997), 141; see also C. Brennan, *Inside Edge* (New York: Knopf Doubleday, 1997), 69.

41.   K. Kaufman, "So They're All Gay, Right?: *Salon.com*, 22 February 2002, www.salon.com/2002/02/22/galindo/.

42.   Brennan, *Inside Edge*, 57.

43.   "TV Crew Upsets Gay Rights Group," *Toronto Star*, 21 February 2010.

44.   A. Picard, "Skating with an Olympic-Sized Dream," *Globe and Mail*, 15 February 1994, A7.

45.   M. Garber, "Victor Petrenko's Mother-in-Law," in C. Baughmann (ed.), *Women on Ice* (New York: Routledge. 1995), 98.

46.   D. Amaechi, *Man in the Middle* (New York: ESPN Books, 2007), 140.

47.   Ibid., 271.

Questions For Critical Thought

1.   What does Jefferson Lenskyj mean by white femininity? How does this concept correspond with theories on colonialism and critical whiteness? Give three examples of white femininity practices that athletes and/or officials have displayed during the Olympic Games.

2.   What is performative regulation? How have these regulations impacted male and female athletes throughout the history of the Olympic Games?

3.   What types of sexual harassment and sexual abuse do athletes experience? Should athletic coaches, trainers, therapists, and sports officials be monitored at all levels of amateur competition? Why or why not?

4.   What cultural, racial, religious, geographic, economic, physical, social, and gendered barriers do aspiring athletes face in regional, national, and international competitions? How can these barriers be systematically eliminated?

5.   Should men and women be allowed to compete together in Olympic sports such as synchronized swimming and skating? Why or why not? Is the Gay Olympic Games an adequate alternative to the Olympic Games?

Fruits of Injustice: Women in the Post-NAFTA Food System

....*Deborah Barndt*

Precious Human Cargo

As we approached the Toronto airport in the still-dark dawn, I asked Irena which terminal her plane was leaving from. I expected her to say Terminal Three, which is the main departure point for international flights and by far the most elegant, with sky-lit boutiques and chic restaurants. When she said "Terminal One," I questioned her, especially as the sign for Terminal One said "Cargo." "But I'm going as cargo!" she jokingly explained.

I was well aware of the Foreign Agricultural Resource Management Services, known as the FARMS program, established in 1974, that brings Jamaican and Mexican farm workers such as Irena to Canada every summer to pick our fruit and vegetables.

I knew it was considered the "crème de la crème" of migrant worker schemes, selecting the heartiest who tolerate a few months of backbreaking work in our fields, twelve hours a day, six and half days a week, because they can make more in an hour here than they make in Mexico in a day. And while I knew that they are brought en masse by plane in the spring and sent home en masse in the fall, no reading or interviews prepared me for the sight I faced as we entered Terminal One that day: a sea of brown and black bodies, primarily men, in massive lineups, pushing carts bursting with boxes of appliances they were taking home. Security guards surrounded this precious human cargo, moving less freely than goods now move across borders in the post-NAFTA context. I imagined lighter-skinned Mexican professionals boarding planes in Terminal Three, briefcases in hand, having just completed a new trade deal with Canadian-based companies, or even middle-class and upper-class students now availing themselves of increased exchanges among North American universities.

For the past seven years, I have been involved in a unique cross-border research program involving feminist academics and activists in Mexico, the United States, and Canada, that has taken advantage of this deepening economic and cultural integration of the continent, and the privilege of university research monies to move academics and graduate students across borders much more easily than Irena can move. We have been mapping the journey of the corporate tomato from a Mexican agribusiness to a Canadian supermarket and US-based fast-food restaurant as a device for examining globalization from above (the corporate agendas) and globalization from below (the stories of lowest-waged women workers in these sectors). We met Irena during this tracing of the tomato's trail, discovering a piece of the story that did not fit into any straight line or simple South–North axis. While most people are aware that our winter tomatoes are planted, picked, and packed by Mexican workers, few realize that locally produced summer tomatoes are also brought to us by Mexican hands, borrowed for the summer as cheap labour. This is one of the less visible stories of trade within the new global economy.

One of the environmental activists advocating for the human rights of Indigenous migrant workers in the Mexican fields calls the tomatoes they pick the "fruits of injustice." We began to realize that not only have the tomatoes become increasingly commodified in the neo-liberal industrialized food system, but the most marginalized workers are also commodities in this new trade game. In fact, tomatoes—a highly perishable, delicate fruit and one of the winners for Mexico in the NAFTA reshuffle—are often treated better than the workers.

In this article, I will focus exclusively on the Mexican women workers in the tomato food chain,[1] and primarily those who would never dream of boarding a plane for Canada, but move in and out of seasonal production processes, key actors in the deepening agro-export economy of post-NAFTA Mexico. Their stories will reveal the increasing participation of young women, the deepening exploitation of Indigenous women, the worsening working and living conditions among workers in chemically dependent agribusinesses, and the triple workloads of women who combine salaried work, subsistence farming, and domestic labour to meet the survival needs of their families. While Canadian women workers in the tomato chain also experience increasing inequities, Mexican women are clearly the most marginalized and invisibilized.

Interlocking Analysis of Power

The increasingly **globalized food system** builds on and perpetuates deeply rooted inequalities of race and ethnicity, class, gender, age, urban–rural, and marital status. As we followed the tangled routes of women workers along the tomato trail, we evolved an interlocking analysis that took into account five key dimensions of power that emerged as the most salient to understanding hierarchies within this food chain.

Figure 1 locates our gender analysis first within a context of *North/South* asymmetries, and in the case of the food system, the dynamic that the South (ever more dependent on agro-exports for foreign exchange) increasingly produces for consumption in the North. We do not want to perpetuate a simplistic North/South analysis. We recognize its limitations by revealing the dynamics within Mexico whereby southern impoverished regions feed cheap migrant labour to the richer industrial North of that country. As a result disintegrating rural communities are sucked into the demands of an increasingly urban Mexico. Poor Indigenous *campesinos* are now salaried labour serving the food needs of a wealthier *mestizo* population as well as consumers in the North. In the continental food system, this North–South axis has allowed us to compare the similarities and differences between women who plant, pick, and pack tomatoes in Mexico and those who scan and bag, or slice and serve tomatoes in Canadian retail and fast-food industries.

Class: There are clearly different socio-economic statuses among women in the food system, even among the lower-waged workers in each sector that we are studying here and in each of the three NAFTA countries. Each company constructs its own hierarchy of workers, sometimes though not always related to educational level, but usually defined by skill levels, disparate wage levels, and working conditions.

Race/ethnicity: Also interacting with class and gender are race and ethnicity, shifting in meaning from one place and time to another. In Mexico ethnic differences are perhaps most pronounced between the Indigenous workers that the agribusiness brings by truck to pick tomatoes under the hot sun and the more skilled and privileged *mestiza* women they bring in buses to pack tomatoes in the more protected packing plant.

Age and family status: The interrelated factors of age, marital status, and generational family roles are clearly significant in the Mexican agricultural context, where the workforce is predominantly young and female (a relatively recent phenomenon based on necessity but challenging patriarchal practices). The family wage has become critical, too, as family members combine their salaries as well as unsalaried work for subsistence production to survive a deepening economic crisis.

Rural/urban: In the context of food and agriculture, the rural–urban dynamic is central. Development strategies in both Mexico and Canada have favoured urban dwellers, but still depend on rural workers to feed populations of the burgeoning cities. Mexican *campesinos* are migrating to both rural and urban areas in Mexico, and the survival of most families depends on the migration of some family members(s) to the United States or Canada, even if temporarily, as in the case of Irena.

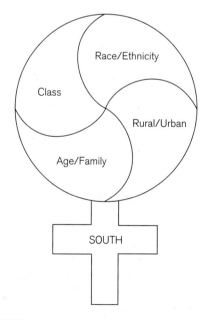

FIGURE 1

It is almost impossible to describe the above dimensions of power in isolation. The stories of the women in the tomato chain reveal the complex interaction between these categories of identity and power and thus enrich our understanding of gender and women's experience as plural, diverse, and constantly changing.

The Tomasita project is by definition a feminist and an ecological project. First, it is a feminist act to make visible the women workers in the food system, redressing their invisibility in other studies of global agriculture and trade regimes as well as in the public consciousness. Beyond filling in the gaps left by male-dominated perspectives, this study benefits from the rich development of diverse feminist theories over the past decade. I have drawn from a wide array of fields, ranging from political economic labour studies to feminist ecological economics, from socialist feminism to feminist environmentalism, from gender and sustainable development to social ecofeminism.[2] My own positions have also been shaped by three decades of research and activism in the United States and Canada, as well as in Peru, Nicaragua, and Mexico.

The complexity of the work and home lives of the women workers in the tomato food chain can only be understood, I believe, by considering particular social constructions of their relationship with nature, and, in Donna Haraway's terms, their situated knowledges (1995). These are inevitably contradictory given that the women workers featured here are immersed in diverse contexts where competing notions of development and globalization are at play. My analysis attempts to weave, like tangled roots and routes, an ecology of women and tomatoes that respects local contexts while acknowledging broader social and historical processes in constant interaction with them.

Profiles of Women in Three Contexts

I will introduce six women who work for Empaque Santa Rosa, the Mexican agribusiness at the production end of the tomato chain. The differences among the Indigenous and *mestiza* workers, the pickers and the packers, will challenge any notion we might harbour in the North of a singular or monolithic Mexican woman worker.

Picking and Packing for the North: Mexican Women Agricultural Workers

Job categories and divisions of tasks within tomato production have evolved over decades (indeed centuries) to reflect and reinforce institutionalized classism, sexism, racism, and **ageism**. According to Sara Lara, the restructuring and technologization of tomato production during the 1990s—promoted by **neo-liberal trade policies**—has not changed the sexual division of labour, but has, in fact, exploited it even further. By employing greater numbers of women, companies contract skilled but devalued labour that is not only qualitatively but quantitatively flexible (Lara 1998b).

A Moving Maquila: The "Company Girls"

The packing plant is one of the places where entrenched gender ideologies clearly reign. Women are considered both more responsible and more delicate in their handling of the tomatoes; and because the appearance of the product is so critical to tomato exporters, there is at least some recognition of this work as a skill, even if managers consider it innate rather than part of female socialization, as Lara argues it is (1998b).

Women who sort and pack tomatoes for Santa Rosa are drawn from two sources: local girls living in the town and mostly young women hired permanently by the company and moved from site to site, harvest to harvest. The latter are the most privileged, and are clearly "company girls," a kind of "moving maquila." They provide the flexible labour and the skills needed by Santa Rosa at the important stage of sorting and packing tomatoes for export.

Juana, Packer

I'm 37 years old now, I've been following the harvests for 23 years. We go from here to the Santa Rosa plant in Sinaloa, and from there we go to San Quintin, Baja California, and then back to Sinaloa—every year we make the round.

We are brought from Sinaloa with all expenses paid, the company covers the costs of transport, food, and once here, we get a house with a stove, beds, mattresses. Our house is close to the plant, and we share it with 16 other workers. In the end, we're all a family.

Yolanda, Sorter

I'm 21, and have been working for Santa Rosa for six years. My father was a manager at the packing plant in Sinaloa, and I began working there during school vacations. I liked packing work better than school. The atmosphere is different, it's more fun and you can make money.

I came here from Sinaloa, and share an apartment with my mother, sister, and brother-in-law. He works in the Santa Rosa office and gets special living expenses. I earn almost 1,000 pesos ($200) a week. I'm saving money for a house I'm building back in Sinaloa.

Many young women Yolanda's age see this as temporary work, a good way to make some money, travel, and perhaps find a husband, so that they can then get on to the "real" business of settling down and raising their own families. Older women like Juana, who do not marry and leave the job, have become virtually wedded to the company, with no time or space for creating their own lives. They move from harvest to harvest, like swallows, returning annually to their hometown.

None of the sorters or packers are Indigenous but rather are lighter-skinned *mestizas*. They are the women who are in greatest contact with the company management. The most privileged, in fact, seem to be women with close connections to men who have administrative jobs with Santa Rosa, such as Yolanda's brother.

There is, however, a hierarchy of skills and of treatment between the two main jobs of sorting and packing, with the packers being the more privileged in several senses.

> The sorters have to sign in, but we packers don't. The sorters have to stand all the time. Packers can sit on wooden boxes.

The sorters start at 9:00 a.m., the packers at 10:00 a.m. Perhaps the biggest and most crucial difference is the wage level and the form of payment. Sorters are paid by the hour, while the box pays packers. At 33 cents a box, a packer might average 200 to 500 boxes a day, earning 66 to 150 pesos, or 13 to 30 US dollars a day; a sorter, earning 5 pesos an hour, would average 35 to 60 pesos, or 7 to 12 US dollars a day. Both of these far surpass the fieldworker's wage of 28 pesos (5 or 6 US dollars) a day for backbreaking work under a hot sun.

Male workers in the packing plant are still the most privileged, however. Most *cargadores* or carriers (who move boxes), make up to 1,200 pesos a week, or 240 US dollars, while packers average 600 to 900 pesos a week (120 to 180 US dollars).

On Saturdays, when workers go to the office to get their weekly pay, the queues themselves reveal the ultimate divisions. In the words of one of the packers,

> When we go to get our money, there are three lines: one for sorters, one for packers, and one for the men.

Factories in the Fields: Hi-Tech Greenhouse Production

The future of tomato production in Mexico appears to be in greenhouses, which allow year-round production and almost total control of key factors like climate, technology, and labour.

Greenhouse production can be seen as the epitome of the "maquila" model, which since NAFTA has now moved from the northern border to be applied to businesses throughout Mexico. Maquila industries are characterized by four dimensions: feminizing the labour force, highly segmenting skill categories (majority unskilled), lowering real wages, and introducing a non-union orientation (Carillo cited in Kopinak 1997). The only Mexican inputs are the land, the sun (the company saves on electricity and heating), and the workers. And like most maquilas, 100 per cent of the produce is for export (10 per cent going to Canada but most to the United States).

Only in recent years has it become culturally acceptable for young women in patriarchal rural communities to enter the paid labour force at all, and then only out of necessity. Most young people have taken these jobs because there is nothing else available and because their income is needed for the family wage.

Greenhouse work offers a new form of employment that combines planting and packing, and in terms of wages and status, falls somewhere between the fieldworkers and the packers at the larger plants. For women, there are basically two different kinds of roles: working in the greenhouses planting and picking tomatoes, or working in the packing house in a more sophisticated process that combines selecting and packing. The next two profiles feature one in each area: Soledad who works in the greenhouse and Yvonne in the packing house.

Soledad, Greenhouse Planter

While Soledad is a very feisty and social 15-year-old, her name means "loneliness or solitude." Ironically, when she was three years old, her parents moved to Los Angeles, and she hasn't seen them since. They have had five more kids there and they send home money, about $500 every two weeks, to support Soledad, her sister and brother, and grandparents, with whom she lives. This is not an uncommon family configuration, as relatives share childrearing on both sides of the notorious border, and those who remain in Mexico are tied both emotionally and financially to their families in the North. Soledad has been working at the greenhouse since she was 13. She makes 180 pesos (US$26) a week, 30 pesos (US$4–$5) a day for six days, or 4 pesos (under $US1) an hour—only slightly more than fieldworkers.

Yvonne, Greenhouse Packer

Yvonne undertakes the other major task assigned to young women, work in the enormous packing house. In her three years working at the greenhouse, the 20-year-old has witnessed the move into hi-tech packing. The pressure that the computerized process on the lines creates within and among the workers is palpable. The French manager's strategy has worked on people like Yvonne who has succumbed to the competitive dynamic:

> I was depressed at first because they would tell me "you're below the quota." I would be ashamed, because this means you're not worth anything. So I was very tense, concerned about getting faster, so they'd have a better impression of me.

Yvonne's efforts to keep up with the new technology and to prove herself a productive worker also reveal the internalization of new work values. "Good workers" are being shaped in Mexico by the combination of controlling technology and foreign management. Yet sexism reigns as once again the male workers are paid more: "If we make 100, men make 175," explains Yvonne.

Into the Fields

The women workers who are closest to the land, the plants, and the tomatoes themselves are also the lowest paid and least skilled in the hierarchy outlined here. They are the most exposed to the hot sun and the rain, as well as the pesticides sprayed incessantly in the fields. Two stories here will reveal two major sources of tomato fieldworkers: local *campesinos* and Indigenous migrants from the south.

Tomasa, Local Fieldworker

As an older woman (68 years old), Tomasa is perhaps not a typical fieldworker. But her story reflects many important characteristics of migrant labour in Mexico. First her personal history growing up as a *mestizo campesino* girl in the countryside reveals the deeply rooted sexism that produces and reproduces the gendered division of labour in the agricultural sector. Second, like many other peasant families, she and her husband combine subsistence farming with salaried work for agribusiness. Finally, her story reveals the **family wage economy**, which is the major strategy of survival for poor Mexicans.

We raised ourselves, that is, my father died when I was two and so my mother was left alone to raise us. She had to work to feed us. As a child, I played around the house, but when I was eight or nine, my mother put me to work—sweeping, fetching water from a faraway stream. When I became older, I helped grind and mix the corn meal to make tortillas.

My kids helped me with the housework and they still help. Two of my sons have gone to work in the US and send money back. My other sons work in the lumber business, cutting pine trees nearby. The women don't work in the field, they stay at home with their family. I'm the only one who runs around like a fried chile, picking tomatoes! My youngest daughter stays at home, and has food ready for us when we return from the fields.

The unpaid domestic work that keeps Mexican *campesino* families alive is not accounted for in any of the official calculations. Tomasa, in fact, works a triple day: as a salaried worker for agribusiness, as a subsistence farmer on their family *milpa* (literally, cornfield or family plot), and as the cook and caretaker of her family.

In either case, they remain dependent on capitalist agribusiness, whether owned by Mexicans or foreigners; both are taking advantage of their cheap labour. And the companies benefit not only from their low wages, but from the family wage economy, which incorporates family remittances, subsistence farming, and Tomasa's domestic labour. While they may represent a triple burden for Tomasa, not even these options are open to most Indigenous migrant women, the most exploited in the hierarchy of workers.

If gender discrimination is entrenched in the tasks offered women workers and in their double or triple days, racism is manifested particularly against the Indigenous migrant workers who are brought in packed trucks by contractors, without certainty of getting work, and with even worse living and working conditions than local *campesinos*. Housed in deplorable huts, without water, electricity, stores, or transport, they come as families to work in the fields and move from harvest to harvest. The women bear the brunt of this lack of infrastructure—cooking and washing, taking care of kids (even while working in the field), and dealing with their own exhaustion and the poor health engendered by the conditions of extreme poverty. Because their own regions offer even less opportunity, they are forced to suffer these jobs and the racist treatment built into them (Lara 1994).

Reyna, Indigenous Migrant Farm Worker

We're from Guerrero. Contractors came to our town to find people to work here. After we finish our contract, they take us back in trucks.

Some women carry their children on their backs while they're working, because they don't have anyone who can take care of them.

We earn 28 pesos a day. It's never enough to save anything. Sometimes the children need shoes and it's not enough. They give us some clothes, because 28 pesos is nothing. There is no union and no vacations.

While children are paid the daily rate, it is often the case that their parents, especially mothers, will rush to fill their own quota, so they can help their children complete theirs. This dynamic makes the fieldwork much more intense and more like piecework (Barrón 1999). Mothers must also carry their babies on their backs as they work in the fields. In breastfeeding her child, Reyna passed the pesticides from the plants to her hands, which then got into his mouth, and almost poisoned him. Indigenous women, as well as men and children, are clearly in the most precarious position of all who bring us the corporate tomato.

In the six stories above, the multiple strategies for survival become clearer. Women are key protagonists for their families, in their triple functions: as salaried workers (with varying status and wage levels), as subsistence farmers (where they have access to land), and as domestic labourers (with a wide range of living conditions, from the horrific camps of Indigenous migrants to the better-equipped but transient homes of the mobile packers). But no one woman's story can be understood in isolation from her family's story, nor separately from her ethnicity, age, marital status, and experience. Globalizing agribusinesses such as Santa Rosa have built their workforces on these historically entrenched inequalities and differences.

Tangled Roots and Routes

The interlocking dimensions of power are even more complex than I was able to reveal here, however, and are constantly changing. The cases of Canadian supermarket cashiers and fast-food workers also demonstrate the growing phenomenon of flexible labour strategies with women bearing the brunt of part-time work schedules. One shift in the Mexican labour force, for example, has been toward younger and younger workers; in a context of oversupply, 15 to 24 is the new ideal age, so a woman's career as a salaried agricultural worker may be finished before she reaches the age of 30. Deepening impoverishment in the countryside has meant that a *campesino* family now needs five rather than three members of the family working in order to eke out their collective subsistence.

Epilogue

The continental economic integration promoted by neo-liberal trade policies and agreements such as NAFTA has also pushed groups working for social and environmental justice to consider the connections between workers in the border-crossing production of food and other goods. There have been spaces within our collaborative research project that women workers have read each other's stories and expressed solidarity with their sisters responsible for moving the tomato along its trail from South to North.

In one example of this growing exchange, Irena, the Mexican farm worker introduced at the start of this essay, extended her stay in Canada in order to spend a week working at the Field to Table Centre, an initiative of FoodShare, which works with low-income communities in Toronto to improve access to affordable and healthy food. Ironically, a woman who knew more about agriculture from her own practice both in Mexico and in Ontario fields, wanted to learn from the urban agricultural experiments on rooftops, greenhouses, and community gardens in this northern city. These are the stories of resistance, of the creation of alternatives, of the building of links of solidarity that have also been invisible in both academic works as well as in the public consciousness.

Notes

1. The stories of women in three different sectors—the agribusiness workers as well as Canadian supermarket cashiers and fast-food workers are featured in my book, *Tangled Routes: Women, Work, and Globalization on the Tomato Trail.*
2. Feminist theorists I have drawn upon include Jacqui Alexander, Kirsten Appendini, Bina Agarwal, Isabella Bakker, Antonieta Barrón, Rosi Braidotti, Patricia Hill Collins, Donna Haraway, Kathy Kopinac, Sara Lara, Elga Martinez Sakazar, Swasti Mitter, Chandra Mohanty, Ellie Perkins, Carolyn Sachs, Catriona Sandilands, Vandana Shiva, and Dorothy Smith.

References

Agarwal, Bina. 1991. *Engendering the Environmental Debate: Lessons Learned from the Indian Subcontinent.* CASID Distinguished Speaker Series, Monograph 8. East Lansing: Michigan State University.

Alexander, Jacqui M., and Chandra Mohanty. 1997. *Feminist Genealogies, Colonial Legacies, Democratic Futures.* New York: Routledge.

Appendini, Kirsten. 1999. "From Where Have All the Flowers Come? Women Workers in Mexico's Non-Traditional Markets." In Deborah Barndt, ed., *Women Working in the NAFTA Food Chain: Women, Food, and Globalization.* Toronto: Sumach Press, 127–40.

Bakker, Isabel, ed. 1996. *Rethinking Restructuring: Gender and Change in Canada.* Toronto: University of Toronto Press.

Barndt, Deborah. 2002. *Tangled Routes: Women, Work, and Globalization on the Tomato Trail.* Toronto: Garamond Press.

Barrón, Antonieta. 1999. "Mexican Women on the Move: Migrant Workers in Mexico and Canada." In Deborah Barndt, ed., *Women Working in the NAFTA Food Chain: Women, Food, and Globalization.* Toronto: Sumach Press, 113–26.

Braidotti, Rosi, Ewa Charkiewicz-Pluta, Sabine Hausler, and Saskia Wieringa, eds 1994. *Women, the Environment, and Sustainable Development: Toward a Theoretical Synthesis.* London: Zed Press.

Collins, Patricia Hill. 2000. *Black Feminist Thought: Knowledge, Consciousness, and the Politics of Empowerment.* New York: Routledge.

Haraway, Donna. 1995. *Simians, Cyborgs, and Women: The Reinvention of Nature.* New York: Routledge.

Kopinak, Kathy. 1997. *Desert Capitalism: What are the Maquiladoras?* Montreal: Black Rose Books.

Lara, Sara. 1994. "La Flexibilidad del Mercado del Trabajo Rural." *Revista Mexicana de Sociologia* 54 (1) (January–February): 41.

———. 1998a. "Feminizacíon de los Procesos de Trabajo del Sector Fruti Hortícultura en el Estado de Sinaloa." *Cuicuilco* 21 (April–June): 29–36.

———. 1998b. *Nuevas Experiences Productiva y Nuevas Formas de Organizacion Flexibile del Trabajo en la Agricultura Mexicana.* Mexico City: Pablos.

Martinez-Salazar, Elga. 1999. "The Poisoning of Indigenous Migrant Women Workers and Children: From Deadly Colonialism to Toxic Globalization." In Deborah Barndt, ed., *Women Working in the NAFTA Food Chain: Women, Food, and Globalization.* Toronto: Sumach Press, 100–9.

Mitter, Swasti. 1986. *Common Fate, Common Bond.* London: Pluto.

Perkins, Patricia E. (Ellie). 1997. "Introduction: Women, Ecology, and Economics: New Models and Theories." Special issue on Women, Ecology, and Economics. *Ecological Economics* 20 (2): 106–9.

Sachs, Carolyn. 1996. *Gendered Fields.* Boulder, CO: Westview.

Sandilands, Catriona. 1999. *The Good-Natured Feminist: Ecofeminism and the Quest for Democracy.* Minneapolis: University of Minnesota Press.

Shiva, Vandana. 1994. "Development, Ecology, and Women." In Carolyn Merchant, ed., *Ecology: Key Concepts in Critical Theory,* p. 272–80. Atlantic Highlands, NJ: Humanities.

Smith, Dorothy. 1987. *The Everyday World as Problematic: A Feminist Sociology.* Boston: Northeastern University Press.

Questions for Critical Thought

1. How do gender, race, and class intersect in the oppression of Mexican workers in the tomato trade? Of Canadian workers in the supermarket? What hierarchies are established in the various workplaces linked to the corporate tomato? How has the North American Free Trade Agreement contributed to this issue?

2. How does the directive for efficiency and competitiveness affect workers in the supermarket? How does it affect consumers? How does it affect the food industry?

3. How does agribusiness in Mexico affect traditional cultures? How has agribusiness changed Mexican cities, towns, rural communities, households, families, and citizens' lives? How has agribusiness affected the lives of people living in communities throughout the world, especially in the global South? How has agribusiness affected you and your family and the community that you live in?

4.   What are some alternatives to agribusiness and globalization? How could its consequences of exploitation, environmental harm, threats to health, and control over women's labour be rectified? Would this require changes by the producers? Consumers? Unions? Marketers? Food chains? Do social movements to heighten consumer awareness and change the conditions for workers have an effect? What is Fair Trade? What can you do to support Fair Trade initiatives in your community?

Conclusion

The emancipation of all people in the spirit of justice and egalitarianism is the general objective of the feminist movement. In its attempts to eradicate social inequality, the feminist movement stands in opposition to globalization, which embodies the principles of neo-liberalism, advocates a free market economy, and limits social and/or moral obligations to contest homophobia and trans discrimination and to regulate the labour practices and the working conditions of its international supply of workers. In the final section of this book, each chapter has examined how the politics of globalization and belonging has affected the lives of women and men throughout the world. Each author raises questions about the global increase in social inequality, and proposes that the future is uncertain for minorities who are homeworkers, manual and skilled labourers, caregivers, and international athletes. Racialized and gendered minorities living and working in the global North and South have been affected by the politics of economic restructuring and have had to become, out of necessity, a more flexible labour force, often causing themselves great physical, psychological, and social distress.

Recommended Readings

Kevin Bales and Becky Cornell. 2009. *Slavery Today: A Groundwork Guide*. Toronto: Groundwood.

- Most people think that slavery is a social system that no longer exists. Kevin Bales and Becky Cornell trace the global social and political origins of bondage that enslaves 27 million people—men, women, and children—throughout the world today. Due to increasing rates of absolute poverty, many people are turning to agriculture, the fishing industry, small factories, and the sex trade, where they work under inhumane, brutal conditions. The authors explain how the global market has created this form of modern slavery and how the growing anti-slavery movement seeks to inform citizens and aims to stop the sale of human beings.

Joyce Green, ed. 2009. *Making Space for Indigenous Feminism*. Halifax, NS: Fernwood.

- This collection of readings by Aboriginal feminist writers argues that the feminist movement has much to offer Aboriginal women in their struggle to contest global oppression and social inequality. The volume includes contributions about feminist activism and the shared political consciousness that is developing among activists from Canada, the United States, Sapmi (Samiland), and Aotearoa/New Zealand.

Thomas Lines. 2009. *Making Poverty: A History*. London: Zed Books.

- The work of giant food corporations in creating and regulating the global food chains that have displaced farmers across the world, especially in the poorest countries, has created a global interdependence that is highly correlated with high rates of rural poverty. Thomas Lines argues that we must examine broader economic policies in order to understand the interaction between global markets and the division of power.

Saskia Sassen. 2007. *A Sociology of Globalization*. New York: W.W. Norton & Company.

- Saskia Sassen examines the roles that global cities, transnational communities, and commodity chains play in moving the world economy into a form of hyper-capitalism, which she suggests is dominated by a form of glocalization. According to Sassen, glocalization is an intricate form of social and political networking, in which major corporations weave local and global economies together to form a global network that is based on a form of economic, political, and social global interdependence.

Adrian Smith, Alison Stenning, and Katie Willis. 2009. *Social Justice and Neo-Liberalism*. London: Zed Books.

- This rich and theoretically grounded volume of readings examines the links between neo-liberalism and social justice, and the material manifestation of this duality in the global world. The authors examine how communities may, through contestation and protest, empower themselves to challenge the unfair practices of a form of capitalism that marginalizes people, places, and communities all over the world.

Soni-Sinha Urvashi and Charlotte A.B. Yates. 2013. "'Dirty Work?' Gender, Race and the Union in Industrial Cleaning." *Gender, Work & Organization* 20, 6: 737–51. doi:10.1111/gwao.12006.

- In this article, Soni-Sinha Urvashi and Charlotte A.B. Yates examine janitorial work and the gendered division of labour in a large cleaning company in Toronto. This study is based on an intersectional analysis of narratives that explores the meaning of janitorial labour. The authors propose that men's work for the company is considered to be heavy duty and subsequently more valuable than the "lighter" cleaning jobs that women are assigned to. The authors conclude that in an effort to deal with the social stigma of doing "dirty" work, the union not only empowers cleaners in the workplace, but it enables janitorial workers to develop a more positive social identity.

Glossary

1982 Constitution Act This legislation was originally called the British North America Act (BNA Act) of 1867. The act was revised in 1982 to introduce several new amendments.

affirmative action policies Affirmative action policies favour groups (mainly ethnic groups and women) that have experienced discrimination, usually in the fields of employment and education.

age of migration Stephen Castles, Hein de Haas, and Mark J. Miller have used this term to explain the changes that have taken place in global migration patterns during the post–Cold War years.

ageism This is a form of age-based discrimination. Irrational and prejudiced beliefs or stereotypes about the abilities and behaviours of the elderly or very young are upheld.

agentic capacity The ability of individuals to empower or enable themselves.

AIDS crisis In June 2001 the United Nations held a General Assembly and declared that HIV/AIDS is a global pandemic and that resources needed to be mobilized to resolve this global crisis.

androcentrism The practice, conscious or not, of putting men (or the masculine point of view) at the centre of the view of the world, including culture and history.

Anishinabek This term is used by the Odawa, Ojibway, and Algonquin peoples who all speak the closely related Anishinaabemowin/Anishinaabe languages of the Algonquin language family.

anti-Davos The annual winter meeting of the World Economic Forum is held in Davos, a mountain resort in Graubünden, in the Swiss Alps. This independent global organization is comprised of 2,500 international leaders in business, intellectuals, and politicians who wish to influence global economic and political interests. The anti-Davos movement is comprised of political activists who have, since 2000, held alternative meetings in Davos at another location where they annually award the Public Eye Award. The Public Eye Award is given to the least socially responsible global corporation in the world.

apartheid A form of racial segregation that was practised in South Africa. This system of racial segregation prevented individuals or groups from interacting with each other and it held sway over marriage laws, area of residence, employment, and in public and private services.

Assembly of First Nations (AFN) The AFN was once called the Canadian National Indian Brotherhood. Every First Nation in the AFN is represented by their Chief. The goal of the AFN is to protect Aboriginal and treaty rights and to support the interests of First Nations people in Canada.

asylum-seeking legislation This is legislation that seeks to protect refugees and asylum seekers who need legal protection while they are living in Canada. Many asylum seekers fear that if they are deported back to their home country, they will experience social, cultural, or political persecution.

autochthonic   This term means that a group of people or animals may originate from, or are native or indigenous to, an area, territory, or geographical region.

band members   Historically First Nations peoples had complex social and political governing bodies. Indian Bands were created by Canadian colonial policy. Many band members in Canada live on reserves, but, they do not actually "own" the land as the legal title, or deed to the land, is held by the Crown.

biopsychological endowment   This is an interdisciplinary medical model that combines biological variables with psychological, socio-economic, and environmental factors. This model is used to determine if a person is healthy.

blank spot   A historical era, epoch, period, or event that may be consciously (or unintentionally) misrepresented, ignored, or not reported in history texts and the dominant discourse of a society or group due to the politically and socially sensitive nature of the event.

Bretton Woods   An international method of monetary management was developed by political and financial leaders from the leading industrial powers of the world at the Bretton Woods Conference in New Hampshire, US, on 22 July 1944. This system of banking was created in order to establish rules and to lay the foundation for an integrated international banking system, that would rebuild the world economy in the post–World War II era.

butch   This term is used to usually describe masculine characteristics of gay, bisexual, transgender, and cross-dressing subcultures and gender identities. Conversely the word *femme* is associated with feminine characteristics.

Canada Pension Plan/Quebec Pension Plan (CPP/QPP)   Every person who works in Canada contributes to the Canada Pension Plan (CPP), or if they live in Quebec, the Quebec Pension Plan (QPP). The CPP/QPP is a social welfare program that supports individuals and their families when they become disabled, retire from their place of work, or if they die.

Canadian Census of Population   The Canadian census is held every five years in Canada. Census data provide the Canadian public with demographic information that is drawn from every Canadian household in Canada. These data include information about health care, public services, housing, education, and transportation.

caste   The caste system is a method of social categorization that is used by Indian Hindus. The five categories in a caste system include the Brahmin, Kshatriya, Vaishya, Shudra, and Dalit (or Untouchable) groups. Social interaction between these five groups of people are monitored by rules that stipulate methods of food preparation and consumption, intermarriage, and spatial segregation.

charismatic powers   Max Weber developed this term in his writings on power, social domination, and authority. The term *charismatic powers* has been used to describe men and women who have the ability to influence large groups of people due to their heroic and/or spiritual qualities.

clash of civilizations   Samuel P. Huntington used this phrase in 1992 proposing that the major source of conflict in the post–Cold War era would be between religious groups. In 1996 he published his popular book *The Clash of Civilizations and the Remaking of World Order* in which he develops this argument.

classism   This is a form of discrimination that denies (or gives) an individual access to wealth, scarce resources, and power, due to his/her socio-economic position in society.

Colonial, colonialism, neo-colonial discourse, and colonial agents   Between the fifteenth and nineteenth centuries, Spain, Portugal, Britain, France, The Netherlands, and Belgium exported natural resources from various countries in the Americas, Africa, and Asia. The systematic destruction of the regional cultures and languages of the Indigenous peoples of these colonies was part of the process of colonialism that was carried out by Eurocentric colonial agents.

colourism   This form of racism is the legacy of slavery. Slave owners created a hierarchy among their slaves by favouring mulattos, who were men and women from racially mixed backgrounds and who had lighter skin tones than other slaves. Lighter-skinned slaves were often employed as domestic servants in the homes of the slave owners.

Confederation   Canadian Confederation took place on 1 July 1867 when the Dominion of Canada was formed. Essentially, the three founding British colonies formed an alliance and were subsequently divided into four separate provinces. Thus, the new Dominion included the provinces of Ontario, Quebec, New Brunswick, and Nova Scotia.

construct validity   Construct validity is a research method that seeks to clarify the codes that are used to represent the subject of the research by taking themes or ideas that are collected in interviews or during other forms of fieldwork and recording and cross-referencing explanations and definitions that are given throughout the research study.

content analysis   This is a research technique that is considered to be an objective, systematic, and quantitative or qualitative descriptive analysis of a written text or other mediums such as films, music, or art work.

creolization   Due to the European colonization of Africa and the Americas, inter-marriage between people of Indigenous and European descent became known as creolization.

crie du coeur   This is a term that is used to describe a passionate outburst that may take place in the form of a protest or an appeal.

cultural heterogeneity   Cultural heterogeneity may occur when two (or more) distinctly different cultural groups live in the same community, region, or country.

Cushing's syndrome   This disorder is the result of problems in the adrenal cortex. The syndrome includes hypertension, obesity, and diabetes mellitus.

decolonization   Decolonization means literally the reverse of colonization (please see *colonialism* above). When an occupying power or nation-state leaves a region, the Indigenous peoples of the region may then reclaim their original cultural identities, languages, and religions.

deinstitutionalization   This term is used to describe the process of releasing individuals from a public care facility who had been under state care.

deregulated neo-liberal economic markets   Neo-liberalism advocates suggest that the privatization of industries, free trade across international borders, the deregulation of government spending, and less taxation will improve the overall efficiency and productivity of the global economy.

disabling barriers   Disabling barriers are due to physical or mental challenges that prevent people, because of prejudices both on an institutional and individual level, from interacting with other people in social, political, and economic situations.

disposable income   This is the amount of money that a person has after she/he has paid their annual taxes to the government.

division of domestic labour   In many societies in the world, domestic tasks in and around the home are assigned by the gender of the person. In "traditional" households, women often work inside the home while men will complete chores such as painting, mowing the lawn, and yard maintenance outside the home.

domestic labour   This work is unpaid work that is mainly done inside and around the home. Domestic labour tasks include child care, preparation of meals, yard work, and cleaning.

domestic workers   Domestic workers are people who work in a home that are not members of the family. Non-family women are paid to do housework and to take care of children in the domestic sphere.

doping policy   The international Anti-Doping Program was developed by governments to cope with the ongoing problem of athletes using performance-enhancing drugs while competing in either amateur or professional sporting events. Global policies have been developed to coordinate anti-doping policies by governments throughout the world.

embedded agency   As feminist critics suggest, women who live and work within hegemonic patriarchal societies can enact various forms of resistance, which are a form of agency.

empowerment   The process of empowerment takes place when people gain social and political control over their lives. When "just social practices" and laws are put into place by states, individuals and groups of people are then empowered or given the ability to "freely" make decisions about issues that they feel are important in the societies in which they live.

epidemic   An epidemic is the rapid transmission of a socially communicable disease among a significant portion of a population.

essentialism/anti-essentialism, essentialized   The term *essentialism* suggests that the explanation of a social phenomenon may be described as natural, biological, or primordial. An anti-essentialist argument suggests that a social phenomenon is not natural, biological, or primordial—it is socially and culturally constructed.

essentialist colonial discourse   Colonialism takes place when more industrialized countries establish a form of formal political authority over less industrialized countries. The nineteenth-century discourse of European domination over various countries in the global South focused on the idea of the "civilizing mission" of converting Indigenous peoples to European languages, religions, and cultures. The rise of racism is one of the legacies of the colonial period of the nineteenth century.

ethnicization   The process that takes place when a cultural cue is used as a symbolic marker to establish a visible boundary between two groups of people.

ethnoracial   This classification has been used by governments as an administrative categorization of people along "ethnic" and/or "racial" lines.

eugenics   This term comes from the Greek words *eu* ("good") and *gens* ("breeding"). Eugenics is the belief that a population can be improved through a program of selective breeding that can increase the occurrence of certain desirable characteristics in a population. The practice of "positive" eugenics ensures that certain individuals and groups of people are encouraged by the state to have children. "Negative" eugenics either prevents (through sterilization) or eliminates individuals or groups of people because they are considered to be "unfit."

Eurocentrism   Eurocentrism is the social and political orientation of history books, historical narratives, and literature on the heroic deeds of the European peoples, whose ancestors are from the European continent. While the European groups are heralded, Eurocentric histories often exclude other geographical, cultural, religious, and ethnic groups from their texts.

European Union   The European Union (EU) is comprised of 28 member states that are located in Europe. The EU was built upon the foundation of the European Coal and Steel Community (ECSC) and the European Economic Community (EEC), which were formed by six European countries in 1951 and 1958.

"ex-pat" or ex-patriate   People who live outside of their country of origin are often considered to be ex-pats or ex-patriates. Ex-patriates may be living in exile, they may be political or social refugees, or they may be immigrants who have "voluntarily" left their countries of origin due to political, economic, or social problems.

extended families   Members of an extended family are relatives who are not part of the nuclear or immediate family, which generally includes parents and their children. Grandparents, aunts, uncles, and cousins are called extended family members.

family wage economy   This is an economic system of sustenance that requires that each member of a family pools all their earnings from subsistence farming in order to survive.

female genital mutilation   This is a surgical procedure that is sometimes called "female circumcision." This procedure may partially or totally surgically remove the labia majora and/or minora and/or the clitoris from the female genitalia.

feminist political economy   The feminist critique of the structures of the capitalist state focuses on the political economy of exploitative working conditions that women experience in both the public and private spheres of capitalist societies.

feminist post-structuralism   Feminist post-structuralism is a systematic critique of the social and political constraints that women experience living in patriarchal societies. This form of theorizing examines how social identities are shaped through cultural representations and social relations.

feminization   The feminization of an area of work refers to a job or profession that was traditionally dominated by men and which has, over time, become increasingly dominated by women. Sometimes when this takes place, the work becomes less prestigious due to male chauvinistic attitudes about the abilities of women who work at these jobs.

feminization of migration   A trend in migration studies, beginning after the Cold War ends in the early 1990s, that refers to a gendered pattern of migration characterized by women migrating from their home countries in search of work or marriage partners.

fiscal restraint   Fiscal restraint is an economic policy that is used by governments to reduce spending money on, for example, social welfare programs, which economists argue will then subsequently reduce the need for higher taxes.

framing   The sociologist Irving Goffman used the term *framing* to describe and understand the "experience" that an individual or a group of people may have while living within a certain social organization or social context.

fundamentalism   A fundamentalist social movement calls for a return to more orthodox or ancient religious texts or teachings that are the "fundamental" core or foundation of a religion.

gay stigma   Gay stigma is a negative label that is placed on those who hold non-heterosexual attitudes, beliefs, identities, or behaviours.

gaze   Laura Mulvey first used this term in 1975 to describe how women are objectified and stereotyped by men who create, direct, and view films. This concept has been used to describe the general social interaction between women and men, where women are considered to be performers who engage in certain behaviours. These behaviours may include speech, style of dress, and forms of bodywork that appeal to men who are considered to be the consumers. Cultural studies scholars argue that there is also a "female" gaze, which may be less obvious but is nevertheless present in films, media advertisements, and the visual arts.

Gemeinschaft   Max Weber the sociologist used this term to describe an "organic social relationship" in which a small group of people who have strong kinship, cultural, social, and regional ties to one another are bonded to one another through community networks.

gender-bending   Gender-bending is a social, political, or cultural activity that individuals or groups take part in to challenge established norms and social values that may be overgeneralizations about each gender.

gender segmentation in the labour market   The global labour market may be described as being divided according to the different types of work that women and men do.

gender socialization   Ann Oakley introduced this term to describe the socially and culturally constructed behaviours that women and men are taught to engage in by society. Gender identities are reinforced by the family, education systems, peer groups, the media, the state, and religious organizations.

gendered racializaton   This is a double form of discrimination that women who are visible minorities experience. A woman is marginalized because of her gender and her ethnicity.

General Social Survey on Victimization   (GSSV) The GSSV was developed to understand how Canadians perceive crime and how their understandings relate to their experiences of victimization.

genetics   Genetics is a scientific field of study in which the biological basis of an individual's physical and social characteristics may be explained by the biological material or genes that have been genetically transmitted from earlier generations.

Gesellschaft   According to Max Weber, this type of community is based on a rational economic foundation. The commitment to this form of community is characterized by impersonal rules and rational means of communication between members of the community.

globalization   This paradigm is comprised of a set of theories that examine the emergence of a neo-liberal global social, political, economic, and cultural system that is the product of a variety of social, technological, and cultural developments.

globalized food system   The globalized production of food by one region of the world for consumption in another part of the world generates a form of economic integration and interdependency in which less wealthy countries become increasingly dependent upon the export of their agricultural products for foreign exchange.

glocalization   Glocalization is a global process in which a product or service is introduced into a new local or regional market from another part of the world and it is eventually adapted and/or incorporated into the local culture of the community.

government downsizing   A government may decide to "downsize" or lay off workers in response to an economic recession.

grounded theory   This form of theorizing uses an inductive form of reasoning to examine and explain the social significance of research data after it has been collected.

Guaranteed Income Supplement (GIS)   The GIS is a non-taxable benefit that is given monthly to Old Age Security (OAS) recipients who are living in Canada.

harbingers   Harbingers are forerunners or warnings of something that will happen in the future.

Hawthorn Report   This 1967 report authored by anthropologist Harry B. Hawthorn followed an inquiry that was carried out in order to assess why Aboriginal peoples were less successful in the Canadian education system than their peers. It also examined how First Nations people could be more successfully assimilated into industrial white society.

healing   This term is used by Aboriginal communities and it refers to the restoration of a person's social, physical, and spiritual vitality. It has also been used by the Canadian government as a form of restitution and correction of the historical injustices committed against Aboriginal people currently and during the period of European colonization.

hegemony   According to Antonio Gramsci, historical materialism includes a form of domination that he calls hegemony. Hegemony is the social relations in which the interests of the ruling class are represented as universally desirable.

hegemonic femininity   In a patriarchal society, the ideal form of femininity is the woman who is an unpaid middle-class homemaker.

heteronormativity   This term is used to describe the social practices that promote heterosexual norms and values. Heteronormativity is enforced by agents of socialization that include the family, schools, religious organizations, and places where people work.

hijab   A hijab is a veil that covers the head, neck, and hair of a woman. It is worn by Muslim women for religious and cultural reasons.

home care   Home care is a form of caregiving that is carried out in the place of residence of an individual who is physically challenged, elderly, or chronically ill.

homophobia   Homophobia consists of a broad range of negative attitudes and behaviours toward people who identify themselves as being lesbian, gay, bisexual, or transgender (LGBT). Homophobia can be expressed in various forms such as contempt, inappropriate humour, or hatred. People who engage in homophobic actions may have irrational fears about the LGBT community.

honour killing   In orthodox Muslim communities, if a woman is suspected of "dishonouring" her husband and his family, for example, by having an extra-marital affair, then the husband's family may kill the wife in order to restore and preserve the family's honour.

House of Commons   The 308 members of the House of Commons are the popularly elected members of the Canadian Parliament. They attend to their political duties during sessions in the House of Commons.

husband's stitch   The husband's stitch is a surgical procedure that is done to tighten a woman's vagina after she has given birth.

human trafficking   Human trafficking, or global slavery, is the illegal buying and selling of women, men, and children for the purpose of sexual slavery, forced labour, commercial sexual exploitation, or for providing a spouse in the context of forced marriage.

hybridization   Hybridization is the ongoing process of blending cultures within a global world.

hydroquinone   This highly toxic industrial product is used to suppress the natural production of melanin in the skin.

hypercapitalism   Neo-Marxist scholars use this term to describe an advanced form of capitalism that is enhanced by the speed and intensity of technological innovations that enable the exchange of material and immaterial goods, people, and information to take place in the globally connected marketplace.

Indian Act   The Indian Act is a law that was established in 1876 and is still in force today in Canada. The act outlines how the Canadian state should interact with 614 Indian bands and all of the status Indians who live in Canada. The legislation has been amended several times, especially since 2002. The Indian Act oversees the use of reserve land, health care, and the education of Aboriginal peoples. The two most important functions of the act are that it establishes rules for governing Indian reserves and it defines who is and who is not recognized as a status "Indian."

Indian status   See Indian Act.

Indigenous people   The First Nations or Indigenous peoples of Canada are recognized by international and national legislation as having specific human rights that are linked to territorial, kinship, and regional ties. Indigenous peoples are groups of culturally and historically distinctive cultures and they have often been exploited, marginalized, and oppressed by politically and culturally aggressive populations.

Indigenous revitalization   Many Aboriginal communities in Canada are involved in several language and cultural revitalization projects. The goal of the Indigenous revitalization project is to educate young people about their ancestral cultures and to teach them how to speak and to write in 52 different Indigenous languages, which have not been spoken for several decades.

integrative anti-racism studies   Integrative anti-racism studies seek to understand how the dynamics of social difference are mediated in people's everyday lives. The studies suggest that multiple, shifting, and contradictory identities are linked to struggles against oppression.

International Monetary Fund (IMF)   The IMF is an international organization that was created in 1944 at the Bretton Woods Conference (see **Bretton Woods**). The IMF was developed to aid in the reconstruction of the world's international loans and payment system that was a product of the post–World War II period. The IMF oversees national economies through a system of reports and other forms of economic and political surveillance. It may demand self-correcting policies to be put into place by some of its 188 members in order to improve the economies of all its member countries.

intersectional theorizing   This form of inquiry examines the social reality of women and men and their interaction with social, cultural, and economic relationships that affect them at various significant points in a social organization.

Kwakwaka'wakw   The Kwakwaka'wakw nation is primarily living on the Pacific Northwest Coast of British Columbia. The majority of the 5,500 members of this First Nation live on or near northern Vancouver Island.

liposuction   Liposuction is a surgical procedure in which an incision is made in a person's body and fat deposits are "sucked" out of the body through a vacuum hose.

low-income cut-off (LICO)   LICO is a measure used by Statistics Canada to indicate whether a person is living on a "low" income.

matrix of violence   In societies that sustain high rates of poverty, the oppression of women is manifested in a web or interlocking matrix of violence in which women experience high levels of emotional, economic, and physical abuse.

mechanical and organic solidarity   In a mechanical solidarity society, Emile Durkheim suggests that people are connected to one another in "traditional" small-scale communities due to their common education, religious, and work experiences. In larger industrialized communities that are not based on kinship networks but on economic and political ties, he proposes that an organic solidarity or cohesiveness will emerge that is based on a specialization of skills and a complex division of labour.

metrosexual image   A metrosexual man is someone who is meticulous about his appearance, spends more time, money, and energy on grooming and clothes than men have been said to spend traditionally. Although the term is sometimes thought to apply to heterosexual men who adopt fashions stereotypically associated with homosexual men, a metrosexual can be straight, gay, or bisexual.

miscegenation/anti-miscegenation   This is a racist term that literally means the "mixing of races," thus denoting sexual relations between different races, especially between light- and dark-skinned people. Anti-miscegenation laws were created to prevent white and black people from having sexual relationships.

modernization   This term originally was used to distinguish between "traditional" agrarian societies and industrial societies. Due to a specialization of labour and other social functions, traditional societies have been reorganized into larger indus-trialized cities.

moral panic   The result of heightened social concern over an issue, usually identified or created by the mass media.

narratives   In qualitative research, these are in-depth personal interviews with an unstructured format, allowing the interviewee to choose the subjects and concerns that are most relevant to him/her and to speak in a free manner or narrative.

neo-cons   Neo-cons are politicians who are part of a conservative political social movement that developed in the United States during the 1960s. The neo-cons sup-port a democratic form of government and they promote the "American national interest" in foreign affairs.

neo-liberal trade policies   Policies, such as the North American Free Trade Agreement (NAFTA), which promote economic integration by restricting barriers to trade among nations.

neo-liberalism   Neo-liberalism most commonly refers to a set of economic policies, including privatization, deregulation, and free trade, that have become widespread in the Western world since the 1980s. These economic policies have been criticized for privileging individualism and the rule of the market over the public good and the concept of community.

network society   This term was created by the social theorist Georg Simmel in the 1980s. A network society is one in which social, political, and cultural ideas are communicated through a process of cultural exchange between individuals and/or communities. Network societies have developed due to the technological revolution and the information highway in the industrialized world.

non-status Aboriginals   This term refers to people of mixed ancestry who will not or cannot be registered as status Indians.

North American Free Trade Agreement (NAFTA)   This neo-liberal agreement, which was implemented in 1993, enables goods, services, and production to move freely between Canada, the United States, and Mexico.

ochronosis   A medical disorder that occurs after a person has used a chemical whitening substance such as hydroquinone, which reduces the production of melanin. When the chemically treated skin is exposed to sunshine, gray and blue-black discoloration of the skin may occur.

off-reserve First Nations communities   Many status Indians live in urban centres and not on reserves. Access to federal social services is difficult for status Indians who are living off of the reserve. In addition, maintaining familial, social, economic, and political connections with status Indians living on reserves is difficult due to the geographical, social, and political isolation of reserve communities.

Ojibway   Ojibway, Anishinaabe, or Chippewa are one of the largest groups of First Nations people living on the North American continent. The Ojibway Nation is the second largest Aboriginal nation in Canada.

Old Age Security Program (OAS)   The OAS is a monthly payment given to Canadian citizens who have lived in Canada for at least 10 years, and are at least 65 years old. The OAS payments are not based upon whether a person has ever worked in the public sector or not.

ontological   This term is used in metaphysics and it suggests that there is a relationship in the material world that is based on the relative existence of another object or body.

Orientalist/Orientalism   The term *Orientalism* has been used by Eurocentric historians, artists, and writers to describe certain aspects of Middle Eastern and East Asian cultures. In 1978 the social theorist Edward Said argued that the term *Orientalism* is a pejorative and patronizing Western attitude towards Middle Eastern, Asian, and North African cultures and societies. Said argues that the West describes these societies as traditional, less civilized, and underdeveloped and, conversely, Western societies as progressive, rational, and ultimately superior.

other-gendering   A form of social control that discourages women or men from taking on different gender roles in society. Women who fail to meet the criteria of being traditionally "feminine," such as being slim, docile, and passive, are sometimes subjected to critical comments that imply they are less feminine, less attractive, and subsequently more masculine than they "should" be. Conversely, men may be criticized for being too "feminine."

outsourcing   Outsourcing is a form of contracting work out to a third-party of workers. The workers who receive the contract may or may not reside in the country where the business is actually located.

overrepresentation of Aboriginal peoples in the justice system   The fact that Aboriginal people constitute roughly 4 per cent of the Canadian population but 17 per cent of all people incarcerated in Canadian prisons. In Saskatchewan Aboriginal people make up 75 per cent of the province's total prison population.

palimony suit   This term refers to cases where a same-sex couple has lived together for a long period of time but never married. If the relationship ends, often the major dispute in a palimony case is establishing whether one partner should financially support the second person who had performed domestic labour that contributed to the social and economic welfare of the common-law home.

pandemic   A pandemic is an outbreak of a disease throughout a country, region, or continent.

pedagogy   The science or the art of teaching. Some sociologists of education use the term *pedagogical practices* or *needs* in reference to methods and principles that inform educational techniques.

periphrastic space   Residential spaces, found in urban centres, that are characterized by racial marginality, slum-like conditions, and pollution.

performative regulation   In the world of sports, the athlete's body has been regulated by dress and conduct codes in order to de-sexualize the body so that social encounters at sporting events will not be misconstrued as sexual in nature by athletes, the media, and the audience.

phenomenology   A mode of inquiry that suggests that our life experiences and our knowledge about the world are shaped by the common discourses of the social and cultural structures of our social world.

postmodernism   A philosophical perspective that rejects the "metanarratives" of liberation and of truth, which legitimated scientific (including social scientific) activity in the last 200 years.

poverty gap   The distance between the poverty line and the actual income of poor people.

primordial   This term is used to describe the earliest form or natural state of an individual or organ.

prohibitionist   A prohibitionist is a person who believes in or practises a particular religious or moral philosophy of life, and lobbies other citizens to abstain from actions which she/he deems are unlawful and/or immoral.

promiscuity   Term used to describe the inappropriate behaviour of individuals who do not conform to society's standards, norms, or expectations when they are engaging in social and sexual relations with other people.

Public-Use Microdata File (PUMF)   The Canadian government has created these files that are a compilation of microdata from Statistics Canada. Anonymity and confidentiality of the respondents' personal information is guaranteed by Statistics Canada.

qualitative research   Research generally associated with an interpretative (non-numeric and non-experimental) methodology, in which data collection and analysis emphasize the understanding of experience. It includes such forms of inquiry as ethnography, case study research, naturalistic inquiry, ethnomethodology, life history methodology, and narrative inquiry.

racial othering   The construction of negative images and/or stereotypes of a particular social, cultural, or ethnic group by another group that wishes to view itself or be viewed as separate. Negative images are meant to make a group of people appear to be less similar to the group that is constructing and propagating the images.

racialization, racialized   The social process in which an individual or group may be categorized by their racial characteristics.

raison d'être   This is a French term that means "the reason for one's existence."

residential schools   A school system that attempted to assimilate Canadian First Nations children into the Euro-Canadian cultural and economic system through a process of isolation and gradual integration.

respatialization   James Rosenau has argued that due to changing migration patterns, technology and telecommunications, economic and labour markets, a process of deterritorialization or respatialization is occurring throughout the world. He proposes that due to these changes, geographic and political borders are disappearing during this age of transition.

rights-based approach   A rights-based approach is the pro-active idea that through the process of empowering members of a society who are poor and/or vulnerable, citizens will be able to collectively hold governments accountable for their actions.

securitization   Securitization is the process of taking an illiquid asset, or group of assets, and through a form of economic manipulation changing them into, for example, a mortgage-backed security, which is secured by a group of mortgages.

sedentarism   Sedentarism is measured by people using less than 10 per cent of their daily energy to perform moderate- and high-intensity activities.

self-fulfilling prophecy   A false view or definition of a situation that, once it is expressed or acknowledged, can lead the people involved to behave in ways that bring about their expectations.

sex workers   Sex workers are women and men who work in the sex work industry. They provide sexual services and related services, such as massage, for a set price or wage.

Sharia law   In orthodox Muslim communities all legal matters are decided by a system of Sharia law. These tribunals are organized and carried out by religious leaders who make decisions about such matters as the custody of children in divorce cases.

situated gaze   Similar to the "gaze," a situated gaze takes place between the subject who realizes that she/he is being observed and the observer. During social, political, cultural, and athletic events, the subject and the observer may be engaged in a form of situated gaze, which takes place within the context of the event.

skin atrophy   A condition where the skin begins to waste away and not grow and replenish itself as it would in a healthy person.

skin bleaching   The practice of using cosmetics and/or chemical treatments to make the colour of a person's skin lighter.

skin lighteners   Products, usually a cream, that produce lighter, brighter white skin when applied. Some skin lighteners contain toxic elements such as mercury. (See **hydroquinone**.)

social dynamics   The social interaction that takes place between individual members of a group or between different social groups is referred to as social dynamics.

social engineering   Social engineering is a governmental or institutional plan to develop or to alter certain social characteristics of a population.

social reproduction   Social reproduction is a Marxist feminist term that is used to describe the unpaid domestic labour or home work that women and children do in a traditional patriarchal home.

South Asian   South Asian groups live in southern countries on the Asian continent. This vast geographical area includes many different ethnic, linguistic, and cultural groups that may be from the sub-Himalayan countries and from territories that are west and east of the continent.

standpoint theory   This is a postmodern practice of understanding the intersubjective nature of social interaction. Standpoint theory proposes that an individual's perspective on reality is shaped by his or her social, political, and cultural experiences in various social locations, and social groups throughout his or her life history.

stereotype   A preconceived image of a group that is usually oversimplified, pejorative, and generally resistant to change.

sterilization   A medical procedure to prevent pregnancy. For example, women's Fallopian tubes may be tied shut; men's vas deferens is surgically cut.

stigmatization, stigma   A form of social rejection or devaluation, shunning, or marginalization due to a person's physical or social characteristics. Irving Goffman refers to three types of stigmatization: bodily, moral, and tribal.

straitened circumstances   A person who is living in poverty or has few assets or possessions may be described as living in straitened circumstances.

stressor   A positive or negative event that causes typical bodily reactions to stress, such as migraine headaches.

symbolic capital   Symbolic capital is a material commodity or a symbol of economic potential or wealth in the marriage market. For example, in some traditionally patriarchal societies such as in India, women who have lighter-coloured skin are considered to be more attractive and subsequently more desirable marriage partners.

systemic barriers   Systemic barriers are boundaries and/or rules that may limit job opportunities and life chances of certain groups of people. Barriers may exclude people who are from various cultural, religious, or racial backgrounds from fully participating in social activities.

systemic discrimination   The standard policies, procedures, and practices that result in the disadvantaging of a disempowered group.

systemic racism   The term *systemic racism* was introduced in the 1960s. Due to the iron cage and the bureaucratic nature of large institutions, it is suggested that regulated forms of discrimination are embedded in a tangled web of government practices, policies, rules, and standards that often exclude and marginalize disadvantaged individuals and groups of people.

temporary work visa   A temporary work visa is a document that is authorized by the Canadian government. It gives a person who is not a Canadian citizen the right to work for a specific length of time at a job in Canada.

terrorism   Terrorism is an act of violence and/or the use of threats by individuals, groups of people, or states to scare or coerce other people to comply with political, economic, social, religious, or cultural threats or demands.

tiger economies   There are four countries in the world that have been described as "tiger economies": Hong Kong, South Korea, Taiwan, and Singapore. From the 1960s to the 1990s, these countries developed rapidly into advanced industrial societies with non-democratic governments that had low tax rates and limited social welfare policies.

transnational   Goods, services, and people that cross borders between countries either legally or illegally are a form of transnational trade.

transgender people   A person who is transgender may exhibit traits of one gender but identify with another. There is a broad range of identities on the gender spectrum, including people who identify as agender, gender-neutral, third gender, genderqueer, or non-binary.

Trudgen   The Trudgen is the name of a swimming stroke that is named after John Trudgen. It is usually called the sidestroke in Canada, as a person swims on his or her side.

two-spirit people   In many Indigenous communities in North America in the nineteenth century, there were men and women who were called bedarche or mixed gender. These men and women would wear both men's and women's traditional clothing and take part in social and work activities and rituals that were carried out by both men and women.

ultra-feminine   Women who act in an ultra-feminine manner are usually characterized by passive and submissive behaviour.

United Nations   The United Nations (UN) was created on 24 October 1945. Originally, it was an intergovernmental organization comprised of 51 nations that replaced the former League of Nations and was created to promote world peace. Currently, there are 193 member states in the United Nations. The UN headquarters is in New York City. It has six major organs, including the General Assembly, the Security Council, the Economic and Social Council, the Secretariat, the International Court of Justice, and the now inactive Trusteeship Council. Agencies that are affiliated with the UN include the World Bank Group, the World Health Organization, the World Food Program, UNESCO, and UNICEF.

virilizing   Virilizing is the process of enabling the body to develop sex differences through the use of androgens.

white femininity   In a patriarchal society, the hegemonic standards of beauty and womanhood are often defined by the "ideal" middle-class white woman. Women who have darker skin tones, and who may come from lower income backgrounds, or from non-European religious groupings, are compared and negatively contrasted to this dominant ideal type.

whiteness   Whiteness or critical whiteness studies is an interdisciplinary area of study that examines the historic role that white or light-skinned people have played in promoting their own racial superiority by systematically oppressing people who come from cultural, religious, and class backgrounds and racial backgrounds that are non-European in origin.

World Bank   The World Bank is an agency that is affiliated with the United Nations. Its headquarters is located in Washington, DC. The World Bank is an international bank that lends money to countries throughout the world.

World Social Forum   This counterhegemonic organization was founded in Brazil. The organization meets annually to propose economic and social policies that could create an alternative future that is not based on neo-liberalism. The forum is a type of global civil society that offers opportunities for international non-governmental organizations to network. It also offers support to formal and informal global social movements and to regional and local economic initiatives throughout the world.

yellow peril   During the nineteenth century this term was used to describe immigrants who had come to the United States and Canada from China and other Asian countries. Many of these immigrants were labourers, who were considered to be a social, economic, and cultural threat to European groups of immigrants who dominated North American society.

YMCA, YWCA, YWHA   The Young Men's Christian Association was created on 6 June 1844 by George Williams, who was a draper living in London, England. The YMCA was created to encourage the development of the "mind, body and spirit" of young men in a Christian environment. The organization provided affordable housing to young men who had moved from rural areas to urban centres in search of work during the period of the industrial revolution. The YMCA and the Young Women's Christian Association (YWCA), and the Young Women's Hebrew Association (YWHA) developed during the next few decades into large multi-facility complexes, which included economical housing, gymnasiums, swimming pools, recreational centres, meeting rooms, and conference halls.

Acknowledgements

Sedef Arat-Koç, "Whose Social Reproduction? Transnational Motherhood and Challenges to Feminist Political Economy," in *Social Reproduction: Feminist Political Economy Challenges Neo-Liberalism*, eds Kate Bezanson, Meg Luxton, and Sedef Arat-Koç. Montreal, MQUP, 2006.

Deborah Barndt, "Fruits of Injustice: Women in the Post-NAFTA Food System," pp. 82–8 in *Canadian Woman Studies* 21, 4 (2002). Reprinted by permission of the author.

Henry M. Codjoe, "Fighting a 'Public Enemy' of Black Achievement: The Persistence of Racism and the Schooling Experience of Black Students in Canada," December 2001, Taylor and Francis Ltd. http://www.informaworld.com

George Sefa Dei, "The Intersections of Race, Class, and Gender in the Anti-Racism Discourse," in *Anti-Racism Education* (Halifax, NS: Fernwood Publishing, 1996). Used with permission of Fernwood Publishing Co. Ltd.

Ann Duffy and Nancy Mandell, "The Growth of Poverty and Social Inequality: Losing Faith in Social Justice," in *Canadian Society: Meeting the Challenges of the Twenty-First Century*, 2nd edn, eds Dan Glenday and Ann Duffy. Copyright © Oxford University Press 2001. Reprinted by permission of the publisher. Excerpts from Patrick Burman, *Killing Time, Losing Ground: Experiences of Unemployment*, reprinted by permission of Thompson Educational Publishing.

Evelyn Nakano Glenn, "Yearning for Lightness: Transitional Circuits in the Marketing and Consumption of Skin Lighteners," *Gender & Society*, June 2008. Reprinted with permission from Sage Publications.

Jana Grekul, "Sterilization in Alberta, 1928 to 1972: Gender Matters," *Canadian Review of Sociology/Revue canadienne de sociologie*, 18 December 2008. Reprinted with permission from John Wiley and Sons.

Sarah Hunt, "Decolonizing Sex Work: Developing an Intersectional Indigenous Approach," reprinted from permission of the Publisher from *Selling Sex*, edited by Emily van der Meulen, Elya M. Durisin, and Victoria Love © University of British Columbia Press 2013. All rights reserved by the publisher.

Helen Jefferson Lenskyj, "In the Pool, on the Ice: Contested Terrain," pp. 87–107 in *Gender Politics and the Olympic Industry* by Helen Jefferson Lenskyj, published 2012 (Basinstoke: Palgrave Macmillan Press), reproduced with permission of Palgrave Macmillan.

Anna C. Korteweg, "The Sharia Debate in Ontario: Gender, Islam, and Muslim Women's Agency," *Gender and Society*, 2008. Reprinted with permission from SAGE publications.

Kari Krogh, "Redefining Home Care for Women with Disabilities: A Call for Citizenship," in *Caring for/Caring about: Women, Home Care and Unpaid Caregiving*, edited by Karen Grant, Carol Amaratunga, Pat Armstrong, Madeline Boscoe, Ann Pederson, and Kay Willson. University of Toronto Press, Higher Education Division © The authors, 2004. Reprinted with permission of the publisher.

Marianne MacKinnon and Laura Lee Howard, "Affirming Immigrant Women's Health: Building Inclusive Health Policy," in *Race, Ethnicity and Women's Health*, ed. Carol Amaratunga.

Patricia A. Monture-Angus, "Lessons in Decolonization: Aboriginal Overrepresentation in Canadian Criminal Justice," in *Visions of the Heart: An Introduction to Canadian Aboriginal Issues*, 2nd edition © Oxford University Press Canada. Reprinted by permission of the publisher.

Jennifer J. Nelson, "The Space of Africville: Creating, Regulating, and Remembering the Urban 'Slum,'" © 2002, in *Race, Space, and the Law: Unmapping a White Settler Society*, Sherene H. Razack, ed. (Toronto: Between the Lines, 2002) 211–232. Used with permission of the publisher.

Valerie Preston, Ann Kim, Samantha Hudyma, Nancy Mandell, Meg Luxton, and Julia Hemphill, "Gender, Race, and Immigration: Aging and Economic Security in Canada," pp. 91–106 in *Canadian Review of Social Policy/Revue canadienne de politique sociale*, no. 68/69 (2012/2013).

Colleen Reid and Robin A. LeDrew, "The Burden of Being 'Employable': Underpaid and Unpaid Work and Women's Health," February 2013. Reprinted with permission from Sage Publications.

Goli Rezai-Rashti, "The Persistence of Colonial Discourse: Race, Gender, and Muslim Students in Canadian Schools," in *Journal of Curriculum Theorizing* (Winter 1999), Caddo Gap Press.

Carla Rice, "Becoming 'The Fat Girl': Acquisition of an Unfit Identity," *Women's Studies International Forum*, March-April 2007, with permission from Elsevier.

Bernard Schissel and Terry Wotherspoon, "The Legacy of Residential Schools," in: *The Legacy of School for Aboriginal People* © Oxford University Press Canada 2003. Reprinted by permission of the publisher.

Daiva K. Stasiulis, "Feminist Intersectional Theorizing," pp. 347–85 in *Race and Ethnic Relations in Canada*, 2nd edn, ed. Peter S. Li. Copyright © Oxford University Press Canada, 1999. Reprinted by permission of the publisher.

Wangari Esther Tharao and Linda Cornwell, "Feminist Leadership and Female Genital Mutilation in Canada: A Community Health Centre's Advocacy and FGM Eradication Efforts," pp. 247–65 in *Theorizing Empowerment: Canadian Perspectives on Black Feminist Thought*. Reprinted with permission by the author.

Njoki Nathani Wane, "African Women and Canadian History: Demanding our Place in the Curriculum," in *Theorizing Empowerment: Canadian Perspectives on Black Feminist Thought.* Reprinted with permission by the author.

Nira Yuval-Davis, "Introduction: Framing the Questions," pp. 1–41 (edited down to 20 pages). Reproduced by permission of SAGE Publications, London, Los Angeles, New Delhi and Singapore, in *The Politics of Belonging: Intersectional Contestations*, by Nira Yuval-Davis, (©London: Sage, 2012).

Index